COLLECTED LETTERS OF

Samuel Taylor Coleridge

From an unfinished portrait of Samuel Taylor Coleridge painted by Washington Allston at Rome in 1806 and now on deposit in the Fogg Art Museum. Reproduced by permission of the Washington Allston Trust

COLLECTED LETTERS OF
Samuel Taylor Coleridge

—

EDITED BY
EARL LESLIE GRIGGS

VOLUME III
1807–1814

OXFORD
AT THE CLARENDON PRESS
1959

Oxford University Press, Amen House, London E.C.4

GLASGOW   NEW YORK   TORONTO   MELBOURNE   WELLINGTON
BOMBAY   CALCUTTA   MADRAS   KARACHI   KUALA LUMPUR
CAPE TOWN   IBADAN   NAIROBI   ACCRA

PRINTED IN GREAT BRITAIN
AT THE UNIVERSITY PRESS, OXFORD
BY VIVIAN RIDLER
PRINTER TO THE UNIVERSITY

PREFACE

I⊤ is a pleasure to express my gratitude to the many persons who have so generously contributed to my undertaking. I am especially indebted to Mr. A. H. B. Coleridge, the great-great-grandson of Samuel Taylor Coleridge, for permission to publish the letters; to Lord Latymer for his co-operation and many courtesies of a personal nature; to Professor Herbert B. Hoffleit of the University of California for a critical reading of the Greek and Latin passages in the letters and for identifying a number of the quotations; to Miss Helen Darbishire for her active interest in the progress of this work and for her response to many questions about Coleridge and Wordsworth; to Mr. Bertram R. Davis for sharing with me his knowledge of Bristol and its literary associations; to Mr. W. Hugh Peal for kindly permitting me to use his valuable manuscript collection and for assistance in discovering the whereabouts of Coleridge autographs; to Mr. B. A. Rowley of University College, London, and to Mrs. Edward M. Sayles and Professor Eli Sobel of the University of California for supplying bibliographical information relating to German literature and philosophy; to Mr. Wilbur J. Smith, head of the Department of Special Collections of the University of California Library, Los Angeles, for his help in tracing a number of Coleridge manuscripts; to Sir John Murray for kindly allowing me to print a letter of Byron to Coleridge first published in Mr. Peter Quennell's *Byron, a Self-Portrait*; to Mrs. Lucyle Werkmeister for advice concerning the 1809–10 *Friend*, of which she is preparing an annotated edition; and to Mr. T. C. Skeat and Mr. J. P. Hudson of the Department of Manuscripts in the British Museum for generous assistance in solving textual and bibliographical problems.

I owe a debt of gratitude, too, to the following persons: Mr. F. B. Adams, Jr., the Rev. A. B. Allen, Mr. James T. Babb, Professor Carlos Baker, Mr. Gordon T. Banks, Mr. Francis L. Berkeley, Jr., Mr. Carey Bliss, Mr. Charles S. Boesen, Mr. W. H. Bond, Mr. W. A. Charlotte, Professor Francis Christensen, Miss Virginia L. Close, Mr. D. F. Cook, Mr. Homer D. Crotty, Professor Kenneth Curry, Miss Norma Cuthbert, Miss Emily Driscoll, Sir Ifor Evans, Miss Helen Gardner, Mr. Irving Halpern, Professor George H. Healey, Miss Norma Hodgson, Mr. Geoffrey Hunt, Mr. Sidney C. Hutchison, Professor Frederick L. Jones, Miss Louise F. Kampf, Mr. David Kirschenbaum, Dr. Milton Kronovet, Mr. Edward S. Lauterbach, Dr. Wilmarth S. Lewis, Mr. T. Lyth, Mr. Angus

Preface

Macdonald, Canon Leslie G. Mannering, Miss A. Martin, Mr. Taylor Milne, Miss Winifred Myers, Miss Eleanor L. Nicholes, Mr. Michael Papantonio, Professor Lewis Patton, Mr. Carl H. Pforzheimer, Jr., Professor Elisabeth Schneider, Professor C. C. Seronsy, Mr. H. L. Short, Mr. Raymond Smith, Professor Charles Speroni, Professor Robert Stevenson, Mr. Arthur Swann, Mr. John C. C. Taylor, Professor Geoffrey Tillotson, and Miss Vera Watson.

I gratefully acknowledge the courtesy of the librarians and trustees of the following institutions for granting me permission to use the Coleridge autograph letters in their collections: Bibliothèque Municipale, Nantes; Black Gate Library; Bodleian Library; Boston Public Library; Bristol Central Public Library; British Museum; Colorado College Library; Cornell University Library; Dove Cottage; Folger Shakespeare Library; Harvard College Library; Haverford College Library; Highgate Literary and Scientific Institution; Historical Society of Pennsylvania; Huntington Library; John Rylands Library; Lehigh University Library; McGill University Library; National Library of Scotland; National Portrait Gallery; New York Public Library (Berg Collection, Arents Collections, and Manuscript Division); Pierpont Morgan Library (the Langlais Collection acquired too late for acknowledgement in these volumes); Princeton University Library; Public Library of Victoria, Melbourne, Australia; Royal Institution; Somerville College, Oxford; Sutro Branch, California State Library; Texas Christian University Library; Trinity College Library, Cambridge; University of California Library, Los Angeles; University of Pennsylvania Library; University of Texas Library; University of Virginia, McGregor Library; Vassar College Library; Victoria and Albert Museum; Victoria University Library; Washington Allston Trust; Wedgwood Museum; Wellesley College Library; Dr. Williams's Library; Wisbech Museum and Literary Institute; and Yale University Library.

I gratefully acknowledge, too, the generosity of the following persons in making available to me the manuscript letters of Coleridge in their possession: Lord Abinger, the late Miss Bairdsmith, Lady Cave, Mrs. Sadie Spence Clephan, the late M. G. D. Clive, Miss Kathleen Coburn, the Rev. A. D. Coleridge, Mr. A. H. B. Coleridge, the Rev. Nicholas F. D. Coleridge, Mr. Basil Cottle, the late H. W. L. Dana, Lord Derby, Mr. J. Graham Eggar, Lord Ernle, Mr. John C. Hanbury, Mr. Henry Hofheimer, Mr. Robert G. Hopkins, Mr. Henry Hutchins, Miss Joanna Hutchinson, Lord Latymer, Professor E. L. McAdam, Jr., the late A. H. Hallam Murray, Sir John Murray, Colonel J. W. Nicol, Mr. W. Hugh Peal, the late Carl H. Pforzheimer (the Carl H. Pforzheimer Library,

Preface

New York City), Mr. William Roethke, the late Colonel H. G. Sotheby, Mrs. Frances Gazda Stover, and Mr. H. B. Vander Poel.

I take particular pleasure in acknowledging the painstaking work of my assistants, Miss Ann Haering, Mrs. Alice Dawson MacAller, and Mrs. Harriet Carey Orkand.

The completion of these volumes has been made possible through the generosity of the American Philosophical Society and of the Regents of the University of California. To the former I am indebted for a grant which enabled me to pursue research in England; to the latter for liberal research funds.

My greatest debt of all is to my wife: *Nunc scio quid sit Amor.*

E. L. G.

University of California
Los Angeles

CONTENTS

LIST OF ILLUSTRATIONS

LIST OF LETTERS

List of Letters

List of Letters

(xv)

List of Letters

List of Letters

List of Letters

List of Letters

ABBREVIATIONS AND PRINCIPAL
REFERENCES

Abbreviations

A House of Letters	Betham, Ernest, ed.: *A House of Letters*, [1905]
A Publisher and His Friends	Smiles, Samuel: *A Publisher and His Friends. Memoir and Correspondence of John Murray, . . .* 1911
Biog. Lit.	Coleridge, S. T.: *Biographia Literaria, . . .* 2 vols., 1817; ed. H. N. Coleridge, 2 vols., 1847; ed. J. Shawcross, 2 vols., 1907. (Unless otherwise indicated references are to the Shawcross edition.)
Byron Letters and Journals	Prothero, R. E., ed.: *The Works of Lord Byron, Letters and Journals*, 6 vols., 1898–1901
Campbell, *Life*	Campbell, J. D.: *Samuel Taylor Coleridge, a Narrative of the Events of His Life*, 1894
Campbell, *Poetical Works*	Campbell, J. D., ed.: *The Poetical Works of Samuel Taylor Coleridge*, 1893
Chambers, *Life*	Chambers, E. K.: *Samuel Taylor Coleridge: A Biographical Study*, 1938
E. L. G.	Griggs, E. L., ed.: *Unpublished Letters of Samuel Taylor Coleridge, . . .* 2 vols., 1932
Early Letters	De Selincourt, E., ed.: *The Early Letters of William and Dorothy Wordsworth (1787–1805)*, 1935
Early Rec.	Cottle, Joseph: *Early Recollections; chiefly relating to the late Samuel Taylor Coleridge, . . .* 2 vols., 1837
Essays on His Own Times	Coleridge, Sara, ed.: *Essays on His Own Times, . . . By S. T. Coleridge*, 3 vols., 1850
Frag. Remains	Davy, John: *Fragmentary Remains, Literary and Scientific, of Sir Humphry Davy, . . .* 1858
Gillman, *Life*	Gillman, James: *The Life of Samuel Taylor Coleridge*, 1838
John Hookham Frere	Festing, Gabrielle: *John Hookham Frere and His Friends*, 1899
John Rickman	Williams, Orlo: *Life and Letters of John Rickman*, 1912
Journals	De Selincourt, E., ed.: *Journals of Dorothy Wordsworth*, 2 vols., 1952
Lamb Letters	Lucas, E. V., ed.: *The Letters of Charles Lamb, to which are added those of his sister, Mary Lamb*, 3 vols., 1935
Later Years	De Selincourt, E., ed.: *The Letters of William and Dorothy Wordsworth: the Later Years*, 3 vols., 1939

Abbreviations and Principal References

Letters	Coleridge, E. H., ed.: *Letters of Samuel Taylor Coleridge*, 2 vols., 1895
Letters, Conversations and Rec.	Allsop, Thomas, ed.: *Letters, Conversations and Recollections of S. T. Coleridge*, 1836, 1858, 1864 (cited)
Letters from the Lake Poets	[Coleridge, E. H., ed.] *Letters from the Lake Poets . . . to Daniel Stuart*, 1889
Letters Hitherto Uncollected	Prideaux, W. F.: *Letters Hitherto Uncollected by Samuel Taylor Coleridge*, 1913
Letters to Estlin	Bright, H. A., ed.: *Unpublished Letters from Samuel Taylor Coleridge to the Rev. John Prior Estlin* (Philobiblon Society, *Miscellanies*, xv, 1877–84)
Life and Corres.	Southey, C. C., ed.: *The Life and Correspondence of the late Robert Southey*, 6 vols., 1849–50
Life of Andrew Bell	Southey, Robert and C. C.: *The Life of the Rev. Andrew Bell*, 3 vols., 1844
Literary Remains	Coleridge, H. N., ed.: *The Literary Remains of Samuel Taylor Coleridge*, 4 vols., 1836–9
Memoir of H. F. Cary	Cary, Henry: *Memoir of the Rev. Henry Francis Cary, . . .* 2 vols., 1847
Memorials of Coleorton	Knight, Wm., ed.: *Memorials of Coleorton, being Letters . . . to Sir George and Lady Beaumont, . . .* 2 vols., 1887
Middle Years	De Selincourt, E., ed.: *The Letters of William and Dorothy Wordsworth: the Middle Years*, 2 vols., 1937
Philosophical Lectures	Coburn, Kathleen, ed.: *The Philosophical Lectures of Samuel Taylor Coleridge*, 1949
Poems	Coleridge, E. H., ed.: *The Complete Poetical Works of Samuel Taylor Coleridge, . . .* 2 vols., 1912
Rem.	Cottle, Joseph: *Reminiscences of Samuel Taylor Coleridge and Robert Southey*, 1847, 1848 (cited)
Robinson on Books and Their Writers	Morley, Edith J., ed.: *Henry Crabb Robinson on Books and Their Writers*, 3 vols., 1938
Shakespearean Criticism	Raysor, T. M., ed.: *Coleridge's Shakespearean Criticism*, 2 vols., 1930
Southey Letters	Warter, J. W., ed.: *Selections from the Letters of Robert Southey*, 4 vols., 1856
Thomas Poole	Sandford, Mrs. Henry: *Thomas Poole and His Friends*, 2 vols., 1888
William Godwin	Paul, C. Kegan: *William Godwin: His Friends and Contemporaries*, 2 vols., 1876
Wise, *Bibliography*	Wise, T. J.: *A Bibliography of . . . Samuel Taylor Coleridge*, 1913
Wordsworth, *Poet. Works*	De Selincourt, E., and Darbishire, Helen, editors: *The Poetical Works of William Wordsworth*, 5 vols., 1940–9

INTRODUCTION

I

THE letters in these volumes provide an inimitable record of Coleridge's middle years. So various in subject-matter, so rich in self-revelation, they portray the mind and character of one of the most baffling yet fascinating figures in English literature.

Letter-writing was to Coleridge a means of self-expression, and his epistolary style, now sparkling with poetic language, now burdened with amplifications and qualifications, varies with mood and subject. His formal prose, as Chambers remarks, 'yields but few examples of that swift felicity of phrase which often illumines his private correspondence'. In the present letters, however, Coleridge shows a growing tendency to write long, involved sentences, and his use of parentheses—frequently extended ones— has become habitual. He recognized, indeed, the discursive nature of his mind. 'My Thoughts are like Surinam Toads', he once wrote, 'as they crawl on, little Toads vegetate out from back & side, grow quickly, & draw off the attention from the mother Toad.' The digressions, it is true, may be more arresting than the matter in hand. In a discussion of Anton Wall's *Amatonda*, for example, Coleridge turns aside to speak of 'long & deep Affection suddenly, in one moment, flash-transmuted into *Love*':

> In short, I believe, that *Love* (as distinguished both from Lust and from that habitual attachment which may include many Objects, diversifying itself by *degrees* only), that that *Feeling* (or whatever it may be more aptly called), that specific mode of Being, which one Object only can possess, & possesses totally, is always the abrupt creation of a moment—tho' years of *Dawning* may have preceded. I said, *Dawning*— for often as I have watched the Sun-rising, from the thinning, diluting Blue to the Whitening, to the fawn-coloured, the pink, the crimson, the glory, yet still the Sun itself has always *started* up, out of the Horizon—! between the brightest Hues of the Dawning and the first Rim of the Sun itself there is a *chasm*—all before were Differences of Degrees, passing & dissolving into each other—but this is a difference of *Kind*—a chasm of Kind in a continuity of Time. And as no man who had never watched for the rise of the Sun, could understand what I mean, so can no man who has not been in Love, understand what Love is—tho' he will be sure to imagine & believe, that he does. Thus, Wordsworth is by nature incapable of being in Love, tho' no man more tenderly attached—

This passage not only reveals something of Coleridge's turn of mind but also offers an illustration of his epistolary manner.

Introduction

The letters present a vivid contrast between the unhappy personal life of Coleridge during his middle years and his career as lecturer, political philosopher, journalist, playwright, and critic. From the year 1807, when he spoke of himself as 'penniless, resourceless, in heavy debt— . . . [his] health & spirits absolutely broken down—& with scarce a friend in the world', until 1819, when he was faced with the bankruptcy of his publisher, he suffered many disappointments and misfortunes. For more than nine years he was a wanderer, living at Coleorton, London, Stowey, Bristol, Bury St. Edmunds, Grasmere, Keswick, Ashley, and Calne, never fixed for long in any one place, until he found a refuge at Highgate in April 1816. Opium held him in pitiful bondage. Many of his early friends lost faith in him. An alienation from Wordsworth occurred. Half of the Wedgwood annuity was suddenly withdrawn. Neither Covent Garden nor Drury Lane produced *Zapolya*, and he was forced to abandon all hope of writing for the theatre. Painfully conscious of 'Genius given, and Knowledge won in vain', and knowing that he was openly condemned for the 'want of inclination and exertion' which prevented him from giving 'full scope' to his mind, he roused himself to sustained literary activity only to become the victim of persecution by the critics, who assailed his published works with 'malignity and a spirit of personal hatred'. Justifiably he complained of having 'bitter enemies and not a single friend in the world of reviewers', and declared that the 'studied silence' of the *Quarterly Review* had been 'far more mischievous' to him than the 'Mohawk truculence' of the *Edinburgh*.

On the other hand, these years were rich in achievement. During this period Coleridge delivered twelve courses of lectures. On 1 June 1809 he published the first number of *The Friend; a Literary, Moral, and Political Weekly Paper*, carried his project forward to the twenty-seventh number of 15 March 1810, and in 1818 brought out a rifacimento of that work in three volumes. Between 1809 and 1817 he contributed a large number of essays to the *Courier*. In 1813 his *Remorse* was produced at Drury Lane, and three editions of the play were published in that year. The volume containing *Christabel*, *Kubla Khan*, and *The Pains of Sleep* appeared in 1816, the two *Lay Sermons* in 1816 and 1817, the *Biographia Literaria*, *Sibylline Leaves*, and *Zapolya* in 1817. In the same year Coleridge projected the plan for the *Encyclopaedia Metropolitana*, and in 1818 his *Preliminary Treatise on Method* was published as an introduction to that work. Coleridge's reputation as a foremost literary critic, indeed, rests on the accomplishments of these years.

The 'ACCURSED Habit' of taking opium weighed so heavily on

the mind and conscience of Coleridge during the years represented
in these volumes that it seems desirable to review his early use of
the drug, the establishment of his habit, and his struggles to
'emancipate' himself from 'a Slavery more dreadful than any man
who has not felt it's iron fetters eating into his very soul can possibly imagine'.

Shortly after he arrived at Jesus College, Cambridge, Coleridge
was 'nailed' to his bed with rheumatism, and in sending details of
his illness to his brother in November 1791, he added: 'Opium
never used to have any disagreeable effects on me—but it has upon
many.' This statement suggests not only that he had recently taken
opium at Cambridge, but also that it had previously been administered to him at school. When he was an 'upper boy' at Christ's
Hospital, he suffered a severe attack of rheumatic fever which confined him to the sick-ward, and it is likely that opium was prescribed
at that time. The letters contain no further reference to the use of
opiates until the year 1796. Writing to Edwards on 12 March
Coleridge referred to his wife's illness, the 'blunders' of his printer,
and other anxieties and went on to say: 'Such has been my situation for this last fortnight—I have been obliged to take Laudanum
almost every night.' On 3 November of the same year he took
'between 60 & 70 drops of Laudanum' to relieve a severe attack of
neuralgia. His medical attendant believed the illness to have
originated 'either in severe application, or excessive anxiety'. On
the 5th Coleridge wrote to Poole that he was taking '25 drops of
Laudanum every five hours'. If we accept his own date for the
composition of *Kubla Khan*, Coleridge also used opium in 1797. In
the manuscript of that poem he records that he took 'two grains of
Opium' to check a dysentery 'in the fall of the year, 1797'. A
further allusion to laudanum occurs in a letter to George Coleridge
of March 1798. After describing a 'general fever' caused by inflammation from the stump of a tooth which his 'Surgeon' had been
unable to extract, Coleridge remarked: 'Laudanum gave me repose,
not sleep: but YOU, I believe, know how divine that repose is—
what a spot of inchantment. . . . God be praised, the matter has
been absorbed; and I am now recovering a pace, and enjoy that
newness of sensation . . . which makes convalescence almost repay
one for disease'. On this occasion, as well as during the earlier illness of November 1796, laudanum was undoubtedly prescribed by
the physician in attendance.

The frank and open manner in which Coleridge occasionally
alluded to his use of opium during these early years and the vivid
way in which he reminded his brother of the 'divine' repose
afforded by laudanum indicate that he was wholly unaware of any

imminent danger. In January 1800, indeed, he referred almost casually to the after-effects of the drug: 'Life were so flat a thing without Enthusiasm—that if for a moment it leave me, I have a sort of stomach-sensation attached to all my Thoughts, like those which succeed to the pleasurable operation of a dose of Opium.' In the light of his later addiction, however, it is significant that in February–March 1796 he should himself have resorted to laudanum, not for illness but to relieve the stress of agitated spirits.

In order to determine when Coleridge first began regularly resorting to opium and the 'immediate cause', it will be necessary to consider some of his own after-statements. On 26 April 1814 he wrote to Cottle:

> I was seduced into the ACCURSED Habit ignorantly. I had been almost bed-ridden for many months with swellings in my knees—in a medical Journal I unhappily met with an account of a cure performed in a similar case (or what to me appeared so) by rubbing in of Laudanum, at the same time taking a given dose internally—It acted like a charm, like a miracle! I recovered the use of my Limbs, of my appetite, of my Spirits—& this continued for near a fortnight—At length, the unusual Stimulus subsided—the complaint returned—the supposed remedy was recurred to.

In April 1816 he mentioned to Byron his 'direful practice' of '15 years', thereby identifying the beginning of his drug addiction with the year 1801. On 1 July 1820 he explained to Allsop:

> By a most unhappy Quackery after having been almost bed-rid for six months with swoln knees & other distressing symptoms of disordered digestive Functions, & thro' that most pernicious form of Ignorance, medical half-knowlege, I was *seduced* into the use of narcotics, . . . & saw not the truth, till my *Body* had contracted a habit & a necessity.

In one of his later notebooks Coleridge indicated that his habitual use of opiates began during the first year of his residence at Keswick:

> At last, my knees began to swell—& for some months, after my return from Germany & my establishment at Greta Hall, Keswick, I had been all but bed-ridden; when my old taste returning, for the study of medical works, having borrowed a load of old Medical Journals from my Medical Attendant, Mr Edmondson, I found—i.e. fancied I found—a case precisely like my own—in which a marvellous cure had been effected by rubbing in laudanum, at the same time that a dose was administered inwardly—I tried it—It answered like a charm—in a day I was alive— all alive!—Wretched Delusion!—but I owe it in justice to myself to declare before God, that this, the curse and slavery of my life, did not commence in any low craving for sensation, in any desire or wish to stimulate or exhilarate myself— . . . but wholly in rashness, and delusion, and presumptuous Quackery, and afterwards in pure *terror*—not *lured*, but *goaded!*

Introduction

From these statements it is clear that Coleridge himself associated
the beginning of his opium addiction with an illness of 1801 during
which he was 'almost bed-ridden' for many months with swollen
knees.

As the letters of 1801 show, Coleridge did suffer just such an
illness, which his medical attendant diagnosed as 'irregular Gout'.
The first attack came suddenly on 8 April 1801, after he had enjoyed
more than two months of relatively good health. A letter of the
18th gives an account of his sufferings: 'For the last ten days I have
kept my Bed, exceedingly ill. . . . My complaint I can scarcely
describe—. . . it flies about me in unsightly swellings of my knees, &
dismal affections of my stomach & head. . . . At present, the Disease
has seized the whole Region of my Back, so that I scream mechanically on the least motion.' This attack lasted until 4 May, when he
recovered 'all at once'. Eight days later, however, a relapse
occurred. Further recoveries and relapses continued to the end of
July. Clearly, then, this four months' illness is the one to which
Coleridge referred in the after-statements cited above.

That Coleridge was resorting to brandy and laudanum during the
first attack of gout, which began on 8 April and lasted for three and
a half weeks, is shown by his letter to Poole of 17 May 1801. This
important letter was not published until 1956. J. D. Campbell,
who quotes a few sentences from it, has this to say: 'I think there
can be no doubt that this letter gives the true account of the
beginning of what Coleridge, in after-years, was accustomed to call
his "slavery" to opium.'

There is no Doubt, that it is irregular Gout combined with frequent
nephritic attacks—I had not strength enough to ripen it into a fair
Paroxysm—it made it's outward shews sometimes in one or other of my
fingers, sometimes in one or more of my Toes, sometimes in my right
Knee & Ancle ; but in general it was in my left Knee and Ancle—here the
Disorder has been evidently attempting to fix itself—my left knee was
most uncouthly swoln & discolored, & gave me night after night pain
enough, heaven knows, but yet it never came to a fair Paroxysm. All
this was mere nothing—but O dear Poole! the attacks on my stomach,
& the nephritic pains in my back which almost alternated with the
stomach fits—they were terrible!—The Disgust, the Loathing, that
followed these Fits & no doubt in part too the use of the Brandy &
Laudanum which they rendered necessary—this Disgust, Despondency,
& utter Prostration of Strength, & the strange sensibility to every change
in the atmosphere even while in my bed—enough!— . . . On Monday,
May 4th, I recovered, all at once as it were—my appetite returned, &
my spirits too in some measure—On the Thursday following I took the
opportunity of a return Post Chaise, & went to Grasmere—to do away
doleful remembrances—& I grew better and better, till Tuesday last

Introduction

[12 May]—indeed I was so stout that I had resolved on walking back to Keswick the next morning—but on Tuesday afternoon I took a walk of about six miles, & on my return was seized again with a shivering Fit followed by a feverish & sleepless night, & in the Morning my left Knee was swoln as much as ever. I return'd to Keswick in a return post chaise on Friday Evening—my knee is still swoln, & my left [ankle] in flames of fire, & last night [16 May] these pretty companions kept me sleepless the whole night—hour after hour, . . . but my stomach & head & back remain unaffected, & I am resolved to believe that I am really recovering.

Despite Coleridge's hopes, the recovery was only temporary. Another relapse, 'as severe as it was unexpected', occurred on 23 June. Writing from a sick-bed Coleridge reported that his 'left Knee' was 'swoln & exquisitely sore', but added: 'I can bear even violent Pain with the meek patience of a Woman, if only it be unmingled with confusion in the Head, or sensations of Disgust in the stomach, for these, alas! insult and threaten the steadiness of our moral Being.' On 1 July he was 'again taken ill with fever & the most distressing stomach-attacks', and on the 8th he described himself as 'a poor fellow with a sick stomach, a giddy head, & swoln & limping Limbs'. A further seizure followed on 26 July, when his left knee 'swelled, *pregnant* with agony'. On 1 August it was larger than the 'thickest part' of his thigh. Undoubtedly, he continued to resort to opiates during these attacks.

This long illness caused grave concern at Grasmere, and in July Wordsworth himself wrote of Coleridge to Poole: 'He cannot be said to be much better, indeed any better at all. He is apparently quite well one day, and the next the fit comes on him again with as much violence as ever. . . . He is himself afraid that, as the disease . . . keeps much about his stomach, he may be carried off by it with little or no warning. I would hope to God that there is no danger of this; but it is too manifest that the disease is a *dangerous* one.'

It seems safe to assume that opium first took hold of Coleridge during his recurrent attacks of gout in April–July 1801, but since as early as 1796 he had resorted to laudanum to relieve mental agitation, any account of the beginning of his drug addiction should take cognizance of his domestic situation and the nervous strain arising out of it. Dorothy Wordsworth gives an indication of the incompatibility at the very time Coleridge was suffering his first attack of gout. In April 1801 she and Wordsworth spent eight days at Keswick, where Mrs. Coleridge made them very unwelcome. 'We are never comfortable there after the first two or three days', she wrote to Mary Hutchinson: 'Mrs C. is . . . indeed a bad nurse for C., but she has several great merits. She is much, very much to be pitied, for when one party is ill-matched the other necessarily must be so too. . . . Her radical fault is want of sensibility, and what can such a woman be to Coleridge?' In January 1802 Coleridge himself referred to his difficulties during the period 'before Midsummer' 1801: 'I was struggling with sore calamities, with bodily pain, & languor—with pecuniary Difficulties—& worse than all, with domestic Discord, & the heart-withering Conviction—that I could not be happy without my children, & could not but be miserable with the mother of them.'

A contributing if not the main cause of the dissension between Coleridge and his wife was his growing affection for Sara Hutchinson, whom he had first met in November 1799. During her visit to Grasmere, which began on 18 November 1800 and lasted for several months, he saw much of her both at Keswick and at Grasmere. She had returned to Bishop Middleham before 17 April, since Dorothy Wordsworth wrote to her of Coleridge's health on that date. In July Coleridge went to Durham professedly to read in the cathedral library, but was for several weeks constantly in the company of Sara Hutchinson both at Bishop Middleham in Durham County and at Gallow Hill in Yorkshire. Convinced, however, of the 'indissolubleness' of marriage, he returned home in a state of frustration and despair. It is not surprising, therefore, to find the following terse notebook entry: 'Laudanum, Friday, Septem. 18. 1801.' Although as early as April he had resolved on a temporary residence in a more equable climate abroad, he now proposed to 'move southward' for several months in the hope that 'warm Rooms & deep tranquillity' might restore his health and spirits. 'O Friend!' he wrote to Southey on 21 October, 'I am sadly shattered. The least agitation brings on bowel complaints, & within the last week *twice* with an ugly symptom—namely—of sickness even to vomiting—& Sara—alas! we are not suited to each other. . . . I will go believing that it will end happily—if not, . . . it is better for her & my children, that I should live apart, than that she should be a Widow & they Orphans.' From 15 November to the end of February 1802 Coleridge was in London and Nether Stowey; and on 19 February he told Poole that recently he had had no 'occasion for opiates of any kind'. On his return journey to the north, however, he stopped at Gallow Hill, where he was with Sara Hutchinson from 2 to 13 March, and after his arrival at Keswick 'scarce a day passed' without 'a scene of discord' between himself and Mrs. Coleridge. The first draft of *Dejection*, which is dated 4 April 1802 and is addressed to Sara Hutchinson, gives a painful description of his state of mind. His health grew worse, and as later letters show, he was taking up to 100 drops of laudanum a day. After one 'violent quarrel', when he was suddenly stricken with spasms in his stomach and expected to die, he threatened to leave his wife and live abroad. A reconciliation followed, and for a time there was more 'Love & Concord' between them than he had known for years.

In November, however, strife began anew. Coleridge left Keswick on the 4th to join Tom Wedgwood on a tour of Wales. On his way he spent a day at Penrith with Sara Hutchinson, who was *en route* to Keswick and Grasmere. This visit led to a bitter correspondence between Coleridge and his wife. Even before he arrived in Wales he received a letter from her which 'immediately disordered' his 'Heart and Bowels'. Only a fragment survives of his reply of 13 November. An allusion to it in a later letter suggests something of its subject-matter: 'I did not write to you that Letter . . . without much pain, & many Struggles of mind. . . . Had there been nothing but your Feelings concerning Penrith I should have passed it over—as merely a little tiny Fretfulness—but there was one whole sentence of a very, very different cast.'

Coleridge wrote again to his wife on 16 November. His letter shows that he was uneasy over the amount of opium he had previously taken at Keswick:

I continue in excellent Health, compared with my state at Keswick— my bowels give me but small Disquiet. . . . Once in the 24 hours . . . I take half a grain of purified opium, equal to 12 drops of Laudanum— which is not more than an 8th part of what I took at Keswick, exclusively of Beer, Brandy, & Tea, which last is undoubtedly a pernicious Stimulant—all which I have left off—& will give this Regimen a *fair, compleat* Trial of one month—with no other deviation, than that I shall sometimes lessen the opiate, & sometimes miss a day. But I am fully convinced, & so is T. Wedgewood, that to a person, with such a Stomach & Bowels as mine, if any stimulus is needful, Opium in the small quantities, I now take it, is incomparably better in every respect than Beer, Wine, Spirits, or any *fermented* Liquor—nay, far less pernicious than even Tea.

On 22 November Coleridge received another disturbing letter from Mrs. Coleridge. A sentence from his answer of the 23rd refers to the Wordsworths and Sara Hutchinson: 'I have a *right* to expect & demand, that you should to a certain degree love, & act kindly to, those whom I deem worthy of my Love.' Coleridge also pointed out how much her letter had affected him:

On my arrival at St Clear's I received your Letter, & had scarcely read it, before a fluttering of the Heart came on, which ended (as usual) in a sudden & violent Diarrhoea—I could scarcely touch my Dinner, & was obliged at last to take 20 drops of Laudanum—which now that I have for 10 days left off all stimulus of all kinds, excepting ⅓rd of a grain of opium, at night, acted upon me more powerfully than 80 or 100 drops would have done at Keswick. I slept sound what I did sleep; but I am not *quite* well this morning. . . . You must see by this, what absolute necessity I am under of *dieting* myself—& if possible, the still greater Importance of *Tranquillity* to me.

This extract offers additional evidence of Coleridge's disposition to resort to opiates under the strain of agitated spirits. Obviously, the 'perpetual Struggle' with Mrs. Coleridge and the 'endless *heart-wasting*' over Sara Hutchinson contributed to the 'detestable habit of poison-taking'.

For Coleridge the year 1803 was marked by increasingly bad health and by a further surrender to opium. If in January he was assuring Tom Wedgwood that in spite of a 'sad bowel-attack' he had taken 'no opium or laudanum' and that he had 'no craving after exhilarants or narcotics', on 17 February he was explaining to Southey: 'Brandy, Laudanum, &c &c make me well during their first operation; but the secondary Effects increase the cause of the Disease. Heat in a hot climate is the only regular & universal Stimulus of the external world; to which if I can add Tranquillity, . . . I do not despair to be a healthy man.' On the same day, too, he proposed jestingly to Tom Wedgwood to give a 'fair Trial of *Bang*, . . . opium, Hensbane, & Nepenthe', and said he considered 'Homer's account of the *Nepenthe* as a *Banging* lie'. On 8 April he was curing himself of influenza by 'a grain of opium'. This illness was followed by an attack of rheumatic fever 'severer for it's continuance' than any he had suffered since his first 'terrific' one at Christ's Hospital. On 2 September he wrote to Mrs. Coleridge from Scotland: 'My Sleep & Dreams are distressful—& I am hopeless; I take no opiates but when the Looseness with colic comes on; nor have I any Temptation: for since my Disorder has taken this asthmatic turn, opiates produce none but positively unpleasant effects.' According to his notebook, however, he had recourse the very next night to a 'violent Stimulus', probably opium, to ward off 'another Attack of Gout in my Stomach'. Yet on 11 September he wrote to Southey that he had 'abandoned all opiates except Ether be one; & that only in *fits*'. Five days later he told Tom Wedgwood that he took 'nothing, in any form, spirituous or narcotic, stronger than Table Beer'. In his letter to Southey he included the first version of *The Pains of Sleep* as a 'true portrait' of the 'Horrors' of his 'fiendish' dreams. Professor Elisabeth Schneider (*Coleridge, Opium and Kubla Khan*) suggests that the poem records the 'miseries' resulting from the withdrawal of opiates. Coleridge himself later spoke of the lines 'as an exact and most faithful portraiture of the state of . . . [his] mind under influences of incipient bodily derangement from the use of Opium'. By November, if not earlier, he was again freely using opiates. A notebook entry records that on the 24th he took 'a considerable Quantity of λανδανψμ'; next day he asked Thelwall to purchase 'an Ounce of crude opium, & 9 ounces of Laudanum' for him at Kendal.

On 11 January 1804 Coleridge wrote: 'O dear Southey! my Health is pitiable—so mere a Slave to the Weather. In bad weather I can not possess Life without opiates—& with what aversion I take them, tho' I can not hitherto detect any pernicious Effect of it—nothing certainly compared with the effect of Spirits.' Three months later he was on his way to Malta. He had at last realized a '3-years-old Persuasion' that 'from 12 to 18 months' Residence & perfect Tranquillity in a genial Climate would send . . . [him] back to dear old England, a sample of the first Resurrection'. He had taken laudanum to check an attack of diarrhoea shortly before his departure from London, and his first letter from Malta reports that he took '30 drops of Laudanum' to relieve a fever soon after his arrival there. Ominously perhaps, his correspondence makes no further mention of opiates during his absence of more than two years. His daughter says that at Malta 'his opium habits were confirmed'.

Coleridge returned to England in August 1806, his mind 'halting between Despondency and Despair' over his slavery to opium. 'For years', he wrote to Estlin on 3 December 1808, 'I had with the bitterest pangs of Self-disapprobation struggled in secret against the habit of taking narcotics.' When he attempted to abandon opium, however, the severity of his sufferings convinced him that if he persisted, he would die. Indeed, he declared to Street that the fear of dying suddenly in his sleep had caused him to take 'enormous quantities of Laudanum, and latterly, of spirits too—the latter merely to keep the former on . . . [his] revolting Stomach'. In January 1808 he said that he had sent for John Abernethy, 'who has restored Mr Dequincy to Health', and a month later he proposed to 'open' the whole of his case to Dr. Beddoes. Apparently he did not see either man, but in September of that year, as his letter to Estlin of 3 December shows, he did consult a country physician, who confirmed his fears that opium 'could not be abandoned without Loss of Life—at least, not at once'. Such, however, was 'the blessed Effect upon . . . [his] Spirits of having no Secret to brood over' that he was enabled temporarily to reduce his dose to 'one *sixth* part' of what he had been taking. In June 1809 he reported to Stuart that his medical attendant had forbidden him to try again 'the desperate experiment' of leaving off the 'accursed Drug' all at once, but that he was then taking less than 'one 20th part' of his old doses.

During the years 1810 to 1816 Coleridge was to seek the help of such physicians as Carlisle (1810), Tuthill (1811?), Gooch (1812), Parry (1813), Daniel (1814), Brabant (1815), and Adams (1816). In 1812, for example, he was for a time to benefit by Gooch's prescription of 'a known & measured quantity of Stimulant, with an attempt to diminish the Opiate part of it by little and little, if it were only a single Drop in two days'. Gooch, indeed, entertained 'strong hopes' that Coleridge would be able either wholly to 'emancipate' himself, or if not '*that*', to bring himself to such an 'arrangement' as would not very materially affect his 'health or longaevity'.

In the early months of 1814 Coleridge fell almost completely under the domination of opium. To one correspondent he wrote: 'I was sure that no ease, much less pleasure, would ensue: nay, was certain of an accumulation of pain. But tho' there was no prospect, no gleam of Light before, an indefinite, indescribable Terror as with a scourge of ever restless . . . Serpents, drove me on from behind.' Elsewhere he exclaimed:

> Lur'd by no fond Belief,
> No Hope that flatter'd Grief
> But blank Despair my Plea,
> I borrowed short relief
> At frightful usury!

By his own admission he was taking 'from 4 to 5 ounces a day of Laudanum'; once he took 'near a Pint'. In desperation he suggested confinement in a private 'Establishment', where he could 'procure nothing but what a Physician thought proper' and where a medical attendant would be constantly with him for two or three months. This step was not taken, but William Hood called in a physician, Henry Daniel; and Josiah Wade, with whom Coleridge was then living, employed a 'Keeper' to superintend him. Such was the 'direful state' of his mind that 'every possible instrument of Suicide' was removed from his room. Before long the doses of laudanum had been reduced to 'four tea-spoonfuls in the 24 Hours', and Coleridge was able to say that 'the terror & the indefinite craving' were gone. Daniel was '*sanguine*' of effecting a 'total recovery', but his efforts, like those of other physicians, were to prove unavailing.

In April 1816 Dr. Joseph Adams arranged for Coleridge's domestication in the household of James Gillman, a Highgate surgeon. In early May John Morgan reported: 'Coleridge goes on exceedingly well—he is reduced to 20 drops a dose.' Opium, however, was never given up, and as late as 1832, two years before his death, Coleridge wrote of 'the Poison, which for more than 30 years has been the guilt, debasement, and misery of my Existence'. Some letters which he addressed to T. H. Dunn, a chemist, offer positive evidence that he surreptitiously obtained supplies of the drug during his long residence at Highgate. A statement prepared in 1888 by S. T. Porter, who was apprenticed to Dunn for five years beginning in February 1824, gives more specific information. Coleridge, he says, 'admitted that he ought not to have prolonged his early use of it [opium] after recovery from acute disease, . . . [and] that he had indulged himself very culpably in the subsequent use of it; & he spoke of his thankfulness that the quantity which he now took, was much less'. Porter went on to add that Coleridge found a 'wine-glass-ful' a day of laudanum, or 'a twelve ounce pint' every five days, 'essential to life & usefulness'. Probably, therefore, the following sentence from a letter to Brabant of December 1815 summarizes what was to be Coleridge's final acceptance of 'this most pitiable Slavery': 'All I can do is to be quite regular, and never to exceed the smallest dose of Poison that will suffice to keep me tranquil and capable of literary labor.'

In Coleridge's day opium was regarded as a medicine. Physicians freely prescribed it in the treatment of rheumatism, dysentery, gout, and diarrhoea, disorders which Coleridge frequently mentions in his letters. Opiates, too, were easily obtainable. Consider, for example, the following remark which Coleridge made in 1808: 'If I entirely recover, I shall deem it a sacred Duty to publish my Case, tho' without my name—for the practice of taking Opium is dreadfully spread. Throughout Lancashire & Yorkshire it is the common Dram of the lower orders of People—in the small Town of Thorpe the Druggist informed me, that he commonly sold on market days two or three Pound of Opium, & a Gallon of Laudanum—all among the labouring Classes. Surely, this demands legislative Interference.' In 1816, in speaking of Wilberforce's addiction, Coleridge commented again on the widespread use of opium: 'Talk with any eminent druggist or medical practitioner, especially at the West End of the town, concerning the frequency of this calamity among men and women of eminence.' In the early nineteenth century, likewise, little was apparently known concerning the cure of an opium addict. One physician told Coleridge that he could not abandon opium all at once without loss of life. 'As to leaving it off by degrees', Coleridge himself wrote to Byron from his own bitter experience, 'it is mere ignorance of the nature of the Distemper that could alone inspire the hope or belief'. Dr. Charles W. Tidd,

Professor of Psychiatry, and Dr. Dermot B. Taylor, Professor of Pharmacology, two of my colleagues in the University of California, assure me that even today the outlook for a drug addict seeking a cure is not promising. Deploring a habit he could not master, Coleridge once wrote: 'After my death, I earnestly entreat, that a full and unqualified narration of my wretchedness, and of its guilty cause, may be made public, that at least some little good may be effected by the direful example!' The letters in these volumes give a true picture of the 'dreadful Hell' of his 'mind & conscience & body'.

Coleridge once referred to his alienation from Wordsworth as one of the 'four griping and grasping Sorrows' of his life. The facts concerning the quarrel are so well known that only a brief review need be given here. In an effort to master his opium habit Coleridge had resolved in the autumn of 1810 to place himself under the care of a medical man at Edinburgh, but the Montagus, who were in the Lake Country, invited him to return to London with them, stay at their house, and consult their physician, Anthony Carlisle. Learning of this plan, Wordsworth warned Montagu not to take Coleridge into his house; obviously he said far more concerning Coleridge's character and habits than was wise. On 28 October, two days after the party reached London, Montagu repeated the warning he had received and told Coleridge that Wordsworth had spoken of him as an 'absolute nuisance' and a '*rotten drunkard*'. Montagu 'prefaced his Discourse' with the false assertion: 'Nay, but Wordsworth *has commissioned* me to tell you, first, that he has no Hope of you.' Soon afterwards Coleridge left the Montagu household for Hudson's Hotel, from which place he was 'rescued' by his friend, John Morgan. Montagu, probably uneasy over the turn of events, reported to Wordsworth what he had done and mentioned that Coleridge had been 'very angry'. Wordsworth, however, offered no explanation to Coleridge, and for the next eighteen months there was no communication between the two men.

Montagu's disclosures came upon Coleridge 'with the suddenness of a Flash of Lightning'. Recalling, perhaps, the earlier misgivings of the Wedgwoods, Mrs. Coleridge, Southey, and Poole concerning his 'prostration in regard to Wordsworth', Coleridge confided to his notebook on 3 November:

Now for fourteen years of my life, . . . I am conscious to myself of having felt the most consummate friendship, in deed, word, and thought inviolate, for a man whose welfare never ceased to be far dearer to me than my own, and for whose fame I have been enthusiastically watchful, even at the price of alienating the affections of my benefactors,—and this during years, in which I stood single in my reverential admiration, and while for my own literary reputation I felt but a languid, at all events, a very desultory interest.

Disillusioned and broken in spirit, he regained a measure of tranquillity only after months of 'benumming Despondency' and 'mental agony'.

While on a visit to Keswick in the spring of 1812, Coleridge was to suffer further disillusionment. Earlier he had repeated to Southey the whole of Montagu's talebearing, 'even as the means of transmitting it' to Wordsworth. As he now learned from Southey, Wordsworth had indeed denied using 'certain expressions' but had 'instantly' declared that 'Montagu never said those words', that Coleridge had 'invented them'. Finding even his veracity questioned by Wordsworth, Coleridge was at last convinced that the affair would end in 'compleat alienation'.

On 2 May 1812 Coleridge was suddenly 'plunged into the hot water of that bedeviled Cauldron, Explanation with alienated Friendship'. Wordsworth had come to London determined to 'confront Coleridge and Montagu upon this vile business'. Through Charles Lamb he bluntly proposed that Coleridge should appear before Montagu and himself, with Coleridge's benefactor, Josiah Wedgwood, present as arbiter. He also added the admonition: if Coleridge 'declined' to offer an explanation, he was no longer to 'talk about the affair'. In making this extraordinary proposal Wordsworth was motivated by the conviction that Coleridge had not only been guilty of misrepresentation in reporting Montagu's conversation but was also responsible for the gossip about the quarrel then circulating in London and elsewhere, gossip which placed Wordsworth in a highly unfavourable light.

On 3 May Coleridge flatly rejected Wordsworth's request—'I can submit to such an examination by no one.' Next day he sent Wordsworth a forthright letter in which he repudiated the charge of having spread gossip and promised to write out a 'solemn avowal' of what Montagu had said—'you will make what use of [it] you please'. Wordsworth notified Lamb that he would not open this letter unless he was first assured that it contained nothing but a 'naked' account of Montagu's conversation. Coleridge considered Wordsworth's message '*insulting*', and matters came to a complete standstill.

On 8 May Crabb Robinson was 'interrupted' by a visit from Wordsworth. After the two men had fully discussed the quarrel, Robinson immediately called on Coleridge and conveyed to him Wordsworth's explanations and denials. Coleridge received these belated 'declarations' with 'less satisfaction' than Robinson 'could have wished'; indeed, Wordsworth's conduct since his arrival in

Introduction

London had ended for Coleridge any possibility of a genuine reconciliation. Writing to Southey on 12 May, Coleridge reported the outcome: 'The affair between Wordsworth & me seems settled —much against my first expectation from the message, I received from him, & his refusal to open a Letter from me—I have not yet seen him, but an explanation has taken place—I sent by Robinson an attested avowed Statement of what Mr & Mrs Montagu told me—& Wordsworth has sent an unequivocal denial of the Whole *in spirit* & of the most offensive passages in letter as well as Spirit'. Coleridge's 'attested avowed Statement' has not come to light, but two manuscript fragments of Wordsworth's denial are extant. They are printed for the first time in the headnote to Coleridge's letter to Wordsworth of 11 May 1812.

Looking back on the misunderstanding nearly a year later Coleridge explained to Poole: 'A Reconciliation has taken place— but the *Feeling*, which I had previous to that moment, when the ⅔ths Calumny burst like a Thunder-storm from a blue Sky on my Soul—after 15 years of such religious, almost superstitious, Idolatry & Self-sacrifice—O no! no! that I fear, never can return. All outward actions, all inward Wishes, all Thoughts & Admirations, will be the same—*are* the same—but—aye there remains an immedicable *But*.' In the postscript to his letter Coleridge added: 'I had not space to speak of T. Wedgewood's farewell Prophecy to me respecting W., which he made me write down, & which no human Eye ever saw—but mine.' What Tom Wedgwood's forewarning was one can only conjecture.

On the whole the separation from Wordsworth proved to be beneficial to Coleridge. It freed him from servile idolatry and an unhealthy dependence, and put an end to his association with Sara Hutchinson. No one, it is true, ever laid hold of his affections with the same intensity as Wordsworth; nevertheless, other friends— the Morgans, R. H. Brabant, Byron, the Gillmans, J. H. Frere, J. H. Green, C. A. Tulk, and H. F. Cary—brought him the devotion and sympathy so necessary to him.

Of the many associations formed during Coleridge's middle life that with James and Anne Gillman was outstanding. The Gillmans gave Coleridge a permanent home after his years of wandering. From April 1816, when he placed himself under Gillman's care, until his death in July 1834, they made him a member of their household, ministered to his health and well-being, and welcomed his children and his friends. As far as his self-tormenting spirit would permit, they brought him peace.

Particularly gratifying to Coleridge, too, was his brief association with Byron. The friendship reveals the extent of Byron's generous support of a fellow poet. Acting on the advice of Bowles, Coleridge first wrote to Byron in March 1815 and asked for assistance in finding a publisher for a projected edition of his poems. Byron responded enthusiastically and took the opportunity to urge Coleridge to prepare a tragedy for Drury Lane: 'We have had nothing to be mentioned in the same breath with *Remorse* for very many years.' In October Byron wrote again: 'Last spring I saw Wr. Scott. He repeated to me a considerable portion of an unpublished poem of yours—the wildest and finest I ever heard in that kind of composition. The title he did not mention, but I think the heroine's name was Geraldine. At all events, the "toothless mastiff bitch" and the "witch Lady", the description of the hall, the lamp suspended from the image, and more particularly of the girl herself as she went forth in the evening—all took a hold on my imagination which I never shall wish to shake off.' Byron expressed the hope that this poem would be included in the forthcoming edition of Coleridge's work and added: 'Scott . . . deplored to me the want of inclination and exertion which prevented you from giving full scope to your mind.'

Stung by this criticism from one who was so heavily indebted to his masterpiece, Coleridge made it clear in replying to Byron on 22 October that he had not himself provided Scott with a copy of his unpublished poem: 'Before I went to Malta, I heard from Lady Beaumont, I know not whether more gratified or more surprized, that Mr Scott had recited the Christabel and expressed no common admiration.' Coleridge began his letter by pointing out that the first part of *Christabel* was composed in 1797, the second part in 1800, and added the comment: 'This is all that Mr W. Scott can have seen.' In giving these dates Coleridge was deliberately emphasizing the 'great *priority*' of his manuscript poem to Scott's *Lay of the Last Minstrel* (1805), but he refrained from mentioning the latter work. Instead, he complained of Wordsworth's neglect: 'I have not learnt with what motive Wordsworth omitted the original advertisement prefixed to his White Doe, that the peculiar metre and mode of narration he had imitated from the Christabel. For this is indeed the same metre, as far as the *Law* extends.' Coleridge told Byron that he was having *Christabel* transcribed 'in the form and as far as it existed before my voyage to the Mediterranean', and promised to send it 'tomorrow or next day'. He also thanked Byron for having spoken so favourably of *The Ancient Mariner* and *Love* and for having 'conveyed' to him in so kind a manner 'the Regrets of many' concerning 'the want of Inclination'. Such censure, he assured Byron, had done him 'exceeding Injury'.

On 27 October Byron acknowledged the receipt of the copy of *Christabel*. Whether he had heard again from Coleridge in the meantime is uncertain. From his letter of the 27th, however, it is evident that as soon as he read *Christabel*, Byron recognized the extent of Scott's indebtedness. 'On your question with W. Scott', he wrote, 'I know not how to speak; he is a friend of mine, and, though I cannot contradict your statement, I must look to the most favourable part of it. All I have ever seen of him has been frank, fair, and warm in regard towards you.' Byron also mentioned his own predicament: 'I am partly in the same scrape myself, as you will see by the enclosed extract from an unpublished poem, which I assure you was written before . . . I heard Mr. S. repeat it [*Christabel*], which he did in June last, and this thing was begun in January and more than half written before the Summer.' Afterwards, in a note to his *Siege of Corinth* (1816), Byron mentioned 'a close, though unintentional, resemblance' of twelve of the lines to a passage in 'an unpublished poem of Mr. Coleridge, called "Christabel"', and went on to say: 'It was not till after these lines were written that I heard that wild and singularly original and beautiful poem recited; and the MS. of that production I never saw till very recently, by the kindness of Mr. Coleridge himself, who, I hope, is convinced that I have not been a wilful plagiarist. The original idea undoubtedly pertains to Mr. Coleridge, whose poem has been composed above fourteen years.'

Byron sent John Murray his copy of *Christabel*, asked him promptly to return it—'I have no authority to let it out of my hands'—and urged him to publish it. Murray issued the work in May 1816. Later, in alluding to the infamous review of the poem in the *Edinburgh Review* (September 1816), Byron spoke scornfully of Scott's plagiarism: 'I hope Walter Scott did not write the review on "Christabel"; for he certainly, in common with many of us, is indebted to Coleridge. But for him, perhaps, "The Lay of the Last Minstrel" would never have been thought of. The line "Jesu Maria shield thee well!" is word for word from "Christabel".' On another occasion Byron declared: '"Christabel" was the origin of all Scott's metrical tales. . . . It was written in 1795 [*sic*], and had a pretty general circulation in the literary world, though it was not published till 1816.' After reading these comments in Medwin's *Conversations of Lord Byron* (1824), Scott was led in 1830 to state in his preface to *The Lay of the Last Minstrel*: 'It is to Mr Coleridge that I am bound to make the acknowledgment due from the pupil to his master.' Scott also admitted that Stoddart had repeated *Christabel* to him 'more than a year' before *The Lay* was begun.

Introduction

On 28 October 1815 Byron asked Tom Moore to write for the *Edinburgh* a favourable review of Coleridge's 'two volumes of Poesy and Biography': 'Praise him I think you must, but you will also praise him *well*.' There was, too, a still further gesture of friendship—a very substantial one. Early in 1816 Byron learned from William Sotheby that Coleridge was 'in great distress' and had applied to the Literary Fund for a few pounds. Though he himself 'could not command 150 in the world', he 'immediately' sent Coleridge £100.

Coleridge and Byron met only once. At this meeting Coleridge repeated his *Kubla Khan*. Byron was delighted with the 'perfect harmony of versification'—indeed, it was at his suggestion that the lines were included in the *Christabel* volume. Coleridge himself came away from the meeting deeply impressed: 'I was once in his Company, for half an hour—He has the sweetest Countenance that I ever beheld—his eyes are really Portals of the Sun, things for Light to go in and out of.' Not long afterwards, on 25 April 1816, Byron left England forever.

Coleridge's letter to Byron of 22 October 1815 clearly anticipates statements made in the preface to the first edition of *Christabel*. In that preface Coleridge again records the dates of composition of the two parts of the poem 'for the exclusive purpose of precluding' from himself 'charges of plagiarism or servile imitation'. Remembering, perhaps, that Wordsworth had rejected *Christabel* from the *Lyrical Ballads* of 1800, Coleridge says: 'It is probable, that if the poem had been finished at either of the former periods, or if even the first and second part had been published in the year 1800, the impression of its originality would have been much greater than I dare at present expect.' Not without irony he adds: 'I am confident however, that as far as the present poem is concerned, the celebrated poets whose writings I might be suspected of having imitated, either in particular passages, or in the tone and the spirit of the whole, would be among the first to vindicate me from the charge.' In the last chapter of the *Biographia Literaria*, too, Coleridge gives expression to his feelings: 'During the many years which intervened between the composition and the publication of the Christabel, it became almost as well known among literary men as if it had been on common sale, the same references were made to it, and the same liberties taken with it. . . . From almost all of our most celebrated Poets, . . . I either received or heard of expressions of admiration. . . . This before the publication. And since then, with very few exceptions, I have heard nothing but abuse.' In one of his letters he is even more explicit: 'With the exception of Lord Byron there was not [one] of the many, who had for so many years together spoken so warmly in it's praise who gave it the least positive Furtherance after it's publication.'

Since Coleridge's letters, along with the Bristol printing bills and other unpublished documents, shed new light on the circumstances leading to the composition of the *Biographia Literaria* in 1815 and make clear why the publication of that work was delayed until 1817, a summary may be included here.

Early in 1815 Coleridge proposed to publish two volumes of poems. Being in great financial distress, however, he sent William Hood, a Bristol friend, a collection of manuscript poems 'equal to one volume' as security for an advance of money. Hood consulted Gutch and Le Breton, two of Coleridge's former schoolfellows, and in April sent £45. He also paid Coleridge's insurance premium for 1815. Further advances during that year brought the total indebtedness to £107. 5s. 6d., Gutch and Le Breton each contributing £14. Later Hood arranged to have the two volumes printed under Gutch's supervision in Bristol. The printing costs and Coleridge's personal debt were to be subsequently repaid by the sale of the work to a London publisher.

At the end of March Coleridge told Byron that his work would be ready for the press by the first week in June. He proposed to send the manuscript volumes 'as soon as they are fit for your perusal', and asked Byron to recommend them to 'some respectable Publisher'. He also expressed his intention of prefixing to his poems a general preface 'on the Principles of philosophic and genial criticism relatively to the Fine Arts in general; but especially to Poetry', and to *The Ancient Mariner* and the ballads a 'Particular Preface . . . on the employment of the Supernatural in Poetry and the Laws which regulate it'. This latter preface was never written, though it is promised in the concluding paragraph of chapter thirteen of the *Biographia*. The preface to the poems is mentioned again in a letter to Wordsworth of 30 May: 'I have only to finish a Preface which I shall have done in two or at farthest three days.'

Not long after writing to Wordsworth, Coleridge abandoned all idea of issuing his 'Poems *and* a Preface'. Convinced that a 'detailed publication' of his 'opinions concerning Poetry & Poets' would excite 'more curiosity and a more immediate Interest' than even his poems, he determined to publish a work in two volumes, the first containing a literary autobiography, the second a collection of his poems. Undoubtedly his decision was influenced by his reading of Wordsworth's *Poems* of 1815, and particularly the critical essays 'prefixed and annexed' to them. To the first volume Wordsworth added a new Preface in which he discussed the terms imagination and fancy and objected to Coleridge's definition of the latter term as 'too general'; and at the end of the second volume he reprinted the Preface to *Lyrical Ballads* and the Appendix on Poetic Diction. By May 1815 Coleridge had received Wordsworth's two volumes; by the end of July he had written the account of Wordsworth's 'Poems & Theory' contained in the *Biographia Literaria*.

The first reference to the *Biographia* in Coleridge's correspondence occurs in a letter to Brabant of 29 July. The letter begins: 'The necessity of extending, what I first intended as a preface, to an Autobiographia literaria, or Sketches of my literary Life & opinions, as far as Poetry and *poetical* Criticism is [are] concerned, has confined me to my Study from 11 to 4, and from 6 to 10, since I last left you. I have just finished it, having only the correction of the *Mss.* to go thro''.' The opening sentence of this letter as printed in the *Westminster Review* with the omission of the first two commas has led such scholars as J. D. Campbell and J. Shawcross to assume that Coleridge was referring to a preface to his 'Autobiographia literaria'. Actually, the preface to his poems had been extended, and as the following passage in the letter shows, Coleridge was describing the subject-matter of the *Biographia* itself:

> I have given a full account (raisonné) of the Controversy concerning Wordsworth's Poems & Theory, in which my name has been so constantly included—I have no doubt, that Wordsworth will be displeased—but I have done my Duty to myself and to the Public, in (as I believe) compleatly subverting the Theory & in proving that the Poet himself has never acted on it except in particular Stanzas which are the Blots of his Compositions. One long passage—a disquisition on the powers of association, with the History of the Opinions on this subject from Aristotle to Hartley, and on the generic difference between the faculties of Fancy and Imagination—I did not indeed altogether insert, but I certainly extended and elaborated, with a view to your perusal—as laying the foundation Stones of the Constructive or Dynamic Philosophy in opposition to the merely mechanic.

On 10 August Coleridge's amanuensis, John Morgan, sent the opening chapters of the manuscript of the *Biographia* to Bristol and reported that the work was 'finished', except for 'a metaphysical part of about 5 or 6 sheets which must be revised or rather re-written—this I trust will be done in a few days'. More than five weeks elapsed, however, before the *Biographia* was complete. As Coleridge explained to Gutch on 17 September, the 'philosophical Part', which he had earlier 'meant to comprize in a few Pages', had become 'not only a sizeable Proportion of the whole, . . . but with the exception of four or five Pages of which due warning is given, the most *entertaining* to the general Reader, from the variety both of information and of personal Anecdotes'. He now suggested a more comprehensive title for his first volume than that mentioned earlier to Brabant: 'Biographical Sketches of my LITERARY LIFE, Principles, and Opinions, chiefly on the Subjects of Poetry and Philosophy, and the Differences at present prevailing concerning both.' He had also given a title to his second volume: 'SIBYLLINE LEAVES, or a Collection of Poems.' Coleridge promised Gutch that the remaining manuscript of the *Biographia* would be dispatched to Bristol 'by Tuesday Morning's Mail', 19 September, and on the 27th he reported to John May that the work was in the printer's hands. The 'compleat' manuscript contained the first twenty-two chapters of the *Biographia* and a prospectus of his proposed 'LOGOSOPHIA: or on the LOGOS, divine and human, in six Treatises'. Coleridge estimated that the *Biographia* would make a volume of '500 pages Octavo'—a correct estimate, since the twenty-two chapters when printed came to 478 pages.

Printing of the *Biographia* began in October, that of the volume of poems a month later. By early May 1816 twelve of the twenty-two chapters of the *Biographia* and almost the whole of *Sibylline Leaves* had been printed, and it was obvious that the two volumes would be of unequal size. Indeed, when Morgan paid a visit to Bristol in late April, Gutch called his attention to this disparity. He suggested that the *Biographia* itself be divided into two volumes 'in order to prevent *disproportion*' and gave his 'positive assurance' that the quantity of manuscript was sufficient to make a second volume. Morgan 'conveyed' the proposal to Coleridge and also consulted John Murray, who recommended that the two works be published in three uniform volumes. Coleridge himself was 'incredulous' when informed of Gutch's estimate of the manuscript, but 'acceded' to the plan of dividing the *Biographia*. Accordingly, on 6 May Morgan, who was acting under Coleridge's instructions, directed Gutch to end volume one with 'the distinction between the Fancy & the Imagination' (chapter thirteen) and to begin volume two with 'the prose proof now returned'. This proof contained all of chapter fourteen and the beginning of fifteen. Since chapter twelve had already been printed when the work was divided, the reference to 'the third treatise of my *Logosophia*, announced at the end of this volume' necessarily remained. In chapter thirteen, however, a correction was made in the proof, and the reader is referred to 'the close of the second volume' for a 'detailed prospectus' of the announced treatises on the Logos.

On 6 May Morgan also sent Gutch instructions concerning *Sibylline Leaves*, which had now become volume three of Coleridge's work: 'Christabel is sold to Murray exclusively till finished; therefore must not be *inserted* in the Vol. It will be out on Wednesday.' Apparently Coleridge was supplying additional matter to take its place. 'By this day's carriage', Morgan wrote, 'I send you *all* the Poetry we are able to collect. We have made many efforts to recover those pieces (not very small in number, & not deficient in quality of composition)—which are lost I fear for ever—the Volume must end there. Col. will prefix to it & send this week an essay on the imaginative in Poetry making the whole Volume about 350 pages quite large enough.' The following poems, which were printed in the two concluding signatures (T and U) of *Sibylline Leaves*, must have been those forwarded to Gutch at this time: *The Visit of the Gods, America to Great Britain* (by Washington Allston), *Elegy,* and *The Destiny of Nations*. The promised 'essay' was probably never written. Since most of *Sibylline Leaves* was printed before it was decided to issue the *Biographia* itself as volumes one and two, the register 'Vol. II.' appears in each signature. Thus in the proof-sheet of signature S, which was returned with Morgan's letter, Coleridge altered the register 'Vol. II.' to 'III.', but the printer ignored the correction.

In early July Coleridge was hoping that the *Biographia* and *Sibylline Leaves* would be published 'at or before Christmas'. Almost certainly, too, he thought of Murray as the publisher. Murray had shown him many courtesies. He published the *Christabel* volume in May 1816, advanced £100 in June for *Zapolya* and 'some other Play, or Publication', and suggested the preparation of a volume of 'Specimens of Rabbinical Wisdom'. He also made inquiries concerning a new edition of *The Friend*; but since in 1812 Gale and Curtis (now Gale and Fenner) had issued in book form the sets of the original *Friend* printed on unstamped paper, Coleridge felt himself 'morally obliged' to make the first offer to them. As a result, on 15 July Gale and Fenner not only contracted for the publication of a revised edition of *The Friend* in three volumes, but insisted on being the publishers of all Coleridge's present and future works, including, of course, the *Biographia* and *Sibylline Leaves*. Furthermore, Coleridge agreed 'immediately' to furnish them with a 'Tract on the present Distresses in the form of a Lay-sermon'.

Printing of the second volume of the *Biographia* continued steadily until mid-July when the proof-sheet containing the first fourteen pages of chapter twenty-two was sent to Coleridge. Along with this proof came the disconcerting news from Gutch that he had made a 'mistake about the quantity of the Manuscript' and that the second volume would not, after all, 'make 200 pages'. Thus at the very time Coleridge had agreed to write a lay sermon and to prepare a new edition of *The Friend* for Gale and Fenner, he suddenly found himself under the necessity of adding '*a hundred and fifty pages*' to a work he had completed nearly a year earlier. In his 'perplexity' he held the proof-sheet for three weeks. Thereupon Gutch sent a threatening letter to Gillman. Coleridge himself wrote an emphatic reply on 6 August. He requested a bill for the printing costs to date and assured Gutch that if it were a reasonable one, the London publishers would remit payment when they received 'the Edition in it's present state'. He sent back the corrected proof-sheet but inadvertently neglected to write in the heading for chapter twenty-two. When it was sent a second time 'for this sole purpose', Coleridge failed to return it.

On 18 December Gutch forwarded an 'excessive' printing bill and reminded Coleridge of the missing proof-sheet. Coleridge now filled in the heading for chapter twenty-two and returned the proof. This signature was the last printed in Bristol. Thus as E. H. Coleridge points out in *Letters from the Lake Poets* (1889), 'the first volume, and the second to page 144' of the *Biographia* were printed in Bristol.

Gale and Fenner now began negotiations with Gutch concerning the printing bill. Gutch, however, proved so cantankerous that it was March 1817 before a financial agreement was reached, and he further delayed matters by refusing to release the printed sheets of the *Biographia* and *Sibylline Leaves* until the £107. 5s. 6d. advanced to Coleridge in 1815 was taken into account. Coleridge repaid £14 to Gutch and a like sum to Le Breton, but Hood, who had continued on friendly terms, cancelled the remainder of the indebtedness. In April the printed sheets, 'together with the MS' of the *Biographia*, arrived in London. The sheets, however, were in such disorder that 'upwards of 4 weeks' were spent 'in gathering and collating' them. A proposal further to reduce the printing bill brought an angry outburst from Gutch: 'Had I been aware of the difficulties . . . in arranging with you a Settlement about Mr. Coleridge's Work, I would have put it behind the fire.' An adjustment in the printing bill having been finally agreed upon by 16 May, Gale and Fenner were in a position to complete the printing of chapter twenty-two of the *Biographia*. An examination of the first edition of that work indicates that their printer began work at page 145 of volume two. To 'fill the Gap' in that volume Coleridge inserted *Satyrane's Letters* from the original *Friend*, a series of articles on Maturin's *Bertram* earlier contributed to the *Courier*, and a concluding chapter written in 1817 in answer to the critics of *Christabel*, *Zapolya*, and *The Statesman's Manual*. The prospectus of the *Logosophia* was omitted, though Coleridge had anticipated its inclusion as late as 5 June. The *Biographia Literaria* finally appeared in July 1817, nearly two years after the manuscript had been sent to Bristol. *Sibylline Leaves* was published separately later in the same month.

E. H. Coleridge once remarked concerning his grandfather: 'My own belief is that by the publication of everything, S. T. C. would gain rather than lose.' If in the present letters Coleridge lays bare his weaknesses, he also reveals the fundamental nobility of his nature. 'But take him all in all'—to quote from his own memorable description of Jeremy Taylor—'such a complex Man hardly shall we meet again'.

II

The present volumes contain 580 letters written between 1807 and 1819. The text of 84 per cent. of the letters is drawn from holographs, 6 per cent. from transcripts of the originals, and 10 per cent. from printed sources. One-third of the letters are printed for the first time, and 114 letters previously printed with omissions are now published in full.

In these volumes I have followed the editorial policy outlined in the Introduction to volume one, with the following exceptions. In order to offer a more readable text I have converted the shilling mark (/) into a dash, and in cases where Coleridge left a quotation or a parenthesis unclosed at the end, I have silently inserted the quotation mark or the rounded bracket. I should note, too, that the angle brackets ($<$ $>$) in the postmarks represent additions by the editor.

639. *To Derwent Coleridge*

Address: Mr. Derwent Coleridge | Greta Hall | Keswick | Cumberland
MS. Lord Latymer. Pub. E. L. G. i. 366. The top of pages one and two of the manuscript is cut off.

When he returned from Malta, Coleridge was finally convinced that he could no longer live with his wife, and in December 1806 he took Hartley with him to join the Wordsworths at Coleorton in Leicestershire. While there he determined to continue his domestication with them, and since they wished to return to the north, he thought of Greta Hall, Keswick, as a possible residence. He 'had an idea' that Southey intended to vacate Greta Hall and settle in the south, and it seemed likely, too, that Mrs. Coleridge planned to migrate southward. First, however, it was necessary to know for certain whether Southey was actually leaving Keswick. The part of the manuscript 'cut off from' Derwent's letter, then, contained a letter of inquiry, now no longer extant, to Mrs. Coleridge concerning Southey's plans. See Letter 640 and *Middle Years*, i. 108 and 119.

Stamped: Ashby de la Zouch.

Saturday Night, Feb. 7. 1807. Coleorton.

My dear Derwent!

It will be many times the number of years, you have already lived, before you can know and feel thoroughly, how very much your dear Father wishes and longs to have you on his knees, and in his Arms. Your Brother, Hartley, too whirls about, and wrings his hands, at the thought of meeting you again: he counts the days and hours, and makes sums of arithmetic of the time, when he is again to play with you, and your sweet Squirrel of a Sister. He dreams of you, and has more than once hugged me between sleeping and waking, fancying it to be you or Sara: and he talks of you before his eyes are fully open in the morning, and while he is closing them at Night. And this is very right: for nothing can be more pleasing to God Almighty and to all good people, than that Brothers and Sisters should love each other, and try to make each other happy; but it is impossible to be happy without being good—and the beginning and A.B.C. of Goodness is to be dutiful and affectionate to their Parents; to be obedient to them, when they are present; and to pray for [them, and to write] frequent Letters from a thankful and loving [heart], when both or either of them chance to be absent. For you are a big Thought, and take up a great deal of Room in your Father's Heart; and his Eyes are often full of Tears thro' his Love of you, and his Forehead wrinkled from the labor of his Brain, planning to make you good, and wise and happy. And your MOTHER has fed and cloathed and taught you, day after day, all your Life; and has passed many sleepless nights, watching and lulling you, when you were sick and helpless; and she gave *you* nourishment out

of her own Breasts for so long a time, that the Moon was at it's least
and it's greatest sixteen times, before you lived entirely on any
other food, than what came out of her Body; and she brought you
into the world with shocking pains, and yet loved you the better
for the Pains, which she suffered for you; and before you were born,
for eight months together every drop of Blood in your Body, first
beat in HER Pulses and throbbed in HER Heart. So it must needs be
a horribly wicked Thing ever to forget, or wilfully to vex, a Father or
a Mother: especially, a Mother. God is above all: and only good and
dutiful Children can say their Lord's Prayer, & say to God, 'OUR
FATHER', without being wicked even in their Prayers. But after
God's name, the name of Mother is the sweetest and most holy.—
The next good Thing, and that without which you cannot either
honor any person, or be esteemed by any one, is—*always to tell the
Truth*. For God gave you a Tongue to tell the Truth; and to tell a
Lie with it is as silly, as to try to walk on your Head instead of your
Feet; besides, it is such a base, hateful, and wicked Thing, that
when good men describe all wickedness put together in one wicked
mind, they call it the Devil, which is Greek for a *malicious Liar;* and
the Bible names him *a Liar* from the beginning, and the Father of
Lies. Never, never, tell a Lie—even tho' you should escape a
whipping by it: for the Pain of a whipp[ing] does not last above a
few minutes; but the Thought of having told a Lie will make you
miserable for days—unless, indeed, you are hardened in wickedness, and then you must be miserable for ever!—But you are a dear
Boy, and will scorn such a vile thing; and whenever you happen to
do any thing amiss, which *will* happen now and then, you will say
to yourself—'Well! whatever comes of it, I will TELL THE TRUTH;
both for it's own sake, and because my dear Father wrote so to me
about it.'

I am greatly delighted, that you are so desirous to go on with
your Greek; and shall finish this Letter with a short Lesson of Greek.
But much cannot be done, till we meet; when we will begin anew,
and, I trust, not leave off, till you are a good Scholar. And now go,
and give a loving Kiss to your little Sister, & tell her, that Papa
sent it to her; & will give hundreds in a little Time: for I am, my
dear Child!

your affectionate Father,
S. T. Coleridge

P.S. I find that I cannot write in this space what I wished—
therefore I will send you, my dear Child! a whole Sheet of Greek
Lessons in a few days. In the mean time, learn your Article, ὁ, ἡ, τό;
and the pronoun relative, ὅς, ἥ, ὅ—and then write out, ὁ τελώνης,

putting the English to each case: with 'of' before the Dependent, and 'to' before the motive, (you need not write out the Dual Numbers). Then write out Μοῦσα; then τιμή;—then ὁ λόγος, and τὸ ζῷον. After this *read over* the verb substantive εἰμί, & all τύπτω— putting the English to each—thus τύπτω, I beat, τύπτεις, thou beatest, τύπτει, he beateth; τύπτομεν, we beat, τύπτετε, ye beat, τύπτουσι, they beat. ἔτυπτον, I was beating, &c—ἔτυψα, and ἔτυπον, (Indefinite 1st & 2nd have the same meaning, & so has the 1st and 2nd Future) I beat, or did beat &c—τέτυφα, I have beaten &c; ἐτετύφειν, I had beaten &c; τύψω, and τυπῶ [*sic*], I will beat:—and so on, declining each thro' all the persons, both singular and plural. And then I will send you Lessons, made up of these words put in different cases and tenses, so as to make sense, and to teach you the use and meaning of these various endings.—May God bless you, my darling! Your dear friend, Sara Hutchinson, sends her Love to you!

S. T. Coleridge.

640. *To Robert Southey*

Address: R. Southey, Esqre. | Greta Hall | Keswick | Cumberland
MS. Lord Latymer. Pub. with omis. E. L. G. i. 364.
Stamped: Ashby de la Zouch.

[*Circa* 16 February 1807][1]

Dear Southey

I am neither willing or able to believe, but that my enquiries were tinged by the medium, through which they were transmitted to you: and I entertain the same suspicion as to your answer.—It is possible, that you might have mentioned to me your intention of leaving your Family at Keswick in case of your going to Lisbon, and that in my perplexed and absent state of mind I might have heard you, as if I had not heard you—but I do not even *recollect* your having once spoken to me concerning *any* of your plans, except the *MSS* relative to Brazil—and most assuredly if you had, and I had not been absorbed or bewildered, I should have seized the opportunity, as an opening to do, what I so much wished, but

[1] On receiving Coleridge's letter of 7 Feb. (see headnote to Letter 639) Mrs. Coleridge was 'almost frantic', for she was forced to accept Coleridge's un-alterable determination 'not to live with her again'. In her response she asserted 'that Southey has no thought of leaving Keswick, it is out of the question', and declared that after she had visited Ottery, she intended 'to return to Greta Hall, and remain there as long as the Southeys do'. Her letter arrived at Coleorton on 16 Feb., and Coleridge replied, not to Mrs. Coleridge but to Southey, in an explanatory letter probably written the same day. See *Middle Years*, i. 119. (Mrs. Coleridge's comments are summarized in Dorothy Wordsworth's letter of 16 Feb., misdated the 17th.)

(3)

found no encouragement from you to do—namely, to open my
mind to you as to my friend & family connection concerning my
own plans.[1]—I took it for granted even, that tho' you should not
go to Lisbon, you yet were determined both from motives of Climate
& of literary convenience to settle near London or Bristol, as soon
as your pecuniary circumstances rendered it convenient. This however I merely state in consequence of an angry sentence conveyed
to me, as from you—and indeed, I am persuaded, had you read my
Letter (that which was cut off from Derwent's) I should not have
had occasion to have written at all on this Subject. I wrote to Mrs
Coleridge that I might gain the information I wanted without
speaking to you at all; fearing lest from motives of delicacy you
might have insisted on giving up the House to me, or have been
wounded. I told Mrs Coleridge, that I could chearfully wait a year
or so; but that if you thought of staying longer, I gave up every
idea of it with chearfulness.—It is not necessary, that I should here
speak of any better feeling as guiding me, than my own interest and
convenience. For what in the world, at present, of external affairs
could be more fortunate for me, than your determination to live at
Keswick indefinitely?—Thus respiting me for some years perhaps
from the vexatious & difficult duty of seeking out a convenient
Abode for my little Girl and her Mother: and of course that person's
comforts are of importance to the probability of my own being left
in some sort of tranquillity, even supposing that I did not for her
own sake most ardently desire to see her as happy as is possible,
consistently with her own after welfare and independence, & that
of my children. In short, my sole object in writing to Mrs C. what
I wrote, was—without application to you to know your plans, such
as they were without any reference to me, & to guide my own, as

---

[1] Southey looked with outspoken disapproval on Coleridge's domestication
with the Wordsworths:
What you have heard of Coleridge is true, he is about to seperate from his
wife. . . . His present scheme is to live with Wordsworth—it is from his
idolatry of that family that this has begun,—they have always humoured
him in all his follies,—listened to his complaints of his wife,—& when he has
complained of the itch, helped him to scratch, instead of covering him with
brimstone ointment, & shutting him up by himself. Wordsworth & his sister
who pride themselves upon having no selfishness, are of all human beings
whom I have ever known the most intensely selfish. The one thing to which W.
would sacrifice all others is his own reputation, concerning which his anxiety
is perfectly childish—like a woman of her beauty: & so he can get Coleridge
to talk his own writings over with him, & criticise them & (without amend-
ing them) teach him how to do it,—to be in fact the very rain & air & sunshine of his intellect, he thinks C. is very well employed & this arrangement
a very good one. I myself, as I have told Coleridge, think it highly fit that
the seperation should take place, but by no means so that it should ever have
been necessary. [Southey to Rickman, April 1807. MS. Huntington Library.]

far as habitation is concerned, by them.—Be assured, that nothing can more alleviate the regret, I must ever feel at being constrained to abandon a place so very dear to me as my Study & the country seen from it's win[dows] as the knowlege that you are still in the same house.

I was shocked, but not surprized, at Lord Grenville's Answer respecting the *MSS.*[1]—Good Heavens! what would have been the answer of a French Cabinet?—And as if the Sea Coast could be politically understood without an accurate knowlege of the Interior —the force, & resources, and dispositions of the Inhabitants. Is Buonos Ayres no Warning to them?—I will write to you on my own studies, as soon as my mind is tolerably at ease. I am considerably better in health; and as one proof of it, have written between 4 and 500 Verses, since I have been here; besides, going on with my Travels. I felt as a man revisited by a familiar Spirit the first morning, that I felt that sort of stirring warmth about the Heart, which is with me the robe of incarnation of my genius, such as it is.—God bless

you—I am very sincerely your's,
S. T. Coleridge

641. *To Derwent Coleridge*

MS. Wisbech Museum and Literary Institute. Pub. Poems, *i. 401.*
Stamped: Ashby ⟨de la Zouch.⟩

March 3. 1807.—

[The chi]ef and most common metrical Feet expressed in corresponding [metre.]

ᴗ means a short, – a long syllable.

[–ᴗ] Trochee / trips from / long to / short:

From long / to long / in sol/emn sort

[– –] Slow Spondee stalks—strong Foot! yet ill able

[–]ᴗᴗ Ever to / come up with / Dactyl tri/syllable.

[ᴗ]– Iambics march from short to long:

[ᴗᴗ]– With a Leap / and a Bound the swift Anapests throng!

[1] Late in 1806 Southey offered Lord Grenville his uncle's papers concerning the interior of South America. They were refused on the plea that the 'information seemed to relate to the wrong side of South America'. *Southey Letters*, i. 401–2, 408–9.

[◡–]◡ One Syllable long, with two [one] short at each side,

Amphĭbra/chys hastes with / a stately / Stride!

[–]◡– First and Last / being long, / Middle short / Amphimacer

Strikes his thun/dering Hoofs, / like a proud / high-bred

Racer.

If Derwent be innocent, steady, and wise,
And delight in the Things of Earth, Waters, and Skies;
Tender Warmth at his Heart, with these metres to shew it,
With sound Sense in his Brains, may make Derwent a Poet!
May crown him with Fame, and *must* win him the Love
Of his Father on earth, and his Father above.
My dear dear Child!
Could you stand upon Skiddaw, you would not from it's whole Ridge
See a man who so loves you, as your fond S. T. Coleridge

642. *To George Coleridge*

Address: Revd. G. Coleridge | Ottery St Mary | near | Honiton | Devon
MS. Lady Cave. Pub. E. L. G. i. 369.
Postmark: 4 April 1807. *Stamped*: Ashby de la Zouch.

2 April, 1806 [1807].—

My dear Brother
    The omniscience of the supreme Being has always appeared to me among the most tremendous thoughts, of which an imperfect rational Being is capable; and to the very best of men one of the most awful attributes of God is, the Searcher of Hearts. As he knows us, we are not capable of knowing ourselves—it is not impossible, that this perfect (as far as in a creature can be) Self-knowlege may be among the spiritual punishments of the abandoned, as among the joys of the redeemed Spirits. Yet there are occasions, when it would be both a comfort and advantage to us, if with regard to a particular conduct & the feelings & impulses connected with it, we could make known to another and with the same degree of vividness the state of our own Hearts, even as it exists in our own consciousness. Sure am I at least, that I should rejoice if without the pain & struggles of communication (pain referent not to any delicacy or self-reproach of my own) there could be conveyed to you a fair Abstract of all that has passed within

me, concerning yourself and Ottery, and the place of my future
residence, & the nature of my future employments (all more or less
connected with you)—but after I have been with you awhile, in
proportion as I gain your confidence & confident esteem, so I shall
be able to pour my whole Heart into you—I leave this place (a
seat of Sir G. Beaumont's) on Saturday, March [April] the 4th—&
proceed to Bristol—where I am to meet Mrs Coleridge, & the two
children (for Hartley is with me) and immediately proceed to
Ottery.[1]—If you find reason to believe, that I should be an assistance or a comfort to you by settling there in any connection with
you, I am prepared to strike root in my native place; and if you
knew the depth of the friendship, I have now for ten years (without
the least fluctuation amid the tenderest and yet always respectful
Intimacy) felt toward, and enjoyed from, Mr W. Wordsworth, as
well as the mutual Love between me and his immediate House-hold,
you would not think the less of my affection and sense of duty towards you, my paternal Brother, when I confess that the resolution
to settle myself at so great a distance from him has occasioned one
among the two or three *very severe* struggles of my life. Previously
however to my meeting you, and at the time of thus communicating
to you my resolve, provided it should be satisfactory to you—it is
absolutely necessary that I should put you in possession of the true
state of my domestic Affairs—the agony, which I feel on the very
thought of the subject and the very attempt to write concerning it,
has been a principal cause not only of the infrequency & omission of
my correspondence with you, but of the distraction of all settled
pursuits hitherto—

In short, with many excellent qualities, of strict modesty, attention to her children, and economy, Mrs Coleridge has a temper &
general tone of feeling, which after a long—& for six years at least—
a patient Trial I have found wholly incompatible with even an
endurable Life, & such as to preclude all chance of my ever developing the talents, which my Maker has entrusted to me—or of applying
the acquirements, which I have been making one after the other,
because I could not be doing nothing, & was too sick at heart to
exert myself in drawing from the sources of my own mind to any
perseverance in any regular plan. The few friends, who have been
Witnesses of my domestic Life, have long advised separation, as
the necessary condition of every thing desirable for me—nor does
Mrs Coleridge herself state or pretend to any objection on the score
of attachment to me;—that it will not look *respectable* for her, is

---

[1] Mrs. Coleridge with Sara and Derwent left Greta Hall for Bristol in March;
Coleridge himself left Coleorton in April but lingered several weeks in London
before joining his family in Bristol.

the sum into which all her objections resolve themselves.—At length however, it is settled (indeed, the state of my Health joined with that of my circumstances, and the duty of providing what I can, for my three Children, would of themselves dictate the measure, tho' we were only indifferent to each other) but Mrs Coleridge wishes—& very naturally—to accompany me into Devonshire, that our separation may appear free from all shadow of suspicion of any other cause than that of unfitness & unconquerable difference of Temper. O that those, who have been Witnesses of the Truth, could but add for me that commentary on my last Words, which my very respect for Mrs Coleridge's many estimable qualities would make it little less than torture to me to attempt.—However, we part as Friends—the boys of course will be with me. What more need be said, I shall have an opportunity of saying when we are together.— If you wish to write to me, before my arrival, my address will be— Mr Wade's, Aggs' Printing-office, St Augustin's Back, Bristol.

Make my apologies to my dear Nephews; and assure them, that it will be a great Joy to me to endeavor to compensate for my epistolary neglect by my conversation with them—and that any valuable Knowlege, which it should be in my power to communicate to them, will on their account become more valuable to me.— My Love & my Duty to all, who have to claim it from me. I am, my dear Brother, with grateful & affectionate esteem

your friend & brother,
S. T. Coleridge[1]

---

[1] George Coleridge's reply may be cited here. It is dated 6 April 1807, but Coleridge did not read it until some time after his arrival at Nether Stowey on 6 June. See Letter 705 and *Thomas Poole*, ii. 182.

Your Letter has necessarily added to a load of distress under which I am at present labouring. . . . We have now ten patients in Bed, one in a very *dangerous* state and two others proceeding towards it. Mrs. Luke Coleridge, who has filled her house with the surplus of my family, has likewise some boys sick in her House; among that number is her own son, who from over growing is very delicate, and our poor aged mother is with difficulty convey'd up and down stairs and cannot of course be at this period of her frail existence incommoded. I mention these particulars, as you must observe, to prove to you how impossible and how imprudent on all accounts it would be for you to come at present to Ottery with any of your Family. I need not tell you that Mrs James Coleridge, who has an hereditary nervousness and despondency and who at present is in little less than a state of wretchedness, would be out of her senses at the very approach of a family in addition to her own. Let me therefore recommend you as sober a plan as my confused mind can suggest—as you are going to Bristol and determine to separate from your Wife (a step which in my own opinion no argument in your situation can justify), make your arrangements there among her Friends. To come to Ottery for such a purpose would be to create a fresh expence for yourself and to load my feelings with what they could not bear without endangering my

643. *To Hartley Coleridge*

Address: Hartley Coleridge | Coleorton | Leicestershire
MS. Lord Latymer. Pub. Letters, *ii. 511.*

Coleorton
3 April, 1806 [1807]

My dear Boy

In all human beings good and bad Qualities are not only found together, side by side as it were; but they actually tend to produce each other—at least, they must be considered as twins of a common parent, and the amiable propensities too often sustain and foster their unhandsome *sisters*. (For the old Romans personified Virtues and Vices, both as Women.) This is a sufficient proof, that mere natural qualities, however pleasing and delightful, must not be deemed Virtues, until they are broken in and yoked to the plough of *Reason*. Now to apply this to your own case—I could equally apply it to myself; but you know yourself more accurately than you can know me, and will therefore understand my argument better, when the facts on which it is built, exist in your own consciousness. You are by nature very kind and forgiving, and wholly free from Revenge and Sullenness—you are likewise gifted with a very active & self-gratifying fancy, and such a high tide & flood of pleasurable feelings, that all unpleasant and painful Thoughts and Events are hurried away upon it, and neither remain on the surface of your memory, or sink to the bottom into your Heart. So far all seems right, and matter of thanksgiving to your maker—and so all really *is* so, & will be so, if you exert your reason and free-will. But on the other [hand] the very same disposition makes you less impressible both to the censure of your anxious friends, and to the whispers of your conscience—nothing that gives you pain, dwells

life—I pray you therefore do not so. . . . It is necessary for me now to tell you that I have made my final arrangements for giving up the School . . . so that I cannot offer you to take the children under my care. . . . Whatever I can spare you in the pecuniary way for putting out your children or making you more comfortable shall be at your service—but peace of mind, if it is to be found here below, I must have. Resolve therefore wisely—your situation is no way desperate if your mind does not make it so—I shall be happy to hear from you and will exert myself to the utmost, when I have got rid of my present troubles, to serve you, but it cannot be by your coming here with your family at present—I know not scarcely what I have written, my mind is so agitated from within and from without. . . . For God's sake strive to put on some fortitude and do nothing rashly. Mr Southey and Mr Wordsworth ought surely to have had some weight with you that you might take no sudden Step. Your male children might be properly sent out and a settlement would probably be made by Mrs Coleridge's friends for the maintenance of herself and Daughter, when you might live apart for some time till you had better considered the nature of what you were doing—[MS. Lady Cave.]

(9)

long enough upon your mind to do you any good—just as in some diseases the medicines pass so quickly thro' the stomach and bowels, as to be able to exert none of their healing qualities.—In like manner this power, which you possess, of shoving aside all disagreeable reflections, or losing them in a labyrinth of day-dreams, which saves you from some present pain, has on the other hand interwoven into your nature habits of procrastination, which unless you correct them in time (& it will require all your best exertions to do it effectually)—must lead you into lasting Unhappiness.

You are now going with me (if God have not ordered it otherwise) into Devonshire to visit your Uncle, G. Coleridge. He is a very good man, and very kind; but his notions of Right and of Propriety are very strict; & he is therefore exceedingly shocked by any gross Deviations from what is right and proper. I take therefore this mean of warning you against those bad Habits, which I and all your friends here have noticed in you—And be assured, I am not writing in anger, but on the contrary with great Love, and a comfortable Hope, that your Behaviour at Ottery will be such as to do yourself, and me and your dear Mother, *credit*.

First then I conjure you never to do any thing of any kind when out of sight which you would not do in my presence. What is a frail and faulty Father on earth compared with God, your heavenly Father? But God is always present.

Specially, never pick at or snatch up any thing, eatable or not. I know, it is only an idle foolish Trick; but your Ottery Relations would consider you as a little Thief—and in the Church Catechism *picking* and *stealing* are both put together, as two sorts of the same Vice—'and keep my hands from picking and *stealing*.' And besides, it is a dirty trick; and people of weak stomachs would turn sick at a dish, which a young FILTH-PAW had been fingering.

Next, when you have done wrong, acknowlege it at once, like a man. Excuses may shew your *ingenuity*, but they make your *honesty* suspected. And a grain of Honesty is better than a pound of Wit. We may admire a man for his cleverness; but we love and esteem him only for his goodness—and a strict attachment to Truth, & to the whole Truth, with openness and frankness and simplicity is at once the foundation-stone of all Goodness, and no small part of the super-structure. Lastly, to do what you have to do, at once—and put it out of hand. No procrastination—no self-delusion—no 'I am sure, I can say it—I need not learn it again' &c &c—which *sures* are such very unsure folks, that 9 times out of ten their Sureships break their word, and disappoint you.

Among the lesser faults I beg you to endeavor to remember, not to stand between the half opened door, either while you are speaking or spoken to. But come *in*—or go out—& always speak & listen with the door shut.—Likewise, not to speak so loud, or abruptly—and never to interrupt your elders while they are speaking—and not to *talk* at all during Meals.—

I pray you, keep this Letter; and read it over every two or three days.

Take but a little Trouble with yourself: and every one will be delighted with you, and try to gratify you in all your reasonable wishes. And above all, you will be at peace with yourself, and a double Blessing

to me, who am, my | dear, my very dear Hartley, | most anxiously | Your fond Father,

S. T. Coleridge

P.S. I have not spoken about your mad passions, and frantic Looks & pout-mouthing; because I trust, that is all over.

644. *To William Sotheby*

Address: W. Sotheby, Esqre. | Upper Seymour St | Portman Square
MS. Cornell University Lib. Pub. E. L. G. i. 373.
Postmark: 18 April 1807.

Brown's Coffee House
Mitre Court
Fleet Street.
Saturday afternoon, 2 o/clock [18 April 1807]

My dear Sir

When I tell you that I have but this moment left my bed, having been sleepless and in fever almost the whole of last night, I have made my apology to you. Yester afternoon I had my Hair cut—and too large a portion of my locks taken away—and I suppose, that my Health went the same way with Sampson's Strength. And unfortunately some of my inmost feelings were lacerated about the same time, and the fever within effected a Junction with the bodily Ague. —At present, I am somewhat better.

I read yesterday in a large company, where W. Wordsworth was present, about 150 lines of your Saul,[1] respecting your country, Nelson, & the admirable transition to the main subject, which follows it—and it was delightful to me, to observe that the enthusiasm which had given animation & depth to my own tones, manifested itself with at least equal strength in the faces & voices of all the auditors. I have little or no doubt, that if you publish a second edition in a smaller size with some few alterations, you will have

---

[1] *Saul, a Poem*, 1807.

(11)

established your SAUL, as the best epic poem in our language, the thread & transitions of which are woven *lyrically*: to which system, tho' it be not perhaps the best in itself, yet the character of David and of his age gives an especial propriety. In making my respectful compliments to Mrs and Miss Sotheby you will convey the sincere feeling of,

dear Sir, | your obliged & I trust grateful | Friend & Servant,
S. T. Coleridge.

645. *To William Godwin*

Address: Mr Godwin | Polygon | Somers' Town
MS. Lord Abinger. Hitherto unpublished.
Postmark: 30 April 1807.

348, Strand.
30 April [1807]

My dear Sir

Be assured, no diffidence as to your kindness or punctuality in performance of promise, but a deep sense how mere a trifle my 'Osorio' is in itself, impels me to remind you of my request, that you would take the trouble of rescuing it from any chance rubbish-corner, in which it may have been preserved.[1] It is not merely, that as a work which employed 8 months of my life from 23 to 24 it is interesting to me in the history of my own mind—tho' I owe it to justice & truth, as well as to myself, to say, that it is but an *unfair* specimen; since I was compelled to finish it within a given time, & not to let it exceed 1800 Lines—but a person who loves me more than I deserve, & has been kind to me from an overflow & restless-ness of his own goodness which he construes into my merits, as indeed we all do too often mistake the effect of *impulse* for the influence of *motive*, has, from certain passages he has heard (not from me, on my honor) expressed an unusual anxiety to possess it.

I am so unwell & so languid from—no matter what—others' follies & my own—from hopelessness without rest, & restlessness without hope—that I scarcely dare promise to *go* any where. But as to staying at home I am always right glad of a promise—If either day, but Friday, you will come & breakfast with me at ½ past 9—Saturday or Sunday, I shall be able to enjoy your company till One, at least.

With esteem & sincere good wishes I am, as I always was, if not better yet certainly not worse,

Your's
S. T. Coleridge

[1] See Letters 333 and 646.

Be so good as to give me a few lines—by return of the Penny—nay—to pay some of the Ex-ministers' Places for Life, I suppose—two-penny Post.—I am joking—it is not Taxes, or Places that frighten or disgust me, for themselves; but abandonment of principle in the great, producing utter negation of principle in the public. This, this *frightens* me.—

646. *To Daniel Stuart*

Address: D. Stuart, Esqre. | Courier office
MS. British Museum. Pub. with omis. Letters from the Lake Poets, *64.*

[*Circa* 5 May 1807][1]

Dear Stuart

I have been both vexed and mortified by this money-blunder of mine relative to your loan to Wordsworth. It was, I own, an imprudence, or rather a strange absence of mind, that I did not enquire of him the particulars—but so it was—I had not once connected our Scotch Tour, or indeed any time or occasion whatsoever with this money—I had heard Wordsworth often, and Mrs Wordsworth still oftener, express uneasiness, that the debt had been suffered to remain unpayed so long—and when I spoke to you about it, & found from you that it was borrowed for our journey into Scotland, I could recollect none of the particulars—nor can I now. But I am sure, that if you knew all that had past, and all that I have suffered, during the long Interval, you would not be surprized by this defect and confusion of memory—at least, would feel more pity for the causes, than wonder at the effect.—I only saw Wordsworth in the hurry of packing up, after this, & his Letter to me, by which I learnt that he had talked with you on the business, did not inform me how it was settled: I mean, as to the payment. For the thing itself was abundantly clear—namely, that thro' some mistake or forgetfulness on my part 20£ had been transferred to Wordsworth from my debt.—However it be, whether I owe this to you or to Wordsworth, I will remit this at least instantly on my arrival at Ottery; that no unpleasant feeling may attach to me on this account—And be assured, my dear Friend! that I will liquidate the whole of my heavy debt to you by regular installments in the course of

---

[1] On 28 April Wordsworth said he expected to leave Thornhaugh Street before Sunday, 3 May, for his brother's at Lambeth. Thus, Coleridge's references to seeing Wordsworth 'in the hurry of packing up' and to 'his Letter to me' suggest that this letter was written shortly after Wordsworth left for Lambeth. *Middle Years*, i. 124. Moreover, Coleridge here says he was 'very much pleased' with *Osorio*, which on 30 April he had begged Godwin to rescue from 'any chance rubbish-corner'.

the next year and a half, even tho' in order to do it I should be obliged to take up partnership with my Brother in his School—a thing he has long wished me to do. With me he would take 50 Scholars at 50 Guineas a year—he has at present 40 at that price. Only one Objection weighs against it in my mind; but that one is a millstone—the separation from Wordsworth's society, and from his Family. This may seem mere *Puling* to the World; but alas! it is almost all-the-world to me.

I have been so lucky as to discover among Mr Godwin's Books the Copy of my Tragedy, which I had lent to poor dear Mrs Robinson—the only copy in existence, that I know of. I was very much pleased with it, still more pleased that I could see at once what it's faults were, and that a week's labor would compleatly remove them. Sir George Beaumont read it about 4 years ago; and he expressed his full persuasion, that with a few alterations which any person acquainted with the mechanism of the stage might easily suggest, it would *act* as well as it reads. I certainly will correct it; & changing both the title, & the names of the Dramatis Personae, procure it to be presented to Covent Garden. But one thing is sadly against me—I am pretty sure, that Kemble has taken a prejudice against me and my productions—and tho' Mr Sotheby and Sir G. Beaumont are on terms of Intimacy with him & would exert themselves to the utmost, yet still I fear, that their Interest will be no sufficient counter-weight to his pride & pertinacity.

I discovered the play in an odd way—I was speaking with some asperity of Sheridan's late conduct in parliament; and Godwin with a half-sneer implied that my *resentment* was the cause of my *dislike*, and that I confounded the *patriot* with the *Manager*. I repelled the charge with warmth; and indeed I might have appealed to *your* evidence, whether I ever wrote to you respecting Mr Sheridan, or spoke, for many many years after, with the least vindictive feeling— and whether I had not (till the coalition) always thought, spoke, & stood ready to write, in his praise & support, as a *public* man. Indeed, I distinctly recollect the having written twice to you, desiring you to assure Mr Sheridan that I did not cherish the least resentment on this account; and wished only to free myself from the charge, which *he* had brought against me of vanity & obstinacy.—Undoubtedly I should be less than a man, if I had not been indignant that within the last 12 months he has made me an object of ridicule among persons disposed to think well of me by misquoting a line, ridiculous enough in itself, & then asserting that it was a fair specimen of the whole Tragedy.[1] But I should have felt much

[1] In the Preface to the first edition, 1813, of *Remorse*, a recast of *Osorio*, Coleridge asserted that a 'Person' (Sheridan) cited the line as 'Drip! drip! drip!

more indignation, if any friend had been so treated; because I should then have encouraged a feeling, which, it being my own case, I checked & repressed. As soon as it is altered, I will beg you to look it over, & give me your opinion & advice, with the same sincerity with which I am

Your obliged & affectionate Friend
S. T. Coleridge

647. *To William Sotheby*

Address: W. Sotheby, Esqre. | Upper Seymour Street | Portman Square
*MS. formerly in the possession of the late Colonel H. G. Sotheby. Pub. E. L. G. i.
377.*

Courier office, 348. Strand—
Tuesday, [5 May 1807][1]

My dear Sir

It was my intention to have called on you yesterday morning; but [I] was prevented by the necessity of attending Miss Hutchinson in her different concerns previous to my accompanying her to the Coach. She is gone to Mr Clarkson's, Bury, & Mr and Mrs Wordsworth leave town tomorrow for Cole-orton—and I and my child either tomorrow or the next day for Bristol in our way to Devon.—In settling some money-matters between Mr Stuart and Wordsworth I found myself indebted 30£, of which, either from defect of memory, or from absence of mind at the time—[*sic*] I have made a contract with Mr Longman for 100 guineas to be paid me on the delivery of two volumes of poems[2]—these are all ready, save only two—but these are the two that I cannot with propriety place any where but at the beginning of the first Volume, & I wish of course to give a week's correction & thought to the others—two months however are the utmost (death & sickness out of the question) that will intervene between this & the completion of my Contract—You kindly encouraged me to apply to you in any difficulty—and I therefore (tho' I cannot conceal that it distresses

there's nothing here but dripping', whereas, Coleridge claimed, the words originally were, 'Drip! drip! a ceaseless sound of water-drops'. Coleridge's memory played him false. The following lines from *Osorio*, 1797, were omitted in *Remorse*:

> Drip! drip! drip! drip!—in such a place as this
> It has nothing else to do but drip! drip! drip!
> I wish it had not dripp'd upon my torch. *Poems*. ii. 562.

[1] Writing to De Quincey on 28 April, Wordsworth says the time of his departure from London is uncertain but that he may leave for Coleorton on Tuesday, 5 May. *Middle Years*, i. 124.

[2] Nothing came of Coleridge's plan to publish 'two volumes of poems' with Longman.

me a good deal) have taken courage to ask you, whether it would be inconvenient to you to advance me 50£ for this length of Time. I doubt not, I might get it from Longman; but I feel an insurmountable dislike to asking it, as he is a man for whom I have no other feeling than that of a selling Author to a purchasing Publisher. Yet should it be inconvenient, I assure you, I shall consider your telling me so frankly as a still greater proof of friendship, than your complying with my application—

For I am | unfeignedly, | dear Sir, | your friend with affectionate esteem

S. T. Coleridge

648. *To Daniel Stuart*

Address: D. Stuart, Esqre. | from Mr Coleridge
MS. British Museum. Pub. E. L. G. i. 374.

Friday Night, [8] May 1807

My dear Stuart

I am much affected at this moment by the re-iterated proofs of your (in my experience unexampled) Kindness to me. But I should sink for ever in my own mind, if I did not deliver under my own hand to you what I have not failed to declare to others, namely, that any services, I may have performed for you, were greatly overpaid at the moment—&, that the whole of the money, I owe you, is *morally* as well as *nominally*, a true *debt*—. Deeply indeed am I convinced, that you always, from personal kindness, overrated the very little, which my own defects, and the Harass of domestic misery, permitted me to do. If I were on my death-bed, I should say, that with regard to your paper what I did, must *certainly* have been of *little* Effect, and not improbably of *none*. The only connection, I feel with you as arising from myself, is that I have had from the first a sincere affection for you; and that I have in my inmost [heart] a deep, & honest respect for you, (*increased* by, no doubt, but) by no means *grounded* on my gratitude to you. I should be glad to believe, that there were two on earth as warmly & unmixedly attached to you.—Excuse me, my dear Sir!—I know, this is oppressive to you—but I felt it a duty, that I dared not resist, to declare under my own hand to *you*, what (I trust) I never have been, never shall be, backward in declaring to others, the true nature of your kindness to me, and of our connection in general.—As to the money, I have a chearful confidence that within the time, I stated, I shall have repayed it—but God in Heaven knows, I would never repay it, if I *could suspect* of myself, that the repayment would in the least degree lessen my sense of obligation to you.—I beg, you will keep this Letter—and having requested that, I shall be silent on this subject for the future.

With regard to Wordsworth's affair I have in vain racked my recollection. I can *recollect* nothing—indeed even of our Tour I cannot recall a single Image or Conversation of the first week or more. I can only therefore *wonder*, how it could be *possible* for me receiving money from you, as I did, on my own account, to apply to you for 80£ for Wordsworth, when he only wished & received 60£. It now dawns on my memory, that you sent 80£ on one account, but by what mistake (for I cannot, cannot degrade myself so far as to talk of *motive*) I could have commingled a debt of my own with Wordsworth's unknown to him or to you, is an absolute *Puzzle* to me. I even imagine, that I recollect that W. had 60£ for the Tour, & that 20£ were left for Grasmere concerns. But Dorothy, Mrs Coleridge, & perhaps, your Letters (the greater number of which are extant) may clear it up.—In itself, it is not of the least *pecuniary* consequence, at present, whether *I* owe it to Wordsworth, or W. to me; but it will teach me a lesson worth more than twice 20£, never to receive or give money without taking a memorandum of it. As to yourself, there is not the dimmest probability, that you could be wrong—many causes of confusion might have [taken] place between me & Wordsworth, but no reason is assignable for your mistaking 80£ for 60£. When I brought the draft, I had no *suspicion* of having any concern on my own account in the business—no more, than if you had desired me to take an 100 guineas, & pay 60£ to Sir G. Beaumont: so blank & naked was my mind at the time—which I say, more as a *confession* than as a *justification*.—

When your attention is open to it, in the course of 3 months, I shall avail myself of your opinion & advice as to my Play—if I had seen half as much of the Theatre, as you have, I should have confidence in my own opinion—& I need not say therefore, that I have great confidence in your's. As to Mr Sheridan, I should feel more for an indifferent person than for myself—& I grossly deceive myself, if *Self* has any share in my feelings. But to have desired a young man struggling for bread to write a Tragedy, at 23—to have heard from him an unfeigned acknowlegement of his unfitness—to have encouraged him by promises of assistance & advice—to have received the play with a letter submitting it *blankly* to his alterations, omissions, additions, as if it had been his own *Mss*—yet still expressing the Author's acknowlegement, that it was not likely to suit the Stage, & that a repulse would create no disappointment, nay, that he would even consider himself as *amply rewarded*, if only Mr Sheridan would instruct him as to the reasons of it's unsuitableness—

then to utterly neglect this young man, to return no answer to his letter soliciting the remission of the Copy—(N.B. all this I had forgiven & attributed to Mr Sheridan's general character & complexity of anxious occupations) but *10 years afterwards* to take advantage of a *Mss* so procured to make the Author ridiculous & that among those disposed to be his friends—& by a downright falsehood—suppose, my dear Sir! this had happened to *you*, or to Wordsworth? It is the wanton cruelty of the Thing, that shocks me, & for *itself* too: tho' few will give me credit for it.

S. T. Coleridge.

649. *To William Sotheby*

Address: W. Sotheby, Esqre. | Upper Seymour Street | Portman Square
MS. Cornell University Lib. Pub. E. L. G. i. 378.

[Circa 8 May 1807][1]

My dear Sir

On Wednesday noon I wrote a Letter & left it with Miss Lamb to be instantly forwarded to you, of which the following is from the same copy: for I wrote the letter over again from finding the back of the Sheet inked, with only a few verbal alterations.

My dear Sir

I received your note with the draft late last night; and immediately after breakfast this morning I sallied forth to thank you in person for this proof of your kindness. But I had scarcely got into Bedford Street before I felt myself unwell; and before I reached Holborn found myself under the necessity of calling a coach, and returning. I almost wish, that Davy had been with me—he would then have seen with his own eyes what the seizures were, on which Wordsworth & his family shortly after my arrival at Coleorton grounded and urged their advice & intreaties to me not to proceed to London; but to abandon my plan of lecturing. They are short, thank Heaven! and it is well, they are. Already by Miss Lamb's nursing I am sufficiently recovered—the disease having, as usual, precipitated itself per viscera. A glass of warm brandy and water, and a basin of strong broth are of more use than any medicines.— But as I am obliged to transact some business for Wordsworth with Mr Longman, and fear that this walk, short as it is, will be as much as I ought to risk, I must write to you, my dear Sir! the thanks, I

---

[1] In response to Coleridge's request of Tuesday, 5 May (see Letter 647) Sotheby sent a draft for £50 the same evening. Coleridge's acknowledgement, of which the present letter contains a copy, was written on Wednesday, 6 May, and the letter itself probably two or three days later.

cannot speak. On my arrival at Ottery you shall hear from me at full; and be assured, it will give me great pleasure to prove to you that irregularity in my former correspondence arose from no fault in the *man*, but in the circumstances. Under the impression of feelings honorable, I trust, alike to you and to myself

I remain, | my dear Sir, | with grateful & affectionate esteem | your obliged Friend,

S. T. Coleridge.

This accident has vexed me—as I am to leave Town to day if possible. I shall proceed to Lamb's to enquire about it. Be assured, my dear Sir! to be negligent in respect where I so strongly feel it, is no part of my nature. If it be possible, I will take my chance of seeing you before I leave Town.

650. *To Josiah Wedgwood*

Address: J. Wedgwood, Esqre. | 24. Charles Street | St James's Square| London
MS. Wedgwood Museum. Pub. A Group of Englishmen, *by Eliza Meteyard, 1871, p. 324.*
Postmark: 27 June 1807. *Stamped:* Bridgewater.

N. Stowey
[25 June 1807]

My dear Sir

As to reasons for my silence, they are impossible; and the number of the *causes* of it, with the almost weekly expectation for the last eight months of receiving my books, manuscripts, &c from Malta, has been itself a cause of increasing the procrastination, which constant Ill-health, Despondency, domestic Distractions, and Embarrassment from accidents equally unconnected with my will or conduct, had already seated deep in my very muscles as it were. I do not mean to accuse myself of Idleness—I have enough of self-crimination without adding imaginary articles; but in all things, that affect my moral feelings, I have sunk under such a strange cowardice of Pain, that I have not unfrequently kept Letters from persons dear to me for weeks together unopened.—After a most miserable passage from Leghorn of 55 days, during which time my Life was twice given over, I found myself again in my native Country—ill, penniless, and worse than homeless. I had been near a month in the Country, before I ventured or could summon courage enough to ask a question concerning you & your's—and yet God Almighty knows, that every hour the thought had been gnawing at my Heart. I then for the first time heard of that Event which

(19)

sounded like my own Knell, without it's natural Hope or sense of Rest.[1] O such shall I be, (is the thought that haunts me) but O! not such. O with what a different Retrospect! But I owe it to Justice to say what good I truly can of myself—long, long before I received your message, I had impatiently waited for my effects, which have been most unkindly or injudiciously detained by Stoddart, after having been rescued from the French at Naples by the unusual address & more extraordinary Courage of Mr G. Noble—Among my papers I had a mss. in which I had reduced into form all I had understood of my Benefactor's opinions in psychology—written partly from my sense of the possibility of Sir J. Mackintosh's Death or loss of the only authentic materials in his possession from other accidents, & partly too, I own, in justification of an assertion, I had once made to Mr Sharp & Sir James respecting the main principle of the System. But while shewing that it was only in the main principle, and not in the proofs or in the manner of coming at it, that it agreed with some philosophers of another country, I had drawn at full a portrait of my friend's mind & character.[2] O Sir! if you knew, what I suffer, and am at this moment suffering, in thinking of him—how often the too great pain has baffled my attempts in going over again the detail of past times—and added to it my own bad state of health & worse state of mind—you would be more disposed to pity than wonder at, my day after day procrastination: when I had every right and every reason to expect the receipt of that, which would enable me to do well & with comparatively little Suffering what without them I could not do but most imperfectly. In other respects too I have been a greater sufferer—for I can appeal to Mr Southey & Mr Wordsworth & his family, that no event has happened of any importance in the Mediterranean, the Constantinople Business, the Explosion & Mutiny at Malta, and the occupation of Egypt with inefficient Troops, which I had not distinctly stated the probability of. I was, it is true, sent for by Lord Howick in consequence of my conversa-

[1] News of the death of Thomas Wedgwood on 10 July 1805 was withheld from Coleridge until after his return from Malta. 'It will I fear prove a dreadful shock to Coleridge on his landing', Mrs. Coleridge had written to Josiah Wedgwood, 'for I have not written him an account of it, knowing how much mischief things of that nature occasion him—he kept his bed for a fortnight after being suddenly told of the fate of his friend Captain John Wordsworth.' (MS. letter, 13 Oct. 1805.]

[2] James Mackintosh had renewed his promise to Josiah to edit Tom Wedgwood's philosophical speculations, to which it was proposed that Coleridge should add a memoir. The project came to naught, but Coleridge did include in *The Friend* a beautiful tribute to his 'munificent Co-patron'. See Letters 380, 436, and 492; R. B. Litchfield, *Tom Wedgwood*, 1903, pp. 207–8; and *The Friend*, No. 8, 5 Oct. 1809.

tions with Mr W. Smith; but his Lordship's Porter repelled me
from his door with gross Insult, and took my Letter even with a
broad Hint, that he should not deliver it.—

If I can summon fortitude enough, as I trust I shall, to give you
the detail of my Life from the time of my leaving Portsmouth to
my Return, you would see, that I had been least of all things idle or
ill-employed, tho' for others' credit and advantage more than my
own immediate benefit—& that, as extremes meet, the faultiest
parts of my conduct have arisen from qualities—both blameable
indeed & piteable, but yet—the very opposite of neglect or Insensibility.

In less than a week I go down to Ottery, with my children and
their Mother—from a sense of Duty as it affects myself, & from a
promise made to Mrs Coleridge, as far as it affects her—and indeed
as a debt of respect to her for her many praiseworthy qualities.

Before I went abroad, I had written a long Letter to Miss S.
Wedgewood concerning some very gross misrepresentations of my
conduct respecting Sir J. M. from a very worthy but a very mischievous man, who (I believe, in great measure from causes connected
with his want of sight) is sure to modify whatever he hears into his
own preconceptions & to spread abroad whatever he imagines himself to have heard. But when I understood, that I had been charged
by Miss Wedgewood herself, & by the Miss Allens without [with?]
having talked unkindly & contemptuously of their Relation before
them at Crescelly, I burnt it. For I had connected with Crescelly
& the sisterly kindness with which I was treated there, some of the
warmest feelings of my nature—and so help me God! I cannot
recollect a single conversation, which might enable me to plead
guilty to the charge—unless it were, that admitting him to be at
the very head of the men of great Talents I still could not according
to my own notions consider him, as a man of Genius.—My last
Call on Sir James was, I may truly say, pressed upon me by Mr. T.
Poole—and I certainly understood him to imply that it was a
request or at least a wish of my revered Friend—and I went
thither, expecting nothing more or less than to hear something
concerning his metaphysical Mss. After leaving him I met Mr Tobin
at Mr Davy's (if I recollect aright) and mentioned Sir James's
kindness to me, quietly & respectfully—which, I am led to suppose,
Tobin colored & shaped according to his own antipathies.[1]

I am at present on the eve of sending two Volumes of Poems to
the Press—the work of past years. My Christabel, which had been
the most & most generally admired, I have been told by Davy,
Lamb, Mr Sotheby, Sir G. & Lady Beaumont, and at least a dozen

---

[1] See Letter 598 for Coleridge's rebuke to Tobin.

others, has been anticipated[1]—as far as all originality of style &
manner goes— by a work which I have not read—and therefore
cannot judge, how far the opinion is just. If so, it is somewhat
hard—for the Author had long before the composition of his own
publickly repeated mine.[2] Besides, I have finished a Greek & English
Grammar on a perfectly new plan, & have done more than half of a
small but sufficiently compleat Greek & English Lexicon—so that
I can put both to the Press whenever I can make just terms with
any Bookseller—for if it should succeed, it might be of consequence
to my children & their mot[her w]hen I am no more.[3]

I am, my dear Sir! with unaltered e[steem, gr]atitude & affection
your obliged Friend
S. T. Coleridge.[4]

651. *To Joseph Cottle*

Pub. Rem. *305.*

[Early Summer 1807][5]

Dear Cottle,

On my return to Bristol, whenever that may be, I will certainly
give you the right hand of old fellowship; but, alas! you will find
me the wretched wreck of what you knew me, rolling, rudderless.
My health is extremely bad. Pain I have enough of, but that is
indeed to me, a mere trifle, but the almost unceasing, overpowering
sensations of wretchedness: achings in my limbs, with an indescribable restlessness, that makes action to any available purpose, almost impossible: and worst of all, the sense of blighted utility,
regrets, not remorseless. But enough; yea, more than enough; if

---

[1] Coleridge refers to Scott's *Lay of the Last Minstrel.* See Letters 632, 662,
664, 708, and 845.

[2] Despite the fact that Wordsworth met Scott in 1803, had learned of the
latter's knowledge of *Christabel*, and was struck by the resemblance of the then
unfinished *Lay of the Last Minstrel* to Coleridge's poem, apparently he did not
discuss the matter with Coleridge at that time. Thus, as Letter 981 suggests,
Coleridge probably first learned of Scott's recitation of *Christabel* from Lady
Beaumont in 1804.

[3] A manuscript fragment of a Greek grammar survives and has been published. See *Poems by Hartley Coleridge*, ed. Derwent Coleridge, 2 vols., 1851
(2nd edn.), i, pp. xxxiv–xxxvi, and ccix–ccxviii.

[4] Coleridge's letter, Wedgwood wrote to Poole, 'removed all those feelings
of anger which occasionally, but not permanently, existed in my mind towards
him. I am very sorry for him.' *Thomas Poole*, ii. 185.

[5] Learning in 1807 that Coleridge was at Nether Stowey, Cottle wrote to him
'expressing a hope that his health would soon allow him to pay me a visit, in
Bristol'. The present letter, probably belonging to the early summer of 1807,
was Coleridge's answer.

these things produce, or deepen the conviction of the utter power-lessness of ourselves, and that we either perish, or find aid from something that passes understanding.

Affectionately,

S. T. C.

652. *To Mary Cruikshank*

Address: Miss Cruckshank | Enmore
MS. Yale University Lib. Pub. with omis. Early Rec. *i. 199.*

[August 1807][1]

Dear Mary

I wandered on, so thought-bewildered that it is no wonder, I became way-bewildered—however seeing a road Post with the name, Stowey, in two places—one by some water & a stone bridge, & the other on a Tree on the Top of the ascent, I concluded I had only gone a *new way*—when coming to a dark Hole where four roads met, I turned to my left merely because I saw some Houses— & found myself at *Pla[i]nsfield*.—Accordingly, I turned upward, and as I knew, I must pay a farewell visit to Ashholt, I dined with the Brices—& arrived at Stowey just before dark. I did not lose my way then, tho' I confess that Mr Brice & myself disobedient to the voice of the Ladies had contrived to finish two bottles of Port be-tween us, to which I had added two glasses of Mead. All this was in consequence of conversing about John Cruckshank's coming down —now J. C.'s idea being regularly associated in Mr B's mind with a second Bottle, & S. T. C. being associated with J. C., the second Bottle became associated with the idea, & afterwards with the body, of S. T. C.—by necessity of metaphysical Law:

as you may see in the annexed figure—in which I have *drawn* the Bottle.

Mrs Coleridge's address—at least, where a Letter will be sure immediately to be sent to her—is—Miss Fricker, College Street,

---

[1] Since Mrs. Coleridge and the children left for Bristol on 30 July and Coleridge here says he has not yet heard from her, this letter presumably belongs to August. The reference to 'a farewell visit to Ashholt' indicates that Coleridge intended leaving Stowey very soon. Actually, he lingered there until the second week of September. See Eliza Meteyard, *A Group of Englishmen*, 1871, p. 329, and *Thomas Poole*, ii. 201.

Bristol. I have not heard from her, & till I hear I can say nothing of going to Kingston—but as soon as I hear, I will contrive to go by way of Enmore—give my kindest remembrances to Mrs Band, assure her that I have had the strongest desire to see her, & take upon your own dear self, Mary! the fault of my not having come the day, I intended.— Kind love to Mrs C.—& best respect to Mr and [Mrs] W. Cruckshank, & Miss Boyd—& may

God bless you &

S. T. Coleridge

653. *To Josiah Wade*

Transcript Coleridge family. Pub. E. L. G. i. 379.

[August 1807]

. . . Poole (to whom I have not had courage to tell any thing about you) sends his kind respects. In consequence of absence I did not hear of your request concerning the Poems till last night. Mrs Coleridge's Letter only arrived here 3 or 4 days ago. I have sent them by the coach—& they will arrive, I presume, at the same time with the letter.—

O God! if you knew the weight at my heart, the misery that cleaves to my spirits. The very day after my arrival at Stowey Mr Poole was obliged to go away & be absent for a few days—on his return I was ill—& in getting over a high Hedge entangling my leg in a root just as I had taken the leap I sprained my ancle—which brought on not only a general fever, but every appearance of gout. In the mean time my kind Brother & his Wife, from whose pressing Invitations to Mrs Coleridge to come down, with an implied promise that it should cost us nothing—in consequence of which & because it was Mrs Coleridge's earnest desire, under the idea of giving herself & the children a sort of claim to their protection, I had made the promise to her which I gave & performed with infinite regret; this Brother (by his wife to Mrs C) sent a cool formal Letter that we could not be received, the secret whereof is this: I had received at Coleorton a most affectionate Letter from this Brother (the only one of my family that I had any esteem or gratitude to) in which he spoke of himself as deserted by & distressed by the desertion of my Brother Edward with regard to his School—& dwelt on the hope & idea of my coming to him & being an aid & comfort to him in such affecting language that I was exceedingly moved—& being at that time very unhappy at Coleorton from causes, I cannot men-

---

[1] The reference to the arrival of a letter from Mrs. Coleridge '3 or 4 days ago' indicates that this letter was written after Letter 652.

tion, after a thousand painful struggles I wrote to him to say, that I would come & should be happy to assist him for any number of months that might be of service to his Health. But at the same time partly from the openness of my disposition, partly from W's advice that unless I disclosed my resolves of parting from Mrs C to my relations & our common friends, she would never give up the hope of making me retract, as I had so often done before, from pure weakness, & partly, because my Brother's letter moved me so exceedingly, that I could not bear to come into his presence and bring my wife with me, with such a load of concealment on my heart—I told him my state, & my resolves, speaking in the highest terms of Mrs C & indeed referring to his councils when we met—as this subject was so very, very painful, that I could only hint the outline in a Letter. His pride & notion of character took the alarm and he made public to all my Brothers, & even to their Children, this most confidential Letter, & so cruelly that while I was ignorant of all this Brewing, Colonel Coleridge's eldest Son (a mere youth) had informed Mr King that *he* should not call on me (his Uncle) for that '*The Family*' had resolved not to receive me. These people are rioting in Wealth & without the least feeling add another 100£ to my already most embarrassed circumstances—indeed, an 100£ will not pay all our expenses to & fro.—About the same time I received too much reason to suspect & fear, that I must not much longer expect the continuance of my annuity—so that at the age of 35 I am to be penniless, resourceless, in heavy debt—my health & spirits absolutely broken down—& with scarce a friend in the world. In addition to all this, your Image has been an incessant Torture to me. I start at the sound of your name—not that under my then circumstances it was in my power to have done any thing—for I was even unable to write a line to fulfil my engagement to Longman, altho' I was under engagements of honor to pay to one, who very much wants the money, the sum, I was to have received[1]—nor have I in the world a single person, to whom I could apply for 20£ without an agony, that I should prefer suicide to—I found too, that my being known to have engaged regularly in a provincial Paper would accelerate & ensure (if any thing could) the abandonment of my hitherto Benefactor. . . .

[1] Presumably referring to Wordsworth, who in 1804 had agreed to repay £100 advanced to Coleridge by Sotheby. See Letter 569.

654. *To Thomas Poole*

Address: T. Poole, Esqre | N. Stowey | Somerset
MS. British Museum. Pub. Thomas Poole, *ii. 196.*

[Endorsed September 1807][1]

Relative to a Friend remarkable for *gëorgoepiscopal*[2] Meander-
ings, and the combination of the *utile dulci* during his walks to and
from any given place: composed, together with a book & a half of
an Epic Poem, during one of the *Halts*.

> Lest after this Life it should prove my sad story
> That my soul must needs go to the Pope's Purgatory,
> Many prayers have I sigh'd, 'May T. P**** be my guide',
> For so often he'll halt, and so lead me about,
> That e'er we get there thro' earth, sea, or air,
> The last Day will have come, and the Fires have burnt out.
>   Job junior,
>   circumbendiborum patientissimus.

P.S. Shortly will be published a new road Map of the country
between N. Stowey & Enmore, comprising many pleasant new
roads from the former place to the latter by way of Ferriton, Fair-
field, Cummage,[3] &c.

655. *To Mary Cruikshank*

Address: Miss Cruikshank | Enmore.
Transcript Coleridge family. Pub. Early Rec. *i. 201.*

Sunday, Stowey
[September 1807][4]

My dear Miss Cruikshank
    With the kindest intentions, I fear you have done me some little
disservice, in borrowing the first edition of my Poems from Miss
Brice. I never held any principles indeed, of which, considering my
age, I have reason to be ashamed. The whole of my public life may
be comprised in eight or nine months of my 22nd year; and the
whole of my political sins during that time, consisted in forming a

---

    [1] On the address sheet Coleridge wrote: 'Post Mark From London, viâ
Carlisle and Penzance.'
    [2] An explanatory note for 'gëorgoepiscopal' has been cut off the manuscript.
    [3] Possibly Coleridge meant Perriton and Combwich.
    [4] In *Early Rec.* Cottle suggests that this letter belongs to 1807; in *Rem.* to
1803. Since the paper bears a watermark of 1806 and since Coleridge refers to
his ten years' fight against French ambition, this letter was certainly written
in the summer of 1807.

plan of taking a large farm, in common, in America, with 10 or 12 other young men of my own age. A wild notion indeed, but very harmless.

As to my principles, they were, at all times, decidedly anti-jacobin, and anti-revolutionary, and my American scheme was a proof of this. Indeed at that time, I seriously held the doctrine of passive obedience, though a violent enemy of the first war. Afterwards, and for the last ten years of my life I have been fighting incessantly the good cause against French ambition, and French principles; and I had Mr. Addington's Suffrage, as to the good produced by the Essays written in the Morning Post, in the interval of the peace of Amiens and the second war, together with my two letters to Mr. Fox.[1]

Of my former errors I should be no more ashamed, than of my change of body, natural to increase of age; but in that first edition there was inserted (without my consent) a Sonnet to Lord Stanhope,[2] in direct contradiction, equally to my then, as to my present principles— a Sonnet written by me in ridicule and mockery of the bloated style of French Jacobin declamation, and inserted by the fool of a Publisher[3] in order, forsooth, that he might send the book, and a letter, to Earl Stanhope; who, to prove that he was not mad in all things, treated both book and letter with silent contempt. I have therefore sent Mr. Poole's second edition, and if it be in your power, I could wish you to read the 'dedication to my brother' at the beginning, to Lady Percival,[4] of whose esteem, so far at least as not to be confounded with the herd of vulgar mob flatterers, I am not ashamed to confess myself solicitous.

I would I could be with you and your fair visitors. Penelope,[5] you know, is very high in my esteem. With true warmth of heart, she joins more strength of understanding, and to steady principle, more variety of accomplishment, than it has been often my Lot to meet with among the *fairer sex*. When I praise one woman to another I always mean a compliment to *both*. My tenderest regards to

[1] See *Essays on His Own Times*, ii. 478–585.

[2] See *Poems*, i. 89 and note to Letter 83. In 1796 Coleridge asked Cottle not to reprint the sonnet. See Letter 145.

[3] Cottle altered this phrase to read, 'by Biggs, the fool of a printer', and to make matters worse, he added a comment of his own: 'The wish to obtain the favourable opinion of Lady E. Percival, evidently obscured the recollection of Mr. C. in several parts of the preceding letter. The book, (handsomely bound) and the letter, were sent to Lord S. by Mr. C. himself.' *Early Rec.* i. 204. In *Rem.* Cottle omitted his comment but reprinted the falsification involving Biggs. See also *The Friend*, No. 2, 8 June 1809, p. 20 (1812, p. 32).

[4] Lady Elizabeth Perceval was the daughter of the second Earl of Egmont and a sister of Spencer Perceval, the statesman.

[5] Penelope Poole Anstice, Poole's cousin.

your dear mother, whom I really long to spend a few hours with, and believe me with sincere good wishes,

Yours, &c.

S. T. Coleridge.

656. *To Humphry Davy*

Address: H. Davy, Esqre. | Royal Institution | Albermarle St | London   Single Sheet.
MS. Royal Institution. Pub. E. L. G. i. 382.
Postmark: 11 September 1807.

[9 September 1807]

My dear Sir

Tho' it were contradiction in terms to pretend reasons for con- duct confessedly most blameworthy, yet there may have been causes implying so severe a punishment already suffered by the offender, that little room for resentment can remain with a man of a kind Nature. This has long been my case; indeed bodily derange- ment, a general wretchedness accompanied with a want and seem- ing incapability of the feeling of Hope, had so abstracted me from almost every thing, considered as existing without, that even the knowlege of the loss of your regard and affection would rather have been a relief than an aggravation of what I have suffered within from the consciousness of meriting this & whatever else of the same kind had befallen me. Yet how very few are there whom I esteem, and (pardon me for this seeming deviation from the language of friendship) admire equally with yourself. It is indeed and long has been my settled persuasion, that of all men known to me I could not justly equal any one to you, combining in one view powers of Intellect, and the steady moral exertion of them, to the production of direct and indirect Good—and if I give you pain, my heart bears witness that I inflicted a greater on myself, nor should have written such words, if the chief feeling that mixed with & followed them had not been that of shame and self-reproach, for having profited neither by your general example, nor your frequent and immediate incentives. Neither would I have oppressed you at all with this melancholy statement, but that for some days past I have found myself so much better in body & mind, as to cheer me at times with the thought, that this most unnatural & morbid weight is gradually lifting up, and my Will acquiring some degree of Strength and power of re-action. My bodily Health is certainly improved; and tho' never wholly free from pain, and tho' sound sleep seems for years to have forsaken me, and I daily receive proofs of the weakness & irritability of my stomach & bowels—yet I am for hours together

(28)

of the morning released from that load of overwhelming general
sensations, that unutterable disgust thro' body and soul seeming to
have myself & my very life for it's sole object—'whence Faintings,
Swoonings of Despair, And Sense of Heaven's Desertion.'[1] For a
length of time, that I cannot look back upon but thro' tears of
anguish, I have not only not answered any letters—God help me,
I have been afraid even to open them, even to look at their directions. For during this state so instant was the action of my mind
upon my body, that within a few minutes after having read a painful Letter my heart has begun beating with such violence, that not
only it's motions were visible thro' my cloathes, but I have literally
felt *pain* as from blows from within—& this has ended with an
action on my bowels that both in the sort & place of the pain and in
the nature & acrimony of the evacuation it bore no slight resemblance of a cholera morbus. I have however received such manifest
benefit from horse exercise, a gradual abandonment of fermented &
total abstinence from spirituous liquors, & by being alone with
Poole & the renewal of old times by wandering about among my
dear old walks, of Quantock & Alfoxden, that I have now seriously
set about composition, with a view to ascertain whether I can conscientiously undertake what I so very much wish—a series of
Lectures at the Royal Institution. I trust, I need not assure you how
much I feel your kindness—& let me add, that I consider the application as an act of great & unmerited Condescension on the part of
such managers as may have consented to it.[2] After having discussed
the subject with Poole, he entirely agrees with me, that the former
plan suggested by me is invidious in itself, unless I disguised my real
opinions, as far as I should deliver my sentiments respecting the
Arts, [and] would require references and illustrations not suitable
to a public Lecture Room; & finally that I ought not to reckon
upon spirits enough to seek about [for] books of Italian Prints, &c
—And that after all, the general & most philosophical Principles I
might naturally introduce into Lectures on a more confined Plan—
namely, the Principles of Poetry conveyed and illustrated in a
series of Lectures—1. On the genius & writings of Shakespere,
relatively to his Predecessors & Contemporaries, so as to determine
not only his merits   defects,   the proportion that each merit
bears to the whole, but what of his merits & defects belong to his
age, as being found in contemporaries of Genius,   what belong to

---

[1] *Samson Agonistes*, 631–2.
[2] On 28 Aug. 1807 Davy, not having heard from Coleridge, wrote to Poole:
'The managers of the Royal Institution are very anxious to engage him; and I
think he might be of material service to the public, and of benefit to his own
mind, to say nothing of the benefit his purse might receive.' *Frag. Remains*, 98.

himself. 2. On Spenser, including the Metrical Romances, & Chaucer: tho' the character of the latter, as a manner-painter, I shall have so far anticipated in distinguishing it from & comparing it with, Shakespere. 3. Milton. 4. Dryden, & Pope, including the origin, & after history of poetry of witty logic. 5. On Modern Poetry, & it's characteristics—with no introduction of any particular names.—In the course of these I shall have said, all I know, the whole result of many years' continued reflection on the subjects of Taste, Imagination, Fancy, Passion, the source of our pleasures in the fine Arts in the *antithetical* balance-loving nature of man, & the connection of such pleasures with moral excellence. The advantage of this plan to myself is—that I have all my materials ready, & can rapidly reduce them into form—for this is my solemn Determination—not to give a single Lecture till I have in fair writing at least one half of the whole course—for as to trusting any thing to immediate effort, I shrink from it as from guilt—& guilt in me indeed it would be.

In short, I should have no objection at once to pledge myself to the immediate preparation of these Lectures, but that I am so surrounded by embarrassments. This is so painful a subject, that I have never even hinted this objection to Poole—and certainly should not to you, if I could by any means have otherwise explained to you the cause of my irresolution. These have been in part, but only in a small degree, the result of my indisposition; but for the greater part have been occasioned by a series of misfortunes, wholly out of my power to avoid or foresee—I can prove to you, that what with actual losses or compelled expenditure, and what but for accident or ill-treatment would to a moral certainty have been in my purse, I have lost little less than a thousand Pound—yet still I might have gone on (tho' Stoddart's cruel & almost inexplicable detention of my books & papers, without which I could not write the Results of my Residence abroad, except very imperfectly, & which I have been taught to expect weekly for a twelvemonth & more will have greatly lessened the value of the work—for what would have appeared almost prophetic, as some of my friends can witness from my then conversation, will now look like an artifice, or poetic *vaticination* of the Past) yet still I could have gone on, & gradually retrieved myself—(as if I live, I doubt not, I still shall. My Debts are of no amount, & all of them but about 40£ de[bts of] obligation & honor, to two or three friends) but for the most unfeeling conduct of my Brother towards me—who had in so pressing a manner urged Mrs Coleridge to come down with her family, promising that the expences of the Journey should be made up to us, that tho' sorely against my will I gave her a promise that I would take her & the children down—however having received a letter from my Brother George written in the spirit of the warmest affection & most ardent desire to have me with him, for as long as I possibly could, if I would not consent to settle altogether there—I—in the fullness of my heart & indeed by the advice of a friend—confided to him—rather as a thing to be talked of between us two when together than as an irrevocable resolve—the necessity, I felt, from the alarming state of my health, & the unfortunate & unhealable disparity of our dispositions to live hereafter separate from Mrs C.—stating however my great esteem for her, that it would be done so as to create no appearance in the world, as I should live within a walk of her, & that it really proceeded more from anxiety to leave her independent than for my own sake, &c &c.—To this Letter I received an answer, *when we had arrived at Bristol*—full of reproach at my immoral intentions, of the disgrace to their family, of the unnaturalness &c &c—& refusing to see us. This journey had been so sorely against my nature, and I had been so exclusively impelled to it by a sense of Duty and of awakening affection for my Brother who had described himself as overtoiled in his school, & deserted by my Brother Edward strangely & unexpectedly, that I should have rejoiced at the circumstance relatively to myself, as releasing my conscience wholly from all connection with a family, to whom I am indebted only for misery—if the heavy expence of conveying myself, Mrs Coleridge, and 3 children, of her lodgings at Bristol, and all the et cetera of being absent from home, 4 or 5 hundred miles & the same to go back again, had not fallen upon me just at the very time, when I could only, without this instant pressure, have just brought the year to.—Other & to me far far crueller Calamities, & of more envenomed Sting, had rendered me till very lately incapable of finishing the two or 3 poems, which it was necessary to do previously to my collecting all my poetic scraps into two volumes—. Indeed, I have determined to defer this publication—& immediately to proceed to my Travels, or rather information & reflections given and suggested by them, as well as I can without waiting any longer. In the course of a month, if my Health continue even as it now is , I shall have written enough to tempt a bookseller to purchase the whole, & to go to Press without hazard—advancing me money proportionally—and therefore, it is my present plan to accompany Mrs C. northward as far as Liverpool (she is at present at Bristol— & it would be cruel indeed to let her go such a journey with so many children by herself) as soon as we can receive a letter from Mr Jackson at Keswick, who has a few pounds of our money in his Hands, which with what Mrs Coleridge now has, will with frugality carry us home—from Liverpool Mrs C. can easily go without further protection to Keswick—& I mean to diverge to London, so as to be there in the last week of this month.[1]—For God's sake enter into my true motive for this wearying Detail—it would torture me, if it had any other effect than to impress on you my desire & hope to accord with your plan, & my incapability of making any final promise till the e[nd of] this month.

S. T. Coleridge.

657. *To Mary Cruikshank*

Addressed and franked: London, September Twenty first, 1807. To | Miss Cruckshank | Enmore | near Bridgwater
MS. Harvard College Lib. Pub. E. L. G. i. 387. This MS. fragment was apparently the concluding page of Coleridge's letter.

In a manuscript note J. D. Campbell suggests that Letter 913 may originally have been part of this letter to Mary Cruikshank. There would seem to be no justification for his assumption, especially since the two letters, as E. H. Coleridge pointed out, are not written on the same sized paper.
Postmark: 21 September 1807.

Septr. 1807[2]

My whole & sincere opinion is this: that Miracles are a condition & necessary accompaniment of the Christian Religion; but not it's specific & characteristic Proof. They were not so even to the first eye-witnesses; they cannot be so to us. I believe the Miracles, because many other evidences have made me believe in Christ; & thus, no doubt, the faith in miracles does then react on it's cause, & fills up & confirms my faith in Christ.—

I had no suspicion th[at] the Book was a Society Book— Mr T. P. had repeatedly intreated me to write notes in his Books—and I had written such notes (especially in Stillingfleet's Origines Sacrae)[3] as precluded—to *him*—all possibility of misconception. I regret the accident; because I am aware, that the words were not cautiously chosen—tho' I meant no more than to point out the false logic of the writer—& then passed off to a general reflection, dismissing all immediate reference to the resurrection, of the sensualizing effects of building up faith mainly in relations of miraculous effects, of which I had seen with my own eyes so many degrading instances

---

[1] De Quincey accompanied Mrs. Coleridge and the children to Keswick, Coleridge remaining in Bristol until late November.

[2] Although this letter was franked in London and bears a London postmark, there is no evidence that Coleridge went there before he joined Mrs. Coleridge and the children in Bristol.

[3] Poole's annotated copy of this work is now in the British Museum. For Coleridge's marginalia see the *Athenaeum*, 27 Mar. 1875, p. 422.

in Malta, Sicily, & Italy—& the withdrawing of the mind from exam-
ining it's own nature, & the necessity of a *Redeemer*, & the correspondence of Christ's doctrines, manner of announcing them, &
of his whole character to that necessity, which must strike a morally
predisposed Being almost like a sensation—& prepare the Heart
for that action of God's Grace, by which alone we can acquire a
true & saving & entire Faith in the Redeemer, & a consequent
Redemption.

S. T. Coleridge.

658. *To Joseph Cottle*

Address: Mr Cottle | Brunswick Square
MS. Huntington Lib. Pub. with omis. Early Rec. *ii. 126.*

Late in July 1807 De Quincey met Coleridge at Bridgwater, and after his
return to Bristol, he inquired of Cottle concerning Coleridge's 'pecuniary affairs'
and the possibility of giving him an anonymous gift of £300. In early October
Cottle wrote to Coleridge concerning the matter and on 7 October reported to
De Quincey that he had seen Coleridge, who, after inquiring whether the
'Gentleman' could afford to make the gift, had said: 'I will think in what way,
as an honest man, I can accept it, but I will write to you on the subject.' (A. H.
Japp, *De Quincey Memorials*, 2 vols., 1891, i. 127–30.) The following letter was
Coleridge's reply.

Tuesday Morning [13 October 1807]

My dear Cottle—

Independent of letter-writing and a dinner engagement with C.
Danvers, I was the whole of yesterday till evening in a most
wretched restlessness of body & limbs [from some acrimony in the
bowels]; having imprudently discontinued [the purgative] medicines which are now my anchor of Hope.[1] This morning I dedicate
to certain distant calls on Dr Beddoes & Colson at Clifton, not so
much for the calls themselves as for the necessity of taking brisk
exercise.—But—no unforeseen accident intervening—I shall spend
the evening with you from 7 o/clock.—

I will now express my sentiments to you on the important subject communicated by you.[2] I need not say, that it is [and] has been
the cause of serious meditation with you [me?]—yet I can give no
other answer than what I gave you orally. Undoubtedly, calamities have so thickened on me for the last 2 years & more, that the
pecuniary pressures of the moment are the only serious obstacles at
present to my completion of those Works, which if compleated

---

[1] The words in brackets in this sentence have been inked out in the manuscript, presumably by Cottle, who omitted them in publishing the letter.

[2] It is worth remarking that Cottle's account of the circumstances surround-
ing De Quincey's gift is unreliable.

would make me easy. Besides these, I have reasons for belief, that a Tragedy of mine will be brought on the stage this season—the result of which is of course only one of the *possibilities* of Life, on which I am not fool enough to calculate.—Finally therefore, if you know that my unknown Benefactor is in such circumstances, that in doing what he offers to do, he transgresses no duty, of morals or of moral prudence, and does not do that from feeling which after reflection may perhaps discountenance—I shall gratefully accept it as an unconditional Loan—which I trust that I shall be able to restore at the close of two years. This however I shall be able to know at the expiration of one year—and shall then beg to know the name of my benefactor, which I should then only feel delight in knowing when I could present to him some substantial Proof, that I have employed the tranquillity of mind, which his Kindness had enabled me to enjoy, in sincere endeavors to benefit my fellow-men, now & hereafter—

May God bless you, | &
S. T. Coleridge

659. *To Joseph Cottle*

MS. Mr. Robert G. Hopkins. Hitherto unpublished.

Novr 3 1807

My dear Cottle

I have not been once out of house, since I saw [you]—& tho' somewhat better, am still confined. If possible, I will however see you to night—I have not seen even Mrs Coleridge's Sister since.—I am compelled to send off a sum of money to day—be so good therefore as to deliver for me to the Bearer one hundred and 5£[1]—It is Mr Morgan[2]—

God bless you &
S. T. Coleridge[3]

---

[1] In 1808 Cottle wrote to De Quincey at Oxford giving him an account of the transmission of the £300 to Coleridge: 'When I paid Mr. Coleridge your three hundred pounds, he gave me the following Receipt

"November the 12th 1807.
Received from Mr. Joseph Cottle the sum
of three hundred pounds, presented to me, thro'
him, by an unknown Friend:
S. T. Coleridge
Bristol."

I had previously paid him £166. 17*s.* 2*d.*, for which he gave me an acknowledgement, but on receiving the remainder, he gave me one receipt for the whole. . . .
Altho' you restricted me . . . from mentioning your name, . . . yet *I am satisfied*
[*Notes continued opposite*]

660. *To John Ryland*[1]

Address: Revd Dr Ryland | North Street
MS. Public Library of Victoria, Melbourne, Australia. Hitherto unpublished.

Tuesday afternoon [3 November 1807][2]
Honored Sir

I have read the Numbers, you lent me, with deep Interest: some-times too much disturbed by the fear, that little can be done of permanent effect, unless the Government in India by especial favor shewn to the new Converts undermine the heart-withering Institution of Casts by creating a new one. Exile would lose part of it's Terrors, when the banished man knows that he is going to a land of Brothers, a land better than that which he quitted. But the injurious consequences of our present system of pretended Tolera-tion, i.e. of shewing to Infidels & Romanists that we ourselves think their Religion as good as our own or better—(for so they must, and to my own personal knowlege so they do, understand & construe our conduct) would furnish matter for a long Essay.—

Your own pamphlets I have perused with instruction as well as pleasure—I greatly admire President Edwards's[3] Works; but am convinced that Kant in his Critique of the pure Reason, and more popularly in his Critique of the Practical Reason has completely overthrown the edifice of Fatalism, or causative Precedence as applied to Action. I greatly regret, that my health has been such as

---

[1] John Ryland (1753–1825) was the minister of the Broadmead chapel at Bristol and president of the Baptist college there from 1793 until his death. The author of a large number of sermons, he was also a 'profound oriental scholar'.

[2] The reference in this letter to an inability 'to quit the House' closely parallels a statement in Letter 659, and they were probably written the same day.

[3] Jonathan Edwards (1703–58), the American theologian, was president of Princeton College at the time of his death.

---

that Coleridge entertains *no doubt* of the source whence the money was derived.' [MS. letter formerly in the possession of the late Miss Bairdsmith.] The original receipt which Coleridge gave to Cottle is now in the Cornell University Library.

[2] Coleridge had known John J. Morgan and his mother during his first residence in Bristol in 1795. Later Morgan married Mary Brent, whose sister, Charlotte, made her home with them. During the next few years Coleridge was on intimate terms with the Morgans and for long periods resided with them.

[3] In *Early Rec.* i. 252, Cottle reports that 'in a letter received from Mr. Coleridge, 1807, he says—speaking of his friend Mr. W.—"He is one, whom God knows, I love and honour as far beyond myself, as both morally and intellec-tually he is above me."' The rest of the letter—if there was one—has not come to light. It would seem, however, that the £105 mentioned in the present letter was intended for Wordsworth. See Letters 553 and 569 for the circumstances of a loan made in 1804, and Letter 662 for Coleridge's reference to a 'Draft' recently sent to the Wordsworths.

to make it unfit for me to quit the House, till I leave it—I have not therefore been able to procure the Shanscrit *Mss*—but I mean to write to Mr De Quincy at Oxford, unless I see him in London, and he will give instructions, I doubt not, concerning it's being sent to you for examination.

On some points of the system of Redemption, as distinguished from the doctrine of Salvation, and concerning the adoration of the second & third Persons of the Trinity *separately*, I had cherished hopes of opening my difficulties to you, alone or by letter—I trust, that I shall be permitted to revisit Bristol in the early Spring. If I can be of the least service to you in any respect in London, either as to the Press, or in procuring any Information, you will make me a pleasant Hour by commissioning me—for I respect you,

honored Sir! | with more than ordinary feelings

S. T. Coleridge

661. *To the Morgans*

Address: Mr Jno. Jas. Morgan | St James's Square | Bristol
MS. Lord Latymer. Pub. Letters, ii. *519.*
Postmark: 23 November 1807.

Hatchitt's Hotel, Piccadilly—Monday Evening
[23 November 1807]

My dear Friends!

I arrived here in safety this morning between 7 & 8, coach-stunn'd & with a cold in my head; but I had dozed away the whole night with fewer disturbances than I had reason to expect, in that sort of *whether-you-will-or-no* slumber brought upon me by the movements of the Vehicle— which I attribute to the easiness of the Mail. About one o'clock I moaned & started—and then took a wing of the fowl, & the rum—& it operated as a preventive for the after time. If very, very affectionate thoughts, wishes, recollections, anticipations, can serve instead of *Grace* before & after meat, mine was a very religious Meal—for in this sense my inmost Heart prayed *before*, *after*, and *during*.—After breakfast on attempting to clean & dress myself from crown and sole, I found myself quite unfit for any thing—& my legs were painful, rather my feet, & nothing but an horizontal posture would remove—So I got into bed—& did not get up again, till Mr Stuart called at my chamber—past 3. I have seen no one else, & therefore must defer all intelligence concerning my lectures &c to a second Letter—which you will receive in a few days, God willing, with the D'Espriella[1] &c.—

[1] Robert Southey, *Letters from England: By Don Manuel Alvarez Espriella,* 3 vols., 1807.

When I was leaving you, one of the little alleviations which I looked forward to, was that I could write with less embarrassment than I could utter in your presence the many feelings of grateful affection and most affectionate esteem toward you, that pressed upon my heart almost, as at times it seemed, with a bodily weight—but I suppose, it is yet too short a time since I left you. You are scarcely out of my eyes yet, dear Mrs M. and Charlotte.— To morrow I shall go about the portraits—I have not looked at the profile since, nor shall I till it is framed. An absence of 4 or 5 days will be a better test, how *far* it is a *likeness*.—For a day or two, farewell—my dear Friends! I bless you all three fervently—and shall I trust, as long as

I am

S. T. Coleridge.—

I shall take up my Lodgings at the Courier Office, where there is a nice suite of Rooms for me & a quiet Bedroom without expence— My address therefore, SQUIRE Coleridge, or S. T. Coleridge, Esqre, Courier office, Strand—unless you are in a sensible mood, & then you will write *Mr* Coleridge, if it were only in compassion to that poor unfortunate *Exile*, from the covers of Letters at least, despised *Mr.*—

662. *To Dorothy Wordsworth*

Address: Miss Wordsworth | Grasmere | Ambleside | Kendal | Westmoreland
MS. Dove Cottage. Hitherto unpublished. I am indebted to Miss Helen Darbishire for making a transcript of this letter, the manuscript being too fragile for photostating.
Postmark: 24 November 1807.

24 November, 1807. Tuesday. Hatchitt's Hotel, Piccadilly.

My dearest Dorothy

I arrived here yestermorning in the Bristol Mail, about 7 o/clock; but so coach-fevered, coach-crazed, that I found it proper to spend the greater part of the day in Bed. To-day I am as usual. Some three weeks ago I got wet thro', after having dined out; took a violent cold, which with the wine turning acid, brought on a slight inflammation of the Stomach & Bowels, occasioning diarrhoea & sickness, with frequent non-retention of food. I was therefore a prisoner to the House, which was luckily Mr Morgan's; where had I been a child or favorite Brother, I could not have received more affectionate attentions & indulgences. I never knew two pairs of human beings so alike, as Mrs Morgan & her Sister, Charlotte Brent, and Mary and Sara. I was reminded afresh of the resemblance every hour—& at times felt a self-reproach, that I could not love

(37)

two such amiable, pure, & affectionate Beings for their own sakes.[1]
But there is a time in Life, when the Heart stops growing.—The
Lectures at the R. Institution commence in a fortnight from yesterday—and if I live, and am in a state of health capable of being anything but a discomfort, I shall be in Grasmere in the first fortnight
of March.[2] I found Davy, this morning, in bed, very seriously unwell—and am going to sit by him this evening. He had exposed
himself to too violent alternations of Cold and Heat during the
March of Glory, which he has run for the last six weeks—within
which time by the aid and application of his own great discovery,
of the identity of electricity and chemical attractions, he has placed
all the elements and all their inanimate combinations in the power
of man; having decomposed both the Alkalies, and three of the
Earths, discovered as the base of the Alkalies a new metal, the
lightest, most malleable, and most inflammable substance in nature
—a metal of almost etherial Levity—and which burns under water
by merely being placed by the side of Sulphur. He has proved too,
that by a practicable increase of electric energy all *ponderable* compounds (in opposition to *Light & Heat*, magnetic fluid, &c) may be
decomposed, & presented simple—& recomposed thro' an infinity
of new combinations. I was told by a fellow of the *Royal Society*,
that the sensation produced last week, by the reading of his Paper
there, was more like stupor than admiration—& the more, as the
whole train of these discoveries have [has?] been the result of profound Reasoning, and in no wise of lucky accident. This account
will probably interest William—at all events, it has respited me
some half a page from writing about myself. Davy supposes that
there is only one power in the world of the senses; which in particles acts as chemical attractions, in specific masses as electricity,
& on matter in general, as planetary Gravitation. Jupiter est,
quodcumque vides; when this has been proved, it will then only
remain to resolve this into some Law of vital Intellect—and all
human Knowlege will be Science and Metaphysics the only
Science. Yet after all, unless all this be identified with Virtue, as the
ultimate and supreme Cause and Agent, all will be a worthless
Dream. For all the Tenses and all the Compounds of *Scire* will do
little for us, if they do not draw us closer to the Esse and Agere.—
    I have been indeed very unhappy since I quitted you, & have had

---

[1] On 10 Dec. 1807 Coleridge published in the *Courier* his poem, *To Two
Sisters*, over the signature Siesti. It is an affectionate tribute to Mrs. Morgan
and Miss Brent, and compares them to two other sisters, obviously Sara
Hutchinson and Mary Wordsworth. See *Poems*, i. 410.
[2] Late in 1807 the Wordsworths rented Allan Bank, in anticipation of
Coleridge's domestication with them. See *Middle Years*, i. 162–3.

ample reason for it; but I must leave it to a quieter room than that of a Coach Coffee House, to give you the detail—even if I have any right to make you uneasy. I will not say, how dearly I love you all; as perhaps it is a misfortune, that so enormous is the difference between my Love of you & of others, that it seems as if I loved nothing & nobody else. O God! has there been a single hour of my Life, even in sleep, in which I have not been blending you with my Thoughts!—

My Lectures will be profitable—and I have re-written my play— & about doubled the length of Christabel—2 thirds are finished.[1] I read Walter Scott's Lay of the Last Minstrel—& could not detect either in manner, matter, or metre, a single trace of dishonorable or avoidable Resemblance to the Christabel.[2] I am puzzled, as to how such a notion could have arisen so widely & among persons unconnected with each other, & yet the close tho' coarse Parody in the Thalaba passed unnoticed. I saw two or three very, very strong imitations of your Brother's Poems.—

I was not in the least degree inconvenienced by sending you the Draft[3]—& you may rely on receiving 50£ before Christmas— 25£ I shall send, as soon as I can find time to write a longer Letter.[4]—

My dear little darlings! John, Dorothy, Thomas!—Were I your Father, I could not dwell on you more tenderly!—May God bless you.

My dear Sister & dear dear Friend! be assured I follow you in all your feelings respecting dear Mary's Thinness, & on the other Hand that Sara is so well & so chearful.—Again, Heaven bless you all, and

S. T. Coleridge

[1] Nothing of *Christabel* beyond what Coleridge published in 1816 (Parts I and II) has survived.

[2] Cf. Letter 845, in which Coleridge admits 'the existence . . . of a number of Lines the same or nearly the same in both Authors', and asserts that 'any just ground for the Charge of "stolen feathers" ' . . . must be found in the supposed close likeness of the metre, the *movements*, the way of relating an event, in short, in the general resemblance of the great Features, which have given to the Physiognomy of Mr W. S.'s late Poems their marked originality'. Coleridge acknowledges that 'several persons . . . have been struck with this general resemblance, & have expressed themselves more or less strongly on the subject', but goes on to add: '*If* I had framed my expectations exclusively by the opinions & assertions of others, those whose expressions were most limited would have excited anticipations, which my own after Perusal of the Lay of the Last Minstrel [was] far from [verifying] to my own mind. But I will admit that of this neither I or Mr S. are or can be the proper Judges.'

[3] See Letter 659.

[4] On 1 July 1807 Dorothy Wordsworth wrote that Coleridge had been unable to repay £50 which he had borrowed from Wordsworth in April. (*Middle Years*, i. 123 and 133.) Obviously Coleridge was using the £300 gift from De Quincey to discharge his debts.

663. *To the Morgans*

Address: Mr J. J. Morgan | St James's Square | Bristol
MS. Lord Latymer. Hitherto unpublished.
Postmark: 3 December 1807.

Thursday Morning, 9 o/clock. [3 December 1807]

My dear Friends

I am arrived in safety;[1] but the Coach being quite full, all lusty men but one, & he together with one of the lusty Travellers having great Coats on, or rather *huge* Coats that ought at least to have payed half-price, I was terribly cramped, my shoulders in a pillory and my legs in the stocks—in consequence of which my feet and legs are more swoln than I ever remember them to have been on a similar occasion. The slenderest of our company was a rather well-featured young Frenchman, as I conjectured by his accent and sallow complexion; who had a livery Servant on the outside; & who seemed intent on acting the part of a young English Blood or Jockey—now riding outside, now inside—always going from one to the other by the Coach door on the wheels—& while in the Coach, eternally pulling up and down, and making a noise with, the window— a more restless monkey never played Gambols off and on the Perch, he was tied to.

Fearing that I should not find my old woman up or the parlor in order, and being much exhausted, I have stopped & breakfasted at the Gloucester Coffee House—in order to bathe my legs, and christianize myself all over. Mr Stuart left me at Knightsbridge, but I shall see him in the course of the day at the Courier Office. I do not think, that half a score sentences were interchanged from the time, we entered, to the minute of our arrival—tho' it was the Sleep of Silence, not the Silence of Sleep.

I will write you tomorrow or next day, if I can see Greenough or any other of my parliamentary Acquaintance—or have any thing to communicate worth an *unfranked* Letter.— Farewell, dear Morgan!—dear Mrs M, and dear Charlotte, be assured I am, and trust, ever shall be, with grateful esteem and brotherly attachment

your obliged Friend,
S. T. Coleridge

P.S. I wish, I had known before your relations to Mrs P. I certainly think, that there is the highest propriety in paying her all innocent attentions—and I feel, that I have been deficient.—Then too, *your* face, dear Miss B., is a sad tell-tale—and Mrs M's not the

---

[1] Coleridge returned twice to Bristol before he settled down for several months in London. See Letters 662 and 666.

tightest Strong-box of her inward feelings, that I have seen in the course of my Life.

664. *To Robert Southey*

Address: R. Southey, Esqre. | Greta Hall | Keswick | Cumberland   *Single*
MS. Lord Latymer. Pub. with omis. Letters, *ii. 520.*
Postmark: 14 December 1807.

[14 December 1807]

My dear Southey

I have been confined to my bed room, & with exceptions of a few hours each night, to my bed for near a week past—having once ventured out, & suffered in consequence. My complaint a low bilious fever. Whether contagion or sympathy, I know not; but I had it hanging about me from the time, I was with Davy—it went off however by a journey, which I took with Stuart, to Bristol, in a cold frosty air—Soon after my return, Mr Ridout informed me from Drs Babbington & Bailly,[1] that Davy was not only ill, but his Life precarious, his recovery doubtful. And to this day no distinct symptom of Safety has appeared—tho', to day, he is better. I cannot express what I have suffered—Good heaven! in the very spring tide of his Honors— his? his Country's! the World's! after discoveries more intellectual, more ennobling and impowering human Nature, than Newton's! But he must not die.—I am so much better that I shall go out tomorrow, if I awake no worse than I go to sleep. Be so good as to tell Mrs Coleridge, that I will write to her either Tuesday or Wednesday; and to Hartley & Derwent, with whose Letters I was much both amused & affected. I was with H. & Mrs W. & Mr J. in spirit, at their meeting.—Howel's Bill I have paid, tell Mrs C. (for this is what she will be most anxious about)—and that I *had* no other Debt at all weighing upon me either prudentially or from sense of propriety or delicacy till the one, I shall mention after better subjects: in the tail of this Letter.

I very thoroughly admired your Letter to W. Scott, concerning the Edingburgh R.[2] The feeling & the resolve are what any one knowing you half as well as I, must have anticipated, in any case where

---

[1] William Babington (1756–1833) and Matthew Baillie (1761–1823).

[2] Scott had written to Southey, urging him to consider writing for the *Edinburgh Review* and offering to intercede with Jeffrey, the editor. Southey refused on the grounds of political divergence from Jeffrey and disapproval of that sort of bitterness in criticism 'which tends directly to wound a man in his feelings, and injure him in his fame and fortune'. *Life and Corres.* iii. 122–5. See E. L. Griggs, 'Robert Southey and the *Edinburgh Review*', *Modern Philology*, Aug. 1932, pp. 101–3, for Southey's letter to Coleridge on the subject.

you had room for 10 minutes thinking, and relatively to any person, with regard to whom old affection & belief of injury & unworthy conduct had made none of those mixtures, which perplex the brains of the best men, none but good men having the component drugs, or at least the drugs in that state of composition—*but* it is admirably expressed—if I had meant only *well* exprest, I should [have] said, *and* it is well exprest—but to my feeling it is an unusual specimen of honorable feeling supporting itself by sound Sense and conveyed with simplicity, dignity, and a warmth evidently under the complete control of the Understanding. I am a fair Judge, as to such a sentence—for from morbid wretchedness of mind I have been in a far, far greater excess, indifferent about what is said, written, or supposed, concerning me or my compositions, than W. can have been even supposed to be interested respecting his—and the Edingburgh R. I have not seen for years, & never more than 4 or 5 numbers.—As to reviewing W's Poems, my sole objection would rest on the *time* of the publication of the Annual Review. Davy's Illness has put off the commencement of my Lectures to the middle of January—they are to consist of at least 20 Lectures—& the subject of modern Poetry occupies the last 3 or 4. Now I do not care, in how many forms my sentiments are printed; if only I do not defraud my Hirers by causing my lectures to be anticipated. I would not review them at all, unless I could do it systematically, and with the whole strength of my mind—and when I do, I shall express my convictions of the faults & defect[s] of the Poems & System, as plainly as of the excellencies. It has been my constant reply to those who have charged me with Bigotry, &c—While you can perceive no excellencies, it is my duty to appear conscious of no defects—because even tho' I should agree with you in the instances, I should only confirm you in what I deem a pernicious error, as our principle of disapprobation must necessarily be different.—In my Lectures I shall speak out of Rogers, Campbell, yourself (i.e. Madoc & Thalaba; for I shall speak only of *Poems* not of Poets) & Wordsworth, as plainly as of Milton, Dryden, Pope, &c.—In my next I will tell you an amusing Anecdote of Dr Stock relatively to W's Poems——

I did not overhugely admire the Lay of the last Minstrel; but saw no likeness whatsoever to the Christabel, much less any improper resemblance.

I heard by accident that Dr Stoddart had arrived, a few days ago—& wrote him a letter expostulating with him for his unkindness in having detained, for years, my Books & *MSS*—& stating the great Loss it had been to me—a Loss not easy to be calculated —I have as witnesses, T. Poole, & Squire Ackland (who calls me, infallible Prophet) that from the information contained in them, tho' I could not dare trust my recollection sufficiently for the Press, I foretold distinctly *every* event that has happened of Importance, with one which has not *yet* happened, the evacuation of Sicily.— This however of course I did not write to Dr S.—but simply requested, he would send me my chests. In return, I received yesterday an abusive letter, confirming what I suspected, that he is writing a book himself—in this he conjures up an indefinite Debt, customs, and some old affair before I went to Malta, amounting to more than 50£ (the customs 25£, all of which I should have had remitted, if he had sent them according to his promise)— and informing me that when I send a person properly documented to settle this account, that person may then take away my Goods.[1] —This I shall do tomorrow—tho' without the least pledge that I shall receive all that I left, & tho' all the prints [and] Mss have been exposed in Dr St.'s house month after month.—This will prevent my sending Mrs C. any money for 3 weeks—I mean, exclusive of the 150£,[2] which, assure her, is & for the future will remain, sacred to her.—By Wallis's [ingrati]tude to Allston I lost 30£ in *Customs*— by my Brother's insulting act[ion all] the expences up & down of my family— so it has bee[n a ba]ddish year; but I am not disquieted.—

S. T. C.

Poor Godwin is going to the Dogs, I fear—he has a Tragedy to come out on Wednesday.[3]—I will write again to you in a few days. After my Lectures I would willingly undertake any Review with you—because I shall then have given my Code. I omit other parts of your Letter, not that they interested me less; but because I have no room—& am too much exhausted to take up a second Sheet. God bless you! My kisses to your little ones—& love to your Wife.—

The only vindictive idea, I have to Dr St., is the anticipation of shewing his Letter to Sir Alexander Ball!! O the folly of sinning against our first & pure Impressions!—It is the Sin against *our own* Ghost, at least.

[1] A fragment of Stoddart's letter, dated 12 Dec. 1807 and preserved at Dove Cottage, confirms Coleridge's statement.
[2] i.e. the Wedgwood annuity.
[3] Godwin's *Faulkener* was produced at Drury Lane on 16 Dec. 1807.

665. *To Richard Sharp*

Address: R. Sharpe, Esqre. M.P. | 17, Mark Lane
MS. Cornell University Lib. Pub. E. L. G. i. 388.
Postmark: 18 December 1807.

348, Strand.
Friday Noon [18 December 1807]

My dear Sir

A most afflicting Instance of Distress has this moment been before my eyes—a woman, the widow of a once respectable Citizen, Brewman,[1] the printer & part proprietor, I believe, of a then celebrated paper, who was left 20 or 25 years ago, with a family of children—this woman was after this elected as a Nurse to one of the Wards in Christ's Hospital, at the time that I was an upper boy there—and from her I received the greatest tenderness, a tenderness, which God knows! I had never received before, even from my own family. This poor Woman, from no other fault than that of too much good-nature, by an act of great severity was sacrificed to a Rule just then made, & sent away from her place—with not the least Imputation on her moral character—Since then she has been struggling on, thro' various scenes of distress—I first heard of her a few years ago—just before I went to Malta—and sent her such assistance, as my own embarrassments permitted. Since then her distresses have come to a height of wretchedness, that I—living so much in the country—had no notion that Poverty could rise to. Of course, what I could do, I have done; but a few pounds is gone in a week or so. But if I could exert interest enough to get her into one of the many alms houses in or about London, I should not only be gratified on my own account; but in a much higher degree happy, as in the removal of distress so very shocking.—Having been the Wife of a Citizen, and acquainted with most of the famous political Writers at that time, she seems to have an additional claim too—If such a thing should be in your power, be assured, my dear Sir! that I shall place it among my own especial obligations—&—for I trust, we are both *superstitious* enough to attribute a *charm* at least to the prayers & blessings of a wretched widow—you will have indeed most fervent prayers offered up by her.—I know, how many applications you must have—yet you will at least excuse the present—and believe me, my dear Sir!

with esteem & affectionate admiration, | Your Friend & Servant,
S. T. Coleridge

[1] Presumably D. Brewman, publisher of the short-lived *British Mercury and Evening Advertiser*, 1780.

(44)

666. *To the Morgans*

Address: Mr J. J. Morgan | St James's Square | Bristol
MS. Lord Latymer. Pub. E. L. G. i. 390.
Postmark: 14 January 1808.

348, Strand.
Thursday Noon—[14 January 1808]

My dear Friends

I arrived at the Gloster yesterday morning something more than
an hour after the usual Time, having had a most unpleasant journey
owing to a succession of vicious Horses. The moonlight, tho' not
always of the clearest, lessened the danger, which in a dark night
would have been very serious. My companions were, a youth going
to the artillery School at Woolwich, a mannish Kilcrop—a Colonel
Peacock, the Brother of the Barrack master at Malta, not held
there in high honor from his countenancing General Villettes' In-
timacies with his wife, Lady Dallan's Daughter—this Colonel, a
free & easy proud Fool—very remarkably stupid & uninformed—
and a third—Gentleman or Merchant—whose jokes & general conversation made it charitable toward human Nature to hope, that
his Mother had borne and reared him in a Brothel—all three with
enormous Great Coats.—From being twice obliged to get out in the
Rain, and from the very great confinement of my limbs, I was more
than ordinarily unwell yesterday Morning. However after having
attended Mr Dibdin's Lecture at the R. Institution,[1] I accompanied
Dr Calcott to a sort of Glee or Catch Club, composed wholly of professional Singers—and was much delighted—Bartleman, Harrison,
Cooke, Greatorix, Smith, were the principal Singers—Webb,[2] the
patriarch of the Club, and Father of Catches & Glees in this
Country, was present, & I was much interested by his affectionate
chearfulness under his grievous Burthen of Age & Infirmities—as
well as by the reverential affection payed to him by all the others:
& Bartleman & Harrison pleased me as much as Men as they did of
course as Singers. They either were, or were polite enough all to
appear to be, marvellously delighted with me; & all the musical
Entertainments of the Town are open to me without expence.—

[1] Thomas F. Dibdin (1776–1847) made a public announcement of Davy's
illness at his Introductory Lecture. See John Davy, *Memoirs of the Life of Sir
Humphry Davy*, 2 vols., 1836, i. 387–9.

[2] The musicians with whom Coleridge spent the evening were John W.
Callcott (1766–1821), James Bartleman (1769–1821), Samuel Harrison (1760–
1812), Robert Cooke (1768–1814), Thomas Greatorex (1758–1831), John
Stafford Smith (1750–1836), and Samuel Webbe (1740–1816).

My own Lecture commences to morrow—till that is over, I can think of nothing else—only that I am, my dear Friends,

most affectionately & earnestly | Yours

S. T. Coleridge

667. *To Mrs. J. J. Morgan*

Address: Mrs Morgan | St James's Square | Bristol
MS. Lord Latymer. Pub. with omis. Letters, *ii. 524.*
Postmark: 25 January 1808.

348, Strand.

Friday Morning—[22] Jan. 1808.—

Dear and honoured Mary

Having had you continually, I may almost say, present to me in my dreams, and always appearing as a compassionate Comforter therein, appearing, in short, as your own dear Self, most innocent and full of love,—I feel a strong impulse to address a letter to *you* by name, tho' it equally respects all my three friends. If it had been told me on that evening, when dear Morgan was asleep in the Parlour, and you and beloved Caroletta asleep at opposite Corners of the Sopha in the Drawing Room, of which I occupied the center in a state of blessed half-consciousness, as a drowsy Guardian of your Slumbers;—if it had been then told me, that, in less than a fortnight, the time should come when I should not wish to be with you, or wish you to be with me, I should have *out* with one of Caroletta's harmless *'condemn its!'* commonly pronounced, *damn it! 'that's no truth!'*—And yet since Friday Evening, my lecture having made an impression far beyond it's worth or my expectation, I have been in such a state of wretchedness, confined to my bed, in such almost continued pain of Stomach & Bowels, the strongest purgatives proving ineffectual & seeming only to increase the horrid *sickness*, to which every food, I force myself to take, only serves as fuel—that I have been content to see no one but the unloveable old Woman, as feeling that I should only receive a momently succession of Pangs from the presence of those who giving no pleasure would make my wretchedness appear almost unnatural—even as if the Fire should cease to warm. Who would not rather shiver on an ice-mount than freeze before the fire which had used to spread comfort thro' his fibres, & thoughts of social joyance thro' his Imagination?—Yet even thus, yet even *from* this feeling that your Society would be an Agony, O I know, I feel, how I love you, my dear Sisters & Friends!

I have been obliged of course to put off my lecture of to day—a

most painful necessity—for I disappoint some hundreds!—I have
sent for Abernethie,[1] who has restored Mr Dequincy to Health!
Could I have foreseen my present state, I would have staid at
Bristol, & taken Lodgings at Clifton, in order to be within the power
of being seen by you, without being a domestic nuisance—for still,
still I feel the comfortlessness of seeing no face, hearing no voice,
feeling no hand that is dear—tho' conscious that the pang would
outweigh the Solace.—

When finished, let the two Dresses &c be sent to me—but if my
Illness should have a complete conclusion, of me as well as of itself,
(and there seems to be a direct inflammation of the mesentery) then
let them be sent to Grasmere—for Mrs Wordsworth & Miss Hutchinson—gay dresses indeed for a mourning.

I write in great pain—but yet I deem, whatever become of me,
that it will hereafter be a soothing Thought to you that in sickness
or in health, in hope or in despondency I have thought of you with
love & esteem & gratitude—My dear Mary! dear Charlotte!—May
Heaven bless you! With such a Wife, & such a Sister, my friend is
already blest! May Heaven give him Health, & elastic Spirits, to
enjoy these & all other Blessings!

Once more, bless you, bless you! Ah who is there to bless

S. T. Coleridge?

P.S. Sunday Night.—I do not know when this Letter was written
—probably, *Thursday* morning, not Wednesday, as I have said in
my letter to John.[2] I have opened this by means of the steam of the
Tea kettle, merely to say, that I have—I know not how or where—lost
the pretty Shirt Pin, Charlotte gave me—I promise her solemnly,
never to accept one from any other—& never to wear one hereafter
as long as I live: so that the sense of it's real Absence shall make a
sort of imaginary Presence to me. I am more vexed at the accident
than I ought to be; but had it been either of your Locks of Hair, or
her Profile (which must be by force of association *your* Profile too—
& a far more efficacious one—than that done for you, which had no
other merit than that of having *no* likeness *at all*—& this certainly
is a sort of negative advantage) I should have fretted myself into
superstition, & been haunted with it as by an omen.—Of the Lady
and her poetical Daughter I had never before heard even the name.
O these are Shadows—!—and all my literary Admirers & Flatterers, as well as Despisers & Calumniators, pass over my Heart as

---

[1] Coleridge apparently did not consult the surgeon, John Abernethy (1764–
1831), at this time, since he was seeking an introduction in 1810. See Letters
810 and 812.

[2] This letter has not come to light. On the address sheet Coleridge numbered
the present letter '2' and noted, 'To be read *after* the other'.

the images of Clouds over dull Ice—so far from being retained, they are scarcely made visible there.—But I love you, dear Ladies! substantially—& pray do write at least a line in Morgan's Letter, if neither will write me a whole one—to comfort me by the assurance that you remember me with esteem & some affection. Most affectionately have you & Charlotte treated me—& most gratefully do I remember it. Good night, good night!

668. *To Thomas De Quincey*

Address: T. De Quincey, Esqre. | No. 5 Northumberland Street | Mary bone
MS. Editor. Pub. E. L. G. i. 422.

[*Circa* 25 January 1808][1]

My dear De Quincey

If you should meet with Hermann de Emendatione[2] &c, in the course of a month or two (for I shall certainly not want it for two or three months, even if my Life be continued to me) and it be procurable at any decent price, be so good as to secure it for me. As likewise Longus, Heliodorus, & D'Orville's Chariton. But here I must be distinctly understood—I asked the New Testament from a sincere Desire to have the best good book, as a $Mνημόσυνον$ $ἀντὶ$ $Mνημοσ[ύνου]$—in all the rest, you must consent to be my Commissioner—which when I have better health, I will gladly be for you. I do not want any of these books except Hermann's Hymns,[3] for Months—

And now permit me, my dear young friend! to do Justice to myself as to one part of a character which has not many *positive* bad points in it, tho' in a moral *marasmus* from negatives—from misdemeanours of Omission, and from Weakness & moral cowardice of moral Pain—But I can affirm with a *sense* of *certainty* intuitively distinguished from a mere delusive *feeling* of *Positiveness*, that no man, I have ever known, is less affected by partiality to his own productions or thoughts. It would have been indeed far, far better for me—in some little degree perhaps for society—if I could have attached more importance, greater warmth of feeling, to my own Writings. But I have not been happy enough for that.—So however it is, that the pleasure, the sincere pleasure, of receiving that

---

[1] Writing to Dorothy Wordsworth on 25 Mar. 1808, De Quincey says he did not know of Coleridge being in town until several days after the first lecture of 15 Jan. (H. A. Eaton, *Thomas De Quincey*, 1936, p. 142.) De Quincey had seen Coleridge by 22 Jan. (see Letter 667), and this letter must have been written not long afterwards.

[2] J. G. J. Hermann, *De emendanda ratione Graecae grammaticae*, 1801.

[3] *Homeri hymni et epigrammata*, ed. J. G. J. Hermann, 1806.

proof of friendship—'I cannot say, that this or that satisfied me—
I did not like this for such and such reasons—it appeared to me
slight, not the genuine *Stuff*' &c has often blinded me so far as to
believe at once, & for a long season, more meanly of what I had
done, than after-experience confi[rmed.] I do therefore earnestly
ask of you as a proof of Friendship, that you will so far get over
your natural modesty & timidity, as without reserve or withholding
to tell me exactly what you think and feel on the perusal of any
thing, I may submit to you—for even if it be only your feelings,
they will be valuable to me—far more indeed than those criticisms,
in which the feeling is not stated, & mere objections made, which
being weak have in one or 2 instances prevented my perception of
real defects—which I should soon have discovered if it had been
said to me—there is something amiss in this! I feel it—perhaps, it
may be *so* & *so*—perhaps not; but something I feel amiss.—
God bless you! Be assured of my unfeigned esteem.

S. T. Coleridge.

When I am tolerably recovered, in case of no relapse, I will on the
first opportunity make the Party, we spoke of.

669. *To J. J. Morgan*

Address: Mr J. J. Morgan | St James's Square | Bristol
MS. Lord Latymer. Hitherto unpublished.

Monday afternoon [1 February 1808]

My dear Friend

I must not dare henceforth stir out of doors except in a close
Coach, till the Weather have become a little vernal—Within an
hour after I had sent off my last to you, I had a relapse of the most
dangerous kind—for 48 hours I was not completely relieved, and
for the first 24 the inflammation of the Bowels and Stomach was so
violent, as to occasion an alarm of convulsions—and my medical
attendant saw himself obliged to quiet for awhile the inordinate
action by Hensbane—the latter half of the attack was much milder,
tho' I could not bear the pressure even of a finger on my stomach,
and the lower evacuations were so acrid, as to strip the viscera of
the mucus that cloathes them, & the pain such that my shirt and
under shirt were wet thro' with the violence of the perspiration—
All yesterday I was calm & easy and unusually light; but I was
obliged to keep my bed still all da[y], because it was feared that the
mere pressure of my body on my bowels, stoopingly as weakness
compels me to sit, might re-produce an inflammatory state. Last

night I had a sound sleep—& I got up a little after midday—and feel myself comfortable—and my hands tremble less than they did before this last Relapse. With unsleeping attention I shall probably get over this, nay, be the better for it, both mind and body; but I have sad bodings, of something worse. In short, I suspect calculus. —But enough for the Day is the Evil thereof.—

I have no sort of recollection about the money-bills, as I never keep any account—I hope, the Worthy is not such a Glutton in Roguery, as to swallow two Joints at one Bolt. Peace go with him, unless Disquiet might make him honester.

If you see Southey—and this is indeed my reason for writing to you so soon, having nothing to say but the old dull tale about my own Sufferings—give my kindest remembrance to him, and beg him from me to pass thro' Town on his Return—the small difference in the number of miles will be compensated by the greater convenience of the Conveyances, and I earnestly wish to see him.

I will find out from Byrne, the Editor of the Morning Post, who this Miss Laura *Temple*[1] *is*. I have my *suspicions*, that I have heard of this young Lady under another name. You will of course return her the latter answer, that I sent.

Mr Frend, who has been under a sort of positive engagement to Miss Hayes for a great number of years, has married suddenly,[2] and informed her of it in a dry letter without comment—so poor Miss Hayes is 'still sighing for the domestic state', and sits in poetic despair another Ariadne bewailing the perfidy of another Theseus. She makes out a very black story of it. It is a sad Quandary, when a man must prove himself either a great Rogue, or a monstrous Fool—I suppose, Frend would say, I can repent of the one and *live*; but in the other I should only live to repent.—

The most flattering Compliment I have received for a long time was from my old woman[3]—During my illness a Mr Lanseer[4] (an Engraver, I hear, who lectured last Season at the *R. Inst:*, but was dismissed for personal Invectives against Boydell) called; but of course could not see me—Indeed, no one was admitted. When a little recovered, seeing his Card among many others I asked the old

[1] Laura Sophia Temple published *Poems* in 1805 and *Lyric and Other Poems* in 1808.

[2] William Frend (1757–1841) married a Miss Blackburne in 1808. See Letter 11.

[3] Mrs. Brainbridge. De Quincey says he often saw Coleridge 'shouting from the attics of the "Courier" office, down three or four flights of stairs, to a certain "Mrs. Brainbridge", his sole attendant, whose dwelling was in the subterranean regions of the house'. *The Collected Writings of Thomas De Quincey*, ed. David Masson, 14 vols., 1889, ii. 188–9.

[4] John Landseer (1769–1852).

woman, who is Mr Lanseer (for I had never heard the *name* before).
I am sure, I don't know (replies she) but from what he said, I guess,
he is a sort of a *Methody Preacher* at that Unstintution, where you
goes to *spout*, Sir.

I have been interrupted—and besides, having had occasion to
talk a good deal—am weak & in low spirits.— O would to Heaven
you, and dearest Mary & Charlotte were within a few Streets of
me—

God bless you | and | Your sincere Friend
S. T. Coleridge

670. *To Thomas De Quincey*

Address: T. De Quincey, Esqre | No /5 Northumberland Street | Mary bone
*MS. formerly in the possession of the late Miss Bairdsmith. Pub. with omis.
E. L. G. i. 396.*
Postmark: 3 February 1808.

Tuesday Night. [2 February 1808] 348, Strand.

Dear De Quincey

I have suffered considerable alarm at not having seen you for so
many days: lest you should be ill, or malaccident have befallen you.
I myself have had a Relapse of a very fearful menace. Having
walked to and from Lambe's to procure his Mss selections from the
Dramatists of the Age of Shakspeare,[1] I stopped in our Office below to look over the Courier: and altho' I could not have stayed
above five minutes, yet (in some small part perhaps the wetness of
the Newspaper might have been the $Κακοδαίμων$ $Κακοδαιμονίζων$, as
actual or predisposing cause or both) the street-damp struck up
from my Shoes to my Bowels, and passed like a poison-flash thro'
my nervous system—A violent Inflammation of the Bowels ensued, the Stomach became inflamed by Sympathy, and for four
and twenty hours I suffered from acrid scalding evacuations, and
if possible worse Vomitings (for the latter were accompanied with
more than mere bodily torture) as much suffering as could well, I
think, be compressed into that space of Time.—At length Symptoms of Convulsion threatened me: and by the advice of the
medical attendant I took Hensbane with diminished doses of the
Rhubarb and magnesia. The Prescription answered it's purpose—&
I had both Sleep and quiet—On Saturday the Sickness had ceased,
and the diarrhoea more benignant—and soon ceased altogether.
But so weak was I, and my whole Inside so sore, that I could not
bear the touch of my own finger on any part of the Stomach or

[1] Lamb's *Specimens of English Dramatic Poets* appeared in July 1808.

Abdomen, and I was desired & indeed found myself almost compelled to continue in bed till Monday Morning with the interval of
about an hour each evening while the bed was remaking, in order to
prevent the pressure on the viscera from the weight of the upright
Trunk—as I could not sit otherwise than bow-bent, like an old
Gardener.—All yesterday & today, thank Heaven! I have not only
remained convalescent, but gather strength, and write less trem-
blingly than I did before this Relapse. But alas! I have gloomy
apprehensions of something still worse in my System—I suspect
either the Stone (one of those Calculi which soft and without angles
affects the system chiefly by it's weight)—or at least some morbid
Affection of the Bladder. If it prove to be so— (and I CANNOT bring
myself to the shocking operation of being examined for it, from the
same kind of feeling or false shame, but greater in degree, that
brought my Life twice or more in Hazard on board Ship, from the
encreasing Horror on my mind of submitting to the Clyster—there
being on board no instrument which the Patient might administer
myself [himself?], & it requiring the whole exerted Strength of the
Captain to effect it.) If it be so, if the various Symptoms, which
have haunted me, I scarce know how long, do not disappear on
using exercise—which I cannot do till the weather is quite settled
either into warm, or frosty, fair weather—I shall begin a course of
alkaline Dissolvents—and if they do nothing, I must sacrifice as
meekly as I may τῷ Βιοθανάτῳ Λιθοτεμνονέμῳ [*sic*] (for I believe the
Reflex Form is more appropriate in this case than either the purely
active or purely passive.) O would to heaven! (depressing as this
Suspicion has been to me) Yet would to Heaven! that I had to
utter no less tolerable groans!—There is a passage in Jer. Taylor's
Holy Dying, at the conclusion of one of the earlier Chapters, of
transcendent pathos and eloquence, which my last Sentence recalled to my recollection.—

I write however not to trouble your feelings with useless concern
—indeed, I had not the most distant intention of doing so or even
Thought, till I had already written it, from blind Instinct of the
Heart's Weakness—but first and chiefly to ascertain whether any
worse cause has prevented my seeing you than the distance, the
weather, or pre-occupation—and secondly, to say that (no Relapse
happening to make it absolutely impracticable, or other cause
equivalent) I shall give my Lecture on Friday Afternoon, two
o'clock[1]—& that an admission Ticket will be left for you with the
Door-keeper, unless I hear from you that you cannot come. Should
this be [the] case (quod Di avertant!—relatively, of course, to the

---

[1] Coleridge's second lecture was delivered at the Royal Institution on
Friday, 5 Feb.

occasion not the effect)—be so good as to let me have a Line from you immediately—This indeed I request at all events, for—I do not [know] why—probably from my own low spirits & general Languor of heart—I have had Bodings utterly out of all Proportion to the small number of Days that you have been absent.—I have neither written to or heard from Grasmere for a long time. Should you have occasion to write, you will remember me to them, & that I hope to write soon. I have had to begin such a volume of Letters to them dolefully, that I myself feel an insupportable Disgust by anticipative Sympathy, that I shrink away like a cowed dog from the Task of adding to the number—and having nothing of Joy to communicate to them I would rather they should hear of the contrary from others than from myself. That there is such a man in the World, as Wordsworth, and that such a man enjoys such a Family, makes both Death & my inefficient Life a less grievous Thought to me.—Believe me your's with affectionate Esteem,

S. T. Coleridge

671. *To Mrs. S. T. Coleridge*

MS. Victoria University Lib. Hitherto unpublished. This fragment, on the opposite side of which Coleridge wrote a brief note in the margin to his son Hartley, is all that remains of a letter probably written from London early in 1808. See next letter.

[Early 1808]

. . . man, of . . . love & be a father to the chi[ldren] . . . Enough of serious matters—which will cease to appear hypochondriacal to you sooner than many would wish. Do not think me capable of the abject Baseness of writing words calculated only either to irritate or agitate. I assure you, *on* . . . Brother, besides . . .
. . . [be]tter written by Colerid[ge] . . I will merely send you from vexation about deserved Fame.—Your account of H . . .[1]

672. *To Hartley Coleridge*

MS. Victoria University Lib. Hitherto unpublished.

[Early 1808]

Dear Hartley

I am very, very busy, and for your sake, and that of Derwent and Sara, and my Wife, your dear dear Mother. But soon I will write to you, and, I pray God! that in less than two months I shall be and

[1] *This* I cannot spare. [Note by Mrs. Coleridge written in this manuscript and obviously referring to the next letter.]

remain with you. Meantime, my dear, anxiously beloved Child—
make your Mother happy—think of God—& what *worms* we all are,
& how likely to be wrong in any case, how sure to be wrong in
many.

S. T. C.

673. *To Charles Lamb*

MS. Harvard College Lib. Pub. Notes and Queries, *7 August 1852, p. 117.* This
letter and the one following were written in the fly-leaves of the second volume
of Samuel Daniel's *Poetical Works,* 2 vols., 1718. The work was annotated by
both Charles Lamb and Coleridge; Lamb's notes run through the two volumes,
whereas Coleridge's annotations are found in volume two only and refer solely
to the *Civil Wars.* They were published in full for the first time by C. C. Seronsy,
'Coleridge Marginalia in Lamb's Copy of Daniel's *Poetical Works*', *Harvard
Library Bulletin,* Winter 1953, p. 105.

Tuesday, Feb. 10 [9], 1808. (10th or 9th.)

Dear Charles
   I think more highly, far more, of the 'Civil Wars', than you
seemed to do, on Monday night, Feb. 9th 1808—the Verse does not
teize *me*; and all the while I am reading it, I cannot but fancy a
plain England-loving English Country Gentleman with only some
dozen Books in his whole Library, and at a time when a 'Mercury'
or 'Intelligencer' was seen by him once in a month or two, making
this his Newspaper & political Bible at the same time—& reading
it so often as to store his Memory with it's aphorisms. Conceive a
good man of that kind, diffident and passive, yet *rather* inclined to
Jacobitism; seeing the reasons of the Revolutionary Party, yet by
disposition and old principles leaning, in quiet nods and sighs at his
own parlour fire, to the hereditary Right—(and of these characters
there must have been many)—& then read this poem assuming in
your heart his character—conceive how grave he would look, and
what pleasure there would be, what unconscious, harmless, humble
Self-conceit, self-compliment in his gravity; how *wise* he would feel
himself—& yet after all, how forbearing, how much calmed by that
most calming reflection (when it is really the mind's own reflection)
—aye! it was just so in Henry the 6th's Time—always the same
passions at work—&c—. Have I injured thy Book—? or wilt thou
like it the better there*fore*? But I have done as I would gladly be
done by—*thee*, at least.[1]

S. T. Coleridge

[1] Writing to Coleridge on 7 June 1809, Lamb refers to the '"Daniel," enriched with manuscript notes', and goes on to 'wish every book I have were so
noted. They have thoroughly converted me to relish Daniel, or to say I relish

674. *To Charles Lamb*

MS. Harvard College Lib. Pub. Notes and Queries, *7 August 1852, p. 118.*

[9 February 1808]

Second Letter—5 hours after the First.

Dear Charles

You must read over these Civil Wars again. We both know what a *mood* is. And the genial mood will, it shall come, for my sober-minded Daniel. He was a Tutor and a sort of Steward in a noble Family in which Form was religiously observed and Religion formally; & yet there was such warm blood & mighty muscle of sub- stance within, that the moulding Irons did not distort tho' they stiffened the vital man within. Daniel caught & recommunicated the Spirit of the great Countess of Pembroke, the glory of the North —he *formed* her mind, & her mind inspirited him. Gravely sober in all ordinary affairs, & not easily excited by any—yet there is one, in which his Blood boils—whenever he speaks of English Valour exerted against a foreign Enemy. Do read over—but some evening when I am quite comfortable, at your fire-side—& O! where shall I ever be, if I am not so there—that is the last Altar, on the horns [of] which my old Feelings hang, b[ut] alas! listen & tremble—Nonsense!—well! I will read it to you & Mary—the 205, 206 and 207th page—[1] above all, that 93rd* Stanza[2]—What is there in description

him, for, after all, I believe I did relish him. You well call him sober-minded. [See Letter 674.] Your notes are excellent.' *Lamb Letters,* ii. 75.

Later, in 'The Two Races of Men', Lamb says:

Reader, if haply thou art blessed with a moderate collection, be shy of showing it; or if thy heart overfloweth to lend them, lend thy books; but let it be to such a one as S.T.C.—he will return them (generally anticipating the time appointed) with usury; enriched with annotations, tripling their value. I have had experience. Many are these precious MSS. of his—(in *matter* oftentimes, and almost in *quantity* not unfrequently, vying with the originals)— in no very clerkly hand—legible in my Daniel; . . . I counsel thee, shut not thy heart, nor thy library, against S.T.C.

The Works of Charles and Mary Lamb, ed. E. V. Lucas, 7 vols., 1903, ii. 26.

[1] Book VI, Stanzas lxxxvii–xcvi.

* and in a different style, the 98th Stanza, p. 208: & what an Image in 107, p. 211.—Thousands even of educated men would become more sensible; fitter to be members of Parliament, or Ministers, by reading Daniel—and even those few, who quoad intellectum only gain refreshment of notions already their own, must become better Englishmen. O if it be not too late, write a kind note about him—[Note by] S. T. Coleridge.

[2]   Whil'st *Talbot* (whose fresh ardor hauing got
          A meruailous aduantage of his yeares)
          Carries his vnfelt age, as if forgot,
          Whirling about, where any need appeares:
          His hand, his eye, his wits all present, wrought

superior even in Shakspere? only that Shakespere would have given one of his *Glows* to the first Line, and flatter'd the mountain Top with his sovran Eye[1]—instead of that poor 'a marvellous advantage of his Years'—but this however is Daniel—and he must not be read piecemeal. Even by turning off, & looking at a Stanza by itself, I find the loss.

S. T. Coleridge—

O Charles! I am *very very* ill. Vixi.

Is it from any hobby-horsical Love of our old writers (& of such a passion respecting Chaucer, Spenser, & Ben Jonson['s] Poems I have occasionally seen glaring proofs in one, the string of whose Shoe I am not worthy to unloose) or is it a real Beauty—the interspersion, I mean, (in stanza poems) of rhymes from polysyllables—such as Eminence, Obedience, Reverence?[2] To my ear they convey not only a relief from variety, but a *sweetness* as of repose—and the Understanding they gratify by reconciling Verse with the whole wide extent of good Sense. Without being distinctly conscious of such a Notion, having it rather than reflecting it (for one may think in the same way as one may see & hear) I seem to be made to know, that I need have no fear; that there's nothing excellent in itself which the Poet cannot express accurately & naturally—nay, no good word.—

675. *To Robert Southey*

Address: R. Southey, Esqre. | Greta Hall | Keswick | Cumberland   If Mr S. have left Keswick, it need not be forwarded.
MS. *Lord Latymer. Pub. E. L. G. i. 398.*
Postmark: 10 February 1808.

Dear Southey					Tuesday, Feb. 10th [9], 1808

I received this afternoon your head piece to Mrs Coleridge's Letter, which, as usual, she has not dated. I certainly only meant by

> The function of the glorious Part he beares:
> Now vrging here, now cheering there, he flyes,
> Vnlockes the thickest troups, where most force lyes.

(*The Complete Works in Verse and Prose of Samuel Daniel*, ed. A. B. Grosart, 5 vols., 1885, ii. 248.)

[1] Sonnet 33. Coleridge cites the line in *Biog. Lit.* ii. 17.

[2] Across the top of the page containing this second letter to Lamb, Coleridge wrote: 'p. 217. V. a fine Stanza.' He refers to Book VII, Stanza 5:

> Whether it be, that Forme, and Eminence,
> Adorn'd with Pomp and State, begets this awe:
> Or, whether an in-bred obedience
> To Right and Powre, doth our affections drawe:
> Or, whether sacred Kings worke reuerence,
> And make that Nature now, which was first Law,
> We know not: but, the Head will draw the Parts;
> And good Kings, with our bodies, haue our harts.

my statement of the Difficulty that prest on me respecting a Review of the Poems, to draw forth your advice—and as far as I can recollect asked, as one main datum of the Solution, at what time the Annual was published.¹ But it is probable, that I wrote confusedly, my health even then being far worse than I suffered to be known. However, I wrote soon after my first arrival in town, almost immediately to Longman—& a second time—but received no answer. He treats me cavalierly enough; and tho' I have never wronged him except by disappointing his expectations, yet having done that, I deserve no better of him—or rather, he treats me more civilly than I deserve—& I should be in perfect Charity with him, & that Jew with the Presbyterian name, his Partner—aye—*Rees* I mean—if I could get rid of the more than suspicion, that with all his professed—nay, and I believe, sincere, Regard for you—esteem, as far [as] such a nature is susceptible of such a feeling, he entertains for you beyond doubt—that he has not made fair and liberal Bargains with you. You are the last man in the World, whom I should presume to advise—but for myself, I would rather give a work away than nominally sell it for a share of the net profits. A happy word, that *net* profits—it must be large Fish with a vengeance, such as the Lay of the Last Minstrel, or Pleasures of Memory, or Mr Fox's Sketches of the two 1st Chapters of his intended History, that shall not escape thro' the Meshes.—Some one (I forget who) was saying that you were about to give a new Translation of Don Quixote, taking the very oldest Translation, which Lamb speaks of with Rapture, as the ground-work, & note to which you were to pitch your Style. I am afraid, this is not true. If you do any more job work, O how much glory & respectability would this gain you— If it were only the driving out of reading that damned Thing of Smollett²—but then I would have it printed in a classical manner, so that the paper, and the shape of the book, and the type, should all be in keeping with the Style. I cannot but hope, that there must be other works of Cervantes worthy of admiration—and that he must have had contemporaries of merit. I believe, that most admirable & only not Cervantic work the Spanish Rogue was considerably posterior to him. I have just learned Spanish and Portuguese enough to read a half a dozen easy pages, at times, without difficulty—but not enough to remember whether it is Spanish or Portuguese, without looking & recollecting a bit. If I could get a Spanish & Portuguese Dictionary, i.e. Sp. explained by P. or vice

¹ Concerning Coleridge's proposed review of Wordsworth's *Poems* of 1807, see Letter 664.
² Southey did not translate *Don Quixote*; Smollett's edition appeared in 1755.

versâ, together with a Spanish & Italian Dictionary, I should take
great pleasure in dedicating my after dinner hours to both Languages—. I have a very nice odd Volume of Franciosini; but unfortunately it is the Italian & Spanish, not Spanish & Italian. It is the
most entertaining Dict—I ever looked into, full of Joe Millar jokes.
I have his Grammar too—When you understand a language, that
is nearly related to one you wish to acquire, it must be of great
advantage, both in point of ease, & for philosophical purpose, to
have the Dictionary of the one by the other—I should have mastered the Swedish & Danish before this time, if the cursed French
(War, I was going to say—but spite of Roscoe's whimpering Scotch
Review Pamphlet it is a blessed War for us, compared with any
Peace we can make) [did not] make it nigh impossible to get any
thing from abroad. I know of no means (and I am exceedingly
anxious on my own account to discover any) of even sending a
Letter to Italy. I am not certain, that I ever heard even the name
of Hervas[1]—I have myself many a scrap, illustrating the laws by
which Language would polypize ad infinitum—and a compleat
History of it's original formation.—My Jesuit Volume, 3 in one, the
first Italian, the second Portuguese, and the third Italian, all relate
to Japan or China.—Pray, did you not once mention to me a
History of the Inquisition written by an Inquisitor? What is the
Title? And where am I likely to be able to see it?[2] Likewise be so
good as to inform me whether you know any Catholic Work in any
language defending the punishment of Heretics &c.—If you had
been coming up to London, you would have served me by bringing
up those 3 Books in thin Quarto of old German Poetry, which you
once lent to Sharon Turner—and likewise the Romance in Latin
Hexameters.—

I am writing this worthless Letter without knowing whether it is
to find you at Keswick. Mrs Coleridge's letter last but this of to day
was steeped in Despondency—literally every sentence had it's
Sorrow—and in this last she writes in such high spirits that she has
forgotten to send me any news at all. Are you not going S. west-
ward? Whence originated these various rumours—that you are expected by the Bristolians at Bristol—by the Stowics at Bridgewater— & by the Londoners in London?

In giving my opinion of your answer to W. Scott, I forgot to
mention my regret at one joke, which is too like an Insult—& was

---

[1] Lorenzo Hervás y Panduro (1735–1809), Spanish philologist.

[2] In replying to this letter, Southey gave the title: 'De Origine et Progressu
Officii S. Inquisitionis, ejusque dignitate et utilitate, Antone Ludovico a
Panamo, Boroxense, Archidiaconio et Canonico Legionense. . . . 1598, folio.
The book is in the Red Cross Street Library.' *Life and Corres.* iii. 133.

unworthy the rest of the Letter—that one word, *Judge*, vexed me.[1]

I remain ill—and speak from no fit of despondency when I say that I know, I have not many months to live. I could scarcely read my last Lecture thro'—the animated passages, few as they were, I was obliged to omit—& scarcely took my eyes off the paper. As I went thither from my bed, so I returned thence to my bed—& have never quitted it except for an hour or two, sometimes a little longer, sometimes less, at night to have the bed made.—

As you never write any thing respecting family matters, I expected to have heard from Mrs C—how many children you have, when Mrs Southey lay in, and whether boy or girl.

Lamb cannot get his Printer on—I suppose, Longman who has taken the work on terms which Lamb should not have assented to, had I been in town & tolerably well, has, I suppose, told the Printer, that he need not hurry about [it]— it is of no consequence, &c. It is done with excellent Taste—& the notes, that I have seen (not quite the first Half) are delicious. Mr W. Taylor called again this morning—I regretted, that I was quite incapable of seeing any body, being in great pain with sickness. He seems very amiable— and it would [be] a twofold Sin of Impudence & Uncharitableness to [have] presumed to have gaged a man's understanding in a first conversation, of little more than half an hour. All I dare to say, is that I had anticipated more subtlety, less of the Trot Trot on the beaten road of Hartley & explanations of every thing by nothing—or what is much the same—by the word association. But I doubt not, he would rise rapidly in my opinion if I were with him for any length of Time.—Do not think, from the first lines of this Letter that I am vexed at not writing the Review—it will be far better, that whatever I do should appear in a different form—for I can speak more freely of the Antagonists. But Charles Lloyd's name did give me a feeling of sadness. No human heart can retain anger for a shorter time than mine—all my old acquaintances spite of quarrels are still my acquaintances, and loved in exactly the same proportions; but of that man's character I have an unfeigned Horror.—Cottle who wrote to me & whom I after visited, & was glad to be undeceived, and to find him returned to himself, has finished his Epic Poem[2]—& it is printing as fast as possible. I wished very much to review his Psalms: which I like very much. He has certainly an extraordinary happiness in rhyme versification. O that he would but give up Blank Verse! Some of the Odes in his Epic Poem are very fine.

S. T. Coleridge.

[1] In his letter to Scott, Southey had spoken of 'Judge Jeffrey of the Edinburgh Review'. *Life and Corres.* iii. 125.　　[2] *The Fall of Cambria*, 1809.

676. *To Mrs. J. J. Morgan*

Address: Mrs Morgan | St James's Square | Bristol
MS. Lord Latymer. Hitherto unpublished.
Postmark: 10 February 1808.

                                        Wednesday Evening [10 February 1808]
My dear Madam

   I address this Letter to you, because among the conjectures with
which I have wearied my poor Brain, from what cause or reason I
have not heard from St James's Square, it has struck me as possible
that Mr Morgan may have gone into Wales, or else where on Business.
So very, very ill as I have been—and ill enough, Heaven knows,
I still am, you cannot conceive what strange gloomy notions, half-
formed fancies, and thoughts that one does not dare examine, move
to and fro in the mind, & harrass the feelings worse than the Death-
watch's knocking. If I had offended all or either of those, my kind
Friends; or if any thing had occurred of any kind of a faulty Semblance respecting myself; would they not instantly write and tell
it me ?—To be sure, they would! So my reason answered, and if my
reason had had any thing to do with these suggestions, the answer
would have been accompanied with severe self-reproach. But in
truth, they are the mere involuntary phantoms, the Birth of Sickness nursed in the atmosphere of a lonely sick-room.—I am sorry
to inform you that I went from my bed to the R. Institution on
Friday last, & having with great difficulty read thro' my lecture
with my eyes never off the book, I returned from thence again to
my Bed. I have now, in addition to almost continued pain, & restlessness of Bowels, a hoarseness—if it does not go off, I must give
up the Lectures, & go somewhere or other. Whither God knows, the
Shelterer of the Shelterless! I attribute it in part to a slight cold
caught in consequence of all the Strings but one pair (out of six
pair of Tape Strings) being worn off my undershirt—of the six
Undershirts which I had, I have lost three—one was at the Wash,
and the one, I had on, was not only very uncomfortable, I having
been so long in bed with it; but in washing myself before I set off
for the Lecture—I had put it under my feet, which I had just washed,
& wetted it—so I was forced to put on the other—I had repeatedly desired the old woman to beg the Laundress to tack on
some strings; but she, poor old Lady! forgot it. O it is a sad thing to
be at once ill and friendless. I received from Mrs Coleridge a letter
complaining of approaching need of money—she had overlooked a
line and [a] half in a former Letter, instructing her to draw for four
fifty Pounds, 50£ at a time—just according to her own pleasure—
and that I *had* paid Mrs F.[1] and *would* pay the yearly assurance

                        [1] Mrs. Fricker.

money—so that altogether she has 100£ more than our settlement —but this complaint occupied only the first 5 lines of her Letter. It was of three sides close writing—I preserve it as a curiosity—literally, there was not one sentence in it (excepting the last—'I remain your Well-wisher, S. Coleridge') that did not contain a sorrow, a complaint, or an expression of misery. Hartley had caught the Itch from Robert Lovell—I take it for granted, as none of the rest have it, that he was put to sleep with Robert Lovell, if it were only because I so earnestly intreated that when Hartley left off sleeping with Mrs Wilson, he might always sleep alone—a boy very big & forward of his age, two years older than Hartley, and from one of those Yorkshire Schools, where boys are fed & cloathed for 14£ a year. I only in the grief of my Heart, from fear of a mental, far more than vexation at the bodily, Itch, began to utter a sorrow— But the orphan Boy smote on my Heart instantly, I paused, and completed the sentence which began with, 'As to R. L.' by sending him a loving Message and a one Pound note for Pocket Money. I dare *say* nothing; yet I am anxious. It is no Cruelty to R. or Mrs L., that a Father loves his own Child. Line after Line, word after word —I suppose, such a Dish of Comfort was never before administered to a *sick* bed. She had not however heard at the time of writing it of my late Attack & relapses. But between that and a letter of to Day I wrote her 3 letters, the last of them, almost a farewell to her & to my Children—written with great effort during Pain and desperate weakness, in which I assured her of my forgiveness & begged her's in return for whatever pain I had wilfully caused her—in short, I will venture to say, that that Letter would draw Tears down the face of your Servant—this day I received the answer. From beginning to end it is in a strain of *dancing, frisking high spirits*—jokes about the Itch—quite the letter of a gay woman writing to some female acquaintance in an hour of mirth—and she notices my illness, the particulars of which and the strong & fearful suspicions entertained of the Stone, in these words—neither more nor less— '*Lord! how often you are ill! You must be* MORE *careful about Colds!*' —I shall preserve both Letters, and when I die bequeath them with some other curiosities to some married man who has an amiable wife (at least a woman with a woman's Heart) to make him bless himself! Not a word respecting my tender & tearful advice to her about the Children—not a single acknowlegement for having nearly doubled the sum for the year, which she herself had stated & settled (for it is curious enough that amid all the alarm about money, and 'how long I meant to leave her moneyless,' she has within a few Pounds a hundred Pound in Mr Jackson's Hands) no! not one simple expression, that she was sorry that I was obliged to work and lecture while I was so ill—not one word of thanks for my earnest prayer that I might recover enough of my healthy Looks, as to be able this spring to assure to her an additional 1000£[1]—O shocking! it is too clear, that she is glad that her Children are about to be fatherless!

I do not know whether I ought to send you this Scrawl? or n[ot.] I have indeed no one to speak to—no gentle voice to listen to—no kind face to look at—and the heart aches to utter forth it's sorrows somewhere. Mrs Wordsworth too is unwell—& her Sister is absent, nursing a sick Cousin in a house of sickness.—And yet what right have I to purchase a poor relief by inflicting pain on you? And then again my uneasy thoughts, lest something or other of a painful nature should have happened among you—O folly of human nature! then when we are most overwhelmed with sad realities, then are we the most inclined to conjure up fantoms and fancies of Evil.—For Heaven's sake, my dear madam! do burn this Letter as soon as you have read it. I will however keep it open—perhaps, I may hear from you tomorrow.

God bless you & your's!—
S. T. Coleridge

Another & another Day—& the Post is come in— & no Letter. O surely either something is the matter—or else—yet how can I have given offence?—Did I write with too presuming a familiarity? I remember indeed, that once, & I fear more than once, I made my-self an object of a little under-ridicule to Miss Brent from the earnest affection of my Looks & manners toward her; but that was when she did not know what was at the bottom of my feelings—and that the highest & most holy remembrances of my Heart & Head were flashed upon the Eye of the Mind, yea, and on the mind in my bodily Eyes, by your joint & relative appearance, in a manner irresistible!—I have lain down since that last word—and it came upon me, what a short time in reality had passed since I heard from you, and that very possibly you had waited for the finishing of the Dresses—which Dresses I had utterly *forgotten*. But O! it makes my eyeballs feel as if it would do them good to weep, to think what an affecting instance this is, of the workings of uncomforted & lonely Disease. I lost all the common notion & sense of Time—shall I say, it seemed an *Age* to me? No! that is not exactly the Feeling. But it seemed a measureless depth, a strange indefinite *Mass* of Time—Time out of all account, or reckonable divisions, of Time—it seemed—tho' scarce a fortnight—like a Life of it's self—& no doubt involved in the dim yet deep sensation the whole of my Confine-

---

[1] See Letters 695, 700, and 708.

ment. There is a sublimity in this, if I could develope it!—But you —I pray you, bear with my Weakness—for I am sore-stricken. I shall make a great Effort tomorrow & next day—yet now I tremble at the Lecture Day. Only forgive me this Letter—take it altogether as a proof how entirely I lay myself open to you—how secure I feel, that all is as secure, from divulgement and the Taint of public Talk, or private Scandal, as if it were still in my own Bosom!

O I pray you, love me! I ask no more.—

P.S. I had just put the Wafer in, expecting the old Lady to come up to my bed for it—for the first Bell is on the point of ringing— when up she came indeed, & with her the Parcel!! O bless you! I am so fluttered that I cannot open it. But it will give me spirits to get up, & I hope to sit up for the whole Evening—I will however send this off—whatever relates to yourselves, consider as the mere Gloom of a sick Chamber.

677. *To the Morgans*

Address: Mr J. J. Morgan | St James's Square | Bristol
MS. Lord Latymer. Hitherto unpublished.
Postmark: 12 February 1808.

[10–12 February 1808]
My dear Friend

I must first address a few words to your dear Wife.
Dear Mrs Morgan

I am grieved, that I wrote the last Letter—not grieved that I sent it, save only as far as it shall have given you pain; but grieved that my Being was so unmanned as to make that letter the natural and almost necessary Overflowing of a swelling Heart, of a Heart swelling with *no self*-administer'd Poison. And I should be ashamed too, as well as grieved, if it had ever been my wish or plan to shew myself off to you, as a Hero. But I am as far from the heroic Temperament, as Hylas from Hercules. With an intellect, which by comparison with ordinary minds might in a complimentary speech, without any grossness of flattery, be termed strong and agile, I have the heart of a child, a cowardice of sensibility that even in a woman might be blamed, as excessive. But so it is—the worse for poor me! I cannot help it, now at least; whatever I might once have done. However, permit me to say, that every atom of the Feelings expressed in that Letter was only a mode of *Self*-suffering, and that I had as little consciousness of attributing any, the least blame, to any of *you*, as little thought of any, the most distant reproach, as a darling of three years old thinks of accusing the Clouds or Sky,

when he cries and sobs at the Rain for imprisoning him within
doors.—Secondly, Loneliness, continued Pain, accessory Irrita-
tions, and a sense of morbid Despondency had revolutionized all my
common Sense & sensation of Time—the ten or eleven days acted
on my fancy like a wild unmeasured Period of universal Desertion
—so that I waked up as from a fever-dream, when *the words* brought
back the natural idea to my recollection and feelings of what the
interval had really been. My mind had yearned only for those at
Grasmere, and the society of *your* affectionate Fire-side—and if I
have betrayed a silly querulousness, I have myself been made
certain that I do indeed love you and your Sister, Gratitude and
Affection with an innocent self-delusion mutually passing themselves off for each other.—And lastly, my visitations were recent
and heavy. In that most melancholy Letter I did not give you *half*
—In my best strength I *could* not have, I would not even *wish* to
have, withstood the shock. *One*, out of many remaining, *one* further
instance only—! In her first Letter of 'the Lamentations', she had
expressed herself as '*exceedingly alarmed*' concerning Derwent's
Eyes, and in Terms that to a far less anxious heart than that of a
fond Father must have conveyed a strong apprehension, that his
Sight was in Danger: and she desired me to send to Mr King for
his Advice. I replied—that she must remember, that Mr King had
repeatedly urged me to permit him to apply the extract of the
Bella Donna or Deadly Night-shade to the Child's Eyes, the state
of which *he* considered as demanding effective remedies; but that
his own account of the tremendous power of that Poison, and that
it acted by withering up and partially paralysing a part of the
Pupil, and that so little a mistake might produce such horrid consequences, had so terrified us, that not only she rejected the plan,
but that I myself shrunk back from it—that what we had both
dreaded to permit, when the application would be ministered by
Mr King's own hand, and the Child once or twice or more every day
under his Inspection, it would be madness to think of, when there
was no one who understood the case, either to apply the medicine
or to watch the Effect. (*N.B.* She had expressly said and confirmed
it, as usual, by Southey's opinion, the least Hint of which, often
gratuitously interpreted, she does not hesitate to set up against
any, the most passionate request, or most direct COMMAND from
me—do not think harshly of *that* word, which LOVE would *preclude*, but which must be where neither Love nor Reason nor common Kindness exists—she had expressly said, that Mr Edmondson,
an apothecary, knew NOTHING AT ALL of the case)—I therefore
added, that I had received such proofs of your & your Sister's
general Tenderness of Heart and especial affection for my little Boy,

such proof of Mr Morgan's Friendship for me, of his fondness for
children in general, and his particular Liking for Derwent; that if
any one were coming to London who would take charge of him
hither, I would in the interval from Friday to Friday take him
down to Bristol, put him under Mr King's Care, having first written
to Mr Morgan, from whom I doubted not to receive in his own &
your name an answer warmly in the affirmative.—Observe, that in
a former Letter I had given her a full account of the exceeding
Kindness of him & all of you, toward me, how I had been nursed &
cheered—& had added—(God forgive the small proportion of *in-
gredient falsehood* for the sake of the motive, which prompted it—)
' I have told you all this, as not irrelevant to you, inasmuch as I owe
this kindness more to their affection for the Children & *friendship to
you*, than to any regard for myself, tho' no doubt they did feel as
much regard for me as was likely or possible considering their short
acquaintance even with my person & the mere accident by which I
introduced myself into their affectionate Circle.' To this she *returned
no answer*; but in her last GAY Letter having first, in *spirit* at least
& *almost* in *words*, contradicted all her former account—or rather,
all her former *feelings*—she concludes—' Get directions from Mr
King, & send them to Mr Edmondson. As to his being at Mr
Morgan's—they are estimable people, no doubt—but it is quite
out of the Question.' These are her very words. And this is her
Child! and the medicine is such, that a couple of drops too concentered, not sufficiently diluted, would make his eyeballs start and
shrink up in their Socket. Are they then not *my* children too ? I
have indeed no other proof, and can have none, than their Faces &
their Hearts; but I have to maintain them, to brood over them, to
hope and fear and pray & weep for them. Whether or no they be my
Children, I am quite certain, that I am *their* Father. Did this
Woman bring me a Fortune ? or give me rank ? or procure me intro-
ductions & interest ? or am I now maintained in Idleness by her
money?—O that I had the Heart to do what Justice & Wisdom
would dictate—& bring her to her Senses!—Henceforward, I will
trouble you no more with this hateful Subject. But only think just
enough of it, not to remain too much surprized that my Spirit was
so weighed down by her unfeelingness, her seeming pleasure at the
anticipation of my being speedily got quit of—me, who in the worst
of times had ever felt & expressed as much Joy in her Health, as my
Wife, and mother of my Children, as if I had been married to you,
or Charlotte, or Mrs Wordsworth or Sara Hutchinson—I say,
wonder not that I was overs[et—that I se]emed to look round a
Wilderness, to hear in the distance the yel[l & ro]ar of fierce
animals, & to see no one that would give me even the Help of

Comfort—! Neither wonder nor be wounded, if in this transient Infirmity of Soul I gave way in my agony, and *causelessly* & almost *unknowing what I did*, cried out from on my *Cross*, Eli, Eli lama sabac[h]thani! My friends! My Sisters! why have you for-saken me! For tho' I should be stung to death, yet such is my nature, that let me die when I will, Love will be uppermost—and if there be grief or disquietude, it will be the Grief and disquietude of Love.—

The arrival of Mr Morgan's letter and your kind Doings with it, so revived me that I have sate up the whole afternoon & evening— & feel myself better. Remember me with zealous affection to Charlotte, whom of course I have considered myself as addressing at the same time with you—& be assured, that [this] shall be the last querulous *over doleful* Letter from your most affectionate & grateful Friend & Brother,

                                                          S. T. Coleridge

My dear Morgan

All the above was written on Wednesday Night—I fully intend-ing, of course, to write the remainder to you and send it by Thurs-day's Post. But my Sleep was overcome—my nature had received a Sting— My Children & their Mother haunted me in a hundred horrid forms— and the whole day I remained in a high Fever. I am now, this is 8 o/clock Friday Morning—calm; but hoarse, in part from nervousness—& perhaps from having taken nothing stronger than Tea & a little Broth, for some days past—& I must, I fear, again put off a Lecture. If I could have given, or can give, the to day's Lecture, I had, before I received your Letter, thought of putting off the next till the Friday fortnight, so arranging it as then to give two, one on the Saturday—& to have got out of Town for that fortnight—in order to recompose my shocked and shattered Spirits. O Friend! *you* cannot comprehend how the poison works—to know, that an ungrateful woman has infused dislike of me into the mind of my own child, the first-born & darling of my Hopes.—Need I say, that I shall rejoice to see you in town?—There are rooms enough in this House; but no additional Beds. I must ask about the possibility of hiring a good Bed for 3 months. But O! that I could dare offer to propose to you to take up Mrs Morgan &c—& to take for us a sufficient suite of Rooms, you paying one fourth of the expence that would be over and above your present weekly ex-penditure. Taking it as medicine, and as enabling me to work with chearfulness, it would be economic on my part—and on your part a benefaction. For I am too low to endure mixed Company—& yet this unceasing Loneliness, I know, must be injurious. The greater the dislike becomes of having that Loneliness interrupted, the more dangerous that Loneliness is becoming. But this is but an aspiration, a wishing-sigh.—God bless you all!—But as to my lovely Mantua-makers, if a beautiful Lady with a fine form, a sweet Chin and Mouth and bright black Eyes will tell a *Eff I Bee*, about 14S. instead of at least 5£, and another sweet young Lady with dear meek eyes, as sweet a chin & mouth, & a general *Darlingness* of Tones, manners, & Person, will join with her Sister & swear to the same -ib, what can a gallant young Gentleman do but admit that his Memory is the Fibster, tho' he should tell another Fib in so Doing? —I supposed from your letter that you had sent Miss S. Temple's blush-compelling note. Tho' the Blush might not have benefited my fever, yet I wish you had, in order that I might identify the hand-writing. I will know who she is, by my next—if I am well enough to admit of a visit from Byrne.

S. T. Coleridge

I received a dry fragment of a Letter consisting wholly of book Enquiries from Southey, 3 days ago, from Keswick—not a word about this journey to Bristol or London. Yet *here* too, I find, he *has been expected*—

678. *To Sara Hutchinson*

Transcript Sara Hutchinson. Pub. Literary Remains, *i. 259.*
The copy of Chapman's *Homer* in which this letter to Sara was inserted has not come to light. The volume was first sold along with other books from Wordsworth's library in 1859 ; it was resold in 1901 at the sale of the library of William Harris Arnold. The letter is described in the catalogue of the 1901 sale: ' *The Whole Works of Homer: Prince of Poetts In His Iliads, and Odysses. Translated according to the Greeke. By Geo: Chapman,* . . . (about 1616.) . . . Inserted is a long letter—one of the most interesting literary letters in existence—which was sent by Coleridge, with this book, to Miss Hutchinson.'

[12 February 1808][1]

Extract from a Letter sent with Chapman's Homer—to S. H.[2]

Chapman I have sent in order that you might read the *Odyssey*— the Iliad is fine, but less equal in the Translation, as well as less interesting in itself. What is stupidly said of Shakespeare is really true & appropriate of Chapman— 'mighty faults counterpoised by

[1] In *Literary Remains* H. N. Coleridge dated this letter 1807. According to the 1859 sale catalogue, however, one of Coleridge's annotations in the Chapman volume is dated 12 Feb. 1808. The letter, therefore, was probably written on the same day. It seems likely that Coleridge sent the volume, along with a gift of dresses, to Mary Wordsworth and Sara Hutchinson (Letter 687), about this time.

[2] H. N. Coleridge altered Sara Hutchinson's heading to read, 'Extract of a letter sent with the volume. 1807', and added a footnote: 'Communicated through Mr. Wordsworth.'

mighty Beauties.' Excepting his quaint epithets which he affects to render literally from the Greek, a language above all others 'blest in the happy marriage of sweet words,' & which in our language are mere printer's compound epithets—such as quaff'd divine *Joy in-the-heart-of-man-infusing* Wine—(the undermarked is to be one word, because one sweet mellifluous Word expresses it in Homer)—excepting this, it has no look, no air, of a translation. It is as truly an original poem as the Fairy Queen—it will give you small idea of Homer, tho' a far truer one than Pope's *Epigrams* or Cowper's cumbersome most anti-Homeric *Miltonized* [translation]—for Chapman writes & feels as a Poet—as Homer might have written had he lived in England in the reign of Queen Elizabeth—in short, it is an exquisite poem, in spite of its frequent & perverse quaintnesses & harshnesses, which are however amply repaid by almost unexampled sweetness & beauty of language, all over spirit & feeling. In the main it is an English Heroic Poem, the *tale* of which is borrowed from the Greek—The dedication to the Iliad is a noble copy of verses, especially those sublime lines in the second page beginning at the 5th & ending at the word 'raigning' the last but one[1]—& likewise the 1st—the 11th, & last but one, of the prefatory Sonnets to the Odyssey.[2]—

Could I have foreseen any other speedy opportunity I should have begged your acceptance in a somewhat *handsomer coat*;[3] but as it is, it will better represent the Sender—to quote from myself—

> A Man disherited, in form & face
> By nature & mishap, of outward Grace![4]

S. T. C.

679. *To Robert Southey*

Address: Robert Southey, Esqre. | Greta Hall | Keswick
MS. Lord Latymer. Pub. with omis. E. L. G. i. 391.
Postmark: 13 February 1808.

Saturday Morning, 3 o/clock. [13 February 1808]

Dear Southey

Having tried in vain to sleep, or even to feel inclined to it, I had better sit up and look at something, than enfever my head and eyes

---

[1] Coleridge refers to the lines beginning, 'O! 'tis wondrous much', and concluding, 'Yet still your Homer lasting, living, raigning'.

[2] Professor Raysor says that the sonnets singled out by Coleridge are those to the Duke of Lennox, the Lady Wrothe, and the Lord of Walden. *Coleridge's Miscellaneous Criticism*, 1936, p. 233 n.

[3] The volume must have been later repaired, since the catalogue of the 1901 sale describes it as 'Tall 4to, original stamped calf, rebacked, red edges'.

[4] *To Two Sisters*, lines 8 and 9, *Poems*, i. 411.

either by keeping my eyelids closed, or staring at the Curtains. We have had Storm, and Snow, and Frost, from Thursday Midnight—having been forced to get out of Bed two or three times on Thursday night, I increased my Hoarseness so much, that it became impossible for me to give my Lecture: which at all events it would have been dangerous to do, & yet but for that I had resolved to do it. I have not left my bedroom since my return from the last Lecture. The inflammation of my Bowels has left them so exceedingly irritable and prone to re-inflammation (which even in a slight degree produces an instant prostration of Strength, and Stomach-sickness) that till the weather becomes more vernal, I have little chance of bringing my Health back even to it's former Par impar. Dr Crompton is in town; and I cannot barricado him out—O! O! never mind! He'll see *me*—I must, I must, I must, see him—and in he dashes—rattles away, & when I am near sinking under him, cries—Now—now—you are quite well.—I never saw you look better. God bless him! he is a noble-hearted fellow—and I should like him if it were only that he loves and is loved by that angel woman, his Wife. Besides, I like him too for his constancy to all whom he has ever countenanced—John Thelwall, for instance—nay, and I like his company too very much, only not in hours of Disease or Dejection. On Wednesday I was surprized and much affected by a call from my old School-fellow, School-patron, and Cambridge Friend (during my first Term) Middleton. How much misery should I have escaped, in all human probability, if he had been but one year my Senior, instead of three. He was evidently much affected at seeing me—and ill in bed—we had a long and interesting Conversation—& much I regret, that he quitted Town that very day. He has just published a Volume on the Greek Article[1]—the very sight of the Book did my Heart good. It's size, type, weight, all the Antipodes of the dolus biblio-policus—a weighty plain-printed plain papered Octavo of 700 pages—and a most masterly work it is—the production of a good Logician and a sound Scholar—it does honor to the Church of England—& will raise it's character abroad—. It is the ablest philological support of the Trinity, in existence; and is of almost equal interest to the general Greek Scholar. Not that I entirely adopt his Theory; or that it has overthrown my own Scheme of the Article. No! on the contrary I feel certain that mine will *take in* all his Truths; and it has enabled me to detect several errors in *his* work, & to explain a number of rules which *he* has been obliged to refer to the Idiosyntaxy of the Greek. On the other hand I have received great & various Instruction from it, and see my own

[1] Thomas F. Middleton, *The Doctrine of the Greek Article applied to the Criticism and the Illustration of the New Testament*, 1808.

Scheme in a fuller light. And as to Socinian Textualism, *there* it lies! in shakes and shatters—! not a fragment of the mirror large enough to see an eye in! Dear Mr Estlin, in speaking of me in a large company a few weeks ago, said—His Intellect is all gone, Sir! all his genius is lost, quite lost—he is a mere superstitious Calvinist, Sir!—. If I had spirits, I could tell you a good Story of Dr Stock, whom I had one evening cock-pecked into an opinion of Wordsworth's merit as a Poet, and who came next morning to C. Danvers (at whose House we had met) complaining of my conduct, as immoral or very improper, carrying people's minds away by subtleties & warmth of eloquence, &c &c— the poor man had been hen-pecked out of it again. But Charles Danvers will tell it more accurately. I heard from all quarters of the insolence & overbearing Self-conceit of Mrs Stock—and the poor Doctor who seems by nature good & kind she treats openly, as a mere Insignificant. Tho' I laughed, yet inwardly I had a sick pang—I had from your account, from the deep impression that C. Danvers' acccount of his escape by *his* heroic friendship had made on me (and surely a better good Man than C.D. does not exist in this planet) the knowlege of the pleasure, you had, in making out his happiness to your mind's eye, returned after so long yet instructive Exile, with a high moral & medical character, with an independent fortune, at least one large enough to preclude anxiety and yet leaving him motives & objects; married to the woman of his choice, of whose mind his own had been the mould & model—in all this I had so sincerely sympathized, that when I first saw him, I felt it odd that his face, Voice, & person should be new to me—. Alas! alas! It is a *secular* Bird indeed that is so plumed—and nested in such precious Balms and Spices!—I have no *authority* for it, but it was hinted to me that he himself had misgivings and drawings-back of Heart—that he was not insensible to the broad bold manners of his betrothed Viragin.—I was much pleased with much of John Morgan—it was not necessary to have found out his reverential Regard for your Memory (for so it must be to him) in order to perceive the impression, that your then mind and mood made on his, he being then but a Lad. It is even painful to see, how superior he is in thought and moral tact, to all those, he consorts with—and the living with none out of his household whom he can seriously be in sympathy with has had an effect in making him reserved, & of low spirits. I was surprized at finding his understanding so much superior to my former idea of him.—Bye the by, I was a good [deal] with Cottle comparatively—for I was seldom out of doors at all.—He is quite himself again—nay, better than ever—He explained the past *satisfactorily* to me—for he did not deny or wish to conceal that he

had wrapt up his Imagination in Delusions, that produced, while
they lasted, an undesirable state of moral Feelings—When his
Cambria, or the Conquest of Edward I, comes out, I should like
very much to give a gratifying Review of it—and if it had been a
little, *or so* altered in the plan, so as to have made the distinction of
a Conquest of an uncivilized by a more civilized & larger Part of the
same natural Realm from foreign Conquest, continually *afloat*—
and so as to leave the Conqueror all justified & the Conquest a
complacent thought in the mind, and yet Llewellyn &c in full
possession of your affection & sympathy, it would really claim a
considerable share of honest Praise. The lyrical & dramatic parts
are the best. Indeed, it is to be regretted that he did not compose it
in heroic Rhyme—fluent Rhyme-verse is natural to him, & would
have pleaded in behalf of the Work with a large number of Readers.
It is scarcely giv[en] to one in an age to write blank verse *numerously*
—numero, et pondere.—When I heard by letter that you were
hourly expected at Bristol on your way to Taunton, I wrote
instantly to J. Morgan, to intreat you in my name to return viâ
London—If I can but get about again, my mind was never more
active nor more inclined to steady work. Indeed, I daily do more
than I ought to do. Advise me, which I should learn first as the
groundwork, the Castilian or the Portuguese? If the former, which
is the best Dictionary, Newman's or Stevens'—or is there a third
better than either? Is the French Spanish D. better than the English? But probably, this is out of your Beat, you having learnt the
Languages in the country—& therefore soon used Dictionaries of
the Language. And what is the best of those?—And what is the
name of the Vocabulary you once, I think, mentioned to me, containing solely all the words of Moorish Origin?—How goes on
Brazil with you? I was quite alarmed sometime ago by seeing an
Advertisement with a name which struck me as that which Mr Hill
had mentioned to you as being the only man who possessed the
same materials with those in your hands. Was it so?

I have read the Sheets of the 1st Vol. of dear Mr Clarkson's Hist.
of the Abolition &c[1]—The grave intensely common Common-place,
the mild & genial Dullness, of the first 3 pages, disappoints one
most delightfully—for all the rest is deeply interesting—written
with great purity, as well as simplicity, of language, which is often
vivid & *felicitous* (as the Monthly Rev. would say)—and nothing
can surpass the moral beauty of the manner in which he introduces
himself and relates his own maxima pars in that immortal War—

---

[1] Coleridge refers to Thomas Clarkson's *History of the Rise, Progress, and
Accomplishment of the Abolition of the African Slave-Trade by the British
Parliament*, 2 vols., 1808.

compared with which how mean all the Conquests of Napoleon and Alexander! Percival is about tcsend Commissioners to the Coast of Africa, to see what can be done in the way of virtuous Trade. So deep has been my Despondency, that for many days nothing but my horror of sea-constipations, and the circumstance of my Assurance limiting me to Europe & to Dry Land, prevented me from applying for one to Mr P. thro' his Sister, Lady Elizabeth, & Lord Egmont. If Mrs S. could be happy there, could you endure to spend 5 or 10 years at Rio de Janeiro? I have a notion, that is a divine Country, in point of Climate & Landscape.

Please to say to Mrs Coleridge, that she is quite mistaken as to Mr King's not being alarmed about the possible Deterioration of Dervy's dear Eyes. He spoke and spoke and spoke again to me— for as to calling, what could that have done, when I could not make up my courage to the exhibition of the Bella Donna, the dreadful medicament, from which alone he expected any decisive Effect—. And a drop or two too much, or too little diluted, might make the pupil of his Eye start from it's Holdings, & shrink up like Geraldine's. Is it too late for a philological or theological article to be sent to the Annual?—

Your's truly,
S. T. C.

The Germans are most happy among many other instances of prepositional compounds in their particles, ver and zer (fer and tser): as kochen, reissen, to bear [to boil?], to rend—verkochen, verreissen, to boil *away*, to rend away—zerreissen, to rend *to pieces*.[1] Now our dis = the ver, if we could only make it run thro' the language, as ver does or may do in German—and *formerly* the prefix to[2] = zer—as in met: rom. 'all *to*-torn'.[3]—

680. *To the Morgans*

Address: Mrs Morgan | St James's Square | Bristol
MS. Lord Latymer. Pub. with omis. E. L. G. i. 402. The first half of this manuscript is missing.
Postmark: 17 February 1808.

[17 February 1808]

. . . I have observed indeed in more than one or two instances that Lawyers in their careless hands write more unintelligibly, than any other class of men. Jack Colson's Letters look like a *copy* of a good flowing hand—and yet I could never read three lines together without boggling—and as his Conceptions are not *all* too (as the

---

[1] Cf. Coleridge's note to Klopstock's remarks concerning the English versus the German language, *The Friend*, No. 18, 21 Dec. 1809, and *Biog. Lit.* ii. 172.

[2] Pronounced *toe*. [Note by S. T. C.]

[3] Chaucer, *The Parlement of Foules*, 110.

Germans say) logical, I never wholly decyphered any one of his
Epistles, to me, or to Mr Poole.—My dear Morgan! I am glad to be
able to turn off to any Subject from the mournful one of myself.
The anecdote of Vixen is not only interesting but valuable—Similar
facts are commonly believed; but it is rare indeed to have them so
accurately stated and circumstanced. Were I even in tolerable
strength of body and spirits I would go thro' it analytically, as a
distinct *datum* for canine psychology. As you have rightly observed,
the memory is the least part—and yet even that is important—
because it completely confutes the dogma of Aristotle, which has
been adopted by almost all after metaphysicians, that Beasts and
Infants *remember*, man only *recollects*—i.e. that Beasts only *recognize*,
the Object being presented anew. But here is a clear instance of
reflective recollection, proved by all the passions of distinct anticipation.—

And now again Pain drags me back to my unfortunate Self. It is
my Wish and the Dictate of my Reason to come to you, and instantly to put myself under Dr Beddoes, & to open to him the whole
of my Case—But yet—forgive me, dear dear friends!—but yet
I cannot help again & again questioning myself, what *right* I have
to make your House my Hospital—how I am justified in bringing
Sickness, & Sorrow, and all the disgusts and all the *Troublesome-
nesses* of Disease, into your quiet Dwelling. Ah! whither else can
I go?—To [Keswick? The *sight* of that Woman would destroy me.][1]
To Grasmere?—They are still in their Cottage, one of their rooms is
proved untenantable from damp—& they have not room scarcely
for a Cat—. Not to speak of the distance. And shall I stay here?—
Alas! it is sad, it is very sad. The Noises of the Pressmen at between
4 & 5 in the morning, & continued till 8—the continual running up
stairs by my door to the Editor's room, which is above me—the
frequent calls of persons, who wish too see me, and whom I cannot
see—the forced Intrusions of some—and the Alarm in consequence
of every Knock at the private Door—trifles in themselves—are yet
no trifles to me. Saving a few hours at night, in order to let my bed
be made, I have not been out of bed, I scarce remember when—all
this morning I was so bad, I thought it all over with me—O what
agony I suffered!—Pray, write to me by return of Post—and in the
meantime I will exert myself to the utmost. Be assured, that I feel
the intensest gratitude—I intreat dear Miss Brent to think of what
I wrote as the mere *light-headedness* of a diseased Body, and a heart
sore-stricken—and fearing all things from every one. I love her
most dearly! O had I health and youth, and were what I once was
—but I played the fool, and cut the throat of my Happiness, of my

---

[1] Passage in brackets inked out in MS

genius, of my utility, in compliment to the merest phantom of overstrained Honor!—[O Southey! Southey! an unthinking man were you—and are—& will be.][1] S. T. C.

681. *To Sir George Beaumont*

Address: Sir George Beaumont, Bart. | Dunmow | Essex. (To be immediately forwarded, if Sir G. be not at Dunmow.)
MS. Pierpont Morgan Lib. Pub. Memorials of Coleorton, *ii. 44.*
Postmark: 19 February 1808.

348, Strand.
Thursday Night,
Feb. 18, 1808.

Dear Sir George

For many weeks with only two Intervals, and those but day-long, I have been ill—very ill—confined mostly to my Bed, altogether to my bedroom. In my pain I earnestly wish to die—and in my best hours the only odor of Hope, that remains at the bottom of my Pandora Casket, is a relaxation of that wish—a passiveness of Life —the continuance of which to any useful purpose I have as little reason to expect, as, for any pleasurable end, to desire. I have written this, most reluctantly; but the instinct not wholly to lose the kind thoughts of the two or three, whom in my heart's heart I revere, still works and will be obeyed. Proofs of this feeling, tho' for the greater part fragmentary or not fully polished, will be found by those who may examine my manuscripts when I am no more.

I have left my bed at this time in consequence of a Letter, which has deeply affected me, and of a Name, which would be a Spell to recall me for the time even from the verge of death. Sara Hutchinson's and Mary Wordsworth's Brother after a *romance* almost of strange and perilous adventures and sufferings has been pressed, and is now in great distress on board of his Majesty's Ship, Chichester, at Sheerness. His name is Henry Hutchinson: an unfortunate man, an enemy to himself only, and like all those of that character, expiating their faults by Sufferings beyond what the severest Judge would have inflicted as their due Punishment—Men would rather be deemed Knaves than Fools; and there are reasons for this at the depth of the human Heart, worthy of a miner like Wordsworth to bring up into light.—Well! this Brother, who is an excellent Seaman, was captured in the Betsy, and taken in to Guadaloupe— there a prisoner for 3 months—thence exchanged & sent to Antigua —shipped himself as Master of a small privateer, and for the first month was successful, having carried in an American Ship with French Property, for which he would have received 400 Dollars,

---

[1] Passage in brackets inked out in MS.

had he been fortunate enough to return to Antigua. But taking a Spanish Schooner he was sent by his Owners on board her to convey her a little to windward of Cape Cordera [Codera] on the Spanish Main, where her Owner lived who had engaged to ransom her—here he was driven off Land, provisionless, without water, even without a Compass—was obliged to stand over for the West India Islands, and after passing four days without tasting any thing he & his poor fellows made the West End of Porto Rique together with his Majesty's Ship '*Fortunee*' (I cannot distinctly decypher the Word) —and Henry having no Copy of Commission, Captn Vansittart[1] took the Vessel from him (of course), and pressed him and his two men. However Captn V. promised him some preferment, and gave him the charge of navigating the vessel; but meeting with an absolute Hurricane in the Gulph of Mexico he lost both his Masts, and four men, and was finally compelled to run in under Jury Masts to Vera Cruz, where he and his remaining crew were taken Prisoners, and sent 300 miles up the Country, to Purbla [Puebla]—there kept 18 months—thence to Vera Cruz again, where he was imprisoned 4 months—whence he was [at] length exchanged, & sent home to join the *Fortune* (?) now at Plymouth.—

Dear Sir George! you cannot yourself feel the burthen & indelicacy of employing private friendship to any interruption of public concerns, or the unpleasantness of addressing a private friend in his public official character, more than I do. Few could be the Instances, in which I could have prevailed on myself to urge you to it. But this man's whole Life has been one dream-like Tale of Sufferings—of repeated Imprisonments, of Famine, of wounds—and twice he has had the Yellow Fever—& escaped each time from among a charnel-house of Corses. He has done enough—he has suffered enough.— And to me it is as if it were my own child—far more than if it were myself—for he is the Brother of the two Beings, whom of all on Earth I most highly honor, most fervently love. If thro' the means of Lord Mulgrave or any other you could procure his Liberation, a whole family's Prayers of Gratitude, & Eyes fixed as on the throne of God with thankful & pleading Tears, would form the host that, I *know*, rise up for you and your dear Lady.

S. T. Coleridge

I have been so exceedingly ill, that I have been able to do nothing— save that I have only to write a concluding Paragraph to a moral & political Defence of the Copenhagen Business.[2] I shall disgust many friends—but I do it from my *conscience*. What other motive have I ?

---

[1] Henry Vansittart was commander of the *Fortunée* from 1803 to 1812.

[2] For Coleridge's defence of the bombardment of Copenhagen by the English fleet, see *The Friend*, ed. H. N. Coleridge, 3 vols., 1844, ii. 143–66.

682. *To Daniel Stuart*

Address: D. Stuart, Esqre
MS. British Museum. Pub. E. L. G. i. 404.

Thursday Night—[18 February 1808]

My dear Sir

I inclose the letter as the best explanation and advocate of my
earnest wishes. I have done every thing which in my present severe
sufferings I can do—I have written to Sir G. Beaumont to apply to
Lord Mulgrave, I have written to his Lordship's Brother, whom I
once met in company & who was very attentive to me, and I have
urged Mr Clarkson immediately to exert his Interest with the
Thorntons, & Wilberforce, to procure this poor unhappy Sufferer's
Release. Like most who are enemies only to themselves he has
suffered more than Rhadamanthus or the other Judges of Hell in
their worst humors would have inflicted on him, for his imprudence.
But I well know, that lesser Dignities can do at once what the first
man in power boggles at—& 'really cannot transgress the rule, he
has laid down'—If by any Interest of your's you can procure
Henry Hutchinson's Liberation, you will have the fervent Gratitude
of Mrs Wordsworth & her Sister—whom from some strange circumstance which I am unable to decypher: for unfeignedly I have
the greatest faith in your *tact* as to character—you have been
somehow or other led to misunderstand. It is not very probable,
that two men so unlike as Wordsworth and myself should have fallen
into the same Error, both having known the same Object for 8 or
9 years—& he almost always in the same House. Would to God I had
health & liberty!—If Sense, Sensibility, sweetness of Temper, perfect Simplicity and an unpretending nature, joined to shrewdness
& entertainingness, make a valuable Woman, Sara H. is so—for the
combination of natural Shrewdness and disposition to innocent
humor joined with perfect Simplicity & Tenderness is what distinguishes her from her Sister, whose character is of a more solemn
Cast. Had Captn Wordsworth lived, I had hopes of seeing her
blessedly married, as well as prosperously—but it is one of the
necessary Results of a Woman's having or acquiring feelings more
delicate than those of women in general, not to say of the same
Rank in Society, that it exceedingly narrows the always narrow
circle of their Prospects, and makes it a stroke of Providence when
they are suitably married. O! to a man of sensibility, especially if he
have not the necessity of turmoiling in life, & can really concenter
his mind to quiet enjoyment, there is no medium in marriage
between great happiness and thorough Misery—but that Happiness
is so great, that all outward considerations become ridiculous to a

man who has enjoyed it, if in opposition to the possession of a Woman, who is capable of being at once a Wife, a Companion, and a Friend.

I have within the last fortnight received such a tremendous Proof of what a man must suffer who has been induced to unite himself to a Woman, who can be neither of the three in any effective sense, that (as what sinks deepest most easily comes uppermost) it has led me into a digression very remote from the subject of my Letter, which yet, Heaven knows! has interested me as much as if H. H. had been my own Brother—and specially indeed from considerations of poor Mrs Wordsworth's alarming State of Health, to whom the Liberation of her unfortunate Brother would be a Charm of Healing.

Unfeignedly your obliged & sincere Friend,
S. T. Coleridge

683. *To Mrs. S. T. Coleridge*

MS. Victoria University Lib. Hitherto unpublished fragment.
Postmark: 1 March 1808.

[1 March 1808]

. . . known any woman for whom I had an equal personal fondness— that till the very latest period, when my health & spirits rendered me dead to every thing, I had a PRIDE in you, & that I never saw you at the top of our Hill, when I returned from a Walk, without a sort of pleasurable Feeling of Sight, which woe be to the wretch! who confounds with vulgar feelings, & which is some little akin to the delight in a beautiful Flower joined with the consciousness— 'And it is in *my* garden.' With what . . .

. . . *alarming statement* in the first of your Letters concerning Derwent's Eyes. I cannot but suspect, that you have *forgotten* what you said in that Letter. It was indeed from beginning to end *steeped* in melancholy. But after the receipt of my answer, relating the state of my Health . . . —indeed, you appeared to have written . . . of Derwent's Eyes was . . .

[S. T.] C.

684. *To Thomas Clarkson*

Address: T. Clarkson, Esqre. | Joseph Hardcastle's, Esqre. | Hatcham House |
New Cross | Deptford | Kent
MS. New York Public Lib. Hitherto unpublished.
Postmark: 3 March 1808.

Thursday Morning. [3 March 1808]
My dear Friend

I have received from Mr Byrne, Lord Gambier, and even directly
from Mr Barrow, as Secretary of, and by command of, the
Admiralty, letters informing me of the Discharge of H. H. To him
I sent Letter, money, and various articles of Linen & Clothes, on
Sunday by means of Mr Wright, of Rochester, who promised to
send a man of trust on board the Namur; he left Town 6 o/clock,
Sunday Morning—and still I have received no Answer from him.—

By the bye, your book, and your little map[1] were the only publication, I ever wished to see my name in; but tho' my first public
Effort was a Greek Ode against the Slave Trade,[2] for which I had
a Gold Medal, & which I spoke publickly in the Senate House, and
tho' at Bristol I gave an especial Lecture against the falling off of
zeal in the friends of the Abolition, combating the various arguments, exposing the true causes, and re-awakening the fervor & the
horror, and published a long Essay in the Watchman[3] on the Trade
in general, in confutation of all the arguments, *all* of which I there
stated, besides a Poem, & several Parts of Poems—yet I consider
my own claim, which is feeble in itself as an *Author*, as evanescent
when compared with Robert Southey's,[4] whose twelve Sonnets on
the Slave Trade were not only among his best, but likewise among
his most popular productions. They were very much read indeed;
not merely in his Volume of Poems; but were scattered into almost
all the Newspapers, (especially the provincial Papers) and Magazines
of the Kingdom—They were reprinted in Scotland, and in America
—And besides these there are at least a dozen other poems of his
either expressly on this Subject, or in which it stands in the fore-
ground.—

An Anecdote.—Professor Blumenbach possesses, and shewed to

[1] The 'little map' in Clarkson's *Abolition of the Slave-Trade* is explained in
Chapter XI. It represents the individual efforts towards abolition uniting
in two main streams, one standing for the abolition of the trade by England in
1807, the other for similar action by the United States in the same year.

[2] See Campbell, *Poetical Works*, 476.

[3] No. 4, Friday, 25 Mar. 1796. See *Essays on His Own Times*, i. 137.

[4] I may add, that I preached a Sermon of an hour's length & a few minutes
against the Trade at Taunton. But I really [think] that *Robert Southey* is fairly
entitled [to] have named one streamlet, or feeder of the great River.—[Note
by S. T. C.]

me, a complete little Library, of his own collecting; consisting of
Books written entirely by African Blacks—and there were books in
every Science, Astronomy, pure & mixt Mathematics, Medicine,
Theology, in Poetry, Belles Lettres, &c.

Likewise, [in] his most able disproof of any difference in kind
between Whites & Blacks in his great classical Work de varietate
humani Generis,[1] which is in Latin, and in a separate Essay in
German, he did vast service in the World of learned men—especially, the first work which is in almost every Philosopher's Library
in Europe.—A multitude of little anecdotes I could furnish you
with—. I am better, save that my both legs are very bad, inflamed,
and eruptive. Wordsworth[2] is well.—Our Love to Mrs C.

S. T. Coleridge.

685. *To Mrs. Thomas Clarkson*

Address: Mrs Clarkson | Joseph Hard Castle's, Esqre. | Hatcham House | New
Cross, Deptford | Kent
MS. Yale University Lib. Hitherto unpublished fragment.
Postmark: 10 March 1808.

Wednesday Evening, 9 March, 1808.
348, Strand.

. . . I cannot come to you—what indeed could I bring but Discomfort?—But Wordsworth certainly will spend a day or two at
your Uncle's—and he is a Comforter. God bless him, and *his*! His
friendship and that of his Sister Dorothy's are the only eminent
Events, or *Passages*, of my Life, (among those, wherein my *Happiness* has been involved) in which I have not been cruelly deceived
or deluded: taking however a full Share of the Blame to myself.

R. Southey has been confined by a Cold—and I hope, that this is
the only reason of my not having seen him since his first arrival. I
have particular reasons to wish to converse with him: as he offered
to recite my Lectures for me at the R. Institution. As soon as I have
settled this, I shall (God willing!) go down to Bristol, and place
myself under the immediate Care of Dr Beddoes—more for Duty,
than from any *Hope* of Recovery, or to utter the whole truth, from
any wish of Life.—I trust, dear Tom is going on well, in body & mind.
Bless his beautiful Eyes & Eye lashes! I often see him before me.—

Affectionately, dear Mrs C. | your sincere Friend,
S. T. Coleridge

[1] J. F. Blumenbach, *De generis humani varietate nativa*, 1775.

[2] Wordsworth had come to London, in part to see Coleridge, in part to make
arrangements for the publication of *The White Doe of Rylstone*. 'Wm . . . wants
to push the printing, and to correct the press himself.' Dorothy to Jane
Marshall, 23 Feb. 1808, *Middle Years*, i. 176.

686. *To Robert Southey*

Address: J. Rickman, Esqre. | New Palace Yard | Westminster   *For Mr Southey*
MS. *Lord Latymer. Hitherto unpublished.*
Postmark: 24 March 1808.

[24 March 1808]

My dear Southey

It is so abhorrent from me, partly from nature, but more from calamity, to think or speak of myself, that when you were with me this morning I not only did not tell you what in sincerity I meant to do—that I had been a little wounded at your not contriving to pass an evening with me, who for three months have not been thrice out of my rooms—but what really was more at my heart—that when at Longman's I spoke something rather disrespectful of the Clergy, tho' in a respectful way (perfectly ignorant of course, either of Mr Hill's being a Clergyman or your Uncle)[1]—and tho' I afterwards *knocked under* completely to Heber,[2] & added many things to express my sense of the wide & silently going on, good, which the Clergy effected, in towns & Villages, as a germ or nidus of civilization, yet you well know, that the best plaister cannot prevent the smallest Wound from being a Wound.—Now I assure you (and when I speak reflectingly, I know, I have a right to be believed to the full amount of what I say) that tho' the knowlege, that he is your Uncle & *such* an Uncle, must needs blend with my thoughts, yet that independent of this his manners, & that countenance, which it is impossible, a good man should see & not revere, work far more with me—and I should be heartily sorry, if any thing, I had said, had left a bad Impression concerning me in his mind. I do not remember whether or no I told you—but I was puzzled, *how* such *a Face* & such *a man* came to be at Longman's Table—and that 'Prince of Dry Salters' precluded almost the possibility of my hitting on the truth.—Pray, have you then seen Mr Hill, the Dry Salter,[3] since?—I ask this, because Wordsworth I know, wishes some information about him & the nature of his connection with the Monthly Mirror—as well indeed as myself—in order to understand, with what motives & by what sort of People, these works are carried on—

Do not forget to inform Mr Rickman, that I shall accept his kind Invitation—

[1] The Rev. Herbert Hill.

[2] Richard Heber (1773–1833), book-collector. Wordsworth later wrote to Scott of this dinner party at Longman's and of meeting 'your Friend Heber' (Richard, not Reginald as De Selincourt assumed). See *Middle Years*, i. 458e.

[3] Thomas Hill (1760–1840), drysalter, book-collector, and part proprietor of the *Monthly Mirror*.

I write in exceeding perplexity or rather anxiety of Mind, in consequence of the News from Grasmere—Miss H. having burst a blood vessel, under circumstances symptomatic of pulmonary affection—*They* are not alarmed; but from the best advice *I* know there is too much reason for alarm.

God bless you | &
S. T. Coleridge—

687. *To the Morgans*

Address: Mr J. J. Morgan | St James's Square | Bristol
MS. Lord Latymer. Hitherto unpublished.
Postmark: 29 March 1808.

Tuesday, 29 March [1808]
My dear Friends

Strange and painful Things must you needs have thought of me, but the hereafter will shew, that no appearances ought to make you doubt of my constant attachment, and undying gratitude.—To-morrow Evening, after my Lecture (which I recommence) I will send off a little parcel, which has been made up & ready to go for more than a fortnight; but was delayed for a letter to accompany it. —My dear Friends! I had begun a Letter to you, with more than ordinary chearfulness, informing Mary & Charlotte that the Gowns had reached Grasmere, had quite delighted them, for the patterns, and still more for the Make; and that they never had had a gown made that *fitted* so completely. Dorothy (to whom I sent some rich Silk more than a year ago for a gown, but which she had not made up) was having it made by their joint Efforts exactly after those, I had sent.—Just then, I received a Letter, that Mrs Wordsworth was wasting rapidly—& that her dear Sister had broke a small blood vessel—and knowing the particulars of her constitution, & adding them to the circumstances of the accident, there remained no doubt on my mind, that it was perilously symptomatic, proved a fullness & inflammation of the Lungs, and—in short—that without the utmost care joined to the most favorable Circumstances, comprizable in four articles—Repose of Body—Tranquillity of mind—regular & gentle, daily, Horse-exercise—and the preclusion of febrile excitement by unceasing watchfulness to keep the Body open—by prepared Kali—magnesia vitrioluta—or aromatic Powder—she would vanish away from us, like a blessed Dream.—My opinions had anticipated, & coincided in every respect with the decision of Drs Babbington, Layard, & Messrs Ridouts—to whom I sent a statement, but of course without adding any of my own fears.

5581.3

G

To the Morgans

Never before did I feel the whole weight of Distance! Grasmere is 19 miles from the Post Town; and a Letter thither cannot have been answered, i.e. the Answer not received, in less than 7 days—& commonly it is 10, from accidents.—Added to this, I have been in continual hot water concerning Mrs W's Brother, who after a romance of sufferings in Africa & Mexico, had been pressed—The express Order for his Discharge from the Admiralty has been trifled with—the Scoundrels kidnapped him from one Ship to another, so as to render it impossible [for him to receive] either the clothes or money which I had employed three agents to convey to him—& at last hurried him out to Sea in the Leyden—However, I have seen the Letter of the Lords of the Admiralty in very severe Rebuke & Menace of the persons concerned; and another peremptory Order to Admiral Wells to take care that on the Return of the Leyden he be instantly discharged.—Before the former more serious Anxiety, this latter business had kept me in continual hot water—writing & writing, & fretting & fretting—

Assure yourself, dear Morgan! that I never do, or will, or can forget you—and the loving-kindnesses, I have received from you all—But more in the parcel Letter—I steal this from my Lecture Writing—

God bless you all, | &
S. T. C.—

. . .[1] Independent of the above, I could have enumerated half a score of accidents, that had swallowed up both Time & Feeling, & helped to occasion my procrastination in writing to you—for I forgot it only in the first 3 or 4 days of the intelligence from Grasmere—even as I should have forgotten to have written to them, had I heard the same or similar of Mrs Morgan or Charlotte from Bristol—

688. *To Matilda Betham*[2]

Pub. A House of Letters, *106.*

[3 April 1808][3]

Dear Miss Betham,—Your bearer waits, and a gentleman is with me on business. I can therefore only say, that I am pleased and feel myself honoured by your intention, but will in the course of to-morrow morning write a *real answer* to both your kind letters. Be

---

[1] The bottom of page three of the MS. is cut off.

[2] Mary Matilda Betham (1776–1852), a poetess and miniature painter, to whom Coleridge had some years earlier addressed his lines, *To Matilda Betham from a Stranger, Poems,* i. 374.

[3] This letter was written the day before Letter 689.

assured, it will not be one disappointment that shall prevent me from seeing you, though my poor face is a miserable subject for a painter[1] (for in honest truth I am what the world calls, and with more truth than usual, an *ugly* fellow). Yet the mere pleasure of being in your company for two or three hours will be my compensation.

Sincerely yours,
S. T. Coleridge,

689. *To Matilda Betham*

MS. Huntington Lib. Pub. E. L. G. i. 410.

(*348, Strand*)
Monday, 4 April, 1808.

Dear Miss Betham

At the time, the little girl delivered me your letter and accompanying present, an acquaintance was coming up stairs who had business of importance, & such as would require half an hour or more to settle, & whose time was valuable—yet having, tho' hastily read thro' your note, I could not bear to send back a mere cold acknowlegement of the Receipt.

Tho' I had wholly forgotten the circumstance, to which I owe it, believe me (if you knew me personally, I venture to affirm, that even this 'believe me', would have been superfluous) I was more than pleased, I was much affected by the Letter. It breathed a spirit so unlike that of the Letters, one is in the habit of receiving from people of the World—in short, it reminded [me] of my earliest Letters from my dear friends at Grasmere.

The only word in it, which a little surprized me, was that of '*fame*'. I assure myself, that your thinking and affectionate mind will long ago have made a distinction between fame and reputation; between that awful thing, which is a fit object of pursuit for the good, and the pursuit of which is an absolute Duty of the great; that which lives & is a fellow-laborer of nature under God, producing even in the minds of Worldlings a *sort* of docility, which proclaims, as it were, *silence* in the cant of noisy human

---

[1] Since Coleridge failed to meet Miss Betham in London in 1808 and missed seeing her at the Lakes in 1809, her miniature of him, which is now in the possession of the Rev. A. D. Coleridge, could not have been painted earlier than 1811. (See *A House of Letters*, 110, 115–17, where Mrs. Coleridge's letter is misdated 1808 for 1809, and 124.) 'The miniature was engraved & published for some magazine, I think the European Magazine, but being afterwards unsaleable or at least unsold was used as a bogus or deputy portrait of Lord Cochrane, prefaced as the frontispiece of a pamphlet issued during his trial in 1814.' [Note by E. H. Coleridge.]

passions—& the reward of which without superstition we may
well conceive to be the consciousness in a future state of each
Being, in whose mind & heart the Works of the truly Famous
have awakened the impulses & schemes of after excellence. What
Joy would it not be to you or to me, Miss Betham! to meet a Milton
in a future state, &, with that reverence due to a superior, pour
forth our deep thanks for the noble feelings, he had aroused in us,
for the impossibility of many mean & vulgar feelings & objects,
which his writings had secured to us!—But putting Fame out of the
Question, I should have been a little surprized even at the word
'reputation'—having only published a small volume, twelve years
ago, which as my bookseller well knows, had no circulation—& in
honest truth did not deserve any, tho' perhaps as much as many that
have attained it—a volume given by me to the public, 'My poverty,
& not my will, consenting.'—I *should* have been surprized even at
any *publicity* of my name, if I were less aware of that sad sad stain
of the present very *anti-gallican* but woefully *gallicizing* Age, the rage
for personality—of talking & thinking ever and ever about A. and B.
and L.—names, names, always names! The alliterations, '*Names &
Novelties,*' would go far in characterising the *bad* parts of the present
generation (for, with pleasure I say it, it has many very good ones).
Of me and of my scanty juvenile writings people know nothing;
but it has been discovered, that I had the destiny of marrying the
Sister of Mrs Southey, that I am intimate with Mr Southey, & that
I am in a more especial manner the Friend and Admirer of Mr
Wordsworth. . . . [Remainder of manuscript missing.]

690. *To George Ward*[1]

Address: Mr G. Ward | Paternoster Row.   *From Mr Coleridge*
MS. British Museum. Hitherto unpublished.

Courier office, 348, Strand—
Monday [4 ? April 1808][2]

My dear Sir
    The young man, who delivers this to you, is a countyman of
mine, & very strongly recommended to me by a man of worth and
high respectability. His name, William Meddlecott—his object, to
procure a situation, either as a *compositor* in some respectable
Printing office, or as a Shopman in some Stationary or Bookseller's
House: for either of these, or both combined, his Education (I am
informed) has fitted him. Of his morals & trust-worthiness I have

---

[1] A brother of Thomas Ward, Poole's partner.
[2] Endorsed April 1808.

received a strong testimonial—of his abilities I know nothing—but his countenance is far more intelligent, than ordinarily falls to the Lot of *us* Devonshire Dumplins; for on my conscience, I believe, that both in morals and intellect, Devonshire is the Sink, the *common Sewer*, of England. But really, judging from outward Looks, this young man might have belonged to another County without dishonoring it. However, if you can recommend him to any situation, or give him any useful advice, you will greatly oblige me by enabling me to oblige the man, who has recommended this youth to me, & to whom I am much indebted. My friend tells me, that this William Meddlecott is 'steady, temperate, industrious, desirous of improvement, & trust-worthy'.

Pray, have you any thought of engaging in *Publication*, of any kind?—If so, I *think*, I could set you out with rather a brilliant name: tho' I could not promise you a *rapid* profit. But this would be a subject more suitable for conversation than a Letter. I have been exceedingly ill—& indeed, at present, have little hope of actual recovery. I shall be glad to see you, if you pass by this way, any time after 1 o/clock: for I am seldom up before that Hour—

I am, my dear Sir, | very sincerely your's

S. T. Coleridge

691. *To Mrs. Mary Evans Todd*[1]

Pub. Athenaeum, *18 May 1895, p. 643.*

Coleridge's letter was in reply to the following communication from Mrs. Todd:

April 6th 1808
No 31—Bury Street, St James's—

My dear Sir

On hearing your name announced at the Royal Institution I felt so great a desire to once more behold an old and esteemed friend that I could not resist the opportunity that presented itself—The pleasure however that I experienced was greatly diminished by seeing you in so indifferent a state of health—making myself known to you at such a moment was perhaps ill-timed and I now write to offer an apology—In truth it was the effect of a momentary impulse and not a premeditated act—If I erred I can only say it was an error of judgement—but not intended to give pain—I hope I shall be able to explain myself better when I have the pleasure of seeing you here which I shall expect in the course of a day or two—

In the meantime | Believe me | still your sincere friend

Mary Todd. [MS. Dove Cottage.]

[1] Mary Evans married Fryer Todd on 13 Oct. 1795. Todd subsequently lost his fortune, the home was broken up, and in 1811 a son, Elliott D'Arcy Todd, was placed under the care of a maternal uncle.

To Mrs. Mary Evans Todd

Thursday. [7 April 1808]

Dear Madam,

Undoubtedly the first moment of the feeling was an awful one to me. The *second* of time previous to my full recognition of you, the Mary Evans of 14 years ago, flashed across my eyes with a truth and vividness as great as its rapidity. But the confusion of mind occasioned by this sort of *double* presence was amply and more than balanced by the after pleasure and satisfaction. Truly happy does it make me to have seen you once more, and seen you well, prosperous, and cheerful—all that your goodness gives you a title to.

I shall, as soon as I am a little at liberty, call on you and Mr. Todd,[1] and believe me to be with most sincere regard and never extinguished esteem

Your friend
S. T. Coleridge.

692. To Andrew Bell[2]

Pub. Life of Andrew Bell, *ii. 578.*

[9 ?] April 1808.[3]

Dear Sir,

I have been more than usually unwell; and I trust that it will be of no material result, if I send you, as I assuredly will do, the sheets[4] to-morrow, or (that being Sunday) on the day following. I have another motive, unwell as I am. I am preparing to go out to my

---

[1] Coleridge later called on the Todds, and he wrote to Stuart that he saw in the fate of Mary Evans 'a counterpart of the very worst parts of my own Fate, in an exaggerated Form'. Letter 695.

[2] Dr. Bell (1753–1832) was the founder of the Madras system of education, a system developed during his residence in India. His report, *An Experiment in Education made at the Male Asylum of Madras,* was published in 1797. In 1803 Joseph Lancaster (1778–1838) published his pamphlet, *Improvements in Education.* Lancaster admitted that he had derived 'useful hints' from Bell's work but maintained that he had thought out independently his system of mutual instruction. Coleridge enthusiastically eulogized the system of Dr. Bell and attacked Lancaster in his lecture of 3 May and was thereby plunged into the bitter controversy raging in 1808 between the two educators and their followers.

[3] Beaumont arrived in London early in April. In this letter Coleridge mentions his wish to interest the Beaumonts in Bell's plan, whereas by 15 April he has seen them and speaks of their desire 'to see and consult' Bell. The present letter, therefore, precedes Letter 694 and belongs to early April.

[4] Coleridge had borrowed the sheets of Bell's *The Madras School, or Elements of Tuition: comprising the analysis of an experiment in education, made at . . . Madras . . . to which are added, extracts of sermons preached at Lambeth; a sketch of a national institution for training up the children of the poor; and a specimen of the mode of religious instruction at the Royal Military Academy, Chelsea,* 1808. Letter 694 shows that Coleridge was using these sheets in preparing his lecture on education.

honoured friends, Sir George and Lady Beaumont, and I wish to interest them, who have so great influence on the minds of the higher classes, in this great duty.

Dear sir, no man can either have conceived or realized what you have both conceived and effected, without a good heart. With far less fear, therefore, than if I were writing to most other men, I dare tell you, and I request you to take for granted, that, much as I should be pleased by any diffusion of your deserved fame, my conscience is far more interested in the spread of your utility. I wish to make you acquainted with Clarkson. You and he have given the sublimest proofs I am aware of, how much good one man can effect. Excuse the paper, for I write in bed.

693. *To William Godwin*

Address: Mr Godwin | Juvenile Library | Skinner Street | Snow Hill
MS. Lord Abinger. Hitherto unpublished.
Postmark: 15 April 1808.

Thursday Night. 14 April—[1808]

Dear Godwin

Once shewing this,[1] and afterwards mentioning your own and my name will be sufficient—(which, I assure you, I am well pleased in having *cheek* by *jole*) and much, very much more than when the Flush of REPUTATION was upon you, which you have strength of mind enough, I know, to distinguish from honorable *Fame*, and therefore not to be—except for outward circumstances—disheartened, because weak minds need the stimulation of *Novelty*— something *new*, whatever it be—. In writing to you, I do not much care whether my nominative Cases have or have not any legitimate offspring of Verbs—but I thought the time before last that I saw you, you seemed in low Spirits—. Be assured, that if I were now to publish any work that should gain the reputation of Caleb Williams,[2] that after the same number of years I should—for a while—meet the same neglect—but if you keep up your spirits, the very same Lust of Novelty will create for you a *new run*—And what *Fame* shall be your's, or any one's, Posterity alone can realize, tho' the inward mind may foresee.—

When you introduced Mr C.,[3] I understood you—*Mr Craddock*. I saw, he was no common man—& it would amuse you, if I could make you conscious of the to & fro workings of my mind, thro'

---

[1] Across the top of this letter Coleridge wrote: 'Be pleased to admit Mr Godwin to my Lectures.—S. T. Coleridge.'

[2] Published May 1794.

[3] John Philpot Curran (1750–1817), Irish judge.

Reviews, &c, &c, to recollect *who* Mr Craddock was—Anxious to speak to him, and yet not knowing how to begin, I assumed false spirits, & tho' I noticed your eyes *pointing* at him, as it were, I felt only an increased perplexity. Glad was I, when he began to speak.— But when I at last heard his name, I struggled against an inward Feeling—& did not alter my *tone*, lest I should by any sudden increase of respect & deference more wound his moral feeling, than I could gratify his intellectual sense—lest, in short, he should have reason to think, that I could treat any friend of your's with care- lessness, or insufficient respect—and assume quite a different Feel- ing for the person himself, after I had known him to be an illustrious character.—But, I trust, he has both sense & kindliness enough not to *gauge* a man's head & heart at a first Interview.—

God bless you!—I only wish, that hundreds, whose Intellects you first awakened and put into action, would but feel as respectfully & friendlily toward you, as I do, who at that time was your Zoilus: & to whom, till I knew you, your name was like that of an Enemy.—

S. T. Coleridge

I open the Letter, after having wafered it, to say: that I should be highly gratified, if I could meet Mr Curran again, when with greater Sobriety I might compare my notions with his—and in cooler Logic attempt to prove, that a man may despise France (in the *intellectual* map of the World) without an atom of English Prejudice.—

694. *To Andrew Bell*

Pub. Life of Andrew Bell, *ii. 575.*

15th April 1808.

A concurrence of intelligence from my friends in the North has not only made it difficult for me to force my mind away from dream- ing about them, but has employed me in running about after my friends day after day; yet even this would not have prevented my commenting (according to my judgment, which, on such a work, is but another word for my feelings) on the sheets you have sent me, if I had seen aught which appeared to me likely to diminish its *present utility*. I confess that I seem to perceive some little of an effect produced by talking with *objectors*, with men who, to a man like you, are far, far more pernicious than avowed antagonists. Men who are actuated by fear and perpetual suspicion of human nature, and who regard their poor brethren as possible highway- men, burglarists, or Parisian revolutionists (which includes all evil in one), and who, if God gave them grace to know their own hearts, would find that even the little good they are willing to assist proceeds from fear, from a momentary variation of the balance of probabilities, which happened to be in favour of letting their brethren know just enough to keep them from the gallows. O dear Dr Bell, you are a great man! Never, never permit minds so inferior to your own, however high their artificial rank may be, to induce you to pare away *an atom* of what you know to be right. The sin that besets a truly good man is, that, naturally desiring to see instantly done what he knows will be eminently useful to his fellow beings, he sometimes will consent to sacrifice a part, in order to realize, in a given spot (to construct, as the mathematicians say), his idea in a given diagram. But yours is for the world—for all mankind; and all your opposers might, with as good chance of success, stop the half-moon from becoming full—all they can do is, a little to retard it. Pardon, dear sir, a great liberty taken with you, but one which my heart and sincere reverence for you impelled—as the Apostle said, Rejoice!—so I say to you, *Hope*! From hope, faith, and love, all that is good, all that is great, all lovely and 'all honourable things' proceed, from fear, distrust, and the spirit of compromise—all that is evil. You and Thomas Clarkson have, in addition to your *material* good works, given to the spiritual world a benefaction of incalculable value. You have both—he in removing the evil, you in producing good—afforded a practicable proof how great things one good man may do, who is thoroughly in earnest.[1]

May the Almighty preserve you!

P.S.—If, in the course of a few days, you could send me the same, or another copy of the sheets I now send back, they would be useful to me in composing my lecture on the subject. Sir G. and Lady Beaumont are very desirous to see and consult you about a school at Dunmow. Be assured, while I have life and power, I shall find a deep consolation in being your zealous apostle.

I write in a great hurry, scarce knowing what I write; but, before a future edition, I will play the minute critic with you, and regard your book as a literary work for posterity.

---

[1] Writing to an unidentified correspondent, Coleridge gives a further impression of Dr. Bell: 'That same day, I saw Dr. Bell & was pleased, highly pleased with him—for it is one of the privileges of a virtuous man, who has confined himself to the Society of good & wise men, that he has a sort of intuitive knowledge of an eminently good man, the first hour he is with him.— S. T. Coleridge.' [Transcript Coleridge family. Only this fragment survives.]

695. *To Daniel Stuart*

Address: D. Stuart, Esqre
MS. British Museum. Pub. E. L. G. i. 408.

[*Circa* 18 April 1808][1]

My dear Stuart

If I did not feel and know, how much & how truly I loved and esteemed you, the weight of my Obligations to you would press heavy on my mind.—I write to you now, simply and at once, to ask you to permit me to draw upon you for a sum not exceeding a hundred Pound;[2] if I live, this with the rest will be gradually repaid to you—if I die, the use I am about to make of it, will secure the repayment. I would at once make over to you all my claims on the R. Institution, amounting exactly to this sum—but an, I trust, not immoral Pride prevents me. On the contrary, it is my fixed intention to employ a 40£ due to me in the course of a month to send them back the sum, which I drew upon them for the travelling expences of my Self & Family.[3] I have less Pride than most men, I have known; but I owe it to my sweet Children, & to my friends, not to suffer myself to be treated ignominiously; or to be regarded as an Hireling.[4]—Few things oppress my Conscience so much, as my repeated non-performance of what I had engaged & God knows! both meant and expected to have done for you; but in that instance the delicacy and generosity on your part toward me have always alleviated, often removed, the feeling. If I was not self-satisfied, yet I had another Object before my mind, in whose conduct I found an unmixed satisfaction: and judging of you of myself, I thought, that the sincere & grateful Love, I felt toward you at and from the bottom of my Heart, and my exceeding Anxiety to see you happy, increasingly so, & more and more worthy of being happy, formed a sort of imperfect Recompense. But to be insulted by people, to whom I had been under no Obligation, *for* whom you in reality (which is '*I*' to them) had been paying, and to be treated as a Shoemaker—or worse—namely, with the idea— 'we must not pay him all beforehand, or he may give us the Slip'—

[1] On the MS. Stuart noted: 'I gave 100£ on the 20 April 1808. D. S.'; this letter was probably written a day or two earlier.

[2] Coleridge was apparently not only anxious to pay his insurance premium, which was due on 7 April, but as early as February 1808 he had been planning to increase his insurance by an additional £1,000. See Letters 676, 700, and 708.

[3] According to the records of the Royal Institution, the first payment of £40 was made in February 1808. Bence Jones, *The Royal Institution*, 1871, p. 284.

[4] When Coleridge made application for a further payment for his lectures, he was deeply wounded at receiving £20 by the hand of a servant. See Letter 698.

as if I were a Sharper, supposing my powers to continue—or a Being without friends interested in my Honor, supposing sudden Death or incapacitating Sickness—all this is rather too bad.

Within a day after I have applied the Sum, for which I wish at present and for the best purposes, you shall receive both the right of claim, and the proof that that Right will have been gratefully anticipated.—The rest of my Obligations I must leave to Chance & Futurity.

It is rather unpleasant, that Mr Hardcastle sent word shortly after your note, how eagerly he expected the pleasure of my Company, and that my coming with a Friend was '*a great addition*'; not only from their wish to see & become acquainted with any particular friend of mine, but as it was a proof, that I '*meant to be friendly*'—and that he had therefore forced a point, & sent an apology to the Hibernian Meeting, to which he had previously engaged himself.—I would have gone, of course; but really what I saw yesterday, which I will explain when I see you, such a counterpart of the very worst parts of my own Fate, in an exaggerated Form, in the Fate of the Being, who was my first attachment, and who with her family gave me the first Idea of *an Home*, & inspired my best and most permanent Feelings,—joined with a Letter from Dr Babbington respecting the Wordsworths, and another from poor Morgan at Bristol concerning his Wife's Health—all coming together overpowered me—I had been forced all yesterevening to exert false Looks, & false Spirits, toward one whom I perceived worthy of absolute abhorrence—&—but this is for our confidential conversations—it agitated me however so, that when Clarkson called, he himself said, that however different the Day had been, it would have [been] imprudent for me—for I had lain awake weeping for the greater part of the Night, and when I might have slept, was obliged (at 8 o/clock) to get up, in order to welcome at Breakfast an old Friend & Schoolfellow returning to the Indies, & who had stayed two days in London in order to Breakfast with me.—

S. T. C. —

696. *To Daniel Stuart*

MS. British Museum. Pub. E. L. G. i. 406.

[*Circa* 18 April 1808][1]

Dear Friend—

I feel myself impelled to write to you some ten Sentences on a subject so full of anxious Hope to you, so full of regretful Anguish

---

[1] According to E. H. Coleridge, this letter was enclosed in the preceding letter. *Letters from the Lake Poets*, 76.

to me. Exclusive of Health, Virtue, and respectable Connections, there seem to me to be just four points, on which a wise man ought to make calm and most deliberate questions—and unless he can answer *all* four queries in the affirmative, he has no chance to be happy—and if he be a man of feeling, no possibility even of being comfortable. I. Is A a woman of plain good sense, as manifested by sound judgment as to common occurrences of Life, and common persons, and either possessing information enough, or with an understanding susceptible of acquiring it, enough, I say, to be and to become a companion? In few words, has she good sense with average quickness of understanding? 2. Is she of a sympathizing disposition, in *general*—does she possess the sensibility, that a good man expects in an amiable Woman?—3. Has she that steadiness of moral feeling, that simplicity undebauched by lust of admiration, that sense of duty joined with a constancy of nature, which enables her to concentrate her affections to their proper Objects in their proper proportions and relations— to her Sisters, Brothers, Parents, *as* Sisters, Brothers, Parents, to her children as her Children, to her Husband as her Husband?—N.B. The second & third Query by no means supersede each other. I know a woman of great sensibility, quick & eager to sympathize, yet ever carried away by the present object—a wholly uncentering Being. This Woman is a pleasant companion, a lively Housemate, but O! she would *starve* the Heart, and wound the pride as well as affections, of a Husband—she cannot be a *Wife*.—Again, Mrs Southey is a woman answering tolerably well in affirmative to the third query—She loves her Husband almost too exclusively, & has a great constancy of affection, such as it is. But she sympathizes with nothing, she enters into none of his peculiar pursuits—she only loves *him*;—she is therefore a respectable Wife, but not a Companion. Dreary, dreary, would be the Hours, passed with her—amusement, and all the detail of whatever cheers or supports the spirits, must be sought elsewhere. Southey finds them in unceasing Authorship, never interrupted from morning to night but by sleep & eating.—

4 and lastly. Are all these 3 classes of necessary qualities combined with such manners & such a person, as is striking to you—as suits your feelings, & coalesces with your old associations, as a man, as both a *bodily* and *intellectual* man?—

I feel a deep conviction, that any man looking soberly & watching patiently, might obtain a full solution to all these queries, with scarce the possibility of being deluded. He will see too, whether she is highly esteemed & deeply beloved by her Sister, Brother, oldest Friends, &c—. If there be an atmosphere of true affection & domestic feelings in her family, he cannot help himself breathing it, &

perceiving that he breathes it. But alas! alas! is it because it is the most important step of human Life, that therefore it so often happens, that it is the only one, in which even wise men have acted foolishly—from haste, or passion, or inquietude from singleness, or mistaken notions of Honor leading them to walk into the Gulph with their eyes open! God preserve my friend from this worst of miseries! God guide my friend to that best of earthly goods, which makes us better by making us happier, & again happier by making us better!—

[No conclusion or signature.]

697. *To William Godwin*

Address: Mr Godwin | Juvenile Library | corner of Skinner's Street | Snow Hill
MS. Lord Abinger. Hitherto unpublished.
Postmark: 22 April 1808.

348, Strand.
[22 April 1808]

Dear Godwin

I wrote you a twopenny Post Letter the morning, I think, after you had called with Mr Curran; inclosing an admission ticket for my Lectures.[1] Other parts too of the Letter half-required, at least, by a subintelligitur of feeling asked for, an answer. Did I any way offend *you*? That I may have disgusted your Friend, I should not be surprized to hear—or that I may unintentionally have injured you in his opinion by causing him to think more meanly of your Judgment, than he had been used to do. But this was not my fault—whether you lay the emphasis on 'fault' or on 'my'.

Be assured, that the possible Injury *you* may have sustained in your friend's admiration is the sole cause of any possible Regret *in me*: tho' even this may do you good by teaching you to be more chary of your panegyric on living Characters, than you are wont to be.

However, at present I want only to know whether you received the admission ticket from

S. T. Coleridge

[1] Godwin attended Coleridge's lecture of 22 April. (Information supplied by Prof. Lewis Patton, who is editing the Godwin papers.)

698. *To William Sotheby*

Address: W. Sotheby, Esqre. | 47. Upper Seymour Street
MS. Cornell University Lib. Pub. E. L. G. i. 412.
Postmark: 28 April 1808.

Thursday Morning [28 April 1808]
348, Strand.

My dear Sir

I esteem you; and am therefore desirous of your Esteem. Nor have I ever ceased to feel an interest in your true Fame. Nay, often have I been indignant at seeing your translation of Oberon[1] so popular (too great an honor from a good man, as I have firm faith, you are, to such a work), and the Saul comparatively neglected. The Saul—I will not say, I have read—I *read it*. But for some defect of the metre (pardon my freedom—a few months probably will shew, that I now have no ordinary *motive* for sincerity, even tho' my constitutional character had not furnished the *Impulse* to it) but for some defect in the metre, arising from the shortness of the Periods in part, and in part from the pausing so often at the second Syllable, which Milton never does, as far as I have examined, except when he means to give an unusual Importance to the words—and even then most often a trochaic, not a Spondee or Iambic—

> 'And now his Heart
> Distends with pride, and, hard'ning, in his strength
> *Glories*:'   Book I. 571.—

But when it is an Iambic, it always has & is meant to have some great effect—see book I. from Line 585 to 615—after all this grand preparation of the imaginative power—

> 'He now prepared
> *Tŏ spēāk*:—whereat their doubled ranks they bend,
>   &c'—

Of course, I do not apply this remark in all it's force to Lines beginning periods or paragraphs; tho' even here, it ought to have some attention paid it—

As I have neither the wit or the vanity of the younger Pliny, & do not write Letters *to* my friends *for* the World, as dissenting Ministers *preach* to their congregation in the masquerade of a Prayer to their Maker, so I am not very solicitous whether or no my nominative cases are childless, or my verbs orphans—all I meant to say is, that tho' my Understanding dictates one or two other faults, yet to my *feelings* the metre alone prevents the poem from being *wholly* delightful. Yet great pleasure, & noble sensations has it given me.—

I said, I was anxious of your Esteem; but my Thoughts are like

---

[1] In 1798 Sotheby translated Wieland's *Oberon*.

Surinam Toads—as they crawl on, little Toads vegetate out from back & side, grow quickly, & draw off the attention from the mother Toad—. Now then straight forward[1]—

I hope you did not misunderstand my state of feeling respecting the R. Institution, which I cannot but honor because it has assisted, perhaps enabled Davy, to do the glorious things he has done, & I trust, is doing, and will do—& which assuredly will place him by the side of Bacon & Newton—for his Inventions are Discoveries, and his Discoveries grand general Principles, fruitful, yea creative—but in all other things I deem it most injudiciously managed—nay, perverted.—I felt no pain concerning the *smallness* of the *Sum* sent to me; but at the *manner*—a vexation that partly owing to my giving up my own feeling to Davy's concerning Mr B.,[2] and receiving great civilities & professions from him (which when received will always *tell* for something in a good man's heart, whatever his Judgement may have decided concerning the Bestower) I had been seduced into an open-heartedness respecting my private concerns, & particular motives for having money at the present moment—(which I have procured from a better quarter)—and that instead of a Letter, or *any* thing respectful, a Servant should be sent, with 20£ in *his hand*. Had I been their Shoemaker, what other could they have done? but *I* have never treated even [a] Shoemaker thus.—I had told Mr Barnard, that wha[tever] they meant to give me (about 90£ or an 100£ remains of what he promised), it would be highly convenient to me at the present time—& (O fool!) assigned my family motives—they *sent* a servant with 20£—& a verbal *message* —What am I to deduce—? that if PAYED beforehand, I should not do my duty afterwards with such *briskness*? Gracious Heaven! and if their Hearts did not dictate the contrary as to my motives, yet as men of the world would not a 5 minutes' calculation have shewn them, that taking in my travelling expences, & my necessary expences in town, wholly on account of these Lectures, compared with my cost supposing me at home or at—that too a dear, dear Home—at Wordsworth's, I must necessarily be out of pocket, with

---

[1] Writing in his diary for 24 May 1843, Crabb Robinson says he sat up till eleven reading over some letters from Coleridge to Mrs. Clarkson: 'I make an extract from one of a part only of a parenthesis as characteristic of his involved style:

"Each, I say (for in writing letters I envy dear Southey's power of saying one thing at a time in short and close sentences, whereas my thoughts bustle along like a Surinam toad, with little toads sprouting out of back, side and belly, vegetating while it crawls). Each, I say," etc.' *Robinson on Books and Their Writers*, ii. 632.
The letter from which Robinson was quoting has not come to light.

[2] Thomas Bernard (1750–1818), who set on foot the plan of the Royal Institution.

the 130 or 40£?—But Sickness or Death might prevent me from
giving the whole course—Am I then so friendless, so unhonored in
this World, that there is no one Being who would step forward, &
repay what was to be repayed, & save my Honor?—Wordsworth,
his Wife, his Sister, his Wife's Sister, yea, his very Children, would
all consent to live on bread and water for a year rather than suffer
my name to have such a stain on it.—Besides, I was to have had an
equal sum the former year for half the number of Lectures.—

If my paper had permitted, I would have explained to you the
justifying circumstances, which suddenly drew back the 50£, which
I borrowed from you, & was on the point of paying—it shall be sent
before I quit town.

I seem to feel, that Mrs Sotheby is in some *little degree some little
offended* with me.—O! if she knew, with what heart I look at the
increasing beauty & intelligent Innocence of her Daughter's face,
with what sympathy of [par]ental Pride & earnest Wishes—but this
is too deep a note—God bless you &

S. T. Coleridge

I hope to have you as my Auditor on Friday—as I shall then
finish Shakspere—. My next Wednesday will be the introductory
one to Milton; when I hope Mrs & Miss S. may be present, at all
events.—

699. *To Henry Crabb Robinson*[1]

MS. Dr. Williams's Lib. Pub. E. L. G. i. 415.

Tuesday Morning.—[3 May 1808][2]

My dear Sir

Sexcenti in the Latin writers, if I remember right, stands for an
indefinite number, but dearest Mrs C's Note first informed me, that
'can admit as many as he pleases', is synonimous with twelve
Tickets.—However, tho' these are disposed of, if you will come a
quarter of an hour before two, & find me (as you will) in the appara-
tus room close by the Lecture Room, you shall be sure to have
admittance—not only to day, but during every one of my Lectures,
which you may have time or inclination to attend. *Perhaps*, I may
have to request you for this day only to sit—where Davy, and a
great number of my best & most honored friends sit, some always
from *choice*, others for to day only in order to give me an opportunity
of introducing more than my number, by putting the Ladies *below*,
& sending my male friends above—i.e. in the Gallery.—You will

---

[1] Henry Crabb Robinson (1775–1867), indefatigable diarist.
[2] Endorsed 3 May 1808.

find there (I assure you) the *most respectable* part of my audience—
those that you at least will regard so.—Basil Montague & his friends
will be there—& many others—I should not wonder, if Dr Bell (whom
you will know by his pale pleasant face & spectacles) were to creep
into a corner there, from an amiable curiosity about a subject in
which he must feel so deep and specific an Interest.—I however
shall speak just what I feel, under the supposition that he is not
present—for no man who ever knew me, suspected me of flattery—
and I *feel*, that I have a right to praise[1]—for my Heart on such
occasions beats in my Brain.—Nothing but endless Interruptions &
the necessity of dining out far oftener than is either good for me, or
pleasant to me, joined with the reluctance to move—partly from
previous exhaustion by company, I cannot keep out—for one
cannot, dare not, always be 'not at home' or 'very particularly
engaged' (& the last very often will not serve my Turn)—these
added to my bread & cheese employments+my lectures which are
—bread & cheese—i.e. a very losing bargain in a pecuniary view—
have prevented me day after day from returning your kind calls.
Più vorrei, più non posso.— I will as soon as I can. In the mean time
I have left your name with the old woman, & the attendants in the
office, as one to whom I am always at home when I am at home.
For Wordsworth has taught me to desire your acquaintance & to
esteem you—& need I add that any one so much regarded by
Mrs C. (whom I love even as my very own Sister, whose Love for me
with that of Wordsworth's Sister, Wife, & Wife's Sister, form almost
the only Happiness, I have on earth) can never be indifferent to,

dear Sir, | Your sincere Friend,

S. T. Coleridge

700. *To Mrs. S. T. Coleridge*

MS. Lord Latymer. Hitherto unpublished.

Thursday, May 5th, 1808.

My dear Sara

I assure you solemnly, that for some months I have never *willingly*
delayed opening any Letter, which I have received, for five minutes.
It is true, that your last remained a day unopened; but this was
owing to a most unusual *press* of occupation—the certainty, that
I should only confuse my mind by it, & make myself less capable of
doing what I had to do.—I have been making some hitherto

---

[1] Coleridge's lecture on Education was delivered on Tuesday, 3 May 1808.
Robinson wrote to Mrs. Clarkson that Coleridge 'eulogised Dr. Bell's plan of
education and concluded by a severe attack upon Lancaster for having stolen
from Dr. Bell all that is good in his plans'. *Shakespearean Criticism*, ii. 14.

baffled attempts to leave you a compleat Independence—for—
strange as it may seem, inoffensive a being as I am—I have many
Enemies—from what cause, but Envy, God only knows. Of course,
when I come into the Country, I come to Keswick—that I have not
written all, that my Heart has been urging me to write, I will leave
to your own Solution, after the following Statement—May 1.
(Sunday)—Wrote a long answer to the Duke of Sussex, about poor
Palm's Pamphlet (the Spirit of the Times) for which Buonaparte put
him to Death.[1]—Answered 5 twopenny post Letters.—Was interrupted by 7 people calling on me one after the other.—At 5 o/clock
dined with Mr Barnard, to meet a party, convened to meet me.—
N. B. The greater part of this day is, variously but equally applicable to every other—therefore I shall not repeat it.—Monday—after
the same interruptions dined at 6 o/clock with the Bishop of
Durham—. Tuesday—after a lecture of two hours and a quarter on
Education & Dr Bell's System—had to dine with the Literary
Fund; but by a very droll mistake dined with the *Whig Club*; but
after discovering it had to go to the other huge Room-full.—
Wednesday.—Lecture of an hour and a quarter—& then to dine
with the famous Rout-giving over-rich Mr & Mrs Thompson in
Portman Square, where I met from Sir H. Englefield the severest
Insult, I ever suffered, concerning the Quack Lancaster—. Mr &
Mrs T. and the Family in agonies—& have since sent to me a very
amiable & feeling Letter.—Thursday—to day—preparing tomorrow's Lecture—written a long Letter to Sir H. E.—answered
three others— and am to dine with Mr Sotheby at ½ past 5—to
meet a party—. Friday—to dine with Sir G. Beaumont, after my
Lecture, to meet *a party*.—Saturday—with Miss Ogle (the Dean of
Winchester's Daughter) to meet Bowles, & a party—& in the mean
time to be preparing for the Press the Lecture on Education, in
order to withstand the Bullies of Lancaster's Faction, who come in
upon me unprepared, and, I may almost say, insult me in the
Streets.—Now, my dear! I leave you to judge whether I *can* do
more than I do—having besides all this to prepare William's Poem
for the Press.[2]

I shall put a full stop to all this in a few days—

Your anecdote of little Sara is not only deeply affecting to me, as
a Father; but exceedingly interesting to me as a philosopher.

---

[1] Johann P. Palm, a German bookseller, was shot by Napoleon's orders on
26 Aug. 1806 for distributing a pamphlet, *Deutschland in seiner tiefen Erniedri-
gung*, presumably written by Philipp Yelin. Coleridge mistakenly believed that
it was E. M. Arndt's *Geist der Zeit* for which Palm was executed. Part I of
Arndt's work was first issued in 1806 and republished in 1807. See Letter 708.

[2] *The White Doe of Rylstone.*

I inclose a letter from good dear Mrs Skepper[1] to Hartley—I have been looking about for 20 minutes or more for a Letter of Montague's, . . . [Remainder of manuscript missing.]

701. *To Thomas N. Longman*

Transcript Coleridge family. Hitherto unpublished.

[Early May 1808][2]

My dear Sir

I will take upon me the correction of the Sheets of 'the White Doe.'—

I seriously hope, that nothing in my last, which was wholly intended to amuse you, has given you offence—Upon my honor, you were not even in my Thoughts—I reasoned with A. X. Y. & Z. exactly as a Mathematician—be assured, my dear Sir! I highly respect you—

S. T. Coleridge.

702. *To Matilda Betham*

Pub. A House of Letters, 109.

Saturday, May 7, 1808.
348 Strand.

Dear Miss Betham,—I sallied forth to find you, at least your abode, unfortunately leaving your direction behind me. I went to New Cavendish Street, and after many vain inquiries was positively assured by a man at the corner shop that you had removed from Foley Street to Old Cavendish Street, and that you did not reside in New Cavendish Street. I knocked at every door in Old Cavendish Street, not unrecompensed for the present pain by the remembrances of the different characters of voice and countenance with which my question was answered in all gradations, from gentle and hospitable kindness to downright brutality. I failed, returned home, and in the Exhibition Catalogue found your true address. N.B.—I looked, when I was at the Exhibition on Monday (the first open day), at the numbers, in order that I *might not* look at your works *then*. The crowd was so great—the number of detestable pushers so overpowering. But I shall go on Monday, the very moment the rooms are open, in order that I may look at *them* singly, and as much alone

---

[1] Basil Montagu married Mrs. Skepper later in 1808.

[2] Coleridge's comments in Letter 708 indicate that he formally arranged with Longman to supervise the printing of *The White Doe of Rylstone* not long after 1 May.

as possible. It is quite shocking, that all that is good in the Exhibi
tion is absolutely extinguished by the glare of raw colours put
into wild shapes on innocent much-injured canvas. I write now to
entreat that you would let me know what day you will be at home
and disengaged next week, as I shall keep myself disengaged till
I hear from you, for I am most sincerely,

Your obliged,

S. T. Coleridge.

703. *To the Secretary of the Royal Institution*[1]

Pub. The Jerningham Letters, *ed. Egerton Castle, 2 vols., 1896, i. 317.*

In introducing this fragment Edward Jerningham says that 'a crowd
attended' in anticipation of the lecture but that Coleridge 'sent a Letter to the
secretary to Inform him That coming out a Boat the Day before He fell back
and hurt his head, and the Continuance of the Pain obliged Him to defer his
Lecture. A common personage would have been satisfied with this Information
that He had convey'd to the Secretary; But Mr. Colleridge goes on in this
manner (I read the Letter—and These are the very words).'

[11 May 1808][2]

The pain however will soon subside, for it does not rise from so
recent an Event as yesterday, but from a more distant period. It
was when I was at Malta, Two years ago: a person rushed into my
Apartment and abruptly announced to me the Death of a dear
Friend, this occasioned my falling backwards and gave a contusion
on my head which Brings back the pain occasionally upon any
Exertion or Accident.

704. *To Matilda Betham*

Pub. A House of Letters, *107.*

[*Circa* 11 May] 1808.

Dear Miss Betham,—Not my will, but accident and necessity,
made me a truant from my promise. I was to have left Merton, in
Surrey, at half-past eight on Tuesday morning with a Mr Hall, who
would have driven me in his cha[i]se to town by ten; but having
walked an unusual distance on the Monday, and talked and exerted
myself in spirits that have long been unknown to me, on my return
to my friend's house, being thirsty, I drank at least a quart of

---

[1] James Peter Auriol.

[2] Coleridge's accident, which gave rise to the explanation in this letter and
led to the postponement of his lecture, occurred on Tuesday, 10 May. Letter
702 shows that Coleridge planned to call on Miss Betham during the week
of 8 May, Letter 704 that his accident prevented him from keeping his appointment.

lemonade; the consequence was that all Tuesday morning, till indeed two o'clock in the afternoon, I was in exceeding pain, and incapable of quitting my room, or dismissing the hot flannels applied to my body. However, determining to be in town on that night, I left Merton at five, walked stoutly on till I was detained an hour and a half on Clapham Common in an act of mere humanity —indeed a most affecting one, and not uninstructive, if to know by *facts* the dreadfully degraded and hardened hearts the inhabitants of cities and their suburbs may be called instructive. At Vauxhall I took a boat for Somerset House; two mere children were my Charons; however, though against tide, we sailed safely to the landing-place, when, as I was getting out, one of the little ones (God bless him!) moved the boat. On turning half-way round to reprove him, he moved it again, and I fell back on the landing-place. By my exertions I should have saved my head but for a large stone which I struck against just under my crown, and unfortunately in the very same place which had been contused at Melton [Malta] when I fell backward after hearing suddenly and most abruptly of Captain Wordsworth's fate in the *Abergavenny*, a most dear friend of mine. Since that time any great agitation has occasioned a feeling of, as it were, a *shuttle* moving from that part of the back of my head horizontally to my forehead, with some pain but more confusion. This sensation the accident brought on with great violence, but it is now abating. As soon as I go out at all I will do myself the pleasure of calling on you, for indeed I very much wish to see you.

S. T. Coleridge.

Pray would it be possible to draw the following figures for a seal? In the centre (as a coat-of-arms), a rose or myrtle in blossom, on the right hand, a genius (or genie) holding in the right hand two torches inverted, and one at least recently extinguished; on the other side, a Love with a flaring torch and head averted, the torch in the direction of the head, as one gazing after something going away. In the corner of the left part of the composition a large butterfly flying off; the motto under it, 'Che sarà sarà'—What will be, will be.

705. *To George Coleridge*

Transcript George Coleridge. Pub. with omis. E. L. G. i. 416.

Coleridge wrote to his brother, first, to obtain a copy of his birth certificate, presumably in connexion with his attempts to increase his insurance; and secondly, to pour out his pent-up bitterness over gossip about him, originating in Ottery as a result of his announcement in 1807 of his intention of separating

from Mrs. Coleridge. (See Letters 642, 653, and 656.) In his immediate response
to this letter George Coleridge explained his motive for not receiving Coleridge
in 1807. He considered the separation from Mrs. Coleridge 'an irreligious act,
. . . which the New Testament forbids', and one to which he 'would not be an
accessary'. Then in October 1809, after Coleridge had asked for a loan in
connexion with *The Friend*, George Coleridge indignantly refused financial
assistance and not only returned Coleridge's '*downright red hot letter*' of 11 May
1808 but attempted to answer the accusations made against him. See Letters
783, 788, and 792.

348 Strand. 11 May 1808

You would serve me, Brother! if by return of Post you would be
so kind as to send to me from the Ottery Register, properly authenti-
cated by the Vicar and Reader or Churchwarden [a certificate] of
the date of my Birth and Christening—

Multifold and urgent as late my employment and my calamities
have been for the last 7 or 8 months, yet I have been prevented
from writing to you chiefly by feelings from within concerning
things—

'Which love cannot revenge, nor Truth forgive.'

I merely snatch this opportunity to say, that dear Mrs. Coleridge
wrote to Mrs. George Coleridge without my knowledge, and before I
had time to prepare her (having been laid up in a fit of sickness
at Bristol, so that tho' I received your Letter *there* I had not seen,
much less read it, with very many others, till a few days after my
arrival at Stowey) before I had prepared her for the unmerited
wrong inflicted on us, after such Invitations as she had received.
I pray you do not suppose that poor as I am, the mere expence of
bringing my Wife and all my Children three hundred miles from
their home in order to see their 'Father's Mamma', & that of their
return to the same distance was that which affected me, ill as I
could afford it. No, Sir! conscious before my Maker, that even the
Errors of my Youth have been most grossly exaggerated, and
wanderings attributed to want of principle which proceeded from
excess of sensibility & moral cowardice in affairs which most other
men would have laughed at—yet since my leaving the university,
what deviation from honor or rectitude can be fairly charged to
me? Are not my old College Friends, two of whom are now Tutors
of the College & among the most respected Characters of the
University, my Friends still? Have I ever had a Friend whom I
have lost? Do not those who have known me longest, & been with
me, night & day as it were, for years & years, love and esteem me
most? Have not all calumnies concerning me, saving these from
my own family, proceeded from Persons abhorred by all who know
them intimately as liars, or pitied as madmen? What *have* I done,
that a Letter written to you in the overflowing of Love and grateful

Remembrance (for to a deserted Orphan every kindness appeared great)—that a Letter written, Heaven knows! in the Hope, that your authority & kindness would mediate and produce a happy effect on a mind softened perhaps by being at the Birth-place and among the Family of the Father of the Children—that this should be disclosed? *so* disclosed, that long before I knew it, a mere Youth at Bristol assigned to a family accustomed to revere me, as the reason of his refusal to call on his Uncle and to see his Cousins 'that the Family had resolved not to receive me'.[1] This *resolution* was, perhaps, in your power; the circumstances, that accompanied it, were *not*—that is, not MORALLY. Are my pursuits less moral or useful than those of my—for so I am to name them—Brothers? or (if I may appeal to a [comparison alien] from *my* nature) are my friends & connections less honorable or splendid? O would to God the Omniscient that every hour of my Life could be made manifest with my actions, and all their context & commentary of feelings, impulses, motives—and at the same time the same process take place with those of my Brothers! Before my Maker I should sink down in confusion; but before Men I should not have to wear on my cheeks a Blush from the *comparison*. I speak not that a Richard Hart[2] could reply to a kind Enquiry concerning me from a young Gentleman, 'I know nothing and wish to know nothing about such a Fellow' (these were the words the syntax only somewhat rectified); but I should indeed be ashamed if I had not been deeply wounded, that one honored Individual's feelings had been prejudiced against me by a person whom that Man would never have known but for my enthusiastic praises & expressions of grateful love[3]—When I was with you with Mrs. Coleridge & Hartley, your Wife informed her that I had been a very bad young man—that my Brother had done wonders for me, but she hoped now that I was *reformed*, I should

---

[1] 'Who the mere youth at Bristol could be . . . I cannot augur—except it was James Coleridge in his way to join his Regiment in Ireland—I declare that I never made such a resolution except in the instance which I stated in my letter [of May 1808]—and in *that instance* I still hold my resolution—that for *such a purpose* as your letter set forth, I never would receive you—and while I think the Gospel to be the Word of God delivered by Jesus Christ, I shall continue to be of the same opinion—' George Coleridge to S. T. C., October 1809. [MS. Lady Cave.]

[2] A brother of Mrs. George Coleridge.

[3] 'You may remember that [in May 1808] I . . . requested that you would within a week or fortnight tell me if Mr. Jos. Wedgwood was not the Person alluded to in your Letter—that he might himself vindicate for me what I was not disposed to do for myself under the imputation of such calumny— You never condescended to answer my letter and I therefore sent your Paragraph to Mr. Wedgwood, who informed me that he had . . . amply justified my conduct—' George Coleridge to S. T. C., Oct. 1809.

be able to repay the money.[1]—Poor as I have been (not for want of opportunities to have become perhaps the wealthiest of the Family, but because I did not feel this to be *my* calling) yet had I not judged of your feelings by my own, long ago should I have requested you to permit me to do away the sole reason, you can have for treating me thus, by sending in the amount of my alimony—As to the little pangs I must have suffered from my sweet Children asking me why they must not see their Grandmamma, their Uncles & Cousins— they are over, and I have endeavored to compensate for the disappointment of a fond Mother, who had indulged the venial pride of shewing to you what had been believed by so many strangers to their Blood.—I would not die, concealing my feelings—nor have I any self-respecting motive, at present, even of the most honorable kind, except the Regret that I shall not be able to cultivate the friendship of my Nephew John Coleridge, of whose virtues and faculties I anticipate all I dare anticipate from a mind whose native nobleness is to be counteracted by systems which transmute by negligent alchemy our Virtue & Religion into selfish Prudence, and direct the Conscience to value men for what they do knowably by the Mass, not for what they *are* actually. But he is a noble Being, and to Heaven with Prayers I commit him—

I need no answer; the mere certificate is the last favor I beg— and only add that if you will inform me of the amount of my Debt to the Family, it shall be ultimately paid to you if I live—broken out of years, even tho' I shorten my own and my Children's simple means—and if I die shortly, it *is* still mentioned in my will—Had I not felt a greater reverence for all that bear the name of my revered Father (and whom, I confess, I have a feeling, one third pride & two thirds tenderness in being told that I strongly resemble him in person & mind)—I could by merely stating to some 4 or 5 of my Friends the cause of my Distress, have procured in a few Weeks the sum necessary to liquidate the Debt, with a certainty that it could never have been considered as a justifying cause of either themselves treating my name & me contumeliously or in telling others to do so. Often, and quite irrelevantly to myself, have I noticed the injustice of resting the condemnation of an Individual

---

[1] 'That part of your accusation which refers to a conversation between your Wife and mine will not possibly appear discreditable to the latter, if Mrs. Samuel can recollect what and who led to the Subject of your expences—Is it likely from what you have known of Mrs. G. Coleridge that she would do any thing thro' malice? Is it not more fair to conclude that in the moment of confidential communication nothing was said at the time but what Mrs. Samuel thought friendly? A detached sentence of the most innocent intention in the hand of anger will set a whole Nation in flames—' George Coleridge to S. T. C., Oct. 1809. The conversation alluded to took place at Ottery in 1799.

in testimony derived from his nearest Relations, merely because they were such—without any enquiry how much, or how intimately they had known him, or what opportunities they had had of seeing him or witnessing his habits of conduct, his tone of principle—and withal reflecting, that when Brothers can exert themselves against an Orphan Brother, the latter must be either a mere monster, or the former must be warped by some improper Passion—

I presume that in general it is not difficult to forgive a tedious length of Letter, when the Receiver is assured that it is *once for all*—that it will never recur. With sincere—often with *fervent* wishes for your permanent well being—; that what my understanding compels me to believe may either not be, or may cease to be, I remain

Your Brother
S. T. C.

706. *To Andrew Bell*

Pub. Life of Andrew Bell, *ii. 582.*

17th May 1808.

Dear and truly honoured Sir,

I write these few lines to you for two purposes—1st, To know when, as far as you have intelligence, your system was first known in England; and 2dly, To assure you that I am not so much to blame as, I fear, you think me, in connecting your revered name with that of such a wretched quack as Lancaster. For not two hours before my lecture of Tuesday, (for which I have been made to suffer very disproportionately to the offence, had I been, which I cannot admit, guilty of any,) Lancaster came to my door, with a Quaker with whom I am somewhat acquainted. The latter came up and asked permission to introduce Mr Lancaster, which I refused, and indeed satisfied the friend's reason, that it was very improper that I should go to an extemporaneous lecture of two hours, perhaps fretted and agitated. He, however, repeated the menaces which one of Lancaster's zealots had made to me on the Monday—'Take care of yourself; you are misled by a Mr Bernard, and the *rascally* Bishop of Durham; but only take care of yourself, or you may suffer for it. There is now a pamphlet in the press, which will show that all the merit is Mr Lancaster's;[1] and a mere trifle that of Dr—what's his name?—Bell.' These, dear sir, were the very words, as far as I can remember—assuredly the meaning, and very nearly the words. Can

---

[1] This was presumably Joseph Fox's pamphlet, *A Comparative View of the Plans of Education, as detailed in the publications of Dr. Bell and Mr. Lancaster,* July 1808.

you then wonder, my dear sir, that I was warm, indignant, at a liar—
an ignorant, vulgar, arrogant charlatan, whom (I know) the most
respectable part of his own sect have given up as an unworthy
brother?

However, dear doctor, be assured, and I solemnly promise you,
that though *forced* to publish my lecture[1]—I say, though forced to
publish the substance of it—I shall, as truth and duty dictate, hold
your name sacred, and, in short, *say the truth*—namely, that neither
directly nor indirectly had I ever had any the slightest impulse
from you respecting Lancaster; that the lecture began wholly
independent of you; and that, on the two (or three) times in which
I had had the pleasure of meeting you, you had evidently *waived* all
discussion on that subject, with the dignity belonging to you. What
interest *can* I have? I would not have a *place* if it were offered me;
I dare not go into orders, though, of all other things, the character of
a clergyman would most gratify me; but I *am* desirous to prove that
I am a zealous *subject*, and a convinced and fervent son of the
Church of England. Do not let me lose your esteem. . . .

707. *To Andrew Bell*

Pub. Life of Andrew Bell, *ii. 584.*

May 1808.[2]

My dear Sir,

. . . I thank you for your letter. Your *name* and *character* shall
be ever held *sacred* by me. I was assuredly hurried away by warmth
of provoked feeling, and was guilty of a breach of trust to the Royal
Institution, in my (the most *impersonal*) personality on Lancaster.
This I confess, and will confess; but that, abstracted from *the time*,
and the place, I said any thing false in reason, or in fact, I *cannot*
confess. Having read your work, and then reading Lancaster's
publications, and lastly, hearing that there was a pamphlet in the
press, the object of which was to depreciate you, had I never seen
you, I am quite certain that I should have done, what I am now
compelled to do. Indeed, I almost wish I never had seen you, in
order that vulgar minds might not be able to suppose, what good
minds will be incapable of thinking, that I had been, in the slightest
degree, influenced by you.

I have been openly charged, among other things, and this in a

---

[1] On 15 May Crabb Robinson reported to Mrs. Clarkson that 'C. has begged
a week's holiday, as he is going to publish his lecture on education'. (*Shake-spearean Criticism,* ii. 18.) Coleridge, however, did not publish the lecture.

[2] This letter was apparently written not long after Letter 706.

large company, by a man of high rank and character, with 'base cowardice, in calumniating a man in a place and mode, in which he could make no reply.' This I cannot submit to. But all my reasonings will be perfectly impersonal, and wholly deduced from passages of works in the possession of the public. Surely I have the same right that any Monthly or Edinburgh reviewer has, and, I trust, shall exercise it with honester motives, and more love.

The more I think, the more do I accord, with Daubeny and Mrs Trimmer,[1] (though, Heaven knows, far enough from assenting to all their arguments or notions!) that Lancaster's schools are a very dangerous attack on our civil and ecclesiastical establishments, at a time when they want all that support, which, before God the Omniscient, I declare that, in my belief, your system would give, beyond any plan conceivable by me.

Dear Dr Bell, it is my comfort that, independent of me, you would have been basely attacked. Surely it is better that, wholly independent of you, some other should come forward: as to any controversy between Lancaster's and your system, in its modes and minutiae, there will not be *one word* about it in my publication. I shall nakedly and coolly give the history of the discovery, and then state the value of the additions to it, and what I conceive likely to be the results final of Lancaster's schools. . . .

708. *To William Wordsworth*

MS. Dove Cottage. Pub. Chambers, Life, 347.

Saturday Night. [21 May 1808][2]

At 8 o/clock this evening I received a note from the Longmans' in consequence of one from you to them—I have been hunting for your Sister's Letter, as yet to no purpose; but as I put it up with many others from Grasmere, in some one or other of my repositories, I shall be sure to find it before this can go off to you; & will leave a space for her words concerning the Poem. At present, I can only state how I understood, and what I believe to be the substance of, them.

In my re-perusals of the Poem it seemed always to strike on my feeling as well as judgement, that if there were any serious defect, it consisted in a disproportion of the Accidents to the spiritual Incidents, and closely connected with this, if it be not indeed the

---

[1] Both Charles Daubeny (1745–1827) and Mrs. Sarah Trimmer (1741–1810) attacked Lancaster's plan of education.

[2] This letter was obviously written on the Saturday before Coleridge's letter to Longman, postmarked 23 May 1808.

same,—that Emily is indeed talked of, and once appears; but
neither speaks nor acts in all the first 3 fourths of the Poem: and as
the outward Interest of the Poem is in favor of the old man's
religious feelings, and the filial Heroism of his band of Sons, it
seemed to require something in order to place the two Protestant
Malcontents of the Family in a light, that made them *beautiful*, as
well as virtuous—In short, to express it *far* more strongly than I
mean or *think* in order, in the present anguish of my spirits, to be
able to express it [at] all, that ¾ths of the Work is every thing rather
than Emily; *then*, the last almost a separate (& doubtless most
exquisite Poem) wholly *of* Emily.—The whole of the Rout and the
delivering up of the Family by Francis I never ceased to find not
only *comparatively* very heavy, but to me quite obscure, as to
Francis's motives. And on the few, to whom within my acquaintance the Poem has been read either by yourself or me (I have,
I believe, read it only at the Beaumonts') it produced the same
effect.—Now I had conceived two little Incidents, the introduction
of which joined to a little abridgement, and lyrical precipitation of
the last Half of the third, I had thought, would have removed this
defect—so seeming to me—and bring to a finer Balance the *Business* with the *Action* of the Tale.[1] But after my receipt of your
Letter concerning Lamb's censures[2] I felt my courage fail—and
that what I deemed a harmonizing would disgust you, as a *materiali-
zation* of the Plan, & appear to you like insensibility to the power
of the history in the mind. Not that I should have shrunk back from
the mere fear of giving transient pain & a temporary offence, from
the want of sympathy of feeling & coincidence of opinions—I rather
envy than blame that deep interest in a production, which is inevitable perhaps, and certainly not dishonorable to such, as feel
poetry their calling and their duty, & which no man would find
much fault with if the Object, instead of a Poem, were a large Estate
or a Title—it appears to me to become a foible then only, when the
Poet denies or is unconscious of, it's existence. But I did not deem
myself in such a state of mind, as to entitle me to rely on my
opinion when opposed to your's—from the heat & bustle of these
disgusting Lectures, for which I receive whole Hods full of plaister

---

[1] 'We do not know what Coleridge's "little incidents" were, nor whether he
ever communicated them, and as neither of the extant manuscripts of the poem
preserves the original text we cannot determine the exact character and extent
of W.'s revision; but it must have been considerable, . . . and, far more important, much of Coleridge's criticism, which was doubtless pertinent enough to the
text before him, is not applicable to its published form.' Note to *The White Doe*
in Wordsworth, *Poet. Works*, iii. 546–7.

[2] For Wordsworth's reaction to Lamb's strictures on *The White Doe* see
Middle Years, i. 196–8.

of Paris-flatteries about as pleasant to me as rancid large Spanish Olives—these on the one side—& permanent hatred, and the most cruel public Insults on the other—& all this to cost me at least sixty £, exclusive of Lodgings, for which I pay either by Obligation or by past services or both—2. the necessity of publishing the substance of my Lecture on national Education in a very enlarged form, in order to obviate the charge made against me, most unprovokedly, in a very large Company, by Sir Harry Englefield of 'base cowardice'—& even this was not the severest sentence of his most solemn & yet most wanton attack.—3. for the sake of money, I am at the same time employed every spare hour in a complete '*Rifacciamento*', or '*Umarbeitung*', of the *Geist der Zeit*—the work, for which poor *Palm* was murdered by Buonaparte—I not only add a long Preface, but throughout by notes or marked Interpolations, joined to softenings, omissions, and the lowering of the dytherambic style prevalent in the original, make almost a new work[1]—It is done at the warm recommendation of His R. Highness, the Duke of Sussex, & will be an exceedingly interesting Work—& likely to have a run—. 4. In getting out of a boat at Some[r]set stairs the little Boy stirred it, & I half turning round to bid him be still, had the misfortune of falling backward, & struck the back of my head on the very part, on which I fell at Malta; tho' with no great force, as but for one stone I should have broken my fall entirely, tho' at the price of weakening my wrist a little.—This produced the whole next day such a shuttle-like motion from the part horizontally to my forehead with such odd confusion, that I was unable to give the Lecture —& it returns every now and then tho' but for a few seconds, if ever a Thought agitates me or a sudden Sound—5. I have been sorely vexed in the failure of my plan of increasing my assurance, after I had procured all the money necessary—this was partly from want of foresight, in offering the whole at one place, & that the most scrupulous & stern Office in London—partly, I had no medical man to refer to who had known me continuedly for any length of time— I referred, by permission, to Dr Babbington—However, after waiting 8 days they declined assuring my Life for the increase proposed—. Had I consulted Montague aforehand, this probably

---

[1] Coleridge later offered his translation of Arndt's *Geist der Zeit* to Meyers, a German bookseller in London, but his letter was ignored. Nothing came of Coleridge's plans for publication, and Arndt's work was translated by Peter Will in 1808. See Letters 700, 712, 721, and 739, and *Essays on His Own Times*, ii. 670. For a study of Coleridge's proposed 'Rifacciamento' of the *Geist der Zeit* and for a list of fragments of his translation incorporated into *The Friend* and the *Letters on the Spaniards*, see Lucyle Werkmeister, 'Coleridge and "the work for which poor Palm was murdered"', *Journal of English and Germanic Philology*, July 1954, pp. 347–51.

would not have happened. I had set my heart & hope upon it: and the refusal made me very melancholy. 6. Among other wicked calumnies, & in addition to my Brother's shameful Usage of me, John Wedgewood & his family have shamefully abused me—A friend of mine asked John Wedgwood, whether he had seen me— he replied—'No! nor ever wish to see him. He was ungrateful and inattentive to my poor Brother, Thomas! during his being with him in his sickness.'—I possess one letter from T. W. that tells a different story.—These have all conspired to prevent sorer anguish from going to rest, as a slight Breeze will keep up the working of a ground-swell; and a mere atom of Dirt occasion wounds to rankle—

From most of these causes I was suffering, so as not to allow me any rational confidence in my opinions, when contrary to your's which had been formed in calmness and on long reflection; then I received your Sister's Letter—stating the wish, that I would give up the thought of proposing the *means* of correction, and merely point out the things to be corrected—which as they could be of no great consequence, you might do in a day or two, & the publication of the Poem, for the immediacy of which she expressed great anxiety, be no longer retarded—assigning a reason.—Now the merely verbal *alteranda* did appear to *me too* very few, & trifling— from your letter on L[amb] I concluded that you would not, from your own opinion, have the Incidents & Action interfered with—& therefore I sent it off—but soon retracted it, in order to note down the single words & phrases that I disliked in the books after the two first—as there would be time to receive your opinion of them during the printing of the two first, in which I saw nothing amiss except the one passage, we altered together, & the two Lines which I scratched out, because *you* yourself were *doubtful*; & Mrs Skepper had told me, that *she* had felt them exactly as *I* did—namely, as interrupting the spirit of the continuous tranquil motion of the White Doe—However—tho' somewhat grieved by your Sister's exceeding anxiety about pecuniary matters—grieved, heaven knows! for your sake and for her's, because I thought it not only a decaying of genial Hope & former light-heartedness, but as a recurrence of fears, which had harrassed you at Racedown— Besides, I could not bear to think, that her judgement should be in danger of *warping*, from money-motives in affairs, which con- cern—if not your *fame*—yet your thereto introductory *reputation*— & which too by expediting or retarding the steady establishment of your classical Rank would affect, of course, even your average pecuniary Gains—. Indeed before my *Fall*, &c, &c, &c, I had in- dulged the Hope, that by a division of Labor you would have no occasion to think about—as if I had been to live, with very warm

& zealous patronage, I was fast ripening a plan, which secures from 12 to 20£ a week[1]—(the Prospectus indeed going to the Press, as soon as Mr Sotheby and Sir G. Beaumont had read it.)[2]—However, on the mere possibility of a genial mood coming upon me, in which I should either see the whole *conduct* of the Poem in the light, in which you & she see it; or such a flash of conviction concerning the excellence of *my own* imagined amendment, as would SETTLE me; I wrote out the last 200 lines, or so of the third Book—& then again sent it off, in order that it might be *advertised* as *in* the Press, about the time, when I gave my Lecture on your System & Compositions —which will be, God willing! on Friday *after* next—as my first Lecture on Modern Poetry is to be on *next* Tuesday.[3]—I cannot therefore think my 'misinterpretation' a very strange one—and, but that—(unless when I am reading it to & for myself—) I can not get rid of the Fear, that it will be talked of, as an imitation of Walter Scott—I having such daily experiences, what people are, & how different their abiding thoughts, *if they have any*, from those which even the worthiest EXPRESS, & I dare say, feel when under the influence of some immediate sympathy—(I therefore did not send the little preface,[4] in which *my* name was, because I know, that *the Public* are quick-witted in detecting the most hidden thing that can be made a topic of chit-chat Scandal. If every one, who had seen the Xtabel, believed, without the least suspicion of the difference, that the metre was the same as that of the Lay of the last Minstrel, they will & must, of course, think your metre to be the same with

[1] A year later Dorothy Wordsworth refers to Coleridge's continued determination to be of financial assistance. Wordsworth, she says, had planned 'to write upon public affairs in the *Courier* . . . for the sake of getting money. . . . Coleridge, however, writes to desire that . . . [Wordsworth] will not withdraw himself from poetry, for he is assured that there will be no need of it, as he (Coleridge) can get money enough.' *Middle Years*, i. 294.

[2] This is the first mention in Coleridge's letters of *The Friend*, published in 1809–10. No prospectus was issued at this time. In June, however, with the approval of Davy and Bernard arrangements were made to have William Savage, printer to the Royal Institution, print and publish *The Friend*. As Letter 740 shows, Coleridge understood the terms to be as follows. Savage was to be paid for the paper and printing at the trade price and was to receive 5 per cent. as the publisher. He was, moreover, to be the publisher of any future editions of *The Friend*.

[3] No such lectures were given. See *Biog. Lit.* i. 38, where Coleridge says he had intended to lecture on English poetry 'from Cowper to the present day' but changed his plan and did not do so.

[4] When Wordsworth published *The White Doe* in 1815, he did not include any such preface, a fact which Coleridge noted in a letter to Byron: 'I have not learnt with what motive Wordsworth omitted the original advertisement prefixed to his White Doe, that the peculiar metre and mode of narration he had imitated from the Christabel.' (Letter 981.) 'The little preface' is now lost. See Wordsworth. *Poet. Works*, iii. 546.

that of the L. of the 1. M.—and then your referring the metre of a
Poem composed since the publication of the L. of the 1. M. to a MSS
Poem, will appear strange and almost *envious*, if the great *priority*
of the Mss. to the Publication be not mentioned at the same time—
and if it be, it would then, I fear, be deemed *invidious*, and a covert
attack on Scott's Originality,[1] which for the world I would not,
that *you* should be suspected of—) I say, *but* for this apprehension,
which I am sure is not an *absurd* one, I should most deeply regret
the withdrawal of a Poem so peculiarly your's, and beyond any
other *in rhyme* illustrative of your characteristic excellences—tho' I
may now add, that it being not only sense, but sense that demands
thought in the Reader, & will not leave him to a lax free-will, that
the metre being—as you observed of your poem in general, rather
dramatic than lyric, i.e. not such an arrangement of syllables, not
such a metre, as acts a priori and with complete self-subsistence (as
the simple anapestic in its smoothest form, or the praise of Bacchus
in Dryden's Ode) but depending for it's beauty always, and often
even for it's metrical existence, on the *sense* and *passion*—I have
something like the same suspicion that you entertained concerning
Xtabel, how far this would or would not be an obstacle to it's
popularity—Lamb & Miss Lamb, who evidently read it—he twice
thro', he said—with no genial effort, no exertion from sympathy,
are for the very reason that disqualifies them as Judges concerning
it's *true merit*, no unfair Specimens of perhaps the majority of readers
of Poetry, especially in the perusal of a new Poem, which does not
employ the common excitements of lively interest, namely,
curiosity, and the terror or pity from unusual external Events &
Scenes—convent dungeons &c &c—

I beg to be understood solely as referring to *the Public*, not *the
People*, according to your own distinction—and this only for a
while—and chiefly influenced by the wish, that two publications
should not succeed each other, both failing in their *first general*
Impression—& perhaps in some measure, by comparing it's *chances*
of immediate Sale with the almost *certainty* of the great popularity
of either Peter Bell, or Margaret, or even the Salisbury Plain—

God forbid, your Sister should ever cease to use her own Eyes
and heart, and only her own, in order to know how a Poem *ought* to
affect mankind; but we must learn to see with the Eyes of others in
order to guess luckily how it *will* affect them—Neither do I *wish*
her to learn this; but then I would have her learn to entertain
neither warm Hopes or confident Expectations concerning Events
dependent on minds & hearts BELOW the distinct Ken of her
Sympathies. Let her only reflect that (even *excluding* the effect of

[1] See Letters 632, 650, 662, and 845.

Routs & continued personal gossip, &c &c, yet) the great majority
of the modern Buyers of new Poems read at least 20 whole *Novels*
of 2, 3, 4, 5 Volumes each, for ONE poem—You have slightly
mentioned this in the Preface to the L.B.[1]—but it deserves to be
dwelt on at length—.

In fine, I did it for the best—the extracts on the next leaf will
shew what grounds I had for taking it as granted, that the speedy
Publication of the White Doe had been decided on at Grasmere—
the first extract shews your Sister's opinion & feeling, for and from
herself—and as the next was written since your return, & expresses
the same opinion, and as I had not received any letter to the contrary from you—nor had any reason to expect one—I coincided
with her, that the speedier the better, & for her reasons—I was
concerned, not at her opinion, but at the anxiety that seemed to
have influenced it, from the very beginning.

S. T. Coleridge—

I assuredly was commissioned by you to retalk the matter with the
Longmans'—I did so—and they finally agreed to your own terms,
whether £s or Guineas.[2] As soon as I had revised it in order to be
aware of any little verbal inaccuracies, I promised to send it.—
They must be in a strange Puzzle, and suppose that you had not
authorized me to dispose of the work to them for this Season.

—Extract from a Letter, Grasmere, March 31.

'This letter is intended for William, tho' I have little hope that he
will be in town when it arrives—

We are exceedingly concerned to hear, that you, William! have
given up all thoughts of publishing your Poem. As to the Outcry
against you, I would defy it—what matter, if you get your 100
guineas into your pocket? Besides it is like as if they had run you
down, when it is known you have a poem ready for publishing, and
keep it back. It is our belief, and that of all who have heard it read,
that the *Tale* would bear it up—and without money what CAN we
do? New House! new furniture! such a large family! two servants
& little Sally! we *cannot* go on so another half year: and as Sally
will not be fit for another place, we must take her back again into

---

[1] 'The invaluable works of our elder writers . . . are driven into neglect by
frantic novels. . . .' 1800 Preface.

[2] It is obvious that in April Wordsworth not only knew of the results of
Coleridge's negotiations with the publisher, but approved of the terms. 'The
poem is to be published. Longman has consented, in spite of the odium under
which my brother labours as a poet, to give him one hundred guineas per
thousand copies.' Dorothy Wordsworth to Lady Beaumont, 20 April 1808,
Middle Years, i. 199. As late as 11 May Wordsworth still planned to publish his
poem with Longman. Ibid. i. 213.

the old one, and dismiss one of the Servants, and work the flesh *off our poor bones*. Do, dearest William! do pluck up your Courage—overcome your disgust to publishing—It is but a *little trouble*, and all will be over, and we shall be wealthy, and at our ease for one year, at least.'

The Italics are as in the original.—I thought, that the difference might be met halfway between you & Mr Longman: that you were quite right in not giving up your poem to be decided by any set of Critics, he chose to appoint—and on the other hand, that as the question was not the intrinsic merit, but the immediate saleability of the article (for remember, it was not for a Copy-right, but an Edition of 1000) that he had a right to have some clue to guide his calculation—I proposed, that you should leave it with me, & leave me plenipotentiary—you did—I sent for the Gentleman, on whose judgment Longman most relied, & with whom you had expressed yourself pleased—talked with him, & read near a third of the poem, & explained the *sort* & conduct of the whole—the result was, that Longman acceded to your Terms, whatever they were—for the 100£ instead of *Gns* was a mere mistake of mine—. I wrote—you exprest no dissatisfaction—and I, who had pledged my judgement for the probability of the Sale, yet felt no anxiety on that account, but some, lest it should not be immediately saleable, purely on account of your last 2 Volumes.—I found the Poem in diction exceedingly correct; but feared concerning the flow of the Interest ab extra—from your letter concerning L.,[1] I, tho' agreeing with you fundamentally, in the general principle, yet deduced that you had made up your mind as to the essentiality of the *Business* bearing this, & no other proportion to the internal Action—from many of the circumstances, annumerated in this Letter, I conscientiously did not dare rely on my own persuasions in my so disturbed state of mind—therefore receiving from Dorothy in a letter written May the first, the following—'*We are very anxious* that "the White Doe" should be published *as soon as possible*——if you would simply mention the passages, to which you object, without attempting to alter them, it would be better—&c—Our main reason (I speak in the name of the Females) for wishing that the Poem may be *speedily* published, is that William may get it out of his head; but further we think that it is of the UTMOST IMPORTANCE, that it should come out before the Buz of your Lectures is settled.—The alterations, we trust, will not be of a difficult or troublesome kind.'—

Now having promised Mr Longman, that I would take the trouble of correcting every Sheet—having found so few & so trifling corrigenda or melioranda, in the language, and submitting my own

[1] Charles Lamb.

Judgement to your's, as to the general conduct of the Story, I am at a loss to know—in what way the having sent it to the Press, under the conviction, that any trifling *verbal* defects which might remain after *my* revisal, & which would have been removed by your's, could bear no proportion to the pecuniary advantage of having the poem published before the King's Birth-day—how this can deserve that not to me (let that be as nothing; but) not to Montague, or your Brothers, but to the Booksellers you should write to inform them, that I had proceeded without authority—& so much so, that the poem itself was no longer to be intrusted . . . [Remainder of manuscript missing.]

709. *To Thomas N. Longman*

Address: Messrs Longman, Hurst, Rees & Orme, Booksellers | Paternoster Row.
Transcript Coleridge family. Pub. E. L. G. i. 421.
Postmark: 23 May 1808.

Courier Office.
[23 May 1808]

Dear Sir

I am painfully surprised by the extract from Mr Wordsworth's Letter.

Mr W. came to town, among other motives, to publish his Poem. He offered Terms—did not choose to submit his work to your previous inspection—and of course felt them, as declined. I did not see the matter in exactly the same light, as he did. I thought, that in the purchase, not of a total Copyright, but of a mere first Edition— & that at a very handsome price—and that too from an author, whose last publication had not been so favorably received, as his admirers anticipated—a Publisher had an undoubted *Right* (in the *equity* between man & man, as well as in the vulgar Sense of the word) to have the means of some distinct Information concerning it's nature, and the probability of it's immediate Sale, from some *indifferent* Judge.

As to it's intrinsic merits he might perhaps be disposed to rely on the Author's own opinion and that of his particular friends; but what is this to the persons, who are to purchase a first Edition at a risk, which can be made to answer only by a quick return?—

I advised him to leave the Poem with me, & to appoint me his plenipotentiary & he did so—Mr T. Rees was so good as to pass an hour or two with me; we read part of the Poem & discussed the whole—he made his report to you—& the result was, that tho' still in favor of the prudence of your first proposal you however acceded to Mr Wordsworth's Proposal—I informed him of this—received his full confirmation & found by an after letter that his opinions differed from mine with regard to one essential in the Tale of the Poem—therefore confined myself to the correction of mere verbal inaccuracies which I found very few & very trifling—when I received a letter from Miss Wordsworth, who always, except where she expresses the contrary, writes in her Brother's name of authority, from which the following is an Extract—'We are all *very anxious* that the White Doe should be sent to the Press AS SOON AS POSSIBLE. The corrections cannot be of a very difficult or troublesome kind— We think it of the UTMOST IMPORTANCE, that it should come out before the Buz of your Lectures is settled.'

My Lectures will finish in about a fortnight—I appeal to you, & to common Sense, whether my transmission of the Poem can be deemed a 'misinterpretation' of the above? or whether after having been authorized to negociate, after the result had been confirmed (not to say, received with thanks) and after I had been thus spurred on, it is exactly agreeable with common English to speak of 'Mr Coleridge's having sent A Mss poem of MINE to you—A!' God bless you, my dear Sir | &

S. T. Coleridge.

P.S. I had sent it before; but retracted it, in order to write out the parts which spite of the author's present opinion, I yet wished to alter, in hopes that his opinion might alter—'Tis a strange World, Mr Longman!—especially with those, who have to do with Authors!—

710. *To Francis Jeffrey*

Address:——Jeffray, Esqre. | to the care of Mr Constable | Bookseller | Edingburgh.
MS. New York Public Lib. Pub. Letters, *ii. 527.*
Postmark: 27 May 1808.

348, Strand. May 23.—1808.

Dear Sir

Without knowing me you have been, perhaps rather unwarrant-[ab]ly, severe on my morals and Understanding—inasmuch as you have, I understand—for I have not seen the Reviews, frequently introduced *my* name when I had never brought any publication within your court—With one slight exception—a shilling pamphlet[1] that never obtained the least notice—I have not published any thing with my name, or known to be mine, for 13 years— surely, I might quote against you the complaint of Job as to those

---

[1] This pamphlet may have been the *Conciones ad Populum*, 1795.

who brought against him 'the iniquities of his Youth'—What harm
have I ever done you, dear Sir—by act or word? If you knew me,
you would yourself smile at some of the charges, which, I am told,
you have burthened on me—Most assuredly, you have mistaken
my sentiments, alike in morality, politics, and—what is called—
metaphysics—and I would fain hope that if you knew me, you
would not have ascribed Self-opinion & Arrogance, to me—But be
this as it may, I write to you now merely to intreat—for the sake
of mankind—an honorable review of Mr Clarkson's History of the
Abolition of the Slave Trade—I know the man—and if you knew
him, you, I am sure, would revere him—and your reverence of him,
as an agent, would almost supersede all Judgement of him as a mere
literary man. It would be presumptuous in me to offer to write the
Review of his Work—yet I should be glad were I permitted to
submit to you the many thoughts, which occurred to me during it's
perusal.[1]—Be assured, that with the greatest respect for your
Talents—as far as I can judge of them from the few numbers of the
Edingburgh Review which I have had the opportunity of reading—
and every kind thought respecting your motives, I am, dear Sir,

Your ob. humb. Servt.
S. T. Coleridge

711. *To the Secretary of the Royal Institution*

Transcript Royal Institution. Pub. The Royal Institution, *by Bence Jones, 1871,
p. 284.* According to the minutes for 13 June 1808, William Savage, the assistant
secretary, 'laid before the Managers the following [Letter from Mr Coleridge'.

[*Circa* 13 June 1808]

Dear Sir,
    Painful as it is to me almost to anguish yet I find my health in
such a state as to make it almost death to me to give any further
Lectures.[2] I beg that you would acquaint the Managers that instead
of expecting any remuneration, I shall, as soon as I can, repay the

---

[1] Coleridge's review appeared in the *Edinburgh Review* for July 1808. See
Letters 717 and 732.

[2] There must have been at least one lecture in June, for De Quincey, writing
to his sister on Monday, 20 June 1808, mentions a lecture given 'this day
week'. Coleridge 'had his pocket picked of the main part of his lecture as he
walked from the Strand; but, having notes, he managed to get through very
well'. Jerningham also refers to the incident. (A. H. Japp, *Thomas De Quincey*,
1890, p. 106 and *The Jerningham Letters*, ed. Egerton Castle, 2 vols., 1896, i.
317.) We know from one of his letters of 1818 that Coleridge 'delivered 18
Lectures on Shakespear at the Royal Institution'. See Letter 1118. See also
Shakespearean Criticism, i. 18, for a similar assertion made in January 1819.

sum I have received.[1] I am indeed more likely to repay it by my executors than myself. If I could quit my Bed-room, I would have hazarded every thing rather than not have come, but I have such violent Fits of Sickness and Diarrhoea that it is *literally* impossible.

S. T. Coleridge.

712. *To Francis Jeffrey*

Address: F. Jeffrey, Esqr. | 62 | Queen's Street | Edingburgh
MS. New York Public Lib. Pub. with omis. Letters, *ii. 528.*
Postmark: 20 July 1808. *Stamped*: Bury St. Edmonds.

[Circa 16 July 1808]

Dear Sir

Not having been gratified by a Letter from you, I have feared that the freedom, with which I opened out my opinions, may have given you offence. Be assured, it was most alien from my intention. The purport of what I wrote was simply this—that severe & long continued bodily disease exacerbated by disappointment in the great Hope of my Life had rendered me insensible to blame and praise even to a faulty degree, unless they proceeded from the one or two who love me. The entrance-passage to my Heart is choked up with heavy Lumber—& I am thus barricadoed against attacks, which, doubtless, I should otherwise have felt as keenly as most men. Instead of censuring a certain quantum of irritability respecting the reception of published compositions, I rather envy it— it becomes ludicrous then only, when it is disavowed, and the opposite Temper pretended to—. The ass's Skin is almost scourge-proof—while the Elephant's thrills under the movements of every fly, that runs over it.—But tho' notoriously almost a zealot in behalf of my friend's poetic reputation, yet I can leave it with cheerful confidence to the fair working of his own powers—I have known many, very many instances of contempt changed into admiration of his Genius; but I neither know nor have heard of a single person, who having been, or having become his admirer had ceased to be so. For it is honorable to us all, that our kind affections, the attractions and elective affinities of our nature, are of more permanent

---

[1] Coleridge did not return the £40 received in February, and in Dec. 1808 Thomas Bernard wrote to him: 'We are in your debt at the Royal Institution. The balance due to you, if I recollect right, is £60; which will be paid with some other Sums, as soon as a Sum of money comes in which ought to have been paid us in June last.' At Coleridge's request the £60 was finally paid to Stuart in May 1809. (See pp. 90, 164, 183, 185, and 194.) Several friendly letters from Bernard indicate that Coleridge retained the respect and admira tion of members of the Royal Institution after discontinuing his lectures.

agency, than those passions which repel and dissever. From this cause we may explain the final growth of honest fame, and it's tenacity of Life. Whenever the Struggle of controversy ceases, we think no more of works which give us no pleasure, and apply our satire & scorn to some new Object—and thus the field is left entire to Friends & Partizans. But the case of Mr Clarkson appeared to me altogether different. I do not hold his fame dear because he is my friend; but I sought and cultivated his acquaintance, because a long & sober Enquiry had assured me, that he had been, in an aweful sense of the word, a Benefactor of mankind: and this from the purest motives, unalloyed by the fears & hopes of selfish superstition—*not* with that feverish Power, which Fanatics acquire by *crowding together*, but in the native Strength of his own moral Impulses. He, if ever human Being did it, listened exclusively to his Conscience, and obeyed it's voice at the price of all his Youth & manhood, at the price of his Health, his private Fortune, and the fairest prospects of honorable ambition. Such a man I cannot regard as a mere author. I cannot read or criticize such a work as a mere literary production. The opinions publicly expressed and circulated concerning it must of necessity in the Author's feelings be entwined with the Cause itself, and with his own character, as a *man*, to which that of the Historian is only an accidental accession. Were it the pride of Authorship alone, that was in danger of being fretted, I should have remained as passive in this Instance, as in that of my own, and of my most particular friend, to whom I am bound by ties more close and of longer standing than those which connect me personally with Mr Clarkson. But I know, that any sarcasms or ridicule would deeply wound his feelings, as a veteran warrior in a noble contest, feelings that claim the reverence of all good men.

The Review was sent, addressed to you, by the Post of yesterevening. There is not a sentence, not a word in it, which I should not have written, had I never seen the Author.

I am myself about to bring out two works—one a small pamphlet—the second of considerable size—it is a *rifacciamento*, a very free Translation with large additions &c &c of the masterly work, for which poor Palm was murdered.

I hope to be in the North, at Keswick, in the course of a week or eight days. I shall be happy to hear from you on this or any other occasion—Your's, dear Sir, sincerely,

S. T. Coleridge

713. *To Mrs. S. T. Coleridge*

Address: Mrs Coleridge | Greta Hall | Keswick.
MS. Lord Latymer. Pub. with omis. E. L. G. i. 424.

After visiting the Clarksons in Bury St. Edmunds, Coleridge 'Re-arrived at Grasmere and entered the new House [Allan Bank] for the first time Thursday Night, ½ past eleven, 1 September 1808'. [MS. notebook.] On 5 September he reached Keswick 'about half as big as the house'. (*Southey Letters*, ii. 16.) Wordsworth had come with him, and on 7 September, they returned to Grasmere, taking Coleridge's daughter with them.

Friday Night—[9 September 1808]

My dear Sara

We arrived all three safe. O it was a perfect comedy to see little John on Sara's Entrance—He had screamed with Joy on seeing us come up the Field; but when Sara entered, he ran & crept under the Kitchen-table, then peeped out at her, then all red with Blushes crept back again, laughing half-convulsively yet faintly— at length, he came out, & throwing his pinafore over his face & with both hands upon that, he ran and kissed her thro' the pinafore—. Soon however all was agreed— John has put the Question, & Sara has consented—But (says she) is the Church a far way off?—Nay, replies John—nought but a lile bit—& I'll carry you on my back all the way, & all the way back, after we are married. Sara sleeps with me—She has made the children as happy as happy can be. Every one is delighted with her—indeed, it is absolutely impossible that there can be a sweeter or a sweetlier behaved Child—This is not *my* Speech; but Wordsworth's.—Little John absolutely dotes on her; and she is very fond of him, & very good to all of them. O, she has the sweetest Tongue in the world—she talks by the hour to me in bed—& does not at all disturb me in the night, she lies so very quiet.—Little Catharine[1] is a fine Baby—& the Mother continues well. Dorothy just came in now to say, she was about to write to you; but finding that I am writing, she will defer it to the next Carrier.—O pray, remember to send my bonny red Razor Case, which I left in the room where William slept: and likewise to send my Undershirt that I pulled off—for that which you gave me instead was so scanty that it left the lower belly bare; & I caught cold in my Bowels & was very badly for almost the whole day yesterday so that I could eat neither Breakfast or Dinner—but I am now well again, & have been keen at work and in good Spirits.

Be assured, my dear Sara! that your kind behaviour has made a deep impression on my mind—Would to God, it had been always so on both sides—but the Past is past—& my business now is to

---

[1] Catharine Wordsworth, born 6 Sept. 1808, died 4 June 1812.

recover the Tone of my Constitution if possible & to get money for you and our Children—I trust, I shall never wilfully do any thing to give you the least pain—Heaven knows! nothing is more at my Heart than to be conducive to your Comfort of mind, body, and estate—for you mistake greatly, if you imagine I do not entertain both affection & a very great esteem for you.—May God bless us both.

When you have received an answer from Miss Nevins,[1] pray let me know—Mary's Confinement has prevented my seeing Mr Dawes[2] hitherto—Pray, send me a good lot of books by each Carrier—no odds, with what you begin—as many each time as you conveniently can—& lastly the Shelves.

Little Sara is gone to bed; but left with me her 'loving kind dutiful Love to dear Mama, and to Dervy dear, and Hartley tho' he is sic a wet kisser; and to Edith.' She told me, last night, that Edith and she tell each other a deal of knowlege—and verily, Sara is a deal cleverer than I supposed—She is indeed a very sweet unblameable Darling. And what elegance of Form & Motion—her dear Eyes too! as I was telling a most wild Story to her & John, her large Eyes grew almost as large again with wonderment—

Remember me affectionately to Southey.—And believe me, my dear Sara,

Your affectionate Husband,
S. T. Coleridge

Be pleased to send me a box of Wafers: and give my love to my dearest Hartley and my own MY SOUL, my Derwent. O bless them both.

714. *To John Monkhouse*

MS. Miss Joanna Hutchinson. Hitherto unpublished. Coleridge's letter is written on the opposite side of a letter from Sara Hutchinson addressed to 'My dear John', presumably John Monkhouse, her cousin.

[Thursday, 15 September 1808][3]

To the best of my recollection there is but one Portuguese & English Dictionary—and as to Grammars they are all alike. I advise

[1] On his way north in August, Coleridge had visited Pim Nevins in Leeds; later Mrs. Coleridge wrote to the daughter, Eliza, then on a visit to Kendal, inviting her to Greta Hall.

[2] The Rev. John Dawes, who was soon to be Hartley's and Derwent's schoolmaster in Ambleside.

[3] A reference in Sara Hutchinson's note, dated only Thursday, to Mary Wordsworth and the baby, and Coleridge's mention of Henry Hutchinson, 'to whom I will write when he is in London', establish the date of this letter. See Letter 717, dated 19 Sept. in which Henry Hutchinson is spoken of as the 'Bearer' of the letter to Street.

you to amuse yourself on board Ship with writing out the articles, the terminations of the cases and numbers of the Nouns,—the Pronouns, and all the Verbs regular & irregular—to these you may or may not add the adverbs of Time & Place, and Prepositions—and then throw your grammar entirely aside, and set to on some easy book with your Dictionary—taking every opportunity to talk little sentences of common Life with any one who speaks Portuguese. In this way you will learn the Language in half the Time. When at Lisbon, I advise you to procure the best Portuguese and Spanish Grammar and Dictionary—and study the difference of the two Dialects—you may so not only become Master of both with little Trouble; but each will be better understood by you. With the sincerest wishes & prayers for your health & prosperity; believe me

Your friend & Servt
S. T. Coleridge

My affectionate remembrances to Mary M., to Joanna, & Tom—& to Henry—to whom I will write when he is in London—.

715. *To Mrs. S. T. Coleridge*

Address: Mrs Coleridge | Greta Hall | Keswick   To be left at Miss Crosthwaite's. *MS. Lord Latymer. Hitherto unpublished fragment.*

[*Circa* 15 September 1808]

. . . lie *suspended* till my Health & Constitution are fairly established —the Interval will be employed as much for your benefit, as for my own: I am sure, I think far more of you than of myself.

Our Sariola is a very angel—she is the sweetest quietest Bedfellow, & the dearest little Girl.

Mrs Wordsworth has had the best of Times—I never saw her look so well. She has never been indisposed. She came down stairs for about an Hour this morning.

My dear Love to Hartley—& to 'my Soul'. I shall see Mr Dawes to morrow—& propose to write to Hartley afterwards. I take a little Tour on Saturday by Mr Scambler's Advice.—

And now may God bless you, my dear Sara! and put it into your Head to make a pair or two of Drawers for the thighs and seat of

Your affectionate Friend & Husband,
S. T. Coleridge

Love from all here. Little Dorothy and Sara make a most amusing Contrast—S. so lady-fairy-like, & Dorothy sic a wild one; but so pretty, especially when she is naughty—i.e. some twice in e[very] . . . But she is so droll!

716. To Eliza Nevins

Address: Miss Eliza Nevins | Mr J. Wilson's | Kendal
MS. Miss Kathleen Coburn. Pub. E. L. G. i. 426.

Allan Bank, Grasmere.

Friday Morning. [16 September 1808]

Dear Miss Eliza

I have just received the kind note, you returned in answer to my Wife's Letter—and tho' doubtless she will herself have answered it, I cannot be easy without expressing how much pleasure both I and those dearest to me feel in the prospect of your visit.—First then, let me say, that my wife and the family at Keswick are equally prepared *at all times* to welcome you—whatever day were most convenient to you, would be most pleasing to her—but a literary Engagement, involving a small Tour on the Duddon, compels me to be absent from Keswick till Friday next with my honored Friend, Mr Wordsworth.—Unfortunately I am unable to drive any other Horse, than Pegasus: so that I have no other means of coming into Kendal & returning with you to Keswick but by Post Chaises. Independent of this, there are two modes practicable perhaps—the first, that of my meeting you at Penrith, to which place there is a daily Coach from Kendal; & thence to Keswick in a Chaise, which is but 18 miles—unless you would find it pleasant to pass one day and night at the House of a Family, amiable Friends of our's, at Penrith, during which time I would accompany you to Ulswater, the grandest of our Lakes, & where likewise I have some female Friends, who occupy the House at the bottom of the Lake, built & formerly occupied by Thomas Clarkson—& the next day we might go in the Coach from Penrith to Keswick—Or if Mr J. Wilson[1] could drive you over to Grasmere, both he and you would find there House-room & Heart-room—we might then see the beauties of this most beautiful of all Vales under Heaven *first*—and it's greatest beauties are quite unknown to the Herd of Tourists—and then after a few days' sojourn in this dear House, we shall have plenty of opportunities of going to Keswick, either by Chaise, open Carriage, or Horse-back, as you like best. Mrs Wordsworth has been recently confined; but is so well already, as to sit down Stairs—tho' her little Catharine saw the Light only the Tuesday before last—that this is no Objection—and she, her Sister, & Mr & Miss Wordsworth will be as happy in your society, as myself. I dare acquit myself of all partiality, tho' I affirm, that there does not exist a family in the Island better worth your acquaintance, if Simplicity, delicacy,

---

[1] John Wilson (1785–1854), later the 'Christopher North' of *Blackwood's Magazine*.

purity of mind, affectionateness, & good sense are of any value in this money-making Planet of our's.

As I hope we shall detain you among us some weeks, I deem it premature to plan any thing about your return—of course, I shall be your guide—The Weather is now settling; and the Fern changing it's green for golden Hues is the Harbenger of our autumnal Splendors.—On my return to Keswick next Friday I shall of course know from Mrs Coleridge, what Plan you deem the best—unless I should find you there. At all events, coming or returning, you must see Grasmere, and go back to Leeds in love with it.

When you write to your Father, will you be so good as to request him to send for me to Sheffield for two sets of Razors from Wass, the one the seven shilling Case, the other the 13 or 14 Shilling one. He is the Inventor, grinding them on a four Inch Stone. I beg this on the Supposition that he means to visit Kendal in order to convoy you hence—when I shall contrive to see him, even if I cannot induce him to pass a few days with me—& can then repay him the Cost.

If Mrs Wilson can leave her Household, I need not say, I should consider it as an additional gratification.

Pray, remember me with respectful affection to your Sisters, whenever you write; and believe me to be,

dear Miss Eliza, | very sincerely your obliged Friend,
S. T. Coleridge

717. *To T. G. Street*[1]

Address: G. Street, Esqre. | Courier Office | Strand   from Mr Coleridge.
MS. British Museum. Pub. E. L. G. ii. 3.

19 Sept. [1808] Grasmere.

My dear Sir

The Bearer is Mr Henry Hutchinson, of whom I wrote to you in my last; and who will thank you in person for your kind exertions in his behalf, when he was at Cork. If you can give him any advice or information, I am confident, you will do it, even for my sake; but still more confident should I be, if you had read the History of his Adventures during 1806, and 1807—which I shall shortly insert in my republication of my Review on Clarkson's History of the Abolition in the Edingburgh Review,[2] which was not shamefully

---

[1] According to the Library of Congress, between 1804 and 3 Dec. 1812 T. G. Street is listed as the publisher of the *Courier*, and a manuscript letter from Street to Coleridge is signed, very illegibly, T. G. or T. J. G. Street. Stuart and Street were co-proprietors of the *Courier*; from 1811 Stuart entrusted the management almost entirely to his partner.

[2] Coleridge did not republish his review of Clarkson's book, nor has it ever been reprinted in full.

mutilated; but in two paragraphs added (in a vulgar style of
rancid commonplace metaphors) made to contradict myself—first,
in a nauseous & most false ascription of the Supremacy of Merit to
Mr Wilberforce, & secondly, in an attack on Mr Pitt's Sincerity
substituted for a Paragraph, in which I had both defended it &
him; & proved that of all the parliamentary Friends of the Africans
he was the most efficient.[1] With the exception of these paragraphs,
I trust, you will read the Review with some satisfaction, even as it
now stands—but in the republication it will be augmented, and be
at least double it's present length.—

I am hard at work—and feel a pleasure and eagerness in it, which
I had not known for years—a consequence and reward of my courage
in at length [having] overcome the fear of dying suddenly in my
Sleep, which and, heaven knows! which alone had seduced me into
the fatal habit of taking enormous quantities of Laudanum, and
latterly, of spirits too—the latter merely to keep the former on my
revolting Stomach.—I am still far enough from well—my lungs are
slightly affected, as by asthma, and my bowels dreadfully irritable;
but I am far better than I could have dared expect. I left it off *all at
once*;[2] & drink nothing but Toast and Water, or Lemonade made
with Creme of Tartar. If I entirely recover, I shall deem it a sacred
Duty to publish my Case, tho' without my name—for the practice
of taking Opium is dreadfully spread.—Throughout Lancashire &
Yorkshire it is the common Dram of the lower orders of People—
in the small Town of Thorpe the Druggist informed me, that he
commonly sold on market days two or three Pound of Opium, & a

---

[1] Coleridge's statement here, though somewhat more outspoken, is substantially what he wrote by way of protest to Jeffrey on 14 Dec. 1808. The
two offending paragraphs (*Edinburgh Review*, July 1808, pp. 362 and 366–8) do
give ascendancy to Wilberforce and question the sincerity of Pitt. Coleridge
later told Allsop that 'Clarkson expressed himself gratified and satisfied with
the effect of the review, and would not allow me to expose the transaction'.
Letters, Conversations and Rec. 185.

[2] This is the first positive reference to Coleridge's attempt to break off the
opium habit formed in 1800–1 and, as Sara Coleridge pointed out, confirmed
at Malta. (See Letter 400, p. 731 n. and *Biog. Lit.*, ed. H. N. Coleridge, 2 vols.,
1847, ii. 409.) Early in 1808 Coleridge had thought of laying the whole of his
case before Dr. Beddoes. (Letters 680 and 685.) Subsequent letters in this year
show that he submitted his case to a physician and found that he could not
abandon the habit '*all at once*'. He did, however, temporarily reduce the dose.
After 1808 he was to seek medical advice from such physicians as Anthony
Carlisle, Robert Gooch, Parry, Tuthill, Daniel, Brabant, Adams, and finally
Gillman, but he was unsuccessful in emancipating himself; and as late as 1832,
during a temporary abandonment of opium, he referred to his 'more than 30
years' Self-poisoning'. For a commentary on Coleridge's slavery to opium, see
E. L. Griggs, 'Samuel Taylor Coleridge and Opium', *Huntington Lib. Quar.*,
Aug. 1954, pp. 357–78.

Gallon of Laudanum—all among the labouring Classes. Surely, this demands legislative Interference—

- If I can on any important subject render you service, I can now venture to offer my powers to you without fear of disappointing you—

Your's affectionately & gratefully,
S. T. Coleridge

718. *To Francis Jeffrey*

Address: F. Jeffray, Esqre. | Queen's Street | Edingburgh   *Single Sheet.*
MS. New York Public Lib. Pub. E. L. G. i. 431.
Postmark: 10 November 1808.   *Stamped*: Keswick.

Grasmere, Kendal
[*Circa* 7 November 1808]

Dear Sir

An unfinished Letter to you is now lying before me—and till the Hurry of writing Requests to all my acquaintances is over, I cannot collect my mind sufficiently to say all to you, that I have to say. I would, I could have your society for an evening—For the London Clocks did not more remind me, when I have been listening to count the Hour, of the 'Inopem me Copia fecit', than my proposed Chapter of Contents when I have resolved to repay your late attentions.

I have taken the liberty of sending you a small parcel of Prospectuses,[1] intreating you to disperse them as favorably, as you can, for me. I have received promises of contribution from respectable men; and I shall myself play off my whole Head & Heart, such as they are, in this work, as from the main pipe of the Fountain. Indeed, it is high Time. Hitherto, I have layed my Eggs with Ostrich Carelessness and Ostrich Oblivion—the greater part indeed have been crush[ed under] foot; but some have crawled into light to furnish Feath[ers] for other men's Caps, and not a few to plume the shaf[ts] in the Quivers of my Calumniators.

[1] Coleridge refers to the prospectus of his weekly essay, *The Friend*.
As early as June Coleridge had determined to have William Savage print and publish *The Friend* in London. After arriving in the north Coleridge prepared an inimitable prospectus, which was printed in Nov. by W. Pennington of Kendal; a second issue, with a few variations, soon followed. These prospectuses announced Coleridge's intention to begin publication of *The Friend* on the first Saturday of Jan. 1809, 'if a sufficient Number of Subscribers shall have been obtained'. Savage was also directed to print 1,000 prospectuses, but his unreasonable demands caused his dismissal as the publisher of *The Friend*. This breakdown in the arrangements led Coleridge to turn to Stuart, under whose auspices a prospectus was printed in Feb. 1809. Subsequent letters show that the delay in issuing the first number of *The Friend* was mainly due to circumstances beyond Coleridge's control.

I cannot flatter myself, that the whole Structure of my Philosophy, speculative and moral, will be deemed of legitimate Architecture by you; but to a man of robust and active Intellect there is a
charm in that Diversity of Opinion with unity of purpose, which
constitute the Discordia Concors of the literary World. 'Ad isthaec
(says one of my great Favorites, Giordano Bruno) quaeso vos,
qualiacunque primo videantur aspectu, attendite: ut qui vobis
forsan insanire videar, saltem quibus insaniam rationibus, cognoscatis.'—[1]

Within 8 days I shall trouble you with a *Letter*—for this I ought
perhaps (without meaning a German Pun) to style a Brief. In the
mean time,

dear Sir! | I am, with great respect | Your obliged
S. T. Coleridge

719. *To John Prior Estlin*

Address: Revd J. P. Estlin | St Michael's Hill | Bristol   *Single Sheet*
MS. Bristol Central Lib. Pub. with omis. Letters to Estlin, *101.* This letter and
a number of those which follow are written on the blank pages of the prospectus
of *The Friend.*
Stamped: Kendal.

Allan Bank, Grasmere. 3 Dec. 1808.
My dear Sir

When I was last at Bristol, not only was my Health in a far
worse state than I had resolution to make known; but my mind was
halting between Despondency and Despair. On my return to the
North I summoned up courage and put my case fairly under the
care and judgment of a Physician—and I have now almost recovered
my former nature. If it were in my power to make you conscious of
what passes within me, you would deduce one proof of this from the
distinct images of my early Friends, that now so often rise up
before 'that inward Eye Which is the Bliss of Solitude',[2] and the
lively affections of attachment and gratitude which accompany
them. What I feel toward you, my dear Sir! and that I have never
forgotten or undervalued your warm and zealous friendship when
I was nakedly my own undisciplined Self, friendless, fameless,
fortuneless, I give you now a slight proof of; yet the best in my
power, by unbosoming myself to you. For years I had with the
bitterest pangs of Self-disapprobation struggled in secret against
the habit of taking narcotics. My Conscience indeed fully acquitted
me of taking them from the weakness of Self-indulgence, or for the
sake of any pleasurable sensation, or exhilaration of Spirits—in

[1] Giordano Bruno, *De Immenso et Innumerabilibus*, Liber I, Caput ii, note.
[2] Wordsworth's *I wandered lonely as a cloud*, lines 21–22.

truth, the effects were the very contrary. From the disuse my spirits and pleasurable feelings used gradually to increase to the very Hour, when my circulation became suddenly distur[bed,] a painful and intolerable Yawning commenced, soon followed by a vio[lent] Bowel-complaint—and the evacuations—being chiefly dark blood in the form of . . . Gra[vel—] gave proof that the Liver had ceased to perform it's proper functions—in short, I had the strongest convictions that if I persisted, I should die. Still however, I had no other ground for this conviction than my own feelings—and therefore was never sure, that I was not acting guiltily.—At length, I made a fair Trial under the eye of a Physician, determining whatever might be the result, henceforward never to conceal any thing of any kind from those who loved me and lived with me. The result was, that it could not be abandoned without Loss of Life—at least, not at once—but such has been the blessed Effect upon my Spirits of having no Secret to brood over, that I have been enabled to reduce the Dose to one *sixth* part of what I formerly took—and my Appetite, general Health, and mental Activity are greater than I have known them for years past.—O had you conjectured the inward Anguish that was consuming me (for it is a goodness of Providence to me that I cannot do wrong without severe Self-punishment) both in your Heart and in that of dear Mrs Estlin's, Pity would have suspended all condemnation for my real or apparent neglects of the Duties, which I owed to my friends, my family and my own Soul.—I look onward to my future Exertions with humble Confidence. By the work, of which you have here the Prospectus, I have received strong encouragements to the belief, that I shall do good. As I am almost sure, that in the subjects admissible in such a work, our Principles are the same, I have no immediate motive to detail to you the Tenets, in which we differ—Indeed, the Difference is not as great as you have been led to suppose—and are [is] rather philosophical, than theological. I believe the Father of all to be the only Object of Adoration or Prayer—the Calvinistic Tenet of a vicarious Satisfaction I reject not without some Horror—and tho' I believe that Redemption by Christ implies more, than what the Unitarians understand by the phrase, yet I use it rather as an X Y Z, an unknown Quantity, than as words to which I pretend to annex clear notions. I believe, that in the salvation of man a spiritual process sui generis is required, a spiritual aid and agency, the nature of which I am wholly ignorant of, as a *cause*, and only imperfectly apprehend it from it's necessity and it's effects.—

As to 'THE FRIEND', I make no request to you. You will do me all the good, you can, compatible with the approbation of your own mind. I have received promises of Support from men of very high name in the literary world—and as to my own Efforts, I consider the work as the main Pipe of my intellectual Reservoir.—The first Essay will be—On the nature and importance of *Principles*. The blindness to this I have long regarded as the Disease of this discussing, calculating, *prudential* age—and to prove this & to shew it's consequences in morality, taste, and even in the common goings-on of daily Life is my paramount Object for the whole work.—Remember me to Mrs Estlin, as one who in his inmost Being has never ceased to be her and your obliged, and affectionate Friend, with most unfeigned respect—

S. T. Coleridge.

720. *To Robert Southey*

Address: Robert Southey, Esqre. | Greta Hall | Keswick
MS. Lord Latymer. Hitherto unpublished.

[*Circa* 4 December 1808][1]

My dear Southey

I herewith send you 35 Prospectuses, intreating you to do what you can for me—and if you want more to send for them. The mode of circulation and delivery of the Essays, whether by Post or no, cannot be determined till the nature of the Subscribers' residence has been ascertained. If there should be so many *scattered* Subscribers, that the number of the Places may compensate for the fewness of the Persons in each, The Friend will be stamped and sent by the Post—in which case the Essay will be printed on one Sheet—and by printing 40 lines in each page instead of 35, and on a larger sized paper, the same quantity will be given, and even the market value remain the same. But if almost the whole are furnished by the great Towns & Cities, a pacquet will be sent off by each Saturday's Mail to some Friend or Bookseller in each place—

This you will say for me in your Letters.

I have not the slightest grounds whereon to form a calculation whether I shall obtain 50, 500, or a 1000 Subscribers—nor have I yet made up my mind as to what number I should consent to begin with. I am grieved, for my own sake, that you cannot go to Mr Curwen's—I have no stomach to the Visit; but it would be unkind to let Wordsworth go alone.—Miss H. informs me, that *W.* has given up all thought of going.

As to public matters I am greatly depressed; and yet I think

[1] The approximate date of this letter is established by Southey's letter to William Taylor, which was written on 6 Dec. in response to Coleridge's request concerning the prospectuses. See J. W. Robberds, *A Memoir of . . . William Taylor of Norwich*, 2 vols., 1843, ii. 229.

there is a stirring and heaving in the mind of the People, Populi absque Plebe, which might have a channel made for it by the zealous and united Efforts of 3 or 4 sturdy Thinkers who both think & write *feelingly*—The Ministers are afraid of Parliament even in it's present venal state—which is a great datum of Hope for a Reform in Parliament, imperfect, and meagre as any Act-of-Parliament Reform would be—20 additional honest Senators would do the work of Giants—nor per se, but by at once increasing, steadying, and directing the convictions of the People. There is now but one sentiment respecting the Army, the Effect of Court Patronage, and the pernicious Consequences of a Ministry, absolutely the *menials* of the King, and the absolute Privation of all Responsibility in the great State-agents, from the——& the Duke of York down to Lord Melville & Mr Trotter.—May God bless you!—I have had a slight attack of Dysentery, and was imbedded for two days; but am now pretty well, only weak.

I have ordered 30 Prospectuses to be sent to Dr Southey, Durham; and to W. Taylor, Norwich—and rely on you to write to both of them for me, intreating your Brother to consult with George Taylor of St Helen's Auckland, about sending some to Sunderland —In short, do what you can for me, which I regard as a sort of Lord's Prayer—i.e. Thanksgiving in the Shape of Petition.

S. T. Coleridge—

P.S. Can Mr Calvert do any thing for me at Carlisle? Be so good as to speak to him.

In the Prospectuses desire Mrs Coleridge to alter the word *are* into *is*, the last word but 8 in the fourth article of the Subjects.[1]

721. *To Thomas Poole*

Address: T. Poole, Esqre. | N. Stowey | Bridgewater | Somerset   *Single Sheet*
MS. British Museum. Pub. E. L. G. i. 432.
Stamped: Kendal.

Grasmere, Kendal. 4 Dec. 1808.

My dear Poole

I will make a covenant with you. Begin to count my Life, as a Friend of your's, from 1 January, 1809. I think this not unfair: for if I ask on the one hand an amnesty for all my *Omissions* toward you (for I cannot charge myself with any positive Acts of Wrong), yet on the other I abandon all claim on your remembrance of my never fluctuating Love and Esteem of you, and zeal to see the whole man of God and his Country developed in you.

---

[1] This last sentence is crossed out in manuscript.

In truth, I have been for years almost a paralytic in mind from self-dissatisfaction—brooding in secret anguish over what from so many baffled agonies of Effort I had thought and felt to be inevitable, but which yet from moral cowardice and a strange tyrannous Reluctance to make any painful Concern of my own the subject of Discourse—a reluctance strong in exact proportion to my esteem and affection for the persons, with whom I am communing—I had never authorized my conscience to pronounce inevitable by submitting my case carefully & faithfully to some Physician. I have however done it at last—and tho' the result after a severe Trial proved what I had anticipated, yet such is the Blessedness of walking altogether in Light, that my Health & Spirits are better [than] I have known them for years. But of all this hereafter.

I have ordered some Prospectuses to be sent to you. I earnestly intreat you, to do me what good you can. O I should be made for ever, if *you* would exert for me and this work one fourth of the Zeal, with which you acted for our Friend, Ackland. (Bye the by, send him a Prospectus. But nay I will send one myself.) I have received promises of contribution from many tall fellows of sounding names in the world of Scribes & Scribelings—and even among the Pharisees I have Favourers—I shall have two or 3 Bishops—Can you not get me Drs Fisher and Majendie ?[1]—I promise you on my honor, that 'The Friend' shall be the main Pipe, thro' which I shall play off the whole reservoir of my collected Knowlege and of what you are pleased to believe Genius. It is indeed Time to be doing something for myself. Hitherto I have layed my Eggs with Ostrich carelessness & Ostrich oblivion—most of them indeed have been crushed under foot—yet not a few have crawled forth into Light to furnish Feathers for the Caps of others, and some too to plume the shafts in the Quivers of my Enemies.—My first Essay (and what will be at the BOTTOM of all the rest) is—on the nature and importance of *Principles*. What a beggarly thing your calculating Prudence is without high general Principles, we have lately seen in that confluent Small-pox of Infamy, the Cintra Convention[2]—on which Wordsworth has nearly finished a most eloquent & well-reasoned Pamphlet[3]—.

[1] Henry W. Majendie (1754–1830), bishop of Chester, and John Fisher (1748–1825), bishop of Salisbury, had both earlier been vicars at Nether Stowey.

[2] On 22 Aug. 1808 at Cintra the British and French signed a Suspension of Arms 'for the purpose of negociating a Convention for the evacuation of Portugal by the French army'. The definitive Convention of 30 Aug. provided that English ships were to convey Gen. Junot's army to France.

[3] *Concerning the Relations of Great Britain, Spain, and Portugal, to each other, and to the common enemy, at this crisis; and specifically as affected by the Convention of Cintra . . .*, published in May 1809.

Lander[1] could not stay in Spain—he was so cut at heart by the Questions and remarks of the Spaniards, who, he says, are the noblest People on Earth, and will finally succeed spite of their allies. He is come home to fight our late Envoy, who said in French in his presence—'He is a fool (un fou) and does not possess the money, he is offering.' What a state we are in!—The People (not the Populace) stirring & heaving with an unwonted Sense of Right and Wrong; but no one to form a Channel for their Feelings —no one to retain, steady, and direct them. The Ministers absolute menials of the King—the D. of Y.—of K., of Cambridge & the King himself the actual great State-Agents—and not a shadow of responsibility in them or their Tools. Yet the Dread, Ministers manifest of Parliament, and their Dislike to it—venal as it is—is a datum of Hope—: Three Commanders in Chief in as many Days, two of them Cowards, and one of those Two an Ideot to boot—and yet no calling to account—no examination into the source of the appointment. And in the Court of Enquiry the infamous Terms never made the ground of one Question—but the grave Query is put, over & over again—Did not the allowing the French to go out of Portugal allow the French to go out of Portugal?—The proper? is—Sir! you were sent to deliver Portugal from the French—but instead of this you have basely delivered the French out of Portugal.—

I have translated Palm's Work (rather that for which poor Palm was shot by a military Commission by order of Napoleon)—It is most masterly. It was sent me by the D. of Sussex—but the Bookseller is trifling with me—. It contains a distinct prophecy of the Spanish Revolution—

My Love to Ward—He will do what he can for me.

Hereafter I will be a better Correspondent—Indeed, indeed, I have never been at ease with myself without instantly wishing for a nearer communion with you—for as you were my first Friend, in the higher sense of the word, so must you for ever be among my very dearest—

S. T. Coleridge

[1] Landor's letter to Coleridge concerning *The Friend* may be included here.

Dec. 14. 1808, 9 South Parade, Bath.

Sir

I beg permission to be a subscriber to the publication you announce. Mr Southey sent me the Prospectus. It followed me from Warwickshire to Clifton, and from Clifton to Bath. Hence arises my delay in acknowledging the pleasure I received from it and in offering the congratulations it gives me the liberty to make.

I am Sir, Yours very respectfully, W. Landor.   [MS. Dove Cottage.]

On the address sheet of Landor's letter Coleridge wrote to Mrs. Coleridge: 'Send it back, as I should like to have a specimen of the Handwriting of so remarkable a man, and of a Genius so brilliant and original.'

722. *To George Coleridge*

Address: Revd G. Coleridge | Ottery St Mary | Devon   *Single Sheet*.
MS. Lady Cave. Hitherto unpublished.
Stamped: Kendal.

Grasmere, Kendal.

[*Circa* 5 December 1808][1]

Dear Brother

I can[not] bring myself to believe that you can be indifferent to any virtuous Effort on my part—I have therefore transmitted this Prospectus to you. I have received promises of support from men of the highest present celebrity, and shall have at least three Bishops among my Patrons. I play off my whole mind in this work, as from the main pipe of the Fountain. Indeed it is high time. Hitherto, I have layed my Eggs with Ostrich Carelessness and Ostrich oblivion —most of them indeed have been crushed under—yet some have crawled into Light to furnish Feathers for the Caps of others, and not a Few to plume the Shafts in the Quivers of the Slanderers. I conjecture, that my opinions will not recede from your's in proportion as they draw near to our elder Divines & Moralists—At all events, I ask with the Philosopher of Nola, Giordano Bruno—'Ad isthaec, quaeso vos, qualiacunque primo videantur aspectu, attendite: ut qui vobis forsan insanire videar, saltem quibus insaniam rationibus, cognoscatis.'

My Children and Mrs C. are well. The two Boys a[re at Sc]hool at Ambleside; but are with me on Saturdays & Sundays. Their progress in Greek is commensurate with their eagerness in acquiring it, which is unusually great. They are happy, healthy, and very innocent. I publish my Greek Accidence, Vocabulary of Greek Terminations, Greek & English Lexicon, and philosophical Greek Grammar in Spring.

May the Almighty protect you and | your's!

S. T. Coleridge

723. *To Daniel Stuart*

Address: D. Stuart Esqre. | 348, Strand | London   *Single Sheet*
MS. British Museum. Pub. Letters, *ii. 533.*
Postmark: 9 December 1808. *Stamped*: Keswick.

Grasmere, Kendal.

[*Circa* 6 December 1808]

My dear Stuart

Scarcely when listening to count the Hour have I been more

---

[1] George Coleridge's reply, dated 10 Dec. and written 'immediately' on receipt of this letter, establishes the approximate date.

perplexed by the 'Inopem me Copia fecit' of the London Church
Clocks, than by the Press of what I have to say to you. I must do
one at a time. Briefly, a very happy Change has taken place in my
Health & spirits and mental activity, since I placed myself under
the care & inspection of a Physician—and I dare say with confident
Hope—Judge me from the first of January, 1808 [1809].

I send you the Prospectus—and intreat you to do me all the
good, you can—which like the Lord's Prayer, is Thanksgiving in
the Disguise of Petition. If you think, that it should be advertised
in any way—or if Mr Street can do any thing for me—but I know,
you will do what you can.

I have received promises of contribution from many tall fellows
with big names in the world of Scribes & Scribes, and count even
some Pharisees (2 or 3 Bishops) in my List of Patrons. But whether
I shall have 50, 100, 500, or a 1000 Subscribers I am not able even
to conjecture. All must depend on the zeal of my friends—on which
[I fear] I have thrown more water than oil. But some, like [Greek
f]ire, burn beneath the wave.

Wordsworth has nearly finished a series of most masterly Essays
on the affairs of Portugal & Spain—and by my advice he will first
send them to you, that if they suit the Courier, they may be inserted.[1]

I have not heard from Savage; but I suppose that he has printed
a thousand of these Prospectuses—and you may have any number
from him. He lives hard by some of the Streets in Covent Garden—
which I do not remember—but a note to Mr Savage, R. Institution,
Alb. St. will find him.

May God Almighty bless you! I feel, that I shall yet live to give
proof of what is deep within me toward you—

                                                    S. T. Coleridge

724. *To Humphry Davy*

Address: H. Davy, Esqre. | R. Institution | Albermarle St | London
Single Sheet
MS. Royal Institution. Pub. E. L. G. i. 435.
Postmark: 10 December 1808.   *Stamped*: Kendal.

                        Grasmere, Kendal.—Wednesday, 7 Dec. 1808
My dear Davy
I wrote ten days ago to Mr Savage; requesting him, if he continued in his former purpose and agreement respecting the Printing
and Publishing of a weekly Essay, to print a thousand or more of
these Prospectuses, adding his own name & address, as the Publisher,

----

[1] Two instalments of Wordsworth's *Convention of Cintra* were published in
the *Courier* in Dec. 1808 and Jan. 1809.

and sending certain numbers to certain places (of which I gave the
list) to dispose of the rest according to his own Judgment. Being
ignorant of his proper address, I directed my letter to the R. Institution. I twice urged him to return me a few lines by return of Post—
which I should then have received on Thursday morning last—a
week tomorrow. In the mean time I have written to a number of
Friends, and Wordsworth and Southey to their's—informing them
that they would receive from London such and such numbers of the
Prospectus—to all, who live in the Middle or South of England—
for to the North & to Scotland they have been sent from Kendal. If
this be a designed Neglect, whatever the motive, it is unkind: if it
be accident, it is unlucky. For I do not know what to do—My best
way, I think, is to write to Mr Stuart or Street, and beg him to find
out Mr Savage's Home, which cannot be far from the Exeter Change
—and if he decline the affair, to have the Prospectuses printed
elsewhere & sent off—as before intended—as soon as possible. I
have no other anxiety than to have *some* answer from him: whether
yea or nay is something less than a matter of Indifference to me.
It might be of considerable service to me indeed, if a Prospectus were
put up in the passage of the Lecture-Theatre at the R. I. and in the
Reading Rooms—and to this Indulgence I have perhaps some *claim*.

My Health and Spirits are improved beyond my boldest Hopes—
A very painful Effort of moral Courage has been remunerated by
Tranquillity—by Ease from the Sting of Self-disapprobation. I have
done more for the last 10 weeks than I had done for three years
before. Among other things I wrote what the few persons, who saw
it, thought [a very] spirited and close reasoned Letter to Mr Jeffray
respecting the introductory Paragraph of the Ed: Review of your
Paper:[1] but I was earnestly dissuaded from sending it, as from an
act of undeserved Respect—as from too great a Condescension
even on my part—and 2ndly (and which was of far more weight
with me) as an act involving you more or less, whatever I might
say, and likely to be attributed to your instigation, direct or indirect
—as it is not unknown, that I have been on terms of Intimacy with
you.—Yet I own, I should be sorry to have it lost, as I think it the
most eloquent and manly composition, I ever produced. If you
think it worth the Postage, it shall be transcribed—and I will send
you the original. The Passage in question was the grossest and most
disgusting KECK-UP of Envy, that has deformed even the E. R.
Had the Author had the Truth before his Eyes, and purposely

[1] See *Edinburgh Review*, July 1808, pp. 394–401, for a review of Davy's
*Bakerian Lecture on some new Phenomena of Chemical Changes produced by
Electricity*. The opening paragraph contains a sneering comparison between the
genius of Newton and the 'indefatigable industry' of Davy.

written in diametrical opposition, he could not have succeeded better—. It is high Time, that the spear of Ithuriel should touch this Toad at the ear of the Public.

I would willingly inform you of my chances of success in obtaining a sufficient number of Subscribers, so as to justify me prudentially in commencing the work; but I do not at present possess grounds even for a sane Conjecture. It will depend in great measure on the zeal of my Friends—on which—I confess not without some Remorse—I have more often cast water than oil. Here a Conceit about the Greek Fire might come in; but the Similie is somewhat *tritical*.

Wordsworth has nearly finished a series of masterly Essays on our late and present Relations to Portugal & Spain. Southey is sending to the Press his History of Brazil,[1] and at the same Time (the Indefatigable!) composing a defence of religious Missions to the East &c.—Excepting the Introduction (which however I have heard highly praised, but myself think it shallow, flippant, and *ipse dixitish*) I have read few Books with such deep Interest, as the Chronicle of the Cid.[2] The whole Scene in the Cortes is superior to any equal Part of any Epic Poem, save the Paradise Lost—me saltem judice. The deep, glowing, yet ever self-controlled, Passion of the Cid—his austere Dignity so finely harmonizing with his Pride of loyal Humility—the address to his Swords—and the Burst of contemptuous Rage in his final Charge & Address to the Infantes of Carrion—and his immediate Recall of his Mind—are beyond all ordinary Praise.—It delights me to be able to speak thus of a work of Southey's: I am so often forced to quarrel with his want of Judgment and his Unthinkingness—which, heaven knows, I never do without pain & the vexation of a disappointed Wish.—But I am incroaching on time more valuable than my own—and I too have enough to do. May God grant you Health and the Continuance of your intellectual vigor.

S. T. Coleridge—

725. *To T. G. Street*

Address: G. Street, Esqre. | 348, Strand | London   Single Sheet
MS. British Museum. Pub. with omis. Letters from the Lake Poets, *95.*
Postmark: 10 December 1808.   *Stamped*: Kendal.

Grasmere, Kendal.   Wednesday, [7] Dec. 1808.
My dear Sir

I cannot exactly decypher the exact tone, you wish the Courier to have, respecting the Cintra Convention and Court of Enquiry; but

---

[1] *The History of Brazil*, i, 1810; ii, 1817; iii, 1819.
[2] Southey's translation of the *Cid* was published in 1808.

I see plainly by X Y's admirable Letters that you maintain an independence truly honorable to you: which pleased me the more, because—allow me the privilege of an old friend—I was sadly grieved by three or four Paragraphs written in your own editorial character, especia[l]ly that defence of the Duke of Portland, assuredly the most unprincipled and rapacious State-Invalid, that ever disgraced an Administration. Forgive me this freedom: for it is out of my power not to feel just the same Interest in the Courier, as if it were at once my own property and of my own writing. Yet if I did not greatly like what you write in general, I should neither have the courage nor feel the impulse nor receive any motive for a specific censure. The Court of Enquiry appears to me a process intended *to kill* the Quicksilver of popular feeling by the Saliva of Drivellers. Not a question concerning the *Terms* of this confluent Small-pox of unparalleled Infamy; but an identical proposition gravely worded as a Query—to wit—'Do you not think, that the Convention (i.e. the allowing the French to go out of Portugal) allowed the French to go out of Portugal?' O Shame, shame!— *This* is the true Question—Wretches! you were sent to deliver Portugal from the French—why then did you deliver the French out of Portugal? Sir A. W.'s 'Not a man is yet arrived' stamps his character for ever. Buonaparte were a fool, if he sent Junot's army immediately into Spain—they are doing him more service in France, where every Soldier with his Plunder is acting the part of a Recruiting Serjeant.

Wordsworth has nearly finished a series of most masterly Essays on this Subject—and I shall send the two first to Mr Stuart by the next post—and the others, as soon as ever I hear from him or you. Believe me, dear Street! an aweful Time is coming on with hasty Strides. G. Britain cannot remain altogether in it's present State, the Ministers absolute Menials of the Royal *Person*, and the actual State-agency in those, who are under no actual responsibility. I can despise as heartily as you & every man of sense, the disgusting Trash of Westminster Meetings; but yet it were blindness not to perceive, that in the *People* of England, not the *Populace*—apud *populum*, non *plebem*—there is a heaving and a fermentation, as different from the vulgar seditions of corresponding Societies and Manchester clubs, as A. Sidney from Horne Took[e]—. Never were a nation more uniform in their contentment with, and gratitude for, their glorious Constitution—they are not even earnest about any reform in it's shape—let them but see the actual Managers of their affairs actually responsible, and that most wise Principle—'The King can do no wrong'—restored to it's true meaning—and they have not a public wish ungratified.   But—Whitelock—Burrard—Dalrymple!—So

(137)

much for Politics—Now for myself and my own Concerns.—12 days
ago I wrote to Mr Savage, directing to the R. Institution from
ignorance of his proper Address (which is in some Street near
Covent garden—close by Bedford St, I seem to remember)—herein
I requested him, if he continued in his former mind, to print off a
1000 of these Prospectuses, for the disposal of a certain number of
which I gave him a list of Names and places—and left the rest to his
own Judgment—but earnestly desired an answer by return of Post.
A week has passed since the post by which I should have received
it—If this neglect be intentional, it is unkind; if accidental, it is
most unlucky. I merely wished an answer—whether yea or nay is to
me something less than indifferent. Now you see that this Work is of
the last Importance to me—and if any thing can, this does justify
me in calling on my friends to do me what good they can.—What
I wish is, that Mr Savage should be found out—he is a Printer &
Publisher—his address may certainly be procured at the R. Inst.—
If he have not printed the Prospectus, then to get a 1000 printed
elsewhere—200 to be sent to Mr Shepherd, Bookseller and Stationer,
Wine Street, Bristol—: 100 to the Revd. F. Wrangham, Hunmanby,
near Bridlington, York (by *the York Mail*): 100 to G. Caldwell,
Esqre. Jesus College, Cambridge: 100 to J. Miller, Esqre. Worcester
College, Oxford—: 100 to T. Clarkson, Esqre. Bury St Edmonds—
25 to T. Russel, Esqre. Junior (Russel's Waggon Office) Exeter.—
A few to Motley, at Portsmouth—and do you know any one at
Plymouth, or at Shrewsbury—Should it be advertised?—O dear
Sir! do what you can for me. I have not enjoyed such steady
Quietness of Heart & activity of mind for many years as I am now
enjoying—— and if I can succeed in this, I shall yet live to pay my
Debts of Love as well as Justice to my Friends—

　　　　　　　　　　　　　　　　　　　　　　S. T. Coleridge.

726. *To James Montgomery*

Address: James Montgomery, Esqre.| the Iris Office | Sheffield　Single Sheet
MS. McGregor Library, Univ. of Virginia. Pub. Memoirs of James Montgomery,
by J. Holland and J. Everett, 7 vols., 1854–6, ii. 210.
Stamped: Keswick.

　　　　　　　　　　　　　　　Grasmere, Kendal.
　　　　　　　　　　　　　　[*Circa* 10 December 1808][1]
Dear Sir
　　In desiring a small pacquet of these Prospectuses to be sent to
you from Leeds, I have presumed less on myself than on our common
Friend, Mrs Montague; but believe me, by more than by either have

---

[1] Montgomery's reply, dated 16 Dec. 1808 and preserved at Dove Cottage,
determines the approximate date of this letter.

been encouraged by my Love and Admiration of your works, and my unfeigned affectionate Esteem of what I have been so often & so eloquently told by Mrs M. of your Life and Character. Conscious how very glad I should be to serve you in any thing, I apply with less discomfort to you in behalf of my own Concerns. What I wish is simply to have the Prospectuses placed and dispersed among such places & persons, as may bring the work to the notice of those whose moral and intellectual Habits may render them desirous to become Subscribers. I know your avocations, and dare not therefore ask you for an occasional contribution—I have received promises of support from some respectable Writers, and for my own part, am prepared to play off my whole Powers & Acquirements, such as they are, in this work, as from the main pipe of the Fountain.

If Choice or Chance should lead you this way, you will find both here and at Greta Hall, Keswick, House room and Heart Room: for I can add Robert Southey's and William Wordsworth's names to my own, when I declare myself with affectionate respect,

dear Sir, | Your's sincerely,
S. T. Coleridge

727. *To William Taylor*[1]

Address: William Taylor, Esqre. | St Helen's Auckland | Durham Single Sheet.
MS. Bodleian Library. Hitherto unpublished.
Stamped: Keswick.

Grasmere, Kendal.
[Circa 10 December 1808]

My dear Sir

I am not quite satisfied, that my acquaintance with you has been such as to justify [me] in the freedom of sending you a small pacquet of my Prospectuses; but if it be not, I am sure, your good nature will forgive me—and my friends W. and Mary Wordsworth, and Miss S. Hutchinson must be taken in, as part of my Excuse.

I cannot flatter myself, that the w[hole Structure] of my Philosophy, speculative and practical, will be deemed by you [and your] Brother of legitimate Architecture; but to men of robust and active [Intellect] there is a charm in that diversity of Faith with unity of honest [purpose,] which constitute the Discordia concors of the intellectual World. [I devote] all my powers and stores, such as they may be, to the work: and [I have] received promises of contribution from several of our most cele[brated] literary Characters.

---

[1] William Taylor of St. Helen's Auckland was a friend of the Hutchinsons and is not to be confused with William Taylor of Norwich.

In dispersing them as favorably as you [may] have opportunity you will increase the obligation tho' not [the] respect and esteem of, my dear Sir!

your sincere Friend & Servt
S. T. Coleridge

728. *To William Savage*

Transcript Royal Institution. Hitherto unpublished.

Dear Sir   [*Circa* 12 December 1808][1]

I well remember a Conversation, in which you proposed the same or a similar plan for my consideration with that contained in your Letter: & that repeatedly telling you that all bargaining was hateful to me, I pressed that it should be left to the arbitration of disinterested Friends. At the same time I distinctly refused to consider my Essay as having the least connection with any former one, and obviated your remark of your *Risk* &c, by declaring that I never would commence the work without such a number of Subscribers as would remove all Risk: and could not help noticing to you, that after you had received your profits as a Printer & Publisher, I was at a loss to conjecture on what grounds you claimed half of the net Profits. Accordingly I spoke to Mr. Davy & wrote to Mr. Bernard my opinions a day or two after, as soon as I had had time to re-review the whole business—& the answer which I received from them after, as I understood, a conversation with you, and containing your Approbation, occasioned me to read your Letter with Surprize. I am not certain whether Mr. Bernard wrote to me—I seem to remember that he did—but I cannot find the Letter—I shall not therefore hazard an incorrect Statement of it. It is sufficient, at present, that I do not assent to your proposals, or will assent to any resembling them.[2]

---

[1] Savage's letter, to which this is an answer, bears a postmark of 8 Dec. 1808.

[2] In his letter to Coleridge, Savage had indicated his willingness to print 1,000 copies of the prospectus, but recommended 'at least 10,000' for purposes of publicity. 'In the last conversation which I had with you', he went on to say, 'it was agreed, if my recollection be correct, that the Copyright of the work should be your property; that I should take the risk of the publication; that is defray the expenses of printing, paper, and advertising, and be repaid out of the first proceeds of the sale; and then the profits to be equally divided between us; I having always the printing and the publishing of the work; and the power of printing it . . . in any subsequent editions, if I should think proper; . . . always understanding that the expenses attending these editions will be borne by me; and that I shall be repaid . . . out of the first receipts of the sale of such edition, and then the profit to be equally divided between us.' [MS. Dove Cottage.]

I have desired a Gentleman of my Acquaintance to call on you
concerning the Prospectus.[1]

S. T. Coleridge.

729. *To Daniel Stuart*

Address: D. Stuart, Esqre. | 348 Strand | London   To be forwarded to Mr S.
without delay.
MS. British Museum. Pub. with omis. Letters from the Lake Poets, *106*.
Postmark: 17 December 1808. *Stamped*: Kendal.

[*Circa* 14 December 1808]

Dear Stuart

The Letters, of which the above are copies,[2] explain to you the
cause of my writing to you now. You see, into what a rogue's hands
I was about to have placed myself. With Davy, Mr Bernard, and
the Bishop of Durham Savage had agreed to print and publish the
work on the simple condition, that he should be payed for the
Printing etc the same price that is usually charged to the Trade,
and was to receive five per Cent for the publishing. As to his proposal of having it sold for sixpence, it might answer for him in a
work according to his notions, i.e. one, the Object of which was to
have as many readers as possible, no matter who or of what sort,
in order to make it as profitable [a] Job as possible. My Purpose is
widely different. I do not write in this work for the multitude of
men; but for those, who either by Rank, or Fortune, or Official
situation, or by Talents & Habits of Reflection, are to influence the
multitude—I write to found true PRINCIPLES, to oppose false
PRINCIPLES in Legislation, Philosophy, Morals, International Law.
Cobbet sells his Sheet for 10d—Now he differs from me in two things
mainly—He applies to the Passion[s that] are gratified by Curiosity,
sharp & often calumnious Personality, the Politics and the Events
of the Day, and the names and characters of notorious Contemporaries. From all these Topics I not only abstain as from guilt; but to
strangle these Passions by the awakening of the nobler Germ in
human nature is my express and paramount *Object*. Now three
fourths of English Readers are led to purchase periodical works,
even those professedly literary, by the expectation of having these
Passions gratified, of which we have a melancholy proof in the great
sale of the Edingburgh Review (which, thank God! has received a

---

[1] Stuart called on Savage, dismissed him from the undertaking, and warned
Coleridge that the proposed conditions 'would have led you into a gulph of
debt or obligation; they are most ruinous'. [MS. Dove Cottage.] Thus at the
end of 1808 Coleridge found himself without a printer and publisher for *The
Friend*.

[2] The letter from Savage and Coleridge's reply. See Letter 728.

deadly stab by X Y's Essays in the Courier, as I have just heard from a Friend of the Editor's & himself a writer in the E. R.)—All these Readers I give up.—Secondly, he fills himself not one half of his Journal—the rest is but reprinting, or stupid Letters from Correspondents—And his own Letters—what are they?—In general, conversational Comments on large *Extracts* from the Morning Papers—at all events, the careless passionate Talk of a Man of robust common sense, but grossly ignorant and under the warp of Heat & Prejudice, on the subjects furnished by the Day.—*I* bring the Results of a Life of intense Study, and unremitted Meditation—of Toil, and Travel, and great & unrepayed Expence.—Those, to whom these Reasons (were there no other) would not justify me in selling the work stamped for a Shilling—i.e. two pence more, I neither expect or wish to have among my Subscribers.

Dear Friend! do call on this Savage, Bedford Bury, London, No. 28. If he have printed the Prospectus, and sent it off according to my directions, well & good—If he have not, use the copy I sent to you or Mr Street, and have a thousand or so printed off immediately.[1] It is my Wish to take the whole at once out of his Hands, to have it stamped & circulated just as Cobbet or Bell's Messenger—and if you called on George Ward in Paternoster Row, I doubt not, he would be the London Publisher. But I dare do nothing on a subject so very important without your Advice. But, as Time is so important now, whatever you think adviseable, do it; and be quite certain, that I shall think it the best possible.

If you knew the Quickening and the Throb in the Pulse of my Hope, when I think of you and anticipate that I shall shortly shew myself in every thing what you have a right to expect from me, you would know that it was from the bottom of my Heart that in a late Letter to Perry of the M. Chronicle acknowleging one late, and some former attentions to me (before my marriage) I mentioned you (as from the nature of the occasion of my Letter I was obliged to do) as 'the wisest Adviser, and the most steady, disinterested, and generous Friend, that Heaven ever bestowed on a man'.

S. T. Coleridge.

Wordsworth's first Essay, I hope, the two first, will be sent to you by this or the following Post.—Will you ask Street (if it is not to be a secret) who [X] Y is?

---

[1] Savage had not printed any copies of the prospectus, and it was not until Feb. 1809 that Stuart had a new issue printed in London. See Letter 743.

730. *To Humphry Davy*

Address: Humphey Davy, Esqre. | Royal Institution | Albermarle Street | London
MS. Royal Institution. Pub. with omis. Frag. Remains, *103.*
Postmark: ⟨17⟩ December 1808. *Stamped*: Kendal.

14 Dec. [1808] Grasmere, Kendal

Dear Davy

The above written Copies[1] will explain this, my second application to you. I understood from Mr Bernard, as well as from yourself, that Mr Savage had agreed to print and publish the work on the sole condition, that he was to have five per Cent for the Publisher, and to charge the Printing etc at the Price charged to the Booksellers, or THE TRADE (as they very ingenuously & truly style their Art and Mystery.) To spare me the necessity of troubling Mr Bernard with a fresh Letter, I intreat you to transmit this to him as soon as possible. There is but one part of Mr Savage's Letter, that I can permit myself to comment upon: that of the propriety of pricing the Essay at Sixpence,—and consequently, of not having it stamped —nor finely printed nor on fine paper. For Him, and for a work conducted as he would have it conducted, i.e. one, the Object of which is to attract as many Purchasers as possible, no matter who or of what kind, in order to make it as profitable a Job as possible— this might answer. My Purposes are widely different. I do not write in this Work for the *Multitude*; but for those, who by Rank, or Fortune, or official Situation, or Talents and Habits of Reflection, are to *influence* the Multitude. I write to found true PRINCIPLES, to oppose false PRINCIPLES, in Criticism, Legislation, Philosophy, Morals, and International Law. As giving me an opportunity of explaining myself, I say—Cobbet sells his weekly Sheet for ten pence—Now this differs from mine in two points mainly. First: he applies himself to the Passions that are gratified by Curiosity, and sharp—often calumnious—personality; by the Events and political Topics of the Day, and the names of notorious Contemporaries.— Now from all these I abstain altogether—nay, to strangle this vicious Temper of mind by directing the Interest to the nobler germs in human nature is my express and paramount Object. But of English Readers three fourths are led to purchase periodical works in the expectation of gratifying these passions—even periodical works professedly literary—of which the keen Interest excited by the Edingburgh Review and it's wide circulation, yield a proof as striking, as it is dishonorable to the moral Taste of the present Public. All these Readers *I* give up all claim to. Secondly: Cobbett

---

[1] The letter from Savage and Coleridge's reply. See Letter 728.

himself rarely writes more than a third of the weekly Journal; the
remainder of the Sheet is either mere reprinting, or stupid Make-
weights from Correspondents (with few excep[tions)]] of the very
lowest order. And what are his own Compositions? T[he] undigested
passionate Monologues of a man of robu[st] natural understanding,
but one uninriched by various kno[wlege,] undisciplined by a comprehensive Philosophy, under the warpin[g] influence of rooted
Habits of opposing and attacking, and from thi[s] state of mind
fruitful in thoughts, which a purer Taste woul[d] have rejected so
long that they would cease to occur, and promisc[uous] in the
adoption of whatever such a state of mind suggests to him [of] these
thoughts on subjects furnished ready to his Hand by the occurrences
of the D[ay.] Indeed, more often than otherwise, his Letters &c are
mere Comme[nts] on large *Extracts* from the morning papers, such
as a passi[onate] man would talk at breakfast over a Newspaper
supporting the political party, which he hated. No ONE Thesis is
proposed—there is no orderly origination, developement, & conclusion—in short, none of those qualities which constitute the
Nicety and *Effort* of Composition. But *I* (and if I do not, my work
will be dropt and abandoned) I bring the Results of a Life of intense
Study and unremitted Meditation; of Toil; and personal Travels;
and great unrepayed Expence. Those, to whom these Reasons would
not justify me in selling [the] work (stamped as Cobbet's) for that
part of twopence more which remains when the additional cost of
finer paper & printing is deducted, I neither expect or wish to have
among my Subscribers.—It is scarcely necessary to remark, that in
pointing out these differences I had no intention of depreciating the
Political Journal—the style and contents of the work are perfectly
well suited to the Purpose of the writer—The Labourers' pocket
knives are excellently adapted to the cutting of Bread & Cheese;
but it would be unfair to demand, that the medical Cutler A should
sell his Case of Lancets, at the same price that the Common Cutler
B. sells an equal weight of the Bread & Cheese Knives: supposing
them both equally good in their Kind.

This Letter from Mr Savage added to his long delay in answering
me at all has a good deal perplexed my proceedings; but it shall not
make me abandon my intention.

If any thing new have occurred in Chemistry from your own
Labours or those of others, it would be highly gratifying to me to be
informed of it by you: for hitherto I have not been [able] to afford to
take in any philosophical Journal—or indeed any other. I was told
by a friend, that William Allen had proved that no Oxygen was
absorbed in the Lungs; but that it's action consisted in carrying
off the Carbon from the Blood—consequently, that the old hypo-

thesis of refrigeration was not altogether false. But my Communicant was no Chemist: and his account was so confused that I am not sure that I have given an accurate Statement of it.

My Health & Spirits are far better, than I had dared hope—only from neglect of exercise I remain more corpulent than I ought, tho' I drink nothing but Table Beer, & eat very moderately.

When I was in London, I was shocked at the alteration in our Friend Tobin's Looks & Appearance. Those, who always interpret two Coincidents into Cause and Effect, would surmise that Marriage has been less conducive to his Health, than to his moral Comfort. It would give me serious pleasure to hear a more cheerful account of Him.

As soon as I have a little Leisure I shall send my Greek Accidence & Vocabulary of Terminations to the Press, with my Greek-English Lexicon; which will be followed by a Greek Philosophical Grammar.

Heaven preserve and prosper you—S. T. Coleridge.

731. *To Sir George Beaumont*

Address: Sir G. Beaumont, Bart | Dunmow | Essex
MS. Pierpont Morgan Lib. Pub. Memorials of Coleorton, *ii. 63.*
Postmark: 17 December 1808. *Stamped*: Kendal.

[*Circa* 14 December 1808]

Dear Sir George

If in the goodness of Providence my Health and Spirits continue to be what they have been since my return to Grasmere, I shall not have said unmeaningly to my Friends: Decide on my moral and intellectual character from the products of the year, 1809. I have received promises of contribution from writers of high reputation: and for myself, I consider THE FRIEND as the Main Pipe, from which I shall play off the whole accumulation and reservoir of my Head and Heart. And truly, as I said to a correspondent, it is high Time. Hitherto I have layed my Eggs with Ostrich Carelessness and Ostrich like Oblivion. The greater part have been crushed under foot: but some have crawled into light to furnish Feathers for other men's Caps—and not a few to plume the Shafts in the Quivers of Calumny. Henceforward

> Et nos tela, pater, ferrumque haud debile dextrâ
> Spargimus: et nostro sequitur de vulnere sanguis.[1]

If this appear to you a Confidence too near to Presumption, yet blame it not too severely, first because it is an exception to my

---

[1] *Aeneid*, xii. 50–51.

ordinary and habitual Tone of Self-appreciation, and because it is scarcely possible to succeed in such a work without a quickening and a Throb in the Pulse of Hope—and what if a blush of modest Shame disguise itself amid the Hectic of unusual Self-assertion, increasing the Semblance, while it is modifying the Feeling?

My first Essay will be on the Nature and the Importance of *Principles*—i.e. of the pure REASON, which dictates unconditionally, in distinction from the prudential understanding, which employing it's mole Eyes in an impossible calculation of Consequences perverts and mutilates its own Being, untenanting the function which it is incapable of occupying. This is Infidelity, essential Infidelity, however goodly it's Garb, however seemly it's name—and this I have long deemed the Disease, nay, let me speak out—the *Guilt* of the Age—therefore, and not *chiefly* because it has produced a spirit of enquiry into the external evidences of instituted Religion, it is an Infidel age. Will the Truth of the Tale exculpate me from the crime of personal calumny, if I illustrate—(thus, and to you alone, and in a confidential Letter)—my general Charge by a particular instance? If I tell you, that I know a Bishop, an English Bishop, who professing Socinianism (not indeed all the heresies of Drs Priestley & Co, but absolutely all the distinguishing tenets of Socinus) affirms the innocence & the duty of offering Adoration and *ultimate* Prayer to Christ, whom he yet Zealously contends to have been & to be not only a finite Creature, but a mere MAN! adding—*I* can *see* no harm, in this practice—it leaves untouched all the motives of future reward and punishment, which is the *essence* of Religion. Merciful Heaven! *this* the Essence of that Religion, which permits the degraded man to commence with terror only as the means of enabling him finally to arrive at itself, which is perfect Love shutting out Fear. Shall I hesitate to deem such a man an infidel, who rejects the fundamental *principle* of all Religion, propounded amid the Thunders of Mount Sinai, and revealed even to Heathen Philosophers by 'the still small voice' of Conscience, simply because in counting the Consequences, that people the tiny field of his dim Vision, he had seen *no Harm* from it! No, dear and honored Sir George! I dare not hesitate—nor would a Library of Evidences & Apologies composed by him invalidate my Conviction or annul the Sentence.—If from Heresy in Faith I pass to Error in the Management of Nations— but I shrink from it—The groans of Ruin from amid the Ruins of sunken Europe month after month still repeat the direful Truth— and the sole Hope of afflicted Humanity, if any Hope there be, rises up in a Nation, which essays to build it's Stronghold of Defence and offence on the rock of unconditional *Principle*—which has proclaimed with solemnity that it is a less evil for Man, woman and

Child thro' a whole kingdom to die by the Sword of War, than for the same Persons to exist enslaved and vicious. This heroic Nation, loyal even to Death, the cometary Monster who hides beneath his gorgeous, or within his iron, Crown of Usurpation, Locks still loathly from the putrid Cap of Jacobin Liberty, howls his hoarse Laugh at, as the genuine Descendents of Don Quixote—a rebellious Mob of fanatical Democrats. Don Quixote? I should glory in the Descent if to have the Corsican at the root of my Ancestral Tree were the only alternative! There was more wisdom in the Heart of that illustrious Madman, than that of all France, were it assembled in one Head. But my Track in 'THE FRIEND' confines me to common Life and to Men acting as Individuals in the daily Toils and Pleasures of common Life—And here I see before me an ample Harvest of Facts—and I am well content, that such *is* the Direction of my Road: for I listen with gladness and an obedient ear to Prudence, while it remains subordinate to, and in harmony with, a loftier and more authoritative Voice—that of PRINCIPLE.

I have dwelt thus on the SUBJECT of my first Essay, because this will be, more or less avowedly, the *Object* of all the succeeding papers —for reflect only on the enormous power, which for a small time a mere Individual can acquire (an Hatfield[1] for instance) by a total emancipation of the will from all the Laws of general Morality. What then must be the power, when one pre-eminently wicked Man wields the whole strength and cunning of a wicked Nation? Is there any Strength adequate to resist this? Yes! one and only one. Consistency, energy, and unanimity in national wickedness must be counterbalanced by consistency and undistracted Energy in national Virtue, which fully exerted bring with them, from the recesses of their own nature, a greater consistency, a more enduring Energy. The atrocious Contempt of all moral must be met by an heroic Contempt of all physical Consequences, and Justice must act to the full stretch of it's Rights, where Wickedness admits no other Limit than that of it's Power. If there were ever a Time when the sublime Truth of the Apostle (We live by Faith alone) was more especially important than at any preceding, it is the present aweful Epoch. Without Faith we perish: and without Principle, pure unconditional Principle, there can be no Faith.

May God bless you and your's—I remain, dear Sir George! with unfeigned Respect

your obliged & grateful Friend,
S. T. Coleridge—

---

[1] See note to Letter 594.

732. *To Francis Jeffrey*

Address: F. Jeffray, Esqre. | Queen's Street | Edingburgh
MS. New York Public Lib. Pub. Letters, *ii. 534.*
Postmark: 19 December 1808. *Stamped*: Keswick.

14 Dec. 1808.
Grasmere, Kendal

Dear Sir

The only thing, in which I have been able to detect any degree of hypochondriasis in my feelings, is the reading and answering of Letters: and in this instance I have been at times so wofully under it's domination, as to have left every letter received lie unopened for weeks together, all the while thoroughly ashamed of the weakness and yet without power to get rid of it. This however has not been the case of late—and I was never yet so careless, as knowingly to suffer a Letter relating to money to remain unanswered by the next post in my power. I therefore on reading your very kind Letter of 8. Dec. conclude, that one letter from you during my movements from Grasmere—now to Keswick—now to Bratha & Elleray—& now to Kendal—has been mislayed.—

As I considered your insertion of the Review of Mr Clarkson's as an act of personal kindness, and attention to the request of one a stranger to you except by name, the thought of any pecuniary remuneration never once occurred to me: and had it been written at your request, I should have thought 20 guineas a somewhat extravagant price whether I considered the Quantity or Quality of the communication. As to the alterations, your character and interest, as the known Editor of the Review are pledged for a general consistency of principle in the different Articles with each other; and you had every possible Right to alter or omit ad libitum, unless a special condition had been insisted on of Aut totum aut nihil.— As the writer therefore, I neither thought or cared about the alterations:[1] as a general Reader, I differed with you as [to] the scale of merit relatively to Mr Wilberforce, whose Services I deem to have been over rated, not perhaps so much absolutely, as by comparison. At all events, some following passages should have been omitted, as they are in blank contradiction to the Paragraph inserted, and betrayed a co-presence of two Writers in one article. As to the longer Paragraph, Wordsworth thinks you on the true side; and Clarkson himself that you were not far from the Truth. As to my own opinion, I believed what I wrote, and deduced my belief from all the facts pro and con, with which Mr Clarkson's conversation had furnished [me]; but such is my detestation of that pernicious Mini-

---

[1] Cf. Letter 717.

ster, such my contempt of the cowardice and fatuity of his measures, and my Horror at the yet unended Train of their direful consequences, that if obedience to Truth could ever be painful to me, this would have been. I acted well in writing, what on the whole I believed the more probable; and I was pleased, that you acted equally well in altering it according to your convictions.

I had hoped to have finished a Letter of more interesting Contents to you—but an honest Gentleman in London, having taken a great fancy to two thirds of the possible profits of my literary Labors without a shadow of a claim, and having over-hurried the business thro' over-weening of my Simplicity & carelessness, has occasioned me some perplexity, and a great deal of trouble and letter writing. I will write however again to you, my first leisure Evening; whether I hear from you or no in the Interim.

I trust, you have received my Scrawl with the Prospectus—and feel sincerely thankful to you for your kindness on the arrival of the Prospectuses prior to your receipt of the Letter which was meant to have announced them. But our Post here is very irregular as well as circuitous—but three times a week—and then too we have to walk more than two miles for the chance of finding Letters. This you will be so good as to take into account whenever my Answers do not arrive at the time, they might have been expected from places in general—

I remain, dear Sir, | with kind & respectful feeling | Your obliged
.S. T. Coleridge

I entirely coincide in your dislike of 'speculative Gloom'[1]—it is illogical as well as barbarous, and almost as bad as picturesque Eye. I do not know, how I came to pass it: for when I first wrote it, I

---

[1] The paragraph containing the controversial phrase reads as follows in both Kendal prospectuses: 'Sources of Consolation to the afflicted in Misfortune, or Disease, or speculative Gloom, from the Exertion and right Application of the Reason, the Imagination, and the moral Sense; and new Sources of Enjoyment opened out.' In the London prospectus, 'speculative Gloom' is altered to 'Distress of Mind', with a qualifying sentence: 'By the words "Distress of Mind," I more particularly refer to speculative doubt or disbelief, concerning the Moral Government of the World, and the Destination of Man.' In the prospectus printed in the first number of *The Friend*, the words are again changed to 'Dejection of Mind', with a somewhat different explanatory sentence: 'In the words "Dejection of Mind" I refer particularly to Doubt or Disbelief of the moral Government of the World, and the grounds and arguments for the religious Hopes of Human Nature.'

As early as 1804, in describing his unrealized 'Consolations and Comforts from the exercise and right application of the Reason, the Imagination, and the moral Feelings, addressed especially to those in Sickness, Adversity, or Distress of mind, *from speculative Gloom*', Coleridge used many phrases re-employed in the prospectus. (See Letters 536 and 550.)

undermarked it, not as the expression, but as a remembrancer of some better that did not immediately occur to me. 'Year-long absences'[1] I think doubtful—had any one objected to it, I should have altered it; but it would not *much* offend me in [the] writings of another. But to 'moral Impulses' I see at present no Objection; nor does any other phrase suggest itself to me which would have expressed my meaning.[2]

That there is a semblance of presumptuousness in the manner, I exceedingly regret, if so it be.—My Heart bears me witness, that the Feeling had no place there. Yet I need not say to you, that it is impossible to succeed in such a work unless at the commencement of it there be a quickening and throb in the pulse of Hope: and what if a Blush from inward modesty disguise itself, on these occasions, amid the Hectic of unusual Self-assertion, [and] increase the appearance of that Excess which it in reality resists and modifies? It will amuse you to be informed, that from two Correspondents, both of them men of great literary celebrity, I have received reproof for a supposed affectation of Humility in the Style of the Prospectus—.[3] In my own consciousness I was guilty of neither. Yet surely to advance as a Teacher, and in the very act to declare yourself inferior to those whom you propose to teach, is incongruous; and must disgust a pure mind by it's evident hypocrisy.

733. *To Daniel Stuart*

MS. British Museum. Pub. with omis. Letters from the Lake Poets, *109.*

Grasmere, Dec. 28. 1808.—Wednesday Night.

My dear Stuart

I wish, it were as endurable to you to hear as it would be pleasant to me to express, the various personal feelings with which I read your Letters. Wordsworth coolly observed to me—'You had a wise and kind friend—you were yourself well aware of his general knowlege of the world, and *his* particular familiarity with things of this kind—& you did not avail yourself of it—what else could you expect?' This is true, no doubt; but then I must say, that I had been informed by Davy & Bernard, that Savage had agreed and engaged to the most moderate Conditions—that of charging the Printing at the Trade Price, and receiving 5 per Cent for the Publication. To publish 'The Friend' monthly would not answer

---

[1] 'Year-long Absences' is altered to 'long Absences' in subsequent versions of the prospectus.

[2] 'Moral Impulses' is retained in later drafts of the prospectus.

[3] See *Southey Letters,* ii. 120.

my moral purposes so well: you can judge better than I whether it would be equally profitable to me. If I publish it on one sheet (as I had for some time determined to do) and have it stamped, could I not send off the Sheet by the Post to the Subscribers of my own procuring, who have sent me their names & address? Mr Curwen has offered me his name to frank it with.[1]—What have the News-men to do with these?—But rather, my dear Friend! do you tell me what I should do, that must be done *by me*: and I will immediately do it without a further Question. Where ever my opinion or assent alone is wanted, that is already pre-included in whatever your opinion is or may hereafter be. The future Prospectuses should be printed *from this Copy*; but make any alterations, omissions, or additions, you think right. I wrote in the form of an Extract from a letter to a Correspondent, as the less of two Evils—that is, in some measure to cover over the indelicacy of speaking of myself to Strangers and to the Public—and yet without speaking thus I did not know how to explain my motives, or the grounds of my fitness for this specific Undertaking.—But I *will try to alter it* into the Form of an Address to the Public: and at all events, will draw up the *short Advertisement*, immediately.—I am afraid, that Wordsworth's fifth cannot go off, as was intended, in this Frank—it is finished all but the corrections—but his Head & Bowels have been disordered the whole day till late this Evening. Consequently, such are our Posts, it cannot go off from Kendal till Saturday Morning.

In begging you to write to me article by article what had better be done, I have no wish of evading trouble or thought; but I have unconditional confidence in your opinion, none in my own; and if you think at all, I imagined, it would be easier for you to frame the whole Scheme & Skeleton of Agenda, of the Things to be done and the Things not to be done, than to supply Fragments. I have at present a hundred names, and more—& have reason to believe that I shall procure at least 150 more.—Whenever the Prospectuses are printed, be so good as to order a hundred to be sent to Basil Montagu, Esqre, Lincoln's Inn: and likewise 20 or 30 to Mr T. Monkhouse, 21, Budge Row. Montagu has asked by Letter for a hundred Prospectuses: and both assured me, they expected to procure me a hundred Subscribers. If a 100 be procured between them, it will be well.—As to Politics, I cannot imagine a *definite legal* meaning of the word—'τὰ πολιτικά' signifies in Greek what-

---

[1] The whole issue of *The Friend* was franked by J. C. Curwen, the member for Carlisle. 'In the wrappers,' Coleridge later wrote to his printer, 'you have nothing to do but to copy those of any of the London Papers, putting "THE FRIEND" instead of "the Courier or Star" and taking "J. C. Curwen, Esqre. M.P." as the franking member's name.' Letter 754.

ever relates to the Duties and Interests of the State and it's
Citizens—but as to any thing ordinarily understood by Politics,
I have as little to do with it, as with News. You will tell me, for
what date (you think) I may venture to announce the Essay. I have
as yet received no accounts from any of the chief Towns.—I meant
the Type to be the same sort with that of this Prospectus, 35 lines
in a page, and about 40 letters in a line—to be printed as a Book,
not as Cobbet's or as a Magazine—. May God bless you, and your
obliged & affectionate Friend,

                                            S. T. Coleridge

The Names of the Persons who have been long expecting Prospectuses, & the numbers to be sent, I wrote in my Letter to Mr
Street. I never conjectured X Y till the last but one—and that only
after I had read the last—but was reading again the former. Then
certain phrases all at once suggested to me that you might be the
Author. This was on Monday Night.—The prospectuses that were
to be sent to G. Caldwell, Esqre, Jesus College, Cambridge, are to
be sent to the Revd. T. Cautley, Jesus College, Cambridge—and
those for Mr Clarkson, not to be sent to Bury.

734. *To Sir George Beaumont*

Address: Sir G. Beaumont, Bart | Dunmow | Essex
MS. Pierpont Morgan Lib. Pub. Memorials of Coleorton, *ii. 69.*
Postmark: 2 January 1809. *Stamped*: Keswick.

                                        [*Circa* 30 December 1808]
Dear Sir George
    There is not a sentence in your kind Letter, to which I do not
assent with my whole head and heart. To deny the *fitness* of motives
from a future state to *any* class of men, or the urgent *need* of such
motives for *very many* men, I deem not only unpsychological but
pernicious. Nay, the most exalted finite Being must need the Faith
in Immortality as giving to Virtue an adequate *Object* and *Consequence*, altho' in the very *Idea* of Virtue it should have found a
sufficient *Impulse*, an adequate *ground* of Action.—But, dear Sir
George! as natural and necessary as motives of Hope and Fear
(indefinite) are to vicious men, in the process of leading them to a
nobler state, even so necessary is it for all men, the bad as well as
the Good, that the *Idea* of Virtue should exist, and a Faith in it's
Reality. Else we sacrifice the End to the Means.—But I shall more
clearly convey my meaning when I have in my first Essay shewn
the nature & evinced the power, of *Principles*—. Are we not a
union of Reason, Understanding, and Sense (i.e. the Senses)? As
necessary as *Perceptions* are to the Senses, so necessary are *Rules* to

the Understanding; and as necessary as *Rules* to the Understanding, so necessary are *Principles* to the Reason. For our sensuous nature would give us only Instinct, our Understanding could only superadd Cunning, or Prudence—in REASON lies the possibility of Virtue. The habit of realizing, as far as we can, the practical *Ideas* of Reason by availing ourselves of the powers of the *Understanding* & the *Sense* is human Wisdom.—In my Essay these Thoughts will be developed *popularly*. This is my definition of a *just popular* Style: when the Author has had his own eye fixed steadily on the *abstract*, yet permits his Readers to see only the *Concrete*.

It is a Whim of modern Date to consider Christianity as a mere Code of Ethics. This seems to me a degradation of the New Testament. It is an offer of Redemption from Moral Evil and it's Consequences, with a declaration of the conditions of acceptance. This indeed contains all the great principles of morality, but only as a *part*—it contains *medicines* too for those incapable of immediate Virtue—not only Rules to walk *well*, but means by which the Lame & the Palsied Spirit, may regain the possibility of walking *at all*. But be it remembered, that tho' the vessel must be cleansed before the new wine be poured in, yet the act of washing out the Cup is not the Infusion of the Wine! be it remembered, that the WORD of God did not exclusively bid men avoid the *wrath* to come—*He* likewise said—Be ye *perfect*, even as your Father in Heaven is perfect. And we are assured, that unless that *Fear*, which is the *Beginning* of Wisdom, shall proceed to LOVE, there can be no Union with God: for God is Love. To the *Diseased* Christ says, Love yourselves so as to leave your *Vices*; but to the *Convalescent*, Love your Neighbour as yourselves; and God *above all*. What then do I blame? Him who *couches* the blind Eye? God forbid! Whom then? Him who lets the Light in on the couched Eye slowly and gradually?—As little. But those I blame, who would convert the temporary Curtain before the window into a windowless Wall—a perpetual exclusion of Light. Those who, with Dr Paley in his Chapter on Moral Obligation, annihilate the *Idea* of Virtue by placing it's *essence* in Selfishness: and say *implicitly*—*Obey* God, *benefit* your Neighbour; but *love* YOURSELVES above all. One more observation—a very important one—and I conclude. I more than doubt whether a *mere* feeling of Selfishness would ever be called into action by Christ, or considered as a possible means of leading vicious men to the Capability of Virtue—I recollect no instance in the *New* Testament, in which it is said—Be temperate & chaste, in order that you may enjoy the keen pleasures, of which Health is the necessary Condition—still less any passage which says—Be honest—and God will make you rich.—But I recollect many passages, in which Rewards are offered in a Future State, & Punishments threatened.—Wherein lies the Difference?—In this: that in the belief of the Latter there is *implied* a FAITH, a submission of the fleshly Sense to the Moral Being, which is verily and indeed the *Beginning* of Wisdom; the *ground & condition*, of Virtue. Besides, it is not only the shadowiness of all Prospects beyond the Grave, and the uncertainty accompanying them in the bodily Feelings and Imagination, that remove these Hopes & Fears from mere Selfishness; this removal is further affected by the *generic* nature of these Consequences—What I hope for myself, I hope for all men—I cannot hope Heaven for myself as myself, but for all good men in the number of which *I* may be included. No act of Thought or Feeling necessarily *social* can be absolutely *selfish*—not therefore the *Insisting* on Heaven and the place of Death do I object to, but to such representations of Reward & Punishment as tend to take away the virtuous Leaven, to make them more selfish than they are in their own nature—. Now this bad Process is carried on in two ways, first, by giving the vulgarest & most material Images, not as Images, but as the Truth & the Reality—thus by a most perverse Alchemy transmuting Spirit into grossest Body, instead of leading thro' the Body to the Spirit— secondly, by excluding from Reality & Belief all *nobler* Prospects, and presenting an Image of Christianity, with no *Crown* on the Head, no Sceptre in the Hand. There are fewer men than is generally supposed, so utterly denaturalized as to have no *Dawning* at all of the Truth & the true Idea, of Goodness: and where ever there does exist even a Dawn of that Idea, it lends a *force* to the selfish motives, which we more often underrate than exaggerate. From opposites (say the Logicians) non datur Transitus nisi per intermedium. Now that State, which is selfish, yet not wholly selfish, not virtuous yet not wholly without virtue, is the Intermedium that makes it possible to pass from Vice to Holiness—that state therefore Christianity attempts to produce in the *first* instance—and he who would preach as a Christian dare deprive it of *neither* of it's constituent parts.— Finally, dear Sir George! this is my Faith—that Christianity is a divine *Religion*, which acknowleges the *existing* state of human nature with more than all the *Historic* Truth of the Epicurean Philosophy, and yet establishes an *Ideal* of Virtue in all the severity of the Stoic—at once avoiding the baseness of the one, and the bloating visionariness of the other.—This is a very dull Letter; but even it's prolixity tho' it may tire you, yet will not be unpleasing, as an evidence of the Value, I set on your Esteem.—With affectionate & respectful mind,

S. T. Coleridge

Miss Wordsworth will write to Lady B. in a few days.

735. *To Thomas Wilkinson*

Pub. Letters, *ii. 538.*

Grasmere, December 31, 1808.

Dear Sir,—I thank you for your exertions in my behalf, and—
which more deeply interests me—for the openness with which you
have communicated your doubts and apprehensions. So much,
indeed, am I interested, that I cannot lay down my head on my
pillow in perfect tranquillity, without endeavoring to remove them.
First, however, I must tell you that . . . 'The Friend' will not appear
at the time *conditionally* announced. There are, besides, great
difficulties at the Stamp Office concerning it. But the particulars
I will detail when we meet. Myself, with William Wordsworth and
the family, are glad that we are so soon to see you. Now then for
what is so near my heart. Only a certain number of prospectuses
were printed at Kendal, and sent to acquaintances. The much larger
number, which were to have been printed at London, have not been
printed. When they are, you will see in the article, noted in this
copy, that I neither intend to omit, nor from any fear of offence
have scrupled to announce my intention of treating, the subject of
religion. I had supposed that the words 'speculative gloom' would
have conveyed this intention. I had inserted another article, which
I was induced to omit, from the fear of exciting doubts and queries.
This was: On the transition of natural religion into revelation, or
the principle of internal guidance: and the grounds of the possibility
of the connection of spiritual revelation with historic events; that
is, its manifestation in the world of the senses. This meant as a
preliminary—leaving, as already performed by others, the proof of
the reality of this connection in the particular fact of Christianity.
Herein I wished to prove only that true philosophy rather leads to
Christianity, than contained anything preclusive of it, and therefore adopted the phrase used in the definition of philosophy in
general: namely, The science which answers the question of things
actual, how they are *possible*? Thus the laws of gravitation illustrate
the *possibility* of the motion of the heavenly bodies, the action of the
lever, etc.; the reality of which was already known. I mention this,
because the argument assigned which induced me to omit it in a
prospectus was, that by making a distinction between revelation *in
itself* (*i.e.* a principle of internal supernatural guidance), and the
same revelation conjoined with the power of external manifestation
by supernatural works, would proclaim me to be a Quaker, and
'The Friend' as intended to propagate peculiar and sectarian
principles. Think then, dear Friend! what my regret was at finding
that you had taken it for granted that I denied the existence of an

internal monitor! I trust I am neither of Paul, or of Apollos, or of Cephas; but of Christ. Yet I feel reverential gratitude toward those who have conveyed the spirit of Christ to my heart and understanding so as to afford light to the latter and vital warmth to the former. Such gratitude I owe and feel toward W. Penn. Take his Preface to G. Fox's Journal, and his Letter to his Son,—if they contain a faithful statement of genuine Christianity according to your faith, I am one with you. I subscribe to each and all of the principles therein laid down; and by them I propose to try, and endeavour to justify, the charge made by me (my conscience bears me witness) in the spirit of entire love against some passages of the journals of later Friends. Oh—and it is a groan of earnest aspiration! a strong wish of bitter tears and bitter self-dissatisfaction,— Oh that in all things, in self-subjugation, unwearied beneficence, and unfeigned listening and obedience to the Voice within, I were as like the evangelic John Woolman, as I know myself to be in the belief of the existence and the sovran authority of that Voice! When we meet, I will endeavour to be wholly known to you as I am, in principle at least.

A few words more. Unsuspicious of the possibility of misunderstanding, I had inserted in this prospectus Dress and Dancing among the fine Arts, the principles common to which I was to develope. Now surely anything common to Dress or Dancing with Architecture, Gardening, and Poetry could contain nothing to alarm any man who is not alarmed by Gardening, Poetry, etc., and secondly, principles common to Poetry, Music, etc., etc., could hardly be founded in the ridiculous hopping up and down in a modern ball-room, or the washes, paints, and patches of a fine lady's toilet. It is well known how much I admired Thomas Clarkson's Chapter on Dancing.[1] The truth is, that I referred to the drapery and ornamental decoration of Painting, Statuary, and the Greek Spectacles; and to the scientific dancing of the ancient Greeks, the business of a life confined to a small class, and placed under the direction of particular magistrates. My object was to prove the truth of the principles by shewing that even dress and dancing, when the ingenuity and caprice of man had elaborated them into Fine Arts, were bottomed in the same principles. But desirous even to avoid suspicion, the passage will be omitted in the future prospectuses.[2] Farewell! till we meet.

S. T. Coleridge.

[1] See *A Portraiture of Quakerism*, 3 vols., 1806, i, ch. v.

[2] In the Kendal prospectuses, Coleridge listed, after mentioning the Fine Arts: 'Architecture; Gardening; Dress; Dancing; Music; Painting; Poetry.' In the London prospectus the entire list was omitted. It was restored, with the excep-

P.S. Do you not know enough of the world to be convinced that by declaring myself a warm defender of the Established Church against all sectarians, or even by attacking Quakerism in particular as a sect hateful to the bigots of the day from its rejection of priesthood and outward sacraments, I should gain twenty subscribers to one? It shocks me even to think that so mean a motive could be supposed to influence me. I say aloud everywhere, that in the essentials of their faith I believe as the Quakers do, and so I make enemies of the Church, of the Calvinists, and even of the Unitarians. Again, I declare my dissatisfaction with several points both of *notion* and of *practice* among the present Quakers—I dare not conceal my convictions—and therefore receive little good opinion even from those, with whom I most accord. But Truth is sacred.

736. *To Pim Nevins*

Address: Mr Pym Nevins | Leeds
MS. Lord Latymer. Pub. with omis. E. L. G. i. 438.

[*Circa* 31 December 1808]

Dear Sir

You will excuse me for inclosing what I understand is the price of the two sets of Razors, with thanks for your kindness in procuring them for me. I would, you had been the Bearer! In the honest overflowings of Welcome my Friends would have convinced you, that the Kindnesses shewn by you to me were felt as Kindnesses shewn to themselves.—I would have gladly accepted the Razors, as a present and valued keep-sake from you; if I had not *written, requesting* you to procure them for me. And you, who are all generosity, and who (surely you will not suspect me of the baseness and *filth* of intentional Flattery) have woven into one web a Gentleman's delicacy and a Quaker's Honesty,—*you* will *understand*, that, if I accepted this kindness, I should never dare hereafter trouble a friend or acquaintance with any little commission, lest my request should be interpreted as a Hint for a *Present*—an artifice of decorous Mendicancy. Again, let me express my wish to see you at my Table, and under my Roof!—After a week, I dare promise myself, there would never take place any Pros or Cons between us in Things of this sort.—Now, dear Sir! for a few words on an affair of some importance to me.

The Person, who was to have been the Printer and Publisher of my Essay in London, made an atrocious attempt to trap me into

tion of the word 'Dancing', in the version of the prospectus printed in the first number of *The Friend*.

an agreement that must have enslaved & ruined me. He had seen me often in town; and from my apparent contempt of money in my proceedings with the R. Institution formed an overweening opinion of my simplicity & ignorance of the World. I rejected his infamous proposals, made as if I had forgotten the terms, he had agreed to in the presence of the Bishop of Durham, Mr Bernard (the beneficent and stirring Friend of the Poor) and the celebrated Davy. But the whole of the Iniquity I did not perceive till it was unveiled to me by a man of the most consummate knowlege of the World, managed by a thorough strong & sound Judgment, & rendered innocuous by a good Heart—indeed the wisest, most disinterested, kindest & most constant Friend, I was ever blest with. He had himself made a very large Fortune as Proprietor & Editor of a Paper—and at once saw & layed open the whole villainous Scheme.—The consequence is, a necessary Delay of the Publication—I hope however, that the second week in February will be the latest.—Now for the work itself. If you will have the goodness to re-peruse the Prospectus, (and the copies to be printed in London, which will be as four to one compared with the few printed at Kendal, will be so corrected) [you will see that] I have amplified the obscure phrase 'speculative gloom' so as to leave no doubt as to the religious Tendency of the Work. An article which I was induced to omit as seeming to announce controversy, which of all evils next to falsehood I wish to avoid—was on the necessary Transition of sincere natural Religion or Religion of Reason into a sense of the necessity of Grace, or an internal Voice & Guide—illustrated by Socrates, M. Antonine, &c. This however being to me a foundation Stone, I will not and dare not omit it in the Work itself; altho' I shall cautiously avoid all peculiar & sectarian phraseology. I mention this; because I was shocked by a Letter from an amiable Quaker, having these words—'I understand, thou dost not believe the reality of an internal Monitor.' Would, O would! that my whole Being were as clear in listening to, & obeying that Voice within, as my Convictions are clear in it's existence & divine Nature. In several points I disagree with the present Quakers, & would fain tell them so, if a more suitable occasion presented itself than that of the present Work, which is addressed to *all men*—But when I tell my mind concerning what I deem the errors in belief or practice that seem to exist in your society, I would wish to do it in a private work circulated only among the Fathers of Families—. I have likewise omitted the line containing the words 'Dress & Dancing', for fear of offence—tho' I was alluding wholly to the Decorations & scientific Pantomimes of the ancient Greeks. It were indeed ridiculous to suppose, that the Hopping up and down of a modern Ball-room, or the Paints,

Patches, and Periwigs of a modern Toilet could have principles common to them with Gardening, and Poetry.—I should be glad to hear from you, and of you and your family.

S. T. Coleridge

P.S. The act of Subscription binds to nothing. I understand it only as a determination to encourage the work, if it should be found worthy of Encouragement; and for the purpose of making the Proof possible without serious Loss to the Author. But as the Stamp Duty is such, that that number of Copies alone can be published of which the Sale is assured, it is requested and expected, that a fortnight's notice will be given to the Publisher (whose name will be hereafter announced) of the intention to drop the Work.— After paying the Stamp Duty, the Publisher, and the Newsman, three pence halfpenny will remain to me of the Shilling received; out of which three pence halfpenny I have to pay all the expences of the Paper, the Printing, the Advertising, &c—with all the contingent Losses of neglect, fraud, bad debts & Waste. I wish, this were known where the Price is objected to: and that it were moreover considered, that by religiously abstaining from all excitements of passion from personality and the events of the Day I give up beforehand three fourths of the English Readers of periodical Works. While—let the Truth of what I say screen me from the charge of speaking boastfully—instead of declaiming and railing on topics and large extracts furnished by the Morning Newspapers, instead of pouring out even such a rude and vehement Comment on the momentary Tidings or Measures, as an angry man might talk at his Breakfast Table while reading a Newspaper hostile to his Party—I bring the results of a Life of constant Study and intense Meditation, the Results of personal Toils and Travels, and of heavy unrepayed Expences. O if money were my Object, I could procure 50 Subscribers for one, if I chose to fight the battles of any particular Party—But to convey important Truth is my main Object: and I should scorn to receive for myself a single crown in the course of the year from any man, to whom I had not been honestly endeavoring to give knowlege and motive which cannot be bought or payed for with earthly coin, and the wish to seek from above those Impulses, which can be given only from above; and of which all that the highest earthly Eloquence can effect, is to convince the mind of it's Need! Tho' I cannot give the Medicine, yet I shall not have been useless if I have discovered the Disease, and shewn the way to the Physician.

737. *To Daniel Stuart*

MS. British Museum. Pub. Letters from the Lake Poets, *153.*

Tuesday Morning. [3 January 1809][1]

Dear Stuart

William received your Letter this morning at 11 o/clock—we have been hard at work ever since—it is now nearly 3 in the morning. However, the Essay has probably benefited by the accident— at all events, it has been increased in size[2]—We are very sorry, you should have had so much or indeed any anxiety about the loss of the papers, which has been so easily repaired—You will accept W's best thanks for your kindness as to the Pamphlet—He cannot guess what he ought to expect in justice, being without all grounds on which to form an opinion—but he is willing to take the risk on himself, and thinks that the Price bargained for ought to be conditional, and proportionate to the number of copies sold. The name shall be given; and *that* may be told the Publisher—but W. does not think it necessary to mention *his name* to him during the bargain, as he will have a fair sample of the goods before him—but this however he leaves to your judgment—if you think it will be better, mention it—Advertising, choice of Publisher, (for he is under no obligation or even tie of delicacy to any one[)] he leaves to your kindness and discretion—. So much for William. I am too much tired to write concerning myself—but I shall write tomorrow —May God bless you!—I have received a very severe and very abrupt Blow in the Death of Dr Beddoes—he was good and beneficent to all men, but to me he was tender and affectionate. Few Events have taken out so much Hope from my Life.—Your obliged & affectionately grateful Friend,

S. T. Coleridge

738. *To Basil Montagu*

Address: Basil Montagu, Esqre. | Lincoln's Inn | London
MS. Harvard College Lib. Pub. Chambers, Life, *354.*
Postmark: 12 January 1809. *Stamped*: Kendal.

Grasmere, Kendal

Saturday Night—[7 January 1809]

My dear Montagu

Many thanks both for your and for Mrs Montagu's Letter—If I were to give way to my private feelings respecting you, this sheet

---

[1] The reference to Dr. Beddoes's death, which occurred on 24 Dec. 1808 and of which Coleridge learned from a letter written Sunday, 25 Dec., determines the date of this letter. See Letter 742.

[2] The second instalment of Wordsworth's *Convention of Cintra* appeared in the *Courier* on 13 Jan. 1809.

would leave me no room for business.—What? if in the summer
vacations you & Mrs M. came down hither? and left such of the
children as might be thought advisable. You seem to me so certain
of rising to the summit of your profession, and I am sure, will do so
much good in it, that I dare not let any thing bribe me to consider
as good what might have the effect of distracting your attention—
Good heaven! you know Mrs Montague—can you suppose there
could be an event more delightful in and of itself to me, and to all
of us (but I dare boldly say, to me above all) than her residence
within a walk of us? The Idea of this and of it's accompaniments,
and the whole Form of the Objection to it's realization arising at
the same moment in my mind, so affected me, when I first read her
letter, that I shed tears. But enough of this, at present.

Savage overweening in my simplicity laid a plot for ruining and
enslaving me—His intentional neglect concerning the Prospectuses
has thrown me back a month—Since then great difficulties have
arisen at the Stamp Office—these have been removed—it is
declared, that if I adhere to my Prospectus, the work will be considered as a Pamphlet—But still the difficulties respecting the mode
of dispersing the Work are increased by this decision—for hitherto
two thirds of the Subscribers live in small towns or single Houses,
here three, here two, here one—scarce any where a sufficient number
to make a parcel per coach feasible—and thro' the country booksellers they would only receive it once a month perhaps—Enormous as the deduction is, I should prefer it's being on one sheet and
stamped, from the convenience of sending it per post—But I have
confided the whole to Mr Stuart, a man of the most consummate
knowlege of the world, and of rich experience in periodical works—
and to me as constant, generous, wise, and disinterested friend, as
ever man was blest with—I am waiting with great impatience for a
Letter from him—and hope, that in a week at l[e]ast a hundred or
more prospectuses will have been sent to you.

William is head, heart, soul, and fingers in the Spanish Business
—In the Courier one Essay of his has appeared, signed G.—the
second was lost in London, and so was re-written & sent again—I
trust, it will have appeared by this time—six more are to follow.

I mean to send you, as soon as it can be transcribed, a most
important memorial from Lord Bacon with additions and regular
application to the present state of the Church, in relation to the
Dissenters in general, but chiefly & prominently to the Evangelical
Preachers & Methodists—It is a masterpiece of Wisdom—My additions are about one fourth—exclusive of a short Introduction—.
Either you or Mrs M. will give it a careful Reading—and if you
think as highly of it, and of it's present applicability as I do—of

it's necessity, I might say—you may perhaps be able to make a
bargain for me with some bookseller.

Among my Books I miss several of the small octavos (Montgomery's Poems &c) all bound a like in a handsome purple—a huge
number of dear Mr Clarkson's History of the Slave Trade Abolition
—of which I can dispose of six Copies here—. At all events, send
the books &c—All here are well excepting dear Sara Hutchinson,
whose side is alarming[ly] painful—& myself, whose Chest and
Respiration are distressingly affected—Dr Beddoes's Death has
taken more Hope out of my Life, than any Event I can remember—
I have now no confidence in any medical man breathing. It very
grievously affected me—indeed at first with a strange and womanish violence of sorrow. He was good and beneficent to all men; but
to me he was tender and affectionate—and went out of the way of
his ordinary character to shew it—.

But I have many letters of business to write—so, dear Montagu,
farewell!—God bless you, & your's,

and your very affectionate Friend,

S. T. Coleridge

P.S. We are miserably off in our Post—this Letter cannot leave
Kendal till Tuesday Morning—on Sunday Night at 10 o/clock three
days' posts arrive at Rydale—and the letters in answer cannot be
sent off so as to leave Kendal till Wednesday or perhaps Thursday
—so that it sometimes takes ten days for the To-and-froage of a
Letter from London—Ambleside & Windermere receive such a
Vast of Letters, that we think of making an application to the Post
Master, Mr Freeling, signed by the Bishop, Llandaff—Sir D.
Fleming, &c.—at present we feel this particularly—that character
of Prescience & Prophecy which would have belonged to William's
Essays, had they been published as soon as written, is in good
measure lost by the Delay—

739. *To Daniel Stuart*

Address: D. Stuart, Esqre. | Courier office | Strand | London   *Single Sheet*
MS. British Museum. Pub. E. L. G. i. 442.
Stamped: Kendal.

Sunday Noon. [8 January 1809]

My dear Stuart

Tho' I trust as well as hope, that I shall receive a letter from you
by to night's post, yet we cannot get it till ten o/clock at night—
and then only by walking to Rydale (3 miles from our house); and
can answer it so as to leave Kendal by the *Tuesday's* Post (for all

Monday the Post loiters at Hawkshead) only by writing, as many lines as we can persuade the man to stay minutes, in the cottage at which he leaves the Letters. We receive Letters four times a week— the Letters of one post on Tuesday, of one post on Wednesday, of one on Friday, and of three posts on Sunday Night—so that a Letter written from London on Friday reaches us as soon as one written on Wednesday or Thursday. Therefore if you are writing to us by *Wednesday's* Post, and could recollect to direct *that* Letter to *Keswick* (Greta Hall) we should receive it by the Carrier with our Newspapers on Saturday instead of Sunday Night—and save a day in the answering.—

On the other side I have written (i.e. proposed) a short advertisement for the Newspapers: leaving to you, if you approve of it, to fill up the Blanks.[1] I have received half a dozen Letters complaining of the non-receipt of Prospectuses, in each of which is said—I am sure, I could have got 30—or 50—or 100 Subscribers. But your information concerning the stamp office has sadly perplexed me—first of all I had fully made up my mind to printing 'The Friend' *on one sheet only*—Was the determination of the Stamp office influenced by the proposal of printing it on one sheet & a quarter?—Secondly, and of more importance, of the Subscribers hitherto procured (180) two thirds and more live scattered, or where booksellers' parcels no[w] do not come above once a month—If the Essay be not stamped, how can it [be] delivered to these?—Would the Stamp office *refuse* to stamp the work, & so give it the privilege of being sent by the Post? Would they stamp *a given number*? I have reason to believe, that either from Percival or Lord Mulgrave I could procure any recommendation for any favor not illegal.—[If] stamped, what if I had it printed at Kendal, and sent off as a Provincial [paper so] as to arrive in London on Saturday Morning?[2]

[1] On Saturday___will be published 'THE FRIEND' a weekly Essay, by S. T. Coleridge. The OBJECT of this work generally expressed, is—to uphold those Truths and those Merits, which are founded in the nobler and permanent parts of our Nature against the Caprices of Fashion, and such pleasures as either depend on transitory and accidental Causes, or are pursued from less worthy Impulses. A more detailed account of it's purpose and chief Subjects will be found in the PROSPECTUS of 'THE FRIEND', which may be procured gratis, from the Booksellers undermentioned. The events of the day, and all personal and immediate Politics will be excluded.

Each Number will contain a Sheet of large octavo and will be delivered___

The names of those inclined to take in the work, and all communications, to be addressed (Post-paid) to MR COLERIDGE, Grasmere, Kendal: or___

[Except for the concluding sentence, this proposed 'advertisement' was written out by Sara Hutchinson, who served as Coleridge's amanuensis during the composition of *The Friend*.]

[2] The preceding sentence is crossed out in MS.

To Daniel Stuart

Monday Night

My dear Stuart

So far I had written, when Sara Hutchinson's Illness stopped me both by the necessary attendance on her and by the weight on my Spirits—And a heavy and continued Rain prevented any one's going to Rydale, so that I did not receive your Letter till this evening. You will long ere this (on Friday Morning, I calculate) have received Wordsworth's second Essay re-written by me, and in some parts re-composed—[1] the part of the necessity of military Courage & Zeal, and yet the equal necessity of their subordination to fortitude & patience, and the certainty of Success if the Spaniards are what we hope, and the triflingness of the disappointment if they are not, was written by me, in the first copy, and I hope improved in the new one.—I have twice read your Letter, and have nothing to reply, but that you are [in] possession of all the facts—the principal one, that of the 180 Subscribers already procured by far the greater part are not resident in great Towns—Do you therefore, dear and honored Friend! decide for me at once. Be assured, (from the very inmost of my heart I say it) as beforehand I have no other feeling but that of perfect confidence, so in the retrospect I never shall or can have any other feelings than those of affection and Gratitude. The tears are in my eyes, as I write, so that I can scarce see my paper—I would, I could convey to you as by intuition, how much I love and esteem you.—

I dare say, I have erred in prematurely propagating my Prospectuses—the number however has been so small, that much Harm cannot have been done—and many persons have since written to me, asking for them. When I entered on the plan, I resolved, & have been since employing myself so as to enable me to execute it, that the Printer should always have four Numbers beforehand—. Finally, if it be not (as I suppose, it is not) practicable to have 300 stamped (for I have every reason to believe, that I shall have that number of scattered Subscribers) and the others for London & the Great Cities unstamped, you will decide whether all or none— and according to your decision set the thing agoing, when & how you think proper. Mr Bernard has informed me that 60£ will be paid to my order, as soon as a certain sum has been paid into the R. I.—This is at least 40£ less, than was fairly due to me—. I shall order it to be paid to you. I believe, I have not told you, in what a scoundrel[l]y manner Meyers (the German Bookseller) has treated me with respect to Palm's Book. I had received advice from Mr Hurst (Longman's Partner) that Meyers was a man not to be trusted in money concerns—I therefore wrote to him, a few weeks

---

[1] The remainder of this sentence is crossed out in MS.

after my arrival, that I was ready to go to the Press; and requested to know, on *what terms* he expected to receive the Copy—(not the Translation: for one third at least is of my own writing, & what is not, cost me line by line, three times the trouble of perfectly original composition). He returned no answer—& I have since been informed, has published the work translated by some one else.[1] I am sure, I am not actuated by any vanity, when I declare my belief, that there are not five men in the Kingdom who could translate that work properly.—

To return to 'THE FRIEND'. There is certainly nothing in the work, that could make the numbers more interesting this day than this day fortnight—But then the pleasure of being able to expect it's arrival on a given day, the difference of *one* arriving at a time, instead of *four shillings* at once, in all those places where Booksellers' parcels arrive monthly only, and the comfort of having a thing come as a Newspaper, & with the Newspapers, are great Influencers. Would it be prudent or practicable to have the whole stamped *at first,* and then after 8 or 10 numbers to adopt the other plan, if a *great majority* of the Sale was found to be in London, and the great Cities? That passage in the Espriella of Southey, which I so bitterly reprobated to you, has deprived me of at least a 100 Subscribers in Birmingham.[2] Southey's Life would be in danger, were he in Birmingham & known to be there—

I feel and have not ceased to feel, *how much* I ask in asking you without any further reference to me to decide for me—My private friends living scattered or in small towns, and my Subscribers hitherto having been procured by these friends, are doubtless no fair presumption of the nature of the sale in general—I have about 20 swelling names of Earls & Countesses and Bishops. [I wri]te thus undigestedly, because a person is going off by day-break to mo[rrow to Ke]swick—& I save one post at least—

God bless you & S. T. C.

The very post by [which] your Letter was received, Wordsworth sent the Essay & the a[nswers to] your Questions—.

There is an error of the Press in the former Prospectuses sent to you, uncorrected—

---

[1] See Letter 708, p. 109 and note.
[2] See *Letters from England: By Don Espriella,* Letter XXXVl.

740. *To Daniel Stuart*

Address: D. Stuart, Esqre | Courier Office | Strand | London
MS. British Museum. Pub. with omis. Letters from the Lake Poets, *113.*
Postmark: 23 January 1809. *Stamped*: Kendal.

Grasmere, Kendal
Wednesday Night—[18 January 1809]

My dear Friend

I am so much in the habit—and alas! with too much reason—of believing myself in the wrong, that I often accede to blame without examination. You say, I knew what I now know of Savage in June last; but my dear Friend, after the conversation between me & S. I wrote to Mr Bernard; he & Davy & I believe, the B. of Durham, spoke to Savage—and from both Davy & Mr B. I understood, that Savage had waived all his former pretensions, and had finally agreed to publish the work on these two conditions—that he was to be paid for the Paper & Printing at the Trade Price, with 5 per cent for the publication—& that I was to bind myself to retain him as Printer & Publisher thro' all after Editions, no misbehaviour having been proved on his part. Of course, when I printed the Prospectus and sent him a Copy, with orders for the reprinting & lists of the Persons to whom certain numbers were to be sent, I conceived that all was an understood matter between him and me—and his Answer (delayed for a fortnight) occasioned in me far more Surprize than indignation. My only fault was in not deducing, as I ought to have done from his first conversation with me, that he was a Sharper; and his main blunder has been in considering me as an absolute Simpleton.—So much for the Past.— For the future, the more I reflect, the more am I perplexed, relatively to the question of stamping or not stamping. Wordsworth can find his way out of the difficulty no better than myself. Let me premise, that no arguments, which occur to me on either side, are equal in force & impression on my mind to the deep sense, I have, of my general Ignorance. Otherwise, I confess, the reasons for stamping the work would form the heavier weights in the scale. These reasons I will briefly enumerate to you; but the utter self-distrust, which disturbs the whole Balance, without being either in the one Scale or the other, I cannot convey to you adequately. Yet if these reasons should not appear of due force to your understanding, and yet make you hesitate in determining as you otherwise would have determined, I shall have cause to regret bitterly that I ever mentioned them. On my soul, if every argument, which my experience or reflection could suggest, pleaded for A: and your calm opinion decided for B., it would not only counterbalance all the former in my steady Judgment, but I should instantly proceed to act on the plan, B. with most unclouded and cheerful confidence. To this my nature inclines me: and in this my constant experience abundantly justifies my Nature. Excuse these professions, dear Stuart! The very great importance of the affair alike to my worldly and my moral interests, as they are the main cause & occasion of them, so let them be the apology. I suppress my feelings of esteem & gratitude toward you twenty times for once that I utter them.—

The reasons in favor of stamping are: 1. That my Subscribers hitherto have been, two in three, such as reside where no regular communication exists, except the Post: a fortnight or more often elapses before they procure their reviews or magazines, after their arrival in the monthly book-sellers' parcels. 2. The arrival of four at a time (four shillings for four sheets!) not only will make the price obtrude itself and be felt; but all that particular pleasure of having to expect an amusement on a particular day, and of being able to count upon it among the little enjoyments of the week, is done away. 3. This class of Readers will not only, as I have some reason to think, form a large proportion of my Customers; but they are the very persons, whom I look forward to with most satisfaction, as the most likely to be gratified by my writings, and to be benefited, and to spread the benefit. 4. If the Essay be not stamped, can I without fair imputation of cupidity bordering on dishonesty or mendicancy charge a Shilling for a single Sheet? I might indeed urge much in favor of the costs of Time, Thought, Study, personal Labor in Travels &c, and of money *sunk*, as it were, in the preparing myself for such a work—even as a Counsellor & Physician justify their fees—not by the particular Effort or Time expended in any one particular case, but by the expences & talents previously applied—but this is not an admitted plea in the literary world— The course of the Trade has once for all settled, that the price attached to Books should be proportioned to the quantity & quality of the paper, the printing, and the plates (if any). 5. If the work were printed at Kendal, stamped as the provincial papers are, I could easily procure a young steady man to devote one day in the week, to send them off, each one in it's own involucrum & with it's own direction, as the Couriers from your office—and by having the date of payment at 20 or 40 weeks, and on the week before affixing an advertisement (which would be payed for at the Stamp office) desiring the Subscribers to remit to me the one or two pound note— or where there were many in the same place, to be payed to some one Acquaintance, the money-concerns might perhaps be settled without much trouble, considering, which should not be overlooked, the probable character of those who would take in my work.

6. It appears to Wordsworth as well as to me, that in a work like mine, the Newsmen could do little—it has nothing of the character or the attractions of a Newspaper—it would seldom indeed be taken in [by] chance or indifference—and I must rely chiefly on advertisements.

With regard to the Printer's and Publisher's Bonds I have little doubt, that I could effect this easily—that G. Ward in London has such confidence in my word, that there were to be neither politics or advertisements, that he would undertake the London Publishing. I have not written to him, because I would in nothing interfere with your kind Offices. N.B. On reason 5. I lay no weight. It is indeed not properly classed by me among the reasons—I mean it only as a simple Query or Datum for Deliberation. If there be advantages in the printing & publishing it in the first instance in London, I waive the notion at once. I have desired Mr Clarkson to call on you.—The great point, I would have kept in view, is the distinctive character of 'The Friend'. It is not to be a Newspaper— it is not even a work meant to attract and amuse the ordinary crowd of Readers—it is a work for the developement of *Principles*. And tho' I shall write as eloquently & splendidly as my portion of genius enables me, yet I never will sacrifice groundedness to entertainingness. For the latter I chiefly rely on skill of illustration by similies, facts, and interesting anecdotes.

I have been long most deeply interested in the American Affairs—If I cannot draw out my thoughts in full and orderly Array, I will at all events in a post or two send you the substance of my reflections, irregularly & in hints. I by no means approved either of the matter or the tone of Mr Canning's State paper—it was to me the work of an insolent & womanish Mind—an air of low Triumph in it, that could do no good—& in the present instance would sting & exasperate. Permit me to add, that I very warmly admired the Article in [the] Courier respecting the private Letters calumniating the Spaniards—. Indee[d] many things in the latter papers have much plea[sed] me. What I most desiderate in the Courier, in [truth], is steadiness & consistency—It is an immense . . .[1]—& we are morally answerable in proportion. I certa[inly] would always *lean* toward the Government for m[any] reasons besides the aversion, we both have, to their only effectual Rivals or possible Substitutes—

God bless you—S. T. C.

[1] Word illegible; MS. torn.

741. *To Daniel Stuart*

Address: D. Stuart, Esqre. | Courier office | Strand | London
MS. British Museum. Pub. Letters from the Lake Poets, *119.*
Postmark: 28 January 1809. *Stamped*: Keswick.

Monday Noon, 23 Jan. 1809

My dear Stuart

In answer to that part of your Letter (which I have just now received) respecting Wordsworth's Copy, I thought, I had explained to you the misery of our Post—It is not once in ten times, that we can answer by the same post, that brings the Letter. For instance, your's of Thursday reached me at Monday Noon—for the bitterness of the raw frosty wind made it impracticable for me to walk three miles to & three miles back again so as to meet the Letter-carrier at Rydale, at ten o/clock at night. And unless I can get to Keswick to night, which I meant to do, but begin to fear that I cannot get a horse, this Letter cannot leave Kendal or Penrith till Wednesday Morning. Our other days are on the same scale of Delay—equal delays in receiving & being able to answer Letters. In every instance Wordsworth has sent off his answer the first moment possible—and has twice walked out to the Carrier's House after two in the morning.—He is very busy at his work—

Tuesday Afternoon—

I walked in to Keswick—and shall return tomorrow or Thursday. As to the prospectuses, Heaven knows! I am impatient about nothing—I have neither spirits enough, nor Hope enough. But it is my friends who are impatient—three Letters I have received in as many days, each having words to this purpose—'Without the Prospectuses we can do nothing.—I have procured so many subscribers —but had I prospectuses I could have decupled them.'—

As soon as I received your's, I decided at once in favor of the Newspaper Plan to be printed at Kendal—the Bonds &c I shall find no difficulty in, except perhaps the Printer's—but I shall send off a Letter to night to set that a going.—I would therefore have it advertised immediately in as short a form as you like—Clement, Milford Lane, opposite St Clem: London; Constable, Edingburgh; Soulby, Penrith; Pennington, Kendal; Shepperd, Bristol; Woolan, Exeter; Miss Gales, Sheffield; Ford, Manchester;—more Book-sellers' names, I have not at present; but by calling on Longman, he or his Partners would doubtless mention the Booksellers in the principal Towns.—The Day of it's appearance to be the first Saturday in March—i.e. it is to be in London on that day.—But the same prospectuses should be sent—200 to Mr Clarkson, at Mr W.

Allen's, Plough Court, Lombard Street—and 50 to Mr T. Poole, Stowey near Bridgwater (by any of the Coaches that pass thro' Bridgwater) and an 100 to the Revd T. Cautley, Jesus College, Cambridge—the others as before given, Montagu, T. Monkhouse, &c.

The next thing I must request is to be informed concerning the mode of having down the stamped Paper, and in what way the stamp money is payed; whether always ready money, or whether any credit is given.—Likewise, whether it will be illegal if I print off unstamped Sheets, not for weekly sale; but to be bound up in different sized volumes, so that persons who begin to take in the work in July for instance may six months after [the] first number procure the preceding numbers—

Something perhaps should be said in the Advertisements concerning the mode of payment; but what, i' faith, I do not know. Those living in retired places I would have remit the £1 every 20 weeks; and where there are a considerable number in one place, to the Bookseller perhaps—tho' in most principal places I could procure a private friend to take the trouble—

I shall wait for instructions from you to whom & in what form the Bond and Securities are to be performed—and whatever else may be proper for me to do.—

May God bless you | &
S. T. Coleridge

742. *To Humphry Davy*

Address: H. Davy, Esqre. | Royal Institution | Albermarle Street | London.
MS. Royal Institution. Pub. with omis. Frag. Remains, *107*.
Postmark: 7 February 1809. *Stamped*: Keswick.

Grasmere, Kendal. Monday Morning.
30 Jan. 1809

My dear Davy

I was deeply affected by the passage in your letter respecting **Dr** Beddoes. It was indeed the echo of my own experience. The intelligence of his departure from among us came upon me abruptly, and unexpectedly. I was sitting down to dinner, having quitted an unfinished sheet which I had been writing in answer to a long and affectionate Letter from the Doctor. There was indeed a depth and a flow of feeling in it, which filled me with bodings, but I had no thought that the event was so near at hand. The Note therefore, sent from one of his Patients, who had placed himself at Clifton by mine & Wordsworth's advice, the day after his decease, struck me like a bodily blow, & was followed by long and loud convulsive weeping with scarce any inward Suffering—but when some half hour after I recovered myself, and my tears flowed slowly and with grief more worthy of the cause, I felt that more Hope had been taken out of my life by this than by any former Event. For Beddoes was good and beneficent to all men; but to me he had always been kind and affectionate, and latterly I had become attached to him with a personal tenderness. The Death of Mr Thomas Wedgwood pulled hard at my heart; I am sure, no week of my life—almost I might have said—scarce a day in which I have not been made either sad or thoughtful by the recollection. But Dr Beddoes's Death has pulled yet harder: probably because it came second— likewise too perhaps, that I had not been in the habit of connecting such oppression of despondency with my love of Him. There are two things, which I exceedingly wished, and in both have been disappointed: to have written the Life and prepared the psychological Remains of my revered Friend and Benefactor, T. W: and to have been entrusted with the Biography &c of Dr B.— This latter work (Southey informs me) was first offered to you, and then to Mr Giddy: and is finally devolved on Dr Stock.[1] As my heart bears me full witness, with what unalloyed satisfaction I should have seen this last Duty in your Hands, or D. Giddy's: so I feel myself permitted to avow the pain, yea, the sense of shame with which I contemplate Dr Stock as the Performant. I could not help assenting to Southey's remark, that the proper Vignette for the work would be a funereal Lamp beside an Urn, and Dr Stock in the act of placing an Extinguisher on it. I speak thus, because I passed one morning, and a very long Evening with this man: a more meagre mind, a feebler Judgment, a punier frame of moral feeling have rarely inflicted on me a pain which I am sure does never originate in any defect of humility in my temper—the painful Sense of another's Inferiority. The Subject, on which I am writing, incapacitates me from relating a ludicrous anecdote of him connected with myself, which of itself would afford no ordinary presumption of my accuracy in characterizing Dr Stock—& to speak degradingly of any man, especially an inoffensive man, even in a confidential Letter, is as unpleasant to me as it is unfrequent: and nothing less than the present occasion could have drawn it from me. However what I can do by the utmost exertion of my powers I will.

I have just read a brief account of your first Lecture of this Season—and tho' I did not see, as clearly as I could wish, the pertinence of the religious declaration quoted from you, and am not

[1] John E. Stock published his *Memoirs of the Life of Thomas Beddoes* in 1811.

quite at ease (especially when I think of Darwin) when I find
Theosophy mingled with Science; and tho' I wished to have been
with you to have expressed my doubts concerning the accuracy of
your comparison between the great Discoverers of Science, and the
Miltons, Spinozas, & Rafaels; yet the intervening History—it is
only that I am writing to you that I stopped & hesitate in using the
word—overwhelmed me—and I dare avow, furnished to my
Understanding & Conscience proofs more convincing, than the dim
Analogies of natural organization to human Mechanism, both of
the Supreme Reason as superessential to the World of the Senses;
of an analogous Mind in Man not resulting from it's perishable
Machine, nor even from the general Spirit of Life, it's inclosed
steam or perfluent water-force; and of the moral connection between the finite and the infinite Reason, and the aweful majesty of
the former as both the Revelation and the exponent Voice of the
Latter, immortal Time-piece [of] an eternal Sun. Shame be with me
in my Death-h[our if] ever I withhold or fear to pay my just debt of
d[eserved] Honor to the truly Great man, because it has bee[n my]
good lot to be his Contemporary, or my happiness [to] have known,
esteemed, and loved as well as admired him.

It is impossible to pass otherwise than abruptly to my own
Affairs. I had from the very first informed Mr Savage that I would
not undertake the work at all except I could secure him from all possible Risk. His proposals were such that had I acceded to them, after
years of Toil I should have been his Debtor & Slave without having
received a farthing—or to use the strong tho' coarse illustration of
a friend, a man of consummate good sense & knowlege of the
world, and of 20 years' experience in periodical works—'Savage's
Proposals would have led you into a Gulph of Debt or Obligation—
You would have been like a Girl who gets into a House of ill fame,
& whom the old Bawd always keeps in Debt stripping her of every
shilling, she gets for prostitution.' What my error was after my
first conversation with Mr S., I know but shall not say: but his
Mistake has been in construing my indifference as to pecuniary
matters & *apparent* ignorance of Business into absolute Silliness &
passive Idiotcy.—But this is passed. As soon as I received his
Letter, I made up my mind to another mode of publication—'The
Friend' will be printed as a Newspaper—i.e. not in form or matter,
but under the act of P. and with it's privileges—printed at Kendal
—& sent to each Subscriber by the Post.

I have received 40£ from the R. Institution—If they think more
due to me, the Directors will be so good as to order it to be payed to
Mr Green, the Clerk of the Courier Office, for D. Stuart, Esqre.—
My Health is more regular; yet spite of severe attention to my

Diet &c my Sufferings are at times heavy.—Please to make my best respects to Mr Bernard—

May God bless you!

S. T. Coleridge

743. *To Thomas Poole*

Address: Thomas Poole, Esqre. | N. Stowey | Bridgewater | Somerset
MS. British Museum. Pub. with omis. Letters, *ii. 541.*
Stamped: Kendal.

Grasmere, Kendal
3 Feb. 1809

My dearest Poole

For once in my Life I shall have been blamed by you for silence, indolence, and procrastination, without reason. Even now I write this letter on a *speculation*—for I am to take it with me tomorrow to Kendal, and if I can bring the proposed Printer and Publisher to final Terms, to put it in the Post. It would be a tiresome job were I to detail to you all the vexations, hindrances, scoundrelisms, disappointments, and Pros and Cons, that without the least fault or remissness on my part have rendered it impracticable to publish 'The Friend' till the first week of March. The whole however is now settled, provided that Pennington (a worthy old Bookseller & Printer of Kendal but *a Genius*, and mighty *indifferent* about the affairs of this Life from that cause, and from age, and from being as rich as he wishes) will become as he has almost promised, the Printer & Publisher. The Friend will be stamped as a Newspaper, and under the Newspaper Act—which will take $3\frac{1}{2}$d from each Shilling but enable the Essay to pass into all parts & corners of the Empire without expence or trouble—it will be so published as to appear in London every Saturday Morning, and be sent off from the Kendal Post to every part of the Kingdom by the Thursday Morning's Post. I hope that Mr Stuart will have had the Prospectuses printed by this time[1]—at all events, within a day or two after your receipt of this Letter you will receive a parcel of them.— The money is to be payed to the Bookseller, the agent, in the next town, once in twenty weeks—where there are several Subscribers in the same vicinity—otherwise [it] must be remitted to me direct. This is the ugliest part of the Business; but there is no getting over it without a most villainous diminution of my profits.—You will, I

---

[1] The prospectus printed in London by C. and R. Baldwin is dated 2 Feb. 1809 and announces the first issue of *The Friend* for the first or second Saturday in March. It differs in several respects from the prospectuses printed at Kendal. (Copies of the London prospectus will be found in Dove Cottage; those of the Kendal prospectuses in the British Museum.)

know, exert yourself to procure me as many Names as you can—for
if it succeeds, it will almost *make* me. Among my Subscribers I have
Mr Canning, and Sturges Bourne,[1] and Mr W. *Rose* of whose moral
Odor your nose, I believe, has had competent experience.[2] The first
Prospectus, I receive, I shall send with letters to Lord Egmont, and
Lady E. Percival—and to Mr Ackland.—

You will probably have seen two of Wordsworth's Essays in the
Courier, signed G. The two last Columns of the second, excepting
the concluding Paragraph, were written all but a few sentences by
me—An accident in London delayed the publication ten days—the
whole therefore is now publishing as a Pamphlet, & I believe, with
a more comprehensive Title.—

I cannot say whether I was—indeed, both I and W. W—more
pleased or affected by the whole of your last Letter—it came from a
very pure & warm heart thro' the moulds of a clear & strong Brain.
But I have not now time to write on these concerns—for *my* opinions, feelings, hopes, & apprehensions I can safely refer You to
Wordsworth's Pamphlet—. The Ministers' Conduct hitherto is
easily defined—A great deal too much because not half enough.
Two Essays of my own on this most lofty theme—what we are
entitled to hope, what compelled to fear, concerning the Spanish
Nation, by the Light of History, and psychological Knowlege, you
will soon see in the Courier.[3]—Poor Wardell! I fear, lest his Zeal
may have made him confound that degree of evidence which is
sufficient to convince an unprejudiced private company with that,
which will satisfy an unwilling numerous Assembly of factious &
corrupt Judges. As to the truth of the Charges I have little doubt,
knowing myself similar facts.[4]

O dear Poole! Beddoes's Departure has taken more hope out of
my Life than any former Event except perhaps T. Wedgwood's—.
That did indeed pull very hard at me—never a week, seldom two
days, have passed in which the Recollection has not made me sad
or thoughtful—Beddoes's seems to pull yet harder, because it combines with the former, because it is the *second*, and because I had
not been in the habit of connecting such a weight of despondency

[1] William Sturges-Bourne (1769–1845) was at this time lord of the treasury.
[2] Coleridge obviously refers to George Rose. See Letter 540.
[3] Coleridge's eight *Letters on the Spaniards* appeared in the *Courier* in Dec.
1809 and Jan. 1810. See *Essays on His Own Times*, ii. 593–676.
[4] On 27 Jan. 1809 Col. G. L. Wardle brought charges in the House of
Commons against the Duke of York, whose mistress, Mary Anne Clarke, had
accepted bribes in connexion with military promotions. The Duke was
acquitted of having received any share of the bribes exacted by Mrs. Clarke,
but he was forced as a result of the inquiry to retire as commander-in-chief of
the army. He was reappointed in 1811.

with my attachment to Him as with my Love of my revered & dear
Benefactor.—Poor Beddoes! he was good and beneficent to all men,
but to me he was moreover affectionate & loving—and latterly, his
Sufferings had opened out his Being to a delicacy, a tenderness, a
moral beauty, & unlocked the source of sensibility as with a key
from Heaven.

My own Health is more *regular* than formerly—for I am severely
temperate, and take nothing that has not been pronounced medi-
cally unavoidable—yet my sufferings are often great, and I am
rarely indeed wholly without pain or sensations more oppressive
than definite Pain. But my mind, and what is far better, *my will*,
is active. I must leave a short space to add at Kendal after all is
settled.—

My beloved & honored Friend! may God preserve you & your
obliged
                              & affectionately grateful S. T. Coleridge

I must give a bond for 400£ for Libels—my Printer & Publisher a
double bond both as Pr. and Pubr.—and two Friends (W. W. &
Southey) each a security of 200£ for Stamp Advertisement Duties
—tho' my Work excludes Politics & Advertisements.—

                                                      Kendal.[1]—
My dearest Poole
Old Mr Pennington has ultimately declined the Printing & Publishing—indeed he is about to decline business altogether—There is
no other in this Country capable of doing the work—and to Printing & Publishing in London there are gigantic Objections. What
think you of a Press at Grasmere? I will write when I get home. O
if you knew what a warmth of unusual feeling, what a genial Air of
new and living Hope breathed upon me as I read that casual
sentence in your Letter seeming to imply a chance, we have of seeing you at Grasmere! I assure you, that the whole Family (Mrs
Wordsworth and her all-amiable Sister not with less warmth than
W. W. and Dorothy) were made chearful [and] were a *holiday*
looking the whole day after. O *do, do* come!

We are sadly off in point of post, both in sending & receiving
Letters—it *often* makes the difference of *six* days!!

[1] According to Wordsworth, Coleridge left for Kendal on Sunday, 5 Feb.
Middle Years, i. 258.

744. *To Daniel Stuart*

Address: D. Stuart, Esqre. | Courier Office | Strand | London *Single Sheet*
MS. British Museum. Pub. Letters from the Lake Poets, *122.*
Postmark: 10 February 1809. *Stamped*: Kendal.

Kendal. [*Circa* 7 February 1809]
Dear Stuart

Indeed, indeed, *I* never had any impatience, *I* never did attach
any importance to the *Prospectuses*—But it is my Friends—and
when you consider how large a proportion of my Subscribers are
procured by private Friends, you will agree with me, that I could
say nothing in Objection when they tell me—With Prospectuses
we can do so & so—without them nothing.

The Paper must be stamped & sent down from London direct to
the Printer—The Distributor has nothing to do with it. Will you be
so good as to fix upon such a size & quality as appears proper to
you? But after twice coming in to Kendal, I have now received a
final answer from old Mr Pennington, the only man short of Liverpool capable of executing the work, *declining it*—from no other
objection, than his Age & intention of leaving off Business altogether shortly.

I send you this hasty scrawl—lest you should wonder at my
Silence.

I am very glad indeed, that you are so much pleased with
William's Pamphlet—

When I get home, I will write at leisure—

Dear Friend! may God bless you & your affectionate & grateful
                                                S. T. Coleridge
I am just about to mount my Horse for Grasmere.—

745. *To Daniel Stuart*

Address: D. Stuart, Esqre. | 9. Upper Brompton Row | Knightsbridge | London
MS. British Museum. Pub. with omis. Letters from the Lake Poets, *124.*
Postmark: 13 February 1809.   *Stamped*: Kendal.

Wednesday Morning. [8 February 1809]
My dear Stuart

Had I received less strong proofs of your Kindness, I should have
good reason to fear, that these successive Disappointments would
weary you out. My best comfort is, that I can not attribute them to
any Indolence or Remissness on my part. Thus however the matter
stands at present. Old Mr Pennington, of Kendal, has finally

declined the being Printer and Publisher of 'The Friend': and I have every reason to believe that no one else nearer than Liverpool is capable of undertaking the Work without sending for new Types etc from London. Consequently, my Alternative lies between two Plans, as the only ones possible: the first, that of having the Work printed and published in London, which would occasion a serious deduction from the Profits—(for at Kendal the Publishing, Wrapping up, Directing, and sending off per Post would not have cost me Sixpence) and the second, the setting up a Press at Grasmere, and the procuring a good steady young Man from Liverpool, or London, who would be at once (as is almost universally the case out of London) at once Compositor and Pressman. Independently of 'the Friend,' we had intended to do this. I believe, you have seen Mr De Quincy at the Courier office with me. Ho!—He was the very short & boyish-looking modest man, whom I introduced to you in Cuthell's Shop, and afterwards gave you his character &c. He has been on a Visit at our House for three months, and has now taken Wordsworth's old Cottage, which he is fitting up, and means to tenant for some years. Besides his erudition, he has a great turn for manual operations, and is even to something of old batchelor preciseness accurate, and regular in all, he does. It is his determination to have printed under his own Eye immaculate Editions of such of the eminently great Classics, English and Greek as most need it— and to begin with the poetic Works of Milton. Old Pennington, who is a truly worthy and respectable old Man, highly approved of the Plan—and made out by calculation, that for the Printing of 'The Friend' an hundred Pound would be ample, both for the Fonts of Type, the Press, and the Fitting-up &c. Now the Objections, as far as 'The Friend' is concerned, are these—1. the delay and uncertainty in the procuring and after character of the Compositor—2. the probability, that none of the great Letter Founders may have any Fonts of suitable Types on hand, that no Press—one of Lord Stanhope's construction it should be—can be procured ready-made —and that the delay in the execution of all orders both for Types and Presses is so enormous (from four months to a year, I have been given to understand) that even were I to put off the commencement of the Work to the First of May, I might still meet with a new & heavier Disappointment.—The questions therefore, on which I do indeed need your advice, are—1. *Supposing* that Workman, Types, Press, &c &c were procurable instantly, i.e. as soon as the Waggon could convey them, is the Scheme of printing the Work at Grasmere an advisable one? 2. What are the chances for and [against] such a *Supposition*? This I should hope might be answered [positively] in the course of a forenoon by sending a man [with] proper letters of precise Enquiry to the different Letter-founders and Press Makers.—

If you consider this Scheme as impracticable—at least, at present, and for the first year of 'The Friend'—nothing remains but instantly to procure a Printer and Publisher in London, who will consent to give the proper Bonds; and to make the best Terms with him possible. Depend upon it, if you consider the Plan as unwise, there is not a Soul in this Family who will think otherwise.

I assure you, dear Stuart! that I am faint and sick at Heart with these Alps upon Alps of Hindrances, and Uncertainties.

Wardell's affair turns out just as both myself and Wordsworth foresaw. These weak men do much Harm. But I have no heart to write about any thing at this present moment. God bless you &

S. T. Coleridge

746. *To John Monkhouse*

Address: John Monkhouse[, Esqre.] | Penrith | Cumberl[and]   [Single] Sheet
MS. Miss Joanna Hutchinson. Hitherto unpublished.

Grasmere, Kendal
Wednesday Night, 8 Febry 1809

My dear Sir

Will you be so good on the receipt of this as immediately to make enquiry first of Mr Brown, the Printer, of Penrith (and if he answer in the Negative, then of Soulby) whether he have good Types of the size or little different from those, with which this Prospectus is printed, and in quantity sufficient to compose at once *a whole Sheet* octavo, consisting of 40 lines in each page and 40 letters in each line, consequently 1600 letters the page, and 25,600 for the whole Sheet, subtracting nothing for Breaks, Paragraphs, Verse, Heads, and Tails—and if he have, whether he would undertake to print 'The Friend' weekly, and at what price per Sheet *for the Printing*: for the Paper must be sent down *stamped* from London. *Supposing* the affirmative to all this, you might *then* inform [him] that tho' 'The Friend' neither can or ever will contain either Advertisements or Politics, yet as it is to be entered and stamped as a Newspaper (merely in order to give i[t the] privilege of frank Post to all parts of the Kingdom) it will be ne[cessary] (as a form) that the Printer & Publisher should give a bond as security—but that respecting this I should have no objection to guarantee him. It is indeed in the present instance a mere Form.

It is of such very great importance to me to receive an answer to these enquiries, full and definite, as soon as the Post can possibly convey it to me, that I have not hesitated to trouble you with this commission, relying on your friendly feeling toward me from the consciousness of the affectionate regard, with w[hich]

I am, | my dear Sir, | Your sincere Friend,
S. T. Coleridge

We are disappointed sadly in not seeing you with Mr T. H., who is just arrived—All are as well here as usual, or perhaps better—only we *suspect* that little Dorothy is about to have the Measles.

747. *To Daniel Stuart*

Address: D. Stuart, Esqre. | 9. Upper Brompton Row | Knightsbridge | London
Single Sheet
MS. British Museum. Pub. E. L. G. i. 445.
Postmark: 18 February 1809. *Stamped*: Penrith.

[11–16 February 1809][1]
Dear Stuart

Had I conceived Mr Clarkson's Business to have extended beyond the matter of Subscribers & Prospectuses, he is the last man, God bless him! with whom I should have troubled you—for he has never more than one Thought in his brain at a time, let it be great or small—I have called him the Moral Steam-Engine, or the Giant with one idea—. Heaven knows! how well I love, and how very highly I revere him. He shall be my Friend, Exemplar, Saint—any thing only not my Counseller in matters of Business. That I could not with credit appoint any one my Publisher but Longman, is more than most ridiculous. 'What's Hecuba to Him or He to Hecuba?' Save & except the translation of Schiller's Wallenstein, done by me at Longman's particular request, and printed & published contrary to my repeated Warnings & strenuous Advice, and by which I earned about the tenth part of what the same Toil, Time, and Effort would have procured me from the Morning Post (setting private obligations & supererogatory payments out of the Question), I have never once in my Life touched Longman's Plutus, or He my Minerva. Besides, it was & I trust, *is* to be a *Newspaper*. It would weary us both to repeat the weighty arguments which decided this point in both our Judgments—From the peculiar nature of the work, and from the particular complexion of those who will form the best & perhaps the largest part of my Customers, there can be no other mode of circulating it every where & *weekly*, except by the Post—and to receive 4 at once (in many places 6 or 8) would destroy the very character of the publication. By that decision

---

[1] This letter was begun about 11 Feb. at Grasmere and concluded at Penrith 16 Feb.

therefore, it having met with your concurrence & having been confirmed by unanswerable arguments adduced by you in addition to my own reasonings, I must abide.—Besides, by 5 per cent Longman means 5 per cent in *addition* to the Trade profit, depend upon it. How could *he* supply the Subscribers, otherwise than by the Town & Country Booksellers—& each of these must have their profit. But were it otherwise, I should still remain by my resolution—even tho' I were obliged to defer the work, till Types &c could be procured from London—

There are three plans possible—1. To seek out a Printer & Publisher who will consent to give the legal Bonds—in London, and to make the best Terms with him possible. If Mr Clement will not do this, I think, that George Ward would. 2. To have it printed at Penrith, where there is a very clever young

16 Feb. Penrith. (I return tomorrow)

While writing the last Sentence, I received a letter from Penrith, that Brown was both able & willing to print & publish the Friend—in consequence on Sunday I walked from Grasmere over the Mountains (O *Heaven*! what a *Journey*!) hither—and arrived at last *limping*, having sprained my knee in leaping a Brook, & slipping on the opposite bank twisted my left leg outward—However, I am perfectly satisfied with Brown's character, proposals, & capability, and have accordingly agreed with him to be my Printer & Publisher—His name is Mr John Brown, Printer & Stationer, Penrith—

I have resolved to commence the work on the first of April.

On your kindness, dear Friend! I must now call to find me out the proper paper, which should be of course very good, & the means of procuring it stamped. An attorney (Antony Harrison) informed me that if I procured it from the Stamp Office as a Newspaperist, I should have a drawback of 16 per cent—But of all these things I am ignorant—only I know to a certainty that both Ware (the Whitehaven Paper) and both the Carlisle Papers receive their stamped Paper from London directly—and I am advised, if it can be procured immediately, to have a considerable quantity sent by sea to Stockton, directed to Mr John Hutchinson, with S. T. C. on the corner of the Box.

On what terms, payment, &c it is to be procured, you will be so good as to inform me—I have written to Davy, requesting that the money due to me may be payed at your Office to your name—

I never once dreamt of receiving any money beforehand—It must have been some carelessness in my language which could have suggested this idea to you—What money may be necessary to carry on the work for the first 20 weeks, I doubt not, I shall be able to procure—I write in great pain from my knee which is very seriously injured—Such a passage you can have scarce a conception of, ice, half-frozen Snow, floods, & the impossibility of remitting attention, nay, anxiety, for a single step—I never paused once, except the few minutes I lay sprawling in torture—& yet was 5 hours in reaching Luff's House which is 10 miles from Wordsworth's.—However, I am at ease in mind—and in my next hope to give you some little proof of it.

I was pleased—a little flattered, perhaps, by your letter to Southey—it was almost verbally coincident with what I had written a few days before. May God bless you & your

affectionately grateful
S. T. Coleridge.

748. *To Daniel Stuart*

Address: D. Stuart, Esqre. | No. 9 | Upper Brompton Row | Knights Bridge London
MS. British Museum. Pub. with omis. Letters from the Lake Poets, *132.*
Postmark: 2 March 1809. *Stamped*: Kendal.

Grasmere, Kendal.
[27 February 1809]

My dear Stuart

I hope, you received mine from Penrith, in which I informed you, 1. That I had settled with Mr Brown of Penrith to print the Friend & be the nominal Publisher, at £1 ‖ 3 ‖ 0 for 500, and £1 ‖ 7 ‖ 0 for a number not exceeding a 1000.—2. That the stamped Paper must be had from London; there are stationers, who upon orders provide it —but I am told, that if I order the stamps myself, as a Newspaper, I am allowed a considerable Drawback. Is this the case?—Will you be so good as to choose out a large Octavo size, of good quality— and to direct it to be stamped in the most advisable way—and to let me know how these matters are to [be] carried on between the Paper Merchant, Stamp office, & myself, as to immediate payment or at what date &c.—3. I have resolved to commence it on the 1 of April.—4. I have written to Wilkin, the Distrib. of Stamps for the District—from his neglect & blundering his Letter dated 16 reached me this morning, 27th—and when it came, said—'it could say nothing, because it knew nothing—but that *I* must apply to the Stamp Office in London to send HIM down the necessary directions.' I had been extremely unwell for 8 days preceding this, so as to be incapable of sitting upright for half an hour together—It was well, the Letter did not reach me then—Me unused to business—a succession of these vexations harrass me out of all my philosophy. I find the writing of the Essays quite delightful by comparison with the troubles of *setting up shop*.—Now what can I do ? In what way can *I* apply to the Stamp Directors—All I can say, I write in the opposite Page.

I intreat you, my dear Stuart! to do what you can as soon as possible to relieve me from this Embarrassment. I shall write immediately to Wilkin, to urge him to write himself to the Stamp office, to get the necessary Information—but he is such a decrepit old Dotard, that Heaven knows! whether he will do it. If any application therefore from you in my name can procure the due quantum of Brain-matter to be sent down to this Knight of the Empty Skull, I pray you, make it as soon as possible.—

Then as to advertising, I must leave it to you. I wrote to desire, that 60£ should be payed in to you from the Royal Institution.

I hope, the time is coming when I shall subscribe myself with more ease of mind tho' never with greater depth of heart, my dear Stuart,

Your obliged & affectionate | Friend,
S. T. Coleridge

Please to direct your answer—Mr Antony Harrison, Penrith, Cumberland (for Mr Coleridge).

I, Samuel Taylor Coleridge, Proprietor and Editor of the weekly Newspaper, entitled 'THE FRIEND', reside in Grasmere, in the County of Westmoreland, and intend residing there.

John Brown, Printer & Bookseller, the Printer and the Publisher of the said weekly Newspaper resides in Penrith, in the County of Cumberland, and intends residing there.

William Wordsworth, Esqre., Mr Coleridge's first Security, resides in Grasmere, in the County of Westmoreland, and intends residing there.

Robert Southey, Esqre. (second Security) resides at Keswick, in the County of Cumberland, and intends residing there.

William Wilkin, Esqre. resident at Appleby in the County of Cumberland, and his Majesty's Distributor of Stamps for the District, solicits information of the Board of the Stamp Office, in what manner he is to comply with the written request of Mr Coleridge, containing the above names, as ready to sign, to know when the Bonds &c will be ready for Signature. Mr Wilkin is ignorant of the nature of the Bonds, and of the sum required to be stated in them and the Securities.

749. *To Daniel Stuart*

Address: D. Stuart, Esqre. | Courier office | Strand | London
MS. British Museum. Pub. Letters from the Lake Poets, *135.*
Postmark: 20 March 1809. *Stamped*: Penrith.

Penrith, 17 March [1809]

My dear Stuart

I have waited here in the daily and anxious hope of hearing from you in answer to my last letters—Every thing here is ready—the Printer, the Publisher, the Type, the Bonds, &c—I have more than 300 Subscribers, tho' there have been no advertisements—and eagerly have I hoped to hear from you concerning the *paper*—I am told, that Fourdiniere[1] is the Stationer who commonly supplies stamped paper—Mr Bernard informed me that 60£ was ready to be payed to my order, & I requested it to be paid to you. O dear Friend! on this business my whole of Prospect is set—I pray you, do set me going—I am ready, with Essays full & written out—*I* can begin whenever the paper arrives, & it is deemed adviseable— Should it be said, on the *first of May*?

Forgive me if I write anxiously—for indeed I am ready to sink under the successive anxieties & disappointments, I have suffered —but God knows! I am always

affectionately your not less grateful | than obliged Friend,

S. T. Coleridge

750. *To Basil Montagu*

Address: Basil Montagu, Esqre. | Lincoln's Inn | London
MS. Mr. Carl H. Pforzheimer. Hitherto unpublished.
Postmark: 31 March 1809. *Stamped*: Keswick.

Keswick

Tuesday Night.—[28 March 1809]

My very dear Montagu

I have been severely indisposed. The utter abandonment of Hope & Spirits, which preceded, I attributed to exhaustion from successive and daily disappointments, and constant anxiety. But it was, it seems, a common symptom of the Disease, called *the Mumps*—a contagion brought hither by the Miners. It is now going off—but I am still deaf in the left ear—& my head weighs down with heaviness.

How can I sufficiently thank you for all your exertions in my behalf? God bless you. I feel most grateful to you, I know that I

---

[1] Fourdrinier & Co., Stationers, Sherborne Lane, Lombard Street.

do—but my Gratitude disguises itself in the form of Love & Affection. I dare not trust myself in writing concerning Mrs Montagu. As soon as my Undertaking is pushed off from the shore, and my mind a little at my own command, I shall write to her—

I have been forced to purchase a font of Types from Wilson's of Glasgow, which my Printer told me would cost from 25 to 28£—instead of which the envoice was 38£ odd—with 2£ discount. This I have paid— but if the stamped Paper is to be paid from ready money, God knows whence I am to borrow it! For I am already under a Pelion upon Ossa of Obligations to dear Mr Stuart—& tho' it is but for 20 weeks, I know no one else that I dare apply to. They owe me 60£ (they themselves say—Heaven forgive them!) at the Royal Institution—but tho' I have twice written, have not paid it.

Mrs Southey was delivered of a Girl yester Morning—On Thursday he, I, Wordsworth, & the Printer & Publisher are to go to Appleby to sign the Bonds & Securities.

You have already done so much that I am ashamed to ask you to do more—but could you not serve me at Cambridge?—The Work will certainly appear on the first of May. And do write to Wrangham & intreat him *for your sake* to do what he can for me—& whether I may not rely on him for an Essay once or twice in a year.

Hartley has been unwell—Tom Wordsworth has had the Measles—With love to you & your's | I am, dear Montagu, | your

affectionate

S. T. Coleridge

I return with W. to Grasmere from Appleby.

It is very odd what can have become of all those copies of Clarkson's Abolition—19 or 20, I think. And indeed a number of other books—but it is my own neglect—

751. *To Daniel Stuart*

Address: D. Stuart, Esqre. | 36 Upper Brompton Row | Knights Bridge | London
MS. British Museum. Pub. with omis. Letters, *ii. 545.*
Postmark: 31 March 1809. *Stamped*: Keswick.

Tuesday Night—[28 March 1809]

My dear Friend

I have been severely indisposed, *knocked up* indeed, with a complaint of a contagious nature, called *The Mumps*—preceded by the most distressing low spirits or rather absence of all spirits, and accompanied with deafness & stupifying, perpetual *echo* in the ear—But it is going off. Little John Wordsworth was attacked with it last year when I was in London, and from the stupor with which it suffuses the eyes & look, was cruelly mistaken for Water in the Brain. It has been brought here a second time by some Miners—and is a disease with little danger and no remedy.—

I attributed your silence to it's right cause—and I assure you, when I was at Penrith and Kendal it was very pleasant to me to hear how universally the conduct of the Courier was extolled. Indeed, you have behaved most nobly, and it is impossible but that you must have had a great weight in the displacing of that prime grievance of grievances—Among many reflections that kept crowding on my mind during the Trial this was perhaps the chief—What if after a long long reign some titled Sycophant should whisper to Majesty— By what means do your Ministers manage the Legislature ? By the distribution of Patronage according to the influence of Individuals who claim it. Do this yourself or by your own family, and you become independent of Parties, and your Ministers are your Servants. The Army under a favorite Son, the Church with a Wife —&c &c—Good heavens! the very Essence of the Constitution is unmoulded, and the venerable Motto of our Liberty 'The King can do no wrong' becomes Nonsense and Blasphemy. As soon as ever my mind is a little at ease, I will put together the fragments, I have written, on this subject—and, if Wordsworth have not anticipated me, add to it some thoughts on the effect of the military principle. We owe some thing to Whitbread for his quenching at the first *smell* a possible fire—how is it possible, that a man apparently so honest can talk & think, as he does, respecting France, Peace, & Buonaparte ?

I have again written a pressing letter to Mr Bernard respecting the 60£. Is it not a shame, that I should have occasion ? I was to have had 140£, as I can shew by a letter from Davy—this was jumbled down thro' my bashfulness or hatred of money-conversations to 120£—and now they have brought [it] to an 100£ (for 40£ they sent me down to Stowey for my travelling Expences)—& yet this is to [be] begged & begged for—tho' they knew, how grievously I was out of pocket, or (which is the same thing to them) you for me—indeed both—and that three times the sum would not more than have repayed me—Nay more because I would not consent to be duped by Savage into my Ruin, neither Davy nor Bernard have ever got me a Subscriber—nor tho' I wrote to request it, have my Prospectuses been suffered to appear at the Royal Institution—. This is Friendship & Gratitude—Davy's conduct *wounds* me—I had written a long Poem (the only verses I have made for years) wholly on his Genius and great Services to mankind, about six weeks ago—we have been intimate these 9 years and more—and often has he declared, in times of yore, how much he owed to my conversation & incitements—& yet Savage is the more interesting man, and I and my poor Children are to be beggared rather than he affronted—and yet Tobin (Davy's intimate Friend) in his last farewell words to Wordsworth writes—'Beg Coleridge of all things to have no connection with Savage.'

On Thursday Wordsworth, Southey, and myself with the Printer & Publisher go to Appleby, to sign & seal—which paper, &c will of course be immediately dispatched to London—I doubt not, but that the sixty Pound will be now paid in at the Courier Office in a few days—and as soon as you will let me know, whether the stamped Paper is to be payed for necessarily in ready money, or with what credit, I shall instantly write to some of my friends to advance me what is absolutely necessary. I can only say—I am ready, & eager to commence—and that I earnestly hope to see 'The Friend' advertised shortly for the first of May.—As to the Paper, how & from whom & what, and in what quantity, I must again leave to your Judgment & recommend to your Affection for me.—I have reason to believe that I shall commence with 500 names.

I write from Keswick. Mrs Southey was delivered yestermorning of a Girl.—I forgot to say, that I have been obliged to purchase & have payed for a font of Types of small Pica (the same with the London Prospectus) from Wilson's of Glasgow—I was assured this would cost only from 25 to 28£—instead of which 38£ odd!

God bless you & S. T. Coleridge

752. *To John Brown*

Address: Mr Brown | Printer & | Bookseller | Penrith
MS. Victoria and Albert Museum. Pub. E. L. G. i. 448.

4 April, 1809

Dear Sir

I have been uneasy from the hour, I left you—& had hoped, that an Acquaintance who meant to have passed thro' Penrith, but (it seems) did not, would have brought me word whether you had felt any ill consequences from your fall. I half feared, that I might appear inattentive in not pressing you, at Appleby, to take either wine or spirits & water; but indeed, my sole reason was that I believed, any stimulus might prove injurious to you, to whom perhaps blood-letting would have been adviseable, if any thing— But one thing I have blamed myself for, that I did not press you more, indeed insist on your permitting me to procure some trusty person to take home the horse, yourself to return in the chaise with us—I was really uncomfortable, when it began to threaten snow or sleet.—I hope, I need not desire you to do—what ought to be a matter of course—that is, to place all your little expences for horse, &c to my account. But I should be glad to hear from you, whether you feel yourself any worse for the accident.

You will, I trust, in a day or two receive 1250 stamped sheets[1]— & as soon as they arrive, I shall procure an equal quantity of un-stamped paper of the same kind from Mr Pennington—& want to know from you, what *sort* of paper & what *quantity*, I ought to order from him for the wrappers.—

Likewise, I wish to know from you, 1. Whether you have leisure to wrap up & direct & put into the Post Office, 'the Friends', weekly—& 2. what you think reasonable per annum as the remuner-ation? I can easily procure some one to take the trouble, if you decline it; but think it right to apply to you first.

I suspect, Wilson has not used me well. How comes it that he charges 38 ‖ 13 ‖ 0 ? By what calculation?—And why has he sent the old cut ? As I shall put a Greek Grammar (which will be a large volume) and Greek and English Lexicon to your Press, as soon as ever the Friend is *pushed off* & at plain sailing, I should like to know the real price of Greek Type, in quantity sufficient to print, per half sheet—a work of which perhaps one fourth might be Greek Charac-ters ?—Be so good as to give me a few lines, addressed to me at Greta Hall, Keswick. I am, dear Sir!

with all respect your sincere &c
S. T. Coleridge

I left your Printers' Grammar with Mr A. Harrison. Apply for it, if it has not been returned.—

P.S. Pray be so good as to send over a Lad to Pooley with the Letter, & intrust him with a one pound note—it is to pay a little Bill, which I had left, meaning to return—I suppose, about ten shillings—& to bring back some books, &c—Russel will send the Bill, which I will repay you for by return of Post.—

---

[1] On 30 Mar. 1809 Stuart wrote to Coleridge: 'On Saturday [25 March] 1250 of Stamped Paper left London by the Waggon for Penrith, addressed to Mr John Brown Printer there, & I was assured it would reach Penrith in 8 days.' [MS. Dove Cottage.] It was not until 5 May, however, that Coleridge was able to report the arrival of the paper. See Letter 764.

753. *To Daniel Stuart*

Address: D. Stuart, Esqre. | 38 Upper Brompton Row | Knights bridge | London
MS. British Museum. Pub. with omis. Letters from the Lake Poets, *139*.
Postmark: 7 April 1809. *Stamped*: Keswick.

[*Circa* 4 April 1809]
My dear Stuart

I received your Penrith Letter at Keswick, and should have answered it last night, but that I wished previously to consult Southey & Wordsworth—Having done this, I write with as much satisfaction as it is possible for me to feel on any point in which I do not accede to your advice immediately, that I think, it will not be wise or right for me to commence till the first of May—for these reasons—1. Because I had settled this time with Brown, the Printer—& he has made his arrangements in that expectation— 2. Because I had informed Wrangham, Poole, my Brother, Mr Clarkson, & some others, that it would appear on the first of May, neither sooner or later—Now it is almost impracticable to write to them & receive answers from all, with the lists of names, which they are procuring, by the 15th—and I know enough of some of them to know, that they would be offended at not receiving the first number as soon as published. 3. It would seem proper to give a longer time both for the possible effect of the London Advertisements, and for receiving the Lists from different Towns.—Yet if it should have been advertised before this Letter reaches you, & the 15th announced, as the day—I will sacrifice every thing, & bring it out on that day.—I have not received any letters from Grasmere to day —but think it almost certain, that one has arrived from Bernard in answer to my pressing request, either to inform me that the 60£ has been paid, or explaining the cause (reason there can be none) of the delay.

I thank you, as I ought, for your kindness in proposing to insert the Prospectus entire in the Courier—Once would be enough—and for the others, a simple annunciation of the Work stating only that it is meant to exclude *personal* Politics. But something ought to be said concerning the mode of payment—& this indeed I had intended to have placed as the 4th & strongest reason for delay till the 1 of next month—because till I have the lists from my Friends (which will arrive in about 8 days) I cannot form any plan, as to my Agents in each centre of each vicinity to receive the money—which I wish to have payed every 20 weeks. But if each person were to send the 1£ in a letter, the expence of postage would swallow up the Profits—I therefore wish it to be said in the Advertisements, that the mode of payment will be stated to the Subscribers in the first number.—

Now for a few words of Politics. Cobbett ought to be censured for his unfair attack on Palafox[1]—His remarks on the Supreme Junta are perhaps just—at least, I always thought that their main blunder, the Queen Bee in the Hive of their Mismanagements, has been—the not assembling the Cortes—This I could amply illustrate by facts from the Dutch in their wars against Phillip 2nd (bye the bye, I *have* written & will send you in a few days an interesting parallelism between that war & the present attempt of Spain) & the American Revolution[2]—But mercy! to charge the Commander of a besieged City, so besieged & so defended, as Saragossa, with the crime of not allowing a treacherous trifling minority—certainly, not one in 20—to take advantage of momentary panics by libels & lampoons—why, he might as well recommend the liberty of the pen to a Man of war at the commencement of an Action.—Another point—is not the conduct of the E. India Company cruel & unjust in punishing innocent Individuals for their own neglect—& for a thing not made criminal by law[3]—Is not this ex post facto vengeance?—And is not the whole a mere Tub for the Whale? It may prevent one mode of venality, which is not corruption—& hard to say what harm it can do—but the worst sort of corruption it increases rather than prevents—the purchase of consciences & political dependents. But I will write at large to you on this Subject, for I am convinced, that it is meant to draw the public Mind off from the true desideratum, the re-establishment of an actual dependence of the Officers & Servants of the Government on Parliament, and of the Parliament on the People—*populum* non plebem —the *people*, not the *mob*—If you could meet with Trenchard's famous old Pamphlet on standing Armies,[4] I wish you would send it to me—I could then state what therein was false, what true but obsolete, what true & existing—& what may be said additionally—. The panegyric on the improvements of the army under the D. of Y. is *half* false at least—the omissions are most grievous.—Do you

---

[1] Jose de Palafox y Melzi (1780–1847), heroic defender of Saragossa. On the capitulation of that town, he fell into the hands of the French and was held a prisoner until 1813.

[2] See *Letters on the Spaniards*, ii–v, *Essays on His Own Times*, ii. 600–40.

[3] 'An order had recently been issued by the Directors of the East India Company cancelling civil appointments which had been obtained by purchase, and disqualifying the holders for future service.' Note by E. H. Coleridge. *Letters from the Lake Poets*, 143.

[4] In 1697 John Trenchard published *An Argument showing a Standing Army inconsistent with a free Government* and in 1698 *A Short History of Standing Armies in England*.

remember some anecdotes, I told you, of Devaux at Rome, relative to Wyndham? and W. Smith's account to me of his long Interview with Pole relative to Gardiner, Woodford, Devaux, & *the honorable* Mr Wyndham?—God bless you & your truly grateful & affect.

Direct to me at Keswick.

S. T. C.

754. *To John Brown*

Address: Mr Brown | Bookseller | Penrith
MS. Victoria and Albert Museum. Hitherto unpublished.
Stamped: Keswick.

[*Circa* 9 April 1809][1]

Dear Sir

I have been expecting to hear from you concerning the arrival of the paper—However whether arrived or no I shall send in *copy* for you to begin on Thursday or perhaps by Wednesday's Post—for I am not sure, that I dare rely on the memory or punctuality of the Coachman or Carrier. My chief reason for not sending it before has been the Hope, that your Type may have arrived from London, for I am really a little alarmed at the idea of extending my weekly Task three pages beyond my first calculation—why, it is the addition of a volume per annum! Certainly, if it be possible, I would have it in the larger Type, for my own sake, for the sake of the readers, and for the *look* of the Essay. However, I must beg you to let me know by return of Post whether your Type is arrived; and if not, when you expect it.—The first Number must be put into the Post Office at Penrith by 7 o/clock, Thursday morning, May 5th [4th], in order to arrive in London on Saturday morning, May 7th [6th]. I was thinking of having each No dated, *Saturday*; but as your name & residence must be printed at the end of each Sheet—'*Penrith*, Saturday 7th [6th]', read in London at the breakfast Table, on the *same* day, would require a faith in my possessing a Fortunatus's wishing-cap or Jack's seven-league Boots.—

If the paper have arrived, I should be much obliged to you if you would write to Mr Pennington 1. ordering the paper for the wrappers (for I unluckily mislayed your letter, mentioning the sort)—and 2. to enquire whether he can supply me with paper of the same *size* as that of the London stamped, and of *similar* *quality. I would rather *prefer* it's not being exactly the same—& I am quite sure, that I have seen Paper of Mr Pennington's as good as any book need be printed on—I should take off 150 on unstamped paper,

* The quantity to be ordered from Mr Pennington I leave entirely to your discretion—about a 1000 or 1200 sheets perhaps at first. [Note by S. T. C.]

[1] This letter was written in answer to one from Brown, dated 7 April 1809.

after the stamped ones have been taken off—and certainly not, till
the day after, or even two days, if the Type can be kept so long
standing without great inconvenience. These should be kept in
some safe place by themselves, till a sufficient number for a *Volume*
—26 probably. It is thus that Cobbett manages it.—In the wrappers you have nothing to do but to copy those of any of the London
Papers, putting 'THE FRIEND' instead of 'the Courier or Star' and
taking 'J. C. Curwen, Esqre. M.P.' as the franking member's name—

I am about to negociate with Longman & Rees for 2 Volumes of
Poems,[1] which I shall prepare for the Press, the moment *'the friend'*
is fairly under way—and you may depend upon it, that not only
in this but in every other work of mine I shall make it an absolute
Condition that they shall be printed by you at Penrith.

I hope, your Headache has wholly left you—

I am sincerely | Your's &c
S. T. Coleridge.

755. *To Thomas Poole*

Addressed and franked: Workington April eleven 1809 | T. Poole Esqr | N
Stowey | Bridgwater | Somerset   J. C. Curwen
MS. British Museum. Pub. with omis. Thomas Poole, *ii. 231.*
Stamped: ⟨Wor⟩kington.

Tuesday Noon 11 April, 1809.

My dear Poole

At length, all is settled—and the Friend is announced *finally* for
the first Saturday of May—. I have been myself obliged to purchase
the Type, as well as the stamped paper before hand—but I will not
tire you or annoy myself by retailing the succession of disappointments, vexations, & delays that have harrassed me almost daily
till within the last 10 days—& in that interval, just as I was beginning to enjoy the delight of composing the Numbers (& delightful I
really did find it, compared with the misery of writing & reading
letters of business, of travelling to & fro & hither & thither) but I
was seized with a complaint in my left Ear, heat, confusion, dull
throbbing turbid echo, & deafness, with the most intolerable dejection
—utter despondency—. My medical attendant believed it to be the
Mumps (cynanche parotidaea) which is at this time rife with &
round about us—tho' he had not seen it under the same shape &
form—But this too is nearly gone—& by way of a little motion I
went with R. Southey yesterday from Keswick to Workington, to
spend a couple of days at Workington Hall, with Curwen—whose
character at least you know both as an honest Country Member,

---

[1] See Letter 762.

always on the right side, & as a stirring & enthusiastic Agriculturist. We return on Thursday Morning—and on Friday I shall be once more at Grasmere.

If you think it would be serviceable, send a short advertisement to the Sherborne Paper—On the first Saturday of May, 1809, (and to be continued on the same day in each week) THE FRIEND, a moral, literary, and political Paper, but excluding all personal politics & the events of the day—by S. T. Coleridge. Sent to Subscribers free of expence to all parts of the Kingdom by the Post, as the Newspapers. Each number, price one Shilling. Orders to be sent post paid to Mr Coleridge, Grasmere, Kendal—&c &c &c &c—You may take the other names out of the Advertisement & Prospectus in the Courier of the 5th or 6th (I forget which) & you may perhaps add some name for Taunton, Bridgewater, & Sherborne—The mode of payment will be announced in the first number—I wish it to be paid every 20th week—God knows how I shall get thro' the first twenty weeks—!

But I must not write any more—for I have half a dozen letters of business to write by this Post—& but two hours before Curwen will expect me to go round his farm with him—Therefore do what you can for me,[1] my dear friend! by yourself, & by your influence or the influence of your friends—for this is to make or mar me—and be pleased to let me know the names of those whom you have procured as Subscribers by the 27th of this month at farthest—&

May God bless you | &
S. T. Coleridge

[1] In the spring of 1809 Wordsworth twice wrote to Poole of his apprehensions concerning *The Friend*:

I cannot say that Coleridge has been managing himself well; and therefore I would not have you disappointed if the 'Friend' should not last long; but do not hint a word of this to any body, as any thing of that kind should it come to his ears would completely dash him.—But I must say to you to prevent mortification on your part that I have not much hope.

I am sorry to say that nothing appears to me more desirable than that his periodical essay should never commence. It is in fact *impossible*—utterly impossible—that he should carry it on; and, therefore, better never begin it; far better, and if begun, the sooner it stops, also the better—the less will be the loss, and not greater the disgrace. . . . I give it to you as my deliberate opinion, formed upon proofs which have been strengthening for years, that he neither will nor can execute any thing of important benefit either to himself his family or mankind. Neither his talents nor his genius, mighty as they are, nor his vast information will avail him anything; they are all frustrated by a derangement in his intellectual and moral constitution. In fact he has no voluntary power of mind whatsoever, nor is he capable of acting under any *constraint* of duty or moral obligation. Do not suppose that I mean to say from this that The Friend may not appear—it may—but it cannot go on for any length of time. I am *sure* it cannot. (*Middle Years*, i. 280 and 321.)

By the bye, tho' this is not the time or place to write about it, yet I cannot help forewarning you that you *must* write me a Number for the Friend upon that infamous lace-beslavered Set of Lazaroni, those rascally male Servants in & out of Livery in those stinking gold-&-silver Fish-Ponds, the Squares, & Places & Grandee Streets in London—Likewise, an Essay 'On the means by which a Man may make his *Wealth* conducive to, productive & augmentative of his *Happiness*'—You may call it—Ariadne's Clue improved, or how a *Jason with a golden fleece may thread both Minos's Labyrinth & Jesus's Eye of the Needle—. But sans joking I should like hugely to see an Essay of your's on Wealth as a Means of additional happiness.— Some evening throw yourself into a day-dream, suppose yourself with your present notions, information, & desire of information, at the age of 21, & with 20,000£ a year—*live* thro' 15 years (from 21 to 36)—your biography of this should make the first Essay—then from 36 to 55—the second—from 55 to 70 or 80— or as you like—people it with any probable events—only *be* married & take precious care, *whom*—& have Sons & Daughters. It might make 2 or 3 delightful Essays—

756. *To George Coleridge*

MS. New York Public Lib. Hitherto unpublished.

Workington Hall—
[*Circa* 12 April 1809]
Dear Brother

I have at length settled the business of my weekly Essay, which has been advertised at full in the Courier—A succession of almost daily delays, disappointments, hindrance & unfair Dealings for some months has not improved either my health or spirits; but I console myself, that the task that remains becomes delightful by comparison with that gone thro'—& some times I conceit, that I may have been suffering penance for the negligences, procrastinations & indolence of past times, tho' I cannot justly charge myself with any fault of this kind in the present affair.

My chief anxiety is for the first 20 weeks; because I can receive nothing till after that period, and in the mean time have to pay the heavy price of five pence a sheet for the stamped paper, on which the work is printed, at ready money—I have likewise been under the necessity of laying out forty pound already in the purchase of new Type.

What names you can procure for me, you will be so kind as to let

* Jason pro *Theseus*—a small confusion—[Note by S. T. C.]

me know by the first of May—the first number will appear on May 7th [6th]—that is to say, it will appear in London on that day, and in all other places at the same distance from Penrith—

I trust, I shall be soon at leisure both to learn & communicate our domestic concerns—My 3 children are well, and go on well—I mean shortly to publish a Greek Accidence with a philosophical Greek Grammar—or the Language in the order of Thought.

I shall return to Grasmere to morrow and my address as before— Grasmere, Kendal.

With sincere prayers for your welfare & that of all those who are dear to you I remain

> Your affectionate Brother
> S. T. Coleridge

I have had a dreadful deafness & confusion in my left ear, accompanied at every loud noise or blowing of the nose with vertigo & dizziness, that tho' it is going off I really scarcely know what I write—My medical attendant thinks it a peculiar mode of the *Mumps* which is rife in this country & very contagious.

757. *To Daniel Stuart*

Address: D. Stuart, Esqre. | 38 Upper Brompton Row | Knightsbridge | London
MS. British Museum. Pub. E. L. G. i. 450.
Postmark: 18 April 1809.   *Stamped*: Keswick.

> Keswick.
> Sat. 15 April, 1809.

Dear Stuart

I am sorry to be forced to trouble you with a double postage in order to convey to you the inclosed Receipt.[1] It would have been sent earlier; but I was at Mr Curwen's, Workington Hall, when it arrived at Grasmere—and am just returned, and after 3 days examination of Mr Curwen's Great farm, & of Mr Curwen's not very great mind, an unexpected Convert to Sir F. Burdett's opinions concerning the impropriety of the great Landholders devoting themselves to practical agriculture.—This very moment I have received a striking proof, tho' in a trifling way, of the importance of a leading Paragraph—The Courier has not arrived half an hour, & yet 3 of the family, each unknown to the other, have come in to my Study, exclaiming—'Have you seen the Courier? It has no leading Paragraph—why, there's nothing in the Paper.' That I cannot assent

---

[1] Thomas Bernard had forwarded a receipt for Coleridge's signature, in order that the £60 due from the Royal Institution could be paid to Stuart. In reply Stuart said: 'I have got the receipt on Bernard. The money I shall lay out in Stamps & Paper as soon as you direct. The 60£ will buy nearly 4000.'

to—for I was much struck with the proof, it contained, of one of my old opinions—namely, of the superiority of our naval commanders, as diplomatists, to our Generals. The latter seem always to look forward to the time, when they shall be in the same situation with the capitulators; & always shew far more fellow-feeling for the enemy, however bloody & rapacious, than for the oppressed or for the majesty of their Country—the Sailors act like men with whom to be conquered is an unknown Thought, and who sacrifice their own pride & that of their country to no other claims than those of justice & common humanity. I was much amused with Mellish's speech at the Middlesex meeting. Had I been present, I would have quoted the following apposite passage from an obscure little Tract of the famous De Foe—'*Probability clear—Proof positive—Circumstances concurring*—He that would not hang a Thief on these three Heads, ought to be hanged himself. He that will doubt after these three heads have been thus cleared up, will doubt for ever; & must expect to have all men doubt both his own honesty and his understanding.'

It grieved me to see Wardle blending his yet transparent character with the muddy yet shallow stream of the Whig-club. If his own good sense and a moment's reflection on the necessary Consequences of the infamous Fox & Grenville Ministry had not taught him, he might have learnt even from Cobbett, that the influence of parliamentary Parties is in it's evanescent state, in the mind of the English Nation—and that [he] would be more trusted, & possess more real power, by attaching himself to the existing administration in all ordinary matters—& yet permit me to say, that your opinion of Mr Canning is one of the very very few, in which my present convictions are different from your's. I never can think that statesman a great man, who to defend a measure will assert— not once but repeatedly—that state-policy can not and ought not to be always regulated by morality. I should not hesitate at the promise of proving the Danish Expedition strictly moral & in the true spirit of the Law of Nations.

Curwen told me (but I place no great reliance on his opinions) that it was feared by many honest men in parliament (MANY!!) that Lord Howick hung off, & with Lord Grenville was pioneering a road to Power by the Duke of York & the King, who is said to be highly offended with the present Ministers. Perhaps, Whitbread's Conduct is no presumption of Howick's opinions; but surely Wynne's is a pretty sure Symptom of Lord Grenville's Bearings.[1]

[1] C. W. W. Wynn was Lord Grenville's nephew. In replying to this letter Stuart remarked: 'Out of your Letter I have written a paragraph or two [for the *Courier*].' [MS. Dove Cottage.]

I should think that once at least more a short advertisement should be put into the Times, M. Chronicle, M. [Pos]t, the Courier, & the Star—each on a different day—to this effect—

On Saturday the 7th [6th] of May will be published (to be continued weekly) No. 1. of the *Friend*, a literary, moral, and political Paper; but excluding personal & party politics, and the events of the Day—by S. T. Coleridge. Orders to be sent to—as before—&c &c &c—

When I say published, I mean it will appear in London, & in all other places equidistant from Penrith, on that day: for it will be sent from Penrith by Thursday's Post—but I did not know how to express it with brevity. It would be advantageous too to add, or to the principal Booksellers in each vicinity, who are requested to transmit the names by the 4th of May, if possible.—If any names have been left at Clement's, he will be so good as to send them as soon as possible. I wish, I knew some persons at Plymouth & Portsmouth who would interest themselves for me.—The mode of paying the money will be announced in the first number—.

God grant, my dear Stuart! that I may live & have health to thank you for all the trouble, you have taken for me, in that way which will, I know, most gratify you, by going on resolutely & with honor to myself & friends. I am ever as affectionately as gratefully

your obliged Friend
S. T. Coleridge

I return to Grasmere to morrow.

758. *To George Coleridge*

Address: Revd. G. Coleridge | Ottery St Mary | Honiton | Devon
MS. Lady Cave. Pub. with omis. E. L. G. i. 452.
Stamped: Keswick.

Tuesday Morning [18 April 1809]

My dear Brother

I have this moment received your letter, being at Keswick for the purpose of answering letters by the Post: for at Grasmere we are often (including the receipt & the answer) from 7 to 10 days behind the regular Post-towns.—It was a great oversight in me not to have informed you, that 'The Friend' will be printed on stamped paper, in the same manner as the Newspapers—and indeed has been registered, as a Newspaper, with Bonds, from myself, from my Printer & from my Publisher, and two Securities besides, at a considerable sum—Consequently, it will be circulated throughout the kingdom, free of all expence, even as a franked letter—No agent therefore is absolutely needful—or useful except as a place for persons to leave their names & orders, who would not take the trouble of sending them to me. For every number will come to the Subscriber's House by the Letter-carrier of the Place. In short, in this respect (and I would fain hope, in this alone) THE FRIEND is the very same sort of publication, as Cobbett's Political Journal—It will leave Penrith every Thursday Morning, arrive in *London* every Saturday Morning, & in all other places of the Kingdom proportioned to their distance.

I have been asked if it will be at all *political*. My answer has been—if by political be meant the events of the day, or discussions on the events of the day, or personalities ministerial or anti-ministerial, or *party*-politics in any shape, or disguise, THE FRIEND will not be *political*. But if under 'political' be included Essays on Legislation, international Morality, & the virtues & vices, that found or undermine the well-being of Nations, assuredly it will occasionally in that sense be *political:* for my Object is to draw the attention of my countrymen, as far as in me lies, from *expedients* & short-sighted tho' quick-sighted Expedience, to that grand Algebra of our moral nature, *Principle* & *Principles*—in public as in private life, in criticism, ethics, & religion. For I have long had reason to suspect, that in times of old the *Principles* were better than the men, but that now the men (faulty as they are) are better than their *Principles*.

But if I write 10 lines more, I shall lose the Post—

The first number will appear (in London) by May the 14th [13th] *certainly*, but if the Paper arrive this week, then on the 7th [6th]—There has been unfortunately [a dou]ble delay—[one in the S]tamp-office, & (that got over) a second in the [W]aggon. Each *sheet* of blank paper costs me fourpence half-penny—add to this fo[r the] expences of Printing, Advertising, Agen[ts,] Waste, & (above all) the great probab[le] Losses in the payments, & you will pe[rceive] that a Shilling is the least, at whic[h I] could afford it—the very moral mer[it of] the Plan precluding two thirds of the rea[ders] of periodical works, because excluding Personality & Bitterness & transient Curiosity.

With more enquiries at my heart (& these anxious ones) than I have either spirits or time to make

I remain, | dear Brother, | affectionately your
S. T. Coleridge

The mode of payment will be announced in some of the early numbers—I purpose, once in 20 weeeks—to make the one pound note up, for convenience of transmission—

Please to direct *Greta Hall, Keswick*.

759. *To John Colson*

Address: J. Colson, Esqre. | Clifton Wood | Bristol   *Single Sheet*
MS. Bristol Central Lib. Pub. E. L. G. i. 454.
Stamped: Keswick.

[*Circa* 18 April 1809]

Dear Colson

The first Number of 'The Friend' will appear in London, Bristol,
& places equi-distant from Penrith (where it is printed) on Saturday,
May the 14th [13th], at the latest—It's Object is—by doing as
much good as I can to do some service to my Wife & children. If it
succeed, (i.e. if it sell a 1000) it will put 7 or 8 hundred £, each year,
in my or rather my wife's pocket (for I never keep any *pounds* in
my own) during it's publication.—Therefore remember old Times,
dear Colson! and do me what service you can, in gaining me names.
For the names & addresses procured for me by my friends will just
put all in my pocket that would, if subscribed at the Booksellers',
go into their's— Indeed, it is quite a shame that the Booksellers
should charge any thing—For if the names are known, my directing
them to the Bookseller is an injury to the Subscribers, inasmuch as
they will have to *send* for that which otherwise would come to them
as a franked Letter. Therefore, dear Colson! do what you can for
me—Had you a bird's-eye view of my heart at this moment, you
would see that [it] is far more gratitude from remembrance of
'The Watchman' working there, than Hope or Wish respecting
'*The Friend.*'

If you are asked if the paper is to be *political*, answer—if by
political be meant the Events of the Day, or Discussions thereon;
or personal attacks or defences of Ministers, or Opposition—*No!*
But if by political be meant any Investigation relating to the Weal
& Woe of Nations in general & of this nation in particular, from
national conduct—Yes! for the Object of '*the Friend*' is to establish,
elucidate, & recommend *Principle* instead of *mere Expedience*—&
therefore *Principles:* Principles in Taste, (Poetry, Prose, Painting,
Music, Dress &c &c &c) *Principles* in private morality—Principles
in general *Religion*, as distinct from Superstition, from Enthusiasm,
& from atheism, & common to all who have indeed a *Religion*, in
whatever sect—Principles in Legislation, and the duties of Legis-
lators—especial[l]y Principles for Englishmen whether Electors, or
elected, Governors or Governed—adapted to the present aweful
Times & relative to France—

Mrs Coleridge is well, & looks younger every year—& my children
are well & going on well. By the bye, judging of your feelings by my
own, I deem it will excite no unpleasurable smile in you if I tran-

scribe one short sentence from the letter (received last night) from a friend, who called with me at your House when you were not at home—'So much for what I think of her head & heart—as to her person, I assure you, she is (in *my* eyes) the most beautiful woman, I ever saw, excepting Mrs Colson—I mean, your Bristol Friend's Wife.' This sentence which I read aloud for the edification of our Women produced a long *Discuss*, to my great amusement—who never in my life heard a Woman's Beauty admitted without exception & *sub*traction by two women together in my life time.

Any names of Subscribers (which subscription does not imply the least promise of continuing the work for a single Number after the Subscriber wishes to discontinue it) should be sent to me, S. T. Coleridge, Keswick, Cumberland—or Mr Brown, Printer & Bookseller, Penrith, *Do*.

May God bless you, & all who [are] dear to you, &
S. T. Coleridge

It will be stamped & registered as a weekly Newspaper—rather say, it *has been*—consequently will be brought to the residence of each person ordering it, as a *franked Letter*. Each sheet of blank stamped paper costs me 5 pence—add to this 1. the Carriage from London to Penrith—2. the Printing. 3. the accidental waste, where every sheet mispulled costs 5d. 4. the advertisements which are very heavy. 5. the unavoidable Losses in the final payments: 6. expences &c of agency (to avoid which as much as possible, I write to you) 6th [7th]—the nature of the work which excluding *personalities*, the events & politics of the Day, precludes two thirds of the Readers of a weekly Paper—and then judge whether selling the same quantity at the same price with Cobbett, I do not sell it at a much lower rate—

760. *To Daniel Stuart*

Address: D. Stuart, Esqre. | 38. Upper Brompton Row | Knightsbridge | London
MS. British Museum. Pub. with omis. Letters from the Lake Poets, *149*.
Postmark: 21 April 1809. *Stamped*: Keswick.

Keswick
Tuesday Evening, 18 April 1809.

Dear Stuart

I have this moment heard from Brown at Penrith, that NO stamped paper has arrived. The sharpness of the Frost-wind & the Snow-storms have kept me still at Keswick; but the present clearness of the Sky holds out a sort of promise that I shall be able to walk to Grasmere tomorrow. Your letter, that informed me of the stamped Sheets having been sent off from London for Penrith, happens to be at Grasmere— so that the anxiety which urges me to trouble you with yet another application, rests wholly on my recollection that the Paper was to have arrived in ten days from the date of your Letter. Indeed, I must be accurate, because I now remember you advised me to commence 'the Friend' on the 15th— i.e. last Saturday. Ignorant too, of course, of the size & quality of the paper, you had ordered to be forwarded, I have not been able to write to Mr Fourdiniere—only last night I wrote to Basil Montagu, begging him to learn the size and sort from you, and then to wait on Mr F. in my name, and try to settle with him for the regular Supply.

I have ordered a small quantity from Pennington, in case of an utter failure—and my Printer must take Oath as to the Stamps— but it will be excessively awkward for the first Number—

Indeed, it was very thoughtless in me not to leave word with Brown to inform me of the arrival or non-arrival of the Stamps on the time announced—but at first overwhelmed by the cursed Mumps & accompanying deafness, and since then absorbed in composition, I suffered myself to take it for granted, that the parcel had arrived —I hope they have not mistaken Penrith, Cumberland, for Penruth in Cornwall—.

I inclosed a receipt for the 60£ in a letter to you the last post but one—and at the same time sent a rude sketch of a shorter advertisement to appear on different days in different papers, or according to your better Judgment. All here are well, except that the Imp, Mumps, has got into Southey & into his youngest Girl but one—. How compleatly those letters between Frere & Sir J. M. have justified your opinions concerning the Latter.[1] *Afraid* of every thing, and only still more afraid of being *thought* to be afraid—O God! to read the life of Gustavus Adolphus by Harte (a book, I earnestly recommend to you) or the Memoirs of Col. (or Captn) Tarlton,[2] which contains the best existing account of Lord Peterborough's Campaign in the N. of Spain—& then to think of the very best of our present Soldiers—almost inspires the melancholy idea,

---

[1] J. H. Frere was appointed minister plenipotentiary to the Spanish Central Junta in Oct. 1808. Shortly thereafter he urged Sir John Moore to resist Napoleon, instead of retiring through Portugal. After the disastrous retreat to Coruña, Frere was blamed for his advice. Although Ponsonby's motion in the House of Commons, on 24 Feb. 1809, for an inquiry 'into the causes, conduct, and events of the late campaign in Spain', was defeated, the government determined to recall Frere, and on 29 April Marquis Wellesley (Richard Colley Wellesley, 1760–1842) was appointed ambassador to Spain.

[2] Coleridge refers to George Carleton's *Military Memoirs*, 1728, a work erroneously attributed to Defoe. It was re-edited by Scott in 1808.

that we are predestined to be baffled. O Heaven! my head is thronged with Thoughts, my Heart swells with Emotions, for an hour daily after the receipt of the Courier—

God bless you | & your affectionate Friend,

S. T. Coleridge

Our Grocer here informs Mrs Coleridge that nothing can be more irregular than portages sent per waggon to Penrith thro' the Yorkshire Road—and that for this reason they have their goods always sent by the *Kendal* Waggon, which may then go on to Penrith. In case of the necessity of another parcel it had better be directed Mr Cookson, Kendal; with S. T. C. on the corner—& I shall have written to him to forward it to Brown instantly.—But when things go by Sea by Stockton upon Tees,—Brown, Penrith— is better than any intermediate direction to J. Hutchinson.—

761. *To Daniel Stuart*

Address: D. Stuart, Esqre. | 38. Upper Brompton Row | Knightsbridge | London
MS. British Museum. Pub. with omis. Letters from the Lake Poets, *152.*
Postmark: 27 April 1809. *Stamped*: Keswick.

Greta Hall, Keswick.

Monday Night. [24 April 1809]

My dear Stuart

I have been writing a very long Letter to you in answer to your last, and as suggested by some of the last Couriers—the chief points, on the state of parties in and out of parliament, 2. the question of Reform in the Representation, & supposing it right & needful, whether it can be accomplished without *associations*— what the dangers of these are, & whether by any regulations they may be precluded—3. on Sir J. Moore's Letter, & Mr Frere, and the strange want of wisdom & dignity in our Ministers—1. first having such a letter in their possession to vote swelling unconditional praise & honor to an army who had behaved so infamously except in the mere act of saving their throats from being cut when thrust up into a corner (when a rat will attack a Lion), and having done this 2. to disclose the letter only forsooth because the Moores wished it—!!— But as I cannot finish it by this post, yet am oppressed with anxiety concerning the Paper, which is not yet arrived, I write now merely to request you in the advertisements to announce Saturday, May 14th [13th] instead of the 7th [6th]—if it be not too late—i.e. if you shall not have advertised before this letter reaches you—I shall not now return to Grasmere till the first number is published.

Was ever such a dull worthless mud-headed dung-hearted Speech

made as that by Lord Howick in the Courier of to-day—? Were
there but only *one* man in the Ministry of any thing like commanding Talents, they might set a regiment of such fellows as the
present Opposition at defiance.—Then too Wardle—why, has he
not one friend to whisper him that he *blows* best aloof and alone, &
that Sir F. Burdett will injure him quite as much in the minds of
the sober & respectable, as the Whig Club would have done in the
eyes of the people at large?

But I must conclude.

God bless you | & | Your obliged Friend,

S. T. Coleridge

762. *To Thomas N. Longman*

Transcript Coleridge family. Pub. E. L. G. i. 456.

Greta Hall, Keswick
Thursday Night [27 April 1809][1]

Dear Sir

It gave me much concern, first that contrary to my direction
some books belonging to you were sent hither from London among
my own; and secondly, that after having been properly packed up
for my friend, Mr De Quincey, to take with him to town, they
were, as I find, forgotten and left behind. Immediately on my
return to Grasmere (for I must remain here and at Penrith, till the
first Number of 'The Friend' has been sent off) they shall be additionally secured, and forwarded to you by the waggon, carriage
paid—You will have seen by my Prospectus the general nature of
my weekly paper, which will be circulated to those that order it, by
the General Post, it having been registered etc. as a newspaper. It
has been often asked, whether 'The Friend' is to exclude *Politics*
altogether? My answer is: If by Politics be meant the Events of the
Day, Public Papers, or Discussions thereon, or attacks on or defences of particular measures, or particular men in or out of power,
in short, personal & party politics, Yes! all these the Friend will
exclude. But if the word 'Political' be taken in it's wider sense, so
as to include whatever relates to the public conduct of men and
nations, I must answer, No! for the object of my Work is, as far as
in me lies and in those who assist me, to draw the attention of the
Country to Principle and Principles instead of mere Expedience &

---

[1] At the end of this letter Coleridge mentions 'an attack of the Croup'
suffered by 'Mr Southey's little Boy the night before last'. Since this attack
took place on Tuesday night, 25 April, Coleridge's letter was written on 27
April. See *Life and Corres*. iii. 231.

prudential maxims in *everything*—in Literature, in the fine Arts, in Morals, in religion, in Legislation, and in international Law. The first number will be sent from Penrith by Thursday's Post, May 12 [11], so as to be in London & all places equi-distant on Saturday morning, 14 [13] May. Any service, you might find it in your power to render it, I need not say, will be acknowledged & remembered gratefully by me—

Ill-health, and still more the consequent morbid Low-spirits amounting almost to despondency, joined to the unworthy Reception of Southey's Madoc & Wordsworth's Poems hung such a weight on every attempt I made to finish two Poems, four fifths of which had been written years ago, that I at last gave up the Thought altogether. I once remarked there were Beauties & Excellencies enough in the very *worst* of Shakespere's Plays to ensure it's damnation had it appeared in the present age. Now it is most certain, that my Poems do not contain either in kind or degree the qualities which make Wordsworth's poems so dear to me and many much greater men and so repulsive to others—But it was enough that I am known to be the particular Friend both of Southey & Wordsworth to draw upon me the whole clamor of those who have waged war against them. I told Jeffray that it was rather hard upon me, that for the poems, which I have published, I received the not-undeserved censure that my style was too highly ornamented, and deviating from simplicity by a too constant employment of the strongest words & boldest figures of Poetry. Even the Ancient Mariner, the only poem of any size that has appeared since—& that anonymously—was yet every where criticized in the Reviews, as 'Laboriously beautiful'—and 'over-polished in the diction with *Dutch* Industry'[1]—and now for *no* poems at all but only for my acquaintanceships, I am abused in every Review & Magazine, in time and out of time for the *simple & puerile:* tho' it is a fact, that I was the very first person who commenced the attack on *Mock*-simplicity in the Sonnets (in one of the early Monthly Magazines) signed Nehemiah Higginbottom.[2]

I have however some reason to believe that Jeffray is well inclined to make me the amende honorable (at least, if I may believe his own letters).—These objections however are perhaps the offspring of Low-spirits in great measure—But the alteration, I have made in the plan, I made from sober reflection.—

The poems in my possession are of two sorts—1. Poems of such

[1] Cf. Southey's comments in the *Critical Review*, Oct. 1798: 'Many of the stanzas are laboriously beautiful; but in connection they are absurd or unintelligible. . . . It is a Dutch attempt at German sublimity.'
[2] See Letter 212.

length that either of them with the necessary notes would make a small volume, when completed—of these not a line has ever appeared in any form.— 2. Poems all of which are completed, & corrected for the Press, the longest of which is a thousand lines—a second 700—the others from 300 to 10 lines—which altogether amount to four thousand lines, and printed as the last edition of my Poems would with the notes make near 400 pages—But of these tho' all are my own property, yet several have already appeared, tho' very different from their present form, in the Morning Post—these however are of small consequence from their minor size etc.—and the A. Mariner (which in any future Edition Wordsworth will withdraw from the L. Ballads, now sold out) in the L.B.—

My wish therefore is to publish these, as a second in 2 & 3 Volumes of *my* Poems—the first being 'Poems written chiefly from the age of 17 to 25'—the second—'Poems from 25 to 33'—and hereafter to publish whatever I may publish by the name of the particular Poem as 'The three Graves, a Sexton's Tale, by S. T. C.'—etc. Now as the first Volume is your *property*,[1] I have no objection to dispose of the absolute Copyright of the second, or second & third (as with notes & critical preface it will make, as I find by accurate measurements, two Volumes of the same size with the last Edition of the first) both for that reason, and in order that any defect of immediate novelty from the Ancient Mariner having past thro' several Editions in the L.B. (for the same objection scarcely applies to those that have appeared occasionally & often without my knowledge in different channels & at very distant dates) may be fully counterbalanced by the certainty of the whole advantage (whatever that may chance to be) derived from any present or future reputation, that I may chance to obtain.—It shall be at your own command on which day the Poems shall be put to the Press, and within what time completed—only it is my particular wish, that they should be printed under my own eye by Brown, of Penrith, and the difference in the *Price* will nearly pay the carriage to London if not wholly. He prints excellently, & his Type is quite new from Wilson, of Glasgow.

For the copy-right I ask 120£[2]—Brown could begin any day after May 21st—When you write, be so good as to send my account for Books etc.—Mr Southey's little Boy the night before last had an

---

[1] Longman and Rees published the third edition of Coleridge's *Poems* in 1803.

[2] In a reply dated 4 May 1809, Longman offered little encouragement to Coleridge: 'If you will be so good as to send us the Poems intended for the two volumes when you have them transcribed, we will communicate with you about terms: though we are fearful that £120 is rather more than can be afforded for [them.]' [MS. Dove Cottage.] As Letter 963 shows, Longman offered only £100 for the copyright. According to Wordsworth, Coleridge rightly refused to conclude 'a most injurious bargain'. *Middle Years*, i. 328–9.

attack of the Croup; but thank Heaven! by instant Bleeding at the
Jugular, and a blister on the Throat, the Danger seems past.—

Respectfully, dear Sir,

S. T. Coleridge.

763. *To Daniel Stuart*

Address: D. Stuart, Esqre. | 38. Upper Brompton Row | Knightsbridge | London
MS. British Museum. Pub. Letters from the Lake Poets, *155.*
Postmark: 5 May 1809. *Stamped*: Keswick.

Tuesday Night, 2 May 1809
Greta Hall, Keswick—

My dear Stuart

I both respect and have an affection for Mr De Quincey; but saw
too much of his turn of mind, anxious yet dilatory, confused from
over-accuracy, & at once systematic and labyrinthine, not fully to
understand how great a plague he might easily be to a London
Printer, his natural Tediousness made yet greater by his zeal & fear
of not discharging his Trust, & superadded to Wordsworth's own
Sybill's Leaves blown about by the changeful winds of an anxious
Author's Second-thoughts.—Wordsworth however has received
impressions of a very different sort, which, if I had known, I should
not perhaps have stated my own quite so freely as I did in my
letter to him on my receipt of your's.[1] Mr De Quincey has informed
him that 'the Compositor has been drunk ever since Easter week—
in one of the weeks attending at the Printing Office only two days
during which time he must have been in a state of Intoxication as
the Proofs were sent with the omission of whole sentences—and
Mr Baldwin either could not, or would not set another man to the
work tho' frequently requested to do so. They have certainly had
reason to complain of chopping & changing in *one* instance; but for
these last five weeks there has not been the slightest alteration
made either in the Text or the Notes: nor a word altered in the
proofs when returned, and only the punctuation in six places.' Such
is Mr De Quincey's statement, as given me by Wordsworth in his
Note of this morning; but of what date Mr De Q.'s letter is, I know
not. I have written to W. stating honestly my convictions, that he
will not find Baldwin so much in the wrong as he now believes—and
that he ought to bring before his fancy all his own *Copy* from the
beginning of the work, and compare it in his mind's eye with the
sort of copy & the mode of receiving it, to which Baldwin had been

[1] On 26 April Stuart had written to Coleridge an account of Baldwin's
difficulties in printing the *Convention of Cintra*, the advertisement of which is
dated 20 May 1809.

probably accustomed: that to Mr De Q.'s positive statement it was impossible for me to offer doubts or objections, but yet [I] cannot blame myself for having, anterior to it, received strong impressions from an account so strictly correspondent to my own experience of Mr De Quincey's Particularities—especially, as the wish to excuse the neglect of a vicious drunken Journeyman appeared to me a very unlikely temptation to a respectable Tradesman to impose a falsehood on a man, like you.—That Wordsworth has not been quite pleased with my first letter, & will be still less with my letter of to-day, I know—but that soon passes off—and I do not wonder, that he is very much vexed at the delay—and not easily to admit one's self to be in fault is as often the mark of a valuable as of an obstinate mind—but I am grieved that you should have had any superfluous trouble & uneasiness—& intreat you, if you write to Wordsworth to take no notice of any part of this Letter excepting the bare facts asserted in Mr De Quincey's statement—and simply to divide what has come within your own knowlege (if any thing) from what has been told you by Baldwin—if it be your wish to write on it [at] all—.

After the instances, I saw, of De Q's marvellous slowness in writing a note to the Pamphlet when at Grasmere, the sum and meaning of which I had dictated in better & more orderly sentences in five minutes, and considering the superlative importance of Dispatch—since that time, I can never retract my expressions of vexation & surprize, that *W.* should have entrusted any thing to him beyond the mere correction of the Proofs—but an unwise anxiety to let nothing escape has been the rock, on which W. has split—whereas had he brought it out, such as it was, he might now have been adding all, he wished, to a second Edition. But so it is! We cannot be perfect. I do far worse both for myself and others by indifference about my compositions & what is thought or said of them, than he by over-irritability—His is a more natural fault & linked to better qualities.—

And now for my own affairs. No news of the Paper—none! What must be done, my dear Friend? Would it not be adviseable to send off 600 Sheets by the Penrith Coach, if they could be procured *immediately*. If they were booked & seen sent off on Saturday they would arrive in Penrith on Monday—and as the Sheet will be ready set, I would then by all means advertise in ONE paper, at least, on Saturday it's appearance for the ensuing Saturday—or else I shall be charged with making fools of my Subscribers—. I have sent the Hull Paper, that contains an advertisement, put in by one of my Zealous Friends—and therefore I so much wish that if possible an advertisement should appear in the Saturday's Courier, announcing

it for Saturday, 13 May—supposing that the Paper can be sent off
per Coach on Saturday—at all events, another parcel of paper
ought to be sent off immediately—and by the *Kendal* waggon direct,
directed to Mr Cookson, Manufacturer, Kendal—with I.[J.?]B.
on one corner. Mr C. will be certain of receiving it instantly on it's
arrival, & will forward it to Brown without an hour's delay—I have
420 names, and shall receive at least 20 more, in a day or two. I
think therefore of printing 500—as I am desired to send a dozen or
more to Oxford, to Clement, to Newcastle &c—.

Again and again, my dear Stuart! let me assure [you], how
sensible I am of the multiplied Trouble, I occasion you—and my
best consolation is that it has not been increased by any fault of
mine. To morrow of subjects of more general Interest—

S. T. Coleridge

I go to Penrith on Thursday, & stay there a week. My address at
Mr Brown's, Bookseller—

764. *To Daniel Stuart*

Address: D. Stuart, Esqre. | 38 Upper Brompton Row | Knightsbridge |
London
MS British Museum. Pub. with omis. Letters from the Lake Poets, *160.*
Postmark: 8 May 1809.   *Stamped*: Keswick.

Friday Night—[5 May 1809]
My dear Stuart
  The Paper is come. I have this moment received the tidings. The
original mistake was in sending it by Halifax.—It should have gone
to Kendal direct from the Bull and Mouth. I am so feeble from the
effect of a severe bilious Colic and Diarrhoea, that I can scarcely sit
up in the attitude of writing three minutes together—and yet I do
so earnestly desire to communicate my thoughts & feelings to you
respecting the two last Couriers, relatively to Sir F. Burdett. You
have ample room and reason for attack on him personally, and for
warning both to & respecting the present *Restorers*—and you have
written well in the article to day, in my humble opinion, all but the
first paragraph. It is that of which I am doubtful and anxious—
anxious, lest from what I hear & have heard, it should diminish the
influence & run of the Paper (but this you must attribute to my
love—you must needs be so much better a Judge than I can be)
and doubtful, whether the charge is not strained. Surely, Sir F. B.
will not be believed by the Public to have meant by 'the tearing out
the pages of the Red book' such impracticable nonsense, as that
there was to be no Civil List, no persons employed and payed by

the executive Government—but only to have expressed his abhorrence 1. of the sinecures, pensions, mock places & unnecessary places, and 2. of the general enslaving effect of government Influence from the amount, & modes of collecting, & final distribution, of our Taxes.—At the time that Sir F. B. gave out that Paper to the Westminster Electors, I was indignant, & retain both my feelings & my convictions—but not that he had such definite opinions as those charged against him in the Courier, but that he had purposely exprest himself in language, the general *effect* of which must of necessity be highly inflammatory & bewildering, without definition, and where it was plain, that to have defined his meaning would have destroyed $\frac{9}{10}$ths of the designed effect of the words—this is indeed one of the detestable Tricks of Horne Tooke, so to talk & write that his words WILL be understood seditiously, & convey the most inflammatory falsehoods, and yet when examined according to the necessity of the logical import are harmless—and this is in itself a proof of the bad intentions of the Speaker—for why should he express that which no body had a doubt of ? On the same ground I abominated Mr Fox's assertion of '*the Rights of Man*'— understood in the same sense, in which it was felt by the mob, he would himself have disavowed it—& if *felt* in the sense, in which it *might* be understood & be consistent with Truth, it could have had no effect at all, nor could there have been any motive for a Demagogue to have uttered it. For it were then a mere Truism, not denied by any one of any one party.

But I am too feeble to write more—I disapprove of more in the late public Meetings than I approve—Sir F. B.'s Speech at the meeting is full of dangerous Sophistry—these are the men and these the means, by which the great blessing of a Reform in Parliament will be baffled—. O that I could but have one long Evening's Conversation with you.

First thoughts often prove right after having apparently been disproved—I begin to recall my first apprehension respecting Wardle—He is a Puppet.

Observe, dear Stuart! that it is to the first Paragraph I object— and less for the matter than for the manner, which, I fear, may be thought coarse & inveterate.

I cannot agree with Street that Lord Auckland's Divorce Bill is wise or proper—I think it cruel, & yet nugatory. The Law should be slow to interfere in cases, in which the criminality of the act is so infinitely modified by difference of circumstances, and where the true circumstances can rarely be known except to God & those who either cannot or will not disclose them. But of this I shall discourse in 'The Friend'.

I write in great pain—but I doubt not, I shall be well tomorrow, & perhaps better for the profuse Scouring. Your affection: grateful

S. T. Coleridge

Does not the Law making Brokerage in offices penal frustrate itself by precluding all conviction? For every person concerned will have a *legal right* to withhold his Evidence—as criminating himself. And after all, what is the advantage to the nation? That Lord A. or B. having *no* motive will give a place to his Butler, or employ it as a means of Parliamentary Influence instead of disposing of it to a man of some property who wishes to sink his property in that mode of being useful. Where is the presumption that a man will prove a bad Cadet, whose inclinations have led him to give 1000£ or more in order to become a Cadet?—After all, 'tis but a Tub for the Whale, to divert it from things of real importance to Freedom & Security.

765. *To John Brown*

Address: Mr Brown
MS. Victoria and Albert Museum. Hitherto unpublished.

[May 1809][1]

I will come in as soon as ever the Rain is over—in the mean time I would go on with this—only I am *convinced* that we must lessen the Margin, and add at least 4 or 5 letters to each page. I tremble at the Idea of an enormous Margin in a weekly Paper—

S. T. Coleridge

You will have no pause or delay henceforwards—It should be dated *Thursday*, 1 June—

766. *To Daniel Stuart*

Address: D. Stuart, Esqre. | 38. Upper Brompton Ro[w] | Knightsbrid[ge] | Lond[on] Single Sheet
MS. British Museum. Pub. with omis. Letters from the Lake Poets, *163.* The bottom half of pages one and two and the upper third of pages three and four of the manuscript have been cut off.
Postmark: 6 June 1809.

4 June, 1809
Penrith—

My dear Stuart

It excited no wonder in me, that your Patience was quite exhausted by my frequent applications to you concerning the Friend

---

[1] The MS. of *The Friend* is in the Victoria and Albert Museum. This note is written on copy for the first number, which appeared on 1 June 1809.

—and God knows! how reluctantly and with lingering and often imprudent delays I made each separate request. And if I had indulged my own feelings instead of regarding your's, I should have expressed my deep sense of my obligations to you more frequently and with warmth more proportioned to them. But yet, my dear Friend! in what one instance did I apply to you undriven by an absolute necessity? And was it not my ill-luck, and not my fault, that I was forced to be so troublesome just at the very time when your Kindness had prompted you to take upon yourself the equal or greater Task of superintending the interests of W. Wordsworth's Pamphlet? Nor (if I did not misconceive the intention of the sense) could I deserve to be included in the Question—Are you all Children? I who had anticipated your arguments & given (I well know) some offence to Wordsworth by the warmth with which I had prest them, and pointed out the irrationality of exculpating Mr De Quincey of a known Foible by criminating Baldwin of a serious Immorality.— . . .

. . . me, because at that very time I had just written to Longman, offering him the COPY RIGHT of two Volumes of Poems for 120£ wholly thro' an uneasy desire to repay you the 100£, I last borrowed, and other smaller Bills at the Courier Office—the only sum of my Debt that lay heavy on my heart, especially after the 60£ (which I expected to have been an 100£) from the Royal Institution had been perforce turned from my original purpose into the service of 'The Friend'.—It was by just such another unpermitted & unknown application of Wordsworth some 8 years ago to T. Poole, that there existed for years a healed indeed but yet scarred wound between me, and Poole[1]—the man who with Wordsworth & yourself I have always placed in the upper Class of my attachments.— Forgive me for thus opening out my heart to you—and let it drop. You know me well enough to be assured that it [is] impossible that I should ever cease to love and honor you, or cherish for an hour a feeling inconsistent with sincere friendship and manly gratitude.

I have not seen or heard from Wordsworth for a month past— Southey who past thro' Penrith yesterday on his way to Durham left his Pamphlet for me, which I have not yet read. I rejoice that by your last letter you seem to entertain confidence of it's Success. Just glancing my eye on . . . Paragraphs—were injudiciously few— . . .

. . . My opinions on the subject of Reform differ very widely from Wordsworth's: but they are my sincere Convictions. I detest the Burdettites & Whitbreads. I was half inclined to insert a squib in a provincial paper but did not, in these words—'An ingenious and

---

[1] See Letters 411 and 416.

eloquent Philanthropist is said to be composing prospectively a work in demonstration of the great advantages to be derived by the French Armies by the substitution of Porter for French Wine & Brandy. A contract however for the same is not likely to be effectuated, we believe.'—Still however I think attacks on Burdettism more likely to do good than attacks on Burdett himself, whose private character is said to be very amiable—I have received a most interesting Letter from Captn Pasley,[1] of which hereafter.

I return to Grasmere the day after tomorrow—direct therefore as before—Grasmere, Kendal.

God bless you | & | your affectionate
S. T. Coleridge

767. *To Daniel Stuart*

Address: D. Stuart, Esqre | 36. Upper Brompton Row | Knightsbridge | London   Single Sheet
MS. British Museum. Pub. with omis. Letters, ii. 547.
Postmark: 17 June 1809.   *Stamped*: Kendal.

13 June, 1809.
Grasmere, Kendal.

Dear Stuart

I left Penrith Monday Noon, & prevented by the heavy rain from crossing Grisedale Tarn (near the summit of Helvellyn & our most perilous & difficult Alpine Pass) the same day, I slept at Luff's, & crossed it yestermorning & arrived here by Breakfast Time. I was sadly grieved at Wordsworth's account of your late sorrows & troubles respecting your Sister's illness, and your Brother's Misfortune.[2] Alas! for how many years have you been wasting advice,

[1] See Letter 775.
[2] Wordsworth was in correspondence with Stuart not only concerning the *Convention of Cintra* but about *The Friend* as well, and he may have undermined Stuart's confidence in Coleridge. On 25 May 1809 he wrote: 'Of Coleridge or the Friend I can say nothing satisfactory; it is nearly 3 months since he left us, and I have not heard from him lately.'

A few days later he was no more encouraging: 'Of the Friend and Coleridge I hear nothing, and am sorry to say I hope nothing. It is I think too clear that Coleridge is not sufficiently master of his own efforts to execute anything which requires a regular course of application to one object. I fear so—indeed I am of opinion that it is so—to my great sorrow.'

On 4 June he was still without hope: 'The Friend has at last appeared. I am sorry for it as I have not the least hope that it can proceed.'

In spite of all Wordsworth had written, Dorothy wrote confidently to Mrs. Clarkson on Coleridge's arrival at Grasmere: 'I think it is most probable that Stuart will remove Coleridge's uneasiness of mind respecting money for the stamped paper. It is probable that Stuart has kept back from offering on account of Coleridge's slowness to begin, and now that he has begun I have little doubt that Stuart will come forward.' Wordsworth himself seems to have

assistance, & forewarnings on him! I can not adequately express how much I am concerned lest any thing, I wrote in my last letter (tho' God knows under the influence of no one feeling which you would not wish me to have) should chance to have given you any additional unpleasantness, however small. Would that I had worthier means than words & professions of proving to you what my heart is.—It will not be uninteresting to you to hear, that tho' my Health is rather alarming, yet all my Habits are what they ought to be—I rise every morning at 5, and work 3 hours before breakfast, either in Letter-writing or serious Composition—I am even abstemious in my Diet, taking only one pint of Table-beer in the day—& tho' forbidden by my medical attendant from trying again the desperate experiment of abandoning all at once that accursed Drug, into which the Horrors of Sleep antecedent to my ever taking it seduced me & to which the Dread of sudden Death (for the sake of my children) afterwards fettered me, yet I have, with a far greater endurance of severest Sufferings than I could have dared give myself credit for, reduced to a comparative trifle, less than one 20th part of my old doses—. Still however Sleep or even a supine Posture does not fail to remind me that something is organically amiss in some one or other of the Contents of the Abdomen.

I take for granted that more than the poor 60£ has been expended in the paper, I have received. But I have written to Mr Clarkson to see what can be done; for it would be a sad thing to give it all up

had misgivings about what he had earlier said to Stuart, for on 15 June he wrote again: 'Coleridge arrived here yesterday morning, after an absence of nearly four months. As I thought it my duty some time since, upon substantial grounds, to express my apprehension, that from the irresolution of the author, *The Friend* might not prosper, which opinion I expressed in order to break the force of your disappointment should my forebodings prove true, I now think it right to say that such appear to be the present dispositions, resolutions, and employments of Coleridge, that I am encouraged to entertain more favourable hopes of his exerting himself steadily than I ever have had at any other period of this business. I confess that it looks ill that he should have interrupted the regular publication so early as even the third number; but there is one circumstance which makes me not sorry that this has been done, as I understand that there is no quantity of paper yet arrived to enable him to carry it on regularly for any length of time. I suspect he has some difficulty in this which he has not laid open to his friends. I have myself had no conversation with him upon the subject, but I have reason to believe that there must be a lack of money on his part to advance for this purpose; which is the more probable as (very properly) he has declined concluding a bargain with Longman for his Poems and Essays —which, if concluded, would have put him into immediate possession of a sum sufficient to enable him to carry on *The Friend*, but this would have been bought at a great price, and indeed would have been a most injurious bargain both for himself and his family, for Longman, I am sorry to say, is an arrant Jew, like most of his Brethren.' *Middle Years*, i. 314, 319, 323, and 327–9.

now I am going on so well, merely for want of means to provide the first 20 weeks paper. My present stock will not quite suffice for 3 numbers—I printed 620 of No. 1. & 650 of No. 2[1]—and so many more are called for, that I shall be forced to reprint both, as soon as I hear from Clarkson.—The proof Sheet of No. 3 goes back to day, & with it the Copy of No. 4[2]—so that henceforth we shall be secure of regularity—indeed it was not all my fault before, but the Printer's inexperience, & the multitude of errors tho' from a very decent copy, which took him a full day & more in correcting. I had altered my plan for the introductory Essays after my arrival at Penrith, which cost me exceeding trouble—but the Numbers to come are in a very superior style of Polish & easy Intelligibility.—

The only thing at present, which I am under the necessity of applying to you for, respects Clement. It may be his interest to sell 'the Friend' at his Shop, and a certain number will always be sent; but I am quite in the Dark as to what profit he expects—surely not Book Profit for a Newspaper that can circulate by the Post? And it is certainly neither my Interest nor that of the regular Purchasers of the Friend to have it bought at a Shop instead of receiving it as a franked Letter. All I want to know is his Terms: for I have quite a horror of Booksellers, whose mode of carrying on Trade in London is absolute rapacity—Longman secures full 40 per cent for letting his Lads lift a book over his Counter—& then calls the X Y Z that remains of 30 per cent after advertising expences &c &c the Author's Half of the profits, to be paid him when the whole Edition is sold off—On this ruinous plan poor Southey has been toiling for years with an Industry honorable to human Nature, & must starve upon it were it not for the more profitable employment of Reviewing, a task unworthy of him or even of a man with not one third of his Honor & Honesty.

I have just read Wordsworth's pamphlet—& more than fear that your friendly Expectations of it's Sale & Influence have been too

[1] Coleridge had only his 'poor 60£' to begin *The Friend*, and the problem of obtaining 'the first 20 weeks paper' remained unsolved until ten numbers had appeared. By June Stuart had sent only 2,500 stamped sheets, and after issuing the first two numbers on 1 and 8 June, Coleridge had paper for but one more. On 7 July Stuart belatedly reported that another 2,500 stamped sheets were on the way. He estimated that the 5,000 sent would print eight numbers; and the £60 being exhausted, he offered to furnish paper for two further numbers before it was needed. This he failed to do. Coleridge published the 3rd number on 10 Aug. and resumed the regular weekly issues with the 4th on 7 Sept. Soon in difficulty for lack of paper, he appealed in vain to Stuart, and 'of No. 8 not one half the Copies' were printed on time. On 5 Oct. Street sent 1,500 stamped sheets, thus enabling Coleridge to print the work through the 10th number. Poole, Hutchinson, and Sharp provided paper for the next ten numbers.

[2] An exaggeration. See note to Letter 770.

sanguine. Had I not known the Author, I would willingly have
travelled from St Michael's Mount to Johnny Groat's House on a
pilgrimage to see & reverence him—but from the Public I am
apprehensive, first that it will be impossible to rekindle an exhausted Interest respecting the Cintra Convention, & therefore
that the long Porch may prevent Readers from entering the
Temple—2. That partly from Wordsworth's own Style, which represents the chain of his Thoughts & the movements of his Heart
admirably, for me & a few others; but I fear, does not possess the
more profitable excellence of translating this down into that style
which might easily convey it to the understandings of common
readers—and partly from Mr De Quincey's strange & most mistaken
System of punctuation—. The Periods are often alarmingly long
perforce of their construction; but De Quincey's Punctuation has
made several of them immeasurable, & perplexed half the rest.
Never was a stranger whim than the notion that , ; : and . could be
made logical symbols expressing all the diversities of logical connection.—But lastly, I fear, that Readers even of Judgment may
complain of a want of Shade & Background, that it is all fore-
ground, all in hot tints—that the first note is pitched at the height
of the Instrument, & never suffered to sink—that such depth of
Feeling is so incorporated with depth of Thought, that the Attention is kept throughout at it's utmost Strain & Stretch—&—but
this for my own feeling—I could not help feeling that a considerable
part is almost a self-robbery from some great philosophical poem, of
which it would form an appropriate part, & be fitl[ier] attuned to
the high dogmatic Eloquence, the oracular [tone] of impassioned
Blank Verse.—In short, cold Readers, conceited of their supposed
Judgment on the score of their possessing nothing else & for that
reason only taking for granted they *must* have Judgment, will abuse
the book as positive, violent, & 'in a mad passion'—and Readers of
Sense & Feeling will have no other dread than that the Work, if it
should die, would die of a Plethora of the highest qualities of combined philosophic & poetic Genius. The apple pie, they may say,
is made all of Quinces.—I much admired our young friend's note
on Sir J. Moore & his Dispatches—it was excellently arranged &
argued—. I have had no opportunity as yet to speak a word to
Wordsworth himself about it—I write to you, as usual, in full
confidence.

I shall be not a little anxious to have your opinion of my third
Number.—Lord Lonsdale blames me for excluding Party Politics
& the Events of the Day from my Plan—I exclude both the one &
the other only as far as they are merely *party*—i.e. personal & temporary Interests—or merely Events of To day, that are defunct

in the To morrow—. I flatter myself, that I have been the first who will have given a calm, disinterested account of our Constitution as it really *is*, & *how* it is so—& that I have more radically than has been done before shewn the unstable & boggy grounds on which all systematic Reformers hitherto have stood—. But be assured, that I shall give up this opinion with joy, & consider a truer view of the Question a more than recompense for the necessity of retracting what I have written—

God bless you— | Do pray let me hear from you, tho' only 3 lines.

S. T. Coleridge

768. *To Francis Wrangham*[1]

MS. Bodleian Library. Hitherto unpublished.

[*Circa* 14 June 1809][2]

. . . Wordsworth bade me leave a blank side for him—but that is now on the other side of possibility—He wants, I suppose, to send you an order for his Pamphlet, which I will write about in my next. Only I will say, that the first note is pitched at the height of the Instrument & the after strains never suffered to sink—so that I fear sadly, independent of the dead weight of the departed Cintra Convention—a dead weight to the '*Public*' spite of it's precious embalmment, that it may die of a plethora of the richest qualities of combined poetic & philosophic Genius.

S. T. Coleridge.

769. *To Thomas W. Smith*

Address: Tho. W. Smith, Esqre. | Stockwell Park | Surry
MS. New York Public Lib. Pub. E. L. G. ii. 1.
Postmark: 26 June 1809. *Stamped*: Kendal.

Grasmere, Kendal.
22 June, 1809

Dear Sir

The irregularity and circuitousness of our Grasmere Post is such, that I did not receive your letter till late on yesternight. Accept therefore this Explanation of my apparently slow acknowlegement

---

[1] This letter was probably addressed to Francis Wrangham, to whom Wordsworth wrote in April that he had not sent copies of the *Convention of Cintra* 'to any personal friends as such; therefore I have made no exception in your case'. On 12 June Wrangham wrote to Wordsworth: 'I hear nothing more of your political pamphlet—Is it out? . . . Coleridge promised me a few lines.' [*Middle Years*, i. 290 and MS. Dove Cottage.]

[2] Since the expressions concerning the *Convention of Cintra* in this fragment parallel those in Letter 767, it seems likely that the two letters were written about the same time.

of your kindness, instead of an Apology. I was affected by your Present, and receive it with feelings correspondent to those, with which it was sent; and still more by your approbation of the Principle, on which I have grounded 'The Friend.' Believe me, nothing but a deep and habitual conviction of it's Truth absolutely, and of it's particular Importance in the present generation could have roused me from that dream of great internal activity, and outward inefficience, into which ill-health and a wounded spirit had gradually lulled me. Intensely studious by Habit, and languidly affected by motives of Interest or Reputation, I found in my Books and my own meditations a sort of high-walled Garden, which excluded the very sound of the World without. But the Voice within could not be thrust out—the sense of Duty unperformed, and the pain of Self-dissatisfaction, aided and enforced by the sad and anxious looks of Southey, and Wordsworth, and some few others most beloved by me and most worthy of my regard and affection. Assuredly much happier & more truly tranquil I have already found myself, and shall deem myself amply remunerated if in consequence of my exertions a Few only of those, who had formed their moral creed on Hume, Paley, and their Imitators, with or without a belief in the facts of mere historical Christianity, shall have learnt to value actions primarily as the language & natural effect of the state of the agent; if they shall consider what they *are* instead of *merely* what they *do*; so that the fig-tree may bring forth it's own fruit from it's own living principle, and not have the figs tied on to it's barren sprays by the hand of outward Prudence & Respect of Character. These indeed are aids & great ones to our frailty, & it behoves us to be grateful for them & to use them; but let not the confidence in the gardner or his manures render us careless as to the health & quality of the *seed*. 'Would not the whole moral code remain the same on the principle of enlightened Selfishness, as on that of Conscience, or the unconditional obedience of the Will to the pure Reason?' has been asked more than once of me. My answer was: All possibly might remain the same, only not the men themselves for whom the moral Law was given.—But in truth I admitted more than was necessary, as I shall have occasion to prove at large.

Permit me to recommend to your Perusal a late Pamphlet written by my dear friend & house-mate, W. Wordsworth, 'Concerning the Relations of Great Britain, Spain & Portugal'—as containing sentiments & principles matured in our understanding by common energies & twelve years' intercommunion. The effect of national enthusiasm in the Spanish People is somewhat too much *idealized*—the introductory part respecting the Convention of

Cintra might with great advantage have been written in a more calm & argumentative *manner*—& throughout, the Note is pitched at the very height of the Instrument, and by the constant combination of deep thought with deep feeling the whole work, in order to be both understood & felt, requires more attention & more warmth of sensibility than can reasonably be expected from the Public Mind, effeminated, as it is, by the unremitted Action of great outward Events daily soliciting & daily gratifying the appetite of Curiosity. But still the defects are but the overflowings of Excellence. I have not often met with a book at once so profound & so eloquent.

After the third number of 'the Friend' the Paper will go on secure—as far as the nature of any weekly Essay permits—from interruption. But my finances had been exhausted in the purchase of Types, Advertisements, Prospectuses, and the Paper for the first four numbers, each sheet costing me fourpence half-penny & a small fraction, and all at once I found myself with paper sufficient only for two Numbers more, so suddenly had the Whale of self-offered Services, which I had mistaken for an Island, plunged away from under me—& the carriage of the Paper from London takes up nearly a fortnight. I had therefore to arrange the whole anew, by the agency of my kind friends, Thomas Clarkson, and Basil Montagu.—After the 20th number the Work will be able to move on it's own legs.

I have thought it right on my own account to mention this circumstance, to ward off suspicions of irregularity and (to *coin* a word) *unreliability* from myself, at least as far as relates to this instance.

If Choice or Chance should direct you hitherward, you will find both in this house at Grasmere, & with R. Southey at Keswick (13 miles from hence) house-room & heart- room, and a heaven without to those who have peace within.

That your Health may be restored to you, and your present Blessings preserved, is, dear Sir, the wish & prayer of your obliged & sincere Friend

S. T. Coleridge

770. *To John Brown*

Address: Mr. Brown | Bookseller | Penrith   *Single Sheet*
MS. Victoria and Albert Museum. Hitherto unpublished.
Stamped: Keswick.

[Late July 1809][1]

If there be too much, leave off with (to be continued)—Enough

---

[1] This letter, which accompanied copy for the conclusion of the third and the

for a second Number will be sent by Saturday's post—and a third
Number is already finished, and only waits till I can see whether
before Tuesday, I cannot send a Number to be interposed, or
printed first—Pray, ask Mr A. Harrison (to whom I will write to
morrow) to look over the Sheets, and send it out as soon as finished,
whenever that is—. I shall not rest till you have five numbers before
hand in your own possession.

S. T. Coleridge—

771. *To John Brown*

Address: Mr. Brown | Bookseller | Penrith
MS. Victoria and Albert Museum. Hitherto unpublished.

[Late July 1809][1]

This should have arrived at Penrith on Friday last—I will explain
this accursed accident tomorrow—for the Carrier is waiting—

S. T. C.[2]

772. *To John Brown*

MS. Victoria and Albert Museum. Hitherto unpublished.

[*Circa* 24 August 1809][3]

N.B. The *French* Note is to be placed as a Note to that passage in
which I say, that after reading Milton's Speech on the Liberty of the
Press we shall suspect, that the best argument for Licensing is to be
found in the incompatibility of Knowlege and a bad Government.[4]
—The other Notes according to their marks in the Text.

Pray be so good as carefully to examine the List of names on the
inky Paper inclosed, and see whether there are not some that are
not inserted in the Catalogue—Great Complaints are made of
Shepherd at Bristol.—

beginning of the fourth numbers of *The Friend*, probably belongs to late July,
since on 1 Aug. Dorothy Wordsworth wrote to De Quincey: 'Coleridge . . . has
sent off the 3rd and 4th numbers of *The Friend*'. *Middle Years*, i. 334.

  [1] This note, which accompanied copy for part of the fourth number of *The
Friend*, was probably written not long after Letter 770.

  [2] On the address sheet Coleridge added the following note: 'Mr Coleridge
presents best respects to Mr Janson, and intreats as a particular favor that he
will forward this to Penrith immediately —Mr B. will give the Bearer a Shilling,
if delivered in the course of Tuesday—'

  [3] This letter is written on copy for the last part of the fourth number of *The
Friend*. The copy contains a note on Charlemagne, the conclusion of which was
printed at the beginning of the fifth number.

  [4] Coleridge refers to a footnote on p. 58 of the fourth number of *The Friend*,
7 Sept. 1809.

Mr T. Poole, Nether Stowey, Bridgewater—has not received the third number—

I would not send any numbers to Kay of Liverpool, unless we hear from him. My friend, Mr Crump, is going home to Liverpool, & will enquire about it.—

I am not particularly anxious for the 4th number, till you have at least half of the 5th in possession—I shall send as much again as this, on Saturday, & the two first numbers corrected—

773. *To John Brown*

Address: Mr. Brown | Printer & Bookseller | Penrith
MS. Victoria and Albert Museum. Hitherto unpublished.

Sunday Night—[27 August 1809][1]
Dear Sir

The Subject will be finished in just two more of those pages— which will be sent off tomorrow—I would therefore be much obliged to you to let me know, in what part of a Number it will leave off. That I may fill up the remainder of that Number with some short Essay,[2] and so begin the Essay on the Constitution with a new Number—

You will now proceed as quickly as you can—I write again to-morrow more at full—for the Chaise-boy who is to take this to Keswick is waiting impatiently—

Your's &c
S. T. Coleridge.

[1] On the address sheet of this letter Sara Hutchinson added a note dated Monday Night, Augt. 28th.: 'Mr. Coleridge, being disappointed in sending the Essay off last night, has finished the subject.' Coleridge's letter accompanied copy for the last pages of the fifth and the opening pages of the sixth numbers of *The Friend*.

[2] For 'some short Essay' Coleridge substituted *The Three Graves* to fill out the sixth number. See next letter.

774. To John Brown

MS. Victoria and Albert Museum. Hitherto unpublished.

Monday Night, Grasmere. [11 September 1809][1]

Dear Sir

I assuredly would not have any more sent to Clement,[2] but instead of him to Longman what used to be sent to the former—& an advertisment shall appear to that purport.—I will write for more paper immediately—and therefore have not sent the two first numbers that are to be reprinted—. I have hereby sent what will be sufficient, I imagine, for one number[3]—and at the same time a poem, which with it's introductory matter will fill up the 8 or 9 pages wanting in that which is to precede it.[4]—At all events, contrive to bring it in, and if need be, print the poem not only without the *numbers* of the Stanza, but even without lines between the Stanzas. I shall never hereafter leave you without two numbers before hand, and I hope therefore that we shall hereafter go on regularly, so that they may be in London on Saturday morning.— Hitherto, it has been all my own fault.—I shall send copy every Friday Night by the Keswick Carrier, which will be booked & sent by the Penrith Coach on Saturday—You will therefore be so good, my dear Sir! as to let your Boy go for the parcel every Saturday Night—and it would be well perhaps if the *proofs* were sent to Mr Southey always on some one particular day.—

I remain, | dear Sir, | very sincerely your's,
S. T. Coleridge

---

[1] Coleridge's request to Brown to send to Josiah Wedgwood 'the third & fourth numbers, & so on henceforward' indicates that this letter was written after 7 Sept., the date of the fourth number of *The Friend*, and before 14 Sept., the date of the fifth number.

[2] A brief note from Charles Lamb to Brown explains Coleridge's irritation:

Temple
24 August 1809

[I] request you to send the *fourth number* of [The Fr]iend and *all succeeding numbers* to *Mr. Lamb No. 4 Inner Temple Lane, London* and to send the whole from the beginning, and so on, to *Mr. Rickman, New Palace Yard, Westminister,* & to *Capt. Burney, 26 James Street, Pimlico.* They have been ordered at Clement's in the Strand, & Mr. Clement refuses to send them, because he says it is an irregular publication.

Please to observe that *I* want no numbers before the 4th, but the other Gentlemen are to have all—

Your humble Servant
C. Lamb [MS. Dove Cottage]

[3] Copy for the seventh number, which appeared 28 Sept. 1809.

[4] The poem was *The Three Graves, A Sexton's Tale. A Fragment,* Parts III and IV, which concluded the sixth number of *The Friend,* dated 21 Sept. 1809.

P.S. Please to add at the Bottom of each number after your own name, & by Messrs. Longman, & Co. Paternoster Row, London.[1]—

The conclusion of the introductory matter to the Fragment over-leaf—And please to direct if his name is not down before, the third & fourth numbers, & so on henceforward to

Josiah Wedgewood, Esqre. | Etruria | Staffordshire—

775. *To Daniel Stuart*

Address: D. Stuart, Esqre | 36 Upper Brompton Row | Knightsbridge, London   *Single Sheet*
MS. British Museum. Pub. with omis. Letters from the Lake Poets, *171.*
Postmark: 15 September 1809.

Grasmere, Kendal—
Monday Night [11 September 1809]

Dear Stuart

I pray you, attribute to no other than the true causes my long silence, which indeed has not only not been intentional but most opposite to my intention—But I have been in a constant state of *perplexity*, and this to *me* is always a state of stupor during which day after day vanishes as in a dream.—I have not been idle or mis-employing my Industry: for I have been getting on with THE FRIEND, am months beyond the printer, and have been so far successful that there is no one of the Numbers that is not more entertaining and lively than the very best of the first five.—But I do not know what to do, with regard to the Paper—I have twice written to Brown to send me an accompt of all the stamped Paper which he has hitherto received—and the waiting for this in order to send it to you has been *one* among others of the temptations and *lulling* thoughts that enabled me to put off the writing to you, and indeed to every body else.—When I began the publication, I had foolishly taken it for granted that I could purchase the stamped paper for the first 20 weeks on credit—and so wretched and con-fused were the letters, I received both from Clarkson & Montagu, whom I had over & over again written to, begging & intreating that they would call on Fourdiniere, & settle it for me, that they left me in double darkness—and only by Montagu's last letter did I learn positively, that the paper could not be had but for ready money—

---

[1] The first four numbers of *The Friend* bore the imprint, 'Penrith: printed and published by J. Brown'; to the next four numbers was added, 'and sold by Messrs. Longman and Co. Paternoster Row, London'; beginning with the ninth number, 'and Clement, 201, Strand, London', was further added to the imprint at the specific request of Clement. [Clement's letter of apology, dated 7 Oct. 1809, is preserved in Dove Cottage.] The 'supernumerary' and twenty-first numbers, however, bore only the imprint of J. Brown.

In the meantime I had neither heart nor pretence to write to you who had already done every thing that had been done—Montagu is moneyless—and Clarkson, to whom indeed for very good reasons I had never applied or thought of applying to, and who squanders away his Wife's property as well as [his] own on very worthless Objects but on the other hand Objects & Persons whose Obligations to him feed and flatter his ostentation & love of feeling his superiority & power, had written me a refusal by anticipation in one of the most unfeeling letters, that ever man received: tho' it is & ever will be, I trust, a sacred law of conscience with me to see in Clarkson nothing but the great Agent in the abolition of the Slave Trade.—I have paper for just three Numbers more[1]—Brown informs me—& that CLEMENT refuses to send the work to Subscribers, or the Subscribers' names to me or to Brown—In short, I feel all over me like a Bird whose plumage is beclammied and wings glued to it's body with Bird-lime—What I can do by the exertion of all my intellectual powers, I was never more willing to do—but never less able to bear up against want of outward means aggravated by a consciousness of already heaped up & unrequited Obligations.—But in the letter which I have sent to Penrith to be inclosed in Brown's account of the Paper received & expended I have said all that I could in reply to your's more clearly.[2]—

I suffered great Anguish from the belief of Pasley's Death[3]—In order to make this Letter worth the Postage I have had transcribed certain passages from his three last Letters, written before & since the Expedition, for your own private amusement;[4] & because I see a greater tendency in the Courier to throw the blame on the E. of Chatham than I conceive just.—With a heavy heart I conclude, dear Stuart, your ever grateful & sincerely

affectionate Friend,
S. T. Coleridge.—

---

[1] i.e. through the seventh number of *The Friend*. (See Letter 785, p. 244, n. 1.) In replying to this letter on 25 Sept. from Cheltenham, Stuart said he had already sent 5,000 sheets at a cost of 'somewhere about 90£', and 'calculated' that the supply would suffice for eight numbers—a miscalculation, since Brown was then printing 644 copies of each number. Disregarding Coleridge's immediate need, Stuart filled his letter with advice and censure concerning the distribution of *The Friend* as a weekly newspaper rather than as a monthly publication, the breaking off of a number in the middle of a sentence, and Coleridge's 'anxiety about trifles'. [MS. Dove Cottage.]

[2] This letter Coleridge subsequently 'ordered back again'. See Letter 779.

[3] Charles William Pasley (1780–1861), a distinguished army officer, was present at the siege of Flushing. He led a storming party on 14 Aug. 1809, and was seriously wounded.

[4] As Coleridge promised, parts of three of Pasley's letters were copied out in this letter by Sara Hutchinson.

776. *To John Brown*

MS. Victoria and Albert Museum. Hitherto unpublished.

[*Circa* 14 September 1809][1]

Dear Sir

I hope, that this Copy will begin a number. At all events, if unfortunately this should not be the case (tho' if it can be effected by leaving out that *note* on the Sense, the Understanding, and the Reason,[2] and in what sense I use the words, leave it out by all means) but in case the preceding Copy should perforce overstride the bounds of No. 7—then at the head of this present Copy I would put—ESSAY the fifth[3]—and at the head of the Copy preceding, that on the different Systems of political Justice, *Essay* the fourth: for Nos. 3. 4. 5. & 6 form but one Essay.

Likewise, I should be greatly obliged to you immediately on the receipt of this to inform me whether it will make a *whole number*, that if not I may send off immediately a concluding paragraph that will compleat it.—According to my best calculation two lines of my friend's writing make three of the printed lines: consequently, supposing the same number of lines in the pages of each, 10 of the *MS.* would make 15 of the print—but there are commonly six lines more in the MSS page than in the other—equal to 9—but $10 \times 9 = 90$; equal to two full pages—Therefore 10 full *MSS* pages would make 17 pages print—were it not for the Notes, in which the Print has the advantage over the MSS.—In this Copy the 9 & 10 page[s] are not full—therefore I hope that the result will be just one Number—

I suspect, that Captn Wyatt, my Subscriber, was killed at Talavera—I would not therefore send any more with his Address— if he be alive, we shall soon hear from him—.

It would be well to write to all those who have had 6 or 12 copies sent to them to desire them to send all, that they have not sold or are likely to sell to Messrs. Longman & Co—and to send no more to them—I allude to the Newcastle [&] Liverpool Booksellers principally.—But above all, pray be so good as immediately to send me an account of all the stamped Paper received from the very first,

---

[1] In replying to this letter on 18 Sept. 1809, Brown writes that 'the sudden death of a brother has occasioned a delay of two days in the proof sheet being sent to Mr Southey, and also in answering your letter'. [MS. Dove Cottage.]

[2] This note was retained and appears on p. 107 of the seventh number of *The Friend*.

[3] 'The preceding Copy' did 'overstride the bounds of No. 7' and filled the first page and a third of the next number. Essay V, copy for which accompanied this letter, concluded the eighth number of *The Friend*, dated 5 Oct. 1809.

how much is used, & so forth—for Mr Stuart has written me a letter which I cannot answer without it.

S. T. C.—

P.S. And please to send a list of all the *Booksellers*, to whom the Friend has been sent hitherto, & the Numbers sent to each.—

777. *To John Brown*

MS. Victoria and Albert Museum. Hitherto unpublished.

Friday Night [22 September 1809][1]

Grasmere, Kendal.

Dear Sir

I truly condole with you on your Loss. I have myself suffered a similar Shock in the Death of my dear & highly respected Friend & Landlord, Mr W. Jackson of Keswick.—

The Copy, which I hereby send, I mean for No. 10—the last sent for No. 9.—for as what I intended for No. 7 will more than fill a sheet by about 3 pages or perhaps more with the Note, I shall on Tuesday or before if I have the opportunity, send you an Article to fill up the 12 remaining pages, so as to make No. 8.—Then the Essay on Luther &c will *begin* a Sheet, i.e. No. 9.[2]—

Be so good as to let me know immediately, for I have forgotten it—1. what Number of the Friend you print weekly—2. and what number is sent off—and (3) of those sent off what number is sent to Booksellers on chance of sale, the names of each of these Booksellers with the number sent to them—and be so good as to desire the Leeds Post Master to send back to you all the numbers sent to the imaginary Pearson. I have received a very civil Letter from Kaye of Liverpool, whom I have desired in answer to send back what he has not sold to you—& henceforward I would send one number only to him. The same I shall request of Mitchell—so that you will have enough of 1 & 2 Numbers to supply those who want them—. I pray you, let me hear from you immediately as to the three questions above—and believe me with sincere respect and well-wishing

your's &c

S. T. Coleridge

[1] The references to Brown's loss of his brother and to the death of William Jackson, who was buried on 19 Sept., establish the date of this letter. See Letter 776 and Southey, *Life and Corres.* iii. 251.

[2] The 'Essay on Luther' appeared in the eighth number of *The Friend*, and the copy accompanying this letter was used for the ninth number, dated 12 Oct. 1809.

I have sent back some odd Friends that had been sent to Mr De Quincey & shall send back the rest all but one of each when I can put my hands on them. You will continue to send *one* to him weekly—.

778. *To Daniel Stuart*

Address: [D. Stu]art, Esqre. | Upper Brompton Row | Knightsbridge | London
MS. British Museum. Pub. with omis. Letters from the Lake Poets, *173.* The top and bottom of pages 3 and 4 of the manuscript are cut off.
Postmark: 2 October 1809. *Stamped*: Keswick.

Grasmere, Kendal
Wednesday Night,
27 Septr. [1809]

Dear Stuart

Miss Hutchinson is copying out (what, I trust, you will think) an interesting Article for the Courier on the grounds of Hope and Fear in a War of a Nation against Armies as illustrated by the close analogy between the present Spanish Revolution and that of the Belgic Provinces against Philip the 2nd[1]—I have drawn my Facts from a very scarce & valuable Latin Work[2] written by a Contemporary, during the first 8 or 9 years of the Insurrection, a man of high Trust in the Spanish Diplomacy—consequently in the Hispano–Austrian Interest.—This article alone will convince you how little Watson's History of P. 2nd deserves the name of '*admirable*'—It is in truth a contemptible Book, the style villainous—but as to Industry and Research he is neither worse nor better than Hume & Robertson. It is to me a most painful Duty to be obliged to point out, as if Southey does not, I shall feel myself obliged to do, the shameful Carelessness and Idleness of our English Historians— Could you believe it ?—Yet you will see a splendid naval Victory of the English over the Spaniards recorded by a Spanish Historian, not one word about which is to be found in Hume, Carte, or Rapin!— nor in Watson! History has occupied but little of my attention; yet with my little knowlege derived from contemporary Writers, in the Latin, German, & Spanish Languages (which last I have lately made myself master of) I could fill an Octavo Volume with the blunders & omissions of Robertson & Watson—while Harte's

---

[1] Much of what follows in this paragraph appeared in Coleridge's first *Letter on the Spaniards*, in the *Courier*, 7 Dec. 1809.
[2] Michael Eytzinger: *De Leone Belgico eiusque topographica atque historica descriptione liber . . . F. Hogenbergii centum et XII. figuris ornatus; rerumque in Belgio maxime gestarum, inde ab anno Christi MDLIX. usque ad annum MDLXXXIII. perpetua narratione continuatus.* Coloniae Ubiorum, 1583 fol.

Gustavus Adolphus & Carlton's Memoirs (both of which I earnestly advise you to procure & carefully peruse) lie on stalls unread. That cursed phrase *the Dignity of History* has made our late histories nothing but pompous dull Romances—all must be beat down into one monotonous style, and all the life & reality & character of Men & things destroyed.—At the same time I send you another Letter from Pasley, which however you will be so good as to shew to no one, for reasons for which the Letter itself will present to you.—I shall draw from him immediately all his grounds for his Abandonment of his former opinion concerning Flushing—. One of the geniuses, of whom he gives so doleful a picture, I was introduced to at Gibraltar, & can pledge my own Experience for his being a rotten-ripe Blockhead.—De Quincey is going into Spain with a Mr Wilson, a neighbor of our's.—

And now for myself—. I have waited & hoped till my heart is sick for a Letter from you—I print weekly 644: of which 632 are sent off by the Post—Brown has received 4 separate Parcels of Paper—& there is now only enough remaining for another number. For God's sake do not abandon me now—need I say, that one of my great Objects in carrying on this work is to enable me to repay by degrees what I owe you—? and that after paying Brown, the whole of my receipts for the first 20 weeks shall be paid into your hands for the past paper and that which is to come—. At all events, do send to Brown immediately & *per coach* stamps for two numbers[1]—that I may have time to beg pecuniary assistance elsewhere;—if it be decidedly inconvenient to you to hold me up till I can walk of myself. God knows! it makes me so sick at heart that I must thus importune you, and throw the burthen of my wants on *you* wholly, that I feel my hand sink away from the paper while I write—But the repayment is certain in this case, and at the distance of but a few weeks—& without it I am ruined & disgraced where I might perhaps build myself up & recover the good opinion of all my friends respecting my perseverance & reliability.—It would be of the greatest service to me to have likewise 1500 Sheets of the same paper *unstamped*, in order that . . . & strike off the same num[ber] . . . Do pray let me hear from you.—I am fully aware, that the Numbers hitherto are in too hard and laborious a style; but I trust, you will find Nos. 7. 8. 9. & 10 greatly improved—& that every No.

---

[1] Stuart responded to this appeal on 5 Oct.: 'Last night I received your Letter & this day I have written to Green to send you 1,250 Stamps for 2 numbers as I promised. This will enable you to publish 10 numbers.' [MS. Dove Cottage.] Since Street sent Coleridge 1,500 stamped sheets '*per coach*' on the very day of Stuart's letter, this order was not filled when it reached the *Courier* office. See Letter 779, p. 228 n. 2.

after these will become more & more entertaining. I informed you of Clement's strange Behaviour—and to day I have received a Note from him complaining of the Non-receipt of *The Friend,* which *Lamb* informed Brown, he had refused to send out as 'an irregular work which he would have nothing to do with'.—

Be so good as to have the next Number advertised in the Courier, & some one other paper on some other day— . . .

We are all greatly dejected by the present state of men & measures, & the utter hopelessness of better—Good God! what a disgrace to the nation—a *Duel* between two Cabinet Ministers on Cabinet Disputes!![1] And not a Breathing of it's hideous Vulgarity & Immorality in any one of the Papers!—Is it possible, that such minds can be fit to govern the one of the two . . .

779. *To Daniel Stuart*

Address: D. Stuart, Esqre. | Stiles's Boarding House | Cheltenham *Single sheet.*
MS. British Museum. Pub. with omis. Letters from the Lake Poets, *178.*
Stamped: Kendal.

Saturday Night, 30 Septr. 1809. Grasmere, Kendal.

My dear Stuart

I received your's, of the 25th, this evening: just in time to direct my answer to Cheltenham. The Article on the Belgic & Spanish Revolutions I will send forthwith to Mr Street—.[2] Neither I nor any one of us can make out what letter you allude to as your *last* and as containing a plan of proceeding for me—The letter, which I sent to Brown for you, I ordered back again—indeed all my latter letters to you have been written in far too tumultuous & uneasy a state of mind.—With regard to the Work, the running of one Number into another I shall carefully avoid for the future, and if I cannot include the whole Subject in one No., I will take care to divide it, polypus-like, so that each part may have a head & tail of it's own— & I feel confident, that my Essays will increase in Interest. It was in the necessity of the Plan, and I stated it as such in the first No. p. 7, that my foundations could not be as attractive as I hoped to make the super-structure—My 12th Number will be on the vulgar

---

[1] The duel between Canning and Castlereagh took place on 21 Sept. 1809. Castlereagh was unharmed, Canning only slightly wounded.

[2] Coleridge refers again to his *Letters on the Spaniards,* which were published in the *Courier* on 7, 8, 9, 15, 20, 21, and 22 Dec. 1809, and 20 Jan. 1810.

Errors respecting Taxation, which I trust will be both interesting &
useful. For there are so many & such grievous evils in the constitution of our Government in all things relating to foreign affairs & our
external Empire, that it is of first-rate importance that the public
Discontent should not be diverted to false Objects.

The Letter, to which you refer, has been found—dated the 25th
of June last. As I read it, to my astonishment I found the most
important passages quite new to me—and on expressing this discovered that this was the letter which had been read to me one day
when I happened to be very unwell & in bed, and that these had not
been read under the notion of not agitating me at that time—& that
they had forgotten to apprize me of them afterwards.—I was additionally misled too by some mistake of both Wordsworth, Mrs, &
Miss Wordsworth, who had told me that you had written to W.
that you would after the 60£ advance the paper as far as the 20th
number—which yet I never *relied* on because you had never given
me any reason to suppose it, & the letter to W. so interpreted had
been destroyed or mislaid—Still in this your letter of June 25th you
were so good as to say that you would advance the paper for two
numbers beyond the 8th—which comes out on Thursday next, if
indeed there be paper even for that.[1] I print only 12 more than are
on the list—& of these 12 all have been sold to chance Customers.—
You are at Cheltenham—I think of writing immediately to Street,
asking him on my own account to send off paper for two numbers
per coach[2]—& in the course of the next 3 weeks, I trust, that I
shall be able to raise the money, from my Brother or from Poole—
My very bowels quiver at the thought of begging it—enough both
instantly to repay him & to get on till the 15th number when I will
call on my Subscribers.—Surely, tho' one third should not pay
me at the 20th Number, yet enough will do so to repay the stamps—
and then if it appears advisable, I may change the plan. But I

---

[1] No such letter has come to light, but Stuart's letter of 7 July 1809 makes
the same point: 'On Wednesday last went off by the Kendall Waggon directed
Mr Cookson Kendall, as the preceding Parcel, 1250 Stamps; and on Friday went
off another Parcel containing 1250 more, so that you have now enough for 8
numbers in all, & I will send sufficient for 2 more before it is wanted.' [MS.
Dove Cottage.]

[2] Coleridge did write to Street, who replied on 5 Oct.: 'I could not get any
Paper stamped for you till today: having been obliged to send it into the
Stamp Office—It is gone off by the Coach this Afternoon & I hope you will re-
ceive it safe—I am much obliged to you for the Article you promise me which
I expect with Impatience—The remainder of your Note to [*The Friend*] No. 4
[on Charlemagne] I shall quote soon in the Courier.' [MS. Dove Cottage.]
See p. 244 n. 2. Street's remarks seem to disprove a misleading sentence of
Stuart's in the *Gentleman's Magazine* for June 1838: 'In the Courier Mr. Street,
the editor, . . . did not require or encourage his [Coleridge's] services.'

am so agitated that I must defer what I have to say to another time—

God bless you & your's most affectionately

S. T. Coleridge[1]

780. *To Daniel Stuart*

Address: D. Stuart, Esqre. | Styles' Boarding House | Cheltenham *Single Sheet*
MS. British Museum. Pub. E. L. G. ii. 8.
Stamped: Keswick.

2 Octr. 1809

My dear Stuart

I am confident, that in the present Business you will confine the Right and Wrong as far as it concerns me to the present business. The mortification, I endure, in consequence of my *misapprehension* (which I am sure you would think very venial if you could, as I have just now done, read over again all your letters to me from the first starting of the plan of THE FRIEND) is a sufficient proof, how little I could have been capable of wittingly & foreknowingly bringing myself within the possibility of pressing upon you against & beyond your own inclinations. It never occurred to me to make you, or to wish, or even to permit you, to be responsible for the Paper & Stamps *in general*—the utmost of my expectations, and these not formed by myself but arising out of your own letters (misapprehended, it appears; but so *I* understood them) was: that as you had kindly made me a present of the first 1250 sheets, and had allowed me to appropriate the 60£ received from the R. Institution to the purchase of the stamps, that you might have helped me out till the 15th or 20th number—as subtracting the 1250 stamps & the 60£, it seemed scarcely possible that out of 600 Subscribers & odd, enough should not pay me to settle the balance with you immediately after the 20th week. *Beyond* that time, I never dreamt of either soliciting or even accepting assistance: because if the Work did not then move forward on it's own legs, I of course should either give it up or alter the form & plan of publication.—It is not quite accurate, dear Stuart! that I was well aware of my present embarrassments—on the contrary, I did fully expect that after I had purchased a number of stamps & continued the publication a sufficient time to invest me with a sort of trades-man's character, that I should be able to purchase the remainder at

---

[1] In pages 2, 3, and 4 of the MS. Sara Hutchinson copied out a letter from C. W. Pasley. After her transcript Coleridge added, 'I need not say, that you will not shew this Letter to any one'.

a quarter of a year's Credit.—And after various commissions at length from Montagu's half intelligible Letter I half understood, that they must be paid for in ready money, & fully understood that Montagu was the last man, I ought to have applied to, on a matter of Business. And yet I had no one else to whom I could write.—

Still however, in your letter of the 25th [June], you say you will advance me the Stamps for two numbers beyond the 8th—while in another part of the letter but for that passage you seem to *imply* that you would go a little farther—yet if those two Numbers—i.e. 1300, had been sent, I should not be in my present state of perplexity & distress.—I have been begging hard, & doubt not that tho' dearly, very dearly earned by sufferings of sickening humiliation, I shall receive the means of going on, after the 10th Number—but if Street does not comply with my request, & send down paper for the 9th & 10th, all is as good as over.

As I am so far beforehand with The Friend I should have been right glad to have worked for THE COURIER & have sent it two Essays weekly on a variety of subjects too much connected with persons & immediate Events to fit them for my own work—so as to have greatly reduced at least the final balance at the 20th week—& Street will see from the Article sent to him how far I should be likely to serve the paper. But I suppose, the great sale of the Courier raises it above the want of literary assistance; and I could not write in any strict harmony with the tone predominant in the leading paragraphs of late. However, if he thought that what *I* with my principles as Anti-jacobin, Anti-buonaparte &c as his own, but with a dread & contempt of the present Ministry only less than that of the last, would be serviceable, I would undertake to furnish him two Columns twice a week for the next 12 weeks—sometimes taking the events of the Day & sometimes retrospective matter—for instance, the State of Sweden & the causes of it's present condition —of Russia, concerning which I have received valuable information [from] a gentleman lately arrived who had been resident in Petersburgh [for] years—of Germany in general—of Spain—& the Mediterranean.—Whatever you may think of this plan, you will agree with me that the Courier need a little *brightening up.*—

But whatever may or may not come of all this, the Friend inclusive, let me conjure you, dear Stuart, not to suffer any of these things to connect permanent feelings of displeasure or diminished kindness with my name in your mind—indeed, indeed, if you could read my heart, it would be impossible—For I am, as I always have been,

most sincerely & affectionately your obliged & grateful Friend,

S. T. Coleridge

781. *To Daniel Stuart*

Address: D. Stuart, Esqre. | Stiles's Boarding House | Cheltenham
MS. British Museum. Pub. with omis. Letters from the Lake Poets, *184.*
Stamped: Keswick.

9 Oct. 1809—

My dear Stuart

Among my faults that of feeling offence, even at the moment,
from advice given me with any tolerable kindness, was never one:
and from you I have never received any advice without a sense of
affection & pleasure.—But indeed, indeed, in the present instance
you have supposed a motive in my mind, of which I had never
dreamt. From the commencement of the Friend to the present hour
I have never heard one word concerning it, either by letter or by
word of mouth, except some *raptures* from Lady Beaumont, and a
passage in Mr Wedgewood's letter corresponding with your's concerning it's occasional Obscurity, & the error of running one number
into another.—In Grasmere, & with such a circuitous post, & seeing
the Courier only very irregularly, never seeing any review, & having
no literary correspondence, what difference could there be between
a week & a month to my vanity—supposing it interested—whereas
heaven knows! I have been agitated by too many painful thoughts
to have room for so pleasant a feeling, as I rather guess than know
it to be, with respect to literary Matters.—I have read over all your
letters—at first, your advice was decisively in favor of the present
plan—afterwards, you doubted—in a third letter, your opinions
were balanced—but the trembling of the Scale was rather against
it—but by that time I had four hundred Subscribers on the present
plan, without the least certainty that they would continue so on
any other—and this was my sole motive added to the conviction,
which some of your former arguments had produced both on my
mind and on Wordsworth's[1]—And still, I confess, that if the Work

---

[1] The Stuart letters preserved at Dove Cottage substantiate Coleridge's statement. On 26 Jan. 1809, for example, Stuart wrote: 'I received your Letter a
few days ago, in which I see you prefer the Newspaper to the Pamphlet,—
quite with my concurrence. I had no other reason for enlarging about the
Pamphlet, than that it seemed to have been your own original Plan, which I
had led you from, that it came nearer to the idea of a *Book*, your ultimate object,
that there would be less risk or loss in printing a number on speculation, and
that the inconveniences of a Newspaper in giving Bonds &c would be avoided.
The expence of the Stamp is in reality nothing to you. If you had printed as a
Pamphlet you must have been at the expence of [one] and the half sheet, which
would have been equivalent to the Expence of the Stamp. And the Newspaper
has this great convenience, great indeed it is, that one man can put your whole
publication into the Postoffice, & in a minute say,—there ;—all your Customers
are served, served regularly & infallibly.' Stuart went on to assert that $3\frac{1}{2}$ pence
for the stamp, 1 penny for the paper, and $\frac{1}{2}$ penny for the publisher would leave

goes on, it seems to me the better—to mention one among others more important—because there are a number of persons who like to have the *Newspaper feeling* of receiving a paper at their own doors without trouble on a particular day. The error of running one number into another I shall avoid as much as possible—& yet how often does Cobbett break off & recommence—or did at least— for I have not seen his Journal for many many months. Any other Lapses will never recur from any fault of mine—& were pardonable in the commencement of a work under so many disadvantages.— So with regard to the Prospectuses, as I have more than once told you, it was not *I* or *my* restlessness; but the number of Letters which I received—'Without prospectuses I can do nothing; with them I am sure of gaining you 30—50—one said, 100—subscribers' —Now, my dear Stuart! I appeal to yourself, whether being new to an Undertaking & receiving such boisterous requests, you might not have mildly echoed them, without any restlessness, or precipitancy of idle *doingness*, in your own mind.[1]

O dear friend! it would be far, far better for me if I had a little more of that vanity, a little more interest in the opinions, people entertain of my talents &c—instead of it's being all up hill work with me! I once was fond of feeling my power perhaps in conversation—tho' even then it was more than one half a pleasure in

'7d each number' to pay the printer and for profit. Later, Stuart was less certain about the advantages of the newspaper. 'I observe', he wrote on 14 Feb., 'that I still think the Pamphlet plan has its advantages. (I *do not say beyond* the Newspaper Plan.) If Longman printed & published as a Pamphlet, taking only 5 per cent & his profits as a Bookseller, you would have no sort of trouble beyond producing your MS. & you would require no money to go on with. For Longman would no doubt deem himself well served by seeing a List of your Subscribers & knowing that they were to pay their money to him. . . . I merely state these circumstances, hoping they will not bewilder you. Either plan has its advantages. For my own part I cannot decide.'

[1] Stuart had written to Coleridge on 5 Oct.: 'The Plan I proposed was that you should constitute Longman or some such Person your Agent in London for receiving Subscriptions, that he should provide the Stamps for the next 5 numbers & that in the 15th number you should request payment of your Subscribers for 20 Numbers, a step which would soon reimburse your Agent & enable you of yourself to go on. . . . I have been from the beginning of opinion & am now more confirmed in it, that your plan is a bad one. You should publish once a month without a Stamp. You see the difficulties arising from printing on Stamps & what good purpose does it answer? Why, that the numbers as soon as printed go instantly to the hands of the Customer. . . . Excuse me for saying that this desire of instant circulation seems to me to arise from a fee[ling] unworthy of you, a desire of producing on the public and receiving on yourself an instant impression. . . . I once or twice had almost likened your anxiety about the Prospectuses before your plan was thoroughly settled, to a gig horse I had. . . . He was extremely restless & eager to proceed while waiting at the Door . . . but before he had gone a mile he became quite sluggish.' [MS. Dove Cottage.]

sympathy, as was proved by my never taking but one side of a question & always talking in full earnest—but be it what it will, even that is past away!—

I doubt not, I shall be able to get on till the 20th number— before that time, I shall address my Subscribers & at the time of their payment collect their suffrages whether they would prefer the work monthly at a hundred pages & subtracting the stamp—but surely, you are not aware of the *rapacity* of the London Book- sellers—35 per cent is the least, they take away from the Author— & supposing I sold 100 pages at 2S—6D—& 35 per cent were taken from it—what should I gain, when the very nature both of my work & of my mind precludes an extensive sale ?—

Would to God, I could but *talk* with you tho' it were only for an hour—for Letters do little more than multiply misunderstandings.

My heart aches at the state of the Country! Two cabinet mini- sters *duelling* on cabinet measures—it is wringing the dregs for the last drops of degradation. But to combine a constitution altogether fitted for legal freedom, tranquillity, & commercial activity *at home* with the production of individual greatness, & with the choice of the very man for the very place in all departments—both which are necessary for maintaining our empire & dignity *abroad*—is a state-riddle, that yet remains to be solved. The sole good in the power of individuals is to enlighten the mind of the public as far as they can, & to draw off the well-intentioned from false scents.

God bless [you] & your affectionate & sincere

S. T. Coleridge[1]

[1] As if to compensate for the tone of his recent letters and for the dilatory way in which he had sent stamped paper, Stuart wrote on 10 Nov.: 'Green is getting 1250 ready for you, which with 1250 unstamped Paper go off on Tuesday by the Waggon.' This letter ends Stuart's connection with *The Friend*.

Stuart had sent 5,000 sheets of stamped paper in Mar., May, and June, Street 1,500 in Oct.—6,500 in all. Since the first 1,250 forwarded by Stuart were a gift, they are not included in the *Courier* account now in the British Museum. This account shows:

3,750 stamps, paper, etc. (Stuart)	£73.	13s.	6d.
1,500 ,, ,, ,, (Street)	£31.	2s.	5d.
5,250 ,, ,, ,,	£104.	15s.	11d.
Cash from the Royal Institution	£60.		
Balance due	£44.	15s.	11d.

It would seem that Coleridge cancelled this indebtedness by contributing to the *Courier* his eight *Letters on the Spaniards*.

Below the *Courier* account Stuart added: '1250 Stamps & Paper *previously* —£24 9 2. Subsequently Novr.—£38.' (The latter amount should be £31. 11s. 8d., the cost of 1,250 stamps and 2,500 sheets of paper.) A second note of Stuart's reads: 'It appears D. S. advanced upwards of 100£ for Stamps & Paper . . . beyond the 60 rec'd.' This estimate includes the *Courier* balance and the cost of both the *gift* parcel and the *unsolicited* paper sent in Nov.

782. *To Thomas Poole*

Address: T. Poole, Esqre. | N. Stowey | Bridgewater | Somerset
MS. British Museum. Pub. with omis. Letters, *ii. 550.*
Stamped: Keswick.

9 Oct. 1809

My dear Poole

I received your's late last night—& sincerely thank you for the contents. The whole shall be arranged as you have recommended.[1] Yet if I know my own wishes, I would far rather you had refused me & said you should have an opportunity in a few days of explaining your motives *in person*—for O! the autumn is divine here—You never beheld, I will answer for it, such combinations of exquisite *beauty* with *sufficient* grandeur & elevation, even in Switzerland.— Besides, I sorely want to *talk* with you on many Subjects.

All the defects, you have mentioned, I am perfectly aware of and am anxiously endeavouring to avoid. There is too often an *entortillage* in the sentences & even the thoughts, which nothing can justify; and, always almost, a stately piling up of *Story* on *Story* in one architectural period, which is not suited to a periodical Essay or to Essays at all (Lord Bacon, whose style mine more nearly resembles than any other, in his greater works, thought Seneca a better model for his Essays) but least of all suited to the present illogical age, which has in imitation of the French rejected all the *cements* of language; so that a popular Book is now a mere bag of marbles, i.e. aphorisms and epigrams on one subject. But be assured, that the Nos. will *improve*—indeed, I hope that if this dire stoppage have not prevented it, you will have seen proof of improvement already in the 7th & 8th numbers—still more in the 9,10,11,12,13, 14, 15th.—Strange! but the three Graves is the *only* thing, I have yet heard generally praised & enquired after!!—Remember, how many different guests I have at my round Table.—I *groan* beneath the *Errata*; but I am 30 miles, cross post, from my Printer & Publisher, and Southey, who has been my corrector, has been strangely oscitant—or—which I believe is sometimes the case, has not understood the sentences, & thought, they might have a meaning for *me* tho' they had not for him.—There was one direful one, No. 5. p. 80.

---

[1] Letter 798 shows that Poole, 'in order that he might be more sure of his money', agreed to 'advance a third of the stamps wanted' on condition that Coleridge arrange to have the subscriptions for the first twenty numbers of *The Friend* paid to George Ward in London. Poole further insisted that Coleridge advise his subscribers of this mode of payment in a future number of *The Friend*. Coleridge did so in the sixteenth number, ignorant of the fact that Poole had neither sought Ward's permission nor apprised him of the proposal. See also Letters 789, 793, and 799.

l[ines] 3 and 4.—Read—it's *functions* being to take up the *passive affections* of the Senses into distinct THOUGHTS and JUDGEMENTS, according to it's own essential *forms:* formae formantes, in the language of Lord Bacon in contradistinction to the formae formatae.—

My greatest difficulty will be to avoid that GRIEVOUS defect of running one No. into another: I not being present at the Printing. To really cut down or stretch out every subject to the Procrustes Bed of 16 pages is not possible without a sacrifice of my whole plan —but *most often* I will divide them polypus-wise, so that the first Half should get itself a new Tail of it's own, and the latter a new Head—& *always* take care to leave off at a paragraph.—With my best endeavors I am baffled in this respect of making one Essay fill one number. The 10th No. is—W. thinks—the most interesting— 'On the errors of both Parties: or extremes meet'—& do what I would, it stretched to 7 or 8 pages more—but I have determined to take your advice *in toto* and shall announce to the public that with the exception of my Volume of political Essays & State-Memorials, & some technical works of Logic & Grammar I shall consider THE FRIEND as both the Reservoir & the living Fountain of all my mind, i.e. of both my powers & my attainments—& shall therefore publish all my poems in THE FRIEND, as occasion rises.—I shall begin with the Fears in Solitude & the Ode on France which will fill up the remainder of No. 11[1]—so that my next Essay on vulgar Errors concerning Taxation, in which I have alluded to a conversation with you, will just form No. 12 by itself—

I have been much affected by your efforts respecting poor Blake —Cannot you with propriety give me that Narrative?—But above all, if you have no *particular* Objection, no *very* particular & *insurmountable* reason against it—do, do let me have that divine narrative of Robert Walford, which of itself stamps you a Poet of the first Class in the *pathetic* & the *painting* of Poetry, so very rarely combined[2]—

As to politics, I am sad at the very heart. Two Cabinet Ministers *duelling* on Cabinet Measures, like drunken Irishmen—O heaven, Poole! this is wringing the Dregs in order to drink the last drops of degradation. Such base insensibility to the awefulness of their situation & the majesty of the Country!—As soon as I can get them transcribed, I will send you some most interesting letters from the ablest Soldier, I ever met with—Extra-aid de Camp to Sir J. Moore

[1] Instead of these poems, Coleridge printed his *Hymn before Sun-rise* in the eleventh number of *The Friend.*

[2] In the manuscript Poole altered Robert to John. For extracts from his narrative of John Walford, see *Thomas Poole,* ii. 234–7.

—& shot thro' the Body at Flushing, but still *alive*![1] —they will serve as a Key to more than one Woe-trumpet in the Apocalypse of national Calamity.—But the truth is: that to combine a government every way fitted, as our's is, for Quiet, Justice, Freedom, & commercial Activity *at home* with the conditions of raising up that individual Greatness, and of securing in every department the very man for the very place, which are requisite for maintaining the safety of our Empire & the Majesty of our Power, *abroad*, is a state-riddle which yet remains to be solved.—I have thought myself as well employed as a private Citizen can be, in drawing off well-intentioned Patriots from the wrong Scent & pointing out *what* the *true* Evils are & *why*—& the exceeding difficulty of removing them without hazarding worse—

I have written to Brown concerning the Bishop of Bath & Wells —I will take care when all the Numbers have been reprinted, to have a copy sent to him, with my respectful &c—. To day, I shall write to Charles Danvers at Bristol—Shepherd has used me most cruelly—the fault is entirely with him who has not sent the names—. I was asked for a motto for a *market*-clock—I uttered the following literally without a moment's premeditation—

> What now, O Man! thou dost, or mean'st to do,
> Will help to give thee Peace or make thee rue,
> When hovering o'er the Dot this Hand shall tell
> The moment, that secures thee HEAVEN or HELL![2]

May God bless you!—My kindest remembrances to Mr Chubb— & to Ward—& pray remember me when you write to your Sister & Mr King.—O but, Poole! do stretch a point, & come.—If the F. rises to 1000, I will *frank* you. Do, come—never will you have layed out money better.

783. *To George Coleridge*

Address: Revd G. Coleridge | Ottery St Mary | Honiton | Devon
MS. Lady Cave. Pub. E. L. G. ii. 10. This letter drew from George Coleridge an angry refusal of assistance on the basis of Coleridge's own bitter letter of 11 May 1808. See Letter 788 for Coleridge's efforts to effect a reconciliation.

Grasmere, Kendal.
Oct. 9th. 1809.

Dear Brother

It would have been well if I had answered your kind letter on the day of it's arrival, as I meant to have done; but I was prevented by

---

[1] C. W. Pasley.   [2] *Poems*, i. 414.

the old cause, the wish of writing to you at large, and the having so
many things in my mind, all of which I equally desired to communicate. I was pleased and affected by the letter; tho' the phrase
of 'taking the liberty' was not becoming for me to read, and out of
your character & relation to me to write. I am, & was at the very
first number of The Friend, sensible of my defect in facility of
Style, and more desirous to avoid obscurity than successful in the
attempt. Habits of abstruse and continuous thought, and the
almost exclusive perusal of the Greek Historians & Philosophers,
of the German Metaphysicians & Moralists, and of our English
Writers from Edward VIth to James IInd, have combined to render
my sentences more *piled up* and *architectural*, than is endurable in
so illogical an age as the present, in which all the cements of Style
are dismissed, and a popular Book is only a sequence of epigrams
and aphorisms on one subject. Too often my Readers may justly
complain of involution and *entortillage* in my style, tristem nescio
quam et impexam antiquitatem.[1] But I flatter myself, that the
Numbers have already become less faulty in these respects, and
that as I proceed, not only will the Essays themselves become more &
more interesting and even entertaining, but the style likewise more
graceful, and equally remote from the long-winded periods of our
thoughtful Ancestors and the asthmatic sententiolae of the French
School, syllabis perpetuo ad eundem numerum distributis, modu-
lationi similiores quam sermoni. This is what I have to adduce in
palliation of myself, and acknowlegement of the defect from excess;
what I have to say in *defence* of myself, will appear shortly as the
introduction to my ethical disquisitions. It should not however be
forgotten, that I am making an experiment whether throughout
the Kingdom a sufficient number of readers can be found for a
periodical Work, which does not appeal to Curiosity, or Personality; that it is essential to my plan, that I should first lay the
foundations well, but the merit of a foundation is it's depth and
solidity—the ornaments and conveniences, the pictures, and gilding,
and stucco-work, the Sunshine and the sunshiny Prospects will
come with the superstructure, if it be the will of Providence that I
should live & possess the means of carrying the work forward.

I can scarcely conceive a man so fully employed as not to have
time for writing a letter, which he ought to write; but I know that
he may easily want the *leisure* of thought & feeling to do it. This has
been my case for the last month and more. When I commenced THE
FRIEND I had taken it for granted, that after I had continued it for
a sufficient length of Time, and purchased a sufficient quantity of

---

[1] Tacitus, *Dialogus*, 20, 3.

the stamped paper (each sheet costs me, carriage included, five-pence) to invest me with a sort of *Tradesman's character*, that I should then be able to purchase the rest on credit—especially as I required only credit for 15 weeks, and this only for the first 25 weeks. Besides, I had received the warmest promises from a gentleman who owes—(& he used to acknowlege it to others as well as in his letters to myself)—a very large fortune not indeed *exclusively* to my efforts but so far that without them he could have done nothing—& what I did for him was shewn by the fact, that when I began to undertake the literary part of the concern, the sale was 1100, & barely paid itself—when I left it, it was net 8000£ a year, and the sale exceeded what had ever been known in a similar Concern.—I had to purchase my own Types—and bought with my own money 70£ worth of stamped paper, and I had 1250 sheets sent to me, as a *present*, in addition to the 70£s' worth—& in a letter to Mr Wordsworth the Gentleman above mentioned promised that he would advance the stamped paper for the remainder of the first 20 numbers, when the work would go on on it's own legs—no very great stretch of Friendship—as if out of 640 subscribers, a hundred and ten only paid me at the appointed time (20th No.) he was certain of the repayment in 12 or 13 weeks.—After this promise I received a letter from him blaming my plan, which he himself had advised as the better on the whole, and limiting his assistance to four or 5 numbers beyond what the 70£+the 1250 Sheets extended to—i.e. 7 numbers and a half—and now has left London on a tour without sending me a single sheet, and I myself absolutely penniless, and what has affected me more, under the necessity of suffering Mrs Coleridge to pay for Hartley & Derwent's Board & this year's annuity to her worthy and almost bed-ridden Mother (a pious & afflicted woman who forty years ago brought 10,000£ as her marriage dowry, & yet has drank up the Cup of affliction for three fourths of that Time to the very dregs). I have no one to apply to except Mr T. Poole—& tho' I never received a pecuniary loan from him but once, and that duly repaid, yet I have no reliance that he will step forward—tho' he is a truly good and indeed excellent man;—but in the *natural* man of the very best of us there is a *speck!*

Not only does The Friend promise to succeed, and bring in a net profit—even tho' the Sale should not increase when I have the means of advertising it properly—of 500£ annually, allowing a 100£ for bad debts &c; but I have a large volume of Poems, another of political Memoirs & Statistic Papers on Naples, Malta, Sicily, Egypt and the Coast of Africa, my Greek & English Accidence, Vocabulary of Terminations, & Gr. & E. philosoph. Grammar, and Introduction to Logic with the History of Logic from Zeno to the French Pseudologicians, Condilliac &c,[1] which are ready for the Press as soon as I can procure the Paper—for it is a hard & indeed to Mrs C. and my Children an unjust thing to sell the Copy-rights for a mere trifle perhaps, when I have a fair chance of selling the Editions, after they are printed, to the Booksellers, at a price little [short] of what they would advance as the Copy-right—especially a[s the] latter [work]s are of a Nature to sell regularly rather than in a Gu[st,] and as the sale will be favored by every increase of my literary repu[tation.] In the meantime I lose 30 shillings every week for want of un-stamped paper of the same size & sort with the stamped, to work off 120 copies of each number for Book-sale & in order to supply New Subscribers—the whole of the 8 numbers must be reprinted—for (on account of the stamps) I print at present six only beyond the names on the List—& there is not a single compleat set at the publisher's.

What I wish, is to have 120£ advanced, between two or three friends, in the first place—and immediately to arrange all the pay-ments to be made to Mr Poole's Partner's Brother (G. Ward, Book-seller, Skinner Street, Snow Hill, London) with instructions to repay [them] out of the first receipts—and to supply the paper for the next numbers with the remainder—and this being repaid, to borrow 100£ on interest for one year, in order to print the two Volumes of Poems & Political Essays—which however I would repay *immediately*, if I succeeded in obtaining a hundred Sub-scribers for the volumes, or if the Booksellers purchased the first Edition at half the Sale price, allowing me 100 copies for the Subscribers.—

It is *bitter* for a man with children, & a wife likely to survive him many years, to see others reap the main harvest of his efforts, and those who are already opulent. I might, doubtless, free myself from all these embarrassments by signing over the Property of The Friend to Longman, and receiving a salary of 300£ a year, as the Author, during it's continuance—but how could I answer this to my family? Especially, as the after-sale, when the work is finished, will probably increase & become of importance: as was the case with the Rambler, and as excepting the Grammatical & Logical Works above stated, the Friend will be the outlet of my whole *reservoir* as well as of the living Fountain—till it shall be dried up.—I might too help myself on, (but for this immediate stoppage which will be a cruel injury to the Work, & will be supposed my own fault—and it is not amiss, that I should be punished for former faults of

---

[1] In 1803 Coleridge had outlined a projected work on logic, under the title, *Organum verè Organum, or an Instrument of practical Reasoning.* See Letters 504 and 505.

procrastination &c when I should most feel it—i.e. in a case where
I was not in fault—unless belief of written promises is a fault,
promises to the breach of which no neglect, no irregularity, no
offence whatever, of my own, has contributed—) I might, I say, if
I can but raise the money for two or three numbers only, help myself on by writing for a party Newspaper for the next quarter of a
year—as I am *so far* beforehand with the Friend—at five guineas
an Essay, but I can hardly reconcile it to my Conscience, tho' I hope,
I need not say that my own Essays would be written in the spirit of
Sincerity & Good will: but what then? I am wittingly assisting
with all my powers the sale & influence of what I do not approve on
the whole—and I cannot at all reconcile it to my feelings, in this
precious & ripe time of my intellectual Manhood to waste the
powers which the Almighty entrusted to me, & the knowlege
which he has permitted me to acquire by a life of Study & Meditation with all the advantages of Travel & various situations, on the
events & passions of the Day.

I hope, you receive the Friend regularly and please myself by
anticipating that you will be gratified by the 7th, 8th, 9th, 10th,
13th & 14th numbers.—As soon as I am in a state of tolerable
tranquillity I will write to my nephews—I passed a *happy* day with
the Tutor of Baliol on Windermere, the enthusiastic manner in
which he spoke of John Coleridge, & the high praise he gave to both
the Cousins had raised my spirits so much beyond their common
pitch!—I should be very glad t[o rec]eive my school-boy poems, as
my friends here are ve[ry anxio]us to see them as curiosities.

With every feeling of [love to] all I remain, dear Brother,
[Y]our affectionate & obliged
S. T. C.

784. *To Richard Sharp*

MS. Cornell University Lib. Hitherto unpublished.

10 Octobr. 1809
My dear Sir

This is not the time to obtrude on you, busy and anxious as you
must needs be in these days of ministerial imbecillity and national
jeopardy. A friend of mine, at once a gallant soldier, and a man of
great and various erudition, has communicated to me information
respecting our movements at Flushing, (where he was first bayonet-
ted in the thigh, and still pressing onward in storming a fort, shot
thro' the body, but thank God! is still alive—) information, that is
a key to more than one Woe-trumpet in the Apocalypse of British
Dishonor. But I suspect, that to combine a government altogether

fitted for tranquillity, legal freedom, & commercial activity *at home*
with the causes and conditions of that individual Greatness and that
selection, in every department, of the very man for the very place,
which are requisite for maintaining our *external* empire, and the
splendor of our Arms *abroad*, is a state-riddle which yet remains to
be solved. At least, every means, I have yet seen suggested for
removing the Evils, we all groan under, seem[s] to me necessarily
super-inductive either of pure Democracy, or pure Oligarchy. And
yet the present circumstances of Europe demand no ordinary
sacrifices.—Of the existing ministry the People think with a contempt and indifference truly alarming: for mean as the *men* may be,
their *situations* cannot but be objects of deepest solicitude to every
thinking patriot.—Good God! two CABINET Ministers *duelling* on
CABINET Measures!! Why, it is wringing the Dregs for the last drops
of Degradation. Depend on it, the Country at large is a *moral*
Country, and tho' ordinary statesmen may sneer with contempt at
causes, which cannot be reduced to local or personal facts, yet this
base insensibility to the awefulness of their ministerial character
will work and is working. 'There is an invisible power (says one of
our elder Biographers) in Right and Wrong', and the opinion of the
people is more operant when it acteth like a silent Epidemic in the
air than when it foameth & roareth like a Torrent: to which every
man can point, and cry: *There* it is!—Lords Grey & Grenville
appear to me to have acted with equal Wisdom & Dignity. Yet I
tremble at the report, that these Statesmen deem a peace with the
French PANTARCH necessary—or to speak more properly, POSSIBLE.
—When the present men came into power, I exclaimed—'God
preserve us from the vigor of Impotence and the bustle of Incapa-
city!' With the same words (substituting *redeem* for *preserve*) I shall
accompany their Exit. As my friend, P. well remarked, the History
of our military Failures is short and palpable—For how should
Expeditions not fail, which with a true *preposterousness* are planned
by Rashness and executed by Procrastination?—If you have not
already perused them, do let me recommend to you three books,
Harte's Gustavus Adolphus, Carlton's Memoirs (containing the best
account of Lord Peterborough's Campaign) and David Lloyd's
State-Worthies: which latter book should be the Manual of every
public man, tho' there are scarcely 20 pages in succession which do
not contain a contradiction, and though the Author is a mere ape
of Bacon & Machiavel—but he, who cannot select what suits himself and the times, is not destined to *rise* in the World—tho' alas!
under an old Monarch he may be *raised* by the pullies of Court
Favor and that Spirit of Panic, which never fails to haunt the
Philo-despotists of a mixed Constitution.

So much for public affairs.—The Friend goes on well. The first six numbers are justly chargeable with obscurity and a too frequent *entortillage* of Style—and my readers have right to complain of 'tristem nescio quam et impexam antiquitatem'. However, be assured, it will improve both in lightness of style and interest of subject. But without any fault of my own, unless the Belief of written promises be a fault, I have been all at once left like a stranded Fish by one who for many reasons ought not to have deserted me at all—much less without warning, and just at the time that I had spent my last shilling in the purchase of the stamped paper—each sheet of which, carriage included, costs me 5d.—Either therefore I must give up the work, which would be a bitter calamity to me, as I have 640 Subscribers on my list, & the Names increase weekly—or I must apply to my friends to assist me till the 20th Number, when the work will go forward on it's own legs. All the Receipts will be paid into the hands of Mr G. Ward, Bookseller, Skinner Street—and as I have purchased the paper for the first 8 numbers with my own money, there remain but 12 to be provided for: so that if but an hundred and twenty of the 640 pay at the due time, the money advanced will be returned at the end of 12 weeks: the numbers for which are all ready, so that even my Death could not prevent it.

I have therefore written to three friends, beside yourself, entreating them to advance to Messrs. Fourdiniere & Co the money for 2500 stamped Sheets for '*the Friend.*' I need not an admonisher, how little claim I have—and that I am using a freedom with you, which no ordinary emergence would justify. But when I am about to lose 500£ a year (& may I not be permitted to add, the means of doing some good to my fellow-creatures?) merely for the want of credit for 120£ for 12 weeks, I cannot justify myself to Mrs Coleridge & my children—not to make one effort at the cost of a few pangs of pride.—

If it should be convenient to you, there will be no occasion for your advance for two months to come, so that the money will be punctually repaid to you within 5 weeks from the time, you need advance it.[1] Alas! dear Sir—to borrow from the Poor is a heart-withering pain and to attempt to borrow from the Wealthy a heart-sickening humiliation—and if I know my own Will, nothing short of a sense of duty could make either endurable to me. Yet there is

[1] Coleridge's plea brought from Sharp a prompt and cordial response dated 16 Oct. 1809: 'If either or all of your three other friends desire to give you the aid I will join them—If it be inconvenient to them to do any part, or if you prefer receiving the assistance from one of us, I will advance the money to Fourdrinier & Co—I shall wait for your answer before I do any thing more than go to Fourdrinier & Co & tell them that the paper is to be sent—' [MS. Dove Cottage.]

one feeling still more painful to me—the being compelled to remember one's own services by the unkindness of the person, for
whom they were zealously & disinterestedly exerted. It makes one
afraid, that there was a selfishness at the bottom of them, of which
we were not conscious at the time. Therefore I have suffered more
from the occasion of the present necessity than from the necessity
itself.—

On re-calculating I find that 2000 Stamped Sheets will do = 36£,
or near it; 3000 stamped Sheets costing 53 ‖ 3 ‖ 6.—But I ought to
have 1000 Sheets, (that is, two Reams) of unstamped paper of the
same kind = £5 ‖ 12 ‖ 0: sent down with it. Fourdiniere & Co know
the sort, & that it is to be sent to 'Mr Cookson, Kendal', by Hargrave's Kendal Waggon—with S. T. C. on the corner of the parcel—
and if it be sent off by the 25 of November, will arrive in time: and
Mr Ward will pay back the sum at your Counting House from the
first receipts in the first week of the new year.—Should this accomodation, however, be inconvenient to you, let me intreat of you not
to suffer this application to diminish your regard for one whose
esteem for you is neither built on nor capable of being affected by
the *outside things* of the World—for I am,

dear Sir, very sincerely your obliged Friend,
S. T. Coleridge

P.S. Wordsworth desires to be remembered to you. I have not
room or I would transcribe a sonnet, he has composed this morning—
but I will inclose it under cover.—Be so good as to let one of your
people drop the inclosed in the two penny Post—unless they should
be passing by Longman's in the course of the morning.—

785. *To Samuel Purkis*

Address: S. Purkis, Esqre. | Brentford | London
MS. Yale University Lib. Pub. E. L. G. ii. 18.
Postmark: 16 October 1809. *Stamped*: Kendal.

Wednesday Night—[11 October 1809]

Dear Sir

Your counter-order of Mr Hutchinson's originated in your not
having seen my letter to Poole, in which I informed him that I had
divided the burthen of advancing the money for the stamped paper
for the next 13 numbers of the FRIEND between him & my other
friends—and am with reason most anxious to have the whole at
Penrith, that I may be out of the reach of future disappointments.—
It is especially unlucky because part of Mr Hutchinson's Order was

for 2000 unstamped Sheets—for the want of which I lose 30 shillings every week—which the reprinting of each No. will cost.—However to bring good out of evil, when you counter-order the counter-order, which you will be so good as to do *immediately* (for I un-luckily am ignorant of Fourdiniere's Address), I would thank you to desire that instead of sending 2000 *unstamped* Sheets by the Hargrave's Kendal Waggon to Mr Cookson, Kendal, he should send only 1500—& send off 500 with the 650 *stamped* Sheets by the Penrith Coach (N.B. not the Mail) to Mr Brown, Printer, Penrith.—Unless this be done immediately, I shall be just as ill off as before—for of No. 8 not one half the Copies could be printed for lack of Paper[1]—so that out of the 650 Copies (and by the bye I print 654) near 400 must go for No. 8.—If however *Mr Street's* should have been sent, as he promised, & have been sent by the Coach, then only the 500 unstamped Sheets need be sent per coach—& the rest stamped & unstamped by the Waggon. Excuse this hasty Scrawl.—

What think you of two Cabinet Ministers *duelling* on *Cabinet* Measures? Is it not wringing the Dregs for the last Drops of Degra-dation? But this Country is on the whole, spite of the beastly *Dinner*ites of the London Common Council, a *moral* Country: and whatever these vulgar statesmen may think, & however they may sneer at causes which cannot be reduced to local particulars & palp-able single *facts*, this base insensibility to the awefulness of their situation will *work* and is working. 'There is an invisible Power in Right and Wrong'—says one of our old sterling Biographers—and be assured, my dear Sir! the opinion of the People is more operative when it acts like a silent Epidemic in the Air than when it roars and foams like a Torrent, to which every one can point & cry: *There* it is!

If you were pleased (and I think, you must have been) with my historical document in illustration of Buonaparte's affectation of imitating Charlemagne,[2] you will see shortly in the Courier another

---

[1] It would seem that Coleridge printed and sent off as many copies of the eighth number of *The Friend* as he had paper for. On 9 Oct. De Quincey wrote to Mrs. Wordsworth from Westhay, Somerset: 'This afternoon we have re-ceived the *Friend*—No. 8.' Since the eighth number is dated 5 Oct. 1809, De Quincey's copy must have left Penrith on time. See H. A. Eaton, *Thomas De Quincey*, 1936, p. 187. See also next letter.

[2] See *The Friend*, No. 4, p. 64 n. Coleridge begins his first *Letter on the Spaniards* (*Courier*, 7 Dec. 1809) with the following comment: 'SIR, ACCEPT my thanks for the compliment you have paid me, by extracting from THE FRIEND the parallel of Charlemagne and Bonaparte, or rather the *factitious* resemblance of the latter to the former.' This extract was reprinted in two instalments in the *Courier* for 12 Sept. and 25 Nov. 1809. See *Essays on His Own Times*, ii. 593. Sara Coleridge erroneously dates the second insertion 1811 for 1809. Ibid. iii. 1024.

& perhaps more interesting Parallel between the present affairs of Spain & the Struggle of the Netherlands against Philip the second.— I would not however, that you should think me an Approver of the Courier—on the contrary, I can scarcely persuade myself, that it is not a *venal* print—tho' I am sure, that if it be, Mr Stuart (the half-proprietor) is not aware of it. But it has manfully fought the good fight for Spain & against Peace-men—or rather your manufacturers of *Truces*, or rather (excuse the pun) parchment *Trusses* for suspending incurable Ruptures.—

The Friend—the first six numbers at least—is justly chargeable with obscurity & heaviness of movement in it's periods—too often with an entortillage or intertwisting both of the thoughts & sentences—But be assured, it will improve with every number in interest of Subject as well as style.—The grievous error of running one No. into the other is chiefly owing to my distance from the Press—the utmost efforts will be used to prevent it for the future.—

Any exertions you can make in my favor will be felt most gratefully by me—the former numbers will be reprinted with all possible speed, & may then be had either at Longman's or Clement's, at 8½ the No—subtracting the stamp duty—But it is a great disadvantage to me that persons should buy the Friend regularly at the Booksellers, instead of sending their Names & Address & receiving it at their own houses by the Post.—

Remember me with respectful affection to Mrs Purkis—and with sincere good wishes for you & your's—

I remain, | dear Sir, | Your's as ever,

S. T. Coleridge

786. *To John Brown*

Address: Mr Brown | Printer | Penrith
MS. Victoria and Albert Museum. Hitherto unpublished.
Stamped: Keswick.

[*Circa* 14 October 1809][1]

Dear Sir

A fatality seems to attend us. So anxious was I concerning your receiving of the Motto[2] (which by the bye had a 1000 times better have been omitted altogether than have occasioned additional

---

[1] This letter contains a note printed at the end of the tenth number of *The Friend* and must have been written not long before that number appeared on 19 Oct. 1809. The note explains 'The delay in the delivery of Nos. 8 and 9'.

[2] The delay in issuing the ninth number of *The Friend*, which should have appeared on 12 Oct., 'was owing', according to Southey, 'to a ridiculous cause. The rats eat up the motto at the printer's.' (*Letters from the Lake Poets*, 415.) New copy for the mutilated passage accompanied this letter.

delay) that two several letters, each containing the passage wanted, were sent to Keswick, by two several Chaise-drivers, together with other important letters—on the very day, I received your's. Several orders, which I cannot recollect, were in those two letters to you— but I have written to Mr Janson to enquire of the two Drivers what they did with them—. In future, I pray that you will on any occasion of equal emergence send off a man express—at present, all that can be done is to print two numbers, as quick as possible, and send them off as soon as possible—adding as a note immediately before your name, in the end of the first,

> The Delay in the delivery of No. 8, & 9 has been occasioned, in the first instance, by the miscarriage of the stamps from London, and in the second, by an accidental mutilation of the Author's *MSS.* in the printing Office.

I doubt not, that in a few days you will receive paper enough for 4 or 5 numbers—& within a week after enough for the next ten Nos.— It is therefore earnestly to be desired, that as soon as possible there should be one Number printed a week before hand; but at present, it is of the greatest consequence that two numbers should be printed, and sent off in the same week.—

Be likewise so good as always to acknowlege the receipt of the Mss sent you—the last sent were—'On the errors of Parties: or Extremes meet'[1]—containing 14 pages of MSS—&—'On the vulgar errors respecting Taxation'[2]—containing 10 pages.

Lady E. Spenser's—to be stopped.

James Burton, Esqre—Bloomsbury Square—(N.B. not Lincoln's Inn) to be sent henceforward to *Tunbridge.*

Send all the Numbers from the beginning as far as you have them to Charles Bardswell, Esqre. Liverpool: & continue them—

Your's sincerely,
S. T. Coleridge.

Not to make any further delay, I must entrust the correction of these Numbers to yourself—if Mr A. Harrison should not be at home or too much engaged—

[1] This essay filled all of the tenth number of *The Friend* and the first 4⅓ pages of the eleventh.

[2] This essay formed the twelfth number of *The Friend*, which appeared a week late on 9 Nov. 1809. Stuart thought it ' a most brilliant one', and wrote to Coleridge that he would 'make a long extract from it in the Courier and another in the Morning Post'. [MS. Dove Cottage.]

787. *To Thomas De Quincey*

MS. formerly in the possession of the late Miss Bairdsmith. Pub. E. L. G. ii. 5.

[*Circa* 16] Octr. 1809[1]
Grasmere.—

My dear Mr De Quincey

If I felt myself competent to offer a decisive opinion on your present plan,[2] even the hazard of offending you would not make me with-hold it: for advice from one better qualified to give it you may easily receive, but hardly from one who esteems you more or who has reflected on the subject with a more affectionate anxiety. But I am too little acquainted with your views, inclinations, and motives, and not sufficiently master of other important circumstances, to offer you *advice*. Yet a few general remarks, I am sure, you will take kindly from me, tho' all on one side of the question: not, my dear Sir! that I see no arguments in favor of your expedition but because, I presume with good reason, that all these have already occurred to you—besides, that these being more *subjective* than *objective*, and grounded on facts which you know either exclusively or better than any other person can, you must be far more competent to count, weigh, and measure them than I. Therefore I will write wholly on the selfish side of the question, tho', heaven knows! without selfishness, much as the prospect of your passing the winter here had delighted me.

It has always been my opinion, that you would do wisely in travelling on the continent some time or other. The question at present is, whether you should do it at this time, and under the present circumstances. Independent of the temporary amusement (which, I take for granted, will not weigh much with you, it's balance over that which you would have at Grasmere being an uncertain thing, subject to the deduction of two Sea-voyages, & after all, only post-poned not abandoned) all the reasons pro and con may be reduced to your Instruction (in which I include all your remembrances, whether of eye, heart, or understanding) and to your Health.—I am to plead *in contra*: and instead of pleading I will merely put down Hints as in a memorandum Book.

1. Instruction.

A most interesting period, I grant—but are you likely to be able to stay long enough to become Master of the Spanish Language, without which you can learn little more than the outsides of Things, here bustle, there quiescence? With two English Companions &

---

[1] This letter was written not long after De Quincey returned to Grasmere in mid-Oct. 1809. See *Middle Years*, i. 344.

[2] De Quincey's proposed journey into Spain.

two English Servants are you likely to acquire it *conversationally?*—
But a far more important objection, and which I scarcely know how
with perfect comfort to my own feelings to press upon you in all the
force, in which my own experience represents it to me—It is, that
three of you together are far far too many & *must*—I speak with
confidence, for I tried it both in Sicily & in Germany—exclude you
from all particular conversations & the best means of acquiring
knowlege. The Natives cannot act towards such a party, as the best
of them would toward you alone or with one companion only—The
number of your suite will even tend to produce an alienating
influence—I travelled for a month in Germany with a German—
for 5 weeks with three Englishmen—in the latter Tour I had a
hundred more advantages a priori, letters of introduction &c, & the
objects were far more interesting, both the places, we visited and
the literary characters to whom we were introduced—and yet the
remembrances & valuable knowlege which I bore away from the
former outweighed the latter a hundredfold—. Depend upon it,
two persons a man can talk to; but three make a visiting party.
And will not the number of English officers & officiaries in Cadiz and
other chief towns be an additional Obstacle?—One other remark,
& I finish this head.— Is not Spain at present too much unsettled,
and the Government too close as well as unjointed, to permit you
to see, hear, & acquire as much as you would do—should you go at
the close of next summer, if the Spaniards hold out—then the Cortes
will have assembled, then Debates will be discussed in every company, and furnish you with a hundred heads of Inquiry & the means
of making them without hazard—then too the Country will have
been organized and the character of the nation drawn forth out of
all it's hiding Holes—and then too the Press will doubtless be
unfettered, & you will have the opportunity of bringing away with
you the best productions of Spanish Wisdom.

And now a few words respecting your Health. It gave me great
pleasure to see how much stronger you seem. Your Constitution is
evidently strengthening, & with care and regulated Exercise I have
little doubt, that in another year you will have left all your complaints behind you, and have muscularized into as steady good
health & strength as a man who thinks & feels as much as you, can
expect. The rapid motions of the French—the roads cleared of
mules—a mountainous Country—the chance, almost my fears
dictate, the probability of your being obliged to travel night and
day, perhaps on foot—the known fact, that the least intemperance
of Exercise in the mountainous parts of Spain will lay the seeds of
a fever—for all these reasons I cannot but wish, that when you
travel, you should do it with a better prospect of it's more essential

aids & conveniences than can be hoped for at present, especially for so large a party.

These are the heads of what my Reason suggests to me, kept as much aloof from my fears & wishes as I can—You will doubtless talk on the subject with our dear & honored Friend, W. W.—I have never discussed the Subject with him—but as I shall have more confidence in my arguments if they strike him too with the same force, so if the contrary should prove to be the case, I shall be inclined to think that my own bad health & increasing low spirits have been playing the Medlers with my Understanding—

Go you or stay you, | May God bless you—& | if you go, speedily & safely restore you | to your friends—among which | think with kindness of

S. T. Coleridge

788. *To George Coleridge*

Address: Revd G. Coleridge | Ottery St Mary | Honiton | Devon   *Single Sheet*
MS. *Lady Cave. Pub. E. L. G. ii. 15.*

Wednesday Night [18 October 1809]
Grasmere
Kendal.—

My dear Brother

The state of emotion, into which the first sentences of your letter threw me, the interval of time between my perusal of them and of the remainder, the reflections—&—why should I hesitate to say what I had been a wretch indeed had I not done—the act of prayer that intervened—rendered it impossible for me to feel even a momentary resentment, or even any grief not mixed with tenderness. Let me first say, earnestly intreating you not to suspect the least intention of conveying a reproach—that but for the nature of our post I should have sent off yester evening a letter informing you that I had no need of the loan, I had begged—for that one of three persons to whom I had written in my distress, had supplied the quotum, I had asked—and each of the other two had replied by taking the whole on himself.—

I am most willing, in the depth of my heart, to take upon myself & attribute to my own past errors, your present mistake—But I fully believe, that of all, who have ever been acquainted with me, even my worst enemy—if any such I have—would disclaim for me the congruity with my habits or dispositions of the base motive, which you assign to my having transmitted you the Prospectus of the Friend. The character of excessive carelessness about worldly interests, the difficulty of acting at all even on motives of duty when they have been cloathed in the form of pecuniary advantage for myself, is so well known to every human being who knows me at all, even to those the most embittered against me for faults of indolence, neglect or self-indulgence; that from any one but yourself I should have received the charge with a smile instead of tears. Deeply wounded by very disrespectful words used concerning me, and which, struggling as I had been thro' life and still maintaining a character & holding connections no ways unworthy of my Family, I felt more warmly than I ought—I wrote you a letter, the contents of which I have wholly forgotten as is commonly the unfortunate case with things said or written in passion—they are soon forgotten by the Aggressor & for ever remembered by the Receiver—but which, I doubt not, was an unwise & in every sense improper letter.[1] But—and let my present emotion apologize for the awefulness of the adjuration—God be my witness! I never uttered a disrespectful word concerning you to another person, nor even for a day together ever thought—much less spoke of you—without gratitude and remembrance of former times. When therefore I commenced 'The Friend', not doubting that the principles, I had pledged myself to support, would meet your full approbation, & flattering myself that the devotion of my talents, such as they were, to so good a purpose, would give you pleasure—I transmitted my plan to you—not perhaps without some anticipation, that it might be the means of renewing a friendly and brotherly correspondence with you. The letters, I had received in consequence, confirmed me in that hope—and when I wrote last—in much agitation and great flutter of spirits and rashly despairing when I had no ground of despair—I was actuated by two considerations— the first, that the loan, small as it was—for it could not have exceeded 50£—there was a moral certainty of repaying in 12 weeks —and secondly, that as it would have removed an obstacle to my obtaining such an income as would enable me to provide for my children, there was a something in family connection that gave a propriety to the application.—Much more I could say, and of motives more delicate & removed from self-interest, which it were now unbecoming to make known—

I repeat that I doubt not but that the Letter, to which you refer, was an unwise one & such as it becomes me to beg your forgiveness for; but that it could deserve all that you have said of it, or by any interpretation be made to imply the contemptuous meanings, in which you have rendered it—what shall I say & not offend?—this only—that if it were so, it conveyed thoughts that never before

[1] Coleridge refers to his letter of 11 May 1808.

that time & never since had a moment's sojourn in my mind or feelings—Permit me to add—and as the Son of your father, I have some claim on your sympathy in my desire of possessing your esteem when I deserve it—that for 14 years I have passed thro' a variety of scenes, never with a spare guinea in my house, & often sorely wanting it—have never been in any instance extravagant tho' habitually careless of money—yet never been in debt—& that I never applied to you all this time, nor ever should have done it except where the Loan appeared to me a mere accomodation, without the least hazard, and the amount trifling in comparison with the temporary advantage—.

Indeed, dear Brother! but for my long estrangement from you, you could not think thus of me—Much you might & would have to blame—but *thus* you could not think. I feel as certain as of any thing not in my own being, that were we together but for a month, you would not think so. If impulses base as those you have ascribed to me had been compatible with my nature, I should have been a rich man long ago: for few men have had more opportunities—. The anxiety to remove from your mind such a mistake will not, I trust, be confounded with pride or vanity.

I should be happy to hear from you again[1]—& most happy if forgetting the past as far as kind feelings imply a moral forgetfulness, I should be able in return to subscribe myself with as much pleasure as now with sincerity

Your grateful & affectionate Brother
S. T. Coleridge

789. *To Samuel Purkis*

Address: S. Purkis Esqre. | Brentford | London
MS. British Museum. Pub. E. L. G. ii. 21.
Postmark: 24 October 1809. *Stamped*: Keswick.

Friday Night—20 Octr. [1809] My birth-day—

Dear Sir

I am confident, that I must have either written illegibly or expressed myself unintelligibly. I had informed our friend, Poole, that I was under the necessity of applying to my friends for the Advance of the Paper for thirteen Numbers—i.e. from No. 7 to No. 20 inclusive, making in all about NINE thousand stamped Sheets; and intreated *him* to advance TWO thousand five hundred

---

[1] Coleridge's letter drew from George a reply beginning: 'Polluted, as the best of us are, with selfishness, I almost shudder at the task of vindicating myself... and I therefore refer the cause of offence—your own letter—to you for reconsideration.' See Letters 705 and 792.

as *his* friendly contingent: a similar request I sent to Mr Hutchinson, (viz. 650 per Coach, & 2000 by the waggon) but desiring of Mr H. an order for some *un*stamped paper *in addition*—. Both Mr H. and Mr Poole acceded to my requests: and consequently *both* orders should have been compleated, *in toto*.—Still near four thousand stamps would be wanting: and for two thousand of these I applied to my Brother—for the first time since I became of age, having never received either accomodation or present from any one of my family during all my hard struggle thro' Life, and I received a refusal so couched that it would require an Œdipus to determine whether the baseness, the inhumanity, or the insolence of the answer was the greater—For the remainder I applied to my friend, Mr Sharp, who in the kindest & handsomest manner not only complied with my request; but begged me to inform him, if I met with a negative from any other quarter, and he would advance to Fourdiniere for the whole *four* thousand—.

The division, I alluded to, between Poole & Hutchinson was of 5150 stamped sheets—or rather a division of 9000 Stamps between Mr Sharpe; Mr Hutchinson; Mr Poole, my Brother by gift of God; and the Revd G. Coleridge, my Brother by accident of Midwifery.

You will now, my dear Sir! understand, that unless I receive both Mr Poole's contingent of 2500, and Mr Hutchinson's of 2650 (the unstamped paper not included in this calculation) I shall be in my former state of anxiety for three Numbers and a half out of the thirteen, the Stamps for which I had to procure.

It is of the utmost importance to my success, that I should be free from all anxiety as well as placed out of any further hazard of having to stop The Friend for want of Paper—I am employed in arranging the mode of payment according to the different Towns, so as to receive the sums in the least expensive way; but all will be paid into the Hands of Mr G. Ward, to whom I shall write as soon as the arrangement is compleated.[1]—

I am very sorry that I must thus put you to the expence of another letter; but for the loss of Time I would send it to Mr Curwen to be franked—However, I will send you a couple of Sonnets, just written by my friend, Wordsworth: the second of which, I am sure, you will rate at sixpenny worth of pleasure[2]—

[1] This Coleridge failed to do. 'I am sorry', George Ward later wrote to Coleridge, 'that neither you nor Mr Poole said anything to me on the subject of collecting your monies. I would have at once explained to you the impracticability of my being able to undertake it.' [MS. Dove Cottage.]

[2] At the end of this letter Sara Hutchinson copied out two sonnets, one beginning, 'Of mortal parents is the Hero born', the other, 'Advance—come forth from thy Tyrolean ground'. Both appeared in the eleventh number of *The Friend*, 26 Oct. 1809. Wordsworth, *Poet. Works*, iii. 129.

I feel even to an occasional despondency the truth of what you say concerning the unfitness of the Friend hitherto for the general Public—it would not depress me so much, if I thought that any efforts of mine at all compatible with the hope of doing any real good or with the sense of the Duty, I owe to myself & to my permanent reputation would remove the complaint—I shall assuredly do my best—I will make every sacrifice in my power—I will frequently interpose Numbers of pure entertainment—& the Work itself according to it's plan will become more interesting when the Foundations have been laid—but still I feel the sadning conviction, that no real information can be given, no important errors overthrown in Politics, Morals, or Literature without requiring some effort of Thought—& that the aversion from this is the mother Evil of all the other Evils, that I have to attack—consequently, I am like a Physician who prescribes exercise with the dumb bells to a Patient paralytic in both arms—. Did not the 7th & 8th Numbers somewhat improve in this respect?—

God bless you &
S. T. Coleridge

790. *To Robert Southey*

Pub. Life and Corres. *iii. 259.*

October 20. 1809.

My dear Southey,

 . . . What really makes me despond is the daily confirmation I receive of my original apprehension, that the plan and execution of *The Friend* is so utterly unsuitable to the public taste as to preclude all rational hopes of its success. Much, certainly, might have been done to have made the former numbers less so, by the interposition of others written more expressly for general interest; and, if I could attribute it wholly to any removable error of my own, I should be less dejected. I will do my best, will frequently interpose tales and whole numbers of amusement, will make the periods lighter and shorter; and the work itself, proceeding according to its plan, will become more interesting when the foundations have been laid. Massiveness is the merit of a foundation; the gilding, ornaments, stucco-work, conveniences, sunshine, and sunny prospects will come with the superstructure. Yet still I feel the deepest conviction that no efforts of mine, compatible with the hope of effecting any good purpose, or with the duty I owe to my permanent reputation, will remove the complaint. No real information can be conveyed, no important errors radically extracted, without demanding an effort of thought on the part of the reader; but the obstinate, and now contemptuous, aversion to all energy of thinking is the mother evil, the cause of all the evils in politics, morals, and literature, which it is my object to wage war against; so that I am like a physician who, for a patient paralytic in both arms, prescribes, as the only possible cure, the use of the dumb-bells. Whatever I publish, and in whatever form, this obstacle will be felt. The Rambler, which, altogether, has sold a hundred copies for one of the Connoisseur, yet, during its periodical appearance, did not sell one for fifty, and was dropped by reader after reader for its dreary gravity and massiveness of manner. Now, what I wish you to do for me—if, amid your many labours, you can find or make a leisure hour—is, to look over the eight numbers, and to write a letter to The Friend in a lively style, chiefly urging, in a humorous manner, my Don Quixotism in expecting that the public will ever pretend to understand my lucubrations, or feel any interest in subjects of such sad and unkempt antiquity, and contrasting my style with the cementless periods of the modern Anglo-Gallican style, which not only are understood *beforehand*, but, being free from all connections of logic, all the hooks and eyes of intellectual memory, never oppress the mind by any after recollections, but, like civil visitors, stay a few moments, and leave the room quite free and open for the next comers.[1] Something of this kind, I mean, that I may be able to answer it so as, in the answer, to state my own convictions at full on the nature of obscurity, &c. . . .

God bless you!

S. T. Coleridge.

791. *To R. L.*[2]

Pub. The Friend, *No. 11, 26 October 1809.*

[23 October 1809][3]

Dear Sir,

When I first undertook the present Publication for the sake and with the *avowed* object of referring Men in all things to PRINCIPLES or fundamental Truths, I was well aware of the obstacles which the

---

[1] Southey complied with Coleridge's request, but he did not think his letter, which is included in *Life and Corres.* iii. 261, very successful. In a cover letter to Coleridge he said that after he had re-read the first eight numbers, 'the truth is, they left me no heart for jesting or for irony. In time they will do their work.' Ibid. iii. 264.

Coleridge did not insert Southey's letter but instead wrote and printed in *The Friend* a long letter of his own to R. L.

[2] Possibly Robert Lloyd, a younger brother of Charles Lloyd. See Chambers, *Life*, 230.

[3] A note in Sara Hutchinson's handwriting to Brown, dated 23 Oct. 1809, accompanied copy for Coleridge's letter to R. L.

plan itself would oppose to my success. For in order to the regular attainment of this object, all the driest and least attractive Essays must appear in the first fifteen or twenty Numbers, and thus subject me to the necessity of demanding effort or soliciting patience in that part of the Work, where it was most my interest to secure the confidence of my Readers by winning their favour. Though I dared warrant for the pleasantness of the Journey on the whole; though I might promise that the road would, for the far greater part of it, be found plain and easy, that it would pass through countries of various prospect, and that at every stage there would be a change of company; it still remained a heavy disadvantage, that I had to start at the foot of a high and steep hill: and I foresaw, not without occasional feelings of despondency, that during the slow and laborious ascent it would require no common management to keep my Passengers in good humour with the Vehicle and it's Driver. As far as this inconvenience could be palliated by sincerity and previous confession, I have no reason to accuse myself of neglect. In the Prospectus of THE FRIEND, which for this cause I re-printed and annexed to the first Number, I felt it my duty to inform such as might be inclined to patronize the Publication, that I must submit to be esteemed dull by those who sought chiefly for amusement: and this I hazarded as a *general* confession, though in my own mind I felt a chearful confidence that it would apply almost exclusively to the earlier Numbers. I could not therefore be surprized, however much I may have been depressed, by the frequency with which you hear The Friend complained of for it's abstruseness and obscurity; nor did the highly flattering expressions, with which you accompanied your communication, prevent me from feeling it's truth to the whole extent.

An Author's pen, like Children's legs, improves by exercise. That part of the blame which rests in myself, I am exerting my best faculties to remove. A man long accustomed to silent and solitary meditation, in proportion as he encreases the power of thinking in long and connected trains, is apt to lose or lessen the talent of communicating his thoughts with grace and perspicuity. Doubtless too, I have in some measure injured my style, in respect to it's facility and popularity, from having almost confined my reading, of late years, to the Works of the Ancients and those of the elder Writers in the modern languages. We insensibly imitate what we habitually admire; and an aversion to the epigrammatic unconnected periods of the fashionable *Anglo-gallican* Taste has too often made me willing to forget, that the stately march and difficult evolutions, which characterize the eloquence of Hooker, Bacon, Milton, and Jeremy Taylor, are, notwithstanding their intrinsic excellence, still less suited to a periodical Essay. This fault I am now endeavouring to correct; though I can never so far sacrifice my judgement to the desire of being immediately popular, as to cast my sentences in the French moulds, or affect a style which an ancient critic would have deemed purposely invented for persons troubled with the asthma to read, and for those to comprehend who labour under the more pitiable asthma of a short-witted intellect. It cannot but be injurious to the human mind never to be called into effort: the habit of receiving pleasure without any exertion of thought, by the mere excitement of curiosity and sensibility, may be justly ranked among the worst effects of habitual novel reading. It is true that these short and unconnected sentences are easily and instantly understood: but it is equally true, that wanting all the cement of thought as well as of style, all the connections, and (if you will forgive so trivial a metaphor) all the *hooks-and-eyes* of the memory, they are as easily forgotten: or rather, it is scarcely possible that they should be remembered. Nor is it less true, that those who confine their reading to such books dwarf their own faculties, and finally reduce their Understandings to a deplorable imbecility: the fact you mention, and which I shall hereafter make use of, is a fair instance and a striking illustration. Like idle morning Visitors, the brisk and breathless Periods hurry in and hurry off in quick and profitless succession; each indeed for the moments of it's stay prevents the pain of vacancy, while it indulges the love of sloth; but all together they leave the Mistress of the house (the soul I mean) flat and exhausted, incapable of attending to her own concerns, and unfitted for the conversation of more rational Guests.

I know you will not suspect me of fostering so idle a hope, as that of obtaining acquittal by recrimination; or think that I am attacking one fault, in order that it's opposite may escape notice in the noise and smoke of the battery. On the contrary, I shall do my best, and even make all allowable sacrifices, to render my manner more attractive and my matter more generally interesting. All the principles of my future Work, all the fundamental doctrines, in the establishment of which I must of necessity require the attention of my Reader to become my fellow-labourer; all the primary facts essential to the intelligibility of my principles, the existence of which facts I can prove to others only as far as I can prevail on them to retire *into themselves* and make their own minds the objects of their stedfast attention; these will, all together, not occupy more than six or seven of my future Essays, and between each of these I shall interpose one or more Numbers devoted to the rational *entertainment* of my various Readers; and, partly from the desire of gratifying particular requests, and partly as a specimen of the subjects which will henceforward have a due proportion of THE FRIEND allotted to them, I shall fill up the present Paper with a miscellany. I feel too deeply the importance of the convictions, which first impelled me to the present undertaking, to leave unattempted any honourable means of recommending them to as wide a circle as possible; and though all the opinions which I shall bring forward in the course of the Work, on politics, morals, religion, literature, and the fine arts, will with all their applications, be strictly deducible from the principles established in these earlier Numbers; yet I doubt not, that being Truths and interesting Truths (and such, of course, I must be supposed to deem them) their intrinsic beauty will procure them introduction to the feelings of my Readers, even of those whose habits or avocations preclude the fatigue of close reasoning, and that by the illustrations and the auxiliary and independent arguments appropriate to it, each will of itself become sufficiently intelligible and evident.

Hitherto, my dear Sir, I have been employed in laying the Foundations of my Work. But the proper merit of a foundation is it's massiveness and solidity. The conveniences and ornaments, the gilding and stucco work, the sunshine and sunny prospects, will come with the Superstructure. Yet I dare not flatter myself, that any endeavours of mine, compatible with the duty I owe to Truth and the hope of permanent utility, will render THE FRIEND agreeable to the majority of what is called the reading Public. I never expected it. How indeed could I, when I was to borrow so little from the influence of passing Events, and absolutely excluded from my plan all appeals to personal curiosity and personal interests? Yet even this is not my greatest impediment. No real information can be conveyed, no important errors rectified, no widely injurious prejudices rooted up, without requiring some effort of thought on the part of the Reader. But the obstinate (and toward a contemporary Writer, the contemptuous) aversion to all intellectual effort is the mother evil of all which I had proposed to war against, the Queen Bee in the Hive of our errors and misfortunes, both private and national. The proof of the Fact, positively and comparatively, and the enumeration of it's various causes, will, as I have already hinted (P. 75) form the preliminary Essay of the disquisition on the elements of our moral and intellectual faculties. To solicit the attention of those, on whom these debilitating causes have acted to their full extent, would be no less absurd than to recommend exercise with the dumb bells, as the only mode of cure, to a patient paralytic in both arms. You, my dear Sir, well know, that my expectations were more modest as well as more rational. I hoped, that my Readers in general would be aware of the impracticability of suiting every Essay to every Taste in any period of the work, and that they would not attribute wholly to the Author, but in part to the necessity of his plan, the austerity and absence of the lighter graces in the first fifteen or twenty Numbers. In my cheerful moods I sometimes flattered myself, that a few even among those, who foresaw that my lucubrations would at all times require more attention than from the nature of their own employments they could afford them, might yet find a pleasure in supporting The Friend during it's infancy, so as to give it a chance of attracting the notice of others, to whom it's style and subjects might be better adapted. But my main anchor was the Hope, that when circumstances gradually enabled me to adopt the ordinary means of making the Publication generally known, there might be found throughout the Kingdom a sufficient number of meditative minds, who, entertaining similar convictions with myself, and gratified by the prospect of seeing them reduced to form and system, would take a warm interest in the work from the very circumstance, that it wanted those allurements of transitory interest, which render particular patronage superfluous, and for the brief season of their Blow and Fragrance attract the eye of thousands, who would pass unregarded

Flowers

Of sober tint, and Herbs of med'cinable powers.[1]

I hoped that a sufficient number of such Readers would gradually be obtained, as to secure for the Paper that small extent of circulation and immediate Sale, which would permit the Editor to carry it on to it's conclusion, and that they might so far interest themselves in recommending it to men of kindred judgements among their acquaintances, that the alterations in my list of Subscribers should not be exclusively of a discouraging nature. Hitherto, indeed, I have only to express gratitude, and acknowledge constancy; but I do not attempt to disguise from myself that I owe this, in many instances, to a generous reluctance hastily to withdraw from an Undertaking in it's first struggles, and before the Adventurer had had a fair opportunity of displaying the quality of his goods, or the foundations of his credit.

* * * * * —the one tantum vidi: the other I know by his works only and his public character. To profess indifference to their praises would convict me either of insensibility or insincerity. Yet (and I am sure, that you will both understand, and sympathize with, the feeling) my delight was not unalloyed by a something like pain, as if I were henceforward less free to express my admiration of them with the same warmth and affection, which I have been accustomed

---

[1] *To the Author of Poems*, lines 26–27. *Poems*, i. 103.

to do, before I had even anticipated the honor of such a communication. You will therefore not judge me too harshly, if so confirmed and cheered, I have sometimes in the warmth of composition, and while I was reviewing the materials of the more important part of my intended Essays, if I have sometimes permitted my Hopes a bolder flight; and counted on a share of favour and protection from the soberly zealous among the professionally Learned, when the Principles of The Friend shall have been brought into clear view, and Specimens have been given of the mode and the direction in which I purpose to apply and enforce them.

There are charges, the very suspicion of which is painful to an ingenuous mind in exact proportion as they are unfounded and inapplicable. I can bear with resignation a charge of enthusiasm. Even if accused of presumption, I will repay myself by deriving from the accusation an additional motive to increased watchfulness over myself, that I may remain entitled to plead, Not guilty! to it in the Court of my own conscience. But if my anxiety to obviate hasty judgements and misapprehensions is imputed to a less honorable motive than the earnest wish to exert my best faculties, as to the most beneficial purposes, so in the way most likely to effectuate them, I can give but one answer, that however great my desires of *profit* may be, they cannot be greater than my ignorance of the world, if I have chosen a weekly paper planned, as the Friend is, written on such subjects, and composed in such a style, as the most promising method of gratifying them.

S. T. C.

792. *To Robert Southey*

Address: R. Southey, Esqre.
MS. Lord Latymer. Pub. E. L. G. ii. 23.

[Early November 1809]¹

My dear Southey

I was obliged to write a letter myself, as you have seen—tho' I shall certainly insert your's in a few weeks, only I shall put something for the middle part, as fearing that it will supply the groundlings with too *hard hits* against me.—There has been a sort of quarrel between me and Stuart—the long and the short of the matter is, that he left me suddenly in the lurch, and declined assisting me very abruptly, and somewhat inconsistently with a former promise to Wordsworth—But when I come in to Keswick, I

¹ This letter was written after 26 Oct. 1809, when the letter to R. L. appeared in *The Friend,* and before Coleridge learned of his mother's death, which occurred on 4 Nov. 1809.

will bring all his letters—I was much pleased with his last, tho' his account about myself & the Copenhagen Business is not quite accurate. But in the name of wonder whence has St. derived, on what does he ground his high opinion of Marquis Wellesley?—who besides the delay from ministerial intrigue stayed a full month in town in consequence of a Squabble about his taking out in great pomp & in a separate Vessel hired for the purpose, a common Whore, called Sally Douglas whom he has in keeping—the King heard of it & expressed his displeasure—& the Marquis took Huff—at length, however, consented to take her more *clandestinely*—She went however, & with a grand establishment, & is now with him in Spain—to the edification of that—O I am sick of my Country—and give up our Great Britainers Cat & Kittens, Sow & Litter!—we are a base people—of that calumniated, infamously calumniated people—. So I have been told by a man who pretended to actual knowlege of the facts—And Mr Canning was one of Stuart's Statesmen of real Ability—in what? and what proof?—These are things, that perplex me in a man of Stuart's consummate good sense.

I shall take your advice with regard to the Friend—Nos. 13 & 14 will be pure Amusement—No. 15—the Constitution as it really *is*, not more *dry* than the Subject compels: but yet of the old sort—16. France & the Character of Buonaparte—17. & 18. The foundations of Morality—Taste—in short, all the *principles* in order to get them over & to be able to say—Now, Gemmen!—all the Brain-work is over—with introduction on the Causes that weaken the public mind—19 & 20 as entertaining as I can[1]—If it will not do after all, I must try at a Monthly Friend, & make it half miscellaneous, half on the former plan.—

I have received a long vindicating letter from my Brother, softened by my very gentle answer[2] to his former one, & inclosing

[1] While Coleridge did not follow this plan for future numbers of *The Friend*, it is evident that he had yielded to the complaints of his friends and correspondents and was determined to give his work a lighter tone. 'In Truth', he wrote in *The Friend* on 11 Jan. 1810, 'since my twelfth Number I have not had courage to renew any Subject which *did* require Attention.' Indeed, forthcoming issues included such diverse topics as the gruesome tale of *Maria Schöning, Satyrane's Letters*, John Wilson's letter signed Mathetes and Wordsworth's answer, some lines translated from the French by Francis Wrangham, and Wordsworth's essay on *Epitaphs*. Thus the steady and purposeful character of the early numbers was abandoned, and *The Friend* became more miscellaneous.

The thirteenth number appeared on 16 Nov., the fourteenth on 23 Nov., the fifteenth on 30 Nov., the sixteenth on 7 Dec., the seventeenth on 14 Dec., the eighteenth on 21 Dec., the nineteenth on 28 Dec., 1809, and the twentieth on 4 Jan. 1810.

[2] Letter 788, which Richard Sharp forwarded from London to Ottery on 24 Oct.

in his defence a *downright red hot letter*[1] which I wrote him on his disappointing poor Mrs C. and our little ones when we had got 300 miles to visit him—I had quite forgotten it—as is the case with works of Anger—the memory is all on the side of the Affrontee. But the most important part of his Letter is, that my poor Mother is near her end, and dying in great torture, death eating her piece-meal, her vital stamen is so very vigorous—& she wishes to see me before her death—But tho' my Brother knows I am penniless, not an offer of a Bank note to en[able] me to set off. In truth, I know not what to do—for [there] is not a shilling in our whole House—

Brown wishes to give his whole time & attention to Printing—My Poems are now getting ready for him—I would, that you could have some one of your works printed by him—He is a worthy creature, & you will see by my Poems whether his Printing is such as you would approve—If you have any interest, pray, exert it for him—if no higher claims stand in the way.—Have you seen the Simpliciad[2]—if not, it shall be sent to you—Such a thing!—O Jesus!—

Mrs Lloyd told Hartley, she had written to Mrs C.—God bless you—I should have written more at length to you, & have written to Mrs C. but that I have to answer three letters all of importance by tonight's Carrier besides sending off The Friend—Pasley's letter will interest you—I begin to be alarmed at not hearing from him.

You will grin at my *modest* account of Satyrane, the Idoloclast,[3] in No. 14—but what can I do?—I must wear a mask—and it is not quite so good a joke either as Godwin's meaning the sublime Visionary and most lofty Poet in Caleb Williams for William Godwin['s] own very Self!—

S. T. Coleridge

793. *To John Brown*

Address: Mr Brown | Bookseller | Penrith
MS. Victoria and Albert Museum. Pub. E. L. G. ii. 26.

Monday Night. 4 December, 1809.

I have received, my dear Sir, your very sensible and satisfactory Letter. Wordsworth and Mr De Quincey were no less delighted with

---

[1] Letter 705.

[2] *The Simpliciad; a satirico-didactic poem. Containing hints for the scholars of the new school, suggested by Horace's Art of Poetry, and improved by a contemplation of the works of the first masters* (anon.), 1808.

[3] Coleridge revised for *The Friend* his letters written from Germany to Poole and Mrs. Coleridge, entitled them *Satyrane's Letters*, and prefixed a semi-autobiographical account of the imaginary Satyrane. See Letters 256, 258–9, 261–2, 269–70, and 276, and *The Friend*, Nos. 14, 16, 18, and 19.

it's judicious, ingenuous, and manly contents than myself—and I shall therefore take the Liberty of sending it to Southey who has far more in his power than any of us. As to myself, and I may add, Wordsworth, your Printing, even as it appears in the Friend under all disadvantages, is quite as good as we want—who have no passion for book-finery, and would be far more flattered by seeing our poems in a shilling Edition on the same paper &c as Reading Made Easy, in the Shelves of Country Booksellers & Stationers, than arrayed in all the Silks & Sattins of Mr Ballantyne's Wardrobe, with engravings to boot. As to *my* poems therefore, and all my other works, I neither need or shall ask the opinions of any: and if the Friend should ultimately fight it's way into a decent & regular Sale, I shall be most happy to assist you in *any* way that may forward your plans. I heard from Mr Cookson, that a parcel of paper had been forwarded by him to you on Monday last—I hope fervently, that you have received it. Would it be painful to you, if for this *first* Volume of the Friend, I had three or four of the Numbers reprinted by Pennington? I ask this, first, because I am anxious to have a Volume ready by the 26th Number, and because in Case Pennington did this, you might begin earlier with the Poems—which are ready for you whenever you wish to begin.

We have had many a fanciful Day-dream that if you *should* confine yourself to the Printing Line (of which the Profits seem to me terribly little compared with other Trades, & of necessity irregular) and were it not for Job Work, how much we should like to see you settled at Grasmere, where De Quincey would add a Lord Stanhope Press, and 200£ worth of Types to your Stock. There is not the least doubt, that we could find you & a Journeyman & an apprentice ample Employment—but what are our Lives? Accidents. I write this therefore for no other end than first to make you smile, & secondly, as a proof how much you have all our best good wishes. The last number was printed as well as any work of the kind could be in any part of the Kingdom—& in correctness far above the London work. There were but two errata in the whole, both mere trifles—one, the omission of (*4thly*) p. 231., the other, of *the* before Duty—last line but four of the last page, both in all probability errors in the MSS.— I take for granted, that the Copy now in hand, Satyrane's second Letter, is not quite enough for a Number—at least, that you can contrive to annex to it the accompanying poem, & Advertisement. If *both* cannot be inserted, at least, insert the Advertisement.[1]

---

[1] The sixteenth number of *The Friend*, which is dated 7 Dec. 1809 and which contains Satyrane's second letter, concludes with the following Advertisement:

The Subscribers, who have not remitted their payment by other means, are respectfully requested, after the 20th Number, to order the money to be

Whenever you can make it convenient, we shall be all most happy to see you, as the Friend as well as Co-adjutor of, dear Sir,

Your's with sincere esteem

S. T. Coleridge

P.S. There should now be on the road 4 or 5 thousand Stamps—I have written to change the waggon.

P.S. Be so good as on the Friend sent to Grasmere to mark the Letter written on the Copy received by you—thus, if I mark the Copy, A, be so good as to write A in some part of the next No. that I may know, that it has arrived.

794. *To Cantab*[1]

Pub. The Friend, *No. 18, 21 December 1809.*

[*Circa* 10 December 1809]

I thank the '*Friend's friend and a Cantab*' for his inspiriting Letter, and assure him, that it was not without it's intended effect, of giving me encouragement. That this was not needless, he would feel as well as know, if I could convey to him the anxious thoughts and gloomy anticipations, with which I write any single paragraph, that demands the least effort of attention, or requires the Reader to enter into himself and question his own mind as to the truth of that which I am pressing on his notice. But both He and my very kind Malton Correspondent, and all of similar dispositions, may rest assured, that with every imaginable endeavour to make THE FRIEND, *collectively,* as *entertaining* as is compatible with the main Object of the Work, I shall never so far forget the duty, I owe to them and to my own heart, as not to remember that mere amusement is *not* that main Object. I have taken upon myself (see No. 11.)[2]

paid to Mr. George Ward, Bookseller, Skinner Street, Snow Hill. The Author takes the liberty of suggesting to his Readers, not resident in London, that it would be of very great advantage to him, especially under the heavy expences and many losses of an infant publication, if they could contrive, in the ordinary course of their Correspondence, to have the money paid by their friends in town, instead of remitting it by the post, which must needs subtract so large a part from the Sum Total of the Subscription.

[1] This letter was written in answer to one dated 4 Dec. 1809 from an unknown correspondent, who assured Coleridge that his object was encouragement, who declared that he admired *The Friend* 'not only for the principles which are its basis . . . but for the manner & Spirit in which they are conveyed', and who felt that he 'must earnestly exhort & entreat' Coleridge 'to press forward steadfastly to the mark of permanent utility & the salvation of right principles'. 'With every hope & wish', this correspondent concludes, 'for the success of the Friend, & entreaty for your perseverance in the plan you have adopted, I am, dear Sir, your very obedient servant, . . . the Friend's friend, & a Cantab.' [MS. Dove Cottage.] [2] Letter 791.

all the blame that I could acknowledge without adulation to my readers and hypocritical mock-humility. But the principal source of the obscurity imputed must be sought for in the want of *interest* concerning the truths themselves. (REVEL. III. 17.) My sole Hope (I dare not say expectation) is, that if I am enabled to proceed with the work through an equal number of Essays with those already published, it will gradually find for itself it's appropriate Public.

S. T. Coleridge.

795. *To John Brown*

Address: Mr Brown | Printer
MS. Victoria and Albert Museum. Hitherto unpublished.

Friday Night Decr. 22 [1809]

My dear Sir

I have sent as much copy as can be set up on Sunday Morning— and on Sunday Afternoon I shall send a Lad to Keswick with the remainder which you will, of course, receive by Monday Morning's Post.—Or by the Kendal Post on Sunday Night.[1]

The Poems[2] are to be printed first—in an openish, handsome manner— and then the Essay, with this Motto.— N.B. this Motto before the *Essay*, not before the Poems.—

> Ma pianger non si dee, come per tempo
> Dal Mondo uscito. Voi, Mortali, errate,
> Per vero dir, nel conto della vita—
> Sol numerate gli anni, e non guardate
> All' opre gloriose di Virtute.
> CHIABRERA.

And in a note below.

LITERAL TRANSLATION. But we ought not to lament, as if he had departed early from the World: It is you, Mortals, in truth, that err in your calculation of Life: you count the years only, and do not look to the glorious works of Virtue.—

I shall do, as you desire. When you receive more paper, inform me. Was it the reprinted 1 & 2 No. you sent Mr Donne?—

S. T. Coleridge

In Page 5th take care not to substitute *Foundling* for 'Fondling'.[3]
There is no need to prefix the word ESSAY—

[1] This sentence and the two sentences which follow the signature are in Sara Hutchinson's handwriting.

[2] Two *Epitaphs translated from Chiabrera* by Wordsworth opened the nineteenth number of *The Friend*, dated 28 Dec. 1809; the motto quoted in this letter and Coleridge's essay followed.

[3] See *The Friend*, p. 296.

796. *To Robert Southey*

Address: R. Southey, Esqre | Greta Hall | Keswick
MS. Lord Latymer. Pub. with omis. Letters, *ii. 554.*

[*Circa* 24 December 1809][1]
My dear Southey

I suspect, you have misunderstood me and applied to the Maltese Regiment what I said of the Corsican Rangers—both are bad enough— but of the former I know little, of course, as I was away from Malta before the Regiment had left the Island—But in the Essays (2 or 3) which I am now writing on Sir A. Ball[2] (the *introductory* matter comes *this* week—then the conclusion of W's remarks on Mathetes,[3] and for the next Numbers Sir A. B.) I shall mention it as an exemplification among many others of his foresight—It was a *job*, I have no doubt—merely, to get General Villette[4] a lucrative Regiment—but G. V. is dead, and it was not such a job as that of the Corsican Rangers which can be made appear glaring—. The long & short of the story is—that the men were ⅘ths married, would have fought as well as the best, *at home* & behind their own walls— but could not be expected to *fight* abroad, where they had no interest—. Besides, it was *cruel, shameful,* to take 1500 men, as Soldiers for any part of our enormous empire, out of a population, man, woman, & child, not at that time more than 100,000.—There were 2 Maltese Militia Regiments, officered by their own Maltese Nobility—these against the intreaties & *tears* of the men & officers, (I myself saw them *weeping*) against the remonstrances & memorial (written by myself) of Sir A. B. &c, were melted into one large one, officered by English Officers—& a general affront given to the Island, *because* General Villette had great Friends at the War office, Duke of York &c!—This is the whole—but do not either expose yourself or me to judicial enquiries. It is one thing to *know* a thing, & another to be able to *prove* it in a Law-court—This remark applies to the DAMNABLE Treatment of the Prisoners of War at Malta.—

[1] In this letter Coleridge mentions the essays he is writing on Sir Alexander Ball. Thus his statement that 'the *introductory* matter comes *this* week' establishes the approximate date of this letter, Ball's name first appearing in the nineteenth number of *The Friend*, dated 28 Dec. 1809.

[2] Coleridge's 'Essays' on Sir Alexander Ball, who died on 20 Oct. 1809, appeared in the nineteenth, twenty-first, twenty-second, twenty-sixth, and twenty-seventh numbers of *The Friend*.

[3] Mathetes' letter appeared in the seventeenth number of *The Friend*; Wordsworth's reply in the seventeenth and twentieth numbers.

[4] General W. A. Villettes, who succeeded to the chief command of the troops in Malta in 1801, died 12 July 1808.

I should have thought your facts, with which I am familiar, a confirmation of Miss Schoning[1]—Be that as it may, take my word for it, that in *substance* the story is as certain as that Dr Dodd was hung—to mention one proof only—Von Hess,[2] the celebrated Historian of Hamburg, and since Lessing the best German Prosist, went himself to Nuremburg, examined into the facts, *officially &* *personally*—& it was on him that I relied—tho' if you knew the Government of Nuremburg, you would see that the first account could not have been published as it was, if it had not been too notorious, even for concealment to be hoped for—After I left Germany, Von Hess had a public controversy, that threatened to become a *Diet*-concern, with the Magistrates of Nuremburg, for some other bitter charges against them—I have their defence of themselves, but they do not even [attempt?] to deny the *fact* of HARLIN & SCHONING. But indeed, Southey! it is almost as bad, as if I could have mistaken e converso Patch's Trial for a Novel[3]—

Your remark on the Voice is most just—but that was my purpose —not only so, but the WHOLE passage was inserted, and intertruded, after the rest was written, reluctante Amanuensi meâ, in order to *unrealize* it even at the risk of *dis*naturalizing it—Lady B. therefore pleased me by saying—never was the golden tint of the Poet more judiciously employed &c—For this reason too I introduced the similie of the Leaf &c—I not only thought the Voice part & Philomel out of place, but in *bad* taste per se.[4]

May God bless you all!—

S. T. Coleridge—

797. *To John Brown*

Address: Mr. Brown | Printer | Penrith   *Single Sheet*
MS. *Victoria and Albert Museum. Hitherto unpublished.* This letter is in Sara Hutchinson's handwriting.

Sunday Night 24th Decr. [1809]

Dear Sir

The Errata to be printed if you have room not otherwise—The Epitaphs and concluding Poem[5] to be printed in the same Type

[1] The story of Maria Schöning was included in the thirteenth number of *The Friend*, dated 16 Nov. 1809.

[2] Jonas Ludwig von Hess (1756–1823).

[3] Richard Patch was found guilty of the murder of Isaac Blight and executed on 8 April 1806.

[4] The passage on Maria Schöning's voice is on p. 195 of *The Friend*, that on the withered leaf on p. 201.

[5] An extract from Wordsworth's *Prelude* concluded the nineteenth number of *The Friend*.

with the Essay which I would always wish to be done with all Poems
—If there should be too much you may omit the shorter of the two
Epitaphs—i.e. the second—& if there be still too much omit both
of them—But I hope you will not find that necessary—I took it for
granted you would not work on Xmas-Day which made me defer
sending the Copy yesterday to Keswick—In the Copy last sent by
the Coach on Saturday you will be pleased to omit the sentences
after the words 'Political oppression'. I mean that bit of a *beginning*
of a Paragraph 'Sir Alexander Ball understood Mankind too well'
& go on with the Copy now sent. Pray be so kind as [to] inform me
at what No. you began to take off on unstamped paper—what No.
of Copies you have taken off—what No. you have printed of No. 1.
& 2.—how many of the other Numbers you have on hand—and
how long the Stamps you have on hand will last you—and also
what number you strike & send off? And lastly what other Subscribers have given up since you sent the List?

S. T. C.

The Copy for No. 20 will be sent you by Tuesday's Coach.

798. *To George Ward*

Address: Mr G. Ward | Bookseller & Stationer | Skinner Street | Snow Hill |
London   Double Sheet.
MS. British Museum. Pub. E. L. G. ii. 28.
Postmark: 10 January 1810.   *Stamped*: Kendal.

Grasmere, Kendal.
Saturday Night. [6 January 1810]

My dear Sir
  I should never have presumed to have published your name as
the Receiver of the Money for the friend, if I had not been desired
by Mr T. Poole so to do, and of course taken for granted that he had
gained your consent, and that I should have heard either from him
or from you if there had been any difficulty.[1] What I am now to do,
God knows—& he only, I believe!—I had no conception that persons would have been so unthinking & unfeeling as to have written

---

[1] Coleridge refers to his 'advertisement' in the sixteenth number of *The
Friend*. See Letter 793, p. 262 n., and Letters 782, 789, and 799.

His experiences in receiving payments for *The Friend* soon led Ward to
decline the business: 'As I am a good deal from home myself I am fearful
your interest may not be properly attended to by those who would represent
me to your "friend" Customers, & as you have other agents in Town
with your permission I will refer those who may call at my House to either
Longman or Brett—the enclosed are all the communications I have at present
received & in future I will hand them over to Messrs Longman & Co.' [MS. Dove
Cottage.]

to *you* desiring you to *call* on any person—I was in hopes, that a considerable number in consideration of the difficulties of the publication would have desired their Correspondents to have left the money at your shop, and that as there must always be some person there to attend the Shop, that person might have received the 1£ note without any other trouble, than that of putting a mark to the name in the List of Subscribers, & giving the Receipt—and that the others would send the 1£ note inclosed.[1]—Who is Mr Brett? Is he a Bookseller? My dear Sir! for God's sake feel for me. I am, as you well know, neither by my habits, or by my nature, a man of Business. I was under the necessity either of giving up THE FRIEND, or of procuring 3 or 4 of my Acquaintances to advance the money for the Stamps to Fourdrinier, for the numbers from 8 to the 20th—I applied to our friend, Poole, among others—and he agreed to advance a third of the stamps wanted, on condition that I had the Subscriptions after the 20th number paid in to you, in order that he might be more sure of his money. Tho' it would have been abundantly more convenient to me to have first got what I could collected for me in London, and the great Towns, by some one Friend in

---

[1] Without waiting for an answer from Ward, Coleridge prepared a 'supernumerary' issue of *The Friend*, dated 11 Jan. 1810, in which he included the following paragraph:

From the same unacquaintedness with business and delusory hopes, I had suggested to the Subscribers, that by desiring their acquaintance in London—not by an especial Letter, but in the course of their other correspondence, to pay in the £1 at Mr. G. WARD's instead of inclosing the note in a letter, they would without any loss to themselves very considerably lessen my expences. The Blame be upon myself! But I certainly had not anticipated, that this suggestion would have occasioned such a number of letters (and those not post-paid) desiring my friend to call on persons, each residing in some different part of the eight square miles occupied by the metropolis and it's suburbs: for this so far from diminishing any expence, must be double to that of receiving the £1 note by the post—which letter would detract ten per cent from the whole sum payed. I am not surprized, that my respected Friend has declined so troublesome a commission: greatly as so unexpected a circumstance has embarrassed me. I can only at present request those who have not paid their Subscriptions, to pay it to the Post-master of the place, at or near which they reside, with instructions to forward it to the Post-master at Kendal: when the receipt which they receive from the Post-master, will be a receipt for the Friend.

Coleridge went on to say that if the number of subscribers remaining on his list should be sufficient barely to pay expenses, he would continue *The Friend* to 28 or 30 numbers and complete the subjects already begun. His list, however, was in London; since he would probably not receive it within less than ten days, and since without it he would remain ignorant of the names of those who had given orders for the discontinuance of *The Friend*, he was 'obliged to suspend the Publication for one Week'. The twenty-first number, therefore, appeared a week late on 25 Jan. 1810.

each, and then to have desired all who had not *so* paid their Subscriptions, to pay them to the Post master of the Place, at or near which they lived, & by him sent with the usual per centage to the Post master at Penrith; yet as Beggars must not be chusers, and the advance was absolutely necessary for me—and my reputation both as a *man* and a Writer depended on my carrying on the work as long as the Number of Subscribers was sufficient to defray it's expences—(and taking in the losses of various kinds, it has never been much more) I assented at once to Mr Poole's Proposal. I earnestly therefore intreat you to help me out of this as well as you can—either by hiring some man, on whose honesty you can rely, for a week, or in whatever other way may strike you as better. I have sent the List of Subscribers to you—at all events, if you really *cannot* have any thing to do with it, the money ought to be paid to some *one* place, and *there* the list of Subscribers ought to be—in order, that I may know as soon as possible what number of the Subscribers have given up the work at the 20th, and that I be able to judge whether the work can go on or must be dropped.—If it be necessary to call at the houses of A. B. and C. and so forth, how can I expect this of Mr Longman's people—? or of Mr Brett, whose name I have now first heard of?—

I know not what to do or what even to ask you—except that, if you *cannot* have the money received at Skinner's Street, you will at all events be so good as yourself to call at Mr Longman's, and to make my best respects either to him or to Mr Rees, and that I intreat that for this once (for there neither will or can be a recurrence of the same difficulties) he will be so good as to let One of his Clerks receive the money and note down the receipt of it—but again I must intreat you, if possible, to hire a man & let him give the receipts, &c—for good God! what can it be less than ruin to me to have persons sent by advertisement first to you, and then to be sent back to Mr Brett, who knows nothing about [it], & thence to Mr Longman? —You will perceive in what distress of mind I write, and will make allowances for it. I intreat you to take nothing amiss, or interpret any word as deficient in respect—I pray you, be so good as to write to me immediately, directing to me—Grasmere, Kendal. And be assured, that whatever you do for me, will be remembered by me with heart-felt gratitude. It is my intention as soon as possible, if the work can go on at all, [to] change it into a fortnightly miscellany, & have it circulated in the ordinary way of Trade without stamps.

If instead of sending the persons to Brett or Messrs Longman & Co, you had simply sent them back, I should have thought it better to advertise in the next Friend, and in the London Newspapers, that all but the Londoners were to send the Subscriptions by the Postmasters, & to have got some private acquaintance to have collected the London ones; but this is too late, I fear.—You will be so kind as to let me know whether any sums have been received,[1] anywhere, and whatever other particulars that may throw any light upon my mind, & enable me to form some feasible plan—

With sincerest good-wishes & respect, believe me, my | dear Sir, | your affectionate Friend,

S. T. Coleridge

P.S. I need not say, that all expences of Postage &c shall be paid you from the first receipts.

799. *To Thomas Poole*

Address: T. Poole, Esqre. | Nether Stowey | Bridgewater | Somerset   Single Letter
MS. British Museum. Pub. E. L. G. ii. 30.
Stamped: Keswick.

12 Jany., 1810. Grasmere, KENDAL.

My dear Poole

I suffer, and have suffered, so much from your long silence, that I can no longer bear the anxiety of suspense, and must intreat you to let me know, if there have been any other cause than your avocations or want of any thing particular to say. I have put both my memory and imagination to the Rack, and cannot even conjecture any ground of offence, unless it should be the trouble I was compelled to give Mr Purkis, in consequence of his own friendly but unlucky interference in counter ordering Mr Hutchinson's Advance to Messrs. Fourdrinier & Co. The persons to whom (as I informed you) I applied conjointly with yourself were Mr J. Hutchinson, and (after my Brother's blank refusal) Mr Sharpe— Mr H. and Mr S. acceded at once to the taking a third of the Stamps on themselves for the 12 or 13 numbers—and Mr H. first sent his order for 2000 St. &c. Mr P. who supposed this to be *all*, that I wanted, instead of being only the *third* part, *substituted* instead of *adding* your order—& to the very last the affair remained so perplexed, that of £137 ‖ 11 ‖ 5d paid, Mr H. payed 53 ‖ 19 ‖ 9; Mr S. 46 ‖ 17 ‖ 8, and Mr Purkis for you 36 ‖ 19 ‖ 0.—But I am not conscious that in my endeavors to explain the case to Mr P., I was deficient in respect: how little it could have been my intention, was

---

[1] In two letters postmarked 3 and 10 Jan. 1810 Ward's firm forwarded statements showing that £9. 15*s.* 4*d.* and £9. 10*s.* 0*d.* had been received on Coleridge's account.

evident by my endeavors to make each letter, I was forced to trouble him with, somewhat less unworthy the Postage by general remarks, on the style of the Friend, the causes of it's unpopularity &c—and in one instance, a couple of Sonnets.—This excepted, which would never have occurred to me except from solicitude to discover if there could be *any* thing, I wonder in vain after a cause on my part for your discorrespondence. Assuredly having sate down in good earnest to exert my best faculties in the way dictated by my best judgment under the prescript of conscience, I should have been glad to have received occasional encouragement or advice from you. I have but slender expectations that THE FRIEND can be continued. The very Essays, you so much admired (3, 4, 5, & 6) occasioned the discontinuance of 70 Subscribers at the 7th No. and as far as I can judge from the 30 or 40 persons, whose payments of I have yet received any account of, three in four will now give it up—This was the effect of the method, by which the original Subscribers were for the greater part obtained, namely, by solicitation of acquaintances, each desirous to oblige me with as large a number as they could—One half therefore of my Subscribers, I am well assured, said Yes! merely to avoid the greater immediate unpleasantness of saying, No!—They not only did not serve me in the way, on which alone I had any reliance from the beginning, namely, as a mode of making the work generally known, as the ordinary plan of advertising on a large scale was out of my power— but they did me disservice by giving out every where that it was an *unreadable* work, dry, obscure, fantastical, paradoxical, and God knows what else—according to each man's taste, and as if they wished to revenge themselves on *me* for the loss of their Shillings.— On the other hand, I have received from some half dozen the warmest acknowlegements, and assurances that if THE FRIEND were more generally known, it's circulation would become considerable. If these good and amiable Folks knew half as much of the present *Public* as even I do, they would think very differently.—My purpose is not to give up the Friend till it gives up itself[1]—& I will go on even tho' it should only barely pay it's expences, till I have brought it to some kind of completeness—however short of my

---

[1] In spite of Coleridge's discouragement, seven more numbers of *The Friend* appeared; the twenty-first on 25 Jan., the twenty-second on 31 Jan., the twenty-third on 8 Feb., the twenty-fourth on 15 Feb., the twenty-fifth on 22 Feb., the twenty-sixth on 1 Mar., and the twenty-seventh on 15 Mar. 1810. Unstamped paper was not obtained until Nov. 1809. As a result, the 100 or more 'sets' of *The Friend* available on unstamped sheets on 15 Mar. consisted of revised reprints of the first 12 numbers and original copies of the last 16 (including the 'Supernumerary'). An edition of these sets was issued in 1812. See pp. 190–1, 239, 243–5, 264, 267, 327, and 385.

wishes—and enable myself to do it by working over hours for the
Newspapers—For Reviewing, which is more profitable & abundantly more easy, I cannot engage in, as I hold it utterly immoral—
and was confirmed in it by the changes, Jeffray made, in my Review
of Clarkson's Hist. of Ab. in the ED. REV., the *only* case in which I
thought myself warranted to make an exception.

Have you seen my seven Letters in THE COURIER—? The 8th &
last will soon appear.[1] They have been highly extolled by *a few*—
the best reward, I can venture to expect, from any thing, *I* can &
at the same time may write—and for my *feelings* a very sufficient
remuneration; but alas! to eat & drink is a necessary condition of
Writing no less than of every other Labor.

One thing half provokes me—that the Friend is called *dear*, tho'
at the same price as Cobbett's, which seldom contains more than a
third of original matter. The *quality* I put out of the question, or the
difference of the powers, motives, previous acquirements, and ex-
penditure of *Thought* requisite in the Friend & a Journal on the
party-politics of the Day—but the *quantity* surely ought to be measured by the matter not by the paper. The 20 numbers of the Friend
cost stamp included (which ought to be taken as a species of
postage, & has nothing to do with the Author but wholly with the
convenience of the Purchasers) £1. Mr Fox's History £1 ‖ 16—take
6s for the Print & call it 30—Now the 20 Nos. of the Friend contain
as many syllables as would fill *two* quartos of the same size so printed,
tho' each quarto should have one fifth *more* matter than the existing
one has. By the bye, tho' I never over-rated Mr Fox, I was grievously
disappointed in his work[2]—The good heart of a sensible English
Gentleman pervades it—rather lax in some parts—but on the
whole a well-thinking amiable man—but of the Philosopher, the
high-minded & comprehensive Historian, I see scarce a trace—.
The names on the other side[3] were written out in the hope of receiving a letter from you, and that you might collect the Sum—which
if I could have procured any friend to have collected the Bristol
ones, would have more than repaid you the advance. But now I fear
it is too late.

I mean to publish, as a Supplement to THE FRIEND, on the same
paper, type &c, not stamped, but in a pamphlet, all my philosophical
principles of Morals & Taste—of all, 'quorum populis tam nulla

---

[1] The last of Coleridge's *Letters on the Spaniards* was published in the
Courier on 20 Jan. 1810.

[2] Charles James Fox's *History of the Early Part of the Reign of James II . ..*
was published by Lord Holland in 1808.

[3] The names of 26 subscribers to *The Friend* living in or near Bridgwater
were copied out by Sara Hutchinson.

cupido'[1] as 'The Mysteries of Christianity grounded in, & correspondent to, the Mysteries of Human Nature.'

I have since (this moment) received a letter from G. Ward, in answer to my earnest request—& he has kindly agreed not to persevere in his declining to receive the payments[2]—

All, whom you know here, are pretty well. It is our intention, as soon as we must quit this House, i.e. before next Winter—to retire to some cheaper part of the Country (for Grasmere is the dearest place in England, out of London, the expence of coals & of carriage for every trifle, included in the additional prices on meat, &c) and live in the cottage style in good earnest—i.e. exactly as Cottagers live. Our only luxury at present is *Tea*: and of that we shall immediately [drink none with] Sugar, & have it only for Breakfast, at which time it is, for *me*, an absolute necessary, if not of Life, yet of literary exertion. We drink (*none of us*) any thing but water—but so great a House, & three servants, make it impossible to bring down our *dinner fare* to the plan which we shall adopt in a Cottage with only one country Maid.—I put myself wholly out of the question. But let any man worthy of that name, contemplate William Wordsworth, let him only read his Pamphlet, assuredly the grandest politico-moral work since Milton's Defensio Pop. Anglic.—and then say, that men of genius make no sacrifices in order to benefit their fellow-creatures. Richard Wordsworth, the attorney, is not worth less than 50,000£ made in business—Christopher is Dean of Bocking (1300 per annum) Chaplain to the Archbishop of C. and likely to obtain the theological Professorship of Cambridge (when the Bishop of Llandaff shall have made the experiment whether an avowed

---

[1] Cf. Virgil, *Georgics*, i. 37 and *Aeneid*, vi. 721.

[2] Ward's letter has not come to light, but a letter postmarked 10 Jan. 1810, from Middleton, Ward's partner, conveys much the same information: 'In Mr Ward's absence I have opened your Letter addressed to him [Letter 798]— he will not return from the Country for some Days but will I am certain be happy to meet your wishes—as far as it lays [*sic*] within his power.' [MS. Dove Cottage.] Thus in the twenty-second number of *The Friend* Coleridge announced: 'Those Subscribers who have not remitted the sum for the first twenty Numbers are solicited to pay the same either to Mr. G. Ward, Bookseller, Skinner-Street, or to the Post-master of the town at or near which they reside; to be repaid by the Post-master at Kendal, or inclosed in a letter (post paid) to Mr. Coleridge, Grasmere, Kendal; or (if containing orders) to Mr. Brown, Penrith.' On 29 Jan. Ward himself wrote: 'I will cheerfully receive any sums that may be brought to me . . . but I cannot undertake to have them collected.'

Ward and Middleton continued to accept payments for *The Friend* until 5 Mar., when they requested that the arrangement be discontinued and reported to Coleridge that an additional sum of £102. 6s. 0d. had been collected. Presumably this money was used to repay in part those who had advanced funds for stamps and paper, though two years later the debt to Sharp weighed heavily on Coleridge. See Letter 863.

Socinian acted honestly in becoming & remaining a Bishop of the Church of England)—After this, Mrs C. Wordsworth (Priscilla Lloyd that was) declares [in a] Letter to her Brother—she shall resign herself wholly to Providence and repel from her mind all anxious discontent concerning the advantages of this transitory World!—How exemplary!—What a [model] of Christian Piety. With 2000£ a year she will take up the Cross [of] the Lord, and mortify the pomps & vanities of the World! Quere. Are such People *conscious* of their Hypocrisy? Answer. No! They take good care, they shall not—& that is the worst sin of the two! God bless you.

S. T. C.

P.S. I must intreat you for reasons explained in my *Supernumerary* to pay the Postage of your letters during the continuance of THE FRIEND.[1] I had no conception of the folly & (far worse) of the malignity of the human heart before.

800. *To Lady Beaumont*

Address: Lady Beaumont | Dunmow | Essex   *Single Sheet*
MS. Pierpont Morgan Lib. Pub. Memorials of Coleorton, *ii. 96.*
Postmark: 24 January 1810.   *Stamped*: Kendal.

Sunday, 21 Jany. 1810, Grasmere, Kendal.

Dear Madam

I have not been insensible of your kind remembrances of me, in your various Letters to Miss Wordsworth, and of the unremitted Interest, which your Ladyship has taken in my weekly labors. Not a letter has arrived from your Ladyship which did not awaken and re-awaken the design of writing to yourself, or to Sir George: and that I have not realized it, I will not attribute to want of *Time* (tho' that is pretty fully occupied, my health and the habits that result from it considered) but to a truer cause, the want of tranquillity. For since the re-commencement of THE FRIEND at the 3rd No., scarcely a fortnight has passed, in which I have not been compelled to struggle with some fresh and unforeseen difficulty: and more than once what I had taken for an Island plunged away downward from under my feet, and left me to providence and my own efforts, to swim or sink.—My Subscribers drop in so slowly with their payments, that at this moment I am as unable to determine,

---

[1] In the 'supernumerary' issue of *The Friend* Coleridge had requested his correspondents to send post-paid letters only—'I have no other resource left, during the publication of the Friend, than to return all not post-paid, unopened'.

whether the Work can be continued, as I was at the publication of the 20th Number. I will, if it please God to permit me, carry it on with increased zeal and spirit, as long as it pays it's own expences: and enable myself to do this by working *over-hours* for the News-papers—which and Reviewing are the only modes of literary Labor, the pecuniary results of which can be relied upon. From the latter I am precluded, as I deem anonymous Criticism altogether immoral, and our *Reviews* without any exception among the most pernicious publications of the age, and as aggravating the Disease, of which they are the symptoms. (One among many reasons for this opinion your Ladyship will see in the introduction to my 21st No.; but I shall hereafter treat the subject at large.) My own hopes con-cerning THE FRIEND are at dead low water. Of the small number, that have payed in their Subscriptions, two thirds nearly have discontinued the work. My House-mates expect better things, and would fain persuade themselves, that those, who meant to discon-tinue the work, would for their own sakes have given the earliest intimation. I should have thought the same myself, two months ago—but my reliance on any argument, which supposes any *delicacy* of conscience in that class of persons, who form perhaps the major part of my List of Subscribers, is very feeble. One instance among *many*—Among the names given in to me at the commencement of the Friend was that of the Earl of Cork.[1] On the appearance of the advertisement, where and to whom the money was to be paid, a Letter came from his Lordship, informing me in very uncourtly language that he had never ordered the work, and therefore should not pay for it—but the Numbers, which he had *quietly* received week after week, he never thought proper to send back or even to hint that he was ready to do so. The true secret of the ill-success of the Friend hitherto (I would be understood as speaking of causes *external* to the *kind* and *execution* of the work itself) is this: the majority of the original Subscribers, who were quite *numerous* enough to have made the work generally known, if it had pleased or suited them, was procured by private solicitation, and at least one Half, I am well assured, answered, Yes! merely to avoid the greater immediate unpleasantness of saying, No!—What *minds*, or rather what *bodies*, I had to deal with, your Ladyship will find no difficulty in conjecturing from a phrase contained in a letter to me from Mr Clarkson, to whose application I owed from sixty to seventy Names—(it was after the appearance of the 5th Number that he wrote to me) 'You ought to consider, that THE FRIEND is a very *dear* work—what if I had charged a shilling per sheet for *my* work?—and that fifty two shillings a year is a serious sum for a person to *bestow*

[1] Cf. *Biog. Lit.*, ch. x.

upon one Author.' Pity that Mr C. had not added—'when there are so many other *Objects* of Distress that have equal or stronger claims on the charitable.'[1] Now I will say nothing of the powers and acquirements (and the sums sunk in the means of developing the one and making the other), the previous possession of which is supposed in such a work: tho' as we always admit this in favor of Lawyers and Physicians, why should it be denied to the Expounders of the Law of the mind, to the Physicians of the Spirit?—But the Friend is sold at the same price as Cobbet's journal, of the same size as that, & stamped like it—and the whole is original matter, while two thirds of Cobbett's is reprinted—and what is original, does for the greater part consist in angry comments on large extracts from the Morning Papers of the week, and the speeches in Parliament. I have not the slightest desire to detract from Mr Cobbett's merits —he is, assuredly, a man of great natural vigor of mind—but he himself, I doubt not, would allow, that this is the very easiest of all possible modes of composition, and that the very *choice* of the *Subjects* in a work, like the Friend, demands a greater effort of Thought, than is required for the *writing* of one of his Letters.— The Spectator, at the time that the value of money was considerably more than double it's present value, was sold at *twopence*. Wordsworth has amused himself with making the calculation, and finds that each No. of the Friend contains the quantity of *five* Spectators —remove the duty from each (each Spectator was taxed one farthing) and the *nominal* Sum remains the same, the real value more than one half in favor of the SPECTATOR. Sixteen Numbers of the Friend would make two quarto Volumes of the size of Mr Fox's posthumous Work, if printed in the same manner.

It is not wholly from weakness of mind that I have troubled your Ladyship with a detail so remote from your habits of thinking and feeling; but for that very reason, because it is so remote—for the wider our sympathies, the more enlarged do our spirits become, and it is only by the knowlege of concerns remote from our own that our Sympathies can be widened. But to finish the Subject, the Subscribers thus gained not only did not serve the work but were of serious Disservice to it. Many abandoned it without any previous warning—and both these, and those who from motives of civility continued it to the 20th, alike joined in giving out THE FRIEND as an *unreadable* Thing—dull, paradoxical, abstruse, dry, obscure, & heaven knows what else! as if they had wished to take revenge on *me* for the Shillings, they had lost in consequence of their own weakness. For the Prospectus bears witness, that I gave them no reason to expect that it would be more amusing than it has been.

[1] Cf. *Biog. Lit.*, ch. x.

I am myself compleatly at rest. I have done my Best—and have received many letters which furnish proof, not by empty praise, but by the feelings which they develope, that even in it's infancy THE FRIEND has done some good—and an unspeakable comfort it is to me to reflect, that what good it does must be of a permanent kind. I dare affirm, after long, repeated, & most religious self-examination, that my sole motive in the undertaking has been, and still is—to enable myself *to* do what good I can *by doing* what good I can; and that I receive a deeper delight from the knowlege that I have half a dozen readers, like your Sister, than I should have from as large a promiscuous sale, as Avarice could crave or Vanity dream of. Early in Life I had my share of Vanity—tho' at the worst it appeared greater than it was, from my natural Open-heartedness, and from being so mixed with the necessity of sympathizing and being sympathized with, and likewise with another pleasure, quite distinct from vanity, that of witnessing *outward proofs* of a power, of which I had attained no steady conviction in my own mind, much less any comparative scale. One mark of this was, that I never in my life defended or attacked any opinion except for itself: nor ever, that I remember, took different sides of a question in different companies to *shew off* my 'colloquial prowess'.—At present, I am more inclined to shun than seek *Reputation,* for it's own sake, and exclusive of it's contingent consequences in the increase of my utility—using the word, Reputation, in it's etymological sense, as the opinions of those who *re-suppose* the *suppositions* of others. Quod Hic *putavit,* ille *reputat*: re-echoes an echo. FAME (from the Greek φημί=the Latin, fari) is indeed a worthy object of pursuit for all men, and to seek it is even a solemn Duty for men endowed with more than ordinary powers of mind: first, as multiplying the ways and chances by which a useful work comes into the hands of such as are prepared to avail themselves of it; secondly, as securing for such a work that submissiveness of Heart, that *docility,* without which nothing really good can be really acquired; and lastly, because the *individuality* of the Author, with all the associations connected with his name & history, adds greatly both to the pleasure & the effect of a work. Who does not read Othello with greater delight from the knowlege, that it was written by the Author of Hamlet, &c &c—that it is SHAKESPERE's! Besides (a more subtle but not unimportant reason) Individuality is essential to the exercise of our moral *freedom*: and if the latter be a most sacred duty, it must likewise be our duty to secure for it it's best and most natural *sphere* of action. FAME is truly the synonyme of *Fatum* (quod optimi homines *fati* sunt)—the fate-like Sentence of the good & wise in a succession of generations, who inevitably decide the ultimate character of Works & actions, from the *permanence* of clear insight, and the *fidelity* of disinterested Love compared with the craving after Novelty, and with those malignant Passions which are under an equal necessity of changing & varying their Objects. But from this, your Ladyship will perceive, it follows as a corollary, that the party of Evil and of Weakness will in the natural course of things be the more operative in and for their generation; because the aching sense of inward infirmity, want of all deep & thorough Conviction, and the necessity of roaming abroad first for new Objects and then for proselytes to confirm them in their own half-belief, will goad the children of folly to ceaseless activity—thence parties are formed —& so a party-spirit—& clamour and bustle, & *hardness* of feeling secure them a temporary victory—Good men shy, and modest; and being satisfied with their own deep convictions they spread their opinions slowly and quietly, just where they chance to find openings of Sympathy. But good men ought to think of this—and the examples of Dr Bell and of Mr Clarkson are therefore invaluable— so much so, that I struggle to forget that the latter would be a case more in point, if an original coarseness of mind had not made the labors & toils of Beneficence less difficult to him, than they would have been to a man of equal Benevolence but of a finer Tact and more exquisite Sensibility. Still his example shews what *one* good man may do, when he goes to the work in right earnest—. Were Virtue as active by energy of Will, as Vice is by the necessity of it's own restlessness, it would be plenipotent.

Miss W. will probably have informed your Ladyship, how deeply I was interested with the account of the Hermit. If it have not been published, I should like to publish it in the Friend, with remarks. Of Jacob Behmen[1] I have myself been a commentator, from Plato, Plotinus, Proclus, & some Catholic Writers of the Vie Intérieure.— But for myself I must confess, I never brought away from his Works any thing I did not bring to them—It is a maxim with me, always *to suppose myself ignorant of a Writer's Understanding, until I understand his Ignorance.*[2] This I have not yet decyphered to myself in the Teutonic Theosopher: yet I conjecture that being ignorant of Logic & not versed in the Laws of the Imagination, he rendered many *Intuitions* in his own mind, perhaps of very profound Truths, and, as it were, *translated* them into such *Images* and *bodily* feelings as *by accident* were co-present with his Intuitions. It is plain, that the words and phaenomena of certain chemical experiments with Quicksilver, and Sulphur (which he learnt from Fludd,[3] or disciples

---

[1] See *Biog. Lit.* ch. ix for Coleridge's remarks on Jacob Boehme.
[2] Ibid., ch. xii.
[3] Robert Fludd (1574–1637), English physician and rosicrucian.

of Fludd) were present to his fancy while he was delving into the possible state of *Being* prior to *Consciousness*—(See the Three Principles,[1] p. 10, 11 etc.) and of the association of bodily feelings, voluntarily forced, with thought, see the ridiculous Analysis of the word, Mercurius, with the separate meanings of Mer, Cu, Ri, and Us. To doubt that this is pure phantastic wilfulness would not be modesty, but ingratitude to the Light of Reason. Yet Jacob Behmen was an extraordinary man. I do not think, you will derive any advantage from his works—the worst and most suspicious circumstance in them is that they dwell so much in *shapes* and *fancies* & things which if true would delight the *curiosity*—whereas *to act* is the duty of man & his essential character—and the most important of all truths can be revealed only *by* and *in* action.—If it please God, I shall shortly publish, as a Supplement to the first Volume of the Friend, a work of considerable size & very great Labor—the toil of many years—entitled, The Mysteries of Religion grounded in or relative to the Mysteries of Human Nature: or the foundations of morality laid in the primary Faculties of Man.—Some parts of the Aurora,[2] and of the Three Principles, may possibly become somewhat clearer to you, after the perusal of my work. Either in this or in some after Number of the Friend I shall give the character of Jacob Behmen & compare him with George Fox—and both with Giordano Bruno.—The most beautiful and orderly developement of this philosophy, which endeavors to explain all things by an analysis of Consciousness, and builds up a world in the mind out of materials furnished by the mind itself, is to be found in the Platonic Theology by Proclus. A Part of it has been translated by Taylor;[3] but so translated that difficult Greek is transmuted into incomprehensible English.—

One observation I must make concerning the plan & style of the Friend in answer to Sir George's kind advice to me , or rather suggestion, concerning Addison. I both love & admire Addison—& deem him inimitable in his own kind of excellence, & that a very high one. But it has *done* it's work—nay, more—it has gone beyond it, & produced a passion for the unconnected in the minds of Englishmen. But for myself, I say—the plan of the Friend is such as I can do best—2. Many can write popularly far better than I can—3. These are *aweful times*! and tho' there is some good done by every additional source of innocent pleasure, yet at present any knowlege,

---

[1] Jacob Boehme, *Beschreibung der drei Prinzipien Göttlichen Wesens*, 1619.

[2] Jacob Boehme, *Aurora oder Morgenröthe im Aufgang*, 1612.

[3] Coleridge's annotated copy of Thos. Taylor's *Philosophical and Mathematical Commentaries of Proclus, . . . and a Translation . . . of Proclus's Theological Elements*, 2 vols., (1792 reissue) is in the British Museum.

which leaves men ignorant of their Ignorance, tends to increase that Ignorance. With most respectful remembrances to Sir George & your Sister, I remain, dear Madam,

your Ladyship's grateful & affecti[onate Friend] & Servant,
S. T. Coleridge.

Miss W. has received the one half of the 10£ note, for which your Ladyship will please to accept my acknowlegements.

801. *To Thomas Poole*

Address: T. Poole, Esqre. | N. Stowey | Bridgewater | Somerset   Single Sheet.
MS. British Museum. Pub. with omis. Letters, *ii. 556.*
Stamped: Keswick.

28 Jan. 1810.
Grasmere, Kendal.

My dear Friend

My 'Man-traps and Spring-guns in this garden'[1] have hitherto existed only on the painted Board, in terrorem. Of course, I have received and thank you for both your letters. What Wordsworth may do, I do not know; but I think it highly probable, that I shall settle in or near London. Of the fate of THE FRIEND I remain in the same ignorance nearly as at the publication of the 20th No.—It would make you sick were I to waste my paper by detailing the numerous instances of meanness in the mode of payment & discontinuance, especially among the Quakers. So just was the answer, I once made in the presence of some '*Friends*' to the ? What is genuine Quakerism? Answer. The Antithesis of the present Quakers. —I have received this evening together with your's one as a Specimen—N.B. Three days after the publication of the 21st No.—and 16 days after the publication of the Supernumerary—A Bill upon a post master—an order of discontinuance and information that any others, that may come, will not be paid for—: as if I had been gifted with prophecy—and this precious Epistle directed—To Thomas Coleridge, of Grazemar.—And yet this Mr Newman would think himself libelled, if he were called a dishonest man. There is one important subject, on which I mean shortly to write—on the influence of the Laws of the Land on the practice and moral feelings of men.—We will take for granted, that the Friend can be continued.

---

[1] 'We talked of a work . . . written in a very mellifluous style, but which . . . contained much artful infidelity. I said it was not fair to attack us thus unexpectedly; he should have warned us of our danger, before we entered his garden of flowery eloquence, by advertising, "Spring-guns and men-traps set here." ' *Boswell's Life of Johnson*, ed. G. B. Hill, 6 vols., 1887, ii. 447–8.

On this supposition, I have lately *studied* the Spectator—& with increasing pleasure & admiration. Yet it must be evident to you, that there is a class of Thoughts & Feelings, and these too the most important, even practicably, which it would be impossible to convey in the manner of Addison: and which if Addison had possessed, he would not have been Addison. Read for instance Milton's prose tracts, and only *try* to conceive them translated into the style of the Spectator—or the finest parts of Wordsworth's pamphlet. It would be less absurd to wish, that the serious Odes of Horace had been written in the same style, as his Satires & Epistles.—Consider too the very different Objects of the Friend & of the Spectator: & above all, do not forget, that these are AWEFUL TIMES!—that the love of Reading, as a refined pleasure weaning the mind from grosser enjoyments, which it was one of the Spectator's chief Objects to awaken, has by that work, & those that followed (Connoisseur, World, Mirror &c) but still more, by Newspapers, Magazines, and Novels, been carried into excess: and the Spectator itself has innocently contributed to the general taste for unconnected writing— just as if 'Reading made easy' should act to give men an aversion to words of more than two syllables, instead of drawing them *thro'* those words into the power of reading Books in general.—In the present age, whatever flatters the mind in it's ignorance of it's ignorance, tends to aggravate that ignorance—and I apprehend, does on the whole do more harm than good.—Have you read the Debate on the Address? What a melancholy picture of the intellectual feebleness of this Country!—So much on the one side of the Question. On the other, 1. I will preparatory to writing on any chosen Subject consider whether it *can* be treated popularly, and with that lightness & variety of illustration which form the charm of the Spectator—if it can, I will do my best. If not, next whether yet there may not be furnished by the *results* of such an Essay Thoughts & Truths that may be so treated, & form a second Essay—3rdly. I shall always, *besides* this, have at least one No. in 4, of rational entertainment, such as were Satyrane's Letters: as instructive as I can, but yet making entertainment the chief Object in my own mind—. But lastly, in the Supplement of the Friend I shall endeavor to include whatever of higher & more abstruse meditation may be needed as the foundations of all the Work after it—and the difference between those, who will read & master that Supplement, & those who decline the toil, will be simply this—that what to the former will be *demonstrated Conclusions*, the latter must start from as from *Postulates* and (to all whose minds have not been sophisticated by a Half Philosophy) *Axioms*. For no two things, that are yet different, can be in closer harmony than the deductions of a profound Philosophy, and the dictates of plain Common-sense—Whatever tenets are obscure in the one, and requiring the greatest powers of abstraction to reconcile, are the same which are held, tho' in manifest contradiction, by the common sense, and yet held and firmly believed, without sacrificing A to —A, or —A to A. There is a beautiful remark on this in Beattie's Immutability,[1] concerning the faith of Sailors in Predestination, & yet equally in their free-agency & moral responsibility.—After this work, I shall endeavor to pitch my note to the Idea of a common well-educated thoughtful man, of ordinary talents; and the exceptions to this rule shall not form more than one fifth of the work—. If with all this it will not do, well! And *well* it will be, in it's noblest sense: for *I* shall have done my best.—Of Parentheses I may be too fond—and will be on my guard in this respect—. But I am certain that no work of empassioned & eloquent reasoning ever did or could subsist without them—They are the *drama* of Reason —& present the thought growing, instead of a mere Hortus siccus. The aversion to them is one of the numberless symptoms of a feeble Frenchified Public.—One other observation—I have reason to *hope* for contributions from Strangers—some from *you* I *rely* on— & these will give a variety which is highly desirable—so much so, that it would weigh with me even to the admission of many things from unknown Correspondents tho' but little above mediocrity—if they were proportionally short, and on subjects which I should not myself treat.

The Supernumerary was printed before I received Ward's third letter. The account of Fourdrinier, which I sent you, was transcribed from Fourdrinier's Letter, stating my Debt, & the manner in which it had been paid.—I daresay, it will be found accurate— but if not, it must surely be, that Mr Purkis has sent down paper since that account, which yet is not likely—for F. says, 'I have this day presented your whole account as finally settled to Mr Sharp &c'—.

You once asked me, what I thought of Grenville Sharpe's Greek Articles.[2] My old School-fellow, & the first Friend, I ever had, the Revd Mr Middleton, has written a thick Octavo on this Subject, deeply interesting—& with some few exceptions, most accurate—It is evident even from *him*, tho' a sort of Advocate, that the rule must be so modified, & so hemm'd in by exceptions, anticipations of mind, &c, as to render it of little practical value. On the first appearance of Christopher Wordsworth's Book on the Subject I

---

[1] James Beattie, *Essay on the Nature and Immutability of Truth in opposition to sophistry and scepticism,* 1770.

[2] See Letters 447 and 679.

studied the matter seriously; [and] but for accidents should have published on it—One fact I *suspected* at [first,] and on research found my suspicion right—viz. that admitting G. Sharp['s] Rule, it is altogether nugatory in the case to which it is applied—He *states* the rule as not applying to Proper names—Now I can prove by a multitude of Instances that from the earliest Ages of Christianity the word Κύριος, = Lord equally with Θεός, Χριστός, &c was used as a proper name—the characteristic of which in the Greek Language is, that you may use it indifferently with or without the article—Δημοσθένης or ὁ Demosthenes, just as we say—Siddons or *the* Siddons—except that what is significant and of course rare in English is common & evidently of perfect indifference in the Greek —*exactly* as in English, Almighty God, or *the* Almighty God—The English is superior to the Greek in point of Articles—The Greek can say—Θεός, which means *a* God, or ὁ Θεός, = *the* God, it depending on the context whether *the* God means some God who was spoken of before, as Apollo for instance, or the Supreme Being—& they have no other way of avoiding this equivocation but by using the neuter adjective, and instead of ὁ Θεός writing το Θεῖον = the divine nature. Now in English we say—*a* God (not a man) *the* God (he of whom we spoke last) and *God*. Consider too, my dear Poole! how little an argument derived from any strict grammatical rule of pure Greek can apply to the Christian Scriptures, when Origen & all the Greek Fathers without exception appeal to the impurity, grammatical barbarisms, & Hebraisms as a proof [of] their authenticity—What becomes of their *Idiōtai*, = illiterate men, applied by them even to St John & to St Paul?—But consult common sense & the philosophy common to all languages, & you will find that even admitting such a rule, it's observation must depend on the ideas connected with the words to which the article is or is not prefixed—that is, in order to apply it, you must first know the very thing which was to be proved by it. For instance, I met in the Lane yesterday the Plumber and Glazier—here *we* know that one person only is meant—I met yesterday the Parson and Clerk—Here are two. Doubtless, it would be better & more accurate to say, the Parson and the Clerk—but where there can be no mistake, what nation even in their common language, even their common writing, is scrupulous in observing such an accuracy? Now, I could produce 20 instances like these of the Plumber & Glazier, and the Parson & Clerk out of the purest Greek Authors—how little then can the Rule be applicable to the Syro-Greek of the New Testament?—Thank God! the doctrine does not want tali auxilio—& I feel convinced, that after a fair perusal of my Supplement you will perceive that Socinianism has not a pin's point to ground itself upon: and that No Trinity, no God—is a

matter of natural Religion as well as of Christianity, of profound
Philosophy no less than of Faith.

May God bless you, and your affectionate
S. T. Coleridge.

802. *To Mrs. S. T. Coleridge*

Address: Mrs Coleridge | Greta Hall | Keswick
MS. Lord Latymer. Pub. E. L. G. i. 429.

[*Circa* 19 February 1810][1]

My dear Sara

Miss Hutchinson, indeed, I believe, all of us wrote to you last
week—& informed you of the safe arrival of the 10£ & that it was
disposed of for paper.—Mr John Monkhouse arrived on Wednesday
Night, with a frightful cut in his chin and (we suspect) a fractured
Jaw, from his Horse's Hoof, as he was walking beside his Horse
between this House & the Blacksmith's Shop. He is going on well—
wonderfully so—but it will confine him a fortnight at least.—
Hartley and Derwent came to the Ball on Friday Night, and
returned on Saturday Morning, to be at some balloon-sport &c at
Mr Lloyd's—They go on better. Mr De Quincey asked Hartley, if
they had quarrelled for the last week—'Why, we had one rather
violent difference—it was a dispute between Derwent and me on
the present state of Agriculture in France. I am very sorry for it—
but indeed Derwent is very tyrannical in his arguing.'—The stumpy
Canary!!—Venerable State-Economists!—What a strange world
we live in! And what a quaint Brace of Doglets these Striplings of
our's are!—And lile Darran[2] too so childish & simple even *under*
his age!—Did you ever tell the story of his grave correcting of me
about the Reptiles &c preserved by Noah?—'O yes, indeed, Father!
there were—there was a Gra[s]shopper in the ark—I saw it myself
very often—I remember it very well.'—O there is a treasure in this
anecdote for a man disposed to examine into the real state of what
is called *Belief* in Religion!—

I am not well—more than usually weak and languid—but it lies
most in my spirits. I do my best to fight up against them; but
indeed bad spirits are a heavier affliction, than folks in general
suppose.

---

[1] The reference to John Monkhouse's accident, which occurred on 14 Feb.,
establishes the approximate date of this letter. See *Middle Years*, i. 357.

[2] Little Derwent was called stumpy Canary, from his short fatness, & wearing a yellow cotton frock. Lile Darran—the name given him by the country
people—who call the Lake 'Darran-water'. [Note written in the manuscript by
Mrs. Coleridge.]

Pray, give my kind Love to Southey, and tell him, that I am sticking in the Mire for the want of the Annual Register, or some equivalent work of the kind, for the year 1800. Indeed, I wish very much to see the volumes from the first treacherous Delivery of Villette [Valletta] to Buonaparte to the recommencement of the war after the Peace of Amiens—i.e.—I imagine, from 1798 to 1802 inclusive; but I absolutely want the volume which contains the delivery of the Island to the British—a nice little prelude of the Cintra Convention in respect of principle & honesty.—If therefore S. have these desideratissima, he will be so good as to let me have them by return of Carrier: and he may rely on receiving them back, spank and spotless, on the same day of next week.

I was delighted with Sariōla's kalligraphical Initiations—and I long to kiss her. As soon as ever I can look a fortnight in the face, i.e. have 2 or 3 Numbers before hand, and there comes a fit of pleasant weather, I will unrust my toes and perform a walk to Greta Hall.

I give my best wishes to Robert Lovell; and should be most happy to do any thing better, that is in my power—by sharing any expences, as soon as ever my chin is above water in the Friend Line.—

Love to all—& kisses, if he will let you, to that darling little Rotondello,[1] whom I more often think of than of any of his sort and standing in Christendom. He is indeed a very, a remarkably engaging child.—

Your's faithfully & affectionately,
S. T. Coleridge

803. *To John Brown*

MS. *Victoria and Albert Museum. Hitherto unpublished.*

[*Circa* 28 February 1810][2]
Dear Sir
The rest tomorrow. Pray, strike out Dominus Pilkington's Name from the List, as requested in the Letter inclosed—I have received the Books—

S. T. C.—

[1] Little Herbert Southey, who died at ten years old. [Note written in the manuscript by Mrs. Coleridge.]

[2] Coleridge's letter appears on copy for the first part of the twenty-seventh and last number of *The Friend*, 15 Mar. 1810. Its approximate date is established by a note of 24 Feb., from Sara Hutchinson to Brown. Her note included a request for books, presumably those acknowledged by Coleridge.

804. *To Mrs. S. T. Coleridge*

Address: Mrs Coleridge | Greta Hall | Keswick
MS. Lord Latymer. Pub. Letters, *ii. 563.*

[*Circa* 14 April 1810]¹

My dear Love

I understand, that Mr De Quincey is going to Keswick tomorrow:
tho' between ourselves, he is as great a *To-morrower* to the full as
your poor Husband, & without his excuses of anxiety from latent
Disease and external Pressure.—Now, as Lieutenant Southey is with
you, I fear, that you could not find a bed for me if I came in on
Monday or Tuesday—I not only am desirous to be with you & Sara
for a while, but it would be of great importance to me to be within
a Post of Penrith for the next fortnight or 3 weeks.—How long Mr
De Quincey may stay, I cannot guess—He (Miss Wordsworth says)
talks of a week; but Lloyd of a *month!*—However, put yourself to
no violence of Inconvenience—only be *sure* to write to me (N.B. to
me) by the Carrier tomorrow.

I am middling; but the state of my Spirit of itself requires a
change of scene. Catherine W. has not recovered the use of her
arm &c; but is evidently recovering it, and in all other respects
in better health than before—indeed, so much better as to confirm my former opinion, that Nature was weak in her, and can
more easily supply vital power for two thirds of her nervous system,
than for the whole.

May God bless you, my dear! and
S. T. Coleridge

Hartley looks and behaves all that the fondest Parent could wish.
He is really handsome, at least, as handsome as a face so original &
intellectual can be.—And Derwent is 'a nice little fellow'—and no
Lackwit either.—I read to Hartley out of the German a series of
very masterly arguments concerning the startling gross improbabilities of the story of Esther (14 improbabilities are stated). It
really *surprized* me, the acuteness and steadiness of Judgment
with which he answered more than half, weakened many others,
and at last determined that two only were not to be got over—I
then read for myself and afterwards to him, Eichhorn's Solution of
the 14 Im[probabilities,] and the coincidence was surprizing—a[s]
Eichhorn after a lame attempt was obliged to give up the two
which H. had declared desperate—

¹ The reference to Catharine Wordsworth's illness closely parallels an account
in Dorothy's letter to Jane Marshall of Sunday night 13 [15] April. See *Middle
Years,* i. 369.

805. *To Lady Beaumont*

Address: Lady Beaumont | S. Audley Street | Grosvenor Square | London
MS. Pierpont Morgan Lib. Pub. E. L. G. ii. 35.
Postmark: 18 April 1810.   *Stamped*: Kendal.

15 April, 1810.

My dear Madam

What can be neither justified or excused, it remains only for me to explain. I am faint with Shame and self-dissatisfaction—but I will nakedly state the fact.—When your Ladyship's Letter arrived, I do not recollect, and as I write from Ambleside, I cannot enquire— but it arrived with two others at a time, when I was labouring under a depression of spirits, little less than absolute Despondency. It is so difficult to convey to another a state of feeling and it's accompaniments, which one believes and hopes that other has never experienced—I can only say, that one of the symptoms of this morbid state of the moral Being is an excessive sensibility and strange cowardice with regard to every thing that is likely to affect the Heart, or recall the consciousness to one's own self and particular circumstances. Especially, in Letters—. A mere letter of Business or from an indifferent person is received and opened at once; but from any one loved or esteemed seems formidable in proportion to that very regard and affection. The sick and self-deserting Soul, incapable of renouncing it's activity, merges it in subjects the most abstruse and remote from it's immediate Duties and Bearings, and so obtains a *forgetfulness*, a sort of counterfeit of that true substantial tranquillity, which a satisfied Conscience alone can procure for us:— 'I will do it after I have read this Chapter—'—'or tomorrow morning'—& so on—till warned by experience the mind is ashamed any longer to *lie* to it's own self by any positive promise, and procrastinates indefinitely.—There is now in my Desk at Grasmere a very large Sheet of paper, three fourths filled by an answer to Sir George's Letter on Shee's proposal[1]—a second with the first page finished on Milton & Party Spirit to yourself—& doubtless, the silly and childish promise, made to myself—I will just finish these Letters—and then I shall have courage to open the second, after I have done my Duty in having answered the first—had some share in this sad neglect.

This is a very imperfect Sketch of the cause of what I am so thoroughly ashamed of—that to day for the first time—nay, this very hour—I opened your Ladyship's Letter, & found the inclosure

---

[1] Coleridge refers to a letter from Sir George Beaumont, dated 21 Jan. 1810, in which the plans of Martin Archer Shee (1769–1850) for the encouragement of historical painting are set forth and criticized.

—I really can write no more at present—. Merely to lose your esteem would be as severe a punishment, as almost any thing external could inflict—but when I reflect on the possible Consequences of esteem so lost by me not only in the present case, but with regard to so many other friends treated disrespectfully in exact proportion to my actual Respect for them, and it's effect in at least weakening whatever I may write, or even what other better men may write, it is almost more than I can bear.—I must therefore now conclude— but I dare venture to say, that I will write and more collectedly, by the next post—and endeavor to make the best of this painful occurrence by rousing myself up to my *immediate* Duty. For I must not blacken myself—Idle I have not been absolutely—but willing to exert energy in any thing, only not that which the Duty of the Day demanded.

    May God bless you, | my dear Madam! | and make even this a Blessing to me.

S. T. Coleridge

Of course, this is not meant as an answer to your kind Letter—In that answer, I must be permitted to write as tho' nothing had happened, that is, as tho' I had read and answered the Letter at the moment—but the feeling, the recollection, will never die.

806. *To Thomas De Quincey*

Address: T. De Quincey, Esqre.
MS. Mrs. Frances Gazda Stover. Hitherto unpublished.

Tuesday Night,
17 April, 1810.—

My dear Sir

    I came down with the Jena Review,[1] was caught in a hard Shower—and not willing to have got a wetting for nothing, have taken the liberty of carrying away with me the remaining Nos. of the work. I am sure, you will excuse me, if only for that I am

Very sincerely | Your obliged & affectionate | Friend,
S. T. Coleridge

I will bring or send them back the day after tomorrow.

---

[1] *Jenaische Allgemeine Literatur-Zeitung*, 1785–1849. See also Letter 1024.

807. *To Mrs. S. T. Coleridge*

MS. Lord Latymer. Hitherto unpublished.

[29 April 1810]¹

My dear Love

My reasons for not coming were these—First, my very great anxiety in consequence of not hearing from B. Montagu, to whom I had sent the order for money to pay the Assurance—The Letter, in which my request with the order was conveyed, he did receive— for it was added to Dorothy's Letter, which he answered; but without taking any notice of mine.—I have not yet received the receipt—and as you may suppose, not a little uneasy. I have written to him again.—Next, I did not like to leave poor Derwent, especially as I was told by Wordsworth, that Hartley's mode of taking leave of him & putting a stop to all thought of *his* walking was too much of a *triumphant* manner—and that Derwent was depressed by it. However, he has been very happy—and you will be pleased to hear, that after repeated examination, I was quite surprized with his process and with the accuracy of his Knowlege in Greek—There lay upon my table a list of words from the original Greek of the Wisdom of Solomon (in the apocrypha) all which were either new-compounds peculiar to that Work, or at least very unusual—the skill, with which Derwent *went about* each word, to analyse it into it's component parts, and the number of them that he made out the meaning of, was truly admirable.—Thus too in a theological work that I was reading, there was a quotation of ten or 12 Hexameter Lines of a Hymn attributed to Orpheus—and Derwent construed nearly one half—that is to say, he knew the meaning of nearly as many of the words, as he was ignorant of— and never made any mistake in the position of the words or in the cases. To day, I pitched on a Chapter in St Paul (I. Corinth. XV)— and having satisfied myself that Hartley [Derwent?] had not read this Epistle at School, I bade him read it to me—and to my surprize he read it as well as I could have done—and not at all in the words of the common translation—But I asked him many quest[ions] of particular words—and he instantly gave the original, & declined it or conjugated it with grammatical fluency.—I thought it my duty to write a short note to Mr Dawes, expressing my acknowlegements.²

---

¹ Coleridge's statement of his 'present intention' to be with Mrs. Coleridge 'on Tuesday next', together with Dorothy Wordsworth's comment on 11 May that 'Coleridge went to Keswick above a week ago' (*Middle Years*, i. 373), seems to give an approximate date for this letter. Furthermore, since it was customary for Hartley and Derwent to spend their week-ends at Grasmere, he was probably writing to Mrs. Coleridge on Sunday.

² The Rev. John Dawes, in whose school at Ambleside Hartley and Derwent

I assure you, Derwent is a very clever Boy—the rapidity, with which he reads & comprehends, is extraordinary. In the course of three days he read three Plays & half of a fourth, of Massinger—tho' he was with me only in the Afternoon & Evening—and he gave a very intelligent account of the story & characters of each.—May God turn it to good account! It is now time for us to begin to think of Hartley—as to profession or trade—It is my present intention to be with you on Tuesday next—but if I am not in at Breakfast time (i.e. 9 or 10 o/clock) I shall not be in till supper—as I shall set off either at 5 in the morning—or at 4 in the Afternoon—

I will bring in the Reply to Clinton[1] if I can rummage it up—& be sure, I will find it if it be in existence here—

I am pretty middling except the dreadful weight on my spirits, which is greater than I would wish my worst enemy to be able to conceive—

Kiss my sweet Sarakin—& may God | bless [you] & your affectionate

S. T. Coleridge—

808. *To William Wordsworth*

Address: William Wordsworth, Esqre. | Grasmere
MS. Dove Cottage. Pub. E. L. G. ii. 37.

[Early October 1810][2]

I am reading Scott's Lady of the Lake, having had it on my table week after week till it cried shame to me for not opening it. But truly

had been placed, assured Coleridge in a letter of Feb. 1810 that 'H. though he may be sometimes verbally, is never *virtually* deficient in brotherly attachment'; and went on to add: 'I have a little favor to ask of you. . . . It is, that, while I have the honour of having Hartley under my care, you will permit me to do the best, that my humble abilities will allow me, to promote his instruction, without receiving any other remuneration than what arises from the pleasure of the performance. In full confidence that you will acquiesce in what will afford me a real happiness, I have ventured to return half the Sum in a Bill inclosed.'

[1] Presumably, Coleridge refers to an answer to Sir Henry Clinton's *A few Remarks explanatory of the Motives which guided the Operations of the British Army during the late short Campaign in Spain*, 1809.

[2] Scott's *Lady of the Lake* appeared in May 1810. On 10 May Southey received the poem at Durham, from whence he returned to Keswick a fortnight later. (*Life and Corres.* iii. 284.) His copy, therefore, was not available to Coleridge until the end of May. But Coleridge for his part kept it unopened on his table 'week after week'. Since Wordsworth was away from Grasmere, where this letter is addressed, during July and August, it must have been written sometime after his return. On 15 Sept. a communication accusing Scott of being 'guilty of imitation' of Home, Pope, Southey, Spenser, and others appeared over the signature S. T. C. in the *Courier*. On 20 Sept. the editor inserted, at

as far as I can judge from the first 98 pages, my reluctance was not unprophetic. Merciful Apollo!—what an easy pace dost thou jog on with thy unspurred yet unpinioned Pegasus!—The movement of the Poem (which is written with exception of a multitude of Songs in regular 8 syllable Iambics) is between a sleeping Canter and a Marketwoman's trot—but it is endless—I seem never to have made any way—I never remember a narrative poem in which I felt the sense of Progress so languid—. There are (speaking of the first 90 pages) two or three pleasing Images—that of the Swan,[1] p. 25.— is the best—the following seems to me to demand something more for it's introduction than a mere description for description's sake supplies—

> With boughs that *quaked** at every breath   *!
> Gray Birch and Aspen wept beneath;
> Aloft, the ash and warrior Oak
> Cast anchor in the rifted Rock—[2]

I wish, there were more faults of this kind—if it be a fault—yet I think, if it had been a beauty, it would not have instantly struck a perplexed feeling in my mind—as it did, & continues to do—a *doubt*—I seem to feel, that I could have used the metaphor; but not in that way, or without other images or feelings in tune with it.—That the Lady of the Lake is not without it's peccadillos against the 8th Commandment[3] a la mode of Messieurs Scott & Campbell, this may suffice—

Coleridge's request, a denial that Coleridge was the author of the attack on Scott, the final sentence of the statement being unmistakably Coleridgean: 'Neither is Mr. COLERIDGE able to interpret the phrase "guilty of imitation," a sort of *guilt* in which every writer in prose or verse must of necessity be implicated, if we except HOMER, who is himself immaculately original only from the loss of all the writings anterior to the Iliad.' That the charge published in the *Courier* turned Coleridge to *The Lady of the Lake* would seem to be borne out by a long criticism of that poem in a notebook entry dated Monday Noon, Septr 1810. Finally, Coleridge's statement to Wordsworth that 'The Kehama is expected', suggests that this letter was written in early October, since the last proof of *Kehama* did not arrive in Keswick until 27 Sept., when Southey thought his poem would probably appear in six weeks. (*Southey Letters*, ii. 202.)

  [1] *The Lady of the Lake*, Canto I. xx, lines 15–16.
  [2] Ibid. I. xii. 11–14.
  [3] This slighting reference to a violation of the eighth Commandment, an allusion reiterated more emphatically in Letter 886, may have been provoked by a conversation with Jeffrey, who visited the lakes during the summer of 1810 and mentioned Scott's favourable comment on *Christabel* to Coleridge. Scott, Jeffrey informed Coleridge, had said that he was indebted to *Christabel* 'for the first idea of that romantic narrative in irregular verse, which he afterwards exemplified in his Lay of the Last Minstrel, and other works'. *Edinburgh Review*, Aug. 1817, p. 510 n.

To William Wordsworth

> Some feelings are to mortals *given*
> *With less* of Earth in them than *Heaven*.[1]
>   Vide Ruth, p. 110.[2]—

In short, what I felt in Marmion, I feel still more in the Lady of the Lake—viz. that a man accustomed to cast words in metre and familiar with descriptive Poets & Tourists, himself a Picturesque Tourist, must be troubled with a mental Strangury, if he could not lift up his leg six times at six different Corners, and each time p— a canto.—I should imagine that even Scott's warmest admirers must acknowlege & complain of the number of prosaic lines—PROSE IN POLYSYLLABLES, surely the worst of all prose for chivalrous Poetry —not to mention the liberty taken with our Articles, & pron. relatives such as—

> And Malcolm heard his Ellen's Scream
> *As faultered thro' terrific Dream.*
> Then Roderick plunged *in sheath* his sword
> And veiled his wrath *in scornful word*
> 'Rest safe, till morning! Pity, 'twere
> Such cheek should feel the midnight air.
> Then may'st thou to James Stuart tell
> Roderick will keep the Lake & Fell
> Nor lackey, with his free-born Clan,
> *The pageant pomp of earthly man!—
> More would he of Clan Alpine know,
> Thou canst our Strength & Passes shew.
> Malise, what ho!'—his henchman came;
> 'Give our safe conduct to the Graeme!'
> Young Malcolm answered, calm and bold,
> [']Fear nothing for thy favourite hold.
> The Spot, †an Angel deigned to grace,
> Is blessed, tho' *robbers* HAUNT THE PLACE;
> Thy churlish Courtesy for those
> Reserve, who fear to be thy foes.

* Vide Wesley's Hymns for the Arminian Methodist chapel.—[Note by S. T. C.]

† Ellen: an Angel means a beautiful young Lady. I think, I have met with the same thought *elsewhere*! and 'deigned to grace'—N.B. She was residing there by compulsion, her father being under the wrath of '*King James*.' [Note by S. T. C.]

1 *The Lady of the Lake*, ii. xxii. 1–2.
2 'For him, a Youth to whom was given
   So much of earth—so much of heaven.' (lines 124–5.)

As safe to me the mountain way
At midnight, as in blaze of Day,
!!! Tho', with his boldest at his back,
Even Roderick Dhu *beset the Track*!*
Brave Douglas—lovely Ellen—nay—
Nought here of parting will I say.
Earth does not hold a lonesome glen
So secret,† but we meet agen.
Chieftain! we too shall find an hour.'
He said, and left the sylvan Bower.—¹

On my word, I have not *selected* this Stanza—I do not say, that
there are not many better, but I do affirm, that there are some
worse, and that it is a fair specimen of the general style.—But that
you may not rely on my Judgment I will transcribe the next
Stanza likewise, the 36th—

Old Allan‡ followed to the Strand
(Such was the Douglas's Command)
And anxious told, how, on the morn,
The stern Sir Roderick *deep had sworn*,
The fiery Cross should circle o'er
Dale, Glen, & Valley, Down, & Moor.
Much were the Peril to the Graeme
From those, who to the signal came;
Far up the Lake 'twere *safest land*,
Himself would row him to the Strand.
He gave his Counsel to the wind,
While Malcom did, unheeding, bind,
Round Dirk & Pouch and broad-sword roll'd,
His ample Plaid in tightened *fold*,
And stripped his Limbs *to such array*
As best might suit the watery way.
37
Then spoke abrupt: 'Farewell to thee,
Pattern of old Fidelity!'

* What a thumping Braggadocio this youthful Lover is! [Note by S. T. C.]
† S. has been called the Caledonian Comet; but Comets move in ellipses—
and this is doubtless a most eccentric Ellipse, which would frighten Priscian.
—[Note by S. T. C.]
‡ A miserable copy of Bracy the Bard—Allan too has a *prophetic Dream*;
and what is it? The very ancient Story to be met with in all books of second
Sight, that a Gentleman travelling found a dinner prepared for him at a place
where he had never been before (as related in Humphrey Clinker, et passim)!—
—[Note by S. T. C.]

¹ Ibid. II. xxxv. 3–32.

The Minstrel's hand he kindly prest,—
'O! could I *point a place* of rest!
My Sovereign holds in ward my land,
My Uncle leads my vassal band;
To tame his foes, his friends to aid,
Poor Malcolm has but heart & blade.[']

Poor Malcolm! a hearty Blade, that I will say for him!—
The Poem commences with the poorest Paraphrase-Parody of the Hart Leap Well—.

I will add but one extract more, as an instance of the Poet's ear for lyric harmony—Observe, this a poem of the dark Ages, & admire with me the felicity of aiding the imagination in it's flight into the Ages past, & oblivion of the present by—God save the King! & other savory Descants.

Boat Song.   (Canto 2. *19.* p. 69)

Hail to the Chief who in triumph advances,
Honour'd & blest be the evergreen Pine!
Long may the Tree in his banner that glances,
Flourish, the Shelter and grace of our line!
 Heaven send it happy dew,
 Earth lend it sap anew,
Gayly to bourgeon and *broadly to grow*,
 While every highland Glen
 Sends our shouts back agen,
'Roderigh Vich Alpine dhu, ho! ieroe!'

Now, that will tell! that last Gaelic Line is 'a damn'd hard Hit'—as Renyolds [*sic*] said of a passage in King Lear—I suppose, there is some untranslatable Beauty in the Gaelic words, which has preserved this one line in each stanza unenglished—even as the old Popish Translators left the Latin Words & Phrases of the Vulgate sticking, like raisins in a pudding, in the English Text.—

In short, my dear William!—it is time to write a Recipe for Poems of this sort—I amused myself a day or two ago on reading a Romance in Mrs Radcliff's style with making out a scheme, which was to serve for all romances a priori—only varying the proportions——A Baron or Baroness ignorant of their Birth, and in some dependent situation—Castle—on a Rock—a Sepulchre—at some distance from the Rock— Deserted Rooms—Underground Passages —Pictures—A ghost, so believed—or—a written record—blood on it!—A wonderful Cut throat—&c &c &c—Now I say, it is time to make out the component parts of the Scottish Minstrelsy—The first Business must be, a vast string of patronymics, and names of

Mountains, Rivers, &c—the most commonplace imagery the Bard gars look almaist as well as new,[1] by the introduction of Benvoir-lich, Uam Var,

> on copse-wood gray
> That *waved & wept* on *Loch Achray*,
> And mingled with the pine trees *blue*
> On the bold Cliffs of Benvenue[2]—
>
> How should the Poet e'er give o'er,
> With his eye fix'd on Cambus-More—
> Need reins be tighten'd in Despair,
> When rose Benledi's ridge *in air*
> Tho' not one image grace the Heath,
> It gain such charm from flooded Teith—
> Besides, you need not travel far,
> To reach the Lake of Vennachar—
> Or *ponder refuge* from your Toil
> By far Lochard or Aberfoil![3]—

Secondly, all the nomenclature of Gothic Architecture, of Heraldry, of Arms, of Hunting, & Falconry—these possess the same power of reviving the caput mortuum & rust of old imagery—besides, they will stand by themselves, Stout Substantives, if only they are strung together, and some attention is paid to the sound of the words—for no one attempts to understand the meaning, which indeed would snap the charm—3—some pathetic moralizing on old times, or any thing else, for the head & tail pieces—with a *Bard* (that is absolutely necessary) and Songs of course—For the rest, whatever suits Mrs Radcliff, i.e. in the Fable, and the Dramatis Personae, will do for the Poem—with this advantage, that however thread-bare in the Romance Shelves of the circulating Library it is to be taken as quite new as soon as told in rhyme—it need not be half as interesting—& the Ghost may be a Ghost, or may be explained—or both may take place in the same poem—Item—the Poet not only may but must mix all dialects *of all ages*—and all styles from Dr Robertson's to the Babes in the wood—

I have read only two Cantos out of six—it is not that it would be any act of self-denial to send you the Poem, neither is it for the pain, which, I own, I should feel, and shrink *at* but not *from*, of asking Southey to permit me to send it—that I do not send you the

---

[1] 'Gars auld claes look amaist as weel's the new', *The Cotter's Saturday Night*, line 44.

[2] *The Lady of the Lake*, I. v. 9–12.

[3] These lines are, of course, a parody on Scott, ibid. I. v. and vi.

Poem to day—but because I think, you would not wish me to ask Southey, who perhaps would refuse, and certainly would grant it with reluctance & fear—& because I take for granted, that you will have a copy sent you shortly—

I send the Brazil which has entertained & instructed me. The Kehama is expected.

May God bless you!—I am curious to see the Babe; but long more anxiously to see little Catherine—

S. T. Coleridge—

809. *To John Monkhouse*

Address: J. Monkhouse Esqre. | Mrs Addison's | 38 Bernard St | Russel Square
From Mr Coleridge
MS. Miss Joanna Hutchinson. Hitherto unpublished.

Since the quarrel with Wordsworth, beginning in October 1810 and concluding with a kind of reconciliation in May 1812, played so great and tragic a role in Coleridge's life, a brief résumé of the circumstances will, perhaps, clarify a good many references and allusions in the letters which follow.

After leaving Grasmere in May 1810, Coleridge settled down for five months at Greta Hall, Keswick. By October he had resolved to go to Edinburgh and place himself 'in the House, and under the constant eye, of some medical man', in an effort to gain a conquest over his opium habit. In the meantime, the Basil Montagus, who were visiting the Wordsworths, invited Coleridge to accompany them to London in their carriage, stay at their house at 55 Frith Street, Soho, and consult their friend and physician, Anthony Carlisle. Yielding to pressure from both Mrs. Coleridge and the Montagus, Coleridge 'acquiesced'.

Convinced that such a domestication would end in 'mutual dissatisfaction', Wordsworth intervened. According to Dorothy, he 'used many arguments to persuade M. that his purpose of keeping Coleridge comfortable could not be answered by their being in the same house together.' When Montagu remained unconvinced—'He would do all that could be done for . . . [Coleridge] and would have him at his house'—Wordsworth 'spoke out and told M the nature of C's habits. . . . Montagu then perceived that it would be better for C to have lodgings near him.' Nothing at all was said to Coleridge. The party set off for London on 18 Oct. and arrived there eight days later.

On Sunday night the 28th, Montagu brought forward 'William's communications as his reason for not wishing to have C[oleridge] in the house with him'. There exists no exact record of what Montagu said to Coleridge, but extant letters and Crabb Robinson's diary repeat some of the more objectionable expressions: 'Wordsworth *has commissioned* me to tell you, first, that he has no Hope of you'; that 'for years past [you] had been an ABSOLUTE NUISANCE in the Family'; and that you were '*in the habit* of running into debt at little Pot-Houses for Gin'. Likewise, Wordsworth was reported to have spoken of Coleridge as a '*rotten drunkard*' who was 'rotting out his entrails by intemperance'.

Although Coleridge had been aware, both at Coleorton and later at Grasmere, that his association with the Wordsworths was no longer on the old footing and that their attitude toward him had undergone a change, nevertheless, he seems not to have realized either that they felt hopeless of him or that they would reveal confidential details of his habits to others. Montagu's disclosures, therefore, came upon him 'with all the aggravations of surprize'. Disillusioned and broken-hearted he retired to Hudson's Hotel, Covent Garden.

Here he was to suffer a second shock. 'A most intimate & dear Friend' of the Montagus went to John Morgan and urged him to call 'at the Montagues in order to be put on his guard' against Coleridge. Instead, as Coleridge later reported, Morgan 'came to me instantly, told me that I had enemies at work against my character, & pressed me to leave the Hotel & to come home with him' to Hammersmith. Even the plan to receive medical assistance had fallen through, for Coleridge had laid bare the facts of his opium habit, only to have Carlisle violate professional confidence by revealing 'to a Woman, who made it the subject of common Table Talk, . . . every thing . . . confided to him as a Surgeon'. Small wonder that Coleridge was to complain of the 'series of anxieties, cruel disappointments, and sudden Shocks' which overwhelmed him from the first week of his arrival in London.

Undoubtedly troubled by Coleridge's precipitate departure for Hudson's Hotel, Montagu wrote to Wordsworth. Dorothy briefly summarizes the letter: 'On their road . . . [Montagu] had seen so much of C's habits that he was convinced he should be miserable under the same roof with him, and . . . had repeated to C what William had said to him and . . . C had been very angry.' It is clear from this summary that Montagu gave only the barest details, and certainly he made no allusion to his false statement that Wordsworth had 'commissioned' him to speak. Wordsworth said nothing to Coleridge but contented himself 'with telling M that he thought he [Montagu] had done unwisely'.

In the next year and a half there was total silence between the two men, but in the households at Grasmere and Keswick and among mutual friends the affair was much discussed. Certainly the activities of others tended to deepen the rift. As word reached Grasmere of Coleridge's state of mind and sufferings, Wordsworth bitterly resented the 'implication' that he was responsible for them; and when he finally heard from Southey the actual words used by Montagu—'Nay, but Wordsworth *has commissioned* me to tell you'—he expressed the 'conviction' that 'Montagu never said those words', that Coleridge 'had invented them'—indeed he came to regard himself as the injured party and to believe that Coleridge was 'glad of a pretext to break with . . . [him] and to furnish himself with a ready excuse for all his failures in duty to himself and others'. Coleridge, on the other hand, waited in vain for an explanation; instead, finding that his sufferings were deemed 'pretence', that even his veracity was questioned, he was led to call Wordsworth his 'bitterest Calumniator' and finally became convinced that Wordsworth had spoken to Montagu 'as an intentional mean of putting an end to our long Friendship'.

Wordsworth's arrival in London in April 1812 precipitated a crisis. Persuaded that Coleridge rather than Montagu was at fault, anxious to put a stop to the gossip circulating in London, and further angered by new disclosures from Mrs. Clarkson and Sharp, Wordsworth proposed that Coleridge should stand trial in the presence of Montagu and himself, with Josiah Wedgwood as referee. 'Woe is me', Coleridge exclaimed on learning of Wordsworth's proposal, 'that a friendship of 15 years should come to this!—and such a friendship'; but he emphatically refused to accede to such a plan—'I can consent to submit to such an examination by no one'. Nor was the matter settled until Wordsworth assured Coleridge that Montagu's statements contained 'absolutely NOTHING of the *spirit* of truth'. See Letters 815, 821, 823, 831, 836 n., 856, 858–9, 863–9, 871, 881, and 888; *Middle Years*, i. 397, 447–9, 454–5, ii. 480–1 and 496; and *Robinson on Books and their Writers*, i. 71 and 75.

To John Monkhouse

Hudson Hotel

Thursday Afternoon—[1 November 1810][1]

My dear Sir

That you did not hear from me last night, was no fault of mine—owing partly to accident, but chiefly to a very painful affair with which I need not trouble you, it was past eleven o'clock before I could get any answer at all—this morning my first business was to arrange every thing as I flattered myself would be most agreeable to your Sister—and accordingly, it has been arranged, that Mrs Montagu will call on your Sister tomorrow morning—and then will introduce the Subject to Carlisle, as of her *own* friend—without any intervention of my name.[2]—

It is impossible, but that Miss Monkhouse should be pleased with Mrs Montagu—She is indeed a very rare instance, of the union of a very superior Intellect with winning kind-heartedness and easy, matronly, confidence-winning manners.—

Believe me, the vexation at not being able to send you any satisfactory account last night, indeed any account at all till too late for a Porter, kept me awake till 3 o/clock this morning—

I have a chearful Presentiment, that Carlisle will restore your Sister to you & to herself an *entire* Machine, without a single creak in any one of the movements of that marvellous piece of Clock-work, which our Souls are shut up in & obliged to act thro'. God knows! I would gladly give up half a dozen years out of my Life if it could secure to Mary a frame of body as good & perfect in *it's* way, as the Soul is pure & lovely that tenants it—O that but one human Being loved me, but half as well as to *my* knowlege three (or four) love & value your Sister—who is the only woman, of whom I ever heard

[1] Since Coleridge retired to Hudson's Hotel shortly after Montagu's revelation of 28 Oct. and left it to join the Morgans at Hammersmith on 3 Nov., the date of this letter must be 1 Nov. See *A House of Letters*, 132–3.

[2] This reluctance to have his name mentioned suggests that Coleridge had already become the victim of Carlisle's unprofessional disclosures. Not having, as he later said, 'the *power* of being vindictive', Coleridge seems merely to have discontinued his consultations with Carlisle—an inference borne out by Mary Lamb's comment of 13 Nov., that 'two days ago' Coleridge 'had not begun his course of medicine & regimen under Carlisle' and by Coleridge's own attempt to gain an introduction to Abernethy on 14 Nov. There is no evidence to confirm Dorothy Wordsworth's statement: 'C had a violent quarrel with Carlyle who refused to attend him as a surgeon after C had slighted his prescriptions.' See Letters 810, 869, and 951; *Lamb Letters*, ii. 106; and *Middle Years*, i. 449.

Carlisle not only discussed Coleridge's case in London but wrote of it to Southey, who reported to Charles Danvers on 13 Nov.: 'Coleridge is in London —gone *professedly* to be cured of taking opium & drinking spirits by Carlisle— *really* because he was tired of being here, and wanted to do both more at his ease elsewhere. I have a dismal letter about him from Carlisle. The case is utterly hopeless.' [MS. Huntington Lib.]

Wordsworth deliver *entire* praise, & without *any* drawback, his own Wife excepted: of whose virtues he considers your Sister, as a Duplicate.

I can only plead in behalf of the above, that it came *direct* from my Heart—and therefore it is no wonder, if it should be a little silly—for want of making the proper circumbendibus thro' the Brain, & calling in on the Understanding on it's way.—

Believe me, | my dear Sir, | with unfeigned & very affectionate | Regard | Your friend

S. T. Coleridge

810. *To John Rickman*

Address: J. Rickman, Esqre | Palace Yard | Westminster
MS. Huntington Lib. Pub. E. L. G. ii. 42.

14 Novemb[e]r 1810.—

My dear Sir

The Report of the Bullion Committee was sent down to me at Keswick & either was lost on the road or missed me—and it is now out of print & not to be bought—I am at present writing on this Subject in opposition to these Scholars of the Edingburgh Review, and cannot go on without it—Now I hope, you may have it in your power to lend it me or to procure me the loan of it—you may depend on it's being restored to you within ten days—and at the same time if you should happen to have the last 15 or 20 Numbers of Cobbett, & will entrust them to me for the same time, I shall have all I want[1]—.

Indeed—you are no friend to *civil* speeches—but indeed I was very much vexed that I was forced off from our mountains so as to cross you in the road—for I had promised myself to have taken (perhaps my last) climb up Skiddaw with you and dear Southey.— His History in the Ed. Ann. Register does him credit—does it not? —Damn the *Edingburgh* in the title page—it is an honor, that that pandaemonium of Impudence, Vanity, Envy, & Ignorance in that it's worst Shape, Sciolism, had no right to.—

Should you be able to lend me the above books, especially the Report, will you be so good as to have them left for me at the Courier office. I would have called myself at your House, but for the fear of interrupting you even for a moment at so busy a time—

Believe me, | dear Sir, | with perfect respect | Your obliged

S. T. Coleridge

[1] Coleridge was apparently writing for the *Courier*, although no contributions for this period have been identified. In a letter to Hazlitt of 28 Nov. Lamb says: 'Coleridge is in Town, or at least at Hammersmith. He is writing or going to write in the Courier against Cobbet & in favor of Paper Money.' *Lamb Letters*, ii. 112.

I am at present at No 7, Portland Place, Hammersmith; but mean to take lodgings as soon as I have fixed on a medical man— Do you happen to know any one who is intimate with Mr Abernethie? And who would introduce me so far as to secure me a little attention?[1]—You may fancy yourself in Ireland again from such a sorites of Requests, one atop of another—Best Compliments to Miss Rickman.

811. *To William Godwin*

MS. Lord Abinger. Hitherto unpublished.

[Endorsed perhaps Nov. 15, 1810][2]

My dear Godwin

I have been of late in a *very low way* as the phrase goes—but I will without fail spend Sunday next with you, & will come, if it be convenient, an hour or two before dinner—or if you will permit, will come very early, taking only such part of your time as would be otherwise unemployed by you, & taking pen, ink, & paper in the other room for the remainder—

May God bless you!

S. T. Coleridge

My Love & kindest wishes to Mrs Godwin—

812. *To the Morgans*

Address: J. J. Morgan, Esqre. | No. 7 | Portland Place | Hammersmith
MS. Lord Latymer. Pub. Letters, *ii. 564.*
Postmark: 21 December 1810.

[21 December 1810]

My dear Friends

I am at present at Brown's Coffee House, Mitre Court, Fleet-Street: my Objects are, to settle something by which I can secure a certain sum weekly, sufficient for Lodging, Maintenance, and Physician's Fees—and in the mean time to look out for a suitable Place near Gray's Inn. My *immediate* plan is, not to trouble myself further about any introduction to Abernethie, but to write a plain, honest, and full account of my state, it's History, Causes, and

---

[1] In Dec. 1810 and again in Feb. 1811 Coleridge was still planning to consult John Abernethy. See Letter 812 and *A House of Letters*, 133.

[2] Since Coleridge was at Godwin's on Sunday, 18 Nov. 1810, the endorsed date is probably correct. See *Blake, Coleridge, Wordsworth, Lamb, etc. being Selections from the Remains of Henry Crabb Robinson*, ed. Edith J. Morley, 1922, p. 32.

occasions, and to send it to him with 2 or 3£ inclosed, and asking him to take me under his further care. If I have raised the money for the inclosure, this I shall do to morrow. For indeed, it is not only useless, but unkind and ungrateful to you & all who love me, to trifle on any longer: depressing your spirits, and spite of myself gradually alienating your esteem & chilling your affection toward me.

As soon as I have heard from Abernethie, I will walk over to you: and spend a few days before I enter into my Lodgings & on my dread ordeal—as some kind-hearted Catholics have taught, that the Soul is carried slowly along close by the walls of Paradise on it's way to Purgatory, and permitted to breathe in some snatches of blissful Airs, in order to strengthen it's endurance during it's fiery Trial by this Foretaste of what awaits it at the conclusion & final goal-delivery.

I pray you, therefore, send me immediately all my Books & Papers with such of my Linen as may be clean, in my Box, by *the errand Cart*, directed—Mr Coleridge, Brown's Coffee House, Mitre Court, Fleet-Street:—A couple of Nails & a Rope will sufficiently secure the Box.

Dear dear Mary! dearest Charlotte!—I entreat you to believe me, that if at any time my manner toward you has appeared unlike myself, this has arisen wholly either from a sense of Self-dissatisfaction, or from the apprehension of having given you offence—for at no time and on no occasion did I ever see or imagine any thing in your behaviour which did not awaken the purest and most affectionate Esteem & (if I do not grossly deceive myself) the sincerest Gratitude. Indeed, indeed, my affection is both deep and strong toward you: & such too that I am proud of it—

And looking t'ward the Heaven, that bends above you,
Full oft I bless the Lot, that made me love you![1]—
Again & again, & for ever | May God bless & love you!

S. T. Coleridge

813. *To George Mitford*

Facsimile Autographic Mirror, *vol. i. 20 February 1864, p. 14.*

George Mitford was the father of Mary Russell Mitford (1787–1855), poetess, novelist, and dramatist. Early in 1811 Mitford sought Coleridge out and persuaded him to look over and revise the proof-sheets of his daughter's poem, *Christina, the Maid of the South Seas*, which appeared in late March or early April 1811. Miss Mitford's letters show that Coleridge went over her poem with meticulous care. He not only struck out an Invocation to Scott, which he felt

---

[1] See *Fragment 26*, lines 7–8, *Poems*, ii. 1002.

contained 'bad lines', but he also added certain 'beautiful lines' of his own. He encouraged her to write a tragedy, perhaps thus launching her on her later career, and in October 1811 a second poem, *Blanch*, was sent to him. Apparently, he was dilatory in returning the manuscript, for on 29 Nov. Miss Mitford hoped she could 'get Blanch back out of his hands', and said she would 'never trouble him' with any more of her manuscripts. [Mitford MSS. Reading Public Lib.; *The Life of Mary Russell Mitford*, ed. A. G. K. L'Estrange, 2 vols., 1870, i. 98–99, 104–5, 123, 126, and 130; and Vera Watson, *Mary Russell Mitford*, n.d., 91–97.] I am indebted to Miss Watson for making available to me a series of extracts from the Mitford manuscripts at Reading.

Dear Sir	Thursday Morning—[14 February 1811][1]

I am sorry that my Health and those engagements which called me suddenly into town should have delayed the Printer.—The last Sheets which I now send back corrected are exceedingly beautiful. Your Daughter like a spirited charioteer has driven in at full gallop, with untired Steeds.—If you will send me the poem entire, I will then give Miss Mitford my sincere opinion of the work, and what those points are in which she appears to me to have something yet to effect in the formation of her poetic style & the principles of construction. In short, I will write as *severe* a review as I can, & let none but the Authoress see it—and praise the poem as warmly as it deserves to all, but the Authoress.—

Accept my thanks for your kind present of the Hare—& believe me, dear Sir, | Your's faithfully,

S. T. Coleridge

814. *To Henry Crabb Robinson*

Address: Henry Robinson, Esqre. | ——Collyer's, Esqre. | 59 | Hatton Garden.
MS. Dr. Williams's Lib. Pub. E. L. G. ii. 44.
Postmark: 12 March 1811.

34, Southampton Buildings—
[12 March 1811]

I have to thank you, my dear Robinson! for the pleasure, I have enjoyed in the perusal of Anton Wall's delightful Tale.[2] I read it

---

[1] On 16 Feb. 1811 Mrs. Coleridge wrote to Miss Betham that Mrs. Morgan had reported Coleridge's removal from Hammersmith to London 'about a week' ago—apparently the sudden journey to town mentioned in this letter. On 14 Feb. Miss Mitford noted that Coleridge had not yet seen the 3rd Canto of *Christina*, and on 20 Feb., possibly as a result of Coleridge's letter, she wrote to a friend that 'the proofs are sent from me to Mr. Coleridge (the Poet) who is so kind as to devote a very large share of his time and attention to them, & who has full liberty to add, omit, or alter at his pleasure'. [*A House of Letters*, 132–3, and Mitford MSS. Reading Public Lib.]

[2] *Amatonda, a Tale from the German of Anton Wall* (C. L. Heyne), translated by H. C. Robinson, 1811.

first with my eyes only, & only for myself—but the second time aloud & to two amiable Women—& both times I felt myself in the embrace of the Fairy Amatonda. The German *Recensent* has noticed as a defect and an oversight what I regard as one of the capital Beauties of the Work; & thus convinced me that for Reviewers the world over & for Readers whose Intellects are commensurate with their's, an Author must write under his best conceptions, This is excellent & I mean so & so by it: even as to the *bodily* dim-sighted, Apelles himself might be under the necessity of saying, This is a Sheep—& this is a Woman. I allude to the omission of Murad. I recollect no fairy tale with so just and fair Moral as this of Anton Wall's—Virtue itself, tho' joined with outward competence, cannot give that happiness which *contents* the human heart, without Love; but *Love* is impossible without Virtue.—Love, true human Love—i.e. two hearts, like two correspondent concave mirrors, having a common focus, while each reflects and magnifies the other, and in the other itself, is an endless reduplication, by sweet Thoughts & Sympathies.—Now Hassan finds content at the outset—in Beneficence, (the emancipation of his Slaves) the social sense (his household henceforward contains only affectionate friends & fellow-labourers), local attachment, chearful Industry— & lastly, virtuous *Love. Him* Amatonda kisses thrice in the first week of his pursuit.—Solmar & Selim wander ten years in the pursuit; they are, however, OFTEN most *honorably*, ALWAYS *innocently* employed—their hearts remain pure—and they *merit* their Biribi and Tabuna.—But Murad sets out on a vile pursuit, & continues it by vile means—He marries a woman, he does not love—neglects her—is a debauchee & a systematic flatterer—he would 'die of ennui' at Beitul Salam—but cuique sua praemia— *his* industry was to wealth, as means to their material ends—& such pleasures, as Wealth & a city Life can confer, let Murad enjoy! What a frightful Incongruity would it not have been, if an Amina had been awarded to the ministerial [Shelter?] of the governing Sultanas!—Defects however there must be in all mortal works.—From Hassan's watching of Algol's countenance we of necessity anticipate some wicked purpose—as well as from the magician's desertion of Bator in his adversity—but no such Thing appears—the fairy Amatonda meets those who deserve her. Algol allegorizes the Hopes & Wishes of the youthful Imagination, which, like Dreams, betoken or betray the innate moral character, out of which they proceed. For all prophecies are the first effects of some Agent, whose presence is not yet seen: as I have heard a friend calling to me by the echoes of his voice among our rocks in Cumberland, before I heard the voice itself or saw *him*.—Perhaps,

I may be as dull in this as the Reviewer was in his Objection;
but I cannot help conjecturing, that Wall in the first floating
plan of his Work had intended to have introduced Algol again—
& his not having done so seems to me almost as great a fault, as if
a character of consequence were to disappear in the first Act of a
Tragedy.—

Secondly, instead of admiring the scanty portion of the supernatural in the Tale, I think this the only important Fault in it's construction—Neither the Hair Girdle, the Ring, the Sword, or the
gold pin do any thing which might not have been done without
them, or in any way carry on the Story. Nay, in Solmar's case, it is
worse than nothing—it is *privative* & not merely negative—for as
far as it is recollected, it detracts from Solmar's Courage—& like
enchanted armour, which the Knights of Chivalry forswore, blends
cowardice with valour. The best of it is, that one does not recollect it.

Thirdly (bless us! here's one of James the first's subdividing
chaplains resurgent in the shape of a Reviewer!) Thirdly—and
(O word of comfort!) *Lastly*—I do not understand the meaning of
the four Houris, & the untasted Banquet in the magician's Palace.
I have tried, over and over again, to make out some allegorical
Substrate; but really have been able to find nothing but a French
Hamiltono-Voltairish Cantharadine, grossly inconsistent with the
character of Hassan, whose Love for Amina is beautifully described as having had a *foundation* from early Childhood—and
this I many years ago planned as the subject-matter of a poem, viz
—long & deep Affection suddenly, in one moment, flash-transmuted into *Love*. In short, I believe, that *Love* (as distinguished
both from Lust and from that habitual attachment which may
include many Objects, diversifying itself by *degrees* only), that
that *Feeling* (or whatever it may be more aptly called), that specific
mode of Being, which one Object only can possess, & possesses
totally, is always the abrupt creation of a moment—tho' years of
Dawning may have preceded. I said, *Dawning*—for often as I
have watched the Sun-rising, from the thinning, diluting Blue to
the Whitening, to the fawn-coloured, the pink, the crimson, the
glory, yet still the Sun itself has always *started* up, out of
the Horizon—! between the brightest Hues of the Dawn and the
first Rim of the Sun itself there is a *chasm*—all before were Dif-
f[er]ences of Degrees, passing & dissolving into each other—but
this is a difference of *Kind*—a chasm of Kind in a continuity of
Time.—And as no man who had never watched for the rise of the
Sun, could understand what I mean, so can no man who has not
been in Love, understand what Love is—tho' he will be sure to

imagine & believe, that he does.—Thus, Wordsworth is by nature incapable of being in Love, tho' no man more tenderly attached— hence he ridicules the existence of any other passion, than a com- pound of Lust with Esteem & Friendship, confined to one Object, first by accidents of Association, and permanently, by the force of Habit & a sense of Duty. Now this will do very well—it will suffice to make a good Husband—it may be even desirable (if the largest sum of easy & pleasurable sensations in this Life be the right aim & end of human Wisdom) that we should have this, & no more—but still it is not *Love*—& there is such a passion, as Love— which is no more a compound, than Oxygen, tho' like Oxygen, it has an almost universal affinity, and a long & finely graduated Scale of elective Attractions. It combines with Lust—but how ?— Does Lust call forth or occasion Love ?—Just as much as the reek of the Marsh calls up the Sun. The sun calls up the vapor—at- tenuates, lifts it—it becomes a cloud—and now it is the Veil of the Divinity—the Divinity transpiercing it at once hides & declares his presence—We *see*, we are conscious of, *Light* alone; but it is Light embodied in the earthly nature, which that Light itself awoke & sublimated. What is the Body, but the fixture of the mind ? the stereotype Impression ? Arbitrary are the Symbols— yet Symbols they are.—Is Terror in my Soul—my Heart beats against my side—Is Grief ? *Tears* form in my eyes. In her homely way the Body tries to interpret all the movements of the Soul. Shall it not then imitate & symbolize that divinest movement of a FINITE Spirit—the yearning to compleat itself by Union ?—Is there not a Sex in Souls ? We have all eyes, Cheeks, Lips—but in a lovely Woman are not the eyes womanly—yea, every form, every motion, of her whole frame *womanly* ? Were there not an Identity in the Substance, man & woman might *join,* but they could never *unify*— were there not throughout, in body & in soul, a corresponding and adapted Difference, there might be addition, but there could be no combination. One *and one* = 2 ; but one cannot be multiplied into one. $1 \times 1 = 1$—At best, it would be an idle echo, the same thing needlessly repeated—as the Ideot told the Clock—one, one, one, one &c—.

It has just come into my head, that this Scrawl is very much in the Style of Jean Paul.[1] I have not however as yet looked into the

---

[1] In his translation of *Amatonda* Robinson says the author told him that the poet Selim in the story was meant 'to satirise the celebrated romance-writer Jean Paul'. Thus Robinson was led to include in his volume a critical estimate of Johann Paul Richter, which begins with a contrast between the German writer and Sterne, and to add a few specimens translated from Richter. See pp. 260 n., 275–88.

Books, you were so kind as to leave with me—further than to see
the Title page. If you do not want it, for some time, I should be
glad to keep it by me—while I read the original works themselves—.[1]
I pray you, procure them for me—work by work—and I will promise you most carefully to return them, you allowing me three
days for two Volumes.[2] I am very anxious to have them—& shall
fill one volume of the Omniana with the extracts, quoting your
criticism as my Introduction[3]—only instead of the *shelves* or
steps I must put the Ladder of a Library—or whatever name those
moveable Steps are called which one meets with in all well-furni-
tured Libraries[4]—

I have been extremely unwell—& am indeed—tho' rather better.
George Burnet's Death,[5] told too abruptly, & in truth exag-
gerated, overset my dear, most dear & most excellent Friend &
Heart's Sister, Mary Lamb—& her Illness has almost overset me—
Troubles, God knows! have thronged upon me—Alas! alas! all my

---

[1] Undoubtedly Coleridge refers to Robinson's copy of *Jean Pauls Geist oder
Chrestomathie der vorzüglichsten, kräftigsten und gelungensten Stellen aus seinen
sämtlichen Schriften; mit einer Einleitung und einzelnen Bemerkungen begleitet,*
2 vols., 1801. Robinson's copy, which contains annotations by Coleridge, is now
in the Dr. Williams's Library.

[2] For Coleridge's interest in Richter, see Letters 907 and 1089; *Blake,
Coleridge, Wordsworth, Lamb, etc. being Selections from the Remains of Henry
Crabb Robinson,* ed. Edith J. Morley, 1922, p. 31; and *Robinson on Books
and Their Writers,* i. 26, 106, and 150.

In addition to *Jean Pauls Geist* Coleridge also annotated Richter's *Das
Kampaner Thal oder über die Unsterblichkeit der Seele; nebst einer Erklärung der
Holzschnitte unter den 10 Geboten des Katechismus,* 1797 (now in the Princeton
University Library); *Palingenesien,* 2 vols., 1798 (whereabouts unknown);
and *Museum,* 1814 (now in the Dr. Williams's Library).

[3] *Omniana, or Horae Otiosiores,* the joint work of Coleridge and Southey, was
published anonymously in two volumes in 1812. No extracts from Richter
appear in the work.

[4] Coleridge refers to a sentence in Robinson's estimate of Richter: 'It was
acutely observed to the translator by an excellent English critic of German
literature, that it seemed to him as if Jean Paul's works were composed while
the author was standing on the steps of a bookcase; as if he opened his volumes
promiscuously, and, having noted down some recondite fact of art or science,
then sought for a moral analogy; and, having collected a number of these
materials, afterwards strung them together as he pleased!' *Amatonda,* 279–80.

[5] In Feb. 1811 George Burnett 'died wretchedly in a workhouse', the
Marylebone Infirmary. According to Robinson, Burnett 'had applied a little
while before to Charles Lamb for money which Lamb had not sent him, for he
had before received relief from him, with a promise not to apply again for six
months'; and from Mrs. C. Aikin, Robinson learned that Burnett had made a
similar application, to which the Aikins 'had shown no attention'. Rickman,
too, had received 'begging letters' a year earlier and had reported that Burnett
was starving. *Robinson on Books and Their Writers,* i. 24, and *John Rickman,*
152.

dearest Friends I have of late either suffered *from*, or suffered *for*. 'Tis a cruel sort of World we live in!—

God bless you | & | Your's with affectionate Esteem,

S. T. Coleridge

P.S. I began with the Scrap of Paper—meaning only to write half a score Lines—And now I have written enough for half a dozen Letters, unnecessarily—when to have written to half a dozen Claimants is a moral (would it were, a physical) necessity. But moral obligation is to me so very strong a Stimulant, that in 9 cases out of ten it acts as a Narcotic. The Blow that should rouse, *stuns* me.

Do not forget whenever you write to Bury, to recall my name to Mrs Clarkson. May God eternally bless her! To feel, not only how *much*, but *how* I love and esteem her, reconciles me to my own nature, when I am least contented with it. Had she been my Sister, I should have been a great man. (Excuse a Vanity which struggles forth out of the pangs of Humility.) But I have never had any one, in whose Heart and House I could be an Inmate, who loved me enough to take pride & joy in the efforts of my power, being at the same time so by me beloved as to have an influence over my mind. And I am too weak to do my Duty for the Duty's Sake. All honorable Things would be dear to me, if they were only lovely—as reputation, fame, competence, Health of Mind & Body —but then in order to become lovely to me, I must be able to think of them as adding to the happiness of some other Being who found her happiness in mine—and under whatever name that might be, with all the duties belonging to that name, Wife or Sister, I *know* that I could not only be content, but be happy. I never saw a woman yet, whom I could so imagine to have [been] born of one parent with me at one Birth, as Catharine Clarkson—She has all, that is good in me, and all that is innocent in the peculiarizing parts of my nature—Would to God! I had what she has besides— & which I have not—her sacred *magnanimity*!

815. *To Matilda Betham*

MS. Lord Derby. Pub. with omis. A House of Letters, *129.*

Thursday afternoon—[14 March 1811][1]
34, Southampton Buildings,
Chancery Lane.—

Dear Miss Betham

True History will be my sufficient Apology. After my return
from Lady J., on Monday night or rather morning, I awoke from
my first short sleep unusually indisposed—and was at last forced to
call up the good daughter of the House at an early hour to get hot
water and procure me medicines. I could not leave my bed till past
six Monday Evening: when I crawled out in order to see Charles
Lamb, and to afford him such poor comfort, as my society might
perhaps do, in the present dejection of his spirits & loneliness.—
This did not mend the matter with me—I became worse, and kept
my bed all Tuesday and the greater part of yesterday—. But
thinking myself a little better yesterday morning, I determined
to keep my engagement with you—and accordingly got up about
4 o/clock & attempted to dress myself for an evening visit. Half
an hour's experience however was enough to shew me the imprudence of the attempt—To walk would have been out of my power
—& had I gone & returned in a coach, I should have only brought
an alarm, instead of a visitor—too unwell to have conversed, and
agitated by the apprehension of being taken sick & giddy, in the
presence of strangers perhaps, and 3 miles from my Lodgings.—
It was too late to send you a note by the twopenny Post, and I
have no servant.

I am a little, and only a little better, at present—if it be possible,
I shall put myself in the Hammersmith Stage this evening—as I
am not fit to be in Lodgings, by myself.

In truth, I have had such a series of anxieties, cruel disappointments, and sudden Shocks, from the first week of my arrival in
London, that any new calamity suffices to overset me—The tidings
of George Burnet's Death with it's circumstances, told me in the
most abrupt manner, and then as abruptly & before I could prevent it, told to Mary Lamb, had agitated me violently—& the
extreme efforts, I made, to suppress the bodily effects of my agitation in her presence, injured me still more—She dropped certain

[1] The allusion to Coleridge's visit to Lady Jerningham's, which took place
on Sunday evening, 10 Mar., and the reference to the illness of Mary Lamb,
who was placed under confinement on 9 Mar., establish the date of this letter.
The Jerningham Letters, ed. Egerton Castle, 2 vols., 1896, ii. 7, and *Robinson
on Books and Their Writers,* i. 24.

ominous words at the time—and on Saturday Night, when I was somewhat recovering my spirits, having received a cheerful & humorous Note from Charles Lamb inclosing a scrap of your Letter, with Lady Jerningham's Address, but informing my hospitable Friends that he and his Sister would come & dine with them, notwithstanding—on the Saturday Night, as I was walking out with Mrs Morgan & her Sister to meet Mr Morgan as he returned from Town, and just as my whole tone of feeling was harmonized & become genial by the mild vernal air & the almost gay moonlight, Mr Morgan replied to our welcoming with the sad news, that Mary Lamb had been attacked with her complaint at 5 o/clock that morning, & taken into the country by Charles at 7—!—On the Sunday Mr Godwin called on me, to inform me that Miss Lamb had been at their house on Friday, & that her manner of conversation had greatly alarmed them (dear excellent creature! such is the restraining power of her Love for Charles Lamb over her mind, that he is always the last person in whose presence any alienation of her understanding betrays itself)—that she talked far more & with more agitation concerning me than about G. Burnett, had urged him to come over to me, & told Mrs Godwin, that she herself had written to Mr Wordsworth, exhorting him to come to town immediately, for that my mind was seriously unhinged.[1]—After

---

[1] Mary Lamb's letter, which was written on the verge of a relapse, has not come to light, but Dorothy Wordsworth, Crabb Robinson, and Coleridge all allude to it. In her reply Dorothy sent Mary Lamb an account of 'what had passed between M[ontagu] and Wm and assured her of the truth that there was no coolness on William's part'; but Wordsworth's 'cold answer'—for there seem to have been two letters—was such that Lamb 'deemed it unadvisable' to show it to Coleridge, who nevertheless learned of its contents and was later to rebuke Wordsworth for having written it.

As early as Nov. 1810 the Wordsworths heard from the Montagus that Coleridge 'has his hair dressed and powdered by a hairdresser every day'; from Mary Lamb that he has been 'very chearful'; and from Lamb that he 'has powdered his head, and looks like Bacchus, Bacchus ever sleek and young'. Thus Mary Lamb's letter urging Wordsworth to come to town immediately drew from him a 'Sneer' on Coleridge's 'reported high Spirits & . . . wearing Powder'. The '*wearing Powder*', Wordsworth asserted, was 'proof positive' that Coleridge 'never could have suffered any pain of mind from the affair— . . . that it was all pretence'.

Although Mary Lamb had aroused the Wordsworths, Lamb himself carefully refrained from communicating any message which would aggravate the quarrel. Yet his sympathy for Coleridge is clearly revealed in several entries in Crabb Robinson's diary for 1811.

'[8 January] We spoke of Wordsworth and Coleridge. Lamb, to my surprise, asserted Coleridge to be the greater man. He preferred the *Mariner* to anything Wordsworth had written.'

'[21 July] Lamb . . . intimated that Wordsworth had lately treated Coleridge

To Matilda Betham

Mr Godwin's departure Lamb came—I had just time enough to have half an hour's mournful conversation with him—he displayed such fortitude in his manners, and such a ravage of mental suffering in his countenance, that I walked off, my head throbbing with long weeping—& the unnecessary Haste, I made, in the fear of being too late, and the having to act before the Curtain, as [it] were, afterwards—for the more I force away my attention from any inward distress, the worse it becomes after—& what I keep out of my mind or rather *keep down* in a state of under-consciousness, is sure to act meanwhile with it's whole power of poison on my Body—This, my dear Miss Betham—waiving all connection of sentences—is the history of my breach of engagement, of it's cause, and of the occasions of that cause.

Remember me to your Brother—& be assured that I am | with unfeigned and affectionate Esteem | Your's most respectfully,

S. T. Coleridge.

816. *To Daniel Stuart*

Address: D. Stuart, Esqre | Courier office
MS. British Museum. Pub. Letters from the Lake Poets, *208*.

[15 March 1811][1]

Dear Stuart

I did call at Brompton on Sunday Afternoon on my way to old Lady Jerningham's, and took with me a letter for you—but just at your door I discovered that in the flurry and agitation of my mind, having just left Charles Lamb, I had not wafered the letter—and

with great unkindness and made him quite wretched. He had warned Montagu not to take him into his house. This had afflicted Coleridge, and Wordsworth had not taken any notice of it, though he knew how much he had been affected by the circumstance.'

'[3 August] Chatted till eleven with Charles Lamb. . . . He corrected me not angrily, but as if really pained by the expression "poor Coleridge", I accidentally made use of. "He is a fine fellow, in spite of all his faults and weaknesses. Call him Coleridge—I hate '*poor* Coleridge.' I can't bear to hear pity applied to such a one."'

When in May 1812 Lamb was asked to convey Wordsworth's demands to Coleridge, he reluctantly assumed the unhappy role of intermediary, but even then he did not repeat one message, 'from the anxiety not to add fuel to the flame'. See *Middle Years*, i. 416 and 448; *Robinson on Books and Their Writers*, i. 17, 40, 43, and 78; *Lamb Letters*, ii. 106 and 108; and Letters 856 and 866–7.

[1] This letter was written on the morning after Coleridge's return to Hammersmith on 14 Mar. See preceding letter.

as it contained several remarks on the second Article on the Abuse of Prisons,[1] which I would by no means have had seen by any one but yourself, I resolved to call again at night: still I not only fully expected but had engaged to be back again at Hammersmith by half past 9, and Lamb actually waited for me till half past 10. It was not so much that I feared, my letter would not be kept sacred if I had left it with your Servant at the time I delivered my message to her, as that it might appear disrespectful or at least any indelicacy to you, considering the nature of the comments.—

For the 4 preceding days I had been kept continually agitated, my head and eyes were throbbing with long weeping at the time I quitted Hammersmith—fearing I should keep the dinner waiting, which would have been an unkind thing to Miss Betham for whose sake alone grievously against the grain I had engaged to go before the unhappy events took place, I walked very hard—arrived in a violent heat—and then had to wait dinner for an hour and twenty minutes—after Coffee I was going, when a Mrs Jerningham sat down to the Piano, & her Mother in law, the old Lady, informing me that she was without doubt the first player in the Kingdom, & allowed to excel her Master, Cramer, I could not in civility not sit down to listen, tho' little inclined to your very superfine Music— the Lady herself however was wondrously so: for she continued playing a long hour—it was now eleven o/clock—as soon as I got out of the house I found myself indisposed, & endeavored to get a bed at Pulsford's & at Hatchett's—but could not—which was lucky: for I was obliged to call up the people at my lodgings at daylight on Monday—& have kept my bed ever since till last night when I forced myself out into the Stage, finding that I ought not to remain by myself—.

I am a good deal better this morning.—I am much obliged to you for your kindness with regard to the Tickets—if Cato is acted tomorrow, I should certainly like to see it, should your Tickets be disengaged—Mr Morgan will leave this at the Courier office, & should he find you there, you will be so good as to let me know thro' him whether or no they are—.

Your obliged
S. T. Coleridge.

[1] Two long articles entitled 'Abuse of Prisons' appeared in the *Courier* on 4 and 7 Mar. 1811. They were probably written by Stuart, who visited the Cold Bath Fields Gaol in the company of Coleridge. The purpose of this visit was to see whether Gale Jones, who was imprisoned for libel, was being mistreated, as he had asserted in the newspapers. Sara Coleridge suggests 'that the article in the *Courier* of Saturday, February 16, on the conduct of Government with respect to libels, was written or dictated by . . . [her] Father', but she did not reprint it. See *Essays on His Own Times*, iii. 1032–4.

817. *To William Godwin*

MS. Lord Abinger. Pub. with omis. Letters, *ii. 565.*

Monday, 1 o/clock—. [18 March 1811]

My dear Godwin

　I receive twice the pleasure from my recovery, that it would otherwise have afforded, as it enables me to accept your kind invitation, which in this instance I might with perfect propriety and manliness thank you for, as an honor done to me. To sit at the same table with GRATTAN[1]—who would not think it a memorable Honor, a red letter day in the Almanach of his Life? No one certainly, who is in any degree worthy of it. Rather than not be in the same room, I could be well content to wait at the Table, at which I was not permitted to sit—and this not merely for Grattan's undoubted great Talents, and still less from any entire accordance with his political opinions, but because his great *Talents* are the Tools & vehicles of his *Genius*—and all his speeches are attested by that constant accompaniment of true Genius, a certain *moral* bearing, a *moral* dignity—His love of Liberty is ἀκαδήμου—it has no smatch of the *mob* in it.

　Assure Mrs Godwin of my anxious wishes respecting her Health. The Schola Salernitana says—

　　Si tibi deficiant medici, medici tibi fiant
　　Haec tria: MENS HILARIS, REQUIES, moderata Diaeta.[2]

The regulated Diet she already has—and now she must contrive to call in the two other Doctors.—

　The night, after I quitted you, I was myself taken ill—& continued, with one imprudent exception, in bed, till Thursday Evening—when I put myself in the Hammersmith Stage, & by care & the social feeling, and that *approach* to the domestic which alone is in *my* power, I am getting about again.

　　　　　　　　　　　　　　　　God bless you | &
　　　　　　　　　　　　　　　　　　S. T. Coleridge

　I have this moment received your note–

---

　[1] Henry Grattan (1746–1820), the Irish statesman. After the Union Act of 1800, Grattan devoted his efforts chiefly to the question of Roman Catholic emancipation.
　[2] See Letter 409 and note.

818. *To William Godwin*

Address: Mr Godwin | Juvenile Library | Skinner Street
MS. Lord Abinger. Pub. with omis. William Godwin, *ii. 222.*
Postmark: 26 March 1811.

Tuesday Noon—[26 March 1811]

Dear Godwin

Mr Grattan did me the honor of calling on me & leaving his
Card on Sunday afternoon, unfortunately a few minutes after I had
gone out—and I am so unwell, that I fear, I shall not be able to
return the call to day, as I had intended, tho' it is a grief even for
a brace of days to appear insensible of so much kindness & condescension. But what need has GRATTAN of Pride?

> Ha d' uopo solo
> Mendicar dall' *Orgoglio* onore e stima,
> Chi senza lui di vilipendio è degno.

Chiabrera.

I half caught from Lamb that you had written to Wordsworth,
with a wish that he should versify some tale or other—& that
Wordsworth had declined it.[1]—I told dear Miss Lamb that I had
formed a complete plan of a Poem with little plates for children,
the *first* thought, but that alone, taken from Gesner's First
Mariner:[2] and this thought I have reason to believe was not an
invention of Gesner's—It is this—that in early times in some island
or part of the continent the Ocean had rushed in, overflowing a vast
plain of 20 or 30 miles, & thereby *insulating* one small promontory
or Cape of high Land—on which was a Cottage, containing a man
& his wife & an infant Daughter——This is the *one* thought—all
that Gesner has made out of it (for I once translated into blank
verse about half of the poem, but gave it up under the influence
of a double disgust, moral & poetical) I have rejected—& strictly
speaking, the tale in all it's parts, that one idea excepted, would be
original—the tale will contain the cause, the occasions, the process,
with all it's failures & ultimate success, of the construction of the
first Boat, and of the undertaking of the first naval expedition——
Now supposing you liked the idea (I address you and Mrs G. and,
as *Commerciants*,[3] not you as the Philosopher who gave us the first
system in England that ever dared reveal at full that most important of all important Truths, that Morality might be built up on

---

[1] For Wordsworth's letter declining Godwin's proposal see *Middle Years*, i.
427.

[2] See Letters 444 and 445 for Coleridge's earlier preoccupation with Salomon
Gessner's *Der erste Schiffer*.

[3] In 1805 Godwin had established a publishing business in his wife's name.

it's own foundation, like a Castle built *from* the rock & *on* the rock, with religion for the ornaments & completion of it's roof & upper Stories—nor as the Critic who in the life of Chaucer has given us if not principles of *Aesthetic,* or Taste, yet more & better Data for Principles than had hitherto existed in our Language)—if (we pulling like two friendly Tradesmen together, for you & your Wife *must* be one flesh, & I trust, *are* one heart) you approve of the plan, the next question is—whether it should be written in prose, or in verse—& if the latter, in what metre—Stanzas, or 8 syllable Iambics, with rhymes (for in rhyme it must be) now in couplets and now in quatrains, in the manner of Cooper's admirable Translation of the Ververt of Gresset[1] (N.B. *not* Cowper, *the*)—

Another thought has struck me within the last month, of a School-book in two octavo volumes, of *Lives* in the manner of Plutarch; but instead of comparing & coupling Greek with Roman, Dion with Brutus, & Cato with Aristides, of placing ancient & modern together—Num[a] with Alfred, Cicero with Bacon, Hannibal with Gustavus Adolphus, & Julius Caesar with Buonaparte—or what perhaps might be at once more interesting & more instructive, a series of Lives from Moses to Buonaparte of all those great Men, who in states or in the mind of man had produced great revolutions, the effects of which still remain, & are, more or less distant, causes of the present state of the World.

I ought to apologize to you for not having repaid you the 2£ you were so good as to lend me—The truth is, I have not been able, having been cruelly unfortunate in losing my only book of accounts, & unsuccessful in collecting the money owed me—Not one half of the Subscribers, scarcely more than a third, have payed me[2]—a job however has been offered me to day, & I shall soon be able to repay you with convenience to myself—My Love to Mrs Godwin, & with kindest wishes for her's & your's I remain with unfeigned & affectionate

esteem, your's, dear Godwin,
S. T. Coleridge

[1] John Gilbert Cooper published a translation of J. B. L. Gresset's *Vert-Vert* in 1759.

[2] From the time of his arrival in London in Oct. 1810, Coleridge had been desperately trying to collect money from the dilatory subscribers to *The Friend.* 'One thing is certain', Dorothy Wordsworth wrote to Mrs. Clarkson of Coleridge in Dec. 1810, 'that he is in great want of money, for he had been with Tom Monkhouse to ask him to help him to collect.' *Middle Years,* i. 416. See also Letters 826, 828, 842, 852, and 863.

819. *To William Godwin*

Address: Mr Godwin | Skinner Street—
MS. Lord Abinger. Pub. with omis. William Godwin, *ii. 224.*

Friday Morning—[Endorsed Mar. 29, 1811]

Dear Godwin

My chief motive in undertaking 'The first Mariner' is merely—
to weave a few tendrils around your destined Walking-stick, which
like those of the wood-bine (that, serpent-like climbing up, and
with tight spires embossing, the straight Hazel, rewards the lucky
School-boy's Search in the winter copse) may remain on it, when
the wood-bine, root and branch, lies trampled in the earth. I shall
consider the Work, as a small plot of ground given up to you, to be
sown at your own hazard with your own seed (gold-grains would
have been but a bad Pun & besides have spoilt the metaphor)—if
the Increase should more than repay your risk and labor, why, then
let me be one of your guests at *Harvest-home.*

Your last Letter impressed and affected me strongly. Ere I had
yet read or seen your works, I at Southey's recommendation wrote
a Sonnet in praise of the author.[1] When I had read them, religious
bigotry, the but half-understanding your principles, and the *not*
half-understanding my own, combined to render me a warm &
boisterous Anti-Godwinist. But my Warfare was open; my unfelt
and harmless Blows aimed at an abstraction, I had christen'd with
your name; and you at that time if not in the World's *favor* were
among the Captains & Chief men in it's admiration. I became your
acquaintance, when more years had brought somewhat more
temper and tolerance; but I distinctly remember, that the first
turn in my mind towards you, the first movements of a juster
appreciation of your merits, was occasioned by my Disgust at the
altered tone & language of many, whom I had long known as your
Admirers and Disciples—some of them too men, who had made
themselves a sort of reputation in minor circles, as your acquaintances and therefore your *Echoes by authority*—who had themselves
aided in attaching an unmerited ridicule to you and your opinions
by their own Ignorance, which led them to think the best settled
truths, and indeed *every* thing, in your Political Justice, whether
Ground, or Deduction, or Conjecture, to have been new thoughts,
downright creations! and by their own vanity, which enabled them
to forget, that every thing must be new to Him who knows *nothing*
—others again, who tho' gifted with high talents had yet been

---

[1] *To William Godwin*, first published in the *Morning Chronicle*, 10 Jan. 1795.
See *Poems*, i. 86.

indebted to you and the discussions occasioned by your work for
much of their developement, who had often and often styled you
the great Master—written verses in your honor—&—worse than
all—had brought your opinions—with many good & worthy men—
into as unmerited an Odium, as the former Class had into contempt,
by attempts equally unfeeling and unwise to realize them in private
life, to the disturbance of domestic peace—and lastly a third Class,
—but the name of Mackintosh spares me the necessity of describing it!—In all these there was such a want of common sensibility,
such a want of that gratitude to an intellectual benefactor, which
even an honest reverence for their past Selves should have secured,
as did then, still does, & ever will, disgust me.—

As to Southey,[1] I cannot justify him; but he stands in no one of
the former Classes. When he was young, he just looked enough
into your books to believe that you taught Republicanism and
Stoicism—ergo, that you were of his opinion, & he of your's and this
was all. Systems of Philosophy were never his Taste or Forte.—
And I verily believe, that his conduct originated wholly & solely in
the effects, which the Trade of Reviewing never fails to produce
at certain times on the best minds—presumption, petulance, and
callousness to personal feelings, and a disposition to treat the
reputations of their Contemporaries as play-things placed at their
own disposal. After Southey had quarrelled with me, during my
first absence from England—and with Hartley playing in the same
room with him—he wrote & published a far more contemptuous
Review of my Poem[2] in the Lyrical Ballads, than of your Age of
Chaucer[3]—'A Dutch Imitator of German Sublimity,' he gave as
my character.—Most certainly I cannot approve of such things;
but yet I have learnt, how difficult it is for a man who has from
earliest Childhood preserved himself immaculate from all the
common faults and weaknesses of human nature, and who never
creating any small disquietudes has lived in constant and general
esteem & honor, to feel remorse or to admit that he has done wrong.
Be[lieve] me, there is a bluntness of Conscience superinduced by a
very unusual Infrequency, as well as by the Habit & Frequency,
of wrong Actions. Sunt, quibus cecidisse prodesset, says St Augustin.
—To this add that *business* of Review-writing carried on for 15
years together—and which I have never hesitated to pronounce an

---

[1] In a letter dated 27 Mar. 1811, Godwin complained to Coleridge of Southey,
who 'treat[s] my efforts, not only with disdain, but with something like
abhorrence. Thank God, I have never had the persuasion as to the singleness of
heart of that man, with which you have been impressed'. [MS. Lord Abinger.]

[2] *Critical Review*, Oct. 1798.

[3] Southey reviewed Godwin's *Life of Chaucer* in the *Annual Review* for 1803.

immoral employment, unjust to the Authors of the Books reviewed, injurious in it's effects on the public Taste & Morality, and still more injurious in it's influences on the Head & Heart of the Reviewer himself. The *Praegustatores* among the luxurious Romans soon lost their Taste; and the verdicts of an old Praegustator were sure to mislead, unless when, like Dreams, they were interpreted into contraries. Our Reviewers are the genuine Descendents of these palate-sered Taste-dictators.—

I am still confined by indisposition, but mean to step out to Hazlitt's, almost my next door neighbor—at his particular request. It is possible, that I may find you there.

With kind remembrances to Mrs Godwin, your's, dear Godwin, affectionately,

S. T. Coleridge

820. *To Unknown Correspondent*

MS. Bodleian Library. Hitherto unpublished.

Dear Sir   Tuesday Morning. [23 April 1811][1]

I have just returned from Richmond: or your very kind Letter would have received an earlier reply. I will write to Mr Southey, who leaves Keswick for London early in May, to bring up with him the deficient Numbers, 3, 6, 16, 19, and the two or three after 25— and will take care, that they shall be forwarded to you at your Father's—The amount is either 27, or 28 Shillings; but you will see by the Numbers. It is my wish to continue The Friend to No. 40, on the same plan: except that after the 30th Number, I shall not print it on Stamped Paper, reducing the Price to 10d.—After the 40th Number, it will probably go on on a new plan, monthly.[2]— But all this you will learn more fully from the next Number. If you please, you may inclose the £1 note for the first 20 numbers, addressed to me at my Lodgings, 34, Southampton Buildings, Chancery Lane—and leave the rest till the Friend in it's present form is compleated. You will generally find me at home, in South: Build: from 9 in the Morning till 2 or 3—and I assure you, I shall be very glad to see you, if waiving all form of Introduction you will give me an opportunity of talking over Christ's Hospital, and former days with you—Your's, dear Sir, very respectfully

S. T. Coleridge

---

[1] Coleridge was at Richmond on 20 and 21 April 1811. See *Specimens of the Table Talk of the late Samuel Taylor Coleridge*, ed. H. N. Coleridge, 2 vols., 1835, ii. 343–57.

[2] Nothing came of Coleridge's plans to continue *The Friend* as a periodical work. See Letters 826 and 842.

821. *To Daniel Stuart*

Address: D. Stuart, Esqre. | 36 | Brompton Row | Brompton
MS. British Museum. Pub. E. L. G. ii. 50.
Postmark: ⟨28⟩ April 1811.

Sunday Morning. [28 April 1811][1]

Dear Stuart

I arrived safe at my lodgings, about ½ past 12 ; but I have suffered, as I deserved, most severely for my Intemperance. So well too as I was becoming, I can scarce pardon myself for my Incaution— the ground of it all is that vile custom of drinking to each other during dinner, which not only makes a modest or heedless man's inclinations dependent on the habits, or intended civilities & complimentary respects of every one of his fellow-guests, but is, I am persuaded, absolute poison to the whole digestive System. How indeed should Nature withstand two violent actions at the same time, that of the Food on the secretory vessels and that of hot diffusive Stimuli on all the nerves of the Stomach! Besides, how much more cheerful, with what cool and broad-awake Hilarity, our Fathers used to take their first bumper of Port, after the Cloth was removed! The presence of the women too for the first half hour made the bottle circulate very slowly: so that the primitiae and most important part of digestion was performed under the assistance of two or three glasses & of easy leisurely chat & mirth, before the Drinking set in. Whereas now, a man is flustered by the violent processes going on in his stomach; and tho' we drink less wine than formerly, what we drink, injures us more. 'When the Devil, was sick'—he amused himself with writing sermons. And the fact is, that till yesterday I have not been able to keep any thing on my Stomach, with such confusion in the feeling of my Skull and Forehead, tho' not in my thoughts, whenever I bent down to write, as rendered me incapable of writing any thing to any purpose. I vow to God, and I pray, God help me to keep the vow, that I never hereafter will drink a single Glass of Wine during dinner, except in case of sudden faintness when I should have drank it as a medicine at any other time. Perfect Health I do not expect ever to have; but Experience has convinced me, and I shall act most criminally if I rebel against it, that by getting up early, by an entire abstinence from Spirits on all ordinary occasions, and by

---

[1] By 3 May the arrangements for regular work on the *Courier*, as Coleridge outlined them in this letter, had already been made. (See Letter 825.) It should be noted, however, that in addition to the contribution to the *Courier* of 16 Feb. (See Letter 816 n.) Coleridge had also furnished an article on 19 April 1811. See *Essays on His Own Times*, iii. 733–48.

living in a family where my social affections are kept alive, that I
may henceforward and for some years enjoy such a portion of
Health as will enable me to perform all my literary Duties quietly
and systematically. The quickness, with which I pass from Illness
into my best state of Health, is astonishing, & makes many think
it impossible, that I should have been so ill, the day or two before;
but this child-like suddenness of convalescence is, I believe, symptomatic of those whose complaints arise from weakness and irritability of the Bowels, and who have at the same time more power of
the nervous, than strength of the muscular, system.

So much for the Past. For the present and future I wish most
anxiously to have your advice & assistance. I must commence by
telling you, great a weakness as it must appear, that so deep and
so rankling is the wound, which Wordsworth has wantonly and
without the slightest provocation inflicted in return for a 15 years'
most enthusiastic, self-despising & alas! self-injuring Friendship,
(for as to his wretched Agents, the Montagus, Carlisles, Knapps,
&c, I despise them too much to be seriously hurt by any thing,
they for themselves can say or do) that I cannot return to Grasmere
or it's vicinity—where I must often see & always be reminded of
him. Every man must take the measure of his own strength. I may,
I do, regret my want of fortitude; but so it is, that incurable
depression of Spirits, Brooding, Indolence, Despondence, thence
Pains & nightly Horrors, & thence the Devil & all his Imps to get
rid of them or rather to keep them just at arm's length, would be
infallibly the result. Even to have only thought of Wordsworth,
while writing these Lines, has, I feel, fluttered & disordered my
whole Inside. On the other hand, to live by myself would be almost
equally dangerous.—I have however an alternative in my power:
if only I can procure any regular situation, which might employ me
& my pen from 9 to 2, 5 or even 6 days a week—in this case, I could
settle myself with comfort to my own feelings & with perfect propriety, as a member of Morgan's Family.—In this letter I address
you, dear Stuart! in a twofold character—first, as my Friend, &
secondly, as I would any other person, Perry or Walter—as the
former, I am sure you will give me the best advice in your power,
but in the latter character I wish nothing but the mere fact of
advantage or disadvantage, convenience or inconvenience, relatively to yourself. But it struck me, that by devoting myself for
the next half year to the Courier, as a regular Duty, I might prove
useful to the Paper: as, if it were desirable, I could be at the office
every morning by ½ past 9, to read over all the Morning Papers &c,
& point out whatever seemed noticeable to Mr Street,—that I
might occasionally write the leading Paragraph when he might

wish to go into the City or to the Public offices—and besides this, I would carry on a series of articles, a column and a half or two columns each, independent of small paragraphs, poems etc, as would fill whatever room there was in the Courier whenever there was room. In short, I would regularly furnish six Columns to Mr Street, which [he] might suffer to accumulate in busy times—. I have thought, that this might perhaps be pleasing to Street: as I should have no pretence to any controll or Intermeddlement; but merely during a certain space of Time be in part, his Assistant, and in part, a political Writer in the service of the Paper—. Should the Plan seem feasible to you in itself, and your objections rest chiefly on your fears as to my steadiness, I can only say—Give me a month's Trial.

I am very uneasy about the payment of my Annuity Assurance— even in London there is far more owing to me than that amounts to—and this I doubt not, I shall be able to collect as soon as my mind is once at ease, and any thing is but settled. Besides, as soon as Southey brings up my Manuscripts, I am sure of being able to sell them for more or less.—But I am interrupted—I hope to see you tomorrow morning, either at Brompton or at the Courier office—God bless you &

S. T. Coleridge.

822. *To John Whitaker*[1]

Address: Mr Whitaker | 48 | Smithfield . . .
MS. Colorado College Lib. Hitherto unpublished.
Postmark: 30 April 1811.

34, Southampton Buildings—
[30 April 1811]

Dear Sir

I have transcribed three Songs[2] of my composition for you. Should either of them awake in you the wish to increase it's value tenfold by setting it to Music, I shall be flattered: tho', permit me to say, in a far less degree, that I should be mortified, if I could even suspect that you would do it, not for the fitness of the Poetry, but out of delicacy to the feelings of the Poet. Believe me, my feelings are of a hardier nature, and my good wishes for your reputation & the success of whatever you publish are quite strong enough to render any private vanity of my own an evanescent point, when

---

[1] John Whitaker (1776–1847), composer and member of the music publishing firm of Button, Whitaker & Co. of St. Paul's Churchyard and organist at St. Clement's, Eastcheap.

[2] These 'Songs', which precede the letter in the MS., are printed after Coleridge's signature.

brought into competition with more serious things.—By some mistake—whether your Wine & the Pipe were in part guilty of it, I cannot say—I put 'Offspring Fair of Love divine' into my pocket, instead of 'Love will find out a way'—The latter I wish to have, yet take the Liberty not to return the former as I mean to write a song to the Notes, for the expression of my own private Feelings.— Perhaps, you will be so good as to let one of your Sons leave it at my Lodgings for me, 34, Southampton Buildings, Chancery Lane.—

After this week, if you have any thing to communicate to me, you will address me at 'J. J. Morgan's, Esqre., No. 7. Portland Place, Hammersmith.'

I almost fear, that I took an improper Liberty in calling on you on Sunday in Smithfield, instead of seeking you, on some week day, in St Paul's Church yard; but your own kindness and Mrs Whitaker's, were in some measure in fault—or rather, the cause.—

As it will be many months before the proposed Work can commence, had I not better return the Radamisto[1] till then?—Pray, make my kind & respectful Remembrances to Mrs W. & with every good wish for you & your's, I remain, dear Sir,

Your obliged
S. T. Coleridge

The Visit of the Gods[2]

Never, believe me!
Appear the Immortals,
Never alone.
Scarce had I welcom'd the Sorrow-beguiler,
Iacchus; but in came Boy Cupid, the Smiler!
Lo! Phoebus, the Glorious, descends from his Throne!
They advance! They float in! The Olymp[ians] all!
With Divinities [f]ills my
Terrestrial Hall.

How shall I yield you
Due Entertainment,
Celestial Quire?
Me rather, bright Guests! with delicious Upbuoyance
Bear aloft to *your* Home, to your Banquet of Joyance,

---

[1] Probably a reference to Handel's opera, *Radamisto*, presented in London 27 April 1720.

[2] *Poems*, i. 310. 'Imitated from Schiller': sub-title in *Sibylline Leaves*.

That the Roofs of Olympus may echo my Lyre!
Hah!—we mount! On their pinions they waft up my Soul!
O give me the Nectar!
O fill me the Bowl!

Give, give [h]im the Nectar!
Pour out for the Poet!
Hebe! pour free!
Moisten his Eyes with celestial Dew,
That STYX the detested no more he may view,
But like one of us Gods may conceit him to be!
Thanks, Hebe! I quaff it! Io PAEAN, I cry!
The Wine of the Immortals
Forbids me to die.

S. T. C.

The Myrtle Leaf, or Innocence Seduced:
(an *allegory* addressed to an unfortunate Woman.)[1]

Myrtle Leaf, that ill-besped
Pinest in the gladsome Ray,
Soil'd beneath the vulgar Tread
Far from thy maternal Spray.

When the Partridge o'er the Sheaf
Whirr'd along the yellow Vale,
Sad I saw thee, heedless Leaf!
Love the dalliance of the Gale.

Lightly didst thou, thoughtless Thing!
Heave and flutter to his Sighs:
While the Flatterer on his Wing
Woo'd and whisper'd thee to rise.

Gaily from thy parent Stalk
Wert thou danc'd and wafted high,
Soon on this neglected Walk
Flung to fade, to waste, to die!

S. T. C.

SEA BATHING.[2]

God be with thee, gladsome Ocean!
How gladly greet I thee once more!
Ships, and Waves, and endless Motion,
And Men rejoicing on thy Shore.

---

[1] *Poems*, i. 172.   [2] Ibid. 359.

Mildly said the grave Physician,
To bathe me on thy strands were Death;
But my Soul fulfill'd her Mission,
And lo! I breathe untroubled Breath.

Fashion's pining Sons and Daughters,
Who seek the Crowd, they seem to fly,
Trembling they approach thy Waters:
And what cares Nature, if they die?

Me a thousand Loves and Pleasures,
A thousand Recollections bland,
Thoughts sublime and stately Measures,
Revisit on thy echoing Strand:

Dreams, (the Soul herself forsaking!)
Grief-like Transports, boyish Mirth!
Silent Adorations, making
A blessed Shadow of this Earth!

O ye Hopes! that stir within me,
Health comes with you from above!
God is with me, God is in me,
I cannot [die,] for Life is Love!

S. T. C.

823. *To Mrs. S. T. Coleridge*

Pub. Middle Years, *i. 448.* This fragment, which is quoted in a letter of 12 May from Dorothy Wordsworth to Mrs. Clarkson, is all that survives of Coleridge's letter.

[Circa 1 May 1811]¹

. . . If you knew in detail of my most unprovoked sufferings for the first month after I left Keswick and with what a thunder-clap that *part* came upon me which gave the whole power of the anguish to all the rest—you would pity, you would less wonder at my conduct, or rather my suspension of all conduct—in short that a frenzy of the heart should produce some of the effects of a derangement of the brain etc. etc. . . .[2] I leave it to Mrs Morgan to inform you of my health and habits. . . .

---

[1] In introducing this excerpt Dorothy writes: 'The other day . . . Mrs C received a letter from Coleridge about his MSS.' Undoubtedly this is the letter to which Coleridge refers in writing to Longman on 2 May 1811.

[2] Coleridge had mentioned no names in his letter except those of Mr. and Mrs. Morgan, to whose kindness, he said, he owed it that he was in his senses—in short that he was alive; but Dorothy 'burned with indignation that William

824. *To Thomas N. Longman*

Address: Messrs. Longman & Co | Paternoster Row—
MS. Mr. Carl H. Pforzheimer. Hitherto unpublished.

[2 May 1811][1]

Dear Sir

I hereby, if this were a sufficient memorial, should make over to you the full and entire Copy-right of a Volume of 360 pages &c— perfectly agreeing to your terms. Of course, I am to understand the pages & lines in them to correspond to the Lyrical Ballads; yet should be obliged to you to inform me what number of Lines, you would wish in a page, that I may present the Copy to you as it ought to be.—Notes to Poetry are contrary to my notions, however fashionable they may be—there will be therefore scarce any, except a few interesting parallel passages from Greek, Latin, & Italian authors. But a Preface of 30 pages, relative to the principles of Poetry, which I have ever held, and in reference to myself, Mr Southey, and Mr Wordsworth, I should think it necessary to add—but have no objection to your making the volume in consequence, 390 pages.—

I have sent off my Letter to Mrs Coleridge, desiring the immediate Transmission, per coach, of my MSS.[2]

After this Volume which shall be (with the exception, perhaps, of about 200 lines, published once as a fragment, & since finished) all new—I do think, that a Volume with full one half new, yet likewise collecting my scattered poems—especially as Mr Wordsworth means in any future Edition of the Lyrical Ballads, now sold, to publish his own separately, & as therefore the full property of the Poem of Love[3]—(to which I have now written the corre-

should thus (by implication) be charged with having caused disarrangement in his Friend's mind'. She felt it was 'very unfortunate for William that he should be the person on whom . . . [Coleridge] has to charge his neglect of duty'. Wordsworth, she continued, 'wrote to Mrs C immediately and wished her to transcribe his letter, or parts of it for C and told her that he would not write to C himself as he had not communicated his displeasure to him. Mrs C replies that she is afraid to do this as C did not desire her to inform us, and that it may prevent him from opening letters in future. . . .' Hopefully Dorothy added: 'Time will remove the cloud from his mind as far as the right view of our conduct is obscured, and having deserved no blame we are easy on that score. If he seek an explanation William will be ready to give it, but I think it is more likely that his fancies will die away of themselves.'

[1] See the concluding paragraph of this letter.

[2] Coleridge also asked Lamb to write to Dorothy Wordsworth for his MSS. at Grasmere. See *Middle Years*, i. 446 and 455.

[3] *Love* was first published with the title, *Introduction to the Tale of the Dark Ladie*, in the *Morning Post*, 21 Dec. 1799. See Letter 304. For the text of *Love* as published in *Lyrical Ballads*, 1800, see Letter 337.

spondent poem,[1] of which it was to have been the introduction, a poem which it would be mock-modesty in me not to value as I have seen it under Mr Fox's Hand Writing, that he thought it one of the sweetest poems in the Language, tho' he did not know the Author[2]—) the Nightingale, the Dungeon, the Foster-Mother's Tale, and of the Ancient Mariner, now reverts to me[3]—might be, with a certainty of moderate success, published as a second Volume whenever you should be disposed to print another Edition of my first Volume. However, I shall deliver forthwith the work, for which we have agreed—and as soon as that is done, I will prepare the other.—

As I shall be obliged to pay in my annuity tomorrow morning— indeed, it ought to be done to night—might I ask you to favor me with the 20£ this evening, by one of your servants—accepting the following as a memorandum—till I can give a legal receipt.

2 May, 1811. Received 47£, in part of 100£ as Copyright for a Volume of original Poems, in the size of the former volume, consisting of 360 pages—to be delivered within a fortnight.[4]

S. T. Coleridge.

825. *To William Godwin*

MS. Lord Abinger. Hitherto unpublished.

Friday Morning
3 May, 1811.

You will be pleased to hear, my dear Godwin! that I received the money, I wanted, & was so reasonably anxious about, within an

---

[1] Despite this statement, Coleridge first published *The Ballad of the Dark Ladié* in 1834 as a fragment of 60 lines. (See *Poems*, i. 293.) A signed holograph of the poem entitled *The Dark Ladie, a fragment*, is now in the possession of Mr. A. G. B. Randle. This manuscript contains the same number of lines as the published version, but the text differs considerably from that printed in 1834. See Letters 304, 444, and 574 for earlier references to the poem.

[2] See Letter 380.

[3] When in 1800 Wordsworth determined to issue a second edition of *Lyrical Ballads* under his own name, Coleridge gave his enthusiastic support. He not only consented to the inclusion of *The Ancient Mariner*, *The Nightingale*, *The Foster-mother's Tale*, and *The Dungeon*, all of which had earlier appeared in the anonymous *Lyrical Ballads* of 1798, but he greatly revised *The Ancient Mariner* and contributed in addition his poem *Love*. With the exception of *The Dungeon*, all of these poems again appeared in the third and fourth editions of Wordsworth's *Lyrical Ballads* of 1802 and 1805.

[4] The proposal to publish with Longman was not carried out. Apparently Coleridge received an advance of only '20 or 22£', but this tentative agreement was later to expose him to Longman's unfavourable criticism. See Letters 1029 and 1093.

hour after the receipt of your note. And the next time, I call, I trust I shall be able with perfect convenience to discharge my former little debt to you.

I write now, because I am going out to Hammersmith, which will be my home for some time tho' I shall be in London, at the Courier office, almost every day from 9 to 1; & because Mrs Godwin informed me, that you were about to put your Fables again to the Press.[1] What I read of them (and as my reading was here & there in both volumes I may consider it as a fair average of the whole) greatly pleased & interested me—yet, I thought, some little alterations would improve the work, in parts—proceeding always on your own principles, as well stated in the Preface. I should like therefore to have a copy left in the course of the Day at 34, Southampton Buildings, which I will take with me, & making such little changes & additions as suggest themselves, will return you the Volumes within 10 or 14 days.

With heart-felt wishes, that your plans may succeed proportionate to your wants & wishes;—(and I doubt not, they will, & that, every year, you will make a larger & yet larger Stride) that your Health may strengthen as your occasions for anxiety diminish; & that Years may still be reserved for you, in which, with perfect ease of mind as to *the Things without*, you may be able to allow yourself to resume studies analogous to those, on which you have built up your name, & so have prepared for yourself that most chearing of all thoughts in old Age—'I have lived to benefit both Man & Child'—

I remain, my dear Godwin, | with affectionate Esteem & Respect | Your sincere Friend,

S. T. Coleridge

826. *To Daniel Stuart*

Address: D. Stuart, Esqre. | 36 | Brompton Row | Brompton
MS. British Museum. Pub. E. L. G. ii. 53.

Sunday, 5 May, 1811.
7, Portland Place, Hammersmith.—

Dear Stuart

I called on Mr Street, stated and particularized my proposal, and found a full, and in all appearance a warm, assent. I told him, that I had previously spoken to you, not as ignorant that the choice and decision would of course rest on him, as the acting Partner, and

[1] Godwin's *Fables*, issued under the pseudonym of Edward Baldwin and first published in 1805, ran to eleven subsequent editions.

who would suffer all the annoyance from the possible irregularity
or unquiet temper of any Employé in your joint service; but
merely as a mode of applying to him. He expressed himself highly
pleased both at the thought of my assistance in general; and with
the specific plan of assistance—and there was no doubt, he said, it
would be of great service to the Paper. I answered, that I hoped,
it would prove no disservice; but that I calculated more on the
relief, which, I trusted, he would receive from my attendance, and
on the ease of mind which the certainty of having an honest and
zealous Vice-gerent would afford him in case, sickness or other
unforeseen Accidents should keep him away from the immediate
superintendence of the Courier, for two or three days or weeks.—
As to weekly Salary, He said nothing & I said nothing: except that
he would talk with you, & there was no doubt that all this would be
settled to our mutual Satisfaction.[1]—

I shall, therefore, unless I hear to the contrary, commence my
attendance tomorrow at $\frac{1}{2}$ past 8: not that I could not or would not
come earlier, the weather permitting; but because the Stage passes
Portland Place at 20 minutes after 7, and it is well to mention the
latest time as the regular one.

I have written to Keswick to calm Mrs Coleridge's disquietudes
concerning the Annuity: & at the same time, to order my *MSS* up,
and the 100 sets of the Friend—I found Longman willing enough
to make a Jew Bargain with me for a Volume of Poems, which I
acceded to from the same coercive Logic which convinced the
Apothecary in Romeo and Juliet, a fellow for whom from the time,
I first read of him in Shakespere, I have entertained a singular
affection, little as I know of himself or his family.—As to the
Friend, however, he hung back, and croaked wofully about
periodical Publications—now quite a drug, &c &c—and how much
more adviseable it would be for me to publish in Volumes. Aye,
doubtless—saving & excepting the two poor Monosyllables '*for me*'
—*for him* it is evident, who would give me a 100£ for the Copyright
of a Work, from which paying all expences, copy-right-purchase

[1] In *Essays on His Own Times*, iii. 749–938, Sara Coleridge reprinted forty-
five prose contributions to the *Courier* appearing between 7 May and 27 Sept.
1811. The notes to Letters 816 and 821 indicate two earlier articles, and Letter
827 refers to an unidentified contribution of 'Monday last', 6 May. Mr. Taylor
Milne of the Institute of Historical Research has drawn my attention to an
article, 'Superstition, Religion, Atheism: an Allegoric Vision', published in the
Courier 31 Aug. 1811, over the initials S. T. C. This article was not reprinted
by Sara Coleridge, possibly because Coleridge himself included it in a revised
form as 'Allegoric Vision', in the Introduction to his second *Lay Sermon*, 1817.
An examination of the files of the *Courier* for 1811 would probably reveal
further contributions by Coleridge. See also note to Letter 828 for a reference
to Coleridge's suppressed article on the Duke of York.

included, he would clear another 100£ at least, by the first Edition.
—But great as my affection may be for the Angels of Paternoster
Row, that sit in the appropriate Shape of Cormorants on the Tree
of Knowlege, I am selfish enough to have a still greater for S. T. C.
and his three little ones.—I shall, therefore, finish off the next
Number of the Friend, which will contain a full detail of the Plan
of a monthly work, including the Friend continued—with a full
catalogue of chapters, of the Subjects to be investigated in the
philosophical (i.e. metaphysical, moral, & religious) and the literary
departments of the work.—With this, which I will first shew you,
I shall call on Baldwin who some time ago proposed the thing to
me of his own accord.[1]—As soon as this can be settled, I shall then
begin to collect the money due to me, & be able to repay you my
more recent obligations.—

I called in Brompton Row yesterday, a few minutes after you
had left your House—henceforward, the afternoons & evenings I
shall be at Hammersmith.—

Believe me, dear Stuart, | with grateful & affectionate
Esteem | Your sincere Friend,

S. T. Coleridge

827. *To Daniel Stuart*

Address: D. Stuart, Esqre. | 36. Brompton Row | Brompton
MS. British Museum. Pub. with omis. Letters from the Lake Poets, *202.*
Postmark: 11 May 1811.

¼ past 2 o/clock, Courier Office.[2]—

[10 May 1811]

Dear Stuart

My letter will scarcely be worth twopence; but I write to say,
that I hope in another week's time I shall have learnt to compress,
or rather to select, my thoughts, so as to make them more frequently admissible—. You will see the Courier to day. I own, IN
CONFIDENCE, it grieved me—The affair of the Stamford Editor[3]
might have been, as it was in several papers, compressed into a
third of a Column—which took two & more unleaded ones—The
stupid Debate in the Common Council might have been abridged,
at all events, to one half; if the vanity of the Speakers rendered it

---

[1] Gale and Curtis rather than Baldwin issued *The Friend* as a volume
in 1812. See Letter 861.

[2] In the midst of writing this letter, Coleridge left for Morgan's and added
'7, Portland Place, Hammersmith' after his signature.

[3] John Drakard, who was convicted of libel for publishing an article against
corporal punishment in the army .

(as it probably may) adviseable to publish it in the form of a Debate, at all, rather than as a short Narration. Mr St. means, I believe, to insert my §§ on Waithman, occasioned by his Speech, to morrow[1]—which I wrote as quant. suff. for the whole affair.—But in this, I doubt not, he is right, as far as respects the sale among the Common Council themselves—But yet it would have been no difficulty, surely, by compression &c to have made room for General Graham's Letter, from the M. Chronicle,—a letter, not only worthy of general Graham, but such a one as will, I venture to predict, form a part of classical English Literature—inserted in every History of the Times, and selected as a specimen of beautiful, manly, simple, epistolary Writing.[2]—I did not mention it to Mr St. —for it really never occurred to me, that it *could* be overlooked. I venture to say, that for one person throughout the Empire who would read, so as to feel any interest in it, any one column in the Courier of To Day, there are a thousand who would have gone about shewing Graham's Letter. I have this moment looked at the Courier: and write in the first overflow of my Surprize & Regret.

I should like, after a time, and if I feel as if I had Street's Confidence, to propose to him, (*written at Hammersmith*) whenever it is practicable, i.e. whenever the three principal Papers, the M. C., the M. P., and the Times, come out at a tolerably early hour, to employ me for the first half hour in abridging the paragraphs, he means to transfer into the Courier, where it is possible, and to re-write them when they merit it—as, for instance, I did in announcing the deaths of Boscawen & Cumberland.[3] This, supposing it practicable, would have two good effects: it would leave more room for the insertion of very interesting articles which must otherwise be omitted (which 9 times in 10 is the same as lost: for what once goes into the Drawers, seldom finds it's way out again)—and it would give somewhat of an original cast to the paper, at least, *a keeping*, as the painters say, in the style of the third side.

But hitherto the only paper, I can get a sight of, for the first hour and more is that astonishing paper, called the British Press: for it astonishes me, where it finds purchasers—so utterly dry and worthless is it.—

As to what I write myself, that has not once entered my thoughts.

[1] *Courier*, 11 May 1811. See *Essays on His Own Times*, iii. 759–62. Coleridge refers to Robert Waithman (1764–1833), the political reformer.

[2] General Thomas Graham, later Baron Lynedoch (1748–1843), won a memorable victory over the French at Barrosa on 5 Mar. 1811. Subsequently, Graham addressed a letter to Henry Wellesley, the British envoy, exposing the conduct of General La Peña, who claimed credit for the victory.

[3] William Boscawen (1752–1811), author, died on 8 May; Richard Cumberland (1732–1811), dramatist, died on 7 May.

I feel, I have yet to learn how much larger a space my Scraps occupy in the Paper, than I am in the least aware of while writing them. What I had imagined a snug little paragraph turns out to be a column—and considering the press of Debates & Foreign News, I think it a great compliment that Street has inserted what he has. But on just at one glance comparing the M. Chr. of to day with the Courier, I was vexed at the manifest superiority of the former, for which I saw no earthly reason: and what I could, of course, say to no other person in the world, I find a relief in saying to you. For if ever an article appeared likely to become the general Topic of Conversation, it is surely Graham's masterly Letter.

There was a well-written & plausible attack in the M. C. on the remarks in the Courier in my §§ of Monday last;[1] but it owed it's plausibility to mis[-s]tatement: as if the reasons assigned for the Courier's preferring to wait for the Debates in the H. of C. on one very difficult & complex question, from which Debates no one expected any other result but that of knowing distinctly the opinions & arguments on both sides, were meant as a general Principle for all questions; and as if the sneer on Cobbett & his compeers were meant for all who had written previously to the Parliam. Discussion. I wrote about half a dozen lines, in calm and respectful reply, which as there was not room for them, may make the first sentence of my Essay.[2]

As soon as I got sight of the Courier to day, I went up to Mr St.'s room, intending to have chatted a little on Politics, and so to have introduced my admiration of Graham's Letter: in the hopes, that he might have given it out for to-morrow (which, perhaps, he may have done.) But it was past 2, and he had left the Office.

The Volume, which Pasley had left for me at the Courier office, was placed for the first time on my Table this morning.[3]—Your Copy I will leave at Brompton the first time, I walk back from Town: which a lame great Toe prevents me from now attempting. The improved state of my Spirits & Digestion, and the lightness with which I rise every morning at $\frac{1}{2}$ past 6, give me some reason for suspecting this to be Gout—a thing, I should welcome: for I doubt not, it would make a new inner man for me for a while. And if once my Stomach were to become strong, and my Spirits

[1] This contribution was not included in *Essays on His Own Times*.

[2] Coleridge contributed an essay, 'Bullion Commerce', to the *Courier* on 2 Aug. 1811, and continued his discussion on 13 Aug. He had previously commented on the question on 7 and 9 May. See *Essays on His Own Times*, iii. 751, 753–7, 861–6, and 869–76.

[3] C. W. Pasley, *Essay on the Military Policy and Institutions of the British Empire*, 1810.

regular, I dare rely on myself to prevent or retard a second Fit by the strictest Temperance, to any deviations from which I have been driven by fear, despondency, and confusing Pains; not seduced by any, the least pleasure, in the stimulants themselves. If I had, it would not have been possible for me to have so suddenly reduced my former quantities to so very moderate a portion as I now take, without either sinking or craving.

If any thing should occur to you, which I can do, or which I may do better, you will, I know, be, as usual, kind enough to suggest it to me—. The New Friends of the People have occasioned much talk—I have procured the article from the Morning Post, with their 'address,' &c: and shall write a paragraph on it, not as if it had been *omitted* in the Courier, but as recalling the public attention to the Fact as introductory to the reasons grounded on it.

If inclined to a nap, this letter may aid in composing you. Had I met you, I should not have written it—or if my mood had been the same, when I began as now I have finished it. But a letter is a sort of escape-valve; & serves to cool, by evacuating, the writer, however it may tire the Receiver.—May God bless you, my dear Sir!

and your affectionately grateful Friend,
S. T. Coleridge

828. *To Daniel Stuart*

Address: D. Stuart, Esqre. | 36 Brompton Row | Brompton
MS. British Museum. Pub. Letters, *ii. 566.*

Tuesday, 4 June 1811.

Dear Stuart

I brought your Umbrella in with me yestermorning: but having forgotten it at leaving Portland Place sent the Coachman back for it, who brought what *appeared* to me not the same. On returning, however, with it, I could find no other: & it is certainly as good or better, but looks to me as if it were not equally new, & as if it had far more silk in it. I will however leave it, at Brompton—& if by any inexplicable circumstance, it should not prove the same, you must be content with the Substitute.—The family at Portland Place laugh at my doubts as to the identity of it.—

I had hoped to have seen you this morning, it being a leisurely time in respect of fresh Tidings—to have submitted to you two Essays, one on the Catholic Question,[1] and the other on Parlia-

---

[1] Two articles on the Catholic question were published on 5 Aug. and 3 Sept., and three letters to the Editor of the *Courier* on the same subject on 13, 21, and 26 Sept. See *Essays on His Own Times*, iii. 867–9, 882–8, 891–6, 920–32.

mentary Reform addressed, as a Letter (from a Correspondent)
to the Noblemen & Members of Parliament who had associated for
this purpose. The former does not exceed two columns; the latter
is somewhat longer. But after the middle of this month it is
probable, that the Paper will be more open to a series of Articles,
on less momentary, tho' still contemporary, interests.—Mr Street
seems highly pleased with what I have written this morning on
the Battle of the 16th (May): tho', I apprehend, the whole cannot
be inserted. I am, as I ought to be, most cautious & shy in recommending any thing: otherwise I should have requested Mr St. to
give insertion to the §§s respecting Holland & the nature of Buonaparte's resources; ending with the necessity of ever re-fuelling the
moral feelings of the People as to the monstrosity of the Giant-
fiend, that menaces them; in *allusion* to Judge Grose's Sentence on
Drakard—before the occasion had passed away from the public
memory.[1] So too, if the Duke's return is to be discussed at all, the
article should be published before Lord Milton's Motion.[2] For
tho' in a complex & widely-controverted Question, where hundreds
rush in to the field of Combat, it is wise to defer it till the Debates
in Parliament have shewn what the arguments are on which most
stress is laid by men in common, as in the Bullion Dispute—yet
generally, it is a great honor to the London Papers, that for one
argument, they borrow from the Parliamentary Speakers, the
latter borrow two from them—at all events, are *anticipated* by
them. But the true prudential rule is, to defer only where any
effect of *freshness* or novelty is impracticable; but in most other

[1] The *Courier* on 4 and 5 June contained articles on the Battle of Albuera;
and on 29 June on Buonaparte. *Essays on His Own Times*, iii. 796–805, 818–25.

[2] Following the reappointment of the Duke of York as commander-in-chief
of the army in May, Lord Milton brought forward on 6 June a motion of censure
which was rejected in the House of Commons.
Coleridge's suppressed article in criticism of the Duke's appointment was
probably ready when this letter was written, for on 11 June Crabb Robinson
recorded in his diary: 'Coleridge read me a very beautiful essay on the reappointment of the Duke of York, which, however, had not been inserted in the
Courier, though promised long since.' On 5 July Coleridge's essay was finally
included in the *Courier* and about two thousand copies were struck off, but
'the government heard of it, & by the interposition of Mr. Arbuthnot of the
Treasury the article was suppressed. This made Mr. C. very uncomfortable'.
Robinson on Books and Their Writers, i. 34–35 and 37; *Blake, Coleridge, Words-
worth, Lamb, etc. being Selections from the Remains of Henry Crabb Robinson*, ed.
Edith J. Morley, 1922, p. 42; and manuscript letter of 1849 from Robinson to
Sara Coleridge, now in the editor's possession.
Two versions of Coleridge's article have come to light. Neither is complete.
The shorter was printed by Sara Coleridge in *Essays on His Own Times*, iii.
850–3; the longer one was included in the *Collection of Alfred Morrison*, 1895,
ii. 254–9.

cases to consider *freshness* of effect as the point which belongs to a NEWSPAPER, & distinguishes it from a *Library* Book; the former being the Zenith, & the latter the Nadir, with a number of inter-mediate Degrees, occupied by Pamphlets, Magazines, Reviews, Satirical & occasional Poems, &c &c.—Besides, in a daily News-paper, with advertisements proportioned to it's large Sale, what is deferred must 4 times in 5 be extinguished. A Newspaper is a market for flowers & vegetables, rather than a Granary or Conservatory—and the Drawer of it's Editor a common Burial-ground, not a Catacomb for embalmed Mummies in which the Defunct are pre-served to serve in after times as Medicines for the Living.

To turn from the Paper to myself, as candidate for the place of *Auxiliary* to it. I drew, with Mr Street's consent & order, 10£: which I shall repay during the week, as soon as I can see Mr Monkhouse, of Budge Row, who has collected that sum for me—This therefore I put wholly aside, & indeed expect to replace it with Mr Green tomorrow morning. Besides this, I have had 5£ from Green, chiefly for the purposes of Coach-hire. All at once, I could not venture to walk in the heat & other accidents of weather from Hammersmith to the office; but hereafter I intend, if I continue here, to *return* on foot—which will reduce my Coach-hire for the week from 18S. to 9.—But to walk in, I know, would take off all the blossom & fresh fruits of my Spirits.—I trust, that I need not say, how pleasant it would be to me, if it were in my power, to consider every thing, I could do for the Courier, as a mere return for the pecuniary as well as other obligations, I am under to you—in short, as working off old Scores. But you know, how I am situated: and that by the daily labour of the Brain I must acquire the daily demands of the other parts of the Body. And it now becomes necessary, that I should form some settled system for my support in London, & of course, know what my weekly or monthly means may be—. Respecting the Courier, I consider you not merely as a private Friend, but as the Co-proprietor of a large concern, in which it is your Duty to regu-late yourself with relation to the Interests of that Concern, & of your Partner in it: and so take for granted, & indeed wish no other, than that you & he should weigh, whether or no I can be of any material use to a paper already so flourishing, & an evening paper. For all mock-humility out of the question, (& when I write to you, every other sort of Insincerity) I see that such services, as I might be able to afford, would [be] more important to a rising, than to a risen, paper, to a Mo[rn]ing, perhaps, more than to an evening one.—You will however decide, after the experience hitherto afforded & modifying it by the temporary circumstances of Debates, Press of Foreign News, &c, how far I can be of actual use; by my attendance in order to help in the things of the Day, as are the §§s, which I have for the most part hitherto been called to contribute; & by my efforts to sustain the literary character of the Paper by longer articles on open days, & more leisure Times.

My dear Stuart! knowing the foolish mental cowardice, with which I slink off from all pecuniary Subjects, & the particular weight, I must feel, from the sense of existing Obligations to you, you will be convinced, that my only motive is the desire of settling with others such a plan for myself, as may, by setting my mind at rest, enable me to realize whatever powers I possess, to as much satisfaction to those who employ them, & to my own sense of Duty, as possible.—If Mr Street should think, that the Courier does not require any auxiliary, I shall then rely on your kindness for putting me in the way of some other Paper, the principles of which are sufficiently in accordance with my own.[1] For while Cabbage-stalks rot on Dunghills, I will never write what, or for what, I do not think right—all that Prudence can justify, is *not* to write what at certain times one may yet think.—God bless you &

S. T. Coleridge

---

[1] There is no evidence that Stuart attempted to find Coleridge a position with another newspaper. According to Crabb Robinson it was Stuart's compliance with the ministry in the cancellation of the article on the Duke of York which led Coleridge to wish to 'exchange his situation for that of *The Times*'. Robinson approached John Walter, the proprietor of *The Times*, on Coleridge's behalf, but nothing materialized. (*Robinson on Books and Their Writers*, i. 37.) There is preserved in Coleridge's handwriting, however, a proposal intended for Walter. It is endorsed July 1811.

1. To be attendant at the office any six hours of the Day, from 8 of the Morning to 8 o/[clock] of the Evening: & to supply any number required of small Paragraphs or the *leading* Paragraph,—when nothing occurs of paramount Interest after 8 o/clock in the Evening.

2. To supply two Essays a week, on the great Interests of the Time, of from two to three Columns: still letting these in busy & crowded times accumulate, according as their Subjects are less temporary, to keep up a constant Fire from the Paper in more open & leisure Months.

3. The Above, always supposing the Paper to be truly independent, 1. of the Administration, & 2. of the Populace—and that it's fundamental Principle is, the due proportion of political Power to Property, joined with the removal of all obstacles to the free circulation & transfer of Property, & all artificial facilitations of it's natural tendency to accumulate in large & growing Masses.—
[MS. transmitted to Sara Coleridge by Crabb Robinson in 1849, and now in the possession of the Coleridge family.] See also Letter 841, p. 348, n. 1.

829. *To William Godwin*

MS. Lord Abinger. Hitherto unpublished.

Saturday, 5 Octr. 1811
Courier office

Dear Godwin

I have not been at the Courier office for near a week past, having been obliged to spend my mornings in Westminster Library. I have thence literally but this moment received your Letter, and shall avail myself of your kind Invitation for Tuesday next, not insensible of the Regard which prompted it. It is not every man's lot to say, that he had been deemed worthy by one, qui etiam inter posteros nominabitur,[1] to dine at his table first with Grattan, and then with Curran.—Among those little coincidences of Life that always amuse the mind (perhaps by the mockery of cause and effect) it has happened, that for the last two or three days I have been reading the best documents, I could procure, of the Debates of the Irish Parliament from the earlier period of the American War to the Union, and was so impressed with the distinction of Irish from English Eloquence, in Flood, Curran, and Grattan compared with Fox, Pitt, and Wyndham, and so much pleased with the specific differences of Genius in the two latter tho' under one genus, that I was passing up to my Room here in order to finish an Essay on this Subject when your Letter was put into my hand.—I hope, you are all well. Except one evening at Lamb's, and I have visited no where since I last saw you. God bless you!

S. T. Coleridge

P.S.—Please to address me always at 7, Portland Place, Hammersmith: for I am then sure of receiving it in the course of 24 Hours at farthest.

830. *To T. G. Street*

Address: T. J. Street[2] Esqre.
MS. National Portrait Gallery. Pub. with omis. Canterbury Magazine, *January 1835, p. 34.*

[5 October 1811][3]

Dear Sir

I have finished Pitt, Buonaparte, Fox, and Sir A. Ball—Pitt's divided into two parts, the character and a revisal of and commentary on the character.—Considering the variety of Books, I

---

[1] Quintilian, x. i. 94.
[2] This name has been inked out in the MS. but is decipherable.
[3] Coleridge's reference to dining with Curran on Tuesday establishes the date of this letter. See Letter 831.

had to look into for Dates, Names & events, I regard this as a
Week's work, which I shall look back on with pleasure.—My next
will be Lord Wellington, of course in a very different line of Thought
from the former, as Lord W. is but a personification of Great
Events—it will therefore consist of an historical Parallel—& you
will be so good as to let me have the two Volumes of Gustavus
Adolphus.—Then will follow Wyndham, then Dundas—the one
including tho' without *name* Wilberforce, the other Whitbread—
and lastly, an Essay for which I have collected all the thoughts and
materials, on the distinct character of English & Irish Eloquence,
ex. gr. that of Pitt, Fox, & Wyndham, compared with Flood,
Grattan & Curran—& again, the specific differences of the two
latter, Grattan's from Curran's——The Day before the publication of the first Character, I should wish to address a Letter to you
on the nature and uses of character-writing, relatively to the Lives
of Plutarch.—This I am now about to write—it will not extend to
more than a column & a half—& I will give it in to you on Monday
Morning by a quarter after nine, together with Pitt's & Fox's—
and you may rely on having the whole set given in so as never to
delay the publication, provided they come out no oftener than
every other Day—i.e. 3 times a week.[1]—

　　Mr Green informed me that Gold was of great convenience to you
—I therefore changed with 5 or 6 Guineas for Notes—and I can
now let you have 19 guineas & a shilling for 20£.—Had I known it
but a day earlier, I could have procured you sixty guineas or more
—and I will try to procure another 20 as it is—

　　　　　　　　　　　　　　　　Your's most | respectfully
　　　　　　　　　　　　　　　　　　　S. T. Coleridge
I dine with Curran on Tuesday at Godwin's.

831. *To J. J. Morgan*

Address: *Private* | J. J. Morgan, Esqre. | 7. Portland Place | Hammersmith
MS. Lord Latymer. Pub. E. L. G. ii. 56.

　　　　　　　　　　　　　　Saturday Night [12 October 1811][2]
Dear Morgan
　　On the Tuesday Night, after I had returned from Mr Godwin's
& his party of Mr Curran, his Daughter, & Peter Pindar, I found a
letter, or rather a letter found me, in addition to one received the
day before—It is no odds, what. Suffice, it was such as made me

　　[1] The characters of Pitt, Buonaparte, Fox, Wellington, &c., were probably
never written. See Letter 875, in which they are again promised.
　　[2] This letter was enclosed in Letter 832.

desirous not to see you: for I knew, I must either tell you falsehoods, which would answer no end, could I have endured to tell
a deliberate falsehood—& if I had told you the Truth, it would
probably have made you restless to attempt for me what you could
not do with prudence or justice to yourself, & what at all events
I could not have received from you—. That this, my disappearance
from you, will have afforded Sign & Seal to all the unfavorable
Judgements prompted by feelings . . .[1] which, Heaven knows how!
I have excited for the last 8 months or more in your Wife & Sister,
I am well aware. I say, Heaven knows how!—because I cannot
torture my memory into a recollection of a single moment, in which
I ever spoke, thought, wished, or felt any thing that was not consistent with the most fondly cherished Esteem, & a personal &
affectionate predilection for them, rendered worthy to my own
thoughts by a sense of Gratitude. I dare affirm, that few men have
ever felt or regretted their own infirmities, more deeply than
myself—they have in truth preyed *too* deeply on my mind, & the
hauntings of Regret have injured me more than the things to be
regretted—Yet such as I am, such was I, when I was first under
your hospitable Roof—and such, unfortunately, when I revisited
you at Portland Place. But so it is. Our feelings govern our notions.
Love a man, & his Talking shall be Eloquence—dislike him, &
the same thing becomes Preaching. His quickness of Feeling & the
starting Tear, shall be at one time natural sensibility—for the
Tears swelled into his eye not for his own pains, or misfortunes,
but either for others' or for some wound from unkindness—the
same at another time shall be loathsome maudlin unmanliness.
Activity of Thought scattering itself in jests, puns, & sportive
nonsense, shall in the bud & blossom of acquaintanceship be
amiable playfulness, & met or anticipated by a Laugh or a correspondent Jest—: in the wane . . .[2] of Friendship, an object of Disgust, and a ground of warning to those better-beloved, *not to get
into that way.*—Such, however, is Life. Some few may find their
happiness out of themselves in the regard & sympathy of others;
but most are driven back by repeated disappointments into themselves, there to find tranquillity, or (too often) sottish Despondency. There are not those Beings on earth, who can truly say
that having professed affection for them, I ever either did or spoke
unkindly or unjustly of them. . . .[3]
My present distracting difficulties, which have disenabled me
from doing what might have alleviated them, I must either get

---

[1] Six words heavily inked out in MS.
[2] Several words heavily inked out in MS.
[3] Two and a half lines heavily inked out in MS.

thro', or sink under, as it may happen. Some Consolation—nay, a great Consolation—it is, that they have not fallen on me thro' any Vice, any extravagance, or self-indulgence; but only from having imprudently hoped too highly of men—that if I had been treated with common tradesmanlike Honesty by those, with whom (ignorantly blending the Author with the Publisher) I had traded —or with common humanity by a *Mecaenas* worth 50,000£, who yet knows I have not received back . . .[1] what he lent me on the prospect of my receiving in money what I sent out in paper & stamps— this could not have been.—In the mean time, what with those clamorous Letters, [from Mrs Coleridge,][2] & what with the never-closing, festering Wound of Wordsworth & his Family, & other aggravations, I own to you that Fortune seems to be playing 'More Sacks on the Mill' with me—and who in the agonies of Suffocation would not wish to breathe no more, rather than to have his Breath Stifled?[3]

I pray you, send my Books & other *paucities* directed to No. 6. Southampton Buildings—for thither I have gotten—As to seeing you, if I could give comfort to you by receiving it from you, I would request it—but that is out of the Question.—Therefore think of me as one deceased who *had been* your sincere Friend,

S. T. Coleridge

Burn this after you have read it.

Private.—If I get thro' these difficulties—(& that done, I doubt not, that tranquillity of mind will enable me to mend all the rest) it will be my first Desire to meet you. Till then what is the use of it? —Pray send the books &c: for something I must *make up* in a hurry—for I have tried in vain to compose any thing anew. To transcribe is the utmost in my power.

832. *To J. J. Morgan*

Address: J. J. Morgan, Esqre. | 7. Portland Place | Hammersmith
MS. Lord Latymer. Hitherto unpublished.
Postmark: 15 October 1811.

[15 October 1811]

Dear Morgan

I intreat (and beg you to intreat for me) Mrs Morgan's and Charlotte's Forgiveness for the gross disrespect, which my absence

---

[1] Several words heavily inked out in MS.

[2] Words in brackets inked out in MS.

[3] It was about this time that Coleridge wrote in Lamb's copy of Beaumont and Fletcher: 'N.B. I shall not be long here, Charles!—& gone, you will not mind my having spoiled a book in order to leave a Relic. S. T. C. Octr. 1811.—'

& silence render me guilty of. I am truly and to my very heart sensible, that it has been such behaviour, as they & you had little merited from me—and that the rudeness is a trifle compared with the apparent Ingratitude. I can only palliate it by saying what is the Truth & the whole Truth, that my intentions have not been guilty—that the agitation & distraction of my mind have been the causes—that it was intolerable to me to bring back to your Home of Peace & Love a spirit so disquieted—that I feared the probable effects of vexation on my bodily health & had solemnly vowed that I would never be ill 24 hours together in your House—and lastly, that if I had not esteemed you all and felt you very near my heart, had you been mere acquaintances, such as Mr Godwin & others, I should then have found easily a plausible pretext for leaving you & have been able to take my Leave.—I wrote the inclosed on Saturday—& I can neither bear to write or even read it over again —I am afraid, there is a great deal of peevish feeling in it, which attribute not to me but to my state of mind at the time of writing it—& burn it.

May God bless you all—and if I pray for better times, it is among the uppermost motives that I may be able to demonstrate otherwise than hitherto, that

> I am sincerely your no less affectionate & grateful than |
> obliged Friend,
>
> S. T. Coleridge

833. *To John Rickman*

Address: J. Rickman, Esqre. | Palace Yard | Westminster
MS. Huntington Lib. Pub. E. L. G. ii. 55.

Saturday Noon—[26 October 1811][1]

Dear Sir

On Tuesday next Mr Morgan and myself will avail ourselves of your kind invitation. I was (and am) in town on the arrival of your letter—& have this moment received it. My business has been to bring about a Lecture Scheme—the Prospectus of which I shall be able to bring with me on Tuesday.[2] On the subject of dining

---

[1] Since Crabb Robinson saw Coleridge's 'annunciation' of a proposed course of lectures on Wednesday, 30 Oct., the reference in this letter to the prospectus being ready on Tuesday establishes the date. See *Robinson on Books and Their Writers*, i. 49.

[2] On 29 Oct. Coleridge outlined to John Payne Collier his plan for a course of lectures to be given in the Coachmakers' Hall, and the next day Robinson noted in his diary: 'Coleridge showed me an annunciation of lectures on poetry, etc., to be delivered this winter, fifteen of them; subscription, a lady two

with Lamb I had a long conversation with him yester-evening—
and only blame myself, that having long felt the deepest convictions of the vital importance of his not being visited till after
8 o/clock & this too, rarely except on his open nights, I should
yet have been led to take my friend M. there, at dinner, at his
proposal, out of a foolish delicacy in telling him the plain truth—
that *it must* not be *done*.—I am right glad, that something effective
is now done—tho' permit me to say to you in confidence, that as
long as Hazlitt remains in town I dare not expect any amendment
in Lamb's Health, unless luckily H. should grow moody and take
offence at being desired not to come till 8 o/clock.—It is seldom
indeed, that I am with Lamb more than once in the week—and
when at Hammersmith, most often not once in a fortnight—and
yet I see what Harm has been done even by me—What then if
Hazlitt—as probably he will—is with him 5 evenings in the Seven?[1]
Were it possible to wean C. L. from the Pipe, other things would
follow with comparative ease—for till he gets a Pipe, I have regularly observed that he is contented with Porter—& that the unconquerable Appetite for Spirit comes in with the Tobacco—the
oil of which, especially in the gluttonous manner in which he
volcanizes it, acts as an instant Poison on his Stomach or Lungs.

Believe me, | dear Sir, | Your's with affectionate | Esteem

S. T. Coleridge

P.S. I return to Hammersmith this Evening—

guineas; gentleman, three guineas, with power to bring a lady, four guineas.'
(*Shakespearean Criticism*, ii. 46, and *Robinson on Books and Their Writers*, i. 49–
50.) Apparently, Coleridge had a prospectus printed, though no copies of it in
this form have come to light. A week later he had ready a revised prospectus, in
which Scot's Corporation Hall was designated for the lectures and reduced
subscription prices were announced. See Letter 835. A third prospectus of
Coleridge's lecture of 21 Nov. also survives. See headnote to Letter 845.

[1] Hazlitt, for his part, thought Coleridge's presence in town injurious to
both the Lambs, but Lamb himself made no complaint of Coleridge and sought
his companionship, especially during Mary's confinement. Lamb was, however,
positive about other visitors and not only warned Hazlitt that Mrs. Hazlitt was
not to stay overnight, but also spoke of the harm which Dorothy Wordsworth's
visit and the coming of 'that damn'd infernal bitch Mrs. Godwin' had done to
Mary. *Robinson on Books and Their Writers*, i. 24, and *Lamb Letters*, ii. 112.

834. *To Thomas J. Pettigrew*[1]

Address: T. Pettigrew, Esqre | Fleet Street
MS. Wellesley College Lib. Hitherto unpublished.

[*Circa* 4 November 1811][2]

Dear Sir,

I came posting into Town with the intention of asking your advice whether I might not take the Liberty of introducing the words—'By Permission of the London Philosophical Society'— or others equivalent[3]—I need not say, how much therefore I was gratified by the Contents of your Note to Mr Pople.[4]

As to the introductory Lecture being given gratis, I have two objections—the first, that after having lectured on similar Subjects at the Royal Institution, for nearly three months, to the most numerous Auditory ever collected in the Lecture theatre (except by my friend, Professor Davy) and having received both verbally & by letter the warmest expressions of Approbation from the Bishops of Durham & Norwich; & from several Noblemen, I think it would be *impolitic* to *imply* that my name & character as a Man of Letters or as a public Speaker were so far among [the] incognita rerum, as to need a sample. If you knew more of me, you would find no difficulty in believing, (indeed it would have been superfluous to have assured you) that the reason here assigned is *prudential*, and no ebullition of Conceit & Self-opinion—Still stronger is my second objection—that it would be tantamount to an advice to all who read the Prospectus, not to take a ticket till after the first Lecture—or should my Friends be numerous (& no small number, I know, will attend me from the West End of the Town, tho' the majority of those most interested in me are yet at their Country Seats) it would be a great injustice to them to subject them to the chance of a Crowd, and would effectually keep away all Ladies of Rank, or even of respectability. To this let me add, that it appears to me as detracting from the dignity of the London Philosophical Society—Most assuredly my own Wish would be expressed in the Motto—'*Fit* Audience f[ind,] tho' few.'

Be pleased to accept my sincere thanks for the kindness with which you have assisted, and the candor with which you have communicated your thoughts. I am at present with my friend,

[1] Thomas Joseph Pettigrew (1791–1865), surgeon and antiquary, was one of the founders of the Philosophical Society of London in 1810.

[2] This letter must have been written two or three days before Coleridge announced his change of lecture halls to Robinson on 6 Nov.

[3] The printed prospectus bore the heading, London Philosophical Society.

[4] W. Pople, 67, Chancery Lane, printer of the prospectus. In 1813 he issued Coleridge's *Remorse*.

'J. J. Morgan, Esqre., 7, Portland Place, Hammersmith'—who
with me would be gratified, if any business or leisure walk should
lead you to take a cup of Tea, or a family dinner with us. On Sundays
we are always all at home, & dine at 3 o/clock—When I return to
my house at Keswick (a large mansion occupied in common by me
& Mr Southey, the husband of my Wife's Sister) should choice or
chance lead you to the Lakes, you will find House-room & a glad
Welcome there—in the mean time I remain, dear Sir,
          with strong anticipations of Esteem & Regard, your obliged
                                                              S. T. Coleridge

835. *To Henry Crabb Robinson*

Address: H. C. Robinson, Esqre   from S. T. Coleridge
MS. Dr. Williams's Lib. Pub. Blake, Coleridge, Wordsworth, Lamb, etc. being
Selections from the Remains of Henry Crabb Robinson, *ed. Edith J. Morley,*
1922, p. 96. The prospectus, on the blank pages of which this letter was written,
is headed: 'London Philosophical Society, Scot's Corporation Hall, Crane
Court, Fleet Street, (entrance from Fetter Lane.)' It announced a course of
fifteen lectures beginning Monday, 18 November, 'On Shakespear and Milton,
in illustration of the Principles of Poetry, and their Application as Grounds of
Criticism to the most popular Works of later English Poets, those of the Living
included', and fixed the price of admission 'for the whole Course' at 2 guineas,
or 3 guineas 'with the privilege of introducing a Lady'. For a reprinting of this
prospectus, see *Shakespearean Criticism*, ii. 26–27.

                                                      6 November 1811
My dear Robinson
    The Coachmakers' Hall having no literary or philosophical
Redolence, or rather smelling somewhat unsavory to the nares
intellectuales of all my wealthy acquaintance, partly from past
political spouting clubs, and partly from it's present assignment to
Hops & the Instruction of Grown Gentlemen in Dancing, I have
at length procured another Room every way answering my purposes—a spacious handsome room with an academical Stair-case &
the Lecture room itself fitted up in a very grave authentic poetico-
phi[losophic] Style with the Busts of Newton, Milton, Sha[ke-
speare,] Pope & Locke behind the Lecturer's Cathedra. I have,
likewise, lowered the prices from 3 & 4 to 2 and 3 Guineas.—I am
sure, you will say what you can for me among your Friends—but
what I more particularly wish you to do is to see it advertised in the
Times—if by *favor*[1] it can be done so as to *advertise* only as many
lines as will not exceed the price of an ordinary advertisement, &

---

[1] Robinson had previously been attached to *The Times* as foreign correspondent in Germany, foreign editor in London, and special correspondent in
Spain.

to let the rest appear as a part of the Paper itself—I certainly should do my best to repay it by sending occasional articles to the Times, prose or verse.[1] Perhaps, you may have it in your power to conciliate Mr Walter's good will towards me in this Business.— Likewise, do you know any Member of the Russel Institution, to whom you could entrust a few Prospectuses to be placed in their Library or Chatting Room?—I have left two or three at the Westminster Library—At present my Dormitory at least is at Mr Morgan's, Portland Place, Hammersmith—

I am very anxious to see Schlegel's Werke before the Lectures commence[2]—May God bless you, my dear Sir, | & Your sincere Friend,

S. T. Coleridge

836. *To Henry Crabb Robinson*

Address: G. C. Robinson, Esqre | ——Collier's Esqre | 56 | Hatton Garden
MS. Dr. Williams's Lib. Hitherto unpublished.

Friday Afternoon ½ past 4
[Endorsed Novr. 8—1811]

Dear Robinson

I received your kind Letter this day noon—I am myself [in town], tho' sadly indisposed from Cold & it's Consequents, a bowel complaint—& a sickishness, the consequent of a medicine to remove the complaint—in order, *prudentially*, to attend a Lecture on Taste by a Mr Clarkson of the London Phil. Society, in which he divides it into Novelty, & a deal of other -ties!—O Lord!—

Now however the main thing is to advertise—I have therefore inclosed one prospectus, containing as *cheap* an advertisement as is practicable—& all, I request of you, is to desire and intreat, that it may be inserted on Monday morning next, in a conspicuous manner, & so every day for the whole of the next week[3]—& if you will be so good

---

[1] See Letter 841.

[2] See Letter 845 for evidence of Coleridge's first acquaintance with A. W. von Schlegel's *Vorlesungen.*

[3] When Lady Beaumont learned from the advertisement that this course of lectures was to include a discussion of contemporary poets—an intention which was not carried out—she expressed 'apprehension & alarm' lest Coleridge should launch an attack on Wordsworth. Agitated that he should even be suspected of 'feeling *vindictively*' toward Wordsworth, Coleridge immediately sent her a copy of his lines, *To William Wordsworth*, '& desired her to judge whether it was possible that a man, who had written that Poem, could be capable of such an act'. Coleridge's letter has disappeared, but the sheet in which the poem is written survives. It is addressed to Sir George Beaumont at Dunmow and has a postmark of [15?] Nov. 1811. In another letter Coleridge

as to be responsible for the payment, I will repay you and ante-pay you in the middle of next week. Should it be in your Power to have a Paragraph inserted comprizing the purport of that omitted in the inclosed Prospectus—so much the better—but at all events procure for me the regular Insertion of the ordinary Advertisement, which surely needs no great Interest.

I have sent you a numb[er] of Prospectuses, which you w[ill] distribute as your judgement dictates—& more you may have tomorrow morning by calling on Mr Pople's, *Bookseller*, 67, Chancery Lane, a few doors from the Holborn End—

In short, my dear fellow! do what you can for me—as I would most *heartfully* do for you—for we are of one Kind, & Aliens in the World of Wor[l]dlings—I did not ask Mr Collier[1] about the M. C.; but Godwin whom yet I have little reason to rely on, for He+She = SELF.

S. T. Coleridge—

837. To William Godwin

Address: Mr Godwin | Juvenile Library | Skinner's Street
MS. Lord Abinger. Hitherto unpublished.

Friday Evening
[Endorsed Nov. 8, 1811]

My dear Godwin

Forgive my perhaps unnecessary Anxiety—but I send you a Prospectus so marked as I would have it appear in the M. C., printed of course in the ordinary lineal form of an Advertisement[2]—Now all I can ask of you is no great matter, viz—to be responsible for the expence of it's Insertion regularly from Monday Morning the 11th to Monday 18th inclusive, for which I will at once repay and ante-pay you in the course of the next week—and all I ask of Mr Perry is to have the Advertisement inserted regularly in some conspicuous part of the Paper—What else can be done, I put to the score of a real feeling of Obligation. But only remember, my dear Godwin! that to delay in this is far worse than to have declined it at once—for it is a matter of great importance to me, as far as I am

assured Beaumont that it was not the 'facts disclosed' but 'the manner & time & the person by whom & the persons to whom they had been disclosed' which formed 'the whole ground' of his complaint against Wordsworth. See Letter 867, p. 400.

[1] John Dyer Collier, the father of John Payne Collier, was employed by the *Morning Chronicle*. At this time Robinson made his home with the Colliers.

[2] This letter is written on the blank pages of a prospectus, which Coleridge altered into an advertisement of his lectures.

unfortunately a husband, Father, &—not thro' any fault of my own—a Debtor. Otherwise, from any lesser dictate than that of Duty, I would not have humbled myself to solicit favors from Newspaper People while such Luxuries, as Cabbage Stalks, lay rotting on Dunghills—No, nor then—for there are worse Deaths than Starving, even if much easier ones were out of our power—

S. T. Coleridge

838. *To William Godwin*

MS. Lord Abinger. Hitherto unpublished.

Wednesday Evening
[Endorsed Nov. 13, 1811]

Dear Godwin

A severe Bowel-attack, occasioned by Cold, and producing extreme soreness to the outward touch, has at once prevented me from thanking you personally for past Efforts, and forces me to ask yet another good office from you—namely, to procure in the M. C. as speedily as possible an addition to the advertisement in these words, so printed as to meet the eye obviously:—Tickets for any one single Lecture may be had by application to Mr Murray, Bookseller, Fleet Street, or to W. Pople, 67, Chancery Lane: price, 5S. 6D.—

I begin very much to doubt, whether my scheme will answer, for few if any of my Friends at the West End of the Town will condescend to attend a Lecture in the City.—

May God bless you & your's—I have been so ill that tho' I reached Chancery Lane, I have been quite unable to extend my Walk to Skinner Street—

S. T. Coleridge

839. *To Henry Crabb Robinson*

Address: G. C. Robinson, Esqre. | 56 | Hatton Garden |—Collier, Esqre
MS. Dr. Williams's Lib. Hitherto unpublished.

Wednesday Evening
[Endorsed 13 Novr 1811]

My dear Robinson

I stopped at Mr Pople's at 2 o/clock with an intention of calling on you, & with a *prose* Essay in my pocket—but within a few minutes I was attacked by so severe a pain in my Bowels with such extreme soreness to the outward touch, that I could not stir without such pain as spite of one self makes grimaces on the Mind's flesh-Vizard.—The same cause compels me to request one other exertion of your Friendship—that you will immediately procure an addition to the Advertisement in these words (obviously printed)—

Tickets for any single Lecture may be procured by application to Mr Millar [Murray?], Bookseller, 32 Fleet Street, or to Mr Pople, 67, Chancery Lane.—

I am quite, & not irrationally, despondent concerning the quantum sufficit of my probable Audience—My Acquaintance at the West End of the Town recoil from the LONDON PHILOSOPHICAL SOCIETY, SCOT'S CORPORATION HALL, CRANE COURT ENTRANCE FROM FETTER LANE—

O Christ! such a PHIL. SOC. ! ! ! ! !

S. T. Coleridge

840. *To William Godwin*

Address: Mr Godwin
MS. Lord Abinger. Hitherto unpublished.

[Endorsed Nov. 16, 1811]

My dear Godwin

I have been very ill during the whole Week—For seven days I have had no passage from my Bowels, tho' night after night I have taken strong aperient medicines—The last, however, has removed, at least it has suspended, the pain & horrible restlessness, & lessened the sickness—I am in hopes therefore, that the obstruction, wherever it may be, or perhaps inflammation, is on it's departure—It has happened very unluc[kily], for I *could* not stir out yesterday or Thursday—indeed, [I could] not *sit* upright 10 minutes together—& to day I dare [not.]

I have inclosed your Ticket & hope that the youthful members of your Family may receive amusement—The Room is far far smaller than I had been led to believe; yet, I fear, will look too spacious for my purposes—

Best regards to Mrs G.—

S. T. Coleridge

841. *To Henry Crabb Robinson*

MS. Dr. Williams's Lib. Pub. with omis. E. L. G. ii. 59.

[Endorsed Nov. 18—1811][1]

My dear Robinson

Stuart was yesterday with me to see how I was—for truly for 8 days together the Trunk of my poor Body was or seemed to be a Trunk which Nature had first locked, and then thrown away the Key. When on Saturday Morning the incessant & racking pain all at once ceased, and a most delightful Ease ensued, I began myself to be not perhaps alarmed, but strongly suspicious of an incipient Mortification, no relief, no *exit*, having preceded—tho' I had been for several days taking the strongest aperient medicines, first every six, & latterly every three, hours. But, thank God! on Saturday Night the *reality* of an old Woman added to the *idea* of a Clyster proved so vehement a stimulus on my morbid delicacy, that flash! like lightning, and roar & rumble! like thunder, it (i.e. the proximate cause) plunged down thro' me—& to the Music loud and visceral and cataractic I sang out, 'I do not want the old Lady!—Give her half a crown & send her away!'—just as I heard her aged feet's plump and tardy echoes from the Stairs, I lying in dressing Gown, unbreeched save by Drawers, in fearful scarce resigned expectance of the dire execution.—Marvellous Beings are we! An Enɳma is not attended with the slightest pain—it is even rather a pleasant sensation—and yet such is the force of thought & intellectual repugnance that I am convinced, I should submit to a Lithotomy with less revulsion & less fortitude.—

A Digression this was—and now to business.—Stuart seemed to wonder at Walter's making any thing of a favor of inserting in the tomorrow's Times an account of the Lecture at this dead Time of the year; & added, that if a Birth day Entertainment had permitted him to be present, he would have written a paragraph of 20 or 30 lines, sent it to Walter with his Compliments, and should have been surprized as at a mark of unusual Discourtesy, if it had not been inserted—there being nothing political or personal in the Subject.—Much more then to me, who have always thought & written in the same Tone of Feeling with the Times, & when the chief

---

[1] In his endorsement of this letter Robinson added: 'Coleridge before his first lecture.' Coleridge's lectures were delivered Monday and Thursday evenings, 18, 21, 25, and 28 Nov.; 2, 5, 9, 12, 16, 19, and 30 Dec. 1811; and 2, 9, 13, 16, 20, and 27 Jan. 1812. In all, Coleridge gave seventeen rather than the fifteen lectures announced in the prospectus. See *Robinson on Books and Their Writers*, i. 51–61. For an account of this course of lectures, see *Shakespearean Criticism*, ii. 24–230.

Writer in it has sometimes quoted & very often written in the exact spirit of Wordsworth's Pamphlet—& twice quoted sentences which I myself wrote.—The only prose Essay I have & which I fully determined to send to Mr Walter when I had polished the style a little, merely as a mark of my high Esteem for a Paper which I not only think incomparably the best Journal that is or has been in G. Britain, but the only one which without impudence can dare call itself independent or impartial—And this I assuredly shall do still: because the compliment was intended to the *Times* itself and was not personal.[1] But yet I do not quite like the notion of chaffering a work of my most serious thoughts, & of my inmost convictions against a compliment or disguised Advertisement for the sake of *money*—tho' this is perfect purity in my feelings, compared with doing it from *Vanity*. Heaven knows! I never feel my Poverty so painful as when I see my name & a puff tacked to it, & know that I knew it beforehand

My Poverty & not my Will consenting—

I am convinced, my dear R., you will do all you can for me—After the Lecture write about 20 lines—notice that it was not in etymologic severity a Lecture—for tho' the reasoning, the arrangement, the &c bore the clearest marks of long premeditation, yet the language, illustrations &c were as evidently the children of the Moment——in short, what strikes yourself. A precious Recipe for a Puff!—O Jesus! Embarrassment like misery, makes us bedfellows with strange Meannesses, but that my Soul will not allow herself to be so reviled, I should have said, basenesses.—This paragraph should be in Tomorrow's Times, or not at all.[2] Doubtless, it [will] be of the greatest service to me—I brought the Essay with me, & if you wish it, will give it you, rude as it is, at the Lecture—God bless you!

S. T. C.—

Pray, tell Mrs C.—how I am & have been—

[1] This proposed essay for *The Times*, which Coleridge also mentions in Letter 839, was probably not acceptable to Walter, for on 20 Nov. Robinson wrote in his diary: '[Fraser, "the writer of great leaders" in *The Times*,] is of opinion, but I can't believe it to be well founded, that Stuart has tried to influence Walter's mind against Coleridge. . . . He believes Walter will not accept anything Coleridge will send him!' *Robinson on Books and Their Writers*, i. 51–52.

[2] Robinson obviously consulted Walter on receiving Coleridge's letter, for he recorded in his diary for 18 Nov.: 'With Walter to request he would put in a paragraph for Coleridge this evening. He hesitated and I was hurt. He consented, not with a good grace; and after the lecture I sent an article.' (*Robinson on Books and Their Writers*, i. 51.) Robinson's article appeared in *The Times* on 19 Nov. It is reprinted in *Shakespearean Criticism*, ii. 199–200.

842. *To Andrew Bell*

Pub. Life of Andrew Bell, *ii. 645.*

Mr Pople's, 67, Chancery Lane, Holborn,
30th November 1811.

My dear Sir,

. . . The room I lecture in is very comfortable, and of a grave academic appearance; the company highly respectable, though (unluckily) rather scanty; but the entrance, which is under a short passage from Fetter Lane, some thirty doors or more from Fleet Street, is disagreeable even to foot-comers, and far more so to carriages, from the narrowness and bendings of the lane. This, and in truth the very name of *Fetter* Lane, renowned exclusively for pork and sausages, have told against me; and I pay an exorbitant price in proportion to the receipts. I should doubtless feel myself honoured by your attendance on some one night; but such is your distance, and such is the weather, that I scarce dare *wish* it, much less ask or expect it.

I wrote a long letter to you concerning the sophistications of your system at present in vogue, the inevitable consequences on the whole mass of moral feelings, even of the dissenters themselves, and the courage, as well as fortitude, required for the effort to do one's duty. But I asked myself why I should give you pain, and destroyed it. Yet come what will come, the subject shall be treated fully, intrepidly, and by close deduction from settled first principles, in the first volume of the recommencing *Friend*, which I hope to bring out early in the spring, on a quarterly or four-monthly plan, in partnership with a publisher, who is personally my friend; and who will take on himself all the *business*, and leave me exclusively occupied in the composition. Even to this day I have not received nearly one-half of the subscriptions for the former numbers, and am expiating the error by all sorts of perplexities and embarrassments. A man who has nothing better than prudence is fit for no world to come; and he who does not possess it in full activity, is as unfit for the present world. What then shall we say? Have both prudence and the moral sense, but subordinate the former to the latter; and so possess the flexibility and address of the serpent to glide through the brakes and jungles of this life, with the wings of the dove to carry us upward to a better.

May the Almighty bless and preserve you, my dear sir! With most unfeigned love and honour, I remain—and till I lose all sense of my better being, of the veiled immortal within me, ever must remain—your obliged and grateful friend.

[S. T. Coleridge]

843. *To William Godwin*

MS. Lord Abinger. Hitherto unpublished.

[Endorsed Dec. 4, 1811]

My dear Godwin

Little Griefs become great vexations when they happen at a time when the Best of our Good Spirits and tranquillity are no more than we need. These have affected my Health—and my ill-health re-acted on them.—But for this, I should have called on you long ago, & this alone prevented me from spending the Day with you on Sunday last, as a Volunteer Visitor.

I write now to intreat you to take care that my advertisement should appear in the M. Chronicle, with the alteration, over leaf. If you have no money in hand, you shall have whatever is requisite for the remaining Lectures (two Advertisements per week) tomorrow night.—I pray you, let it appear if possible, tomorrow morning— It's non-appearance manifestly thinned my Auditory—

Kind respects to Mrs G. God bless you | &

S. T. Coleridge

844. *To Sir George Beaumont*

Address: Sir G. Beaumont, Bart | Dunmow | Essex
MS. Pierpont Morgan Lib. Pub. with omis. Letters, *ii. 570.*
Postmark: 7 December 1811.

J. J. Morgan's, Esqre., 7, Portland Place, Hammersmith.
Saturday Morning 7 Decembr. 1811

Dear Sir George

On Wednesday Night I slept in town, in order to have a Mask taken, from which or rather with which Allston means to model a Bust of me.[1] I did not, therefore, receive your Letter and the inclosed till Thursday Night, 11 o/clock, on my return from the Lecture: and early on Friday Morning I was roused from my first Sleep by an agony of Tooth-ach, which continued almost without Intermission the whole Day, and has left my Head and the whole of my Trunk 'not a man but a Bruise.' What can I say more, my dear Sir George, than that I deeply feel this proof of your continued friendship, and pray from my inmost Soul that more perseverance in efforts of Duty may render me more worthy of your kindness than I at present am? Ingratitude, like all *crimes* that are at the same time *Vices*, bad as Malady and worse as Symptom, is of

[1] Coleridge must have meant to write Dawe and not Allston. George Dawe (1781–1829) exhibited his bust of Coleridge at the Royal Academy in 1812. See Letter 861.

From a crayon sketch of Samuel Taylor Coleridge drawn by George Dawe in 1811 and now in the possession of Lord Coleridge

so detestable a nature that an honest man will mourn in silence under real injuries [rather] than hazard the very suspicion of it: and will be slow to avail himself of Lord Bacon's remark, much as he may admire it's profundity—'Crimen Ingrati Animi, quod magnis Ingeniis haud raró Objicitur, saepius nil aliud est quám Perspicacia quaedam in causam beneficii collati.'[1] Yet that man has assuredly tenfold reason to be grateful who can be so, both head and heart, who at once served and honored knows himself more delighted by the motive that influenced his Friend than by the Benefit received by himself: were it only perhaps for this cause, that the consciously [consciousness?] of always repaying the former in kind takes away all regret that he is incapable of returning the latter.

Mr Dawe, Royal Associate, who plaistered my face for me, says that he never saw so excellent a Mask, and so unaffected by any expression of Pain or Uneasiness. On Tuesday at the farthest, a Cast will be finished, which I was vain enough to desire to be packed up and sent to Dunmow—with it you will find a chalk drawing of my face,[2] which I think far more like than any former attempt, excepting Allston's full length Portrait of me,[3] which with all his Casts, &c, two or three valuable Works of the Venetian School, and his Jason almost finished, and on which he had employed 18 months without Intermission, are lying at Leghorn— with no chance of procuring them. There will likewise be an Epistolary Essay for Lady Beaumont, on the subject of Religion in reference to my own Faith: it was too long to send by the Post.—

Dawe is engaged on a picture (the figures about 4 feet) from my Poem of LOVE[4]—

> She leaned beside the armed man,
> The Statue of the armed Knight—
> She stood and listened to my Harp[5]
> Amid the lingering Light.—
>
> His dying words—but when I reached &c—
>
> All impulses of Soul & Sense &c—[6]

[1] *De Dignitate et Augmentis Scientiarum*, Liber VI, Caput iii. 15, reads: 'Crimen ingrati animi nil aliud est, quam perspicacia quaedam in causam beneficii collati.'

[2] In 1812 Dawe exhibited a portrait of Coleridge at the Royal Academy. The head was drawn in 1811, the remainder in 1812. See p. ix.

[3] See frontispiece.

[4] Dawe exhibited *Genevieve: from a poem by S. T. Coleridge, entitled 'Love'*, at the Royal Academy in 1812. See Letter 861.

[5] song [Cancelled word in line above.]

[6] *Love*, lines 13–16, 65, and 69.

His Sketch is very beautiful & has more expression than I ever
found in his former productions—excepting indeed his Imogen.—

Allston is hard at work on a large Scripture Piece, the dead man
recalled to Life by touching the Bones of the Prophet. He models
every figure—Dawe, who was delighted with the Cupid and
Psyche, seemed quite astonished at the facility and exquisiteness
with which Allston modelled—Canova[1] at Rome exprest himself to
me in very warm terms of admiration on the same subject.—He
means to exhibit but two or at the most three pictures, all poetical
or history painting—in part, by my advice—it seemed to me
impolitic to appear to be *trying* in half a dozen ways, as if his
mind had not yet discovered it's main current.—The longer I live,
the more deeply am I convinced of the high importance, as a
symptom, of the Love of *Beauty* in a young Painter—It is neither
honorable to a young man's Heart or Head to attach himself year
after year to old or deformed Objects, comparatively too so easy,
especially if bad Drawing & worse Coloring leaves the Spectator's
Imagination at lawless Liberty—& he cries out 'How very like!'
just as he would at a coal in the centre of the Fire, or at a Frost-
figure on a Window-pane. It is [on] this added to his quiet unenvious spirit, to his lofty feelings concerning his Art, and to [the]
religious Purity of his moral character that I chiefly rest my hopes
of Allston's future Fame. His best productions seem to please
him principally because he sees and has learnt something which
enables him to promise himself—'I shall do better in my next.'—

I have not been at the Courier office for some months past—I
detest writing Politics, even on the right side—and when I discovered that the Courier was not the independent Paper, I had
been led to believe, and had myself over and over again asserted,
I wrote no more for it. Greatly indeed do I prefer the present
Ministers to the Leaders of any other Party—but indiscriminate
Support of any class of men, I dare not give—especially when there
is so easy and honorable an Alternative as not to write Politics at
all—which, henceforth, nothing but blank Necessity shall compel
me to do. I will write for the PERMANENT, or not at all. 'The Comet'
therefore I have never seen—or heard of it[2]—yet most true it is
that I myself have composed some Verses on 'the Comet'—but I
am quite certain, that no one ever saw them—for the best of all
reasons, that my own Brain is the only substance on which they
have been recorded.—I will, however, consign them to Paper and

---

[1] Antonio Canova (1757–1822), a celebrated Italian sculptor.

[2] Wordsworth had written to Lady Beaumont that he half suspected a
poem on the comet published in the *Courier* on 16 Nov. 1811 to be Coleridge's.
Middle Years, ii. 478.

send them to you with the Courier Poem as soon as I can procure it—for the curiosity of the thing.—

I write in some pain from the extreme soreness at the surface of my Chest and Stomach—My most affectionate respects to Lady Beaumont—and believe me, dear Sir George, with heart-felt regard

Your obliged & grateful Friend,
S. T. Coleridge

P.S.—Were you in town, I should be very sorry indeed to see you in Fetter Lane. The Lectures were meant for the young men of the City.—Several of my Friends join to take Notes[1]——and if I can correct what they can shape out of them into any tolerable Form, I will send them to you.—On Monday I lecture on Love & the Female character as displayed by Shakespear.—

Good Dr Bell is in town—He came from Keswick, all delight with my little Sara, & quite enchanted with Southey. Some flights of admiration in the form of questions to me—('Did you ever see any thing so finely conceived?—so profoundly thought? as this passage

[1] Among the friends who took notes on Coleridge's lectures were John Payne Collier (1789–1883), the Shakespearean critic; J. Tomalin; and Henry Crabb Robinson. Collier made a shorthand record of the first, second, sixth, seventh, eighth, ninth, and twelfth lectures, and published his notes in 1856 as *Seven Lectures on Shakespeare and Milton. By the late S. T. Coleridge*. Tomalin made extended reports of the first eight lectures. These notes were formerly in the possession of E. H. Coleridge, who says in a manuscript note that his 'unique Tomalin was lost . . . on the Railroad'—a reference to the theft of his box of MSS. and papers *en route* to Torquay. Fortunately J. D. Campbell had previously made transcripts of Tomalin's reports of the third, fourth, and fifth lectures. See *Shakespearean Criticism*, ii. 24–25 and 56–230.

Mary Russell Mitford heard several of Coleridge's lectures. The fifth lecture of 2 Dec. 1811 she attended in the company of Frances Rowden, author of *The Pleasures of Friendship*, 1810; and since her report is not included in *Shakespearean Criticism*, it may be given here:

'I had the satisfaction of seating . . . [Mrs. Rowden] close by my side in the lecture room. It was very full, the orator was more than usually brilliant. I had just got Mrs. R. to confess "that he really was tolerable" (a wonderful confession considering she was *a lady* & determined to dislike him) when to my utter dismay he began a period as follows. "There are certain Poems,—or things called poems—which have obtained considerable fame—or that which is called fame—in the world.—I mean the Pleasures of Tea Drinking & the Pleasures of Wine drinking & the Pleasures of Love & the Pleasures of Nonsense & The Pleasures of Hope"—There thank God the list ended for it was only aimed at Campbell whom he proceeded to abuse—but think what I felt while he was going on with his Pleasures, & I expected the Pleasures of Friendship to come out every moment. Mr. Rogers was just by, so that Mrs. Rowden had the comfort of company in her sensations, whatever they might be—but they had both the wit to keep them to themselves.'

[MS. Reading Public Lib. and *The Life of Mary Russell Mitford*, ed. A. G. K. L'Estrange, 2 vols., 1870, i. 131–2.]

in his Review on the Methodists?—Or on the Education?'—&c—)
embarrassed me in a very ridiculous way—and I verily believe,
that my odd way of hesitating, left on Bell's mind some shade of a
suspicion as if I did not like to hear my Friend so highly extolled—
Half a dozen words from Southey would have precluded this,
without diminution to his own fame—I mean, in conversation
with Dr Bell.

845. *To Unknown Correspondent*

MS. British Museum. Pub. E. L. G. ii. 61. This letter is written on the backs
of several printed prospectuses of the lecture of 21 November 1811. Coleridge
twice endorsed his letter, the first endorsement reading: 'Rough Draft of a
Letter written to a Man (–, $\delta - y\kappa\ o\mu\theta$) who offered to review W. Scott's poems
to his injury.' The cryptogram is indecipherable. The second endorsement,
which is crossed out in the manuscript, reads: '[intended?] to have been copied
[and] sent to Lord B.' If Lord B. refers to Byron, this endorsement was almost
certainly added several years after the letter was composed. Although Byron
was probably an auditor at Coleridge's ninth lecture of 16 December, and
certainly attended the sixteenth lecture of 20 January 1812, the two men were
not acquainted, and there would be no reason for sending Byron the letter at
this time. In 1815, however, a correspondence between Coleridge and Byron
began; and as the question of Scott's indebtedness to *Christabel* arose, Coleridge
may very well have planned to send a transcript of the present letter to Byron.
Coleridge again recalled this letter in writing to Allsop in 1820. *Byron Letters
and Journals*, ii. 90, and iii. 228; *Robinson on Books and Their Writers*, i. 60;
Letters, Conversations and Rec., 27; and Letter 981.

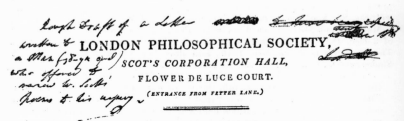

LONDON PHILOSOPHICAL SOCIETY,

SCOT'S CORPORATION HALL,

FLOWER DE LUCE COURT.

(ENTRANCE FROM FETTER LANE.)

MR. COLERIDGE

WILL DELIVER

ON THURSDAY, NOV. 21,

HIS SECOND LECTURE ON SHAKESPEAR AND MILTON,

IN ILLUSTRATION OF

THE PRINCIPLES OF POETRY,

AND THEIR

*Application as Grounds of Criticism to the most popular Works of later English
Poets, those of the Living included.*

Sir   [*Circa* 15–21 December 1811][1]

As I am bound to thank you for your good-will and the high opinion, you have been pleased to express of my Genius, so I ask in return that you should give me credit for perfect sincerity in the motives and feelings, which I shall assign for my inability to comply with your request.

Excuse me, if I say that I have ever held parallelisms adduced in proof of plagiarism or even of intentional imitation, in the utmost contempt. There are two Kinds of Heads in the world of Literature. The one I would call, SPRINGS: the other TANKS. The latter class habituated to receiving only, full or low, according to the state of it's Feeders, attach[es] no distinct notion to living production as contra-distinguished from mechanical formation. If they find a fine passage in Thomson, they refer it to Milton; if in Milton to Euripides or Homer; and if in Homer, they take for granted it's pre-existence in the lost works of Linus or Musaeus. It would seem as if it was a part of their Creed, that all Thoughts are traditional,[2] and that not only the Alphabet was revealed to Adam but all that was ever written in it that was worth writing.—But I come to the point. I can scarcely call myself an Acquaintance of Mr Walter Scott's; but I have met him twice or thrice in company.[3] Those who hold that a Man's nature is shewn in his Countenance would not need the confident assurance, which all his Friends & Acquaintance so unanimously give, that he is of the most frank and generous disposition, incapable of trick or concealment.—The mere expression of his Features, and the Tones of his Voice in conversation, independent of the matter, sufficiently attest the fervor & activity of his mind.—The Proofs must be strong indeed, Sir! which could convince me that such a man could consciously make an unfair and selfish use of *any* Manuscript that came by accident into his

---

[1] This letter refers to a conversation which occurred 'only last week, ... after the close of my Lecture on Romeo and Juliet'. Since Coleridge's seventh and eighth lectures of 9 and 12 Dec. both deal with that play, the present letter was written during the following week of Sunday, 15 Dec.

[2] Cf. Coleridge's Preface to *Christabel*, 1816, p. vi: 'For there is among us a set of critics, who seem to hold, that every possible thought and image is traditional; who have no notion that there are such things as fountains in the world, small as well as great; and who would therefore charitably derive every rill, they behold flowing, from a perforation made in some other man's tank.' See also Letter 981 for several passages equally close to the Preface.

[3] Coleridge must have first met Scott when in London with his son Hartley and Wordsworth in 1807. 'Walter was certainly in London in the Spring of 1807', wrote Hartley in a reminiscent mood, 'for well do I remember his accompanying a bard [Wordsworth] . . . and my too happy self to the Tower.' *Poems by Hartley Coleridge*, ed. Derwent Coleridge, 2 vols., 1851 (2nd edn.) i, p. ccxxii.

possession—least of all, one of a known Contemporary.—What then are they the Facts that are to weaken this presumption?— First, that the Fragment, entitled Christabel, was composed many *years*, and known & openly admired by Mr Scott some time, before the *publication* of the Lay of the Last Minstrel. (For be pleased to observe, it is no part of the known *Fact* that the Lay of the Last Minstrel was not composed in part at least or at least *planned*, before Mr S. had seen the Fragment in question.[)]¹

Secondly, that of those who had seen or heard the Fragment a large proportion were struck with certain lines the same or nearly the same in the L.L.M., with similar movements in the manner of narration and the arrangement of the Imagery, and lastly with that general resemblance which is exprest by the words—the one still reminded them of the other.—Before I proceed to the argu-

¹ The confusion over the date of Scott's first acquaintance with *Christabel* will justify, perhaps, a brief review of the facts. In an Introduction to *The Lay of the Last Minstrel* written in 1830, Scott intimated that Stoddart recited *Christabel* to him in the summer of 1800. A letter from Stoddart to Scott, dated 26 Dec. 1800, shows, however, that Stoddart visited the Lakes *after* his tour of Scotland. Moreover, he tells Scott that 'Coleridge is engaged on a poetical Romance called Christabel, of very high merit'—a remark he would not have made had he previously repeated the poem to Scott. Stoddart arrived in Grasmere soon after Coleridge had completed Part II of *Christabel* and heard the poem read on 22 Oct. 1800. On 12 Jan. 1801 he wrote urging Coleridge to come to London and to bring *Christabel* with him. [MS. Lord Latymer.] It must have been in this year that Stoddard obtained a copy of the poem. References in Lamb's letters show that Stoddart made a second journey to Scotland in Sept.–Oct. 1802, again stopping at Keswick on his return southward; and it seems safe to assume that *Christabel* was read or recited to Scott during this excursion.

The Wordsworths visited Scott in 1803, and at that time he told them that when he heard Stoddart recite *Christabel* 'he had begun his poem and was much delighted to meet with so happy a specimen of the same kind of irregular metre which he had adopted'. In his Introduction of 1830, however, Scott openly admitted that 'the singularly irregular structure of the stanzas [of *Christabel*], and the liberty which it allowed the author to adapt the sound to the sense, seemed to be exactly suited to such an extravaganza as I meditated. . . . It was, to the best of my recollection, more than a year after Mr. Stoddart's visit, that . . . I composed the first two or three stanzas of "The Lay of the Last Minstrel".'

Scott's tardy acknowledgement in 1830 of his indebtedness to *Christabel*— an 'acknowledgment due from the pupil to his master'—was undoubtedly prompted by his displeasure on reading the following charge in a conversation of Byron published in 1824: 'I hope Walter Scott did not write the review on "Christabel"; for he certainly, in common with many of us, is indebted to Coleridge. But for him, perhaps, "The Lay of the Last Minstrel" would never have been thought of. The line "Jesu Maria shield thee well!" is word for word from "Christabel".' *The Poetical Works of Sir Walter Scott*, 1833, vi. 23–27; Wilfred Partington, *Sir Walter's Post-Bag*, 1932, p. 12; *Journals of Dorothy Wordsworth*, i. 69–71 and 184; *Lamb Letters*, i. 313 and 323; *Early Letters*, 533; and Thomas Medwin, *Conversations of Lord Byron*, 1824, p. 309.

ments on the other side, I will examine these, and if I can rely on my own feelings at the present moment, exactly as I would wish a friend of mine to do if I had been the fortunate Author of the Lay of the last Minstrel and the Marmion, & Mr W. S. the earlier Writer of the Christabel.

Now it must be obvious on the first calm reflection, that Mr W. S. could have had no previous intention of using the Christabel —from the very fact which has furnished the main strength of the contrary presumption—For before the appearance of the Lay of the L. M. he not only mentioned the Christabel repeatedly to persons who had never before heard of it, not only praised it with warmth, but *recited* it.—In order to evade or weaken this fact, we must make the arbitrary supposition, that he had not at that time planned his Poem as it now appears: and that the purpose was formed in his mind afterwards, & while he was composing.—A purpose, of course, implies consciousness.—Now this again is rendered in the highest degree improbable by another of the Facts above stated, & by one too that has assuredly had no small share in occasioning the suspicion—the existence, I mean, of a number of Lines the same or nearly the same in both Authors. I have not the Poems by me; but I distinctly remember, that the greater part consisted of Phrases, such as Jesu Maria! shield thee well,[1] &c— which might have occurred to a score of Writers who had been previously familiar with Poems & Romances written before the Reformation or translated from the Spanish—and the small remainder contain nothing remarkable either in language, thought, feeling or imagery. From long disuse I cannot have the tenth part of the fluency in versification as Mr Scott or Southey have: & yet I would undertake in a couple of Hours to alter every one of these Lines or Couplets, without the least injury to the context, to retain the same meaning in words equally poetical & suitable, & yet entirely remove all the *appearance* of Likeness.—And this, Sir! is what an intentional Plagiarist would have done—He would have *translated*, not transcribed.

If then there be any just ground for the Charge of 'stolen feathers' (say rather, for an imitation of the mode of flying), it must be found in the supposed close likeness of the metre, the *movements*, the way of relating an event, in short, in the general resemblance of the

---

[1] *Christabel*, lines 54 and 582: 'Jesu, Maria, shield her well!' *The Lay of the Last Minstrel*, I. i. 5: 'Jesu Maria, shield us well!' Scott never acknowledged this borrowing. In 1830 he merely said that in the first and discarded draft of the poem a line, 'Mary, mother, shield us well', was taken 'a little softened' from Coleridge. Actually Scott's rejected line was close to *Christabel*, line 69: 'Mary mother, save me now!'

great Features, which have given to the Physiognomy of Mr W. S.'s late Poems their marked originality, in the public Feeling. Now that several persons, and these too persons of education, and liberal minds, at several times, and without any knowlege of each other's opinions have been struck with this general resemblance, & have expressed themselves more or less strongly on the subject, I do not pretend to deny: for it is a fact of my own knowlege.[1] But it would be most dishonorable in me if I did not add, that *if* I had framed my expectations exclusively by the opinions & assertions of others, those whose expressions were most limited would have excited anticipations, which my own after Perusal of the Lay of the Last Minstrel were [was?] far from veriyfing [verifying?] to my own mind. But I will admit that of this neither I or Mr S. are or can be the proper Judges. A Poet may be able to appreciate the merit of each particular Part of his own Poem as well, or (if he have a well-disciplined mind) better than any other can do; but of the *effect* of the Whole as a Whole he cannot from the very nature of Things (from the foreknowlege of each following part, from the parts having been written at different times, from the blending of the pleasures & disgusts of Composing with the Composition itself, &c) have the same sensation, as the Reader or auditor to whom the whole is new & simultaneous.—The Case must then be thus stated. Put aside the fact of the previous acquaintance with the Christabel —suppose that no circumstances were known, that rendered it probable—Would the resemblances in and of themselves have enforced, or at least have generally suggested, the suspicion that [the] later Poem was an intentional Imitation of the elder? In other words, is the general Likeness, or are the particular resemblances, such as a liberal and enlightened Reader could not with any probability consider as the result of mere Coincidence between two Writers of similar Pursuits, and (argumenti causâ loquor) of nearly equal Talent? Coincidence is here used as a negative—not as implying that the Likeness between two Works is merely accidental, the effect of chance, but as asserting that it is not the effect of imitation. Now how far Coincidence in this sense and under the supposed Conditions is possible, I can myself supply an instance, which happened at my Lectures in Flower de Luce Court[2] only last week, and the accuracy of which does not rely on *my* evidence only, but can be proved by the separate testimony of

----

[1] See Letters 632 and 650.

[2] The prospectus of the lecture of 21 Nov. 1811 specified: 'Scot's Corporation Hall, Flower de Luce [now Fleur-de-Lis] Court. Entrance from Fetter Lane.' The earlier prospectus had designated Crane Court, Fleet Street. Cf. headnote to Letter 835 and Letters 839 and 842.

some hundred Individuals—that is, by as many as have attended
& retained any distinct recollection of my Lectures at the Royal
Institution or at Fetter Lane. After the close of my Lecture on
Romeo and Juliet a German Gentleman, a Mr Bernard Krusve,
introduced himself to me, and after some courteous Compliments
said, Were it not almost impossible, I must have believed that you
had either heard or read my Countryman Schlegel's Lecture on
this play, given at Vienna: the principles, thought, and the very
illustrations are so nearly the same—But the Lectures were but
just published as I left Germany, scarcely more than a week since—
& the only two Copies of the Work in England I have reason to
think, that I myself have brought over.[1] One I retain: the other is
at Mr Boosy's[2]—I replied that I had not even heard of these
Lectures, nor had indeed seen any work of Schlegel's except a
volume of Translations from Spanish Poetry,[3] which the Baron
Von Humboldt had lent me when I was at Rome[4]—one piece of
which, a Translation of a Play of Calderon I had compared with
the original, & formed in consequence a high Opinion of Schlegel's
Taste & Genius.—A Friend standing by me added—This cannot
be a question of Dates, Sir! for if the gentleman, whose name you
have mentioned, first gave his Lectures at Vienna in 1810[5] I

---

[1] The lectures of A. W. von Schlegel (1767–1845) were delivered at Vienna
in 1808. The first two volumes (vol. i and Part I of vol. ii) of his *Ueber dramatische Kunst und Litteratur. Vorlesungen* were published in 1809; the third
volume (Part II of vol. ii), which contained Schlegel's lectures on Shakespeare
and which was probably the 'Work' Krusve had brought from Germany, bears
the date 1811 on the title-page. Actually, this third volume was published late
in December 1810. (See J. Körner, *Die Botschaft der deutschen Romantik an
Europa*, 1929, pp. 17–18, 24; and *August Wilhelm Schlegels Briefwechsel mit
seinen Heidelberger Verlegern*, ed. E. Jenisch, 1922, pp. 69, 73, and 75.) According to his own testimony, however, Coleridge first read the third volume of the
Vorlesungen in December 1811. Robinson, too, was reading this work, apparently for the first time, in Feb. 1812: 'Read evening at home Schlegel's
lectures on Shakespeare. Coleridge, I find, did not disdain to borrow observations from Schlegel, tho' the coincidences between the two lecturers are for the
greater part coincidences merely and not the one caused by the other.' (*Shakespearean Criticism*, ii. 221.) In a letter of 25 Oct. 1813 Coleridge mentions his
ownership of 'the three Volumes of *Schlegel's Vorlesungen*', and his use of them
at the Surrey Institution in 1812–13. J. L. Haney says: 'The late Professor
Dowden informed me in 1906 that he had in his library a copy of . . . Schlegel's
Ueber Dramatische Kunst und Literatur (Heidelberg, 1811), containing Coleridge's marginalia.' ('Coleridge the Commentator', *Coleridge* . . . , ed. Edmund
Blunden and E. L. Griggs, 1934, p. 124.) The present whereabouts of this copy
is unknown.   [2] Thomas Boosey, Broad Street bookseller. See Letter 1023.
[3] The first volume of Schlegel's *Spanisches Theater* was published in 1803.
[4] Karl Wilhelm von Humboldt (1767–1835), Prussian minister in Rome
1801–8. See *The Friend*, ed. H. N. Coleridge, 3 vols., 1844, iii. 198.
[5] Coleridge apparently wrote 1809 and then altered the date to 1810. Indeed,

can myself bear witness, that I heard Mr Coleridge deliver all the *substance* of to night's Lecture at the Royal Institution some years before.—The next morning Mr Krusve called on me & made me a present of the Work;[1] and as much as the Resemblance of the L. of L.M. fell below the anticipations which the accounts of others were calculated to excite, so much did this Work transcend.— Not in one Lecture, but in all the Lectures that related to Shakespear, or to Poetry in general, the Grounds, Train of Reasoning, &c were different in language only—& often not even in that—. The Thoughts too were so far peculiar, that to the best of my knowlege they did not exist in any prior work of Criticism—Yet I was far more flattered, or to speak more truly, I was more confirmed, than surprize[d]. For Schlegel & myself had both studied deeply & perseverantly the philosophy of Kant, the distinguishing feature of which [is] to treat every subject in reference to the operation of the mental Faculties, to which it specially appertains—& to commence by the cautious discrimination of what is essential, i.e. explicable by mere consideration of the Faculties in themselves, from what is empirical—i.e. the modifying or disturbing Forces of Time, Place, and Circumstances. Suppose myself & Schlegel (my argument not my vanity leads to these seeming Self-flatteries) nearly equal in natural powers, of similar pursuits & acquirements, and it is only necessary for both to have mastered the spirit of Kant's Critique of the Judgment to render it morally certain, that writing on the same Subject we should draw the same conclusions by the same trains [of reasoning] from the same principles, write to one purpose & with one spirit.

Now, Sir! apply this to Mr W. Scott. If his Poem had been in any sense a borrowed thing, it's Elements likewise would surely be assumed, not native. But no insect was ever more like in the color of it's skin & juices to the Leaf, it fed on, than Scott's Muse is to Scott himself—Habitually conversant with the antiquities of his Country, & of all Europe during the ruder periods of Society, living as it were, in whatever is found in them imposing either to the

he repeatedly asserted that Schlegel's lectures were given two (in one letter three) years after he had delivered his own lectures at the Royal Institution in 1808. See Letters 1113, 1118, 1165 n., and 1182; *Shakespearean Criticism*, i. 18–19, and ii. 164; *Biog. Lit.* i. 22 n., 102, and 213; *Coleridge's Miscellaneous Criticism*, ed. T. M. Raysor, 1936, p. 172.

[1] This statement would indicate that Coleridge obtained the Schlegel volume on Friday, 13 Dec., but in his ninth lecture he says he had received a book by a German critic 'Yesterday afternoon', or 15 Dec.—a discrepancy of two days. *Shakespearean Criticism*, ii. 164. See Letter 1113, in which Coleridge says 'the first Copy [of Schlegel] that arrived in England was presented to me in the [lecture] Room by a German Gentleman'.

Fancy or interesting to the Feelings, passionately fond of natural
Scenery, abundant in local Anecdote, and besides learned in

all the antique Scrolls of Faery Land,
[And all the thrilling Tales of Chivalry.][1]
Processions, Tournaments, Spells, Chivalry—

in all languages from Apuleius to Tam o' Shanter—how else or
what else could he have been expected to write? [If I dared prophecy, I would say that Posterity will blame him, if at all, for
being totus ⟨in toto⟩].[2]—His Poems are evidently the indigenous
Products of his Mind & Habits.—

But I have wearied myself, & shall weary you.—I will only add,
that I have a volume of Poems now before me, compleatly made
up of gross plagiarisms from Akenside, Thomson, Bowles, Southey,
& the Lyrical Ballads—it is curious to observe how many artifices
the poor Author has used to disguise the theft, transpositions,
dilutions, substitutions of Synonimes, &c &c—and yet not the
least resemblance to any one of the Poets whom he has pillaged.—
He who can catch the Spirit of an original, has it already. It will not
[be] by Dates, that Posterity will judge of the originality of a
Poem; but by the original spirit itself. This is to be found neither in
a Tale however interesting, which is but the Canvass, no nor yet in
the Fancy or the Imagery—which are but Forms & Colors—it is a
subtle Spirit, all in each part, reconciling & unifying all—. Passion
and Imagination are it's *most* appropriate names; but even these
say little—for it must be not merely Passion but poetic Passion,
poetic Imagination.—[MS. breaks off thus.]

846. *To Henry Crabb Robinson*

Address: H. C. Robinson, Esqre | J. Collier's, Esqre | 56 | Hatton Garden |
Holborn
MS. Historical Society of Pennsylvania. Pub. E. L. G. ii. 68.
Postmark: 28 December 1811.

My dear Sir   [28 December 1811]
    I have not left the House this whole Christmas Week, fearful of
increasing my stomach disposition—yet I am much perplexed and
in need of good advice respecting the 5 lectures yet to come.—The
advertisement on Monday Morning must be—'Monday Evening,
30 Decembr 1811—Mr Coleridge will deliver his eleventh Lecture
on the English Historical Plays of Shakspeare with the characters
of RICHARD THE THIRD and FALSTAFF'—&c as usual.—
    Now this is a pretty *fistful* for one Lecture—What then of Lear,

[1] This line crossed out in MS.
[2] The sentence in brackets crossed out in MS.; 'in toto' supplied by editor.

Othello, Macbeth, Hamlet—with all the characters as well as the Plays containing them—& my review of Johnson's Preface to Shakespere—*all, all,* in the 12th Lecture?—But if this be impossible, what is to become of Milton &c &c?—Had I not better on Monday at the close of my Lecture mention this difficulty—& put it to the choice of my Audience whether I should finish Shakespere completely in 15 lectures—or leave him incomplete & proceed to Milton?—¹

> God bless you—
> S. T. COLERIDGE

847. *To William Godwin*

MS. Lord Abinger, Hitherto unpublished.

[Endorsed Jan. 8, 1812]

Dear Godwin

Do not forget my Advertisement tomorrow—'On Dr Johnson's Preface, and the criticisms and comments of Shakspeare in general.'²
O that it was over! I should then have some time to shew myself personally.

> Your's affectn.
> S. T. Coleridge

848. *To Robert Southey*

MS. Lord Latymer. Hitherto unpublished.

[*Circa* 9 January 1812]³

Dear Southey

You will have a fair opportunity when you are recording Percival's Masterly Reply to Whitbread—

> the web of Prophecy in vain,
> The creature's at it's dirty work again,⁴

¹ 'He kept to his subject', wrote Crabb Robinson of Coleridge's eleventh lecture, 'and, in conformity with an opinion I gave him, intimated his intention to deliver two lectures on Milton.' *Shakespearean Criticism*, ii. 218. Thus Coleridge added two lectures to the fifteen originally announced in the prospectus.　　² This lecture, the thirteenth, was delivered 9 Jan. 1812.

³ Coleridge's reference to Perceval's speech suggests an approximate date for this letter.

⁴ On 8 Jan. 1812, in speaking on the Lords Commissioners' Speech, Samuel Whitbread noted with gloomy apprehension the cause against France in Spain and Portugal and argued that a failure to consider a peace with Napoleon 'must lead to eternal war; or rather to a war which could only end in the extinction of either power. It might, he thought, be foreseen, which must fall, . . . when it was considered that the greatness of one nation was artificial, while the greatness of the other, such as it was, was natural.' Perceval replied brilliantly. He pointed out 'the state in which the war stood at the beginning of the last session', recalled Whitbread's 'opinions and fears and prophecies', and declared that 'his fears were unfounded, . . . his expectations were falsified, . . . his prophecies were erroneous; and yet the hon. gent. was prepared upon the

or wherever else you come forward as Grigri-mastix, to quote against them, especially against my Lord Futurum Post, Knight of the *vile Grin*—or (perhaps as being the fillet or broad bottom of one of John Bull's Calves, which he has kept far too long, and is now in *a state of complete mortification*, even to Gangrene) *Green Veal*, full of maggots, & like his own Spanish Cause, dead, yet all alive o'—the following witty Stanza of Berni's in his Rifacc: of the Orland. Innam.—I need not say that it is Berni's very own[1]—

> Onde ora avendo a traverso tagliato
> Questo Pagan, lo fè sì destramente,
> Che l'un pezzo in su l'altro suggellato
> Rimase, senza muoversi niente:
> E come avvien, quand'uno è riscaldato,
> Che le ferite per allor non sente,
> Così COLUI DEL COLPO NON ACCORTO
> ANDAVA COMBATTENDO, ED ERA MORTO.

L. II. C. xxiv. St. 60.

S. T. C.

849. *To J. J. Morgan*

MS. Lord Latymer. Pub. E. L. G. ii. 90.

[January 1812][2]

My dear Morgan
I wish you would be my Organ
And when you pass down Piccadilly
To call in at Escher's,[3] who sells books wise and silly
But chiefly in a Lingo by the Learned called German,

same grounds of apprehension, namely, the boasts of Buonaparte, to repeat his prophecies—

> "Destroy the web of prophecy in vain,
> The creature's at his dirty work again."'

Following Perceval's speech, Whitbread arose to 'demand of the right hon. gentleman to explain, whether he meant any personal allusion in some words that fell from him that appeared to me to be of no very delicate description'. Perceval replied: 'I could have meant none. The lines are Pope's [*Epistle to Dr. Arbuthnot*, lines 91–92]—the metaphor is that of a spider spinning a new web after one has been destroyed. I thought it applicable to the pertinacious manner in which the hon. gentleman appeared to me to have been reviving his prophecies over again.' T. C. Hansard, *The Parliamentary Debates*, 1812, xxi. 53–64.

[1] *Orlando Innamorato, composto già . . . Bojardo, . . . ed ora rifatto tutto di nuovo da M. Francesco Berni*, published posthumously in 1541.

[2] Coleridge wrote this note on the back of the address sheet of an old letter directed to him at Portland Place, Hammersmith. His connexion with this address ended in Feb. 1812.

[3] Henry Escher was a bookseller at 201 Piccadilly from 1807 to midsummer 1812.

And who himself looks less like a Man than a Mer-man—
And ask him if he still has a work called Ardinghello,[1]
It was in his Catalogue, I am sure, and of course to sell o—
And if it is, to buy it for me.[2] Don't forget it, my dear Fellow!
                                                    S. T. C.

850. *To Mrs. William Sotheby*

Address: Mrs Sotheby | U. Seymour Street.
*MS. formerly in the possession of the late Colonel H. G. Sotheby. Hitherto
unpublished.*
Postmark: 7 February 1812.

                              7, Portland Place, Hammersmith
                                        6 Febry. 1812.
Dear Madam
    Most happy should I have been to have partaken the always
rememberable pleasures of a party in Seymour Street: for even to
be thankful to you and Mr Sotheby for your perseverant kind notice
of me is itself a pleasure—if indeed that which does our hearts good,
and supplies at once impulse and motive to merit regard do not ask
a still higher name.—But on Saturday Night I leave town for Keswick, to return in the first week of March at the farthest. Be so good
as to inform Mr Sotheby that I will not fail to bring back with me
his Petrarch—for my unintentionally and almost hopelessly long
detention of which any other apology would be idle, but that of
proving hereafter that the Study of the amiable old Moralist has
enabled me to furnish something for the entertainment & perhaps
instruction of others.
    On my return if I can procure at a reasonable price a respectable
Room in any respectable part of the West End of the Town, I shall,
if Health & Power be vouchsafed me, give a course of Lectures on
Dante, Ariosto, Don Quixote, Calderon, Shakspere, Milton, and
Klopstock—assigning, on the average, two lectures to each.[3]
    With sincere respects to Captn and to Miss Sotheby I am,
        dear Madam, | with very affectionate esteem your and
    Mr Sotheby's | obliged & grateful | Friend and Servt,
                                            S. T. Coleridge
P.S. Shortly after my return to town I expect to move to 71,
Berners' Street, Oxford Street.

---

[1] J. J. W. Heinse, *Ardinghello und die glückseeligen Inseln,* 2 vols., 1787.
[2] Evidently Morgan did not obtain this work, for on 21 April 1812 we find
Coleridge asking his wife to send him the imperfect copy which was at Grasmere.
[3] In May and June Coleridge lectured on drama at Willis's Rooms, St.
James's Square. See Letter 863 for his proposal to give two courses of six
lectures each, and Letter 873 for his comment on the first lecture of the second
course.

851. *To Mrs. S. T. Coleridge*

Address: Mrs Coleridge | Greta Hall | Keswick | Cumberland
MS. Lord Latymer. Hitherto unpublished.
Postmark: 8 February 1812.

Friday, 7 Febry. 1812.

My dearest Sara

I shall leave town tomorrow night in the Liverpool Mail, if a place can be taken—if not on Monday at the furthest. I shall stay at Liverpool a day to rest myself—& then proceed to Keswick. All my old Cloathes, coats & breeches & waistcoats will be sent off by the waggon, as it would cost too much to take them in the Mail.—I would have written before, but that it was not till yesterday that my plans were finally settled—& such, as I hope, will please you. They will enable me not only to pay off all Keswick Debts in a few months, but to remit you 200£ a year regularly, independent of Lectures.—

I said, yesterday; but in truth the final settlement was not made till this afternoon. I will write from Liverpool, should I be induced to give a couple of Lectures there—Of course, particulars I defer till we meet—indeed I must miss the Post if I do not now conclude—My Love to all—I will send to Mr Bedford to know if I can take down any thing for Southey—& to Mr Murray. . . . [Remainder of manuscript missing.]

852. *To William Hood*

Address: W. Hood, Esqre | Brunswick Square | Bristol
MS. Huntington Lib. Pub. with omis. E. L. G. ii. 69.
Postmark: 10 February 1812.

Bishopgate Street—
Febry. 10 1812.

Dear Sir

I write from a Shop in which I find only bad pens & what they call *business* paper—i.e. I suppose, paper fit to use when a man is doing his business—or as Catullus calls it, papyrus cacatissima.[1] However, it suffices for one good end, that of conveying to you my unfeigned acknowlegements of your continued kindness toward me—nor do I feel the debt of Gratitude a greater burthen, because your station in life renders it almost impossible that I should ever repay it, otherwise than by affectionate acknowlegement. Yet if in any way, by advice or otherwise, I could be useful to you relative to the education of your Boy, believe me, it would gratify me highly.—

---

[1] See *Carmen* 36, line 1: 'Annales Volusi cacata charta.'

As to the F<small>RIEND</small>, I have informed you of the most untradesman-like confusion in which the Accounts are, from the mysterious disappearance of the Book from our friend's House containing the names, sums due, & sums received. I am therefore at the mercy of the memory & honesty of my Subscribers. All therefore I can say, is that if you should meet with any Subscribers, or hear of any at Shepperd's, to whom I believe, some were sent, I shall be greatly obliged to you to collect it for me—in law phrase, I authorize you to give a receipt.

I leave London for Keswick this Evening, to return hither in the first week of March at latest—when if I can procure at a reasonable price a respectable Room in any respectable part of the West End of the Town, I propose to give a course of Lectures, probably on moral subjects—the causes of domestic Happiness and Unhappiness—the influence of Christianity on Christendom independent of theological differences & considered merely as a part of the *History* of Mankind, revelation wholly omitted—on Education—on the present fashion of reading, & h[ow a man of] business may employ his leisure hours [to his] advantage as well as amusement &c[1]—

Morgan has taken—at least, I hope and trust, nothing will pass between the cup & the lip—a very nice House in Berners' Street, Oxford Street, No. 71—the rent 60£, and the premium 500£: which is very cheap, as houses go. We were house-hunting for a month & more—& the prices really sickened as well as surprized me.—

Should choice or chance ever lead you to the Lake Country, be assured that whether I am there or no, you & your family will find both House room & Heart room at Greta Hall, Keswick—& that Mrs Coleridge will do her best to make your stay comfortable—

for I am, dear Sir, | with grateful regard | Your obliged Friend
S. T. Coleridge

853. *To the Morgans*

Address: J. J. Morgan, Esqre. | 7. Portland Place | Hammersmith | London
MS. Lord Latymer. Hitherto unpublished.
Postmark: 12 February 1812. *Stamped*: Windsor.

Slough, 11 o/clock, Monday Night—[10 February 1812]
My dear Friends

My Companions in the Coach were only for Turnham Green or Brentford—but from one of them I learnt that the said Coach was

---

[1] This proposal varies from Coleridge's later 'Annunciation' of lectures 'On the Drama of the Greek, French, Italian, English, and Spanish Stage, chiefly with reference to the Works of Shakespear'. See Letter 863.

called the Lousy Liverpool, and deemed the worst Coach on the
Road—that it had very rarely inside Passengers except for short
stages—but that the Coachman crammed into the inside such of his
Outsiders as could fee him—& lastly, *which occasions my writing,* &
which the Guard has confirmed, that we shall not be in Liverpool
till Thursday Morning, one or two o/clock—Hitherto, one fellow
has been put inside—O such a fellow. I have time for no more—I
will write when I arrive at Liverpool; but you must not expect the
Letter till Saturday—

> O if you knew how dearly I love you all—!—
> S. T. Coleridge

854. *To the Morgans*

Address: J. J. Morgan, Esqre. | 7. Portland Place | Hammersmith | London
For Miss Brent.
MS. Lord Latymer. Pub. E. L. G. ii. 70.
Postmark: 15 February 1812.

> Saracen's Head, Birmingham—
> Tuesday Night, 9 o/clock. 11th Febry. 1812.

I know you are fond of *Letters* in general, from A to Z,
Charlotte, with the exception of three; but yet don't throw
it into the fire, when you find it from S. T. C.—

My dear Friends
  How pleasant 'tis to travel brisk! At Stratford upon Avon we
were only 9 Hours behind the Mail, having travelled almost but not
quite 4 miles an hour.—I breakfasted at Oxford, & stayed more
than an hour; but was afraid to send for my nephews, lest they
should have been quizzed by their fellow collegiates, such was the
Pothouse at which the Stage landed, such the ridiculous appearance
of the Coach, with 14 distinct gaudy Pictures painted on it—& we
were so followed both in & out of the city by a mob of Boys, shouting out—Lazy Liverpool! Lousy Liverpool—! Here comes long,
lazy, lousy Liverpool—!—And truly the Coach deserves it's honors
—Two *such* wretches were forced in on me all night, half drunk, and
their Cloathes crusted over with dirt, the best portion of it from the
mud into which they had fallen in a squabble, & the worst part
filth of their own making.—Two large *ticks*, i.e. Λουσες, I have found
on me—& I had taken the precaution to put my bank notes into my
breast-plate, but not liking money to lie so near my heart, or to tell
the silly truth, not liking it to touch the little remembrancer of
affection which I wear there, I therefore put the money into my

watch-fob. And sure enough in the night, while dozing, I felt a hand at my small Cloathes—& starting up, the *handy* Gentleman said, he was afraid I was cold, & so was only putting up the straw round my Legs. Kind Creature! Meantime, the Guard & Coachman (the last especially) had such ferocious phyzzes, that I thought it prudent not to complain to the Proprietors—so on my arrival here I quitted the Concern, & have taken a place in the Bang-up for Liverpool at 6 o/clock tomorrow morning. I continued the only inside passenger— & during the day was left pretty much alone— but a precious set would have been crowded in on me during the night. Besides, I itched all over me—& was miserable till I could shift myself, & have my hair combed out by a Hair-dresser.— I was obliged to open the bag in order to get a book— '& *did you not open the Snuff Cannister*?' *Inss*! tcharlotte—!—

I am well & in good spirits—& if you could but take a bird's Eye View of my Heart & all it's movements since I left you, you never could be *very angry* with me again, I am sure——May God bless you!—

Unless something particular happens to detain me, at Liverpool, I shall probably not write again till I get to Kendal—for the Postage of such Scrawls goes against my Conscience.

Blenheim & Woodstock are sweet places—I bought a pair of Gloves at the latter, but found them dearer than in London—

Dear Morgan!—dear Mary & Charlotte | I am with most affectionate Esteem | Your obliged Friend,

S. T. Coleridge

Saracen's Head, Liverpool: Thursday Noon.—

I had a very pleasant passage in the Bang-up, an excellent Coach, which in general reaches Liverpool in 14 hours from Birmingham, i.e. from 6 o'clock to 8; but from an hour's delay at setting off, & the heaviness & badness of the roads we did not arrive till eleven. My fellow-passengers: an anglicized Jamaica German, a rational being; a semi-demi-anglicized Dutch-German, who is a working Jeweller, a most presumptuous overflowing & perennial Coxcomb, whose English splash-dashed on in a true torrent, at once vapid and *broken*; & lastly, a Mr Adam Wilson, either first Mate or Purser of an East-India Man, who has been twice taken Prisoner, & twice ship-wrecked—a well-informed and intelligent young man, about six & 20, handsome & with agreeable & gentlemanly manners —I made but one deep Sleep from ½ past 12 last night to ½ past 11 this morning—& no wonder! for I had a most disturbed & unrefreshing series of Dozes during the night, I slept at Birmingham—

So haunted was my fancy by the two $\frac{L}{I}\ \frac{C}{E}$, which I had found

on my neck! The larger of the two was called Scrubmocreepi, the other Sclawmicraulo—& these during my first Doze had been harnassed to a tiny Plough by a little young Scratch, recently picked out with a needle from a Whelk on old Scratch's Nose—and still as young Nicholini Scratch urged on his Plough and Team over my Back, sowing Cow-itch in the furrows, his little long Tail hung down so as just to come in contact with my Skin, tickling it, as he passed.—But my last Sleep-adventure was still more terrific—for I found myself within view of the Scotch Corner in Hell, the only spot in all Devildom free from Brimstone. It was an angle made by two walls ⌐ , the walls seemingly composed of Thistle-beards and Dandelion-down, of immense thickness & giving way to the least pressure. In this angle sat a solitary Caledonian, writhing & frowning as in the vain hope of making the very frown-wrinkles of his forehead scratch each other. He every minute looked at his hands (which seemed armed with sharp long Nails) with a sort of savage hope, still renewed & as instantly destroyed: for the moment he attempted to apply them to his limbs or shoulders, his fingers & thumbs turned at once into ten rabbits' tails. Pity seized me, tho' in Hell—I determined to relieve him—the strong wish created a large Branch of prickly Holly in my hand, and I was beginning to flog him with it, when up started old Scratch, flew off with me, & threw me into a flaming Oven, but in a second of time I was drawn out, transformed to a large French Roll or Brick with the Crust burnt black—& the Devil was *rasping* me; when I awoke in the Fright & found that I had been furiously sclawing my left Shoulder Bone.—

S. T. Coleridge

Don't spake to henny wun, if u plaze, about them thare two Lousses, as I caut [on] my nek—becaze they may take the *licence* to zay, has h[ow] I has more of the first sillybull in my ed, than the last.

I found that the Birmingham Post did not go out till 4 o/[clock] in the afternoon & so carried this Letter with me to Liverpool.— I am now going out to find Mr Crump & when I return, shall be able to inform you whether I shall stay here another day, or set off immediately for Kendal & Penrith.

P.S. Mr Crump not at home; but I have seen Dr & Mrs Crompton, Mr Roscoe & Son, &c—& must stay all to morrow in order to spend the Day at Dr Crompton's delightful Country Seat at Eaton, 5 miles from Liverpool, & to meet the Roscoes at dinner. Dr C. has commenced Brewer, & has an enormous Brewery in Liverpool—If I can get him to send up to Berners' Street half a Hogshead of his best Ale, such as I drank a glass of to day, I will never taste a drop of Spirit in secula seculorum. How is Mary's Cold? and don't let Charlotte rub her pretty Eye. S. T. C.

[Ch]arlotte! how do you do? [Pre]tty well, I hope. *God be [prai]sed!*—How becoming [the pr]etty Watch-chain looked made of some fair Friend's Hair!—I dare say, She had long promised it him.

855. *To J. J. Morgan*

Address: J. J. Morgan Esqre. | 7. Portland Place | Hammersmith | London
Single Sheet
MS. Lord Latymer. Hitherto unpublished. This manuscript begins with the notes which are here printed after the letter.
Postmark: 21 February 1812. *Stamped*: Kendal.

Kendal, Tuesday, 18 Febry. [1812]
My dear Morgan

Not having time to write more than half a dozen lines, I write at the fag-end of these Notes not intended for anything but private Memoranda for myself, rather than make you pay postage for almost a Blank.—They may, perhaps, so far amuse or inform you as to count for a small fraction above O—for the Taylor of an integral Letter.—Disappointed in the Mail, I could not leave Liverpool till Sunday Evening, ½ past 5—& spent the Interim with Dr Crompton, part at Eaton with his excellent Sister, and Mrs Crompton, that angel without wings, the only thing that seems wanting to her celestial capacity. Mary & Charlotte will smile at my extravagance; but I have never ceased from my first acquaintance (nearly 17 years) to love and venerate in her the heavenliest Vision possible on Earth; viz. the Ideal of Womanhood. O how they both would love her! Tho' her elder children are now men & women, I seem to see no change in her. The Bodily holds in *her* the same relation to the Spiritual, as appropriate *Words* to pure and sweet conceptions—the Mortal is swallowed up in the Immortal, not destroyed but interfused and glorified. She explains to my feelings that most venial, because most beautiful, of all forms of Idolatry, the adoration of maiden Motherhood visualized & realized in the Virgin & Child. But it is more than this.—I must add the commanding Submissiveness, the dignified & elevating Humility of the Matron; the seriousness, the equability, the *for-ever*-ness of the conjugal affection still blended with, never disparted from, the delicacy & wakefulness of First-love! I must add too sincerity & constancy with the truest & justest Subordination in her attachments, from the Acquaintance who is received with courtesy to the Friend who is welcomed with an Interest that transcends while it accompanies gladness. In short, you cannot be with her without becoming *better*, & THEREFORE wiser: & besides this, her very questions improve *my* understanding oftentimes more than the answers of even wise men.—Now as I have written this as if with the blood of my inmost Heart, so let me without suspicion of insincerity conclude by affirming, that few indeed are the women, in my sphere of acquaintance, to whom I could write thus, as confident as I now am, that as far as they credited my description, they would be delighted with it.—

I could only take the Mail to Preston—*there* pre-engaged—in short, off & on, arrived at Kendal in the heavy Coach Monday Night, 12 o/clock; stay here to arrange some affairs till Wednesday Morning, 5 o'clock—proceed to Ambleside & with the Boys hope to reach Keswick by dinner on Wednesday Afternoon, Febry. 19th, 1812. There seems a fair opening for Lectures at Liverpool; but of this when I hear from Dr Crompton.—Greta Hall, Keswick: my address for the next ten days.—God bless you, & Mary & Charlotte, & your & their most affectionate

S. T. C.—

I was ill & in a high fever the whole night at Preston, owing to the wet *seat* in the Coach—otherwise I have been well: & am so.

1. Liverpool supplied with Coals from Wiggan, 25 miles distant by the Coach-road, but far more by the Canal. Yet mark the advantage of Water Carriage. The Coal-merchants in Liverpool receive the Coals from the Wiggan Pits by the Canal, and then cart them in 2 horse Carts to the Inhabitants of the Town, all of whom pay the same stated price: viz, £1 ‖ 7 ‖ 0 for the double Cart-load, weighing 35 Cwt, or a Ton and ¾ths. In the Coal-yards there is a weigh-board with a heap of Coals by it—the Carts that are too heavy have the surplus Coals shovelled off into this heap, and those too light brought up to the proper weight from it. Near Birmingham I observed a cluster of enormous Furnaces, with columns of flame instead of Smoke from their chimneys, the extremity of the column disparting itself in projected Balls and eggs of Fire—on the other side of the road were the Coal mines that supplied them, & observing the pools & puddles of water smoking I at first thought that the mine might have taken fire, as is, and for some 40 years past has been, the case with some acres of Coal near Shrewsbury; but I was informed that it was not so, & that the constant steam was occasioned by the vicinity of the furnaces, tho' I myself (probably, from the motion of the Carriage) did not perceive any increased sensation of Warmth.

2. The Dutch-German Jeweller has discovered a mode of coloring

white & yellow Cornelians of any color—but I observed that the red was far deeper than that of any natural red Cornelian, I have ever seen, which have all a *dilution* of the red by yellow. The artefact Color is a deep sealing-wax red. He has offered to cut my Mary & Charlotte Seal for me gratis, coloring the Letters green or purple.

I mean to have it thus:

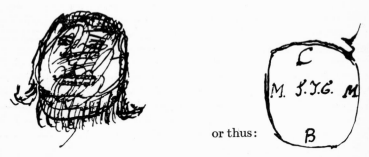

or thus:

the STC in one cypher or else a fish, a die, and a Hill—the fish, a char, the die for lot, and the Hill for Brent = Charlotte Brent—which will have this advantage, that Edipus himself with Catterfelto's Cat[1] whispering him at one ear, and St Athanasius at the other, would be unable to decypher it.

The Brasil pebble is so hard that like Diamond it can only be cut by steel wheel-teeth supplied with oil of brick (i.e. oil of amber with oil of turpentine) & diamond dust sprinkled on it. He uses (he says) thirty pounds worth of diamond dust per week, & asked me if I could suggest any means of recovering it from the waste-tub into which the oil drops.—The Brasil pebble, when cut & set, looks as *bright* as the diamond, but not so *radiant*: and when you look close, is easily detected by it's *glassiness*.

3. The Liverpool Exchange & Custom House are noble Buildings, far surpassing those of London; but so miserable are the streets with one exception, that of the High Street which terminates in these grand Erections, that the whole presented to my fancy the thought of a magnificent Palace rising out of a vast dunghill with one broad clean road made thro' the dung straight up to it.—

4. On my observing that I thought the Pearl was some imperceptibly small grain of Sand or a like particle which had been taken in by the Oyster, & incommoding it, as the Calculus or Gravel does poor *me*, the animal coated it in like manner (and perhaps from the same cause) as it coats the inside of it's Shell with the same secretion from it's own body, which then is mother of pearl—Mr Adam

---

[1] A reference to Gustavus Katterfelto, the conjurer, who employed the services of some extraordinary black cats.

Wilson answered—Ingenious, Sir! but if so, how comes it that the Pearl is peculiar to one or two sorts of Oysters, not edible?—I denied the fact as a general truth: for I had often found them in the common Oyster, & supposed that one sort might be more subject than others to take in particles of Sand, both from it's organization & from the nature of the Oyster-bed—or else why should the same inedible Oyster be pearl-oysters at Ceylon, & not on the Coast of Coromandel? & I retorted, that if it were a natural product, *every* Ceylon Oyster ought to have pearls & the same number—whereas not one in ten has any—& added in confirmation the story of the manner in which the Chinese force a hard paste, round or pear-shaped, into the gaping oyster, & taking it again a year after find it compleatly coated & undistinguishable from the true pearl except by the little hole thro' which the thread past.—Mr A. W. smiled— & owned, that this, if true, would form a very strong presumption in favor of my Theory—but he had never heard of it, tho' several times in China, & tho' the various tricks of the Chinese in pearls had been often the subject of conversation in his presence.

5. Mr A. W. almost convinced me that an open trade to India would be of no advantage to the nation, & would, probably, at first occasion the ruin of hundreds from rash Speculation. He thought Ceylon, Java, &c, of no real use to us—except as exchanges in a Treaty of Peace. It is absurd to suppose, that France, or the Continental Powers even if they should be rescued from French Influence, would consent to make peace with G. Britain, leaving her sole mistress of all colonial property & commerce: & *during* the war what is the use of cramming the Warehouses with 10 times the quantity of Sugar, Coffee, Spice, &c, that we can dispose of?—And as to revenue & the consumption of our own manufactures, from 80 or 90 millions of Inhabitants subject to Great Britain in the East, how can either be expected when these Inhabitants can purchase all they want, of a much better & finer texture & infinitely more suitable to their climate & Habits, at one eighth of the price—& when an immense majority live upon two pence a day? Would you draw blood from a Post, or hope to quench your thirst by sucking a Pumice Stone?—He had the common opinions of the East-India Company's Servants, & the same strength of prejudice against the Missionaries, & the practicability and even the utility of christianizing the natives. None, he affirmed, but the lowest Class with those who from crimes had lost their Cast, would be *christened*: & even these would never be christianized. He admitted Dr Claudius Buchanan[1] to [be] a man of talents, but seemed to suspect

---

[1] Claudius Buchanan (1766–1815), Bengal chaplain and vice-provost of the college of Fort William.

To J. J. Morgan

that he had looked on the subject thro' colored, magnifying, & multiplying Glasses—with great Enthusiasm & some Ambition. Any man *wishing* to believe *any* thing might find plenty of seeming facts to confirm him among the Hindoos, from their system of flattery & assentation, & their habitual disregard of Truth. Veracity is a virtue, of which the *best* of them have no idea—they all regard the Tongue as an instrument given to the Weaker for the purpose of escaping from and over-reaching the Stronger; but especially with regard to Europeans, they regard Falsehood as a duty of Politeness, a part of the respect due to their Superiors. That all the most essential Doctrines of Christian Faith exist, and (as the natives at least believe & as it is impossible to disprove) pre-existed in the Hindoo Religion, such as the Trinity, the Incarnation of the second Person in the Trinity, the necessity of Baptism, the article of original Sin & of redemption & regeneration—this agreement instead of facilitating, he thought, must present an almost insurmountable Obstacle to their Conversion—& the Solifidianism of Christianity, i.e. the dogma of exclusive Salvation by Christ, appeared to them at once unphilosophical, inhuman, & derogatory of the divine attributes of the common father of Mankind.—I could not but assent to his opinion, as far as the ordinary notion of Christianity and the ordinary modes of preaching it extended— but I was desirous to believe, that some progress might be made if in Hindostan it were taught as having the same relation to Brahmanism, as Protestantism has to Popery—namely, as a reformation of their Religion, as the same scummed and drawn off from the Dregs.—And surely, the Hindoos are an acute race: and it requires little or no *reasoning*, (that is, links or chain of arguments) but merely common sense, in order to be made [to] perceive the extreme grossness & cruelty of their present ceremonial rites and sacrifices, not to mention the glaring incongruity of them with their humane & inoffensive character.—O Sir! replied Mr Wilson— common sense they have, & inoffensive & *negatively* humane, they are; but the great & desperate Obstacle is their utter, radical, and constitutional Insensibility. They will not injure a *worm*, but they will let a Cow, their sacred animal, & one from whom they have derived half their nourishment, pine away for hunger without a pang: they will not destroy the deadliest Serpent or Scorpion, but they will stand by and look at a woman or child tortured to [death] without a single Emotion.—Here ended our friendly dis[course—] all his remarks were sensible; but this latter most excellent—for sensibility, and self-introition, which is impossible without great sensibility, is the conditio sine quâ[non] of conversion to Christianity, at least, to aught but the name.—

856. *To J. J. Morgan*

Address: J. J. Morgan, Esqre. | 7. Portland Place | Hammersmith | London
Single Sheet.
MS. Lord Latymer. Pub. with omis. Letters, *ii. 575.*
Postmark: 28 February 1812. *Stamped*: Keswick.

Sunday, Keswick. [23 February 1812]
My dear Morgan

I stayed a day in Kendal in order to collect the Re-prints of the
Friend, & reached Keswick on Tuesday last before dinner, having
taken Hartley & Derwent with me from Ambleside. Of course, the
first Evening was devot[ed] Laribus domesticis, to Southey & his
& my Childre[n. My] own are all, the fondest Father could pray
for: & [li]ttle Sara does honor to her Mother's anxieties, reads
French tolerably & Italian fluently, and I was astonished at her
acquaintance with her native Language.[1] The word 'hostile' occur-
ring in what she read to me, I asked her what 'hostile' meant?
And she answered at once—Why! inimical: only that inimical is
more often used for things and measures, and not, as hostile is, to
persons & nations.—If I had dared, I should have urged Mrs C. to
let me take her to London for 4 or 5 months, to return with Southey
—but I feared, it might be inconvenient to you, & I knew, it would
be presumptuous in me to bring her to you. But she is such a sweet-
tempered, meek, blue-eyed Fairy, & so affectionate, trust-worthy,
& really serviceable! Derwent is the self-same fond small Samuel
Taylor Coleridge as ever. When I sent for them from Mr Dawes, he
came in dancing for joy, while Hartley turned pale & trembled all
over—then after he had taken some cold water instantly asked me
some questions about the connection of the Greek with the Latin,
which latter he has just begun to learn. Poor Derwent, who has by
no means strong health, (having inherited his poor father's tenderness of Bowels & Stomach & consequently capriciousness of animal
Spirits) has complained to me (having no other possible grievance)
that Mr Dawes does not *love* him, because he can't help crying when
he is scolded, & because he an't such a genius, as Hartley—and that
tho' Hartley should have done the same thing, yet all the others
are punished, & Mr Dawes only *looks* at Hartley, & never scolds
him—& that *all* the boys think it very unfair [—but] he *is* a
genius! This was uttered in low spirits & a [bitt]erness brought
on by my petting—for he adores his Brother. Indeed, God be
praised! they all love each other. I was delighted, that Derwent of
his own accord asked me about little Miss Brent that used to play

---

[1] Dorothy Wordsworth, too, thought Mrs. Coleridge 'an excellent teacher *by
Books*' and Sara 'an admirable scholar for her age'. *Middle Years*, ii. 483.

with him at Mr and Mrs Morgan's: adding that he had almost forgot what sort of a Lady she was, only she was littler—*less, I mean* (this he said hastily & laughing at his blunder) than Mama.— A Gentleman who took a third of the Chaise with me from Ambleside & whom I found a well-informed & thinking Man, said after two hours' knowlege of us, that the two boys united would be a perfect representative of myself.—

I trust, I need not say that I should have written on the second day if nothing had happened; but from the dreadful dampness of the House, worse than it was in it's rudest state when I first lived in it, & the weather too all storm & rain, I caught a violent cold which almost blinded me by inflammation of both my eyes, & for three days bore all the symptoms of an Ague or intermittent Fever. Knowing, I had no time to lose, I took the most herculean remedies, among others a solution of Arsenic, & am now as well as when I left you—& see no reason to fear a relapse.—I passed thro' Grasmere; but did not call on Wordsworth. I hear from Mrs C., that he treats the affair as a trifle & only wonders at my resenting it—& that Dorothy Wordsworth before my arrival expressed her confident hope, that I should come to them at once!!!¹—I, who 'for years past had been an ABSOLUTE NUISANCE in the Family.'—

This Illness has thrown me behindhand; so that I cannot quit Keswick till the end of the week. On Friday I shall return by way of Ambleside, probably spend a day with Charles Lloyd who is at present sadly afflicted with a semi-deranging Oppression of Spirits, [and] his excellent Wife just on the point of confinement (i.e. accouchement.) It will not surprize you that the statements respecting me, & Montague & Wordsworth, have been grossly perverted: & yet spite of all this, there is not a friend of Wordsworth's, I understand, who does not severely blame him, tho' they execrate the Montagues yet more heavily.—But the tenth part of the Truth is not known. Would you believe it possible, that Wordsworth himself stated *my wearing Powder* as a proof positive that I never could have suffered any pain of mind from the affair— & that it was all pretence!!²—God forgive him!—At Liverpool I

---

¹ Writing to Poole Mrs. Coleridge said: 'Numerous were the letters and messages I received from Miss W. to urge C. to write to her and not to leave the country without seeing them; but he would not go to *them* and *they* did not come to him.' *Minnow among Tritons*, ed. Stephen Potter, 1934, p. 16.

That the Wordsworths were deeply affected by Coleridge's refusal to call at Grasmere is noted by Crabb Robinson: 'Wordsworth dwelt on this circumstance with more warmth than any other, particularly on the injustice done to his sister, who had been Coleridge's best friend at all times.' *Robinson on Books and Their Writers*, i. 78. See also Letter 858 and note.

² See Letters 815, p. 309 n. and 867, p. 402.

shall either give Lectures, if I can secure a 100£ for them, or return immediately to you. At all events, I shall not remain there beyond a fortnight—so that I shall be with you before you have changed houses. Mrs Coleridge seems quite satisfied with my plans, & abundantly convinced of my obligations to your & Mary's kindness to me. Nothing (she said) but the circumstance of my residing with you could reconcile her to my living in London. Southey is the semper idem. It is impossible for a good heart not to esteem him & to love him too; but yet the Love is ¼th, the esteem all the remainder. His Children are, 1. Edith, 7 years. 2. Herbert, 5—3. Bertha—4. Catharine, a year & a half—& Mrs Southey evidently beginning anew. I had hoped to have heard from you by this t[ime.] I wrote from Slough, from Liverpool, & from Kendal.—Why need I send my kindest loves to Mary & Charlotte? I would not return if I had a doubt that they believed me to be in the very inmost of my being their & your affectionately grateful & constant Friend,

S. T. Coleridge

P.S. Dignum notatu est: uxor mea casta est, modesta, prudens, mater optima, formâ aequè ac moribus eximia, et mihi quidem pulchrior adhuc videtur, quàm primis nostris amplexibus visa est. Ego autem vir iste sum, cui ipsa natura cor totum et tota praecordia amoribus complevit, cujus ipsis in medullis aegra quaedam *necessitas* inest, ut amem aliquam, et ab aliquâ redamer—vir in delicias, blanditiasque faemineas et dulcia cum corporis tum animae coeuntis susurramina natali et ingenitâ proclivitate raptus, in omnia promptus, quae maritum decent, et quae nequeo non cupire—et tamen tanquam uxor mea mea *soror uterina* fuisset, frigesco et horreo vel ipsâ *imaginatione* [con]gressûs conjugalis.—Deo gratias! illa quoque [non vu]lt nec desiderat.

Your Letter is just arrived—I will write to you from Liverpool— if you write, direct to me at the Liverpool Post Office, till called for.—I rejoice that all is settled as to the House. I hope, Charlotte was not offended at my Joke in directing my Letter to her, as the great philo-letterist.—Kind Love from all—.

Τᾶκ θε ρooμ, βι αλ μεανς.[1]

[1] Coleridge wrote this sentence on the address sheet.

857. *To J. J. Morgan*

Address: J. J. Morgan, Esqre. | 7. Portland Place | Hammersmith | London
Single
MS. Lord Latymer. Pub. E. L. G. ii. 74.
Postmark: 5 March 1812. *Stamped*: Keswick.

2 [1] March, 1812
Sunday Night
Keswick.

My dear Morgan

I have been detained here two or three days beyond my first determination by the accidental sending for of Southey by Charles Lloyd, who is in such a state of mind as is little short of Derangement—no Sleep, eternal Restlessness of body & mind (the other day he ran up & down & round & round his Bed room as hard as he could gallop from 12 at night till 4 in the morning)—in short, it is, in my opinion, his old constitutional Disease which I can invent no better name for, than a *diffused* Epilepsy, an Epilepsy that does not concenter itself in the crisis of a full Fit—like the Phlegraean Plain in the kingdom of Naples, that burns and trembles all over, without the power of periodically exhausting itself thro' a given Crater & by a volcanic eruption. Last year he was in the same way, & neither suffered poor Mrs Lloyd either to leave him for a moment or even to sleep while with him—When Nature overpowered her, he would let her remain two or three minutes, and then run to her and awaken her—with—O God! don't go to sleep!—Can you conceive any thing more dreadful—and she is now on the very Eve and Edge of Parturition!—And what is worse is that I have not the least doubt but that these heart-afflicting Self-sacrifices on her part are all injurious to him—and that contradiction & terror are the appropriate medicines. In short, his Parents should contrive to have him placed under Dr Willis or some other Physician of that sort.—He '*would* see Southey'—his 'mind was made up'—Mrs Lloyd mentioned me, and Wordsworth—No! it must be Southey. And so poor Southey who could not find in his heart to return a denial, was forced away from his Study, at a time, when the Loss of Time will be a Loss of at least 30£ to him, to a man to whom he can be of no service, whose manners and conversation annoy & disquiet him even when he is at the sanest!—I expect him home tomorrow— so that as I must have one whole Day to spend with him, to settle certain literary arrangements, I cannot leave Keswick till Wednesday Morning—

As I have collected the Friends, and besides that have ascertained (and it is so understood by Mrs Coleridge) that should any unforeseen event occur between this (3 March) and the 7th of April, to prevent me from either bringing the money to London or receiving it there immediately on my arrival, there is a hundred Pounds at the Bankers of Mrs Coleridge's, which may be drawn upon before the first week of April, & that she will transmit to you (in case, I should not have myself payed it in to you before) an Order for 50£ before the Bill becomes payable, I have not hesitated to draw upon you under the name of Brent and Co, 103, Bishopgate St., a Bill for 50£ at 5 weeks' date which you will be so good as to accept or cause to be accepted.—In truth, having let Mrs C. have the few Pounds, I had with me, I could not have left Keswick without doing it.—

Derwent left us to return in the Carriage with his Uncle—& Hartley goes tomorrow, and we hope, will meet him half way, where Southey means to quit the Carriage, & walk the other—so that it may take back Hartley—tho' he scoffs at the Idea of 18 miles being too long a walk for him, since he walked from Grasmere to Kendal & back again to Ambleside in the same day in order to be confirmed. For he is very religious, and quite orthodox—he says, his Creed and his Father's are the same. He fully believes the Christian *Revelation*, and more than *believes* the Christian RELIGION; but the former for the sake of the latter, not the latter for the former.—

I am quite recovered, & the better for the attack, or at least for the consequences of it.

Mrs Coleridge sends her love and best remembrances to Mary & Charlotte—and so does little Sariola.—Positively, Mrs M. and Charlotte must make up a little Bonnet or something of the kind to be sent down to her and to her Cousin, in order that they may have your names in their thoughts & mouths.—I shall miss a *Post* if I do not end—that firm as *a Pillar* I trust that without end on this side the Grave at least I shall continue

Your Friend,
S. T. Coleridge

858. *To J. J. Morgan*

Address: J. J. Morgan, Esqre. | 71. Berners Street | Oxford Street | London
MS. in the Frederick Locker-Lampson, Paul M. Warburg, Samuel B. Grimson Album, now on deposit in the Harvard College Lib. Pub. E. L. G. ii. 76.
Postmark: 27 March 1812. *Stamped*: Keswick.

Tuesday, Keswick—[24 March 1812]

My dear Morgan

I leave Keswick on Thursday Morning—shall take my place from Penrith all the way for London on Saturday, & of course (neck

& limb safe) shall be in town on Monday Morning.—Nothing can justify my not writing to you; but in very truth I have been dreadfully bewildered—first of all, I was trifled with most egregiously, off and on, about the Liverpool Lectures—secondly, the Grasmere Business has kept me in a fever of agitation—and will end in compleat alienation—I have refused to go over, & Wordsworth has refused to apologize and has thus made his choice between me and Basil Montagu, Esqre—and to omit less matters, lastly, Brown, the Printer of the Friend, who had the Friends, & 20 or 30£ worth of Paper of mine, and 36£ worth of Types, about 14 days ago run off and has absconded.—Every day I meant to write to you—but partly, I was in hopes that by delaying it I might be able to say definitely when I should set off, but chiefly, I have been in such a state of fever and irritation about the Wordsworths, my reason deciding one way, and my heart pulling me the contrary—scarcely daring to set off without seeing them, especially Miss Hutchinson who has done nothing to offend me—& yet—in short, I am unfit to bear these things—and make bad worse in consequence.—I have suffered so much that I wish I had not left London.[1]—As to the Bill, I would not have drawn it if I had not been sure of taking it up before the Time. If every thing else fail, yet I shall take up a Draft with me for 50£ on the Bankers—My dear Friend! forgive me for having made you anxious by my silence—God knows I have been on thorns, with the wish to rejoin you, & the causes of my procrastination in writing, tho' they would not satisfy you as reasons, yet as Sufferings would, I am sure, make you feel any thing rather than displeasure

at your faithful & affectionate Friend
S. T. Coleridge

God bless you all!—

[1] Shortly after Coleridge left Keswick, Sara Hutchinson had this to say: 'We heard from Mrs Coleridge last night [28 March] that C is gone back to London—he came thro' Grasmere without calling but went back by Penrith— He is offended with William, or fancies himself so—and expected Wm to make some advances to him which as he did not he was miserable the whole time he was in Keswick, & Mrs C. was right glad to get him off again, for she had no satisfaction in him—and would have given the world, I dare say, to have had him well again with Wm. We are all very sorry that his visit has ended so; being persuaded that he never would have come down at all but in the hope of a reconciliation.'

It is significant, in the light of what followed in May 1812, that Wordsworth fixed on the date of his journey to London almost immediately after learning of Coleridge's departure from Keswick. *The Letters of Sara Hutchinson,* ed. Kathleen Coburn, 1954, pp. 45–46.

859. *To J. J. Morgan*

Address: J. J. Morgan, Esqre. | 71 Berners Street | (or 81) | Oxford Street | London
MS. Lord Latymer. Pub. E. L. G. ii. 78.
Postmark: 30 March 1812. *Stamped*: Penrith.

Good Friday Night [27 March 1812]
Penrith

My dear Friend

In the haste, I last wrote, I did not mention, as being indeed no excuse for my not writing what yet prevented my setting off ten days ago—that the Roads are blocked up with Snow, so that no Coaches can pass, there being only a way cut thro' for a single Horse by which the Mail is sent from Appleby to Greta Bridge— I left Keswick on yesterday as I informed you, taking for granted that the Road would be open, there having been two fine days— but to night a Traveller has arrived on horse, with a most tremendous account of his adventures, it having snowed here all the day— & it appears that the cut horse-path is snowed up, & that in all the rest of the road the Snow is four yards deep upon Stainmore—It is at this moment *thawing* at Penrith—but even should this be the case likewise at Stainmore, it would be two or three days before the Mail can pass. My first thought was to go to Kendall—but I find that over Shap Hills the road is equally unpassable—I have therefore no alternative but to return to Keswick & so go to Grasmere, Ambleside, & thence to Kendall—which will be an enormous increase of expence, as I must travel by Post Chaises.—As I have nothing to detain me but the weather, I hope still to be in London on Wednesday—but should this be impracticable, I will send you up a Draft for the 50£ to make all secure & your mind at ease.—

I have been with Brown's Assignee, & luckily the FRIENDS (& I hope the Paper) have not been taken into the account of Stock— but the Type has—& I must enter myself as a Creditor to that amount besides the Subscriptions received beyond his Bill—but have, of course, authorized Mr Harrison to receive the Dividend & return it to Brown whenever he can be found. It seems, he took to drinking, got nervous, and went off, more for sensibility than Debts, which are trifling—However this be, money from the unhappy is a hateful Thing—& I am sure you will do me the Justice to believe, that I would not have put my name down among his Creditors but for the purpose of doing him a little service—

O would to Heaven! I were but once more by your fire-side! —I have received four Letters in 3 days about my not having called on Wordsworth as I passed thro' Grasmere—& this morning

a most impassioned one from Mrs Clarkson[1]—Good God! how could
I? how can I?—I have no resentment—and unless Grief & Anguish
be resentment, I never had—but unless I meet him as of yore, what
use is there in it? What but mere pain? I am not about to be his
Enemy—I want no stimulus to serve him to the utmost whenever
it should be in my power.—And can any friend of mine wish me to
go without apology received, and as to a man the best-beloved &
honored, who had declared me a nuisance, an absolute nuisance—
& this to such a Creature as Montagu? And who since then has
professed his determination to believe Montagu rather than me, as
to my assertion to Southey[2] that Montagu prefaced his Discourse
with the words—'Nay, but Wordsworth *has commissioned* me to
tell you, first, that he has no Hope of you,'[3] &c &c &c.—A nuisance!
—& then a deliberate Liar! O Christ! if I dared after this crouch to
the Man, must I not plead guilty to these charges, & be a Liar
against my own Soul?

No more of this! And be assured, I will never hereafter trouble
you with any recurrence to it.

Mention me affectionately to Mary & Charlotte, & unless I am
utterly ignorant of my own heart assure yourself that I am by
every feeling both of choice & of gratitude both your & their
honest and sincere Friend & Brother
S. T. Coleridge

[1] Mrs. Clarkson, whom Coleridge in March 1811 had extolled for her 'sacred *magnanimity*', had long been the recipient of denunciatory letters concerning Coleridge from Dorothy Wordsworth, letters in which 'We have no hope of him' is reiterated. Fully informed of the misunderstanding between Coleridge and Wordsworth, she soon became an active partisan of the latter. If she sent Coleridge an 'impassioned' letter in March 1812, within a month she was writing bitterly of him to Crabb Robinson: 'I trust that Wordsworth will insist upon an explanation. I know so well the power of Coleridge's presence & the effect of his eloquence that something ought to be done by W—— to counteract them. . . . Heaven forgive my hard-heartedness but I think . . . [Coleridge] had better . . . put a pistol to his brains.' Her meddlesome talebearing involved her deeply in the quarrel, and by the spring of 1813 she was to complain of Coleridge's indifference to her. See *Middle Years*, i. 154, 174, 325, 365–7, 409, 447–9, 454, ii. 463 and 480–1; *The Correspondence of Henry Crabb Robinson with the Wordsworth Circle*, ed. Edith J. Morley, 2 vols., 1927, i. 66–68 and 70–76; Letter 814 and notes to Letters 866–7.

[2] At Richmond during the summer of 1811 Coleridge had spoken to Southey concerning 'the whole affair, . . . even as the means of transmitting' it to Wordsworth. See Letter 867, p. 400.

[3] As Southey reported, Wordsworth expressed his 'conviction that Montagu never said those words', that Coleridge 'had forgotten' himself. This 'conviction' probably explains Wordsworth's high-handed treatment of Coleridge in London in May 1812. At that time Wordsworth proposed that Coleridge stand trial in the presence of himself and Montagu. See Letters 866–7.

P.S. Mrs Southey & Mrs Coleridge who have twice debated the matter with Wordsworth as well as with his Sister, are most vehement against Wordsworth—& Mrs C. says, she never in her whole life saw her Sister so vehement, or so compleatly overcome her natural timidity as when she answered Wordsworth's excuses— She would not suffer him to wander from the true point—Never mind, Sir!—Coleridge does not heed *what* was said—whatever is true, his friends all know, & he himself never made a secret of— but that *you*, that *you*, should say all this—& to Montagu—& having never at any one time during a 15 years' friendship given him even a *hint* of the state of your opinions concerning him—it is *you*, Sir! *you*—not the things said, true or false!—Southey never says any thing but only— '*that miscreant, Montagu!*'[1]—whereas (I have nothing to complain of in Montagu) I think him in error——

860. *To Mrs. S. T. Coleridge*

Address: Mrs Coleridge | Greta Hall | Keswick | Cumberland
MS. Lord Latymer. Pub. E. L. G. ii. 80.
Postmark: 15 April 1812.

[15 April 1812]

My dearest Sara

I begin almost to despair of my fate—for some Misery or other either by fault or accident I am for ever causing to my friends.— After a most fatiguing Journey & three sleepless nights I arrived yester morning at 5 o/clock, at the Bull in Mouth Inn—but not able to procure a hackney Coach immediately, I was so ill, & in such a state of high fever with a sore throat that I went to bed—& slept for 8 or 10 hours continuously—so that I did not see the Morgans till just now—And good God!—What a thunderbolt to me—I heard that Morgan had never received the Draft for 50£, which fearful of my being detained I begged you to send to him, & on which you must never have received my Letter.—To the best of my remembrance, it was the third day after Good Friday, that fully intending to set off on the next day if possible but forced to wait for information concerning the passability of the Road, I wrote to you by a Mr Naylor, an elderly Gentleman in a Carriage who was then setting off for Keswick, & politely offered to take

---

[1] Writing to Matilda Betham on 25 April 1812, Southey remarked: 'My own opinion is . . . that Montagu has acted with a degree of folly which would be absolutely incredible in any other person; that W. is no otherwise blameable than as having said anything to such a man which he would have felt any dislike to seeing in the *Morning Post*; that I do not wonder at C.'s resentment.' Campbell, *Life*, 180 n.

any Letter or Parcel for me—as you would receive it sooner than
by the Post—for the Post had gone off for that day——In the
same Letter I told you that instantly on my arrival in London
I would send you an order for 50£ on Gale & Curtis.—I am
certain, you did not receive this Letter—because I stated my
great anxiety, & that if any thing should ever prevent you, that
you should desire Southey to give you the order.—

I am pretty well—tho' the agitation, I am suffering, does not
improve my penmanship.—I declare to God, I would have lost an
arm rather than Morgan should have suffered the Distress of mind
& uneasiness, which he has done—So help me God! as I hereby vow
that I will hereafter never have any thing to do with any other
Money than what I have actually in my possession—

I have seen Gale & Curtis—all goes on well there—they are in
great hopes respecting my Work—but I really can write no more
till to morrow—

God bless you | &

S. T. Coleridge

Love to all—the dear children—

Of course, I shall not want the Draft now—as I can get it from
Gale & Curtis—

Mrs Morgan sends her kind remembrance to you, and bids me
say that as *Table* Spoons are generally used for Soup, she supposes
that Southey would not wish the *Desert* Spoons made larger than
the usual Size—she thinks, it would have an awkward Look—Mr
& Mrs M. think that it would look much handsomer to have the
Motto *over* & not under the black S.—The fashion too is to have the
Motto *over*, not under, the Cypher or Letter.—

P.S. All is well—attribute the beginning Sentence to my agitation—

861. *To Mrs. S. T. Coleridge*

Address: Mrs Coleridge | Greta Hall | Keswick | Cumberland
MS. Lord Latymer. Pub. with omis. Letters, ii. 579.
Postmark: 21 April 1812.

Tuesday, 21 April 1812
71 Bernards' Street.

My dear Love

Every thing is going on so very well, so much beyond my
Expectation, that I will not revert to any thing unpleasant to
damp good news with.—The last receipt for the Insurance is now
before me—the date, the 4th of May—Be assured that before

April is past, you shall *receive* both Receipts, this & the one for the
present year, in a Frank.—In the first place, my Health, Spirits,
& Disposition to activity have continued such since my arrival in
Town, that every one has been struck with the Change—& the
Morgans say, they had never before seen me *myself*. I feel myself
an altered man, and dare promise you that you shall never have to
complain of, or to apprehend, my not opening & reading your
Letters.—Ever since I have been in town, I have never taken any
Stimulus of *any* kind, till the moment of my getting into bed,
except a glass of British White Wine after dinner—& from 3 to 4
glasses of Port, when I have dined out.—Secondly, my Lectures
have been taken up most warmly & zealously by Sir Thomas
Bernard, Sir George Beaumont, Mr Sotheby, &c—& in a few days
I trust, that you will be agreeably surprized with the mode in which
Sir T. B. hopes & will use his best exertions to have them announced. Thirdly, Gale & Curtis are in high Spirits & confident
respecting the Sale of The Friend, & the call for a second Edition—
after the complemental Numbers have been printed[1]—& not less
so respecting the Success of the other Work, the Propaedia (or
Propaideia) cyclica—& are desirous to have the Terms properly
ratified & signed as soon as possible.—Nothing intervenes to over-
gloom my mind, but the sad state of Health of Mr Morgan, a more
faithful, and zealous Friend than whom no man ever possessed.
Thank God! my safe arrival, the improvement of my Health &
Spirits, & my smiling Prospects have already exerted a favorable
influence on him—yet I dare not disguise from myself, that there is
cause for alarm to those who love & value him.—But do not allude
to this Subject in your Letters: for to be thought ill, or to have
his state of Health spoken of, agitates & depresses him.—

As soon as ever I have settled the Lecture Room, which perhaps
will be Willis's in Hanover Square, the price of which is at present
ten guineas a time, I will the very first thing pay the Insurance, &
send off a parcel of Books for Hartley, Derwent, & dear Sara—
whom I kissed 7 times in the Shape of her pretty Letterlet.—My
poor darling Derwent! I shall be most anxious to receive a Letter
from you, or from himself, about him. Perhaps, the Eruption may
prove very beneficial to him, & strengthen the tone of his Stomach
& Bowels, & therewith his nervous system.—Dear Boy! were I

[1] Nothing came of these plans for *The Friend*, Gale and Curtis in 1812
merely issuing in volume form the sets of the 28 numbers printed earlier on
unstamped paper. (See p. 271 n.) They advanced £50 to Coleridge and gave
him credit for a supply of unused stamped paper—'20 or 30£ worth'. Letters
1016 and 1029 throw further light on the arrangements made at this time. See
also pp. 380, 383–4, 392–3, 413, and 503; and E. H. Coleridge's note, *Letters,*
ii. 579.

with you, I would *slobber* him spite of his Eruptions.—In giving my Love to Mrs Lovell tell her, that I have not yet seen Robert; but it has been because I have not since the day after my arrival been able to go into the City, my Business having employed me wholly either in writing or in traversing the West End of the Town.—I dined with Lady Beaumont & her Sister on Saturday—for Sir George was engaged to Sir T. Bernard's. He, however, came & sate with us to the very last moment—& I dine with him to day—& Allston is to be of the Party.—The Bust & the Picture from Genevieve are at the R. Academy, & already are talked of—Dawe & I will be of mutual Service to each other.—As soon as the Pictures are settled—i.e. in the first week of May he means to treat himself with a fortnight's relaxation at the Lakes. He is a very modest man—his manners not over-polished—& his worst point is that he is (at least, I have found him so) a fearful Questionist—whenever he thinks, he can pick up any information, or ideas, poetical, historical, topographical, or artistical, that he can make bear on his own profession. But he is sincere, friendly, strictly *moral* in every respect, I firmly believe even to *innocence*—and in point of cheerful Indefatigableness of Industry, in regularity & Temperance, in short, in a glad yet quiet Devotion of his whole Being to the Art, he has made choice of, he is the only man, I ever knew, who goes near to rival Southey: gentlemanly address, person, physiognomy, knowlege, learning, & Genius being of course wholly excluded from the comparison.—God knows my Heart! & that it is my full Belief & Conviction, that taking *all together* there does not exist the Man who could without flattery or delusion be called Southey's Equal. It is quite delightful to hear how he is spoken of by all good people. Dawe will doubtless *take* him— Were S. and I rich men, we would have ourselves & all of you, short & tall, in one family picture. Pray, receive Dawe as a friend.

I called on Murray, who complained that by Dr Bell's Delays, & Irresolutions, & Scruples the Book 'On the Origin, &c'[1] instead of 3000£ in three weeks, which he has no doubt would have been the Sale had it been brought out at the fit time, will not now sell 500—. I told him, that I believed otherwise—but much would depend on the circumstance whether Temper or Prudence would have most influence on the *Athenian Critic* & his friend, Brougham.[2] If, as I hoped, the former, & the work should be reviewed in the

[1] Coleridge refers to Southey's *The Origin, Nature, and Object, of the New System of Education*, published anonymously in 1812.

[2] Henry Brougham (1778–1868), later Baron Brougham and Vaux, contributed numerous articles to the *Edinburgh Review*. A staunch abolitionist, he was first elected to the House of Commons in 1810.

Ed. Rev., if they took up the gauntlet thrown at them, then there was no doubt, but that a strong tide of Sale would set in. Tho' verily this Gauntlet was of weighty metal tho' of polished Steel—and being thrown *at*, rather than *down*, it was challenging a man to fight by a Blow that threatened to brain him.—I have seen Dr Bell, & shall dine with him at Sir T. Bernard's on Monday next.—The venerable Bishop of Durham has sent me a very kind message —that tho' he cannot himself appear in a hired Lecture Room, yet he will not [only] be my Subscriber, but use his best Influence with his Acquaintance.—I am very anxious that my Books should be sent forward as soon as possible—they may be sent at 3 different times, with a week's intervention. But there is one—scarcely a Book—but a collection of loose Sheets, tied up together, at Grasmere, which I want immediately: & if possible would have sent up by the Coach, from Kendal or Penrith. It is a German Romance, with some name beginning with an A. followed by—oder die glückliche Inseln[1]—It makes two volumes, but several of the Sheets are missing. At least, were so when I put them together. If with this Book the two volumes of Schiller's prosaische Schriften[2] were sent off immediately, it would [be] of serious benefit to me in my Lectures.[3] Miss Hutchinson knows them, & will probably recollect the Sheets, I allude to—and these are what I more especially want.—

One pair only of Breeches were in the Parcel—& I am sadly off for Stockings—but the white & under ones I can buy here cheap; but if young Mr White could procure half a dozen or even a dozen Pair of Black Silk, made as stout & weighty as possible, I would not mind giving 17 Shillings per pair, if only they can be *relied* on—which one cannot do in London.—A double Knock—I meant to read over your Letter again, lest I should have forgot any thing—if I have, I will answer it in my next.—God bless you & your [affec]tionate Husband

S. T. Coleridge

Has Southey read Childe Harold? All the world is talking of it. I have not; but from what I hear, it is exactly on the plan that I myself had not only conceived six years ago, but have the whole Scheme drawn out in one of my old Memorandum Books.

---

[1] Referring to Heinse's *Ardinghello.* See Letter 849.
[2] Coleridge apparently refers to *Kleinere prosaische Schriften von Schiller. Aus mehrern Zeitschriften vom Verfasser selbst gesammelt und verbessert*, 4 parts in 2 vols., 1792–1802.
[3] On Monday, 4 May, Dorothy Wordsworth reported that she had sent off by coach the volumes Coleridge specified and that the remainder of the books had been dispatched to Keswick. See *Middle Years*, ii. 494–5.

Does Southey know the price of Silver Forks—? 20£ per dozen!
—If he chooses, Mr Brent will give him a year's credit for any thing,
he may wish to have.

My dear Edith—& my dear Moon! tho' I have scarce room to
write it, yet I love you very much.

As soon as possible, I will write to dear Hartley.

862. *To George Dawe*

MS. Sutro Branch, California State Lib. Hitherto unpublished.

Thursday Afternoon—[23 April 1812][1]

Dear Dawe

Tell me, if it will be any difference to you whether I return the
10£ on Saturday or to day. I should treat you unkindly, if I did
not say that the difference *may be* about 20£ to me—but which I
would far rather give up than forfeit my promise to your inconvenience.

When I see you, I will explain to you the particulars—in truth, a
mere *Bargain* between Bookseller & Author, in which I honestly
do wish not to be so compleatly *bit*, as I have hitherto been—But
on the other hand I *conjure* you, if it will make the *least* difference,
to let me know it—& you shall have the money this evening—

Your's sincerely,
S. T. Coleridge.

863. *To Richard Sharp*

Address: Richard Sharpe, Esqre. M.P. | Mark Lane
MS. Cornell University Lib. Hitherto unpublished.

71, Berners' Street
Oxford St.—
24 April, Friday Morning. [1812]

My dear Sir

A more favorable Star seems rising for me, and promises to set
me even with the World—that is, the sphere of my Agency. For
the last two years Blow had followed Blow, Loss Loss, bewilderment within had linked with embarrassment without, the majority
of the Subscribers to the Friend had forgotten to *pay* for a work
which had neglected, or been unable, to please, the very Account

---

[1] This letter was probably written about the time Coleridge wrote of Dawe
to Mrs. Coleridge. See Letter 861.

Book, which contained their names & by which alone I could know who had & who had not payed, suddenly disappeared under circumstances not mysterious only because they were of the most suspicious kind—the Printer at Penrith run away, left his Bill, as Creditor, fully made out against me, but the Debtor Side a woeful Fragment, & all my Property confounded with his Stock—& as the consummation of all, I had scarcely arrived in London, last October twelvemonth, before the conviction was forced on me, say rather, pierced thro' my very soul with the suddenness of a Flash of Lightning, that he had become my bitterest Calumniator whom to that very moment I had cherished in my Heart's Heart.[1]—The benumming Despondency relieved by no gleam of Hope, and only alternating with fits of (truly may I call it) mental agony, I even now scarcely dare look back on.—But in the last worst affliction the Cure was involved. I gradually obtained the conquest over my own Feelings—and now dare call myself a freeman, which I did not dare do till I had been at Keswick, & satisfied myself that no possibility remained of my having been deluded.[2]—The effect[s] of this Conquest on my Health, on my activity, & on my very appearance, have been such that the amiable Family under whose hospitable roof I have been sheltered since October, 1810, declare that till this time they had never seen me as *myself*—and as Good comes in Bands no less than Evil, so all outward Affairs have put on a cheerful face of Promise. I have entered into the most liberal Terms with the respectable House of Gale & Curtis—& the Plan of my Lectures has been patronized in a way which I should never have dared hope for.— This last affair contains the motive for the present Letter to you. You will, I am sure, feel as well as understand my reason & motive for having introduced it with so long a preface.—

Sir T. Bernard, Sir G. Beaumont, Mr Sotheby, Sir H. Davy (if he can return to town in time) & (I have some reason to flatter myself) Earl Darnley, are about to announce my Lectures under their Patronage, as a kind of *Committee*—the Account to be opened at Messrs. Morelands in their names. My request confines itself to your permitting *your* name to be placed with their's.[3]—The Committee will be merely nominal, and it's chief purpose to give a *first impulse*

[1] When Wordsworth reached London, Sharp most reprehensibly gave him Coleridge's letter. By early May Dorothy was quoting a part of it with undisguised bitterness. See *Middle Years*, ii. 496–8.

[2] Conversations with Mrs. Coleridge and Southey, as well as Wordsworth's refusal to offer either explanation or apology, convinced Coleridge of Wordsworth's antagonistic attitude. See Letters 856 and 858–9.

[3] The advertisement for the lectures published in the *Courier* on 11 May does not include Davy's, the Earl of Darnley's, or Sharp's name. See *Shakespearean Criticism*, ii. 240.

to the fashionable World, and a respectability to the Lectures.—
The form of Annunciation is as follows—

Lectures on the Drama.

Mr Coleridge proposes to give a Series of Lectures on the Drama
of the Greek, French, Italian, English, and Spanish Stage, chiefly
with reference to the Works of Shakespear, at Willis's Rooms,
King St, St James's, on the Tuesdays & Thursdays[1] in May & June
at three o'clock precisely. Each Course will contain six Lectures,[2]
at one Guinea the Course, the Tickets transferable, & no more
Subscribers admitted than the Room will conveniently accomodate.

An account is opened at Messrs. Morelands in the names of the
Earl of——Sir G. B. Sir T. B.—Richard Sharpe, Esqre. M.P.
Mr Sotheby—where Subscriptions will be received & Tickets
issued—

I trust, you will not refuse me this favor. The influence of your
name will essentially serve me—and in addition to this, Sir T.
Bernard & Sir G. Beaumont take it for granted both that I should
apply to you in the first instance & that you would accede to the
Proposal—so that the loss of your name will be *privative*, & not
merely *negative*. I dare not ask any further exertion of your
influence in my favor, much as the addition of one or two other
distinguished Names would benefit me.—

These Lectures so announced & so attended as in all human
probability they will be, will not only altogether disembarrass me
(that indeed is not of so much importance at present: as my Debt
to you is double the amount of all my other Debts put together)
but they will effectually aid all my plans of more permanent
literature.—I shall wait with great anxiety for a few lines from you
—and am,

my dear Sir, | with unfeigned Regard & Respect | Your obliged
S. T. Coleridge

---

[1] The lecture days were later changed to Tuesdays and Fridays.

[2] Coleridge apparently gave two courses of lectures, as here proposed. The
advertisement in the *Courier* of 11 May announced the first course of six
lectures, to begin on 12 May (actually, the lectures began a week later); Letter
873 and Crabb Robinson's diary offer further evidence of the second course,
the first lecture of which was scheduled for Tuesday, 9 June. See *Shakespearean
Criticism*, ii. 240–4, and *Letters*, ii. 595 n.

864. *To Mrs. S. T. Coleridge*

Address: Mrs Coleridge | Greta Hall | Keswick | Cumberland
MS. Lord Latymer. Pub. with omis. Letters, *ii. 583.*
Postmark: 24 April 1812.

24 April, 1812
71, Berners' Street.

My dear Sara

Give my kind Love to Southey, and inform him that I have,
egomet his ipsis meis oculis, seen NOBS, alive, well, and in full
Fleece—that after the Death of Dr Daniel Dove of Doncaster,[1]
who did not survive the loss of his faithful Wife, Mrs Dorothy
Dove, more than eleven months, Nobs was disposed of by his
Executors to Longman & Clementi, Musical Instrument Manufacturers—whose grand Piano-forte Hearses he now draws in the
streets of London. The Carter was astonished at the enthusiasm,
with which I intreated him to stop for half a minute, and the
embrace I gave to *Nobs*, who evidently understood me, and wist-
fully, with SUCH a sad expression in his eye! seemed to say—Ah
my kind old Master, Doctor Daniel, and ah! my mild Mistress, his
dear duteous Dolly Dove—My gratitude lies deeper even than my
Obligation—it is not merely skin-deep!—Ah what I *have* been!
ah what I *am*!—his naked, neighing, night-wandering, new-
skinned, nibbling, noble Nursling, *Nobs*!—

His legs & hoofs are more than half-sheepified, and his Fleece
richer than one sees even in the Leicester Breed ; but not so fine
as might have been the case had the Marino Cross been introduced
before the surprizing Accident and *more* surprizing Remedy took
place—*More* surprizing, I say—because the first happened to St
Bartholemew—for there were Skinners even in the Days of St
Bartholemew—but the other never before, for there was no Dr
Daniel Dove.—I trust, that Southey will now not hesitate to
record and transmit to Posterity so remarkable a fact—I am
delighted! for now Malice itself will not dare to attribute the story
to my Invention. If I can procure the money, I will attempt to
purchase Nobs, & send him down to Keswick by short Journeys,
for Herbert & Derwent to ride upon: provided, you can but get the
field next us.—

I have not been able to procure a Frank; but I daresay, you will
be glad to receive the inclosed Receipt even with the Draw-back
of Postage.—

Every thing, my dear! goes on as prosperously as you could your-

[1] For the story of Dr. Daniel Dove of Doncaster and his horse Nobs see
Southey's *Doctor*, 7 vols., 1834–47.

self wish. Sir T. Bernard has taken Willis's Rooms, King St, St James for me, at only 4 guineas a week, fires, benches, &c &c included—and I expect the Lectures to commence on the first Tuesday in May.—

But at this present moment I need both the advice & the aid of Southey. The Friends have arrived in town—I am at work on the supplemental Numbers, & it is of the last importance that they should be brought out as quick as possible, during the Flush & fresh Breeze of my Popularity—but this I cannot do, without knowing whether Mr Wordsworth will transmit to me the two finishing Essays on Epitaphs.[1] It is, I know & feel, a very delicate Business; yet I wish, Southey would immediately write to Wordsworth, & urge him to send them, by the Coach, either to J. J. Morgan, Esqre., 71, Berners' Street—or to Messrs. Gale & Curtis, Booksellers, Paternoster Row—with as little delay as possible—or if he decline it, that Southey should apprize me of it as soon as possible.—

Secondly, you, my dear! immediately on the receipt of this Letter will be so good as to write to our good friend, Antony Harrison, to inform him that I will write to him before this Day week—that I shall execute the *formal* part of his Commission tomorrow, & have the articles transferred to 71, Berners' Street; but that *till* the middle of next week it will be out of my power to do more, as every hour of my time is fully occupied.—But that I desire that the Stamps may be sent up to me by the Waggon *immediately*, as Gale & Curtis will give me the full value of them, that of the paper included—if only they come up in time. For they have now an opportunity of exchanging them without any Loss of any kind.

As to the *apparent* Balance against me on Brown's Account, of about £13, I must wait till Brown's Brother sends to you for me

---

[1] Wordsworth, whose first essay on *Epitaphs* had appeared in the twenty-fifth number of *The Friend*, had left London when Coleridge's request arrived in Grasmere. Dorothy did not comply but sent Coleridge a message in the parcel of books she forwarded to London. 'I wrote some Memorandums respecting the Books', she reported to Wordsworth on Monday, 4 May, 'and wrapped the Books in it which we sent to Coleridge—and I therein told him that you were in London therefore he had an opportunity of asking you himself; but that even if I could venture to send off the MS. without your orders I could not do it till another Transcript had been made; which we should do immediately, and have it ready to be sent off at a moment's warning.' *Middle Years*, ii. 495.

The events which followed Wordsworth's arrival in London (see Letters 866–7) certainly precluded any further request from Coleridge. The concluding essays on *Epitaphs* were published posthumously by A. B. Grosart. See *The Prose Works of William Wordsworth*, 3 vols., 1876, ii. 41–75.

such Letters, as may lead to the discovery to whom he had disposed of the 25 Copies of the Friend, which are missing—I will myself enquire of Longman—and likewise endeavor to find out Brown himself in order to question him respecting certain Subscriptions which I have reason to suppose payed to him, but which are not recognized in his account.—But at all events, no Debt can possibly lie against me—for he himself in his Bill charges me with the Reprinting of more than a hundred Copies—& lo! but 74 are to be found—say, 76—yet 24 at 28 Shillings each leaves him to account to me for $24 \times 28 - £13$.—

The sooner you send me what Cloathes you mean to send, the better.—

My Love to all—O that I had my pretty Sara here—The Books will go off next week for Hartley & Derwent, & some for you & Sara—but take care to send me *my* Pastor Fido[1]—& I will send you a handsomer Edition. I want mine for the sake of the minor Poems.—

S. T. Coleridge.

The Morgans desire to be kindly remembered—& Charlotte Brent (tell Derwent) hopes, he has not forgot his old Play-fellow—whose face he made use of to draw ink-pictures on.—

I have inclosed the last receipt only, as it would be idle to make you pay treble postage—& I will transmit the former in a Letter to Southey in one of his Murray Parcels.

865. *To William Godwin*

Address: Mr. Godwin
MS. Lord Abinger. Hitherto unpublished.

Thursday Morning—[Endorsed Apr. 30, 1812]

My dear Sir

If Wednesday be as convenient to you, as Tuesday, it would be more so to me; but if not, I will force my arrangements to the Latter.—I will endeavor to procure Mr Wirgman's Article & to have read it before our meeting—You know, I suppose, that Mr Wordsworth is in town—& I need not hint, that it would be painful to me, & *I trust*, to himself that we should meet—

Your's very truly,
S. T. Coleridge

---

[1] *Il Pastor fido*, 1590, a pastoral drama by G. B. Guarini.

866. *To Charles Lamb*

Address: Mr Charles Lamb | India House
[Readdressed] No. 4. Inner Temple Lane
MS. Dove Cottage. Pub. Letters, *ii. 586.*

In late April 1812 Wordsworth arrived in London determined to put a stop to reports in circulation concerning his conduct toward Coleridge. Convinced that Coleridge had misrepresented Montagu's disclosures of Oct. 1810, and had even 'invented' the more offensive expressions (see headnote to Letter 809), Wordsworth resolved to 'confront' him in the presence of Montagu. Two occurrences confirmed Dorothy's urgent warning that he owed it to himself to 'lose not a moment's time'. He heard from Dorothy, who had the story from Mrs. Clarkson, that Sharon Turner had 'trumpet[ed] abroad at Longman's Table' details of the misunderstanding; likewise, on reading a letter to Sharp of 24 April 1812 (Letter 863), he found himself described as Coleridge's 'bitterest Calumniator' and made responsible for 'benumming Despondency' and 'mental agony'. Now thoroughly aroused, Wordsworth proposed through Lamb that Coleridge appear before Montagu and himself with Josiah Wedgwood present as arbitrator, and added a further blunt request: if Coleridge 'declined an explanation', Wordsworth 'begged' that he would 'no longer continue to talk about the affair'.

The present letter was Coleridge's first shocked reaction to Wordsworth's proposal for a confrontation with Montagu. Next day Coleridge told Crabb Robinson that he had 'no objection whatever to see Wordsworth, either alone or in the presence of friends', but emphatically declared that he would not agree to a meeting with Montagu—'I cannot endure to meet a man like Montagu and to stand a trial with him which of us is a liar'. He was equally emphatic in rejecting the suggestion that Josiah Wedgwood should act as referee: 'Of all men Wedgwood is the most unfit. He is my *benefactor*—he has made me independent. However, I can consent to submit to such an examination by no one.' *Robinson on Books and Their Writers*, i. 70–71; *Middle Years*, ii. 490, 496, 498; *The Correspondence of Henry Crabb Robinson with the Wordsworth Circle*, ed. Edith J. Morley, 2 vols., 1927, i. 68; and Letters 859 and 867.

Postmark: ⟨2⟩ May 1812.

2 May, 1812

My dear Charles

I should almost deserve what I have suffered, if I refused even to put my Life in Hazard in defence of my own Honor & Veracity, and in satisfaction of the Honor of a Friend. I say, *Honor*, in the latter instance, singly: because I never felt as a matter of serious Complaint, *what* was stated to have been said—(for this, tho' painfully aggravated, was yet substantially true)—but *by* WHOM it was said, and *to* whom, & *how* & *when*.—Grievously unseasonable therefore as it is, that I should again be overtaken & hurried back by the Surge, just as I had begun to feel the firm Ground under my feet—just as I had flattered myself, & given reason to my hospitable Friends to flatter themselves, that I had regained Tranquillity, & had become quite myself—at the time too, when every Thought should be given to my Lectures, on the success or failure of my efforts in which no small part of my reputation & future Prospects will depend[1]—yet if Wordsworth, upon reflection, adheres to the Plan proposed, *I* will not draw back.—It is right, however, that I should state one or two things—First, that it has been my constant desire that evil should not propagate evil—or the unhappy accident become the means of *spreading* Dissension.—2—that I never quarreled with Mr Montagu—say rather, for that is the real truth, that Mr Montagu never was, or appeared to me, a man with whom I could without self-contempt allow myself to quarrel.—And lastly, that in the present Business there are but three possible cases—either, 1, Mr. Wordsworth said what I solemnly aver that I most distinctly recollect Mr Montagu's representing him as having said, and which *I* understood not merely as great unkindness & even cruelty but as an intentional mean of putting an end to our long Friendship, or to the terms at least under which it had for so long a period subsisted—or, 2, Mr Montagu has grossly misrepresented Wordsworth & most cruelly & wantoned [wantonly ?] injured me—or (3) I have wantonly invented & deliberately persevered in atrocious falsehoods, which place me in the same relation to Mr. Montagu, as (in the second case) Mr Montagu would stand in to me. If therefore Mr Montagu declares to my face that he did not say what I solemnly aver that he did—what must be the consequence, unless I am a more abject Coward than I have hitherto suspected, I need not say.—

Be the consequences, *what* they may, however, I will not shrink from doing my Duty; but previously to the meeting I should very much wish to transmit to Wordsworth a statement which I long ago begun with the intention of sending it to Mrs Wordsworth's Sister—but desisted in consequence of understanding that she had already decided the matter against me[2]—. My reason for wishing

---

[1] '[Lamb] thinks Wordsworth's arrival at London a most unhappy thing for Coleridge, who apprehend his presence at Sir G. Beaumont's will operate to his disadvantage. Lady Beaumont has taken twenty tickets, but she has procured no other subscribers. Coleridge is certainly disturbed by Wordsworth's being in town, and the effect upon his lectures may be bad.' *Robinson on Books and Their Writers*, i. 78.

[2] Wordsworth speaks of this proposed account in a letter to Mrs. Clarkson: 'C. intimated to me by a letter addressed to Lamb that he would transmit to me a statement, begun some time ago, in order to be sent to Miss Hutchinson, but discontinued on account of his having heard that she had "already *decided* against him". A very delicate proposal! Upon this I told Lamb that I should feel somewhat degraded by consenting to read a paper, begun with such an intention and discontinued upon such a consideration. Why talk about "*deciding*" in the case? Why, if in this decision she had judged amiss, not send the paper to rectify her error? or why draw out a paper at all whose object it was to win from the sister of my wife an opinion in his favour, and therefore to my

this is that I think it right that Wordsworth should know & have
the means of ascertaining, some conversations which yet I could
not publicly bring forward without hazarding great disquiet in a
family, known (tho' slightly) to Wordsworth—2. because common
Humanity would embarrass me in stating before a Man what I and
others think of his Wife—& lastly, certain other points which my
own delicacy and that due to Wordsworth himself & his family
preclude from being talked of[1]—For Wordsworth ought not to
forget that whatever influence old associations may have on his
mind respecting Montagu, yet that *I* never respected or liked him—
for if I had ever in a *common* degree done so, I should have quarreled with him long before we arrived in London.—Yet all these
facts ought to be known—because supposing Montagu to affirm
what I am led to suppose, he has—then nothing remains but the
comparative Probability of our two accounts—& for this the state
of my feelings towards Wordsworth & his family, my opinion of
Mr & Mrs Montagu, and my previous intention not to lodge with
them in town, are important documents as far as they do not rely
on my own present assertions.—Woe is me, that a friendship of 15
years should come to this!—and such a friendship, in which, I call
God Almighty to be my witness, as I ever thought it no more than
my Duty, so did I ever feel a readiness to prefer him to myself, yea,
even if Life & outward Reputation itself had been the pledge required—But this is now vain talking—Be it, however, remembered
that I have never wandered beyond the one single complaint, that
I had been cruelly & unkindly treated—I made no charge against
my friend's Veracity, even in respect to his charges against me—
that I have explained the circumstance to those only, who had
already more or less perfectly become acquainted with our difference or were certain to hear of it from others—& that except
on this one point no word of reproach, or even of subtraction from
his good name, as a good man, or from his merits as a great man,
ever escaped me—May God bless you, my dear Charles! &

S. T. Coleridge—

prejudice, upon a charge of *injuries*, grievous injuries, done by me to him;
before he had openly preferred his complaint to myself, the supposed author of
these injuries? All this is unmanly, to say the least of it.' *Middle Years*, ii.
498–9.

[1] Coleridge said to Robinson that if 'he were pressed he should be obliged to
state how grossly Montagu has calumniated Wordsworth' and that this would
force him 'to involve other persons, a most respectable family'. Coleridge
apparently referred to a conversation at the Butlers in Oct. 1810 when he and
the Montagus were *en route* to London. See *Robinson on Books and Their
Writers*, i. 71, and Letter 869.

867. *To William Wordsworth*

Address: W. Wordsworth, Esqre | Sir G. Beaumont's, Bart | South Audley
Street | Grosvenor Square.
MS. Dove Cottage. Pub. Letters, *ii. 588.*

This letter is a reply to Wordsworth's request that if Coleridge declined to
make an explanation, he was to cease talking about the affair. Tersely remarking that he 'little . . . needed the admonition, or deserved the sarcasm',
Coleridge was quick to point out that he himself had expected and 'had a right
to expect' an explanation from Wordsworth. Nevertheless, he promised to
send a second letter containing a 'solemn avowal of what was said by Mr &
Mrs Montagu', adding that Wordsworth could make whatever use of it he
pleased.

When Wordsworth received the present letter, he did not open it. Instead,
as he wrote to Mrs. Clarkson, he sent Lamb the following message: 'If Coleridge
will assure me that this letter contains nothing but a naked statement of what
he believes Montagu said to him, I will read it and transmit it to Montagu, to
see how their reports accord. And I will then give my own, stating what I
believe myself to have said, under what circumstances I spoke, with what
motive, and in what spirit.' To Mrs. Clarkson herself he was even more specific:
'I shall admonish Coleridge to be more careful how he makes written and public
mention of injuries done by me to him. . . . All I want is to bring the parties for
once to a naked and deliberate statement upon the subject, in order that
documents may exist, to be referred to as the best authority which the case
will admit.' *Middle Years,* ii. 498–9.

Wordsworth's refusal to read his letter had a marked effect on Coleridge,
who considered the action, as he told Robinson, '*insulting* or unfriendly'. He
gave Wordsworth no indication of what his letter contained, and he did not
write out his promised account of the Montagus' conversation of 1810. In fact
he did nothing. Lamb, too, noting the coldness of Wordsworth's manner and
certain that no healing of the breach between the two men was possible, ceased
to take any further part in the affair. There matters rested until Wordsworth
took the initiative by calling on Robinson on 8 May and sending him to
Coleridge with an oral denial of some of the expressions used by Montagu.
See headnote to Letter 869 and *Robinson on Books and Their Writers,* i. 73–78.

Monday, 4 May 1812.
71, Berners' Street.

I will divide my statement, which I will endeavor to send you
tomorrow, into two Parts, in separate Letters. The latter commencing from Sunday Night, 28 October 1810, i.e. that on which the
communication was made to me, and which will contain my solemn
avowal of what was said by Mr & Mrs Montagu, you will make what
use of, you please—but the former I write to *you,* and in *confidence*
—yet only as far as to your own heart it shall appear evident, that
in desiring it I am actuated by no wish to shrink personally from
any Test, not involving an acknowlegement of my own degradation, & so to become a false witness against myself, but only by
delicacy towards the feelings of others, and the dread of spreading
the curse of Dissention. But, Wordsworth! the very message, you

sent by Lamb & which *Lamb* did not deliver to me from the anxiety not to add fuel to the flame,[1] sufficiently proves what I had learnt on my first arrival at Keswick, & which alone prevented my going to Grasmere—namely, that you had prejudged the case. As soon as I was informed, that you had denied having used certain expressions, I did not hesitate a moment (nor was it in my power to do so) to give you my fullest faith, and approve to my own consciousness the truth of my declaration, that I should have felt it as a blessing, tho' my Life had the same instant been hazarded as the pledge, could I with firm conviction have given Montagu the Lie at the conclusion of his Story, even as at the very first sentence I exclaimed—'Impossible! It is impossible!'—The expressions denied were indeed only the most offensive part to the feelings—but at the same time I learnt that you did not hesitate instantly to express your conviction, that Montagu never said those words & that I had invented them—or (to use your own words) 'had forgotten myself.'[2] Grievously indeed, if I know aught of my nature, must I have forgotten both myself & common Honesty, could I have been villain enough to have invented & persevered in such atrocious falsehoods.—Your message was that 'if I declined an explanation, you begged I would no longer continue to talk about the affair.'— When, Wordsworth, did I ever decline an explanation? From you I expected one, & had a right to expect it: for let Montagu have added what he may, still that which remained was most unkind & what I had little deserved from you who might by a single question have learnt from me that I never made up my mind to lodge with Montagu and had tacitly acquiesced in it at Keswick to tranquillize Mrs Coleridge to whom Mrs Montagu had made the earnest professions of watching & nursing me, & for whom this & her extreme repugnance to my original, & much wiser, resolution of going to Edingburgh & placing myself in the House, and under the constant eye, of some medical man, were the sole grounds of her assent that I should leave the North at all.—Yet at least a score of times have I begun to write a detailed account, to Wales & afterwards to Grasmere, & gave it up from excess of agitation,—till

---

[1] Wordsworth had told Lamb that he should feel 'degraded' by consenting to read a 'statement' intended for Sara Hutchinson. This may have been the message which Lamb did not deliver to Coleridge.

On receiving the present letter Wordsworth apparently thought that Coleridge had sent him, as proposed in Letter 866, the statement 'long ago begun with the intention of sending it to Mrs Wordsworth's Sister'.

[2] Coleridge is referring to information gained at Keswick. Wordsworth had professed to Southey his 'determination to believe Montagu' rather than Coleridge, thereby making Coleridge 'a deliberate Liar' concerning Montagu's prefatory remark, 'Wordsworth *has commissioned* me to tell you'. Letter 859.

finally I learnt that *all* of your family had decided against me unheard.—*And that I would no longer talk about it*—If, Wordsworth, you had but done me the common justice of asking those with whom I have been most intimate & confidential since my first arrival in Town in Oct. 1810, you would have received either negative or positive proofs how little I needed the admonition, or deserved the sarcasm. Talk about it? O God! it *has* been talked about—! & that it had, was the sole occasion of my disclosing it even to Mary Lamb, the first person who heard of it from me— and that not voluntarily—but that morning a Friend met me, & communicated what so agitated me that then having previously meant to call at Lamb's I was compelled to do so from faintness & universal Trembling, in order to sit down.—Even to her I did not intend to mention it; but alarmed by the wildness & paleness of my Countenance & agitation I had no power to conceal, she entreated me to tell her what was the matter. In the first attempt to speak, my feelings overpowered me, an agony of weeping followed, & then alarmed at my own imprudence and conscious of the possible effect on her health & mind if I left her in that state of suspense, I brought out convulsively some such words as—Wordsworth— Wordsworth has given me up. *He* has no hope of me—I have been an absolute Nuisance in his family—And when long Weeping had relieved me, & I was able to relate the occurrence connectedly, she can bear witness for me, that disgraceful, as it was, that I should be made the Topic of vulgar Gossip, yet that 'had the whole & ten times worse, been proclaimed by a Speaking Trumpet from the Chimneys, I should have smiled at it—or indulged indignation only as far as it excited me to pleasurable activity—; —but that *you* had said it, this & this only, was the Sting! the Scorpion-tooth!' —Mr Morgan & afterwards his Wife & her Sister were made acquainted with the whole Case—& why? Not merely that I owed it to their ardent Friendship, which has continued to be my main comfort and my only support, but because they had already heard of it, in part—because a most intimate & dear Friend of Mr & Mrs Montagu's had urged Mr Morgan to call at the Montagues in order to be put on his guard against me. He came to me instantly, told me that I had enemies at work against my character, & pressed me to leave the Hotel & to come home with him—with whom I have been ever since, with exception of a few Intervals when from the bitter consciousness of my own infirmities & increasing inequality of Temper I took lodgings against his will & was always by his zealous friendship brought back again. If it be allowed to call any one on earth Saviour, Morgan & his Family have been my Saviours, Body and Soul. For my moral Will was,

& I fear is, so weakened relatively to my Duties to myself, that I cannot act, as I ought to do, except under the influencing knowlege of it's effects on those I love & believe myself loved by. To him likewise I explained the affair: but neither from him or his family has one word ever escaped concerning it.— Last Autumn Mr & Mrs Southey came to town and at Mr May's at Richmond, as we were walking alone in the Garden, the Subject was introduced—& it became my Duty to state the whole affair to them, even as the means of transmitting it to you.—With these exceptions I do not remember ever to have made any one my Confidant—tho' in two or three instances I have alluded to the suspension of our familiar Intercourse without explanation, but even here only where I knew or fully believed the persons to have already heard of it.—Such was Mrs Clarkson, who wrote to me in consequence of one sentence in a Letter to her—yet even to her I entered into no Detail, & disclosed nothing that was not necessary to my own defence in not continuing my former correspondence.—In short, the one only thing which I have to blame in myself was that in my first Letter to Sir G. Beaumont I had concluded with a desponding remark allusive to the Breach between us, not in the slightest degree suspecting that he was ignorant of it—In the Letters, which followed, I was compelled to say more (tho' I never detailed the words which had been uttered to me) in consequence of Lady Beaumont's expressed apprehension & alarm lest in the advertisement for my Lectures the sentence 'concerning the Living Poets' contained an intention on my part to attack your literary merits.—The very Thought, that I could be imagined capable of feeling *vindictively* toward you at all, much more of gratifying the passion in so despicable as well as detestable manner, agitated me—I sent her Ladyship the verses composed after your recitation of the great Poem at Cole-orton & desired her to judge whether it was possible that a man, who had written that Poem, could be capable of such an act[1]—and in a Letter to Sir G. B. anxious to remove from his mind the assumption, that I had been agitated by the disclosure of any till then unknown actions of mine or parts of conduct, I endeavored to impress him with the real truth: that not the facts disclosed, but the manner & time & the person by whom & the persons to whom they had been disclosed, formed the whole ground of the Breach.—And writing in great agitation I once again used the same words which had venially burst from me the moment, Montagu had ended his account—O this is cruel! this is *base*!—I

---

[1] This poem was sent to Lady Beaumont in Nov. 1811. See note to Letter 836. When Coleridge asked for the return of the poem in 1815, he failed to recover it. See Letters 964 and 969.

did not reflect on it till it was irrevocable—& for that one word, the only word of positive reproach that ever escaped from me, I feel sorrow—& assure you, that there is no permanent feeling in my heart which corresponds to it.—Talk about it?—Those who have seen me & been with me, day after day, for so many many months could have told you, how anxiously every allusion to the Subject was avoided—and with abundant reason—for immediate & palpable derangement of Body as well as Spirits regularly followed it.—Besides had there not existed in your mind—let me rather say, if ever there had existed any portion of Esteem & Regard for me since the Autumn of 1810, would it have been possible that your quick and powerful Judgement could have overlooked the gross improbability, that I should first invent & then scatter abroad for Talk at Public Tables the phrases, which (Mr Robinson yesterday informed me) Mr Sharon Turner was indelicate enough to trumpet abroad at Longman's Table?[1]—I at least will call on Mr Sharon and demand his authority.[2]—It is my full conviction, that in no one of the hundred Tables at which any *particulars* of our Breach have been mentioned, could the Authority be traced back to those who had received the account from myself.

[1] On 26 Mar. 1812 Crabb Robinson dined at Longman's, where 'Sharon Turner . . . talked about . . . the late quarrel between Wordsworth and Coleridge in a manner which was unpleasant. Certain things may be whispered *tête-à-tête* which in a party outrage our feelings'. Robinson repeated the story to Mrs. Clarkson, who lost no time in writing of it to the Wordsworths. Her letter, which brought forth indignant replies from Sara Hutchinson and Dorothy, reached Grasmere after Wordsworth had left for London, but in an unpublished letter to Wordsworth of 4 May 1812, she referred again to the gossip at 'Longman's Table':

> I hope you will either see . . . [Coleridge] or at least take some measures to put a stop to the reports which are in circulation respecting your Conduct towards him. . . . There has been downright *lying* somewhere not mere misrepresentations & dressings up of facts but inventions against you—and if I were in your place I would take Mr. Montague & C. Lamb with me & force an interview with C——. I confess that I feel a great repugnance at the thought of my name being brought forward. . . . If it is necessary & not else you may say that you were informed by me—that Mr. Montague had told C. that he was positively *commissioned* by you to inform C. that you had no hope of him. With Respect to the *monstrous* words as dearest Dorothy calls them I gave my Authority, Chapter & Verse for them. H. Robinson heard them at Longman's Table, reported them to Lamb who said they had been used by you. It will be easy therefore for you to trace them to their source. [MS. Dove Cottage.]

See *Robinson on Books and Their Writers*, i. 67–68, and *The Correspondence of Henry Crabb Robinson with the Wordsworth Circle*, ed. Edith J. Morley, 2 vols., 1927, i. 68.

[2] It seems likely that Sharon Turner had learned details of the quarrel from his friend Southey.

It seemed unnatural to me, nay, it was unnatural to me to write to you or to any of your family with a cold exclusion of the feelings which almost [over]power me even at this moment—& I therefore write this preparatory Letter, to disburthen my heart, as it were, before I sit down to detail my recollections simply, and unmixed with the anguish which spite of my best efforts accompany them.

But one thing more—the last Complaint that you will hear from me, perhaps. When without my knowlege dear Mary Lamb, just then on the very verge of a Relapse, wrote to Grasmere, was it kind or even humane to have returned such an answer, as Lamb deemed it unadvisable to shew me; but which I learnt from the only other person, who saw the answer, amounted in Substance to a Sneer on my reported high Spirits & my wearing Powder?[1]—When & to whom did I ever make a merit of my Sufferings?—Is it consistent *now* to charge me with going about complaining to every body, & *now* with my high Spirits?—Was I to carry a gloomy face into every society? or ought I not rather to be grateful, that in the natural activity of my Intellect God had given me a counteracting principle to the intensity of my feelings, & a means of escaping from a part of the Pressure?—But for this I had been driven mad —& yet for how many months was there a continual Brooding & going on of the one gnawing Recollection behind the curtain of my outward Being even when I was most exerting myself—and exerting myself more in order the more to benumb it! I might have truly said, with Desdemona,

> I am not merry, but I do beguile
> The Thing, I am, by seeming otherwise.

And as to the Powder, it was first put in to prevent my taking Cold after my Hair had been thinned, & I was advised to continue it till I became wholly grey—as in it's then state it looked as if I had dirty powder in my hair, & even when known to be only the everywhere intermixed grey, yet contrasting with a face even younger than my real age gave a queer & contradictory character to my whole appearance.—Whatever be the result of this long delayed explanation, I have loved you & your's too long & too deeply to have it in my own power to cease to do so.

S. T. Coleridge.

[1] See Letter 815 for an earlier reference to the correspondence between Mary Lamb and Grasmere and Letter 856 for another allusion to Wordsworth's reaction on learning that Coleridge was wearing powder.

868. *To Daniel Stuart*

Address: D. Stuart, Esqre
MS. British Museum. Pub. with omis. Letters, *ii. 595.*

71 Berners' Street
8 May [1812]

My dear Stuart

I send you 7 or 8 Tickets, entreating you, if pre-engagement or your Health does not preclude it, to bring a group with you, as many Ladies as possible but Gentlemen if you can not muster Ladies: for else I shall not only have been left in the Lurch as to actual Receipts by my Great Patrons (the 500 half promised are likely to shrink below 50) but shall absolutely make a ridiculous appearance. The Tickets are transferable. If you can find occasion for more, pray send for them to me as (what it really will be) a favor done to myself.

I am anxious to see you & to learn how far Bath has improved or (to use a fashionable Slang Phrase) disimproved your Health.

Sir James & Lady Mackintosh are, I hear, at Batt's Hotel, Jermyn Street. Do you think, it will be taken amiss, if I enclosed two or three Tickets & Cards with my respectful Congratulations on his safe Return?—I abhor the doing any thing that could be even interpreted into Servility; & yet feel increasingly the necessity of not neglecting the courtesies of Life.—

Mr Wordsworth is in town: & at a time when I require the most perfect tranquillity of mind, I am plunged into the hot water of that bedeviled Cauldron, Explanation with alienated Friendship.—

God bless you, | my dear Sir, | & your obliged & very |
affectionate Friend
S. T. Coleridge

P.S. Mr Morgan left his Card for you.

869. *To William Wordsworth*

Address: W. Wordsworth, Esqre | Sir G. Beaumont's, Bart. | South Audley Street | Grosvenor Square
MS. Dove Cottage. Pub. with omis. Letters, *ii. 596.*

Negotiations being at a stand-still, on 8 May Wordsworth made an unexpected call on Crabb Robinson and authorized him to convey the following message to Coleridge:

'1. That he, Wordsworth, denied most positively having ever given to Montagu any commission whatever to say anything as from him, Wordsworth, to Coleridge; that he said nothing to Montagu with any other than a friendly purpose towards both Coleridge and Montagu, that he was anxious to prevent Coleridge's going into Montagu's family, because he knew that such an intimacy would be broken as soon as it was formed, and lead to very painful consequences. Under this impression only, he spoke with Montagu. But he takes blame to himself for being so intent upon attaining this object as to forget that Montagu was not a man whose discretion could be safely trusted with even so much as he did say to him.

'2. He denies having ever used such a phrase as *rotten drunkard*; such an expression he could not, as a man of taste, merely, have made use of.

'3. Neither did he ever say that Coleridge *had been a nuisance in his family*. He might, in the course of conversation, and in reference to certain particular habits, have used the word "nuisance," which is a word he frequently makes use of, but he never employed it as the result or summary of his feelings towards Coleridge. He never said *he* was a nuisance.

'4. Further, he wished me to inform Coleridge that he no longer wished to confront him and Montagu. He was content to leave undetermined who had erred, but he expected from Coleridge that when he, Wordsworth, had made this declaration, he, Coleridge, would give him credit for the truth of it.'

Immediately after receiving his instructions, Robinson sought out Coleridge and repeated Wordsworth's assertions. Although Coleridge 'manifested certainly much more feeling than Wordsworth', he received the declarations with 'less satisfaction' than Robinson 'could have wished'. He said: 'Had Wordsworth *at first* denied using the language employed by Montagu, had he stated, " I said what I did say purely out of friendship, and I regret having said so much to a man like Montagu," the . . . affair would have been as a cobweb between Wordsworth and my love of him.' Obviously Wordsworth's recent overbearing conduct and refusal to read Coleridge's letter had had the worst possible effect. As Robinson noted, 'Coleridge evidently believed Montagu, notwithstanding his own bad opinion of . . . [the latter's] veracity'. Coleridge complained of Wordsworth's 'taking part with Montagu, going at once to his house, etc.'. Nevertheless, he agreed to prepare 'a dry statement of the assertions of Montagu'.

On Sunday, 10 May, Robinson called on Coleridge, received the promised statement, in which he found 'the most indubitable internal evidence of truth', and hastened to Wordsworth with it. Next day he met Wordsworth again, and the morning was devoted to the preparation of an answer, the purport of which 'was a denial most direct and comprehensive'. Since Wordsworth had fully revealed Coleridge's habits to Montagu and since he could not deny having said he 'had no hopes of him', he found it difficult 'to reconcile . . . the most exact truth and sincerity with the giving his friend the least possible pain', and though the 'very bad opinion' he now held of Montagu's veracity 'greatly facilitated the writing a conciliatory letter', a 'great part' of the reply was actually written by Robinson.

Neither Coleridge's statement of Montagu's talebearing nor Wordsworth's letter of denial has survived—an ironic circumstance, since Wordsworth had earlier wished to obtain written 'documents' which could 'be referred to as the best authority'. Nevertheless, two unpublished fragmentary drafts of Wordsworth's letter are preserved at Dove Cottage. The first is in Wordsworth's handwriting:

'I shall without preface come to the point upon which our attention ought to be fixed.—

'I solemnly deny that I gave to Montagu a Commission to say to Coleridge that I had no hopes of him. I solemnly also deny that I said Coleridge *was in the habit* of running into debt at little Pot-Houses for Gin. In like manner I do solemnly also deny that I ever said C. had been an absolute Nuisance in my family. I also affirm as sacredly that though [in] some of the particulars enumerated by Coleridge as having wounded his feelings there is *some thing* of the *form* of truth, there is absolutely NOTHING of the *spirit* of truth.—So that in every sense in which these particulars severally and the whole number of them conjointly could, as evidences of unworthy behaviour on my part, give pain to Coleridge, if he knew what I said, under what circumstances I spoke, with what motive, and in what spirit, I do give a *most solemn denial to the whole.*—

'I have with the utmost severity of self-examination looked into my own heart & soul upon this occasion, and I stand acquitted before my conscience of all blame, except that I freely acknowlege an error of judgement, in having suffered myself, from any motives however kind to the parties & however pure, to speak to a man upon so delicate a subject, whose conduct is so little governed by the universally admitted laws of Friendship, and regulations of society, in similar cases. If Coleridge be satisfied, that is, give entire and absolute faith to the above disavowal, I ask no more ; if he is not, in justice to myself I must demand that a meeting take place between C., M., & me, in the presence of some unexceptionable Arbiter.—

'In justice to C. I must not omit to say that I believe that a conviction exists in his mind that M. did express himself in that manner ; but as from C's own statement it appears that he was much agitated from the very opening of the conversation, it is possible that he might be mistaken in some important points. But as to this and other considerations too naturally rising out of the Statement made by C. I do not wish to enter. It is enough for me if I receive from his hand an affirmation to the above effect ; but I do earnestly entreat that it may not be given but with the *perfect consent of his whole soul.* If he have any doubts or misgivings, my wish is that the affair should rest where it now is till he has closed his course of Lectures, and then we will proceed in the manner first proposed, the only one which in such a case can satisfy my mind.

'Should this however be rendered necess[ar]y by the state of C's feelings I beg that no further steps may be taken till he has closed his present course of lectures. [This sentence is in Robinson's handwriting.]

'[I solemnly deny that I gave to Montagu a Commission] to say *any thing* whatever to Coleridge from me. All that I did say had a reference merely to an apprehended Connection between C. and himself which I was convinced must prove injurious to both. Nor did it ever enter my mind that by any possibility what I then mentioned to M. could any way affect the *intimacy* between C. and me. That I may meet C's statement in all detail I proceed to say, I, of course ; as for instance, if I ever said that C. was or had been [a] nuisance [in my] family, which I do not recollect that I did say, and which I think it little less than morally impossible that I should have said, [I certainly never applied such a term in its absolute Sense but must have spoken in reference to particular habits only.]' (The last bracketed passage, which is in Robinson's handwriting, is crossed out in the manuscript. All other bracketed words in this paragraph have been inserted by the editor to make the text readable.)

The second draft, which is a rewriting of the first, is in Robinson's handwriting :

'I shall without preface come to the point upon which our attention ought to be fixed.

'I solemnly deny that I gave to M. a Commission to say any thing whatever to C. from me. All that I did say had a reference merely to an apprehended Connection between himself & M. which I was convinced must prove injurious to both—Nor did it ever enter my mind that by any possibility what I then mentioned could any way affect the friendship & *intimacy* between C. & me. Of course & inclusively and that I may meet C's statement in detail I solemnly deny that I commissioned M. to say to C. that I had no hopes of him—I also solemnly deny that I said C. was *in the habit of* running into debt at little Pot-houses for Gin. In like manner I also affirm as sacredly that tho' in some of the particulars enumerated by C. as having wounded his feelings there is *something* of the form of truth, there is *absolutely nothing of the spirit* in any of them. As for instance: that I asserted that C. had been [an] absolute nuisance in my family. It is little less than morally impossible that I should have used these words, but it is absolutely impossible that either by these words, if used, or by any resembling them, I could mean to express the impression of my mind & heart concerning C. or the feelings of my family in respect to him—So that in every Sense in which the particulars enumerated by C. & the whole of them conjointly could as evidences of unworthy behaviour on my part give pain to C., if he knew what I said, under what circumstances I spoke, with what motive & in what spirit, *I do give a most solemn denial to the whole.*

'I have with the utmost severity of Self examination looked into my own heart & Soul upon this occasion and stand acquitted before my conscience of all blame, except that I freely acknowledge an error of judgement in having suffered myself, from any motives however kind to the parties & however pure, to speak to a man upon so delicate a subject whose conduct is so little govern-able by the universally admitted laws of Friendship & regulations of Society in similar cases.

'Hoping to receive from C. an assurance of his entire & absolute faith in this my disavowal I have to add that fully believe in the truth of his statement as an expression of his Conviction that M. did say all he has ascribed to him— But whether the agitation in which C. represents himself to have been from the first Moment M. touched upon this business, may not have occasioned him to mistake M. in some important points; or whether M. may not have mistaken me; or how the misapprehension which actually subsists, originated:—these are points which I do not deem it necessary to enter into. The Love & Affection which I entertain for C. and which I trust he entertains for me do not need [or] require a solution of these difficulties.

'If however C's mind is still troubled by doubts & misgivings as to the sincerity, simplicity, & integrity of the disavowal which I have hereby made, I must then in satisfaction of my own honour require his consent to the first proposed interview between M. & ourselves, tho' aware that this would of necessity lead to an opening of the points in difference between himself & M. which I think in itself very unadviseable.

'Should this however be rendered necessary by the state of C's feelings, I beg that no further steps may be taken till he has closed the lectures which he is on the point of commencing.'

Robinson left Wordsworth's conciliatory letter at Coleridge's soon after it was ready on 11 May; returning later that same day he found Coleridge at home with the Lambs. He was gratified when Coleridge said 'in a half whisper that Wordsworth's letter had been perfectly satisfactory to him, and that he had answered it immediately'. The present letter was Coleridge's reply to Wordsworth.

A superficial reconciliation followed. Even Robinson was forced to admit that though the wound was healed, the scar remained in Coleridge's bosom. The old intimacy, not only with Wordsworth but also with Sara Hutchinson and Dorothy, was gone forever. Coleridge himself added a fitting conclusion: 'A Reconciliation has taken place—but the *Feeling* . . . never can return. All outward actions, all inward Wishes, all Thoughts & Admirations, will be the same—*are* the same—but—aye there remains an immedicable *But.*' See *Robinson on Books and Their Writers*, i. 73–81 and 84; *Middle Years*, ii. 499; and Letter 888.

Monday afternoon, 3 o/clock—
11 May, 1812.
71, Berners' St.

My dear Wordsworth

I declare before God Almighty that at no time even of my sorest affliction did even the *possibility* occur to me of ever doubting your word. I never ceased for a moment to have faith in you, to love & revere you: tho' I was unable to explain an unkindness, which seemed anomalous in your character. Doubtless, it would have been better, wiser, & more worthy of my relation to you, had I immediately written to you a full account of what had happened —especially, as the person's Language concerning your Family at Mr Butler's was such as nothing but the wild general Counterpanegyric of the same person almost in the same Breath of your self—as a Converser &c—could have justified me in not resenting to the uttermost[1]—from the intuition, I had, that such a man was not to be quarreled with, & from Mrs Butler's intreaties to refer the whole to the Woman, whom her Husband not many Hours after he had been with her denominated the Old Serpent.

All this was full on my mind when he spoke to me; but the particular facts mentioned that could not have come but from you, the seemingly natural Comments of the Woman, as if the whole had been equally known at the same time to both;[2] & (accidentally) his repetition of the very same phrase, which you had used to myself on the last morning as respecting Schiller & as told you by Mr Robinson,[3]—all these & more overwhelmed me.—After that,

[1] E. H. Coleridge omitted the passage from this point through the words 'Mrs Morgan's possession', with the following comment: 'I have followed Professor Knight in omitting a passage in which "he [Coleridge] gives a lengthened list of circumstances which seemed to justify misunderstanding". The alleged facts throw no light on the relations between Coleridge and Wordsworth.' (*Letters*, ii. 595 n.) The reader may not agree.

[2] Coleridge had earlier told Robinson how much he had been affected by Montagu's assertions and such 'circumstances of confirmation' as Mrs. Montagu's saying: 'I thought it not friendly in Mr. Wordsworth to go into such a detail. . . . I thought the facts stated by Wordsworth did not warrant his conclusions.' *Robinson on Books and Their Writers*, i. 77.

[3] In Oct. 1810 Montagu had quoted Wordsworth as saying that 'Coleridge has rotted his entrails out with [intemperance]'. Wordsworth told Robinson he did not 'think' he had used such an expression, though 'the idea might . . . [have been] conveyed in what he said, and Montagu might . . . [have given] that as the conclusion from all he said'. Coleridge, however, emphatically declared to Robinson: 'I could not forget that Wordsworth had on leaving me, reminded [me] of the fact *you* stated concerning Schiller, that when he was opened

Mr Carlisle's most unprofessional Detail to a Woman, who made it the subject of common Table Talk, of every thing, I had confided to him as a Surgeon—(a fact, by which, had I in my nature the *power* of being vindictive, I could have gone near to blast him)[1] —the circumstance of Mr Morgan's being urged to call on Mrs Montagu in order 'to be warned against me'—Montagu's own re-assertions in Letters, one of which I by accident saved (after I had with many others torn it to pieces)—tho' I declare that the phrases used in that wh[ich] was preserved were far less impressive than those destroyed—& the purport of all of which was that given up by all others & against the Admonitions of my warmest Friends he had yet resolved to be 'my Saviour'—the detection of a Spy in the very House, I lived, whose Letter to me acknowleging herself 'a *Liar*', that all, she had written, was devoid of all foundation, & that she had invented it from what she had heard from Mrs Montagu's Friend, in order to ingratiate herself with that friend, is still in Mrs Morgan's possession—all these added to what I mentioned in my Letter to you—may not justify but yet must palliate the *only* offence I ever committed against you in deed or word, or thought—that is, the not writing to you & trusting instead to our common Friends. Since I left you, my Pocket books have been my only full Confidants—& tho' instructed by prudence to write so as to be intelligible to no Being on Earth but yourself & your family, they for 18 months together would furnish proof that in anguish or induration I yet never ceased both to *honor* & love you—

S. T. Coleridge

I need not say, of course, that your presence at the Lectures, or any where else, will be gratifying to me[2]—

his entrails were, as it were, eaten up, while his brain was sound. And Wordsworth used the very same expressions, speaking of Schiller, which Montagu did.' *Robinson on Books and Their Writers*, i. 72, 75, and 77.

  [1] Cf. Letters 809 and 951.

  [2] By 19 May Wordsworth had seen Coleridge 'several times'. He attended at least one of Coleridge's lectures, and 'one morning' the two men had 'a pleasant walk to Hampstead together'. See *Robinson on Books and Their Writers*, i. 84 and 88, and *Middle Years*, ii. 502.

870. *To William Sotheby*

Address: W. Sotheby, Esqre | 47 | Seymour Street
MS. formerly in the possession of the late Colonel H. G. Sotheby. Pub. E. L. G. ii. 82.

[11 May 1812]

Dear Sir

The moment, I heard of the fatal event,[1] I hurried off, with a 3 line letter in my Hand, to Sir T. Bernard to suggest [to] him the propriety of deferring my Lecture[2]—in truth, my own incapability of giving it. O Mercy!—Such a man—he who had knit my very soul not only to my Country (for that it was, always was) but to the immediate Government—I never saw him—yet I loved him as if he had been flesh & blood to me rather than the mere Idea of a great & good, & most simple, great Man!—

Sir T. B. was on his way to me, and on my return from his House I luckily met him—He was coming with the same purpose— & on our return he found a note from Lady Beaumont likewise urging the same—

You, I well know, think the same—the Object therefore of this flurried Letter is to intreat you to let those of the Subscribers, whom I owe to your kind exertions, know that the Lectures are deferred to the Tuesday after next—Lady Beaumont, we trust, will take upon herself another third, & Sir T. Bernard the remainder. Having no Servant, I know no other way of preventing disappointment—

Dear Sir | Your obliged
S. T. Coleridge

871. *To Robert Southey*

Address: R. Southey, Esqre | Greta Hall | Keswick | Cumberland
MS. Lord Latymer. Pub. with omis. Letters, ii. 597.
Postmark: 12 May 1812.

[12 May 1812]

My dear Southey

The aweful Event of yester afternoon has forced me to defer my Lectures to Tuesday, the 19th—by advice of all my Patrons.

---

[1] Spencer Perceval was assassinated by John Bellingham in the lobby of the House of Commons on 11 May 1812.

[2] The first lecture was postponed until Tuesday, 19 May. According to Crabb Robinson, whose scanty notes contain the only information concerning this course, the remaining lectures were given on 23, 26, 29 May and 5 June. If Coleridge kept to his schedule of six lectures he also must have lectured on Tuesday, 2 June. *Shakespearean Criticism*, ii. 242–4.

The same thought struck us all at the same moment—so that our Letters might be said to meet each other—I write now to urge you, if it be in your power, to give one day or two of your time to write something in your impressive way, on that theme which no one, I meet, seem[s] to feel as they ought to do—and of which I [find] scarcely any, but ourselves, that estimate according to it's true gigantic magnitude—I mean, the sinking down of Jacobinism below the middle & tolerably educated Classes into the Readers & all-swallowing Auditors in Tap-rooms &c, of the Statesman, Examiner, Cobbet, &c—I have ascertained that throughout the great manufacturing Counties Whitbread's, Burdett's, & Waithman's Speeches, and the leading Articles of the Statesman & the Examiner, are printed in Ballad Form, & sold at a halfpenny & a Penny each—

I was turned numb, & then sick, & then into a convulsive state of weeping on the first Tidings just as if Perceval had been my near & personal Friend—But Good God! the atrocious sentiments universal among the Populace—& even the lower order of Householders—On my return from the Courier, where I had been to offer my services if I could do any thing for them on this occasion, I was faint from the Heat & much Walking—& took that opportunity of going into the Tap room of a large Public House frequented about 1 o/clock by the lower Orders—. It was really shocking—Nothing but exultation—Burdett's Health drank with a Clatter of Pots—& a Sentiment given to at least 50 men & women —May Burdett soon be the man to have Sway over us!—These were the very words. 'This is but the beginning'—'more of these damned Scoundrels must go the same way—& then poor people may live'—'Every man might maintain his family decent & comfortable if the money were not picked out of our pockets by them damned Placemen'—'God is above the Devil, *I* say—& down to Hell with Him & all his Brood, the Minister Men & Parliament Fellows'—'They won't hear Burdett—No! he is a Christian Man & speaks for the Poor'—&c &c—I do not think, I have altered a word.—

My Love to Sara, & I have received every thing right—The Plate will go as desired and among it a present to Sariola & Edith from good old Mr Brent, who had great delight in hearing them talked of—It was wholly the old gentleman's own thought—Bless them both!

The affair between Wordsworth & me seems settled—much against my first expectation from the message, I received from him, & his refusal to open a Letter from me—I have not yet seen him, but an explanation has taken place—I sent by Robinson an attested avowed Statement of what Mr & Mrs Montagu told me—— & Wordsworth has sent an unequivocal denial of the Whole *in spirit* & of the most offensive passages in letter as well as Spirit—& I then instantly informed him that were ten thousand Montagues to swear against it, I should take his word not ostensibly only but with inward Faith!—

To morrow I will write out the passage from Apuleius & send the Letter to Rickman—It is seldom that want of leisure can be fairly stated as an excuse for not writing—but really for the last 10 days I can honestly do it, if you will but allow a due portion to agitated Feelings. The Subscription is languid indeed compared with the expectations, Sir T. Bernard almost pledged himself for—However, he has done his best & so has Lady Beaumont—who herself procured me near 30 names. I should have done better by myself, for the present—but perhaps the future will be better, as it is.—

Assure Mrs C. that I now instantly read her Letters—& that she will excuse my silence when she knows that no day passes in which I do not write a dozen Letters or more—& I have not been in bed after ½ past 8 since I have been in town.

S. T. C.—

872. *To John Murray*

Address: Mr Murray | Fleet Street   with Mr Coleridge's Complts.
MS. Sir John Murray. Pub. E. L. G. ii. 83.

71, Berners' St.
Saturday, May 16, 1812

Dear Sir

You would oblige & serve me much if you could (and if you *can with propriety*, I feel confident that you *will*) entrust to my Care for two or three days only that Sheet of the unpublished Ed. Ann. Register, which contains the Remarks on the parliamentary Schemes & Labors of Mr Banks, and his Co-adjutors of the Finance Committee, on Sinecures, Audit office &c &c—My whole motive is this—I am writing on the same Subject, & am anxious not to publish any thoughts, even tho' my own many years before Southey read to me that masterly paper, which are to be found in it—but having given such of my own, as have not been anticipated in the Ed. Annual Register, I intend to say—I should add many and much stronger grounds of Dissent, but having by favor of accident seen & perused a most masterly series of Reflections on the same Subject in the yet unpublished third Volume of the E. A. R.

and these reflections supported by a chain of Facts, not less cogent as *proofs* than valuable as matter of general information, I deem it my duty rather to refer the Reader to the Work itself than to repay the obligation for so much interesting Instruction by an ungenerous anticipation. I dare challenge the malignity of party Spirit itself to deny, that the Historical Portion (two thirds of the whole) of this & the former Volumes forms beyond all comparison the noblest Specimen of recent & progressive History in the annals of Literature. In all rival works I have found little or nothing which I had not or might not have previously learnt from the Newspapers; but in this independent of the dignity, perspicuity, and vivacity of the Style, more than half of the most interesting & important Facts, both domestic & foreign, are in the strictest sense new to the English Reader.

My Subscription goes on most languidly.—When I was young, I wrote an Epigram of which I remember the Thought only— namely, that I dreamt, that a great Lord had made me a most splendid Promise; awoke, and found it as much a delusion, as if the great Lord had really made me a Promise.—

If you can do any [thing] for me among your Friends, I am sure, you will.—A guinea for six Lectures is no extravagant Sum—

Your's, dear Sir, | Sincerely
S. T. Coleridge

873. *To Joseph Hardcastle*

Address: Joseph Hardcastle, Esqre. | Hatcham House | London Bridge
MS. Folger Shakespeare Lib. Hitherto unpublished.
Postmark: 8 June 1812.

Monday 8 June, 1812
71, Berners' Street

Dear Sir

I had promised myself the honor of waiting on you in person, to inform you & your amiable Family that my second Course commences tomorrow, (Tuesday) 3 o/clock with an analysis of the Tragedies of Macbeth & Hamlet[1]—but a country Friend leaving town abruptly to day, I am compelled to devote my Morning to his Concerns.[2]

With unfeigned respect | I remain, | dear Sir, | Your very obliged
S. T. Coleridge

[1] At his lecture of 5 June, the last of his first course, Coleridge announced that in 'the future lectures, money is to be taken at the door'. (*Shakespearean Criticism*, ii. 244.) Coleridge's statement in this letter would indicate that at least the first lecture of the second course was delivered. There is no further information concerning this series of six lectures.

[2] Probably Wordsworth, who planned to leave London for Bocking on 8 June. *Middle Years*, ii. 501.

874. *To John Rickman*

Address: John Rickman, Esqre. | Palace Yard | Westminster
MS. Huntington Lib. Pub. with omis. John Rickman, *161.*
Postmark: 17 July 1812.

71 Berners' Street
Friday, 17 July, 1812

My dear Sir

I well know, how little time you have to throw away—and Mr Morgan & myself have therefore long struggled with the desire of inducing you to dine & spend the evening with us & one or two intelligent friends at 71, Berners' Street—. But Mr Morgan has requested me to ask you, whether it is in your power or plan of time to mention any day in the next week, or the week after, which you can afford—and if there were any chance of Mrs Rickman & your Sister's favoring us, Mrs Morgan would not only be most happy to see them, but would previously call on Mrs R. to make a personal Invitation.

In whatever part of Christendom a genuine Philosopher in Political Economy shall arise, & establish a system, including the Laws & the disturbing Forces of that miraculous Machine of living Creatures, a Body Politic, he will have been in no small measure indebted to you for authentic & well guarded Documents. The Prel. Observ. interested me much in & for themselves—and as grounds or hints for manifold reflections they are at least equally valuable.—I am about to put to the press a second Volume of THE FRIEND; & in all points, but one, treated of in the work I seem to myself to be in broad daylight—but in that one, perplexed & darkling & dissatisfied—the Subject is the Constitution of our Country & the Expediency? and (if expedient) the practicability? of an Improvement (for Reform is either a misnomer or a Lie to all our History) of the House of Commons.—A series of weak Ministries; the strange co-existence of little Knots & Sub-parties in the Legislature; the strength of the stronger Party to do harm & it's weakness to effect, even what they themselves consider, good, upon any *system*; & above all, the rapid Increase both of inorganized, and of *self-organizing Power & Action throughout the Kingdom; make a deep impression on me as far as the *wish* for some Improvement goes—while the general laxness & almost *flaccidity* of intellectual manhood, the scarcity of true virile productive strong-Sense, renders me despondent even as to the formation in Parliament of any grand *outline*.—Where shall we find 500 better?—or if I

* Wens, Hydatids, &c under the name of Societies, Committees, Associations, &c. [Note by S. T. C.]

reply—the very same men would be better if sent into Parliament by better means, then comes the yet harder question—What are these means, which effecting this one end would not at the same time reduce the Peerage of the Realm to a Puppet-shew, and the Ministers of the Crown to a Committee of Public Safety reporting to the National Convention ?—If I have been rightly informed, there never was a House of Commons that contained so large a number of men without Estates or known Property as the present—Most certainly there never was one so cowardly *plebicolar.*—I fear, I fear, that it is a hopeless business & will continue so till some fortunate Giant-mind starts up & revolutionizes all the present Notions concerning the education of both Gentry & Middle Classes. While this remains in statu quo, I suspect that good Dr Bell's Scheme carried into full effect by the higher Classes may suggest to a thinking man the Image of the Irishman on the Bough with his face toward the Trunk sawing himself off.—

Excuse my garrulity & believe me, my dear Sir, | Your's with affectionate Respect

S. T. Coleridge

P.S. Next Thursday is the only day, I am engaged out—to dine with a Mr. Saumarez,[1] who has just written a Book, a biggish one, to overthrow Sir Iky's System of Gravitation, Color, & the whole 39 Articles of the Hydrostatic, chemic, & Physiologic Churches—

875. *To Daniel Stuart*

MS. *British Museum. Pub. E. L. G. ii. 84.*

Friday, August 7 1812

Dear Stuart

Since I last saw you, I have been confined to my bed with the alarming symptom of a swoln Leg, Ancle, and Foot, and a painful oppression on my chest which for three days rendered me unable to sit up even in bed & with the pillows behind me more than 10 or 15 minutes at a time. The Morgans were really alarmed, & I myself thought it the commencement of Dropsy on the Chest. I called in a Physician, and a man in whom I have the greatest confidence, who has dismissed these apprehensions in good part—and declared the whole of my immediate Disease to be Indigestion, & Erysypelatous Inflamation—Accordingly, the complaint on the Chest has already disappeared, and tho' my right leg is still visibly larger than the left, yet the swelling is greatly abated.—I informed

---

[1] Richard Saumarez (1764–1835), surgeon, whose *Principles of Physiological and Physical Science* appeared in 1812.

Dr Gooch[1] without the least concealment of the whole of my *general case,* and have put myself under his direction. The two evils produced by the use of narcotics on my constitution are, he says, a secretion of acrid Bile from the Liver and a relaxation of the extremities of the Blood-vessels—but without tormenting myself or imposing on my fortitude a burthen greater than it can bear, he entertains strong hopes that I shall either wholly emancipate myself, or, if not *that,* yet bring myself to such an arrangement as will not very materially affect my health or longaevity.—His prescriptions are—Mercury in very small quantities, in the form of Corbyn's Blue Pill—Nitric Acid, 10 drops in a glass of water, twice a day—& a known & measured quantity of Stimulant, with an attempt to diminish the Opiate part of it by little and little, if it were only a single Drop in two days.—

I have adopted this plan for the last four days, and find it not in the slightest degree burthensome: and were it not for the remaining Inflammation in my Leg, I should feel myself better, livelier, with more steady appetite & more regular Digestion than for some time past. This I attribute, however, in great measure to the Weight having been taken off my spirits by my having at length put a Physician in possession of the *whole* of my Case with all it's symptoms, & all it's known, probable & suspected Causes.

I called at the Courier office on Wednesday, in hopes of the chance of seeing you; but the Walk increased the heat & size of my Leg—& therefore instead of walking over to Brompton I must talk by the Twopenny Post—

I do not know, whether I can be of any use to the Courier; but if I could, it would be of great use to me, who partly from Ill-health, but still more from my anxiety to finish 1. the re-writing of my Play,[2] & 2. the second Volume of the Friend, have thrown myself behind hand—and the sending off a paltry Bill of 2 or 3 pound the second or third time agitates & flutters me so as not only to injure my health but to put a stop for an hour or two to all power of writing or composing.—What I wish, would be this—not to write for any given time for the C. but to send in at once the whole of a stated quantity of articles—all of which I have in a more or less fragmentary form by me, tho' my Lectures joined with the W——business to leave them in that form—

1. Two articles on America in relation to G.B.—and on Maddison's Proclamation.[3] (These Mr Street shall receive, the first to morrow, the second the day after.)

---

[1] Robert Gooch (1784–1830), physician.   [2] i.e. *Remorse,* a recast of *Osorio.*
[3] James Madison (1751–1836), fourth president of the United States, issued his war message on 1 June 1812. War with Great Britain was declared 18 June.

2. The public character of Mr Perceval, & reflections on the consequences of his Fall, and the sentiments & tone of Feeling in & out of Parliament—

3. On the ruinous tendency of all ranks of men to Disorganization or partial Organizations—

4. Is the Church in Danger? And (if so) from what causes?—N.B. The Bible Society—Egyptian Hall! VANSITTART!!![1]

5. The Importance of the Established Church to the State, to Tolerancy, & to the best Interests of the Dissenters themselves.

6. On Toleration—and the question of right & policy as pleaded for the unconditional Equalization of the Irish Papists.

7. The, alas! long promised Characters, of Buonaparte, Commentary on that of Pitt, Mr. Fox, Wyndham, Lord Wellington—& two or three short ones without a name—

The whole will consist of twenty Articles from two Columns to two and a half, on an average; I pledge you most solemnly *my word of Honor*, that Numbers, 1. 2. and 7. (which will form Half of the whole) shall have been delivered to Mr Street within 14 days from the present day, and the Remainder before the end of the following Fortnight—and I ask for the whole 50£—25 now, & 25 on the 21st of the Month. If you have no other Objection than the doubt of my perseverance in the performance, I entreat you to confide in me *this once*—and I will disclaim all pretensions to your Friendship hereafter, if I disappoint you either in Time, Quantity, or Quality.

But if you or Mr Street think, that the Courier will not be adequately benefited by the Essays, then I must beg your assistance, as a Friend, for 8 days—by which Time I shall have been able to submit my re-written Play to Morris [Harris?] or Colman,[2] & if they do not accept it, I will take Gale & Curtis's offer, & repay you.[3]—

Your's affectionately,
S. T. Coleridge

[1] Nicholas Vansittart (1766–1851) was chancellor of the exchequer from May 1812 to Dec. 1822.

[2] George Colman (1762–1836), dramatist and manager of the Haymarket Theatre. *Remorse* was accepted by Drury Lane. See Letter 879.

[3] 'I sent 20£ D.S.' Endorsement in MS. by Stuart.

876. *To John Murray*

Address: Mr Murray |Bookseller & Publisher | Fleet Street
MS. Sir John Murray. Hitherto unpublished.

[*Circa* 7 August 1812][1]

Dear Sir

I have been unlucky in never finding you at home when I have called. I therefore trouble you with a few lines instead. I wish to have *your* opinion concerning the *physiognomy* of a Work, which Mr Mason Good[2] and one or two other literati think promising. In the huge cumulus of my Memorandum & common-place Books I have at least two respectable Volumes, the nature of the Contents of which I can perhaps convey to you in part by the proposed title-page—

EXOTICS NATURALIZED, i.e. impressive Sentiments, Reflections, Aphorisms, Anecdotes, Epigrams, short Tales and eminently beautiful Passages from German, Spanish, and Italian Works, of which no English Translations exist;—the whole collected, translated, and arranged by S. T. Coleridge, with explanatory, critical, and biographical notes and notices by the Collector.

Now what I wish to know from you, is your opinion of the nature of such a work *in general*, taking for granted the execution as adequate. If this should be favorable, I will then copy out 40 or 50 pages, as a specimen—& send them to you.—I dare venture to say, that it will be one of the most *entertaining* Books in our Language.—A single Line will suffice in answer to this—a mere yes or no to the Question—Does the *Idea* of the work appear to you sufficiently promising to induce a wish to see a Specimen of it as realized?—

I am half confined to the house with an inflamed Leg.

Your's, dear Sir, | respectfully

S. T. Coleridge

P.S. I should be obliged to you not to mention this to any one, should it not meet your judgement—

---

[1] The reference to an inflamed leg (see Letter 875) establishes the approximate date of this letter.

[2] John Mason Good (1764–1827), physician and miscellaneous writer, lectured at the Surrey Institution in 1811–12.

877. *To Richard Saumarez*

Address: Richard Saumarez, Esqre | Surry Institution | Blackfriars Road   To
be *given* to Mr Saumarez, when he calls:—not forwarded.
MS. Private possession. Hitherto unpublished. In the manuscript Coleridge's
outline of the 1812–13 lectures precedes the letter.
Postmark: 12 August 1812.

Wednesday, 12 August—[1812]

My dear Sir

I have here sent you a chapter of Contents of my proposed Lectures:[1] in the formation of which I have been desirous to introduce as much variety of matter, as is compatible with unity of Object.

I received your Note this morning, & cannot make out your date; so that not knowing whether the note was written this morning or last night, I think it best to direct this Letter to you at the Surry Institution, for fear that (Newington being off the Stones) it may not arrive in time at your House.—

Of course, I have drawn out this Sketch far more at large (for the satisfaction of the Committee) than it need appear in a printed Annonce[2]—

with unfeigned respect | your obliged
S. T. Coleridge

Lecture 1. That to use each word in a sense peculiarly it's own, is an indispensable Condition of all just thinking, and at once the surest, easiest, and even most entertaining Discipline of the mind. —On the words, Beautiful, Sublime, Majestic, Grand, Picturesque, Fancy, Imagination, Taste.

Lectures 2 & 3. The falsehood of the almost universal opinion, that in the progress of civilized Life the Invention of Conveniences, and Utilities precede the Arts of Ornament proved by Facts, and *a priori* (i.e. from the nature of the Human Being). The fine Arts in the natural order of their Origination—Dress, Orchēsis, (including all the arts of bodily motion, as mimic Dances, gymnastic Sports &c), Architecture, Eloquence, Music, Poetry, Statuary, Painting, Gardening.

---

[1] This lecture course was delivered at the Surrey Institution on Tuesday evenings beginning 3 Nov. 1812. Crabb Robinson mentions lectures on 3, 10, 17, and 24 Nov.; 1 and 8 Dec.; and 5, 12, 19, and 26 Jan. Coleridge himself mentions a lecture of 22 Dec. (Letter 883.) If there were, as planned, twelve lectures, another lecture was given, probably on 15 Dec. (See *Shakespearean Criticism*, ii. 248–51.) It was to this lecture course that Coleridge 'used to take' his three volumes of Schlegel's *Vorlesungen*. See Letter 895.

[2] The only known printed copy of this prospectus, which differs somewhat from that in Coleridge's letter, is among Robinson's papers in the Dr. Williams's Library. See *Shakespearean Criticism*, ii. 246–8.

Lecture 4. *On Poetry* in genere, and as common to ancient Greece & to Christendom. On the Poetry of the Ancients, as contra-distinguished from that of the moderns, or the differences of the Classical from the Romantic Poetry, exemplified in the Athenian Dramatic Poets.

Lecture 5. On the Mythology of ancient Greece, it's Causes and effects—and the worse than ignorance, infused by our School Pantheons, and the mistaken Zeal of religious Controversy. The connection between the Polytheism, Ethics, and Re-publicanism of Greece: and (as thence deduced) the impossibility and (were it possible) the uselessness of modelling our Poetry, Architecture, Music, etc, on the Remains of the ancients. The *Spirit* of Poetry common to all ages—and to *imitate* the ancients wisely, we should do as they did, that is, embody that Spirit in Forms adapted to all the Circumstances of Time, State of Society, &c.—

Lecture 6. The *human* Causes, which the goodness of Providence directed to the Diffusion of Christianity, and it's temporal Effects, abstracted from all higher and purely theological Views—the Deluge of Nations—the Establishment of Christendom—and the formation of mixt Languages, in which the decomposed Latin became amalgamated in different proportions with the Gothic, Celtic, or Moorish—these collectively were called the *Romance*, & in this sense of the *mixed* as opposed to the simple or homogeneous, I use the word *Romantic*—& not *exclusively* with reference to what we now call *Romances*.

Lecture 7. The characteristics of the Romantic Poetry, and the true Origin of the Romantic Drama in Shakespear—. On the false points of view, from which Shakespear has been regarded as wild, irregular, &c &c—and proofs that a profound Judgement in the *construction* of his Plays is equally his Characteristic, as Genius, and deep Insight into human Nature—or rather that they are the same Power variously applied.

Lecture 8. A philosophical Analysis of Romeo and Juliet, and of Hamlet.

Lecture 9—Macbeth, and Othello.

Lecture 10. Hasty Review of the most important of the other Plays—and the character of Shakespear, as a Poet and as a Dramatic Poet.

Lectures 11 and 12.—Milton's Paradise Lost—

878. *To Mr. Spencer*

Address: Mr Spencer | Surry Institution | Black Friars' Road.
MS. Bodleian Library. Hitherto unpublished.
Postmark: 21 October 1812.

71 Berners St.

[21 October 1812]

Dear Sir

I mentioned to Mr Saumarez, when I had first the pleasure of seeing him, the persons & number, I wished to have admitted. In compliance with your desire I have inclosed the form, I shall adopt: adding only, that I shall introduce myself the members of my own Family that may accompany me, which will not be more than three at the farthest.—Might I request the favor of a single Line from you, to inform me whether Joseph Hardcastle, Esqre. or any of his Family of the same name are Subscribers to the S. I., & whether the Revd. Mr Burder is or is not on the List?—

very respectfully, dear Sir, | Your obliged
S. T. Coleridge

879. *To Josiah Wedgwood*

Address: Josiah Wedgwood, Esqre | Etruria | Staffordshire
MS. Wedgwood Museum. Pub. E. L. G. ii. 87. This letter is in answer to one from Wedgwood, dated 9 November 1812:

Dear Sir

When I joined with my brother Thomas, some years ago, in giving you an annuity of One hundred and fifty pounds it was not likely that I should ever find it inconvenient to continue the payment. My circumstances are now, however, so much changed that the payment of my share of that sum annually diminishes my capital, for my expenses have for some time exceeded my income. I mention this to you with perfect openness, and in the same spirit I add that my continuing the payment will depend upon its appearing that I am bound in honor to do so. I hope you will write to me without reserve on this subject.

I am | Dear Sir | Sincerely yours
Jos. Wedgwood.

[MS. Wedgwood Museum.] See E. L. Griggs, 'Coleridge and the Wedgwood Annuity', *Review of English Studies*, January 1930, p. 6.
Postmark: 3 December 1812.

71, Berners' Street
Oxford Street
1 Decemb[e]r, 1812.

Dear Sir

I should deem myself indeed unworthy of your and your revered Brother's past Munificence,[1] if I had had any other feeling than

---

[1] In his will, dated 13 June 1805, Tom Wedgwood provided for the annual payment of £75, his half of the annuity.

that of Grief from your Letter: or if I looked forward to any other or higher Comfort, than the confident Hope that (if God extend my Life another year) I shall have a claim to an acknowlegement from you, that I have not misemployed my past years, or wasted that Leisure which I have owed to you, and for which I must cease to be before I can cease to feel most grateful.—Permit me to assure you, that had *the Friend* succeeded instead of bringing on me embarrassment & a loss of more than 200£ from the non-payment of the Subscriptions, or had my Lectures done more than merely pay my Board in town, it was my intention to have resigned my claims on your Bounty—and I am sure, that I shall have your good wishes in my behalf, when I tell you that I have had a Play accepted at Drury Lane,[1] which is to come out at Christmas, and of the success of which both Manager, Comm-Men, & actors speak sanguinely. If I succeed in this, it will not only open out a smooth & not dishonorable road to competence, but give me heart & spirits (still more necessary than time) to bring into shape the fruits of 20 years Study & observation.—

Cruelly, I well know, have I been calumniated: & even my faults (the sinking under the sense of which has been itself perhaps one of the greatest) have been attributed to dispositions absolutely opposite to the real ones——and I beseech you, interpret it as a burst of thankfulness & most unfeigned esteem, not of pride, when I declare that to have an annuity settled on me of three times or thrice three times the amount, would not afford me such pleasure, as the restoration of your Esteem & Friendship

for your deeply obliged
S. T. Coleridge

P.S. Since the receipt of your Letter I have been confined by illness, till last Tuesday—with a nervous depression that rendered me incapable of answering it, or rather fearful of trusting myself.[2]—

---

[1] *Remorse* was produced at Drury Lane on 23 Jan. 1813 and ran for twenty nights.

[2] Wedgwood's answer, endorsed Dec. 5—1812, may be given here:

Dear Sir

To hear of any good happening to you will never fail to excite the greatest pleasure in me. I have never ceased to feel most kindly towards you, and I believe I shall always retain the impressions that have been made in me by our former intimacy, of your genius and of your tender and deep feelings. We have however lived so long without meeting, and our pursuits and characters are so dissimilar, that I cannot form a hope that we can again feel towards each other as we have done.

I can assure you with perfect sincerity that I do not believe that any communications have ever been made to me respecting you from a desire of injuring your character in my estimation. It would be unworthy of you

880. *To Henry Crabb Robinson*

Address: H. C. Robinson, Esqre. | J. Collier's Esqre | 56. Hatton Garden | Holborn
MS. Dr. Williams's Lib. Pub. with omis. Diary, Reminiscences, and Correspondence of Henry Crabb Robinson, *ed. Thomas Sadler, 2 vols., 1872, i. 222.*

Monday Morning
7 Decr. 1812.

My dear Sir

Excuse me for again repeating my request to you, to use your best means *as speedily as possible* to procure for me (if possible) the Perusal of Goethe's work on Light & Color.[1] In a thing, I have now on hand, it would be of *very important Service to me.*—At the same time, do not forget Jacobi to Fichte[2]—& whatever other work may have bearings on the Neuere, neueste, und allerneueste Filosofie.— At the same time I will return your Magazines &c.—If Mr Ader[s][3] or any other of your German Friends, would entrust me with the works of Goethe in toto, I would bind myslf to send them back on a given day: & I will tell you my motive for making this request. It is my hope & purpose to devote a certain portion of my Time for the next twelve months to theatrical attempts, & chiefly in the melodrama, or *comic opera* kind—& from Goethe (from what I read of his little Singspiele in the volume, which *you* lent me) I expect no trifling assistance—especially, in the songs, airs, &c & the happy mode of introducing them. If one knew a German, at once musical & literary, in all probability he might point out some mode of procuring the music, by Schulz,[4] & others. In my frequent conversations with Whitaker (a composer, & music-seller) I could not find, that he, or the music sellers in general, had any knowlege of those compositions, which are so deservedly dear to the German Public. —Be so good, as not to mention the above to any one. As soon as I can disembarrass myself, I shall make one sturdy effort to understand music myself—so far at least [of] the *science*, as goes to the

& of myself to conceal that I have heard circumstances of your habits which have given me pain with a reference to their effects on your activity & happiness, but they have been called forth by my inquiries & have been told with the delicacy & respect due to you.

Accept my warmest wishes for your welfare and particularly for the success of your play—[MS. Wedgwood Museum.]

1 J. W. von Goethe, *Zur Farbenlehre*, 1810.

2 Friedrich H. Jacobi, *Jacobi an Fichte*, 1799.

3 Charles Aders, a German merchant in London. He and his wife Eliza, the daughter of John Raphael Smith, engraver and painter, became Coleridge's intimate friends.

4 J. A. P. Schulz (1747–1800), German composer, noted for his folk-songs.

composi[tion of a] simple air. For I seem frequently to form such in my own mind, to my inner ear.

When you write to Bury, do not omit to assure Mrs C. of my never altered & unalterable Esteem & Affection.

S. T. Coleridge

881. *To William Wordsworth*

Address: W. Wordsworth, Esqre. | Grasmere | Ambleside | Kendal | Westmoreland
MS. Dove Cottage. Pub. with omis. Letters, *ii. 599.* The occasion for this letter was the death of Thomas Wordsworth on 1 December 1812.
Postmark: 7 December 1812.

71, Berners' Street.

Monday Noon, 7 Decr. 1812

Write? My dearest Friend! O that it were in my power to be with you myself instead of my Letter. The Lectures I could give up; but the Rehearsal of my Play commences this week—& upon this depends my best Hopes of leaving Town after Christmas & living among you as long as I live.[1]—Strange, strange are the Coincidences of Things! Yesterday Martha Fricker dined here— and after Tea I had asked question after question respecting your children, first one, then the other; but more than all, concerning Thomas—till at length Mrs Morgan said, What ails you, Coleridge?

[1] It is clear from Mrs. Clarkson's letters to Crabb Robinson that both Words- worth and Dorothy wrote to Coleridge 'that nothing would do W—— so much good as his company & conversation'. In Jan. 1813 Dorothy said she thought of Coleridge with her 'wonted affection' and was 'confident' he would come to Grasmere 'if his play succeeds'. Later she complained to Mrs. Clarkson that he had sent Southey rather than themselves the first copy of *Remorse*; and while she was hoping for his arrival at Grasmere, she received from Keswick the 'cutting intelligence' of his proposed excursion with Morgan to the seaside. The Wordsworths failed to recognize that the quarrel had completely altered Coleridge's feelings towards them. In a moment of spontaneous grief over the death of Thomas Wordsworth, Coleridge did regret that it was not in his power to be with the Wordsworths, but afterwards he could not bring himself to make the journey. By April 1813 Dorothy seems to have accepted the situation: 'I do not now wish him to come into the North; that is, I do not wish him to do it for the sake of any wish to gratify us. But if he should do it of himself I should be glad as the best sign that he was endeavouring to perform his duties.' Even Mrs. Clarkson gave up trying to force Coleridge to go to the Wordsworths: 'After all I do incline to think with M. L[amb] that there is some thing amongst them which makes it perhaps better that they should not meet just now—I am however quite sure that nothing like indifference towards him exists on their part. And also that it rests with him entirely to recover all that he has lost in their hearts—' Coleridge was never to return to Grasmere again. *The Correspondence of Henry Crabb Robinson with the Wordsworth Circle*, ed. Edith J. Morley, 2 vols., 1927, i. 71–75; *Middle Years*, ii. 536 and 556–7; and Letters 888 and 891.

Why don't you talk about Hartley, Derwent, & Sara? And not two hours ago (for the whole Family were late from bed) I was asked what was the matter with my eyes?—I told the fact—that I had awoke three times during the Night & Morning, & at each time found my face & part of the pillow wet with Tears—'Were you dreaming of the Wordsworths?' she asked.—Of the children? —I said, No! not so much of them—but of Mrs W. & Miss Hutchinson, & yourself & Sister—.

Mrs Morgan and her Sister are come in—& I have been relieved by Tears. The sharp, sharp Pang at the heart needed it, when they reminded me of my words the very yester night—'It is not possible, that I should do other than love Wordsworth's children, all of them; but Tom is nearest my heart—I so often have him before my eyes sitting on the little stool by my side, while I was writing my Essays—& how quiet & happy the affectionate little fellow would be, if he could but touch me, & now and then be looked at!'—

O dearest Friend! what comfort can I afford you? What comfort ought I not to afford, who have given you so much pain?— Sympathy deep, of my whole being, & a necessity of my Being— that, so help me God at my last hour! has never been other than what it is, substantially! In Grief, and in joy, in the anguish of perplexity & in the fullness & overflow of Confidence, it has been ever what it is.—There is a sense of the word, Love, in which I never felt it but to you & one of your Household—! I am distant from you some hundred miles, but glad I am, that I am no longer distant in spirit, & have faith, that as it has happened *but once*, so it never can happen again. An aweful Truth it seems to me, & prophetic of our future, as well as declarative of our present *real*, nature, that one mere Thought, one feeling of Suspicion or Jealousy or resentment can remove two human Beings farther from each other, than winds or seas can separate their Bodies.

The words '*religious* fortitude' occasion me to add, that my Faith in our progressive nature, and in all the *doctrinal* parts of Christianity is become habitual in my understanding no less than in my feelings. More cheering illustrations of our survival I have never received, than from a recent Study of the *instincts* of animals, their clear heterogeneity from the reason & moral essence of Man, & yet the beautiful analogy.—Especially, on the death of Children, & of the *mind* in childhood, altogether, many thoughts have accumulated—from which I hope to derive consolation from that most oppressive feeling, which hurries in upon the first anguish of such Tidings, as I have received—the sense of uncertainty, the fear in enjoyment, the pale & deathy Gleam thrown over the countenances of the Living, whom we love—As I saw bef[ore] me the dear little Boy in his Coffin, it *dim*[*med*?] (suddenly & wholly involuntarily & without any conscious connection of Thought preceding) & I beheld Derwent lying beside him!—

But this is bad comforting. Your own virtues, your own Love itself, must give it.—

Mr De Quincey has left Town, & will by this time have arrived at Grasmere. On Sunday last I gave him a Letter for you; but he (I have heard) did not leave town till Thursday Night, by what accidents prevented, I know not. In the oppression of Spirits, under which I wrote that Letter, I did not make it clear, that it was only Mr Josiah's Half of the annuity that was withdrawn from me.— —My answer, of course, breathed nothing but gratitude for the Past.

I will write in a few days again to you. Tomorrow is my Lecture night, 'on the *human* causes of the spread of Christianity, & it's effects after the establishment of Christendom.'—

Dear Mary! dear Dorothy! dearest Sarah!—O be assured, no thought relative to myself has half the influence in inspiring the wish & effort to *appear* & to *act* what I always in my will & heart have been, as the knowlege that few things could more console you than to see me healthy & worthy of myself!—Again & again, my dearest Wordsworth!!

I am affectionately, & truly your
S. T. Coleridge

882. *To Elton Hamond*[1]

MS. Dr. Williams's Lib. Hitherto unpublished.

71 Berners' Street.
Tuesday 8 Decr 1812

Dear Sir

When I remind you, that Tuesday Nights are my Lecture Nights (& I am then at the Surry Institution from $\frac{1}{2}$ past 6 to $\frac{1}{2}$ past 8) I have only to express my regret at the loss of so pleasant a Day, as I might without compliment & with little risk of Disappointment have anticipated. Imagine a rigid Catholic, yet of keen appetite, & happy mixture of the Gourmand & the Epicure, invited to Turtle and Venison, on a good Friday, and you will have formed no bad notion of the feeling, which your kind Invitation & the names with which it was sauced, impressed on, dear Sir,

Your obliged
S. T. Coleridge

[1] This letter is endorsed by Crabb Robinson: 'Coleridge to E. Hamond.

883. *To Daniel Stuart*

Address: D. Stuart, Esqre. | 36. | Brompton Row
MS. British Museum. Pub. with omis. Letters from the Lake Poets, *216.*
Postmark: 22 December 1812.

Tuesday Morning [22 December 1812]
My dear Stuart

This is my Lecture Day, or I would immediately peruse the work inclosed to me & write or call on Mr Owen.[1] Excepting Tuesday, any day convenient to yourself & Mr Owen, Mr Morgan & myself will be happy to dine with you—only be so good, as to let me know it a day or two before.

You have heard that my Play is in Rehearsal—I find the alterations & alterations rather a tedious business, & I am sure, could compose a new act more easily & in shorter Time than add a single Speech of ten lines.—The Managers are more sanguine far than I am: & the actors & actresses with exception of Miss Smith are pleased & gratified with their Parts. And truly Miss Smith's Part is not appropriate to her Talents, in *kind* at least—& I am labouring with much vexation & little success to make it better. She was offered a part that would have suited her admirably, but (I know not from what motive) refused it.

God bless you & your | obliged & ever affectionate
S. T. Coleridge

Will Wednesday, next week, be agreeable to you?

You remember that for many years a Courier has been sent to Keswick, as a compliment to myself, Southey, and Wordsworth, [of] which we all of us feel the kindness—I have this moment received a letter from Mrs Coleridge with these words—N.B. We observe a different name in the Courier: are you sure that the new Proprietor knows upon what terms? Should you not ascertain this, lest it should be charged hereafter? I am very anxious.

Be so good as to let me know whether Mrs C's anxiety has any foundation. Poor woman! she is sadly out of heart, in consequence of Mr Josiah Wedgewood having withdrawn his share of the annuity settled on me, as far as written promise & assurance could without Law settle. I feel my mind rather lightened—& am glad that I can now enjoy the sensation of sincere gratitude towards him for the Past, & most unfeigned esteem & Affection, without the weight that every year seemed to accumulate upon it.

[1] Presumably Coleridge had an advance copy of Robert Owen's *A New View of Society,* 1813. Little is known of Coleridge's association with Owen, the social reformer (1771–1858), but there is in private possession a copy of *Remorse* inscribed by Coleridge, 'R. Owen Esq., from his sincere admirer, S. T. Coleridge'.

884. *To Miss Smith*[1]

Address: Miss Smith with Mr Coleridge's respects
MS. New York Public Lib. Pub. E. L. G. ii. 90.

Thursday Night—[21 January 1813][2]
Dear Madam

If composition had been an Act wholly in the power of the Will,
you should not have been made uneasy at the Delay of the Epilogue[3]—Here it is, such as it is—I had meant to have added ten or
12 more lines; but as they are somewhat unlicked, & I feared that
it may be already too long, I have not stayed to polish them—You
shall see them tomorrow, & adopt or not as you like—

With sincere respect | dear Madam | Your obliged
S. T. Coleridge

885. *To John Rickman*

Address: J. Rickman, Esqre | &c &c | Old Palace Yard | Westminster
MS. Huntington Lib. Pub. with omis. John Rickman, *164.*
Postmark: 26 January 1813.

Monday Night, 25 Janry. 1813.
My dear Sir

Having stayed at home this Evening from that persecuting
Stomach & Bowel Faintness of mine, and alone too (a delightful
Feeling now & then, even when those, who are for a few Hours
absent, are dearly loved) for Morgan, and the Women, both Par-
lourty and Kitchenty, are at the Theatre, I have time to thank
you for your kind Gratulation, & still more for your remarks, the
greater part of which coincided with my own previous judgments,
and the rest produced instant conviction. All were acted upon this
morning, except that I could not persuade either actor or Manager
to give up Isidore's Description of Alvar's Cottage & the Dell[4]—
and in truth it was somewhat odd, as the world goes, to have the
Writer pleading strenuously for more & more excisions, and the
Actors (& in one or two instances the Manager) arguing for their
retention. Indeed it has been so far from escaping Notice, that

---

[1] Miss Smith acted the part of Donna Teresa in *Remorse*.
[2] Coleridge's Epilogue to *Remorse* was probably transmitted with this letter
just before the play opened on 23 Jan. 1813.
[3] The Epilogue, which was spoken by Miss Smith, was printed in the *Morning
Chronicle* on 28 Jan. 1813 but was not included by Coleridge in any edition
of *Remorse*. See *Poems*, ii. 817–18, and Wise, *Bibliography*, 89.
[4] *Remorse*, Act II, scene i, lines 170–81.

Arnold[1] & Raymond, I hear, have given me the name of '*the Amenable Author*'. But then with Sir Fretful Plagiary in the Critic 'I will print every word of it': tho' that is not true either, for many of the Omissions have improved the piece no less as a dramatic Poem than as an acting Tragedy.

By the bye, that most beastly Assassination of Ordonio by the Moor, that lowest Depth of the μισητέον,[2] was so far from being a deed of mine, that I saw it perpetrated for the first time on Saturday Night. I absolutely had the Hiss half way out of my Lips & retracted it, as I have seen a costive Dog *introsuscept* his *White Greek*. It is, perhaps, almost the only case in which scenic Life is the same as real Life—We can as little endure the *imitation* of absolute *Baseness*, as we can it's reality. It is now altered, or rather *re*formed to my original purpose—& so as to obviate your very just Objection to Alhadra's *Sneak-exit.*—After the words—'those little ones will crowd around and ask me—Where is our Father ? I shall curse thee then!' the cry of rescue! Alvar! Alvar! and the Voice of Valdez is heard from behind the Scenes—and Alhadra with those words—

<blockquote>
Ha! a rescue!—and Isidore unrevenged!
The deed be mine! (stabs Ordonio)
       Now take *my* Life!
</blockquote>

  Alvar.
<blockquote>
Arm of avenging Heaven!
</blockquote>

        &c &c[3]—

I had never once attended the Rehearsal of the last Act, the bowel-griping Cold from the Stage Floor & Weariness from cutting Blocks with a Razor having always sent me packing homeward, before the conclusion of the Fourth. They attempted to justify it by the Death of Coriolanus; but in the first place Shakespear is borne out by the *historical Fact*, in the second place, the Mode of the Murder (in Shakespear at least, for I never saw it acted) is quite different; & lastly, in Morgan's Copy of Shakespear's Works I had some three weeks ago in a note expressed my incapability of explaining the character of Titus [Tullus] Aufidius consistently with the re-creating psychologic (if not omni-, yet) hominiscience of '*the Myriad-minded*' Bard.

This, my only word in it, puts me in mind of the Prologue, of which I have yet nothing to say in addition to *your* remarks. I am a miserable Coward when Pain is to be given—& hesitated & hesitated, till (had I even plucked up Fortitude enough to have declined it) I had no longer time to substitute a better.[4]—It is hard

---

[1] Samuel James Arnold (1774–1852), dramatist and manager of Drury Lane.
[2] Underlined once in MS.   [3] *Remorse*, Act V, scene i, lines 247–55.
[4] The Prologue was written by Charles Lamb. See *Poems*, ii. 816–17.

to say which was worse, Prologue or Epilogue, videlicet, *as* Prologue
& Epilogue to this particular Tragedy—only the Prologue, because
it was *Pro* did harm, & the *Epi* no good—. However, I shall begin
to brave Nemesis by a full Joy, if all go off as well to night as it did
on Saturday—With best respects to Mrs Rickman & to your Sister
I am,

My dear Sir, | with unfeigned Esteem & Regard | Your obliged
S. T. Coleridge

P.S.—If it would amuse Mrs & Miss R—or you deem it right to let
little Anne see the Pantomime at so early an age—I have half a
dozen Box Tickets at their Service for any day of this or the next
week, should 'the Remorse' run so long.—I have not yet read what
the *remorseless* Critics of the 'ano-abstersurae Chartae' (more often
defiled than f[iled]) say of the Play; but I hear that Hazlitt i[n the]
M.C. has sneered at my presumption in [entering] the Lists with
Shakespear's Hamlet in Teresa's Description of the two Brothers:
when (so help me the Muses) that Passage never once occurred to
my conscious recollection, however it may, unknown to myself,
have been the working Idea within me. But mercy on us! is there
no such thing as two men's having similar Thoughts on similar
Occasions—? To all Poetry primaeval Revelation, as I have sometimes laughingly asserted of good Jests, that the very same, mutatis
paraphernalibus, are to be found in all Languages, & were revealed
for the amusement of Noah & his Household during their year-long
See-saw on the 5 mile deep Inundation, which accounts for every
phaenomenon in Geology, only not for that miraculous Olive Tree,
the Leaf from which the tame Pigeon (Pigeon or Raven?) brought
back to the Jewish Ogyges.—This woundy long Letter will, I fear,
remind you of another over copious Correspondent—but it is one
advantage (Postage out of the Question) that Letters have over
Conversation—that a Man may shut his Eyes, but has no Ear-lids,
& may burn an Epistle, when neither to that or to other more
economic uses, he would or could employ a Talker.—

886. *To Mrs. S. T. Coleridge*

Address: Mrs Coleridge | Greta Hall | Keswick | Cumberland *Single*
MS. Lord Latymer. Pub. with omis. Letters, *ii. 602.*
Postmark: 27 January 1813.

Wednesday afternoon [27 January 1813]
My dear Sara

Hitherto the Remorse has met with *unexampled* APPLAUSE—but
whether it will *continue* to fill the *House*, that is quite another

Question—and of this my Friends are, in my opinion, far, far too sanguine. I have disposed not of the Copy right but of Edition by Edition to Mr Pople, on terms advantageous to me as an Author, & honorable to him as a Publisher—The expences of Printing, & Paper (at the *Trade Price*), advertising &c are to be deducted from the total Produce—& the net profits to be divided into three equal parts, of which Pople is to have one, and I the other two. And at any future time, I may publish it in any volume of my Poems *collectively*. Mr Arnold (the manager) has just left me—he called to urge me to exert myself a little with regard to the Daily Press, & brought with him the Times of Monday, as a specimen of the *infernal Lies* of which a Newspaper Scribe can be capable. Not only is not *one* sentence in it true; but every one is in the direct face of a palpable Truth. The misrepresentations must have been wilful. I must now therefore write to the Times—& if Walter refuses to insert, I will then recording this circumstance publish it in the M. Post, M. Chron. & the Courier. The dirty malice of Antony Pasquin[1] in the M. Herald is below Notice.—This, however, will explain to you why the shortness of this Letter—the main business of which is to desire you to draw upon Brent & Co, No. 103, Bishopsgate Street, within—for an 100£ at a month's date from the Drawing, or if that be objected to, for three weeks—only let me know which. In the course of a month I have no hesitation in promising you another 100£—& I hope likewise before Midsummer, if God grant me Life, to repay you whatever you have expended for the Children. My Wishes & Purposes concerning Hartley & Derwent I will communicate as soon as this Bustle, & endless Rat a Tat Tat at our Door, is somewhat over. I concluded my Lectures last night most triumphantly, with loud, long, & enthusiastic applauses at my Entrance, & ditto in yet fuller Chorus as and for some minutes after, I had retired. It was lucky, that (as I never once thought of the Lecture, till I had entered the Lecture Box) the two last were the most impressive, and really the best. I suppose, that no dramatic Author ever had so large a number of unsolicited, unknown, yet *predetermined* Plauditors in the Theatre, as I had on Saturday Night. One of the malignant Papers asserted, that I had collected all the *Saints* from Mile End Turnpike to Tyburn Bar. With so many warm Friends it is impossible in the present state of human Nature, that I should not have many unprovoked & unknown Enemies.—You will have heard, that on my entering the Box on

---

[1] Anthony Pasquin was the pseudonym of John Williams (1761–1818), a satirist who immigrated to the United States not long after losing a suit for libel against Robert Faulder in 1797. Coleridge apparently used the name to denote a scurrilous critic.

Saturday Night I was discovered by the Pit—& that they all turned their faces towards our Box, & gave a treble chear of Claps. I mention these things, because it will please Southey to hear that there is a large number of Persons in London, who hail with enthusiasm any prospect of the Stage's being purified & rendered classical. My success, *if* I succeed (of which, I assure you, I entertain doubts in my opinion well-founded, both from the want of a prominent Actor for Ordonio, & from the want of vulgar Pathos in the Play itself—nay, there is not enough even of *true* dramatic Pathos) but if I succeed, I succeed for others as well as for myself.—

I have just left Martha [Fricker]—All in my power I will do, tho' even the compliment of asking my advice was not paid me previously to her *apparently full settlement* in London—More I will not say—because I could not write sincerely (and otherwise I never will write to *you*) without giving offence & pain. She is a very deserving Woman: and it would be well in you to express to Mrs Morgan your sense of their kindness & hospitable—nay, friendly—attentions to her—attentions wholly originating in themselves.—With Love to all, I am

dear Sara, your anxiously affectionate
S. T. Coleridge.

P.S. I *pray you*, my dear Sara! do take on yourself the charge of instantly sending off by the Waggon Mr Sotheby's Folio Edition of all Petrarch's Works, which I left at Grasmere. I am ashamed to meet Sotheby till I have returned it.—At the same time, my Quarto MSS. Book, with the German Musical Play[1] in it, & the two Folio Volumes of the Greek Poets may go. For I want them hourly—& I must try to *imitate* W. Scott (who has set me the example in a less honorable way, in contempt of the 8th commandment)[2] in making Hay while the Sun shines.

Kisses & heart-felt Loves for my sweet Sara—& scarce less for dear little Herbert, & Edith.—

[1] This 'Quarto MSS. Book' is now in the Huntington Library. It contains Coleridge's transcript of A. F. X. S. Sailer's *Adams und Evens Erschaffung und ihr Sündenfall. Ein geistlich Fastnachtspiel mit Sang und Klang: aus dem Schwäbischen in's Oesterreichische versetzt*, 1783. On the last page of the copy Coleridge wrote, 'Transcribed June 17, 1799'. A second reference to this notebook in Letter 895 shows that Mrs. Coleridge sent it to London.

While in Helmstedt Coleridge also transcribed another play, Hans Sachs's *Die ungleichen Kinder Eve*. See *Shakespearean Criticism*, i. 192–3, and ii. 8.

[2] E. H. Coleridge omits the clause in parentheses. See Letter 808 in which Coleridge refers to the 'peccadillos against the 8th Commandment' in *The Lady of the Lake* and to 'Old Allan' as 'a miserable copy of Bracy the Bard'.

887. *To Robert Southey*

Address: R. Southey, Esqre | Greta Hall | Keswick | Cumberland
MS. Lord Latymer. Pub. with omis. Letters, *ii. 605.*
Postmark: 9 February 1813.

Tuesday, 8 [9] Feby. 1813.   71, Berners' St

My dear Southey

It is seldom, that a man can with *literal truth* apologize for Delay in writing; but for the last 3 weeks I have had more upon my hands & spirits, than my Health was equal to. I have read somewhere or other, of a punishment in Arabia, in which the Culprit was so bricked up, that he could neither turn his eyes to the Right or Left, while in front was placed a large Heap of barren glittering Sand. Some faint analogy of this I have suffered, from the mere unusualness of having my attention forcibly directed to one Object, which precluded both sequence of Imagery and Trains of Thought—. Then the endless Rat a Tat Tat at our black & blue bruised Door— & *my* two Master-Fiends, Letters and Proof Sheets, to which indeed I must add a third, their Compeer—invitations to large Dinners, which I cannot refuse without giving offence, yet never accept without vexation & involuntary bad humour the morning before, & stomach & bowel disturbance the day after.—

The first Copy, I can procure of the Second Edition,[1] I will do my best to get franked for you. You will, I hope, think it much improved, at least as a Poem. Dr Bell, who is all kindness & goodness, came to me in no small Bustle this morning in consequence of 'a censure passed on the Remorse by a man of great Talents, both in verse & prose, who was impartial & thought highly of the Work on the whole'—What was it, think you?—There were many very unequal *Lines* in the Play; but which he did not choose to specify. Dr Bell would not mention the Critic's name; but was very earnest with me to procure some indifferent Person of good sense to read it over, by way of spectacles to an Author's own dim Judgement— Soon after he left me, I discovered that this Critic was Gifford,[2] who had said good-naturedly, that I ought to be whipt for leaving so many weak & slovenly Lines in so fine a Poem.—What the Lines were, *he* would not say—& *I* do not care. Inequalities every Poem, even an Epic, much more a Dramatic Poem, must have & ought to have—the question is, are they in their own place *Dissonances?* If so, I am the last man to stickle for them, who am nicknamed in the Green Room the anomalous Author, from my utter indifference or prompt facility in sanctioning every omission that was suggested.

---

[1] W. Pople issued three editions of *Remorse* in 1813.

[2] William Gifford (1756–1826), first editor of the *Quarterly Review*.

That §§ in the Quarterly Review respecting me as ridiculed in the Rejected Addresses,[1] was surely unworthy a man of sense like Gifford. What reason could *he* have had to suppose me a man so childishly irritable as to be provoked by a trifle so contemptible? If he had never read my Works, how could he justify his applause of the Parody? If he had, how could he think it a *Parody* at all?[2] But the noise, which the 'Rejected Addresses' made, the notice taken of Smith, the Author, by Lords Holland, Byron, &c, give a melancholy confirmation of my assertion in the Friend—that we worship the vilest reptile, if only the brainless Head be expiated by the sting of personal Malignity in the Tail.—I wish, I could procure for you the Examiner, & Drakard's London Paper—they did not dare go as far as *the Times*—for that was one *big Lie* which the Public cried out against—they were force[d] to affect admiration of the Tragedy—but yet abuse me they must—& so comes the old infamous Crambe bis millies cocta of the 'sentimentalities, puerilities, whinings, and meannesses (both of style & thought)' in my former Writings—but without (which is worth notice both in these Gentlemen, & in all our former Zoili), without one single Quotation or Reference in proof or exemplification—No wonder!—for excepting the 3 Graves, which was announced as not meant for Poetry, and the Poem on the Tethered ass, with the motto, Sermoni propriora[3]—& like your Dancing Bear—which might be called a ludicro-splenetic Copy of Verses, with the diction purposely appropriate, they might (as at the first appearance of my Poems they did) find indeed all the opposite vices; but if it had not been for *the Preface* to W's Lyrical Ballads would themselves have never dreamt of affected Simplicity & Meanness of Thought & Diction—. This Slang has gone on for 14 or 15 years, against us—& really deserves to be exposed.

As far as my Judgement goes, the two best Qualities of the Tragedy are: First, the simplicity and Unity of the Plot, in respect of that which of all the Unities is the only one founded on good sense, the presence of a one all-pervading, all-combining, Principle.—By REMORSE I mean the Anguish & Disquietude arising from the Self-contradiction introduced into the Soul by Guilt—a

---

[1] *Rejected Addresses: or the New Theatrum Poetarum*, parodies by James and Horace Smith, was published anonymously in 1812. The contribution attributed to S. T. C. is entitled *Playhouse Musings*.

[2] The passage in the *Quarterly Review* reads: 'Mr. Colridge will not, we fear, be as much entertained as we were with his "Playhouse Musings", which begin with characteristic pathos and simplicity, and put us much in mind of the affecting story of old Poulter's mare.' *Quarterly Review*, Sept. 1812, p. 180.

[3] An error; 'Sermoni propriora' in 1797 formed the motto to *Reflections on having left a Place of Retirement*. Cf. *Biog. Lit.* i. 17 and n. and Letter 459, p. 864.

feeling, which is good or bad according as the Will makes use of it. This is exprest in the lines chosen as the Motto[1]—& Remorse is every where distinguished from virtuous Penitence.—To excite a sanative Remorse Alvar returns—the Passion is put in motion at Ordonio's first entrance by the appearance of Isidore's Wife &c—it is carried still higher by the narration of Isidore, 1 S. 2 A: higher still by the Interview with the supposed Wizard: & to it's ἀκμή by the Incantation Scene & Picture—. Now then we are to see it's effects & to exemplify the second part of the Motto—'but if proud & gloomy, It [is a] poison-tree' &c. Ordonio too proud to look steadily into hi[msel]f catches a false scent, plans the murder of Isidore & the Poisoning of the Sorcerer, perpetrates the one, & attempting the other is driven by Remorse & the discovery of Alvar to a temporary Distraction, & finally falling a victim to the only crime, that had been realized, by the hand of Alhadra, breathes his last in a Pang of Pride—'O could'st thou forget me!'[2] As from a circumference to a centre, every Ray in the Tragedy converges to Ordonio.—Spite of wretched Acting the Passage told wonderfully, in which as in a struggle between two unequal Panathlists or Wrestlers, the weaker had for a moment got uppermost—& Ordonio with unfeigned Love & genuine repentance, says—I will kneel to thee, my Brother! Forgive me, Alvar!—till the Pride, like the Bottom-swell on our Lake, *gusts* up again in—*Curse* me with Forgiveness.[3]—

The second Good quality is, I think, the variety of metres, according as the Speeches are merely transitive; or narrative; or passionate; or (as in the Incantation) deliberate & formal Poetry. It is true, they are all or most Iambic Blank Verse; but under that form there are 5 or 6 perfectly distinct metres.—As to the outcry, that the Remorse is not pathetic (meaning such pathos, as convulses us in Isabella or the Gamester) the answer is easy—True! the Poet never meant, that it should be. It is as pathetic as the Hamlet, or the Julius Caesar.—He woo'd the feelings of the Audience, as my wretched Epilogue said—

> With no *too real* Woes that make you groan
> O'er home-bred kindred Griefs, perhaps your own;
> Yet with no Image compensate the Mind,
> Nor leave 'one Joy for Memory' behind.—

[1] The motto, which was taken from Act I, scene i, lines 20–24, reads:
> Remorse is as the heart, in which it grows:
> If that be gentle, it drops balmy dews
> Of true repentance; but if proud and gloomy,
> It is a poison-tree, that pierced to the inmost
> Weeps only tears of poison!

[2] Act V, scene i, line 264.   [3] Act V, scene i, lines 213–14.

As to my Thefts from the Wallenstein,[1] they were on compulsion
from the necessity of Haste—& do not lie heavy on my Conscience,
being partly thefts from myself, & because I gave Schiller 20 for
one I have taken. I shall, however, weed them out as soon as I
can: & in the mean time, I hope, they will lie snug.—'*The obscurest*
Haunt of all our Mountains'[2] I did not recognize as Wordsworth
till after the Play was all printed. I must write again tomorrow on
another Subject—Martha—who, I assure Mrs C., has neither
shewn Peevishness nor any other unamiable Quality since she has
been in Town—With Love to all, till tomorrow—

S. T. C.

The House was crowded again last night: & the Manager told
me, that they lost 200£ by [susp]ending it on Saturday Night, tho'
Jack Bannister came out.

888. *To Thomas Poole*

Address: T. Poole, Esqre | Nether Stowey | near Bridgewater | Somerset—
MS. British Museum. Pub. with omis. Letters, *ii. 609.*
Postmark: 13 February 1813.

71 Berners' St
Oxford St
[13 February 1813]

Dear Poole

Love so deep & so domesticated with the whole Being, as mine
was to you, can never cease *to be*—. To quote the best & sweetest
Lines, I ever wrote—

Alas! they had been Friends in Youth!
But whisp'ring Tongues can poison Truth;
And Constancy lives in Realms above;
And Life is thorny; & Youth is vain;
And to be wrath with one, we love,
Doth work, like Madness, in the Brain!
And so it chanc'd (as I divine)
With Roland & Sir Leoline.
Each spake words of high Disdain
And Insult to his Heart's best Brother—
They parted—ne'er to meet again!
But never either found another

---

[1] For the borrowings from *Wallenstein* see Campbell, *Poetical Works*, 650–1.
[2] Act I, scene i, lines 116–17, and *The Brothers*, line 140, 'It is the lone-
liest place of all these hills'.

(435)

> To free the hollow Heart from Paining—
> They stood aloof, the Scars remaining,
> Like Cliffs, which had been rent asunder—
> A dreary Sea now flows between!
> But neither Frost, nor Heat, nor Thunder,
> Shall wholly do away, I ween,
> The marks of that, which once hath been!'[1]—

Stung as I have been with your unkindness to me, in my sore Adversity, yet the receipt of your two heart-engendered Lines was sweeter than an unexpected Strain of sweetest Music—or in humbler phrase, it was the only pleasurable sensation which the Success of the Remorse has given me—. I have read of, or perhaps only imagined, a punishment in Arabia, in which the Culprit was so bricked up, as to be unable to turn his eyes to the Right or to the Left: while in front was placed a high heap of barren Sand glittering under the vertical Sun—Some slight analogue of this I have myself suffered, from the mere unusualness of having my attention forcibly directed to a Subject, which permitted neither sequence of Imagery, or series of Reasoning. No Grocer's Apprentice, after his first Month's permitted Riot, was ever sicker of Figs & Raisins than I of hearing about THE REMORSE.—The endless Rat a Tat Tat at our black- & blue-bruised Door— & my three Master-fiends, Proof-Sheets, Letters (for I have a raging Epistolophobia) & worse than these, invitations to large Dinners, which I cannot refuse without offence & imputation of Pride, or accept without disturbance of Temper the day before, & a sick aching Stomach with disordered Bowels for two days after—so that my Spirits quite sink under it.— I have never seen the Play since the first Night—from what I myself saw, and from what an intelligent Friend, more solicitous about it than myself, has told me—the Remorse has succeeded in spite of bad Scenes, execrable Acting, & Newspaper Calumny. In my compliments to the Actors I endeavored (such is the lot of this World, in which our best Qualities tilt against each other, ex. gr. our good Nature against our Veracity) to make a Lie edge round the Truth as nearly as possible[2]—Poor Rae[3] (why poor? for Ordonio has almost made his fortune) did the best in his power—& is a good man— . . .[4] & is an honest man, a moral, & affectionate Husband & Father—But Nature has denied him Person, & all volume & depth of Voice—so that the blundering Coxcomb, Elliston,[5] by mere

---

[1] *Christabel*, lines 408–26.
[2] See the Preface to *Remorse*.
[3] Alexander Rae (1782–1820), who acted the role of Ordonio.
[4] MS. blurred; several words illegible.
[5] Robert W. Elliston (1774–1831), who played the part of Alvar.

dint of Voice & Self-conceit out-dazzled him—It has been a good thing for the Theatre—They will get 8 or 10,000£—& I shall get more than all my literary Labors put together, nay, thrice as much, subtracting my heavy Losses in the Watchman & the Friend— 400£: including the Copy-right.—

You will have heard that previous to the acceptance of Remorse Mr Jos. Wedgewood had withdrawn from me his share of the Annuity! Well—yes, it is well!—for I can now be *sure*, that I loved him, revered him, & was grateful to him from no selfish Feeling. For equally (& may these Words be my final Condemnation at the last aweful Day, if I speak not the whole Truth), equally do I at this moment love him, and with the same reverential Gratitude! To Mr Thomas Wedgewood I felt, doubtless, Love; but it was mingled with Fear, & constant Apprehension of his too exquisite Taste in morals—But Josiah—O I ever did, & ever shall, love him, as a Being so beautifully balanced in mind & heart, deserves to be.— 'Tis well too—because it has given me the strongest impulse, the most imperious Motive, I ever experienced, to *prove* to him that his past Munificence has not been *wasted*!

You, perhaps, may likewise have heard (*in this Whispering-Gallery of* [*the*] *World*) of the year-long Difference between me & Wordsworth—compared with the sufferings of which all former Afflictions of my Life were less than Flea-bites—occasioned *in great part* by the wicked folly of the Arch-fool Montague— . . .[1] A Reconciliation has taken place—but the *Feeling*, which I had previous to that moment, when the ⅔ths Calumny burst like a Thunder-storm from a blue Sky on my Soul—after 15 years of such religious, almost superstitious, Idolatry & Self-sacrifice—O no! no! that I fear, never can return. All outward actions, all inward Wishes, all Thoughts & Admirations, will be the same—*are* the same— but— aye there remains an immedicable *But*.[2] Had W. said (what he acknowleges to have said) to you, I should have thought it unkind, & have had a right to say—Why, why am I, whose whole Being has been like a Glass Bee-hive before you for 15 years, why do I hear this from *a third* Person for the first Time? But to such an

---

[1] Three lines heavily inked out in MS.

[2] Mrs. Coleridge, too, doubted that a genuine reconciliation had been effected: 'I think, I may venture to say, there will never more be *that* between them which was in days of yore—but it has taught C. one useful lesson; that even his dearest & most indulgent friends, even those very persons who have been the great means of his self-indulgence, when he comes to live *wholly* with them, are *as* clear-sighted to his failings, & much *less* delicate in speaking of them, than his Wife, who being the Mother of his children, even if she had not the slightest regard for himself, would naturally feel a reluctance to the exposing of his faults.' *Minnow among Tritons*, ed. Stephen Potter, 1934, pp. 16–17.

acknowleged Wretch, as Montague! to such a Horror of Women, as Mrs M. (a[gain]st whom W. himself had forewarned me)—O! it cut [to the] Heart-core of

S. T. C.—

The first Edition is infamously incorrect—the Second will appear on Monday, & I will try hard to get the first Copy franked to you—

I had not space to speak of T. Wedgewood's farewell Prophecy to me respecting W., which he made me write down, & which no human Eye ever saw—but mine[1]—

889. *To John Rickman*

Address: J. Rickman, Esqre | &c &c | New Palace Yard | Westminster
MS. Huntington Lib. Pub. E. L. G. ii. 89.
Postmark: ⟨16 February⟩ 1813.

Tuesday Morning—[16 February 1813]
My dear Sir

I would give 5£, (and that is a good deal for a Poet, notwithstanding his having got 300£, which has elevated his estate to 0–0 from—0–yx) that the Speaker's Dinner had not pre-engaged you on Saturday—tho' it were but for a fair Chance of prevailing on you to dine with us ¼ before six, on Saturday next. You would meet Caldwell, my earliest College Friend, & a man deservedly loved & esteemed—and what tho' he has been the Tutor, & still is the Friend, of the Marquis of Sligo? Why, it would puzzle an Angel to turn Chick-weed into Wheat: tho' the Marquis himself contrived to turn his lordly *Honor* into Bar(e)-lye—(It won't do—that Pun!) (It looks so ugly upon Paper.)

I expect a second Edition of Remorse tomorrow—which as corrected & augmented I waited for, as better worth your acceptance than the first.—If Southey has any notion of reviewing it in the Quarterly,[2] I should wish him to do it from the second Edition—but I do not know enough of the thing, to ask you to frank a second to him—for should it come near to any thing like an unusual privilege on your part, I need not say, that I should not think of it. But I have some reason to suspect, that Mr Gifford will not permit Southey to review it—for Mockery & abuse are ad libitum delivered

---

[1] For the misgivings of Coleridge's friends concerning his idolatry of Wordsworth see especially Letters 255, 330, 350, and 640 n.

[2] As Coleridge later remarked, the review of *Remorse* in the *Quarterly Review* (April 1814) was 'delayed till it could by no possibility be of the least service to me'. Southey did not write the review. See Letter 951.

up to the Journeymen, but to flatter a friend's Work is a Privilege which the Foreman commonly reserves to himself.—

Should you be able & inclined to drop in in the Evening, on Saturday, I need not say, that it would gratify,

my dear Sir, | Your's with unfeigned respect
S. T. Coleridge

890. *To Mrs. J. J. Morgan*

Address: Mrs Morgan | 71, Berners' Street| Oxford Street | London
MS. Lord Latymer. Hitherto unpublished.
Postmark: 15 March 1813. *Stamped*: Bexhill.

Bex Hill.
Sunday Morning, 14 March 1813.—

My dear Friends

I was sadly afraid of Morgan before we reached the Coach in Fleet Street—he was so dreadfully sick—but the air soon recovered him, and with an unusually pleasant Coach-Company, who all of us collectively & individually declared, we had never passed a more agreeable Day, thro' a sweet Country & delightful Weather, we arrived at Battle at ½ past 4, & found Mr Walker at the Inn Door— but we had found ourselves so hungry at Robertsbridge (the dinner stage, 12 miles from Battle) that we had already dined, off a sirloin of good roast Beef very well drest—boiled Slices of Plum Pudding, & an apple Pie—& I have seldom, if ever, seen Morgan eat so much so heartily, & without the least heaviness or uncomfortable feeling after or since—There was but one Post Chaise, which a Mr Russel, an old man of 70, who has made 10,000£ in the Building Line, one of our Coach Party, had taken before for the Earl of Ashburnham's —It was, however, but 2 miles or a little more, out of our way; & he offered us a share in it. So we paid 10 Shillings additional, (he having payed 9) & had a delightful ride thro' Lord Ashburnham's Grounds & park (layed out by *Capability* Brown) to the great House—returned the same way—& the after five miles, the Dusk coming on, & the road very bad, were the only at-all-unpleasant part of our whole Journey. Walker who had stayed 20 Minutes after us had arrived an hour before us—We were both much pleased with Mrs Walker, who is an agreeable woman at all times, & (Morgan says) a perfect Gentlewoman; & who by Candle Light looked quite beautiful—& reminded me in her face & shape of that Miss Ogle, whom we noticed at Miss Hughes' Concert at Mrs Billington's House—. Little Samuel Henry Walker is a fair fat healthy fellow, very like what Derwent was at 2 years old—certainly, not quite so beautiful, or brilliant—but the very same *Build* of Vessel, & waggles his little Body & Tail in the same way. I shall find him a great amusement.

Morgan bids me remind you of a Bill due on the 18th, of Mr Brent's—Pray, tell Allston that my anxious Wishes go after him where ever I am, & that I hope to hear *Progress reported* & to see it on my return.—We are now going to take a Stroll—. Mr & Mrs Walker send their best remembrances, & Mr W. is rejoiced to hear that there is some Chance of seeing you at Bex Hill—

God bless you both.—I mean to shave infant-smooth the very last Stage, before we reach London.

                                        S. T. Coleridge

891. *To James Kenney*[1]

Address: Mr Kenny   favored by Mrs Morgan
MS. Cornell University Lib. Hitherto unpublished.

                                   [*Circa* 20 March 1813][2]

My dear Sir

I have just returned from the Sea Side, (Bex Hill, 5 miles from Hastings, Sussex) & find that I have at once to congratulate & to thank you. May the Twins prosper, & develope in union the French Wit & the English Humor, with the good Heart, which, thank God! is of no Country & of all Countries.

I need not tell you that I feel myself highly gratified by Mr Harris's[3] Kindness, & even more by the manner of the Bestowal than by the favor bestowed: much as I feel myself obliged for the latter.

I have enclosed a note of acknowlegement, being ignorant of Mr Harris's Address. Should you not be likely to have the opportunity of delivering it to him yourself within a day or two, you will be so good as to add the Initial of his Christian Name, & his address to my Superscription.

I trust, that Mrs Morgan & Miss Brent will bring back good news of all of you: for they will be my Post-man. If two — make a +, why not two pretty Women = one man? An *algebraic* Compliment, for which the Ladies would thank me with a Box on the Ear.—

---

[1] James Kenney (1780–1849), the dramatist, who had married Thomas Holcroft's widow in 1812.

[2] Coleridge and Morgan had returned from Bexhill by 20 Mar. See *Robinson on Books and Their Writers*, i. 124.

[3] Thomas Harris, stage-manager of Covent Garden.

There is a new Comedy to be read for the first time in the Green Room, D.L.T., this morning—By whom written, I know not; by whom to be acted, I do know—& eke the Managers, the Sub & Super Committees of said Theatre, &c, will sooner or later feel. But this is *inter nos.*—

At least 5 Evenings out of 7, I am at home: & should chance or choice lead you our way, Solo or Duality, you will in no slight sort gratify

Your's, my dear Sir, with sincere regard
S. T. Coleridge

My best regards to Mrs Kenny: & as soon as the Twins are nursable by Arms of the masculine gender, I shall be glad to give them a Tossing to diverse Tunes of diverse nursery Lyrics.—

892. *To Daniel Stuart*

Address: D. Stuart, Esqre | Kilburn House | Kilburn.
MS. British Museum. Pub. Letters, *ii. 615.*
Postmark: 25 September 1813.

25 Septr. 1813.

Dear Stuart

I forgot to ask you by what address a Letter would best reach you, whether Kilburne House, Kilburn?—I shall therefore send it to, or leave it at, the Courier Office.—I found Southey so chevaux-de-frized & pallisadoed by pre-engagements that I could not reach at him till Sunday Sennight, i.e. Sunday, October 3— when, if convenient, we should be happy to wait on you. Southey will be in town till Monday Evening, & you have his Brother's Address should you wish to write to him—(Dr S. 28, Little Queen Anne St, Cavendish Square).

A curious §§ in the M. C. of this Morning—asserting with it's usual *comfortable* Anti-patriotism the determination of the Emperor of Austria to persevere in the terms offered to his Son in Law in his frenzy of Power, even tho' he should be beaten to the Dust— Methinks, there ought to be good Authority before a Journalist dares prophecy folly & knavery in union of our Imperial Ally. An excellent article might be written on this Subject. In the same paper there is what I should have called a masterly Essay on the causes of the Downfall of the Comic Drama, if I was not perplexed by the distinct recollection of having myself *conversed* the greater part of it at Lamb's.—I wish, you would read it: & tell me what you think. For I seem to remember a conversation with you, in which you asserted the very contrary—that Comic Genius was the thing wanting, & not Comic Subjects—that the watering Places or rather the characters presented at them, had never been adequately managed—&c—

Might I request you to present my best respects to Mrs Stuart, as those of an old Acquaintance of your's, & as far [as] I am myself conscious of, at all times

with hearty affection | Your sincere Friend
S. T. Coleridge

P.S. There are some half dozen more of Books of mine left at the Courier office—Ben Jonson, & sundry German Volumes—As I am compelled to sell my Library,[1] you would oblige me by ordering the Porter to take them to 19, London Street, Fitzroy Square— whom I will remunerate for his Trouble.—I should not take this Liberty; but that I had in vain written to Mr Street, requesting the same favor—which in his Hurry of Business I do not wonder that he forgot—

893. *To Joseph Porter*

Address: Revd. Joseph Porter | Castle Green | Bristol
MS. Cornell University Lib. Hitherto unpublished. Pages one and two of the manuscript are missing.
Postmark: 15 October 1813.

[15 October 1813]

. . . an 100£ within a week or 10 days at farthest—& then to settle with him as to the security or bill for the remainder. As affairs at present are, I do not hesitate to take on myself to say, that 250£ would settle their affairs: so as to preserve for Miss Brent the unembarrassed Business of Bishopsgate Street, with every favorable presumption of considerable Increase, as soon as it shall be rescued from Lloyd's Tyranny: & the Trade is able to go to Market for itself.[2]

Henceforward the Business will be legally transferred to Charlotte Brent, as the sole Proprietor.—The House in Berners' St *has been* let for a year on advantageous Terms: & the Tenant has no doubt

---

[1] Coleridge evidently pawned rather than sold his books. See Letter 902, in which he asks Charlotte Brent 'to go *to the Depository* . . . [to redeem] 40 Books, Watch, Snuff Box, in for 6£—the Duplicates in the Watch Fob of my old whity-colored Small Clothes—'.

[2] At this time Coleridge devoted much effort and extended considerable financial assistance to Miss Brent and the Morgans. He later said that 'the successive Losses and increasing Distress of poor Morgan and his family while I was domesticated with them—and which being before my eyes, scarcely left me the power of asking myself concerning the Right or Wrong— . . . absorbed and anticipated my resources'. E. L. G. ii. 294.

but that (if Mr M. should not wish to reoccupy it) he shall continue for any number of years settled on.—

You, my dear Sir! will best judge in what manner it will be most convenient to you to realize your friendly offer—I have stated all the main circumstances. As soon as Mrs Morgan's Strength & Spirits make it possible, or rather advisable, she will, I doubt not, convey her own feelings to you in her own words.—Her last Letter from M. brought favorable accounts of his Health.[1]—

Shall we ever, my dear Sir! have the pleasure of meeting in your native & in my adopted, Vales? O believe me, that at Keswick you will find both House-room & Heart-room[2] from my friends, my family, & from

Your's, dear Sir! with affectionate regard & Esteem

S. T. Coleridge.

894. *To Charlotte Brent*

Address: Miss Brent | 19 London Street | Fitzroy Square | London
MS. Lord Latymer. Pub. E. L. G. ii. 91.
Postmark: Bristol, 24 October 1813.

Sunday Afternoon [24 October 1813]
White Hart—

My very dear Friends

I have received your's, & am glad to hear that Mary is better— I will not trouble you with the Detail of my operations, or of the difficulties I have met with, at least not till I can give you middle and end as well as beginning. Suffice it, that I have no doubts of succeeding so far as to secure the B. St Business for the nonce —The proposed Scheme of Lecturing has met with such support, that I have resolved on it—and shall give the first at the White Lion, on Thursday Evening, at 7 o'clock[3]—and hope, I shall be [able to sen]d you within a week . . .[4] account—

---

[1] On 15 Oct. Robinson noted that 'Coleridge's kind friend, Morgan', was 'forced to leave the country by pecuniary difficulties'. Chambers says that 'evidently Morgan was in prison for debt'. Actually Morgan went to Ireland, for in an unpublished letter of 1815 he refers to an Irish family who 'behaved extremely well' to him while he was there. *Robinson on Books and Their Writers*, i. 132, Chambers, *Life*, 260, and MS. letter Coleridge family. See also Letter 902.

[2] As early as 10 Aug. 1813 Dorothy Wordsworth wrote that the Morgans had '*smashed*' and intended 'to settle at K[eswick] for cheapness'. They and Coleridge 'are coming down immediately'. Nothing came of these plans, Coleridge leaving London for Bristol late in Oct. *Middle Years*, ii. 565.

[3] This course of lectures, of which six were on Shakespeare and two on Education, began in Bristol on Thursday, 28 Oct. 1813, and continued on Tuesdays and Thursdays, 2, 4, 9, 11, 16, 18, and 23 Nov. *Shakespearean Criticism*, ii. 252–98.   [4] Half a line cut from MS.

I am pretty well—& have heard an excellent Sermon from Mr
Porter, whose style of reading Prayers however I greatly prefer to
his mode of Preaching, which (like mine) is too uniformly emphatic,
& when he speaks loudest, he is least articulate, i.e. when most
audible, he is least intelligible—. But he is a most respectable
Performer—Dr Small is miraculously recovered—I am ashamed to
say, I have not seen Alston, but his address I learnt from Mr
Morse[1]—viz—5 Richmond Place, Clifton—and that he has sold
both Pictures to Mr Visgar for 160£—Mr King has performed
several operations on him—& it appears, that I was too much in
the Right in fearing it to be an analogous Case to Thomas Wedgewood's—It is a stricture, or thickening of the Colon—but it will
not put a period to his Life, I trust. Indeed, he is very much better
—& out of Pain— . . .[2]

& S. T. Coleridge

895. *To Mrs. J. J. Morgan*

Address: Mrs Morgan | 19, London Street | Fitzroy Square | London
MS. Lord Latymer. Pub. with omis. E. L. G. ii. 92.
Postmark: Bristol, 25 October ⟨1813⟩.

Monday Morning: White Hart, Bristol.
[25 October 1813]

My dear Friends
On Thursday and Friday I dined at Mr Porter's: and spent
Thursday Night in compliment to P. at Mr Wensley's, and Friday
at Porter's & at Half Play, to see the stupid Humbug Elliston's
Dog Gellert, who tho' a better actor than any of the Bipeds did no
more than I would undertake to teach a Poodle in a couple of days.
On Saturday I dined & spent the Evening at Mr Elton's, who has
an amiable Wife, and six [of] the most beautiful Children I ever
saw in my whole Life, i.e. *all together*. One of them is so startlingly
like Sara, only of less flimsy growth, (but the very same eyes with
the very same manner & expression) that (I found) Porter had
often mentioned it to the Mother, herself a bright-eyed Dame. It
was quite curious to see 14 such eyes, all at once, as her's & the
Children's. On Sunday I dined & spent the evening at Mr Clayfield's, York Place—a friend of Tobin's & Sir H. Davy's, & the
gentleman that accompanied Sadler in the Balloon.[3]—To day I

---

[1] Samuel F. B. Morse (1791–1872), artist and inventor of the telegraph,
accompanied Washington Allston to England in 1811.
[2] Half a line cut from MS.
[3] James Sadler, who made his first balloon ascent on 5 May 1785.

am to dine at Kiddle's, tomorrow at Colson's, Wednesday at Mr Hood's—Mr Hood dines with us to day.—I waited on Michael Castle yesterday, who received me very graciously, & enquired after Morgan & you with apparently warm Interest: & to day at one o'clock I am to be presented to Mr Protheroe, & (if possible) to Mr Hart Davies, the two Members, whose names are to head the List of my Subscribers.—I hope, I need not say that *I* at least have not lost a moment in bringing the main (as till I arrived, it was the *sole*) object of my Journey to some satisfactory Conclusion. *'Judge not, lest ye be judged.'* This I bear in mind, & without withdrawing my Esteem from your Friend, say only, yet dare venture to say, that after so unconditional an Offer, as his, twice repeated, & with a long Interval between each, I could have leapt to the Moon *physically* with as much ease, as I could have leapt back from such a promise, *morally*. It is, however, but common Justice to add, that his Conduct has been occasioned wholly by the apprehension imprest on his conviction by his mercantile friends, that he would not only not be serving M. & you permanently, but only Lloyd & the Bill-holders, but likewise be putting it out of his power to serve you afterwards, when it might be of actual service.—After frequent, & long Discussions however I have succeeded in convincing them, that the *B G St Bss* may be saved, ought to be saved, & can only be saved by making some immediate satisfactory settlement with Lloyd—not indeed to the fullness of my own Belief—but as the plan proposed by them, in consequence of their remaining Doubts, appeared to me more delicate, & less oppressive on your feelings, than any other, I have heard, I assented to it—It is, that Porter, Hood, and Kiddle should advance whatever sum is immediately necessary taking Charlotte's Hand for each, so that *in case of* failure they may *appear* as joint Creditors, and so have it in their power at once to serve you & to manage for you.—And now, my very dear Friends! do let me conjure you to do as I do—measure others entirely by what they wish and mean—(which is beyond all doubt to serve M.) and not by the difference between their feelings and our's, each of which depends on the differences of habitual Pursuit, Employment, & perhaps, on the original constructon of the mental frame. I must say, that excepting the expressions of deep Regret, that Morgan had not stayed at Bristol & pursued the Law in good Earnest, I have not heard a symptom of that ordinary indelicacy, *retrospective* Censure & Criticism on a friend in adversity.—This Evening, I trust, all will be settled that can be, in this place: & for the future, we will rely on our own efforts.

And now for my own—nay, why do I say so?—for the second & accidental part of *our* Concerns—the Lectures. The Subscription

promises to go on with a steady Breeze—but you must be so good
as immediately on the receipt of this to hunt out for me the three
Volumes of *Schlegel's Vorlesungen*—they are in Paper Covers, one
of the Volumes thicker & more dirtied than the other two—I think,
they are in pink-coloured Paper—& likewise my two *square* thick
Memorandum Books (not the large Quarto one with the Play &
Music in it)—I am sure, you will be able in the Title pages of the
Books, that are not bound, to distinguish the words Vorlesungen,
at the Top, & *Schlegel* as the Author's name, at the end (excepting
the place & name of the Publisher)—Besides, you will remember
that I used to take them to the Surry Institution. (There are two
other unbound Octavos, in blue Covers, which I have been reading
lately, & taller than the 3 Schlegels—these are *not* what I mean.)
There is likewise another LITTLE *wholly unbound* memorandum
Book of mine, very much rumpled, written all thro', & square: in
the first 5 or 6 leaves there is, I remember, an extract from an old
play of Robin Hood & Marian—'As I am Much, the Miller's Son,
Who left his Mill to go with thee, and nill repent what I have done;
This pleasant Life contenteth me'—&c is part of the extract at the
end of the opposite page to the beginning—. This too I wish. Likewise, I must have a pair of Drawers, one of the best shirts, & two
of the double Cravats—if they have come from the Wash.—They
must be sent by the first Coach, booked, for Mr Coleridge, White
Hart, Bristol: so that I may have them (if possible) on Wednesday
afternoon—& you will be so good as by a Letter by the Post to let
me know, by what Coach they were sent, & at what Inn in Bristol
[it] puts up.—

My Health continues pretty good—[If] possible, I will see Allston
this afternoon—. I said in my last, I was ashamed; but I had no
reason so to accuse myself—For I am like a Boat getting off from a
shoaly Shore—every ten yards I am grounded & detained.

I have not yet been able to see Cottle, Dr Estlin, Mr King (T.
Poole's Brother in law) or King, the Surgeon, or Danvers: tho' I
met the last in the Streets, & Mr King in the grand Commercial
Room, which is very beautiful indeed.

May God bless you & rely on me as

your sincere &
affectionate Friend,
S. T. Coleridge.

P.S. *Pray read all thro'*—and a pair of white Stockings

896. *To Mrs. J. J. Morgan*

Address: Mrs Morgan | 19 London Street | Fitzroy Square | London
MS. Lord Latymer. Pub. E. L. G. ii. 95.
Postmark: Bristol, 29 October ⟨1813⟩.

[29 October 1813]

My dear Loves

I have written to Lloyd, & informed him that by Monday's Post he will receive an 100£, with an arrangement for the rest—. Yesterday Evening's Lecture was tolerably attended, & I doubt not, the Scheme will be profitable—You can scarce conceive how I am hurried—especially, as dining out every day & sitting up every night makes me invisible till 11 o/clock of the Morning—Be assured, I will [neither] neglect nor delay any thing—Pray, write me whether you want any money for yourself. I can send you from 20 to 30£ for your immediate use—& will do so by Sunday's Post —I have not had time to call at the Post Office to day—The Pocket books unfortunately had nothing of what I hoped they would have had—If you would be so good as immediately in the same way as before to send me all my memorandum Books—*except* the little ones with brass clasps & chemical Paper, some black, some red: for these I do not want—but all the others, and should you have an hour to waste in looking over the loose papers, & to send all such as you saw any lecture Hints or notes on—(Poetry, Drama, Shakespear's Macbeth &c &c) you would oblige me—but direct to me at

Josiah Wade's, Esqre
2 Queen's Square
Bristol

I will write at large by Sunday's Post—I shall be too late for the Post if I add more than that I am,

my very dear Mary & Charlotte, | Your constant & affectionate | Friend

S. T. Coleridge

To day I dine with Mr T. King, (Poole's Brother in law).

897. *To Mrs. J. J. Morgan*

MS. Cornell University Lib. Hitherto unpublished.

[Sunday 31 October 1813]

My dear Friends

I write to day for fear you should feel disappointed—but I must write again tomorrow, because I think it better that Charlotte should pay the 100£ to Lloyd, and take his receipt as *C. Brent*—not Brent & Co.—and I cannot procure a Check to day, being Sunday, or even a 100£ bank Note—tho' the latter would, besides, be risking too much—.

I am to dine at Michael Castle's at 2 o/clock, to day—having attended the Pitty Meeting this morning with Mr Wade, & heard the most eloquent Preacher, I ever heard—Robarts.[1]—I must therefore hurry, & only say that on the other side is a check for 20£ for yourselves—and I will send you more in a few days.—Lime Street is near Mincing Lane, some where about Fenchurch Street —[but you had better not present it till Tuesday.][2] I wish, you could take Lodgings for a month at Richmond, or any [oth]er pleasant Retirement—But I will write again—

  Allston & Mrs send their kindest affections to you—May God love you | & your ever faithful

             S. T. Coleridge

I have not received a second parcel as yet—

Some times Mr Smith is not in Town on Monday—but you may be sure of him on Tuesday. I *have* given Mr Wade the 20£ for it —& send the check merely for security's sake—.

898. *To Miss Cottle*

Address: Miss Cottle | Brunswick Square
Transcript Coleridge family. Hitherto unpublished.

           [Endorsed Nov. 1813]

Dear Madam

Permit me to request the honor of your and Mr Cottle's acceptance of the enclosed. Should you not feel inclined or find it convenient to attend yourselves, the Tickets are transferable: and may amuse some of your younger friends.

        With affectionate respect
           S. T. Coleridge

---

[1] The Rev. Thomas Roberts (1780–1841), a Baptist minister in Bristol. See Letter 909.
[2] Passage in brackets crossed out in MS.

899. *To John Colson*

Address: J. Colson, Esqre from *S. T. C.*
MS. Public Library of Victoria, Melbourne, Australia. Hitherto unpublished.

Wednesday afternoon, 3 o/clock
3 Novr. 1813

My dear Colson
I called on you to request you to exert your good offices in my behalf in obtaining for me, at a moderate sum, the use of the Great Room, at Mangeon's Hotel, at Clifton, from one to three on Monday, Wednesday, & Friday afternoons. I have been informed that you are acquainted with Mr Oriel, who is the presiding Influence of the Hotel—. As there will be no Candles necessary, and the Hours such as can not interfere even with a dinner party, I should not like to exceed 2 guineas a time—but if more, we must give it, not exceeding 3—I pay but 2£ for the Room at the White Hart [Lion], Candles &c included—

But if you feel inclined or able to do this, my dear friend! you must do it *immediately*—& let me know the Result, at my old friend, Wade's, No. 2, Queen's Square.

Could I have seen your Wife, I should have preferred her Advocacy to leaving this Scrawl—But I am confident, you will do what you can for

Your old and affectionate Friend
S. T. Coleridge

The subjects of the Lectures, I propose, are:

On the construction, metre, and *distinguishing, characteristic* Merits & Beauties of the Paradise Lost.

On Milton in general, as a man and as a Poet—

On the great distinctions between the poetry of ancient republican Polytheism (the Greek Poets) and the poetry of Christendom since the revival of Letters & the Fine Arts—the Causes & their results—

On the connection of Taste with the moral & religious feeling; the dependence of the former on the latter; that a just Taste may be, and can only be, derived from fixed Principles—and lastly the Rules deduced from these Principles, which will facilitate right & tenable Judgement, both positive and comparative, on poetic Works & the merits of different Poets.—

The Course—from six to eight Lectures—Admission to each, 5 Shillings—Names of those who propose to favor the Lectures with their attendance, it is requested, will be left at the Ma[ngeon] Hotel; or at the Library, Clifton: or at Mr Sheppard's, Corn Street; or Mr Barry's, Bridge Street, Bristol.

Should a sufficient* number of names have been procured, the Lectures will commence on Monday next, 8 Novr. 1813[1]—

God save the King, the | Prince Regent, the Princesses, | and John and | likewise Mrs Colson | who is no small matter handsomer than | all of them put together—

S. T. C.

900. *To Mrs. J. J. Morgan*

Address: Mrs Morgan | 19, London Street | Fitzroy Square | London
MS. Lord Latymer. Hitherto unpublished.
Postmark: Bristol, 5 November 1813.

Friday Morning, 9 o/clock. No. 2. Queen's Square.
[5 November 1813]

Dear Mary

If you have been disappointed in hearing from *me* (as I from *you*), it has not been my fault. I left instructions at the Post office, that all *my* Letters should be put in Mr Wade's Box, and sent by *his* Clerk. Receiving none yesterday, I am anxious—& this is the reason, why I did not send the inclosed piece of Nonsense, the only Object of which was to make you laugh.—My Lecture of yester evening seemed to give more than ordinary satisfaction—I began at 7 o/clock, and ended at half past 9.—*Mercy* on the audience, YOU will say; but the audience did not seem to be tired, and cheered me to the last.—Why do I write these things to you?—Because they flatter my Vanity? O God! MY Vanity, if it exist, is no such Coarse Feeder!—But—nay, *words* will not remove unfavorable Impressions.—

I have this moment heard, that Mr Wade's Clerk did not call at the Post Office—he himself is this moment returned from Caerphilly, Wales—is angry with the Clerk—& I must wait.

11 o/clock, Friday Morning

My dear Mary

I have this moment received your's of the 3rd, which I ought to have had yesterday. You no where mention your receipt of the Check on Joseph Smith, Esqre for 20£. That the 100£ was not sent on Monday, was not my fault—in any other sense, than that I am seldom out of my bedroom till half-past 10 or 11—When you have to see three or four persons of Business, between the Hours of 12 to

---

* say, *40*. [Note by S. T. C.]

[1] The first of the Clifton lectures was delivered on Wednesday, 10 Nov., the second and last on 17 Nov. Coleridge was too ill to lecture at Clifton on Friday, 12 Nov., or on Monday, 15 Nov. See Letters 901–2 and 904.

4, the odds are against you, and I could not have sent it off even on Tuesday, had I added 20£ of my own to make up the 100£.— *That included*, I think, I can now command 80£ more, and, I dare say, an 100£—But do you not remember, my dear! that our proposal to Mr Porter in all the first instances was merely to pay a 100£ immediately, and to give Security for the rest to be payed in two, or 3 months?—I am sorry that the Debt to Lloyd should have increased, and shall not mention it to any one here—because it would be a fact in proof of the direct Contrary of what I had so earnestly lay'd weight, viz—that under all your difficulties the Debt to Lloyd had decreased to 230£.—For the future, we must try to avoid it. I doubt not, that I shall be able to supply you regularly with whatever is necessary for your immediate expences.—

As to Lloyd, I am indignant to the last degree at his Conduct. Shame upon the Wretch! to impose on and act the Bully-Creditor, towards a young Lady ignorant of business! He well knew, that the 100£ Bill could not have been sent, had not the hundred pound in ready Cash been paid in to the Bank that drew the Bill in London—he well knew, that it was the regular, because the only quite secure, mode of transmitting large Sums to London—he knew, that to any and all of his purposes it was the same as ready money—& above all, he ought to have told Charlotte, that by stepping to the Bank, on which the Bill was drawn, they would

instantly have given her 99 ‖ 12 ‖ 6—so that by merely add[ing] seven & sixpence from her own pocket, she might have brought ready money to him.—I will take care that the next 100£ shall be ready money, & Charlotte should ask him, why he had not taken the former with the discount added: tho' there is not a tradesman in London, but himself, that would have [been] guilty of such meanness.

The *reason* for not paying off all at once was to delay it for two months from his acceptance of Charlotte, as the sole Proprietor— after which time M. would be free from all chance of Bankruptcy from the Bill-holders. This is, however, I hope & trust, of no great consequence.—One part of your letter *seems* to contradict the other —in the first you say 'he will not give up M's responsibility till the whole is paid'—& over leaf you say—'he has promised to consider C. as sole Proprietor from to day, if the payments are made once a month &c'—. If this mean only, if you pay me immediately the 290£, & hereafter pay me every month—the Devil thank him.— What is that to him?—I think, that Charlotte might make this Proposal to him—that 100£ should be payed in the course of seven days from the date of her calling, and that he should accept my note of hand, as conjoint responsibility with her own, that the remaining ninety should be payed by monthly installments—. But perhaps, I shall be able to raise 130£—and you had better request Mr Butler to call with Charlotte on him, & before you let him know that you have the money ready, to know whether if the 130£ be paid immediately, & my note of hand given for the monthly payment of the remainder in three months, he will give a receipt to Charlotte, &c—. His Conduct is base & cruel.—I do not expect to raise more than 200£ here—& among the nonsense of the inclosed Letter you will find my reason for being glad that it is *thus* raised instead of your borrowing the money from Porter—who could not, according to his own account, have done more than given security for it to be paid in February, without selling out of the Stocks at an enormous disadvantage.—I dine to day with Kiddle—sup at Cottle's—tomorrow dine at Dr Stock's & so on & so for the whole of next week—this is the [worst] evil—& I will make no new engagements—I wi[ll] write again on Sunday—& pray, tell me what moneys you want for yourselves, by return of Post—

                                                        S. T. C.

901. *To Mrs. J. J. Morgan*

Address: Mrs Morgan | 19 London Street | Fitzroy Square | London   *Post paid*
MS. Lord Latymer. Pub. E. L. G. ii. 96.
Postmark: Bristol, 10 November ⟨1813⟩.

Tuesday Night, 12 o/clock [9 November 1813]
                    Mr Wade's, 2, Queen Square—
My dear Friends
    I can not express the uneasiness, I have suffered, from not hearing from you. It REALLY so deprest my Spirits, and so haunted me, that the Lecture of to Night, which I had expected to have been the best & to have produced the most lively Effect, that on Othello, was the worst, I ever delivered—& a humiliating Contrast to the Lecture before. I so confidently depended on a Letter from you by this day's Post, that since two o'clock, when Mr Wade assured me that no Letter had arrived, I could do nothing else but torment myself with conjectures and fancies. The root of the Evil is, that neither of you ever formed a just appreciation of my Affection toward you. You never believed that I loved you & Morgan, as (God knows!) I have done.—
    But what is most unfortunate is, that tomorrow at one o/clock I must be at Clifton, tho' with no probability of even more than enough to pay the Lecture Room & the Printing. (I have had experience enough to expect nothing but meanness from the fashion-

able World, & therefore shall not be disappointed—tho' I confess, that I am vexed at heart at the inferiority of the Lecture, I delivered to night—tho' all, I spoke to, said, it was a Whim of my own. But I know these things by Tact.) But in consequence of this I must set off for Clifton by 12 o/clock, just an hour before the Post Office is open—& do what I will, cannot expect to return time enough to read and answer your Letter, if Letter there should be. But if not, I must write to Mr Evans, 103, B. G. St—to know what is become of you.—You cannot conceive, how unhappy this has made me—I pray God fervently, that it may be accident, or even your fault—& not Illness or any new Misfortune. Sure, there cannot have been any thing in my latter Letters, that has affronted you?—Pray, pray, write immediately—& let the Letter be circumstantial, first and foremost, as to Mary's Health; 2ndly, as to your private & household Bills, what have remained unpayed; and lastly, as to your immediate Plans, & what you think of my proposal as to settling in or near Bristol for the next 4 months—As I shall not be able to write tomorrow, I bid you Good Night with my old—God love you both &

S. T. Coleridge

Pray, hereafter write every other day: & I will do the same, till things are settled one way or the other—& pray, dear Megrim! be particular about Mary's Health. God forbid, you should have any thing to say of your own!

S. T. C.

902. *To Mrs. J. J. Morgan*

Address: Mrs Morgan | 19 London Street | Fitzroy Square | London
MS. Lord Latymer. Hitherto unpublished.
Postmark: Bristol, 14 November ⟨1813⟩.

Sunday [14 November 1813]

My very dear Friends

When I wrote my last peevish and querulous Letter (for which I am sorry but hope, you attributed it to it's true Cause, the anxiety of Affection) I did not foresee the severe attack of Illness, which I have since suffered, and tho' something better, still labour under. I dined on Wednesday at Mr T. Castle's—felt myself uncomfortable—& whether from that cause I drank more wine, or that the wine acted more on me, I was little less than drunk: tho' on my return Mr Wade did not detect it.—All next day I looked forward with Terror to the Evening's Lecture, but got over it so as to redeem the preceding and with an eclat equal to the third. On

my return I sent for 5 grains of Calomel & 15 of Jalap—& I cannot
but suspect, that some carelessness was used in weighing the former,
and a much larger dose sent—for all the next Day, on which I was
to dine at ½ past 5, & spend the evening with Lady Russel at
Clifton, and the whole of which I had predetermined to your Concerns & writing to & for you—I was alternately sick and griped to
a degree, I had never before any conception [of].—The pain &
still more the state of my skull benumbed & stupefied, by the
violent strainings, alarmed me: & even yesterday I could retain
nothing on my Stomach till late evening. This day I am much
recovered; but still unable to sit down to the dinner-table. And
now for business—as much at least as my past Illness has permitted me to do & my present to write about—.

First, the moment I opened the parcel, & before I had read your
letter, I sent off the inclosed—afterwards on reading your letter I
was so much pleased & so much affected, that I sate musing &
dreaming of you, at the first half—and reading it over again—that I
was interrupted & forced off before I had read the whole, or came
to the request about Mr Tipton—But Mr Wade has carried the 10£,
inclosed in a note from me, stating that I had received it from you,
but in the hurry of company had passed over your direction as to
it's employment.

As you have forbad it (I hope to God! not from false delicacy)
I shall not inclose in *to day's* Letter the 30£ Bank Note, which I
had procured.—Whatever you wish, as to my coming up to Town,
I will most assuredly do—but it would add very, very greatly to
my Happiness, & I may add, to my Well-being, if I could induce
you to let me immediately find out some respectable Family either
at Clifton or at Frenchay where we all three might lodge and board,
and have two bedrooms, and one sitting room private to ourselves.
I can feel & understand your Objections; but I am certain, that
the getting *them* over would greatly smooth the way to Morgan's
comfortable Return & Settlement. M. could come to Bristol quite as
cheap, & within a day as soon from Dunnover,[1] as he could to Keswick.—The Wednesday, on which I went to Clifton, was one series
of such impetuous *Storms* of Wind, and Rain, that there were not
above 8 or 10 persons there—I therefore took a Chair, drew round
the fire, & chatted for an hour & a half—and before Wednesday I
cannot even guess whether they will or will not answer[2]—my Illness precluding me from all the necessary no less than expedient
Courtesies of Morning calls & evening Lady-parties.—

[1] Possibly Dunover House, County Down, Ireland.
[2] This statement would indicate that Coleridge planned to lecture at Clifton
on Wednesday 17 Nov.

Allston was very evidently better when I last saw him; & had I been well, I should have been there yesterday by appointment— as he promised to take a little sketch of me for Mr Wade.[1]—

I hope, I shall be quite recovered by tomorrow, & able in a few days to settle all things—

Lectures are nothing, were they every day—It is dinnering, dinnering that is the Devil—

May God love you both—I do most affectionately.—Tomorrow, if able, I must transmit 10£ to you, and employ Charlotte on a very, very awkward Business—to go to *the Depository* for me—40 Books, Watch, Snuff Box, in for 6£—the Duplicates in the Watch Fob of my old whity-colored Small Clothes—the same *Relation* of our's as before.—How can she do it?—And yet who else can I employ?—C. Lamb? or M. Burney?—

Again & again I bless & love you—
S. T. Coleridge

903. *To J. Eden*

Address: Revd. J. Eden
MS. Huntington Lib. Hitherto unpublished.

Wednesday Evening [17 November 1813][2]

Dear Sir

In order to be sure not to offend in my tomorrow Evening's Lecture, I beg you will lend me that little Book, of Southey's, which you honored me with the acceptance of in London—And as I am in a most unnatural Dearth of Books here, should you have any two or three Volumes that you have found interest in, critical, controversial, or historical, of recent date, you would by entrusting them to me for a day or two oblige

Your respectful & obliged
S. T. Coleridge

[1] This portrait was painted in 1814. See Letter 938 and E. P. Richardson, *Washington Allston*, 1948, pp. 112 and 198.

[2] This letter was probably written the evening before Coleridge's lecture on Education, 18 Nov. 1813. The 'little Book, of Southey's', was probably *The Origin, Nature, and Object, of the New System of Education*, 1812.

904. *To Mrs. J. J. Morgan*

Address: Mrs Morgan | 19 London Street | Fitzroy Square | London
MS. Lord Latymer. Pub. E. L. G. ii. 98.
Postmark: Bristol, 19 November ⟨1813⟩.

Bristol, Wednesday Night. [17 November 1813]

It just happened, as I had stated to those who insisted on my attending at Clifton Hotel to day—some 12 persons present, and among them *one only* of the Score who had overpersuaded me to hazard the mortification & to incur the expence. Is not this shameful?—I am not angry; yet I am vexed not in the most distant kind for or with respect to myself, but because against my will I am compelled to prostrate myself, an unconditional Captive, at the feet of my own Understanding and previous Experience, as to the hollowness of Zealous *Acquaintances*. Zealous *Friends* are among God's prime Blessings: but oh! ever while you live, be suspicious of zealous *Acquaintances*!—(Do you remember poor Hartley's distinction of *Ac-* and In-quaintances—to which by adding *Con-* I affirmed that we might arrange all whom we were in the frequent habit of seeing?—viz. 1. *Ac*quaintances. 2. *Con*quaintances. 3. *In*quaintances.—)

Well, my dear *In*quaintances! I must again express my regret at sending off your Letter, as (from Kiddle) I find, I did; not only without the 10£ inclosed, but even without a wafer—since K. informs me, that Mr Tipton immediately wrote to you, & I fear, may have hurt your feelings. In this instance alone have I been, directly or indirectly, the cause or the occasion of any thing, you or M. could wish otherwise.—I write now, because beginning a Letter does with me ensure, by facilitating, the concluding it—for I shall not send it off, till I can inclose a second 100£, & have heard from you that you have received my eye-fatiguing lengthy Epistle of To Day, with it's Inclosure.—I have not seen Allston again. Yester afternoon (Tuesday) was the first of my re-emersion since Thursday—O mercy! such an account of my last night's (6th) Lecture in Mills's Paper!—it is so strangely throughout the *direct opposite* of what I said, that I triumph in it. It has given *me*, the Philosopher so convincing a proof of the effect of all *un-commonplace* Discourses on the commonplace minds, that admire t'other *me*, the Lecturer. The account is a compleat Lord's Prayer read backwards—of course a most *charming, bewitching* Account.—Gutch[1] & Mills are at daggers-drawing, both as Men and as Newspaperists

---

[1] John Mathew Gutch (1776–1861), proprietor and printer of *Felix Farley's Bristol Journal.*

—Gutch is an old Schoolfellow of mine, & has been ostentatiously civil—but yet because Mills has given account of my Lectures, he will not.—

Thursday Night.

Well, my dear Loves! I have made a famous Lecture to a crowded Room—& all the better, because on account of my mortification at the ill-conduct of those, who had *forced* me against my own ex-prest convictions on the Cliftonian Lecture, I had not prepared one single word or thought, till 10 mi[nutes] before the Lecture com-menced—. It was, therefore, quite in my fire-side way, & pleased more than any.—This was to have been the last. However, I am to go on on Tuesday next—& probably, for an indefinite time I might with advantage. But I can determine nothing till I hear from you, which I expect to do by tomorrow's Post.—This only I can say, that if you were with me, I could make all things answer both for my Family, & for you. But if your feelings are insurmountable, I will take leave of my Bristolian Friends, & instantly go off with you to Keswick: with no other serious repugnance but that of giving up a scheme, hitherto flattering, of making Morgan friends zealous & under promise to do their best for him, should he return to his Birth-place & devote his time (not himself) to his Profession. But I will not say another word about it: only whithersoever you go, I will accompany you, till I re-deliver the goods to the rightful owner, J. J. Morgan, Esquire—N.B. Miss Polly Parker, that charm-ing Nymph! has sent to me, hoping that I will call on '*his old and affectionate Friend*'; these were the very words of the message as delivered to me by Kiddle—the overture to the Farce being a broad Grin on his part.—Kiddle the Immutable! So have I christened him—for he is the *very same* Being, I knew 20 years ago —& a most worthy Being it is.—Good Night! To morrow I shall hear *from* you & *of* Miss Brent. *From* Miss B.? 'O La! no! Write to a man, tho' old enough to be my father—!—my neck-and-breast-kerchief is downright scorched & iron-moulded with the intensity of my *expansive* Blush.'—Well then, be it so!—you, my dear Mary! may have been able to measure one of Megrim's Blushes, I can only swear to from the bare interspace on her head, (formed by her horrid torture of her beautiful Hair) down to *a little* beyond the lowermost end of her tiny pretty Bird's-Neck.—O! while I write, I try to *see* you laughing, or looking as you do, Mary! while sky-larking.—

If I do not receive tomorrow a minute, circumstantial account of your Health, what it *has* been as well as what it *is* at the moment of writing, I shall be deuced angry—

S. T. C.

Friday Afternoon—

No Letter from you!—Did you not receive mine of Wednesday with 20£ inclosed?—Two Posts missing, I am half-alarmed—. Pray write.

905. *To Mrs. J. J. Morgan*

Address: Mrs Morgan | No. 19 London Street | Fitzroy Square | London
MS. New York Public Lib. (Arents Collections). Pub. E. L. G. ii. 101.
Postmark: Bristol, 2⟨1⟩ November ⟨1813⟩.

[Saturday, 20 November 1813]

My dear Mary

Most assuredly I will be with you as soon after Tuesday Night, as Stages can carry me. You will see by Gutch's Paper that I am already *engaged* to give a further Lecture on Education on Tuesday Night—of course, I cannot set off till Wednesday. If your feelings render the vicinity of Bristol out of the question, there is no use of saying any thing further—but my friends here were disposed to exert their utmost influence in bringing about the plan, that I had long so fondly fostered, of a *system* of private Lectures with Discussions afterwards, conveying all the knowlege that a Gentleman ought to have, whether Lawyer, Clergyman, Medical man, Merchant, or Senator—& which if realized would secure me 600£ a year, & yet leave me time for other things.—My *notion* was, if such a thing could be effectuated, instantly to send down for Hartley & Derwent, to take Lodgings answerable till by my own & my friends' efforts we could furnish a suitable House—to take it in Morgan's name, & for Morgan—so as to give him time, opportunity, & increase of connections for resuming his Profession here. However, be it understood that I leave Bristol on Wednesday Evening, unless I hear from you either by Tuesday's (the first possible day) or by Wednesday's Post—In the mean time (N.B. this is Saturday Midnight: for from some neglect Barnard did not bring home the Letter before I was forced to go out to dinner, to Revd. Mr Eden's, & I have therefore just *received* & read it) I will employ my time & efforts (as far as the Lecture permits me) . . .[1] to settle Lloyd's.—

Forgive me, my dear Sisters! but how comes it that when, Mary, you are unwell, that you, Charlotte! do not write to me? Have you no confidence in me? Have I not told you, that I burn every letter as soon as I have done reading it? And that with the exception of the Letters sent in the Parcel I have read every one the moment it

---

[1] Six words heavily inked out in MS.

was delivered—& even those on the same day ?—You write a good
hand, & you express yourself naturally & like an unaffected
Gentlewoman—but in the name of Love & Friendship, have you
known me so long as to fear that my Regard for you, or my respect
for your Understanding, could be increased or diminished by your
Style or your Hand-writing ?—If that were at all possible, it could
only happen from your Style being too blue-stocking fine & correct,
& your Handwriting *too* exquisite. So help me Conscience! I should
always anticipate a more natural Letter, more really wise, & more
unaffectedly affecting, the more ill-spelt Words there were in it;
& the fewer Stops & divided Sentences.—You yourselves *cannot*
write half as sweetly & heart-touchingly, as with *your* thoughts &
feelings you would have done, if you had never heard of Grammar,
Spelling, &c.—O curse them—at least as far as Women are concerned. The longer I live, the more do I loathe in stomach, & de-
precate in Judgement, all, *all* Bluestockingism. The least possible
of it implies at least two *Nits*, in one egg a male, in t'other a female
—& if not killed, O the sense of the Lady will be *Lice*nce! Crathmo-
crawlo!—

I have at the same time with your's received a letter from Allston.
I transcribe—'From your letter I conclude Mrs Morgan is better—
WELL, I hope. Bless her bright Eyes! I wish, they were the illumined
Windows of a *Heart* of Sunshine!—& the inexpressible archness,
yet timidity, shrewdness yet meekness, in her Sister's!—I doubt,
whether the Sun's Beams ever did or will visit any of better Hearts
than their's!—As to my own Health, Mr King told me a few days
since, that if no accident occurred to obstruct my present progress,
I should in short time be *a well man*: and indeed I *seem* such even
now in all but strength.' Mrs A. is but poorly—bashfulness alone
has prevented her (A. says) from writing to you; but she loves you
dearly. They remove on Monday from Clifton to No. 18, Pritchard
Street, Portland Square, Bristol.—

Perhaps, I may receive a Letter from you tomorrow, more fully
explaining your Ideas & Intentions.—I wish it, only because I am
a little puzzled; there existing so general a wish that I should give
the Miltonian Lectures at Bristol.[1] I have made Friends of them

---

[1] On 4 Dec. *Felix Farley's Bristol Journal* announced a new course of lectures,
to begin on 7 Dec.: 'Two on those plays of Shakespeare which were not referred
to in the former course and illustrative of the poetic and romantic character of
our great dramatist, namely, *The Tempest, Midsummer Night's Dream, Merchant of Venice, As You Like It, Twelfth Night*, etc.; and four on the *Paradise
Lost* and the character of Milton as a man and a poet; with an examination of
Dr. Johnson's Preface to Shakespeare and his life of Milton.' (*Shakespearean
Criticism*, ii. 255–6.) Coleridge fell ill at Bath and was not able to give the
course in Dec. See Letters 908–10.

all, even by my sarcastic observations on the contrast between Bristol & Clifton Patronage. Guignette is (as I always thought) a wretched Creature—seemed to have never heard of Morgan, or to have seen me!—I dined yesterday at M. Castle's—played four Rubbers of Whist, and lost only two Shillings—& Michael Castle sent from his table to mine (there were 4 Card tables) to beg a pinch of Snuff & just after came over to me & said—'I have wished a Keep sake of your's—let us exchange Boxes—I assure you, I shall preserve your's as a Relic' (you remember my Miss Fenner 10d one) & presented me with one of the most elegant boxes of richest Tortoise shell mounted in Gold. So rich was the Tortoise shell that till I looked thro' it by Candle Light, I mistook it for jet—. I tell you these things because they pleased me chiefly in the anticipation that they would give you pleasure.—Had your feelings been such, as on the whole I could have wished them, I had proposed to myself after Tuesday to have fetched you from London, to have gone with you to my friend, T. Poole's at Stowey, (a mere half-day's journey from hence) to have procured comfortable Dwelling, Acquaintance &c—till such time as M. could return & settle at Bristol—or if that was too distant, to have taken Lodgings at Wrington, 12 miles from Bristol—where you would have found in Mrs & the Miss De Quinceys unaffected Women prepared* to love & esteem you.—But on Thursday I will be with you, Life & Health permitting.—

S. T. C.

906. *To Josiah Wade*[1]

MS. John Rylands Lib. Hitherto unpublished.

19, London Street, Fitzroy Square—
Thursday Afternoon. [25 November 1813][2]

My dear Friend

I have arrived safe, tho' somewhat nervous from sitting up all night in the constrained posture of a Mail Coach, & with the soreness of the Temples from the Knocks of the side of the Coach while

---

* From Sore Throat's Letters to them: in consequence of which they asked *solicitously* about you, whether you were not CHARMING women. No, Ma'am! (says I) I never saw any thing charming in them. N.B. I said this only to heighten their Surprize when they saw the Beauty, the compleat Woman. [Note by S. T. C.]

[1] The page containing the address is missing, but references to Sally and Barnard indicate that this letter was written to Josiah Wade.

[2] Letter 905 shows that Coleridge planned to leave Bristol for London on Wednesday, 24 Nov.

dozing.—We were but three in all—S. T. C.—& two Officers, who had served in Malta, Sicily, Spain &c—one of them at the breach of Burgos had a blunderbuss applied to the side of his Face, which had taken away all but four of his Teeth, two thirds of his Tongue, & about half of his Jaws—& yet he conversed intelligibly—the other a young man in the Commissariat. Of course, we were quite at home with each other.—The flurry of Joy at seeing me has precluded all conversation that could enable me to settle any thing with my Protégées here: and of course all information of my own plans.—Mrs Morgan had been far, far worse than they thought proper to let me know—& out of London she must go immediately, somewhere or other.—By Saturday we shall have decided—& you will (God willing) receive a Letter from me by Sunday's Post.— To morrow morning I will wait on Mr. Pritt & Mr Holford—.

Be so good as to take off the second Leaf of this Letter, & inclose it to Mr Kiddle—Remember me kindly to Sally, & to Bernard—& be assured that I am in the most serious sense of the words your obliged, your grateful, & your affectionate Friend,

S. T. Coleridge

907. *To Henry Crabb Robinson*

Address: H. C. Robinson, Esqre | Essex Court, | Inner Temple
MS. Dr. Williams's Lib. Hitherto unpublished.

[Circa 26 November 1813][1]

My dear—Robinson—I was going to write; but without any alteration of *old feeling*, & only in *decorum*—I must substitute— Dear Sir!—I am just returned from Somersetshire in order to return thither—at the voice of '*Pflicht*'—if the health & circumstances of two virtuous, pure-hearted, & kind-hearted Women, the Wife & the Sister of a Man, I call my Friend—& whom, in his Prosperity, I found a *Friend*—can constitute Duty—I return you (very reluctantly, I own) the two Volumes of Spinoza—reluctantly, because in England I cannot purchase them—

Pray, give my best thanks to Mr Aders—

You told Mr M. that you did not much regard the Fichte Magazines[2]—If this be the case, pray, send them to me, directed to me— J. Wade, Esqre, No. 2. Queen's Square, Bristol—by the Coach— & if you would add Schelling's Methodologie[3] you would not only

[1] Coleridge left London for Bristol by way of Bath on 29 Nov. See Letter 908.

[2] *Philosophisches Journal einer Gesellschaft Teutscher Gelehrten*, 1797–1800, herausgegeben von J. G. Fichte und F. I. Niethammer, Jena.

[3] F. W. J. von Schelling, *Vorlesungen über die Methode des akademischen Studiums*, 1803.

oblige but really serve me—for I have a plan maturing, to w[hich] that work would be serv[iceable.] To tell the Truth, I sho[uld be] glad to exchange with you almost any of my Books (metaphysics excepted) for the Selections from J. J. Richter[1]—I could explain to you my motive if I were with you—

Pray, give my best & most respectful Love to Mrs Clarkson when you see her or write to her—

Excuse my hurry—

S. T. Coleridge

God bless you & may you be illustrious & useful.

908. *To Josiah Wade*

Address: Josiah Wade, Esqre | 2. Queen's Square | Bristol
MS. Cornell University Lib. Pub. with omis. Rem. *351.*
Postmark: Bath, 8 December 1813.

Wednesday [8 December 1813]

My dear Friend

I left London the Monday before last, in the Reading Stage—to accomodate those with me I stayed Monday Night & Tuesday there—left Reading in a Post Chaise on Wednesday Morning—arrived at Chippenham on Wednesday Night—& at Bath on Thursday. . . .[2] I can only answer sorrowfully—the passions & pride of Women, even of in most respects good & amiable Women! —passions that thwart all I do to serve them—the two Sisters I have lodged at Mrs Smith's, Grocer, Ashley, near Box—about 4 miles from Bath, & ½ a mile from Box.—I could not leave them till they seemed settled—namely, on Sunday—when missing the Stage, & very unwell with a violent cold, I was obliged to walk to Bath thro' *such* a Road, Slip or Slop, Mud or Mire, the whole way—And since my arrival at the Grey Hound, Bath, I have been confined to my Bed-room—almost to my Bed.—. . .[3]

Pray for my recovery—and request Mr Robarts's Prayers—but for my infirm wicked Heart, that Christ may mediate to the Father to lead me to Christ, & give me a living instead of a reasoning Faith!—and for my Health as far only as it may be the condition of my Improvement & final Redemption.—

My dear affectionate | Friend, I am your | obliged & grateful & affectionate | Friend,

S. T. Coleridge

[1] Referring, of course, to *Jean Pauls Geist.* See Letter 814.
[2] Three-fourths of a line heavily inked out in MS.
[3] Two lines heavily inked out in MS.

909. *To Thomas Roberts*

Transcript Cornell University Lib. Hitherto unpublished.

[*Circa* 19 December 1813][1]

. . . You have no conception of what my sufferings have been,
forced to struggle and struggle in order not to desire a death for
which I am not prepared.—I have scarcely known what sleep is,
but like a leopard in its den have been drawn up and down the
room by extreme pain, and restlessness, worse than pain itself.

O how I have prayed even to loud agony only to be able to pray!
O how I have felt the impossibility of any real *good will* not born
anew from the Word and the Spirit! O I have seen far, far deeper
and clearer than I ever saw before the ground of pernicious errors!
O I have seen, I have felt that the worst offences are those against
our own souls! That our souls are infinite in depth, and therefore
our sins are infinite, and redeemable only by an infinitely higher
infinity; that of the Love of God in Christ Jesus. I have called my
soul infinite, but O infinite in the depth of darkness, an infinite
craving, an infinite capacity of pain and weakness, and excellent
only as being passively capacious of the light from above. Should I
recover I will—no—no may God grant me power to struggle to
become *not another* but a *better man*—O that I had been a partaker
with you of the discourse of Mr Robt Hall! But it pleased the
Redeemer to appoint for me a sterner, fearfuller, and even more
eloquent preacher, if to be impressive is to be eloquent. O God save
me—save me from myself. . . .

910. *To Mrs. J. J. Morgan*

Address: Mrs Morgan | Ashley
MS. Lord Latymer. Pub. E. L. G. ii. 127.

Sunday December 19th [1813]

Yesterday was the first day, Mary! that I could leave my Bed,
except in a Blanket to have it made—even from the day, I quitted
you—The Terrors of the Almighty have been around & against
me—and tho' driven up and down for seven dreadful Days by restless Pain, like a Leopard in a Den, yet the anguish & remorse of
Mind was worse than the pain of the whole Body.—O I have had a

[1] To her transcript of this letter Mrs. Thomas Roberts prefixed an explanatory note: 'The following extract is from a letter of Coleridge's addressed by
him whilst at Bath to his friend in Bristol, T. R. (probably 1813.)' The similarity
in the description of his sufferings in this and the following letter indicates that
Coleridge wrote to Roberts just before leaving Bath for Bristol in Dec. 1813.

new world opened to me, in the infinity of my own Spirit!—Woe be
to me, if this last Warning be not taken.—Amidst all my Anguish
you and Charlotte were present to me—& formed a part of it.—
Dr Parry,[1] who was called in by accident (for I was too wild with
suffering to direct any thing myself) attended me day after day, &
often twice a day, with parental kindness—. Mrs May says, he did
what she never knew him do—stay with me two & three hours at a
time—& to him under God's Mercy I owe that I am at present
alive. For seven days consecutively I never swallowed a morsel—
Dr Parry said daily—so much the better—why should you take
what you cannot digest?—I shall put myself into a Post Chaise
this afternoon, please God! & proceed to Bristol—from thence I
will write you immediately. Feeble, as I am, & so deprest in spirit,
I dare not come over to you—lest I should not be able to get away:
and Dr Parry says, it is quite necessary that I should be in Company
& drawn away from my own Thoughts—

I will send you word as soon as I have settled myself in Bristol[2]
—i.e. within 3 or 4 days.—

May God protect you both, & | Your severely yet most
deservedly | visited

S. T. Coleridge

P.S. IF POSSIBLE, I will come over on the 24th and spend the
Christmas Eve & Christmas Day with you.—

911. *To Charlotte Brent*

MS. Lord Latymer. Hitherto unpublished.

[Late December 1813][3]

My dear Friends

From a short absence for two days I have just received your
Letter—& am relieved to hear of Mary's convalescence—I have

---

[1] Caleb Hillier Parry (1755–1822), physician and the father of Charles and
Frederick Parry, Coleridge's friends at Göttingen.

[2] Coleridge was returning to Bristol to undertake the lectures originally
planned for early December. (See Letter 905.) On 30 Dec. the following advertisement appeared in the *Bristol Gazette*: 'Mr. Coleridge having been surprised and confined by sudden and severe illness at his arrival at Bath, six days
before the promised commencement of his second course, 7th December, 1813,
respectfully informs his friends that this second course will commence on
Tuesday, 4th January, 1814, at the White Lion.' (*Shakespearean Criticism*, ii.
256.) Although Cottle speaks of a second course of six lectures, 'which was well
attended', no newspaper accounts of the course appeared and it is unlikely
that Coleridge was able to resume lecturing until April 1814. See *Rem.* 354 and
Letters 911–12.

[3] This letter, which is composed of two detached fragments, was apparently
written in late Dec., since the lectures referred to were advertised on 30 Dec.
to begin on Tuesday, 4 Jan. 1814.

been myself far, very far from well—my appetite & digestion
worse, I think than formerly, tho' I am very careful—but
what most afflicts me is the heavy Load on my Spirits which by
no effort I can shake off—. My Lectures are to recommence on
Tuesday Evening, with what success I expect to inform you in
person: for if God permit, I mean to be with you on Wednesday,
tho' I must, perforce, return early on Thursday—. I would go now,
but that I feel it necessary to exert myself in writing the Essay
containing my plan of private Lectures.[1]—. . .

God bless you &
S. T. Coleridge

I have seen none of my Bristol Friends but Mr Hood once, for a
few minutes—& Michael Castle, whom I attempted to dine with
—but was taken ill at his Table—but my after Journey with W.
has done me service—

912. *To John Prior Estlin*

Address: Dr Estlin | St Michael's Hill
MS. Bristol Central Lib. Pub. Letters to Estlin, *107*.

Tuesday, 5 April—1814

My dear Sir

βραδὺς καὶ ὀκνηρός τις ὢν φύσει πρὸς τὸ γράφειν, I have had, alas!
other both external & internal obstacles, and those of a sort the
most heart-appalling, to the realization of a resolve, I had made—
to wit, that of writing to you at large on the deeply interesting
Subject of your Work on universal Restitution. I speak within
bounds, when I say that I have carefully read thro' the *whole*
five times, independent of partial & desultory references: and my
own private judgement is fixed. It is this: that in the Court, which
you have selected, & to the Judges or Opponents, to whom &
for whom you have argued, you have gained the Cause *completely*.
I scarcely know how to *fancy* a mind so obstinately illogical, as
assenting to your premises (the *remedial* ends of all just punishment; the inconsistency of the Adjunct with it's Principal in the
term, '*vindictive* justice'; & it's further incompatibility with the
infinite LOVE, which God *is*; &c) could refuse his assent to your
Conclusions. The writer of the illiberal article in the Eclectic
Review among other uncharitable oversights forgot the first Duty
of a candid Critic—that of asking, to whom & for whom was the
Work written? His proper language, as an orthodox, or (if I might

---

[1] On 20 Nov. 1813 Coleridge wrote of a '*system* of private Lectures', which
'if realized' would secure him £600 a year. See Letter 905.

coin a more modest expression) a pleistodox = ὡς τοῖς πλείστοις δοκεῖ man should have been something like the following:—'The opponents, to whom alone this work is controversial, assume the same premises as the Author: & we cannot conceive, how *they* can object to his deductions. If the Scriptures present difficulties to the advocate of limited & remedial Punishment, they present them tenfold to the annihilators—from whose System nature itself recoils. As Deists, the latter Class might have something plausible to say for themselves; but as Christians, & as deeming themselves, of course, obliged to acknowlege the resurrection of all men, the worst as well as the best, their system becomes monstrous, & represents the supreme Being in a light scarcely less blasphemous to his Wisdom than to his Goodness.—For ourselves, we hold it sufficient to say: Non nobis!—to those of our faith, who deny the premises in toto, the Book was not written—and unless Dr Estlin should address a proof of the Premises (which in his present work would have been superfluous) to all Christians in general, we shall content ourselves with the open declaration of this our Dissent— Considered as a literary work, the arrangement is orderly & natural, the language simple & correct: & the whole Composition breathes a sincere, open, & most affectionate Spirit.'—

This, my dear Sir! is my own Opinion of your Discourses. If you felt inclined to ask, what then my faith is as to this awful subject, I should refer to your own Book, to the quotation from Jeremy— that is my creed. I believe, that punishment is essentially *vindictive*, i.e. expressive of abhorrence of Sin for it's own exceeding sinfulness: from all experience as well as a priori from the constitution of the human Soul I gather that without a miraculous Intervention of Omnipotence the Punishment must continue as long as the Soul—which I believe imperishable.—God has promised no such miracle—he has covenanted no such mercy—I have no right therefore to believe or rely on it—It *may* be so; but wo to me! if I presume on it.—There is a great difference, my dear Sir! between the assertion—'It is so!' & 'I have no right to assert the contrary!'

I take the Liberty of inclosing for your kind acceptance a ticket of admission to my Lectures[1] (which commence this evening) for

---

[1] On 2 April 1814 the following announcement appeared in *Felix Farley's Bristol Journal*: 'Mr. Coleridge informs the former attendants at his lectures, and his friends in general, that being now recovered from his severe and protracted illness, he proposes to give six lectures on the following subjects and in the following order on Tuesday and Thursday evenings . . . : 1st. on the life, character, and prose writings of Milton; 2nd. on the minor poems of Milton; 3rd and 4th. on the plan, metre, characters, and distinguishing beauties of the *Paradise Lost*; 5th on the means of acquiring a just and austere poetic taste and its close connection with religious and moral feelings; and 6th (by particular

yourself, family & friends. Should you or Mrs E., or any of your family, have leisure or inclination, believe me, the more you bring, the more service you will do me. I am asking a *favor* by the same act by which I would give a humble proof, that notwithstanding difference of creeds I can never cease to *remember* that I am your *greatly obliged*, nor, I trust, to *feel* myself your *grateful* Friend,

S. T. Coleridge.

913. *To Joseph Cottle*

Pub. Early Rec. *i. 204.* Cottle describes this letter as a 'Fragment of a Theological letter of Mr. Coleridge, date unknown'. J. D. Campbell, who saw the MS., says that the letter 'is printed, very inaccurately, by Cottle'.

[Early April 1814?]

. . . The declaration that the Deity is 'the sole Operant'[1] is indeed far too bold; may easily be misconstrued into Spinosism; and therefore, though it is susceptible of a pious and justifiable interpretation, I should by no means now use such a phrase. I was very young when I wrote that poem, and my religious feelings were more settled than my theological notions.

As to eternal punishments, I can only say, that there are many passages in Scripture, and these not metaphorical, which declare that all flesh shall be finally saved; that the word *aionios* is indeed used sometimes when eternity must be meant, but so is the word 'Ancient of Days,' yet it would be strange reasoning to affirm, that therefore, the word ancient must always mean eternal. The literal meaning of '*aionios*' is, 'through ages;' that is, indefinite; beyond the power of imagination to bound. But as to the effects of such a doctrine, I say, First,—that it would be more pious to assert nothing concerning it, one way or the other.

Ezra says well, 'My Son, meditate on the rewards of the Righteous, and examine not over-curiously into the fate of the wicked.' (This Apocryphal Ezra is supposed to have been written by some christian in the first age of christianity.) Second,—that however the doctrine is now broached, and publicly preached by a large and increasing sect, it is no longer possible to conceal it from

desire) a philosophic analysis of the *Don Quixote* of Cervantes. It is intended to give the first lecture on Tuesday next, 5th April, 1814.'

Scheduled for 5, 7, 12, 14, 19, and 21 April at the White Lion, this course was apparently given in full. Announcements for the first four lectures appeared in the Bristol newspapers, and Letter 918 implies that the remaining two were also delivered. *Shakespearean Criticism,* ii. 256–7.

[1] Cf. *Religious Musings,* line 56.

such persons as would be likely to read and understand the Religious Musings. Third.—That if the offers of eternal blessedness; if the love of God; if gratitude; if the fear of punishment, unknown indeed as to its kind and duration, but declared to be unimaginably great; if the possibility, nay, the probability, that this punishment may be followed by annihilation, not final happiness, cannot divert men from wickedness to virtue; I fear there will be no charm in the word Eternal.

Fourth, that it is a certain fact, that scarcely any believe eternal punishment practically with relation to themselves. They all hope in God's mercy, till they make it a presumptuous watch-word for religious indifference. And this, because there is no medium in their faith, between blessedness and misery,—infinite in degree and duration; which latter they do not practically, and with their whole hearts, believe. It is opposite to their clearest views of the divine attributes; for God cannot be vindictive, neither therefore can his punishments be founded on a vindictive principle. They must be, either for amendment, or warning for others; but eternal punishment precludes the idea of amendment; and its infliction, after the day of judgment, when all not so punished shall be divinely secured from the possibility of falling, renders the notion of warning to others inapplicable.

The Catholics are far more afraid of, and incomparably more influenced in their conduct by the doctrine of purgatory, than Protestants by that of hell! That the Catholics practise more superstitions than morals, is the effect of other doctrines. Supererogation; invocation of saints; power of relics, &c. &c. and not of Purgatory, which can only act as a general motive, to what must depend on other causes.

Fifth, and lastly.—It is a perilous state in which a christian stands, if he has gotten no further than to avoid evil from the fear of hell! This is no part of the christian religion, but a preparatory awakening of the soul: a means of dispersing those gross films which render the eye of the spirit incapable of any religion, much less of such a faith as that of the love of Christ.

The fear of the Lord is the beginning of wisdom, but perfect love shutteth out fear. It is sufficient for the utmost fervour of gratitude that we are saved from punishments, too great to be conceived; but our salvation is surely not complete, till by the illumination from above, we are made to know 'the exceeding sinfulness of sin,' and that horribleness in its nature, which, while it involves all these frightful consequences, is yet, of itself more affrightful to a regenerated soul than those consequences. To him who but for a moment felt the influence of God's presence, the thought of eternal exclusion from the sense of that presence, would be the worst hell, his imagination could conceive.

N.B. I admit of no right, no claim of a creature on its Creator. I speak only of hopes and of faith deduced from inevitable reason, the gift of the Creator; from his acknowledged attributes. Above all, immortality is a free gift, which we neither do, nor can deserve. . . .

S. T. C.

914. *To Thomas Curnick*

Address: Mr. T. Curnick
Pub. Nation, *21 August 1913, p. 162, and as* The Thorny Path of Literature, *ed. W. E. A. Axon, 1917.*

Bristol, 9 April, 1814.

Dear Sir:

I have been much affected by your letter, and have perused, with considerable pleasure, the poems which accompanied it. But how can I serve you? Gold and silver have I none; but, on the contrary, I am myself sorely embarrassed. Mr. Southey and I married sisters; and I am on terms of intimacy with him. But it was not to Kirke White, but to his family, that Southey could make himself serviceable, by becoming his biographer and editor, after his premature death.[1]

Many thoughts crowded on me during the perusal of your letter, which pressing engagements prevent me from communicating at present; but within a short time I will endeavour to perform that most arduous duty of one sympathizing Christian to another, that of telling what appears to him to be the truth. O that I could convey to you, in all its liveliness, the anguish of regret which I have a thousand times felt (while obliged, for the bread of the day, to be aiming at excellencies which in the most favored natures require health, competence, tranquillity, and genial feelings), that I had not been taught to earn my subsistence mechanically, where, if my fingers were weary, my heart and brain at least were at rest!

From the time of Pope's translation of Homer, inclusive, so countless have been the poetic metamorphoses of almost all possible thoughts and connections of thought, that it is scarcely practicable for a man to write in the ornamented style on any subject without finding his poem, against his will and without his previous consciousness, a cento of lines that had pre-existed in other works; and this it is which makes poetry so very difficult, because so very easy,

---

[1] Henry Kirke White died in 1806; in the following year Southey published *The Remains of Henry Kirke White* in two volumes.

in the present day. I myself have for many years past given it up in despair.

There is much fire and spirit in your Ode on Lord Wellington;[1] and the chief defect is a confusion of mythology. Cherubs have no connection with Mars; and the first stanza is obscure, because the reader does not know whether you mean Lord Wellington or an imaginary god of war. If the latter, the after introduction of the Almighty is irreverent; or (as the painter's phrase is), 'out of keeping.' If the former, the ponderous *spear*, etc., is not translatable into sense and fact. Poetry must be *more* than good sense, or it is not poetry; but it dare not be less, or discrepant. Good sense is not, indeed, the superstructure; but it is the rock, not only on which the edifice is raised, but likewise the rock-quarry *from* which all its stones have been, by patient toil, dug out.

The whole of next week I am unfortunately preëngaged, day after day, and the whole of each day; but, after that, you will generally find me at No. 2. Queen Square, any time from seven in the evening to ten; and if you can point out any mode in which I can be really useful to you, be assured I shall be most ready to attempt it.

Will you forgive a man who has had repeated occasions for mourning that he had not himself pursued the profession of the law, (a profession which needs only to be considered in the light of a manly philosophy to present many charms to a thinking mind, and which, beyond all others, gives an insight into the real state of society, the hearts, morals, and passions of our fellow-creatures,) to ask you why a man of genius should despair of making genius effective and illustrious in the pursuit of the profession in which it has pleased Providence to place him? I do not know your age, but you inform me that you are an attorney's clerk. Even such was Garrow—such was Dunning.[2]

Do I advise you to desert the Muses? No! I give no advice which, I know, would be vain; but my experience does warrant me, 'with a warning and dolorous blast,'[3] (as Milton says,) to exhort all men of genius to take care that they should rely on literature only for private pleasure and solace; or, at most, for the *dessert* to their dinner, not for the dinner itself.

I beg your acceptance of the enclosed ticket, which, should you

---

[1] *Ode on the Victories obtained by the Allied Armies under the command of Lord Wellington.*

[2] Sir William Garrow (1760–1840), later baron of the exchequer, and John Dunning (1731–83), privy councillor and first Baron Ashburton.

[3] See *The Reason of Church-Government*, Book II: 'But when God commands to take the trumpet, and blow a dolorous or a jarring blast.'

have desire or inclination, will admit yourself and a friend to my
course of lectures.

> With sincere good wishes, yours, dear sir,
> S. T. Coleridge.

915. *To John Prior Estlin*

Address: Dr Estlin | St Michael's Hill
MS. Bristol Central Lib. Pub. E. L. G. ii. 104.

Saturday Night. April 9 1814

Dear Sir

And is it possible that you can reject, and drive from your presence 'a friend, once dear to your Heart,' unquestioned? unheard?
—I have this very moment returned home: and on eagerly opening
your note was, as it were, thunder-struck: and I have no reason to
believe that I should have guessed the cause, had it not been for
an accidental Speech of Mr Le Breton's to me, after my Lecture—
'At a certain phrase of your's, (said he) I looked round to see
whether Dr E. was there'—I instantly replied to him—Would to
Heaven, he had been! the very sight of Him would have made it
impossible that so foolish an expression should have entered into
my mind, much less have been uttered by me.—And (I continued)
yet I solemnly declare, that to the best of my Belief I should have
been just as likely to have used it, being in a similar tone of mind,
at the time that I was myself a most sincere & fervent Unitarian.—

First, dear Sir! let me entreat you to consider that my Lectures,
with exception only of the general Plan & leading Thoughts, are
literally & strictly *extempore*—the words of the moment! Next, let
me hope that the expression used by me has not been represented
with all the palliating Circumstances. Whoever was your Informer,
can likewise tell you that the immediately preceding part of the
Lecture had been of a (*for me*) unusually cheerful & even mirth-
exciting nature—& in speaking of a sublime Invention of Milton,
unsupported by the natural and obvious Sense of the Text (for
had it been a mere quotation, like that of 'Let there be Light! &c'
where had been *his* Sublimity?) I said in previous explanation
these very words—'*for Milton has been pleased to represent Satan
as a sceptical Socinian*'—

Now had I said, that Milton had represented Satan as convinced
of the prophetic & Messianic Character of Christ, but sceptical
concerning any higher claims—I should have stated the mere
matter of fact—& can I think it possible, that you should for ever
withhold your affection & esteem from me merely because most

incautiously & with improper Levity, I confess & with unfeigned
Sorrow, I conveyed the very same thought or fact in a foolish
Phrase ?—

Permit me, Sir! to ask you one Question. Have you ever had
reason to suppose or suspect, that in my expressions of Gratitude
& affectionate Esteem toward you, I have been ever influenced by
a single selfish expectation, or the most distant interested motive ?
Has that been *my* Character ?—or if it had been, can it be supposed
that deliberately & with malice *prepense* I could have openly
insulted a body of Christians, not only comprizing a large number of
the wealthiest & most respectable Citizens of Bristol, but among
these full half of all, whom I know most intimately, most respect,
& who have been most kind & attentive to me—as Mr M. Castle &
Family, & Brothers, Mr Danvers, &c. ?

Dear Sir! Let not tomorrow's Prayer offered to our common
Father for forgiveness pass without an inward forgiveness of me
for an offence, which, I call Heaven witness, was never intended—
which was the result of a momentary Levity, for which I should be
most eager to make any Apology, public or private, as far as is
consistent with the truth—namely, that it was a mere Levity, &
not meant to convey any serious sarcasm on the opinions, you
profess. I do again assert, that as far as I know my own heart &
nature, it is my full conviction, that in the same careless mood of
mind I should have been just as likely to have used the same words
to the same purpose at the time that I was myself a zealous Socinian
—And let D'Anvers or any one who knew me then intimately in my
unguarded Talk, decide whether I have said aught improbable in
this assertion.—I hope, I need not say, that it is the desire of being
present to you in your kind wishes, & not any great pleasure, I
find, in *visiting*—except as far as I at once enjoy & gratify friendly
feelings, that has occasioned you the trouble of reading this long
Letter from him, who (however unkindly you may think of him)
will ever be and avow himself with high esteem

Your obliged & grateful
S. T. C.

916. *To Joseph Cottle*

Pub. Rem. *360*.

Mr. Wade's, Queen Square.
[Sunday, 10 April ?] 1814.

My dear Cottle,

It was near ten before the maid got up, or waked a soul in the
house. We are all in a hurry, for we had all meant to go to Broad-

mead.[1] As to dining, I have not five minutes to spare to the family below, at meals. Do not call, for, if possible, I shall meet you at the Meeting.

S. T. Coleridge.

917. *To Joseph Cottle*

Address: J. Cottle, Esqre | Brunswick Square
MS. Harvard College Lib. Pub. with omis. Early Rec. *ii. 147.*

Tuesday Night, 11 o/clock—[12 April 1814]

My dear Cottle
    I have been engaged three days past to dine with the Sheriff at Merchants' Hall tomorrow—As they will not wield knife & fork till near six, I cannot, of course, attend the meeting[2]—but should it be put off, & you will give me a little longer notice, I will do my best to make my humble Talents serviceable in their proportion to a cause, in which I take no common Interest, which has always my best wishes, & not seldom my prayers.—God bless you

& | your affectionate | Friend
S. T. Coleridge

P.S. To you who know that I prefer a roast potatoe and Salt to the most splendid public Dinner, the very *sight* of which indeed always overlays my infant appetite, I need not say that I am actuated solely by my pre-engagement, & by the impropriety of disappointing the Friend whom I am to accompany, & to whom probably I owe the unexpected Compliment of the Sheriff's Invitation—
    I have read two thirds of Dr Pole's Pamphlet[3] with deep Interest —Thoughts on Thoughts, Feelings on Feelings, crowded upon my mind & heart during the Perusal—and which I would fain, God willing, give vent to! *One* word only shocked me—& ever *will* give me severe pain: because I truly honor & love the orthodox Dissenters, appreciate with heart-esteem their works of Love[4]—but anti-Church Bigotry begetting wilful, tho' not conscious, falsehood —O that is sad, sad, sad, dear Cottle!—I allude to the phrase, the

---

[1] John Ryland was at this time the Baptist minister at the Broadmead chapel.

[2] In *Early Rec.* ii. 148, Cottle here added in brackets: 'for the establishment of an Infant School'.

[3] Thomas Pole, *An Address to the Committee of the Bristol Society for teaching the adult poor to read the Holy Scriptures*, Bristol, 1813.

[4] At this point Cottle interpolated two sentences concerning his *Alfred*. They belong to Letter 925.

Lancasterian System—Discovery, &c—I have myself seen Letters of Lancaster written soon after the first publication of Dr Bell's truly Bacon-like Work, in which he in plain words thanks the Dr for the grand & new Discovery of making the children *systematically* each other's Teachers.—I can prove that before Lancaster ever dreamt of *the* System, it was carried into full efficacy at Kendal—Southey's Book is a dilution of my Lecture at the R.I.—Would that he had not interspersed so much bitterness.

918. *To Joseph Cottle*

Address: J. Cottle, Esqre. | Brunswick Square
MS. Mr. Basil Cottle. Pub. with omis. Early Rec. *ii. 146.*

April 24, 1814

My dear Cottle

An erysipelatous complaint, of an alarming nature, has rendered me barely able to attend, & go thro' with, my Lectures[1]—the Receipts of which have *almost* paid the expences of the Room, Advertisements, &c.—Whether this be to *my* Discredit, or that of the good Citizens of Bristol, it is not for me to judge.

I have been persuaded to make another Trial, by advertising 3 Lectures, on the Rise, & Progress, & Conclusion of the French Revolution, with a critique on the proposed Constitution;[2] but unless 50 names are procured, not a Lecture give I.—

Even so the two far, far more important Lectures, for which I have been long preparing myself and have given more thought to than to any other Subject, viz. those on female Education from Infancy to Womanhood, practically systematized, I shall be (God permitting) ready to give, the latter end of the Week after next[3]—

[1] This statement suggests that Coleridge completed his course of lectures on 19 and 21 April.

[2] These lectures, which were advertised in *Felix Farley's Bristol Journal* on 23 April, were planned for 26 and 29 April and 3 May. Only the first was delivered as scheduled. Ill health caused the postponement of the other two, and they were probably never given. On 30 April 1814 *Felix Farley's Bristol Journal* printed a brief report of the first lecture, which 'Mr. C., from severe indisposition, was compelled abruptly to close. . . . He has since continued so indisposed that he was last night also obliged to postpone his second lecture, which if his health permits, he hopes to deliver on Tuesday evening in the ensuing week.'

[3] There is no evidence that these two lectures were delivered. They had been mentioned on 2 April in *Felix Farley's Bristol Journal*: 'MR. COLERIDGE has been desired by several highly respectable Ladies to carry into effect a plan of giving one or two lectures, in the morning, on the subject of FEMALE EDUCATION, of a nature altogether practical, and explaining the whole machinery of a school organized on rational principles, from the earliest age to

but upon condition, that I am assured of 60 names—Why, as these
are Lectures, that I must *write down*, I could sell them as a *recipe*,
for twice the sum, at least. If therefore you or your Sisters are disposed to attend, be pleased to send your names.—

If I can walk out, I will be with you on Sunday.—

Has Mr Wade called on you?—Mr Le Breton, a near Neighbor
of your's, in Portland Square, would (if you sent a note to him)
converse with you on any subject relative to my Interests with
congenial Sympathy—but indeed I think your Idea one of these
Chimaeras, which Kindness begets upon Unacquaintance with
Mankind[1]—'Harry! thy Wish was Father to that Thought.'[2]
Shaksp.

God bless you &
S. T. C.—

the completion of FEMALE EDUCATION, with a list of the books recommended,
&c. so as to evolve gradually into utility and domestic happiness the powers
and qualities of Womanhood. Should a sufficient number of Ladies and
Gentlemen express their design to patronise this plan, Mr. Coleridge will hold
himself ready to realise it, at such time as may be found most convenient to his
auditors.' *Shakespearean Criticism*, ii. 258 n.

[1] Cottle had proposed to raise a subscription for an annuity, in order that
Coleridge, 'his mind . . . relieved by the certainty of a present income', might
produce 'great things'. Southey bitterly opposed this plan and in writing to
Cottle on 17 and 18 April revealed not only his usual propensity to decide what
was best for Coleridge but a deplorable lack of either sympathy or understanding. Emphasizing Coleridge's 'most culpable habits of sloth and self-indulgence',
he declared that the 'embarrassments and . . . miseries of body and mind . . .
[were] all owing to one accursed cause—excess in opium'. He argued that a
subscription should be raised only 'where the object is disabled from exerting
himself—or when his exertions are unproductive', but he found Coleridge 'in
neither of these predicaments'. Southey erroneously assumed that it lay within
Coleridge's power to break the opium habit—'Nothing is wanting to make him
easy in circumstances and happy in himself, but to leave off opium, and devote
a certain portion of his time to the discharge of his duty'. Coleridge, he insisted,
'should return home [to Greta Hall], raising a supply for the present exigencies
of his wife and children by lecturing at Birmingham and Liverpool'. Southey
was specific about his letter of 17 April: 'Do not communicate this letter to
Wade ; he would report it to C. and make mischief.' [MSS. New York Public Lib.]
I am indebted to Professor Kenneth Curry for sending me transcripts of
Southey's letters to Cottle. See *Rem*. 376–9 for Cottle's mangled version of these
two letters.

The effect of his letters was exactly what Southey desired—Cottle abandoned
his plan to provide Coleridge with financial assistance.

[2] *Henry IV*, Part II, IV. v. 93.

919. *To Joseph Cottle*

Address: Joseph Cottle, Esqre | Brunswick Square
MS. New York Public Lib. Pub. E. L. G. ii. 107. See *Early Rec*. ii. 112 and 155,
where Cottle prints this manuscript as two letters.

Coleridge's heart-rending outburst was occasioned by a letter from Cottle of
25 April. Bolstered by Southey's unfeeling letters of 17 and 18 April, Cottle
saw fit to berate Coleridge and to exhort him to renounce opium 'from this
moment', to return to Keswick, and to exert 'the ample abilities which God has
given you'. Like Southey, Cottle assumed that Coleridge could abandon opium
by a mere act of the will. See *Rem*. 361–6, and Letter 918.

April 26, 1814

You have poured oil in the raw and festering Wound of an old
friend's Conscience, Cottle! but it is oil of Vitriol! I but barely
glanced at the middle of the first page of your Letter, & have seen
no more of it—not from resentment (God forbid!) but from the
state of my bodily & mental sufferings, that scarcely permitted
human fortitude to let in a new visitor of affliction. The object of
my present reply is to state the case just as it is—first, that for
years the anguish of my spirit has been indescribable, the sense of
my danger *staring*, but the conscience of my GUILT worse, far far
worse than all!—I have prayed with drops of agony on my Brow,
trembling not only before the Justice of my Maker, but even before
the Mercy of my Redeemer. 'I gave thee so many Talents. What
hast thou done with them'?—Secondly—that it is false & cruel to
say, (overwhelmed as I am with the sense of my direful Infirmity)
that I attempt or ever have attempted to *disguise* or conceal the
cause. On the contrary, not only to friends have I stated the whole
Case with tears & the very bitterness of shame; but in two instances I have warned young men, mere acquaintances who had
spoken of having taken Laudanum, of the direful Consequences, by
an ample exposition of it's tremendous effects on myself—Thirdly,
tho' before God I dare not lift up my eyelids, & only do not despair
of his Mercy because to despair would be adding crime to crime;
yet to my fellow-men I may say, that I was seduced into the
ACCURSED Habit ignorantly.—I had been almost bed-ridden for
many months with swellings in my knees—in a medical Journal I
unhappily met with an account of a cure performed in a similar
case (or what to me appeared so) by rubbing in of Laudanum, at
the same time taking a given dose internally—It acted like a
charm, like a miracle! I recovered the use of my Limbs, of my
appetite, of my Spirits—& this continued for near a fortnight—
At length, the unusual Stimulus subsided—the complaint returned
—the supposed remedy was recurred to——but I can not go thro'
the dreary history—suffice it to say, that effects were produced,

which acted on me by *Terror* & *Cowardice* of PAIN & sudden Death, not (so help me God!) by any temptation of Pleasure, or expectation or desire of exciting pleasurable Sensations. On the very contrary, Mrs Morgan & her Sister will bear witness so far, as to say that the longer I abstained, the higher my spirits were, the keener my enjoyments—till the moment, the direful moment, arrived, when my pulse began to fluctuate, my Heart to palpitate, & such a dreadful *falling-abroad*, as it were, of my whole frame, such intolerable Restlessness & incipient Bewilderment, that in the last of my several attempts to abandon the dire poison, I exclaimed in agony, what I now repeat in seriousness & solemnity—'I am too poor to hazard this! Had I but a few hundred Pounds, but 200£, half to send to Mrs Coleridge, & half to place myself in a private madhouse, where I could procure nothing but what a Physician thought proper, & where a medical attendant could be constantly with me for two or three months (in less than that time Life or Death would be determined) then there might be Hope. Now there is none!'—O God! how willingly would I place myself under Dr Fox in his Establishment[1]—for my Case is a species of madness, only that it is a derangement, an utter impotence of the *Volition*, & not of the intellectual Faculties—You bid me rouse myself—go, bid a man paralytic in both arms rub them briskly together, & that will cure him. Alas! (he would reply) that I cannot move my arms is my Complaint & my misery.—

My friend, Wade, is not at home—& I sent off all the little money, I had—or I would with this have inclosed the 10£ received from you.[2]—

May God bless you | & | Your affectionate & | most afflicted
S. T. Coleridge.—

Dr Estlin, I found, is raising the city against me, as far as he & his friends can, for having stated a mere matter of fact, . . .[3]—viz— that Milton had represented Satan as a sceptical Socinian—which is the case, & I could not have explained the excellence of the sublimest single Passage in all his Writings had I not previously informed the Audience, that Milton had represented Satan as knowing the prophetic & Messianic Character of Christ, but sceptical as to any higher Claims—& what other definition could

---

[1] See Letter 921.
[2] According to Cottle, after one of the lectures Coleridge said that a 'dirty fellow' threatened to arrest him for £10. 'Shocked at the idea' Cottle gave him the money. Then in writing to Coleridge on 25 April Cottle said: 'For opium you will . . . expose yourself to the liability of arrest, by some "dirty fellow," to whom you choose to be indebted for "ten pounds!"' *Rem.* 357 and 363.
[3] Several words heavily inked out in MS.

Dr E. himself give of a sceptical Socinian?—Now that M. has done so, please to consult, Par. Regained, Book IV. from line 196.—& then the same Book from line 500.—

920. *To Joseph Cottle*

Address: J. Cottle, Esqre
MS. Mr. W. Hugh Peal. Pub. Early Rec. *ii. 160.* On receiving Letter 919 Cottle wrote that he was 'afflicted to perceive that Satan is so busy with you, but God is greater than Satan. Did you ever hear of Jesus Christ?' He called upon Coleridge to pray: 'Pray earnestly, and you will be heard by your Father, which is in Heaven.' *Early Rec.* ii. 159–60.

April 26. 1814

O dear Friend!—I have too much to be forgiven to feel any difficulty in forgiving the cruellest enemy that ever trampled on me: & *you* I have only to *thank*.—You have no conception of the dreadful Hell of my mind & conscience & body. You bid me, pray. O I do pray inwardly to be able to *pray*; but indeed to pray, to pray with the faith to which Blessing is promised, this is the reward of Faith, this is the Gift of God to the Elect. O if to feel how infinitely worthless I am, how poor a wretch, with just free will enough to be deserving of wrath, & of my own contempt, & of none to merit a moment's peace, can make a part of a Christian's creed; so far I am a Christian—

S. T. C.

921. *To Joseph Cottle*

Address: J. Cottle, Esqre. | Brunswick Square.
MS. Cornell University Lib. Pub. Collection of Alfred Morrison, *1895, ii. 259.*

[*Circa* 27] April 1814.[1]

Dear Cottle[2]

Christians expect no outward or sensible Miracles from Prayer— it's effects and it's fruitions are spiritual, and accompanied (to use the words of that true *Divine*, Archbishop *Leighton) 'not by

---

[1] J. D. Campbell (*Life*, 202) suggests that this letter, in which Coleridge 'enlarged, very calmly, on the reasonable expectations a Christian may entertain on the subject of sincere prayer', was probably written 'on the day following' Letter 920.

[2] In *Early Rec.* ii. 83, where this letter is printed, Cottle here interpolated the words, 'To pursue out last conversation'.

* Are you familiar with his works? He resigned his Archbishoprick & retired to voluntary Poverty, on account of the persecution of the Presbyterians —saying 'I should not dare introduce Christianity itself with such cruelties—

Reasons and Arguments; but by an inexpressible Kind of Evidence, which they only know who have it.'—To this I would add that even those who (like me, I *fear*) have not attained it may yet *presume* it—1. because Reason itself, or rather mere human Nature in any dispassionate moment, feels the *necessity* of Religion; 2. but if this be not true, there is no Religion, no *Religation* or Binding over again, nothing added to Reason—& therefore Socinianism is not only not Christianity, it is not even *Religion*— it doth not *religate*, doth not bind anew—

The first outward and sensible Result of Prayer is a penitent Resolution, joined with a consciousness of weakness in effecting it (yea, even a dread too well grounded, lest by breaking & falsifying it the soul should add guilt to guilt by the very means, it has taken to escape from Guilt—so pitiable is the state of unregenerated man!).[1] Now I have resolved to place myself in any situation, in which I can remain for a month or two as *a Child*, wholly in the Power of others—But alas! I have no money—Will you write [to] Mr Hood (a most dear & affectionate Friend to worthless me), to Mr Le Breton, my old Schoolfellow, & likewise a most affectionate Friend, & to Mr Wade, who will return in a few Days—desire them to call on you any evening after 7 o'clock that they can make convenient—& consult with them whether any thing of this kind can be done?—

Do you know Dr Fox?[2]—

how much less a surplice, & the name of a Bishop?'—If there could be an intermediate Space between inspired & uninspired Writings, that Space would be occupied by Leighton.—No Shew of Learning! no appearance of Eloquence (and both may be shewn properly & holily) but a something that must be felt even as the Scriptures must be felt.—[Note by S. T. C.]

[1] At this point Cottle inserted as part of the text Coleridge's footnote on Leighton; he then added Letter 922 and dated the whole Bristol, 1807. The remainder of the present manuscript he printed as a separate undated letter. See *Early Rec.* ii. 83–99 and 162.

[2] Although Coleridge's wish to put himself under restraint, as expressed in this and Letter 919, was the wisest course to be adopted for one in so pitiable a condition, Cottle did not act on it; rather he sent Coleridge's letters to Southey, who negatived any plan for confinement. 'You may imagine', Southey wrote, 'with what feelings I have read your correspondence with C[oleridge]. Shocking as his letters are perhaps the most mournful thing which they discover is that while acknowledging the guilt of the habit, he imputes it still to morbid bodily causes, whereas after every possible allowance is made for these, every person who has witnessed his habits, knows that for the greater —infinitely the greater part—inclination and indulgence are the motives. It seems dreadful to say this with his expressions before me, but it is so and I know it to be so, from my own observation and that of all with whom he has lived. . . . This, Cottle, is an insanity of that species which none but the Soul's physician can cure. Unquestionably restraint would do for him as much as it did when the Morgans tried it, but I do not see the slightest reason for thinking it

To Joseph Cottle

I have not yet read your former Letter—for I have to prepare my Lecture[1]—O! with how *blank* a spirit!

S. T. Coleridge

922. *To Joseph Cottle*

Pub. Early Rec. *ii. 85.* Cottle printed this letter as the conclusion to Letter 921, dating the whole 1807. Cottle's text, as J. D. Campbell suggests, is highly suspect. *Life,* 165 n.

Bristol, [Late April 1814][2]

... You ask me my views of the *Trinity.* I accept the doctrine, not as deduced from human reason, in its grovelling capacity for comprehending spiritual things, but as the clear revelation of Scripture. But perhaps it may be said, the *Socinians* do not admit this doctrine as being taught in the bible. I know enough of their shifts and quibbles, with their dexterity at explaining away all they dislike, (and that is not a little) but though beguiled once by them, I happily, for my own peace of mind, escaped from their sophistries, and now, hesitate not to affirm, that Socinians would lose all character for honesty, if they were to explain their neighbour's will with the same latitude of interpretation, which they do the Scriptures.

I have in my head some floating ideas on the *Logos,*[3] which I hope, hereafter, to mould into a consistent form; but it is a gross perversion of the truth, in *Socinians,* to declare that we believe in *Three Gods,* and they know it to be false. They might, with equal justice affirm that we believe in *three suns.* The meanest peasant, who has acquired the first rudiments of christianity, would shrink back from a thought so monstrous. Still the Trinity has its difficulties. It would be strange if otherwise. A *Revelation* that revealed nothing, not within the grasp of human reason!—no religation, no

would be more permanent. . . . The restraint which would effectually cure him is that which no person can impose upon him. Could he be compelled to a certain quantity of labour for his family every day, the pleasure of having done it would make his heart glad, and the sane mind would make the body sane.' Southey went on to repeat his advice that Coleridge should return to Keswick. [MS. New York Public Lib. From a transcript kindly supplied by Professor Curry.] Pub. *Rem.* 373–5.

Coleridge remained at Wade's, and through Hood's kindness Henry Daniel, a Bristol physician, was called in to care for him. See Letters 927–8.

    [1] This lecture must be the one originally scheduled for 29 April. See Letter 918.
    [2] This letter was obviously written shortly after Letter 921.
    [3] This is the first reference in the letters to Coleridge's proposed work on the Logos. See Letter 951.

binding over again, as before said:[1] but these difficulties are
shadows, contrasted with the substantive and insurmountable
obstacles with which they contend who admit the *Divine authority
of Scripture*, with the *superlative excellence of Christ*, and yet undertake to prove that these Scriptures teach, and that Christ taught,
his own *pure humanity*!

If Jesus Christ was merely a Man,—if he was not God as well as
Man, be it considered, he could not have been even a *good man*.
There is no medium. The SAVIOUR *in that case* was absolutely *a
deceiver*! one, transcendently *unrighteous*! in advancing pretensions
to miracles, by the 'Finger of God,' which he never performed; and
by asserting claims, (as a man) in the most aggravated sense,
blasphemous! These consequences, Socinians, to be consistent,
must allow, and which impious arrogation of Divinity in Christ,
(according to their faith,) as well as his false assumption of a
community of 'glory' with the Father, 'before the world was,' even
they will be necessitated to admit, completely exonerated the Jews,
according to their law, in crucifying one, who 'being a man,'
'made himself God!' But in the Christian, rather than in the
Socinian, or *Pharisaic* view, all these objections vanish, and harmony succeeds to inexplicable confusion. If Socinians hesitate in
ascribing *unrighteousness* to Christ, the inevitable result of their
principles, they tremble, as well they might, at their avowed
creed, and virtually renounce what they profess to uphold.

The Trinity, as Bishop Leighton[2] has well remarked, is 'a doctrine of faith, not of demonstration,' except in a *moral* sense. If the
New Testament declare it, not in an insulated passage, but through
the whole breadth of its pages, rendering, with any other admission,
the Book, which is the christian's anchor-hold of hope, dark and
contradictory, then it is not to be rejected, but on a penalty that
reduces to an atom, all the sufferings this earth can inflict.

Let the grand question be determined: Is, or is not the Bible
inspired? No one Book has ever been subjected to so rigid an
investigation as the Bible, by minds the most capacious, and, in the
result, which has so triumphantly repelled all the assaults of
Infidels. In the extensive intercourse which I have had with this
class of men, I have seen their prejudices surpassed only by their
ignorance. This I found conspicuously the case in Dr. D.,[3] the
prince of their fraternity. Without, therefore, stopping to contend
on what all dispassionate men must deem undebatable ground, I

[1] See first paragraph of preceding letter.
[2] Robert Leighton (1611–84), archbishop of Glasgow, for whose writings
Coleridge had an almost reverential admiration.
[3] Erasmus Darwin. See Letter 99.

may assume inspiration as admitted; and, equally so, that it would be an insult to man's understanding, to suppose any other Revelation from God than the christian Scriptures. If these Scriptures, impregnable in their strength, sustained in their pretensions by undeniable prophecies and miracles, and by the experience of the *inner man*, in all ages, as well as by a concatenation of arguments, all bearing upon one point, and extending, with miraculous consistency, through a series of fifteen hundred years; if all this combined proof does not establish their validity, nothing can be proved under the sun; but the world and man must be abandoned, with all its consequences to one universal scepticism! Under such sanctions, therefore, if these Scriptures, as a fundamental truth, *do* inculcate the doctrine of the *Trinity*, however surpassing human comprehension, then I say, we are bound to admit it on the strength of *moral demonstration*.

The supreme Governor of the world, and the Father of our spirits, has seen fit to disclose to us much of his will, and the whole of his natural and moral perfections. In some instances he has given his *word* only, and demanded our *faith*; while on other momentous subjects, instead of bestowing a full revelation, like the *Via Lactea*, he has furnished a glimpse only, through either the medium of inspiration, or by the exercise of those rational faculties with which he has endowed us. I consider the Trinity as substantially resting on the first proposition, yet deriving support from the last.

I recollect when I stood on the summit of Etna, and darted my gaze down the crater; the immediate vicinity was discernible, till, lower down, obscurity gradually terminated in total darkness. Such figures exemplify many truths revealed in the Bible. We pursue them, until, from the imperfection of our faculties, we are lost in impenetrable night. All truths, however, that are essential to faith, *honestly* interpreted, all that are important to human conduct, under every diversity of circumstance, are manifest as a blazing star. The promises also of felicity to the righteous in the future world, though the precise nature of that felicity may not be defined, are illustrated by every image that can swell the imagination; while the misery of the *lost*, in its unutterable intensity, though the language that describes it is all necessarily figurative, is there exhibited as resulting chiefly, if not wholly, from the withdrawment of the *light of God's countenance*, and a banishment from his *presence*!—best comprehended in this world by reflecting on the desolations which would instantly follow the loss of the sun's vivifying and universally diffused *warmth*.

You, or rather *all*, should remember that some truths, from their nature, surpass the scope of man's limited powers, and stand as the criteria of *faith*, determining, by their rejection, or admission, who among the sons of men can confide in the veracity of heaven. Those more ethereal truths, of which the Trinity is conspicuously the chief, without being circumstantially explained, may be faintly illustrated by material objects.—The eye of man cannot discern the satellites of Jupiter, nor become sensible of the multitudinous stars, whose rays have never reached our planet, and, consequently, garnish not the canopy of night; yet, are they the less *real*, because their existence lies beyond man's unassisted gaze? The tube of the philosopher, and the *celestial telescope*,—the unclouded visions of heaven will confirm the one class of truths, and irradiate the other.

The *Trinity* is a subject on which analogical reasoning may advantageously be admitted, as furnishing, at least, a glimpse of light, and with this, for the present, we must be satisfied. Infinite Wisdom deemed clearer manifestations inexpedient; and is man to dictate to his Maker? I may further remark, that where we cannot behold a desirable object distinctly, we must take the best view we can; and I think you, and every candid and enquiring mind, may derive assistance from such reflections as the following.

Notwithstanding the arguments of Spinoza, and Descartes, and other advocates of the *Material system*, (or, in more appropriate language, the *Atheistical system!*) it is admitted by all men, not prejudiced, not biased by sceptical prepossessions, that *mind* is distinct from *matter*. The mind of man, however, is involved in inscrutable darkness, (as the profoundest metaphysicians well know) and is to be estimated (if at all) alone by an inductive process; that is, by its *effects*. Without entering on the question, whether an extremely circumscribed portion of the mental process, surpassing instinct, may, or may not, be extended to quadrupeds, it is universally acknowledged, that the mind of man, alone, regulates all the voluntary actions of his corporeal frame. Mind, therefore, may be regarded as a distinct genus, in the scale ascending above brutes, and including the whole of intellectual existences; advancing from *thought*, (that mysterious thing!) in its lowest form, through all the gradations of sentient and rational beings, till it arrives at a Bacon, a Newton, and then, when unincumbered by matter, extending its illimitable sway through Seraph and Archangel, till we are lost in the GREAT INFINITE!

Is it not deserving of notice, as an especial subject of meditation, that our *limbs*, in all they do or can accomplish, implicitly obey the dictation of the *mind*? that this operating power, whatever its name, under certain limitations, exercises a sovereign dominion, not only over our limbs, but over all our intellectual pursuits? The mind of every man is evidently the fulcrum, the moving force, which alike regulates all his limbs and actions; and in which example, we find a strong illustration of the subordinate nature of mere *matter*. That alone which gives direction to the organic parts of our nature, is wholly *mind*; and one mind, if placed over a thousand limbs, could, with undiminished ease, control and regulate the whole.

This idea is advanced on the supposition, that *one mind* could command an unlimited direction over any given number of *limbs*, provided they were all connected by *joint* and *sinew*. But suppose, through some occult and inconceivable means, these limbs were dis-associated, as to all material connexion; suppose, for instance, one mind with unlimited authority, governed the operations of *two* separate persons, would not this, substantially, be only *one person*, seeing the directing principle was one? If the truth, here contended for, be admitted, that *two persons*, governed by *one mind*, is incontestably *one person*; the same conclusion would be arrived at, and the proposition equally be justified, which affirmed that, *three*, or otherwise, *four* persons, owning also necessary and essential subjection to *one mind*, would only be so many diversities or modifications of that *one mind*, and therefore the component parts virtually collapsing into *one whole*, the person would be *one*. Let any man ask himself, whose understanding can both reason and become the depository of truth, whether, if *one mind* thus regulated with absolute authority, *three*, or otherwise, *four* persons, with all their congeries of material parts, would not these parts, inert in themselves, when subjected to one predominant mind, be, in the most logical sense, *one person*? Are ligament and exterior combination indispensable pre-requisities to the sovereign influence of mind over mind? or mind over matter?

But perhaps it may be said, we have no instance of one mind governing more than one body. This may be, but the argument remains the same. With a proud spirit, that forgets its own contracted range of thought and circumscribed knowledge, who is to limit the sway of Omnipotence? or presumptuously to deny the possibility of *that* Being, who called light out of darkness, so to exalt the dominion of *one mind*, as to give it absolute sway over other dependent minds, or (indifferently) over detached, or combined portions of organized matter? But if this superinduced quality be conferable on any order of created beings, it is blasphemy to limit the power of GOD, and to deny *his* capacity to transfuse *his own* Spirit, when and to whom he will.

This reasoning may now be applied in illustration of the Trinity.

We are too much in the habit of viewing our Saviour Jesus Christ, through the medium of his body. 'A body was prepared for him,' but this body was mere matter; as insensible in itself, as every human frame when deserted by the soul. If therefore the Spirit that was in Christ, was the Spirit of the Father; if no thought, no vibration, no spiritual communication, or miraculous display, existed in, or proceeded from Christ, not immediately and consubstantially identified with JEHOVAH, the Great First cause; if all these operating principles were thus derived, in consistency alone with the conjoint divine attributes; if this Spirit of the Father ruled and reigned in Christ as his own manifestation, then, in the strictest sense, Christ exhibited 'the God-head bodily,' and was undeniably '*one* with the Father;' confirmatory of the Saviour's words: 'Of myself,' (my body) 'I can do nothing, the Father that dwelleth in me, he doeth the works.'

But though I speak of the body as inert in itself, and necessarily allied to matter, yet this declaration must not be understood as militating against the christian doctrine of the *resurrection of the body*. In its grosser form, the thought is not to be admitted, for 'flesh and blood cannot inherit the kingdom of God,' but that the body, without losing its consciousness and individuality, may be subjected, by the illimitable power of Omnipotence, to a sublimating process, so as to be rendered compatible with spiritual association, is not opposed to reason, in its severe abstract exercises, while in attestation of this *exhilarating belief*, there are many remote analogies in nature exemplifying the same truth, while it is in the strictest accordance with that final dispensation, which must, as christians, regulate all our speculations. I proceed now to say, that:

If the postulate be thus admitted, that one mind influencing two bodies would only involve a diversity of operations, but in reality be one in essence; or otherwise, (as an hypothetical argument, illustrative of truth) if one pre-eminent mind, or spiritual subsistence, unconnected with matter, possessed an undivided and sovereign dominion over two or more disembodied minds, so as to become the exclusive source of all their subtlest volitions and exercises, the *unity*, however complex the modus of its manifestation, would be fully established; and this principle extends to DEITY itself, and shows the true sense, as I conceive, in which Christ and the Father are one.

In continuation of this reasoning, if God who is light, the Sun of the Moral World, should in his union of Infinite Wisdom, Power, and Goodness, and from all Eternity, have ordained that an emanation from himself (for aught we know, an essential emanation, as light is inseparable from the luminary of day) should not only

(485)

have existed in his Son, in the fulness of time to be united to a
mortal body, but that a like emanation from himself (also perhaps
essential) should have constituted the Holy Spirit, who, without
losing his ubiquity, was more especially sent to this lower earth, *by*
the Son, *at* the impulse of the Father, then, in the most comprehensive sense, God, and his Son, Jesus Christ, and the Holy Ghost,
are ONE—'Three Persons in one God,' and thus form the true
Trinity in Unity.

To suppose that more than ONE Independent Power, or Governing mind, exists in the whole universe, is absolute Polytheism,
against which the denunciations of all the Jewish and Christian
Canonical books were directed. And if there be but ONE directing
MIND, that Mind is GOD!—operating, however, in Three Persons,
according to the direct and uniform declarations of that inspiration
which 'brought life and immortality to light.' Yet this divine
doctrine of the Trinity is to be received, not because it is or can be
clear to finite apprehension, but, (in reiteration of the argument)
because the Scriptures, in their unsophisticated interpretation
expressly state it. The Trinity, therefore, from its important
aspects, and Biblical prominence, is the grand article of faith, and
the foundation of the whole christian system.

Who can say, as Christ and the Holy Ghost proceeded from, and
are still one with the Father, and as all the disciples of Christ derive their fulness from him, and, in spirit, are inviolately united to
him as a branch is to the vine, who can say, but that in one view,
what was once mysteriously separated, may, as mysteriously, be
recombined, and (without interfering with the everlasting Trinity,
and the individuality of the spiritual and seraphic orders) the Son,
at the consummation of all things, deliver up his mediatorial
kingdom to the Father, and God, in some peculiar and infinitely
sublime sense, become All *in* All!

God love you,

S. T. Coleridge.

923. *To Josiah Wade*

Pub. Early Rec. *ii. 133.*

Tuesday night, i.e. Wednesday morning.

[3–4 May 1814][1]

My best and dearest friend,

I have barely time to scribble a few lines, so as not to miss the
post, for here as every where, there are charitable people, who,

[1] This letter was probably written a week after Cottle's letters of 25 and
26 April and not, as Cottle implies, in 1807. See headnotes to Letters 919 and
920.

taking for granted that you have no business of your own, would save from the pain of vacancy, by employing you in theirs.

As to the letter you propose to write to a man who is unworthy even of a rebuke from you,[1] I might most unfeignedly object to some parts of it, from a pang of conscience forbidding me to allow, even from a dear friend, words of admiration, which are inapplicable in exact proportion to the power given to me of having deserved them, if I had done my duty.

It is not of comparative utility I speak: for as to what has been actually done, and in relation to useful effects produced, whether on the minds of individuals, or of the public, I dare boldly stand forward, and (let every man have his own, and that be counted mine which, but for, and through me, would not have existed) will challenge the proudest of my literary contemporaries to compare proofs with me, of usefulness in the excitement of reflection, and the diffusion of original or forgotten, yet necessary and important truths and knowledge; and this is not the less true, because I have suffered others to reap all the advantages. But, oh! dear friend, this consciousness, raised by insult of enemies, and alienated friends, stands me in little stead to my own soul, in how little then, before the all-righteous Judge! who, requiring back the talents he had entrusted, will, if the mercies of Christ do not intervene, not demand of me what I have done, but why I did not do more; why, with powers above so many, I had sunk in many things below most! But this is too painful, and in remorse we often waste the energy which should be better employed in reformation—that essential part, and only possible proof, of sincere repentance. . . .

May God bless you, and Your affectionate friend,

S. T. Coleridge.

924. *To Joseph Cottle*

Pub. Rem. *360*.

[9 May] 1814.[2]

My dear Cottle,

The first time I have been out of the house, save once at meeting; and the very first call I have made. I will be with you to-morrow by noon, if I have no relapse. This is the third morning, that, thank heaven, I have been free from vomiting. . . .

¹ Probably Cottle, of whose activities Coleridge had certainly written to Wade. See Letter 935.

² As Letter 935 shows, Cottle had burst a small blood vessel in his chest. Since Letter 926, dated 13th May 1814, mentions a call 'last Monday to enquire in person' concerning Cottle's health, the present note, which Cottle says was 'Written on a card' and which was apparently left with Miss Cottle, must belong to Monday, 9 May.

925. *To Joseph Cottle*

Address: Mr Cottle | Miss Cottle's Boarding-School, Corner | House in Bruns-wick Square
MS. Harvard College Lib. Pub. with omis. Rem. *359.*

My dear Cottle   [10 May 1814][1]

On my return home yesterday I was & continued unwell so as to be obliged to lie down for great part of the evening—& my indisposition keeping me awake during the whole night, I found it necessary to take some magnesia & Calomel—& I am at present so very sick at Stomach (the medicine operating both ways) that I have little chance of being able to stir out of doors this morning—but if I am better, I will see you in the evening.—

I have received the C. of *Camb.*[2]—& read with much pleasure the second preface to Alfred,[3] which is very well written,[4] & suited to your intentions. God bless you &

S. T. Coleridge

This note has been detained for want of a messenger a full hour, and more.

926. *To Miss Cottle*

Address: To Miss Cottle, Brunswick Square.
Pub. Early Rec. ii. 164.

Dear Madam,   13th May, 1814.

I am uneasy to know how my friend, J. Cottle, goes on. The walk I took last Monday to enquire in person proved too much for my strength, and shortly after my return, I was in such a swooning way, that I was directed to go to bed, and orders were given that no one should interrupt me. Indeed, I cannot be sufficiently grateful for the skill with which the surgeon treats me. But it must be a slow, and occasionally, an interrupted progress, after a sad retrogress of nearly twelve years. To God all things are possible. I intreat your prayers, your brother has a share in mine.

What an astonishing privilege, that a sinner should be permitted to cry, 'Our Father!' Oh! still more stupendous mercy, that this poor ungrateful sinner should be exhorted, invited, nay, commanded, to pray—to pray importunately! That which great men

---

[1] This letter was written the day after Letter 924.
[2] Coleridge refers to Cottle's *Fall of Cambria*.
[3] The third edition of Cottle's *Alfred* was published in 1814.
[4] These comments concerning the preface to *Alfred* Cottle transferred to Letter 917.

most detest, namely, importunacy: to *this* the GIVER and the
FORGIVER ENCOURAGES *his* sick petitioners!

I will not trouble you, except for one verbal answer to this note.
How is your brother?

> With affectionate respects to yourself and your sister,
>
> S. T. Coleridge.

927. *To J. J. Morgan*

Address: J. J. Morgan, Esqre | Mrs E. Smith's | Ashley Cottage | Box | near
Bath
*MS. formerly in the possession of the late A. H. Hallam Murray. Pub. E. L. G.
ii. 110.*
Postmark: Bristol, 14 May 1814.

> 14 May, Saturday [1814]
>
> 2. Queen's Square—

My dear Morgan

If it could be said with as little *appearance* of profaneness, as
there is feeling or intention in my mind, I might affirm; that I
had been crucified, dead, and buried, descended into *Hell*, and am
now, I humbly trust, rising again, tho' slowly and gradually. I
thank you from my heart for your far too kind Letter to Mr Hood—
so much of it is true that such as you described I always wished to
be. I know, it will be vain to attempt to persuade Mrs Morgan or
Charlotte, that a man, whose moral feelings, reason, understanding,
and senses are perfectly sane and vigorous, may yet have been *mad*
—And yet nothing is more true. By the long long Habit of the
accursed Poison my Volition (by which I mean the faculty *instru-
mental* to the Will, and by which alone the Will can realize itself—
it's Hands, Legs, & Feet, as it were) was compleatly deranged, at
times frenzied, dissevered itself from the Will, & became an independent faculty: so that I was perpetually in the state, in which
you may have seen paralytic Persons, who attempting to push a
step forward in one direction are violently forced round to the
opposite. I was sure that no ease, much less pleasure, would ensue:
nay, was certain of an accumulation of pain. But tho' there was no
prospect, no gleam of Light before, an indefinite indescribable
Terror as with a scourge of ever restless, ever coiling and uncoiling
Serpents, drove me on from behind.—The worst was, that in
exact proportion to the *importance* and *urgency* of any Duty was it,
as of a fatal necessity, sure to be neglected: because it added to the
Terror above described. In exact proportion, as I *loved* any person
or persons more than others, & would have sacrificed my Life for
them, were *they* sure to be the most barbarously mistreated by

silence, absence, or breach of promise.—I used to think St James's
Text, 'He who offendeth in one point of the Law, offendeth in all',
very harsh; but my own sad experience has taught me it's aweful,
dreadful Truth.—What crime is there scarcely which has not been
included in or followed from the one guilt of taking opium? Not
to speak of ingratitude to my maker for the wasted Talents; of
ingratitude to so many friends who have loved me I know not why;
of barbarous neglect of my family; excess of cruelty to Mary &
Charlotte, when at Box, and both ill—(a vision of Hell to me when
I think of it!) I have in this one dirty business of Laudanum an
hundred times deceived, tricked, nay, actually & consciously
LIED.—And yet *all* these vices are so opposite to my nature, that
but for this *free-agency-annihilating* Poison, I verily believe that
I should have suffered myself to have been cut to pieces rather than
have committed any one of them.

At length, it became too bad. I used to take [from] 4 to 5 ounces
a day of Laudanum, once . . .[1] [ou]nces, i.e. near a Pint—besides
great quantities [of liquo]r. From the Sole of my foot to the Crown
of [my h]eart there was not an Inch in which I was not [contin]ually
in torture: for more than a fortnight no [sleep] ever visited my Eye
lids—but the agonies of [remor]se were far worse than all!—
Letters past between Cottle, Hood, & myself—& our kind Friend,
Hood, sent Mr Daniel to me. At his second Call I told him plainly
(for I had sculked out the night before & got Laudanum) that while
I was in my own power, all would be in vain—I should inevitably
cheat & trick *him*, just as I had done Dr Tuthill[2]—that I must either
be removed to a place of confinement, or at all events have a
Keeper.—Daniel saw the truth of my observations, & my most
faithful excellent friend, Wade, procured a strong-bodied, but
decent, meek, elderly man, to superintend me, under the name of
my Valet—All in the House were forbidden to fetch any thing but
by the Doctor's order.—Daniel generally spends two or three hours
a day with me—and already from 4 & 5 ounces has brought me
down to four tea-spoonfuls in the 24 Hours—The terror & the

¹ MS. mutilated by removal of signature. A British pint contains twenty
fluid ounces.
² G. L. Tuthill (1772–1835) had been Mary Lamb's physician in 1810. It is
not clear when Coleridge was under his care. *Lamb Letters*, ii. 112.
In the summer of 1813 Coleridge engaged Tuthill's services for Washington
Allston, who had fallen ill at Salt Hill on the way to Clifton. 'Mr. and Mrs.
Allston left London, accompanied by Morse and myself', writes C. R. Leslie;
'but, when we reached Salt Hill, Allston became too ill to proceed, and it was
determined that Morse should return to town and acquaint Coleridge with the
circumstance. . . . [Coleridge] came to Salt Hill the same afternoon, accompanied by his friend Dr. Tathill [*sic*].' *Autobiographical Recollections. By the
late Charles Robert Leslie*, ed. Tom Taylor, 2 vols., 1860, i. 33.

indefinite craving are gone—& he expects to drop it altogether by the middle of next week—Till a day or two after that I would rather not see you.

[Signature cut off.]

928. *To J. J. Morgan*

Address: J. J. Morgan, Esqre. | Mrs Smith's | Ashley | Box | near Bath
MS. New York Public Lib. Pub. E. L. G. ii. 112.
Postmark: Bristol, 15 May 1814.

Sunday, 15 May, 1814.
2. Queen's Square.

My dear Morgan

To continue from my last—Such was the direful state of my mind, that (I tell it you with horror) the razors, penknife, & every possible instrument of Suicide it was found necessary to remove from my room! My faithful, my *inexhaustibly patient* Friend, WADE, has caused a person to sleep by my bed side, on a bed on the floor: so that I might never be altogether alone—O Good God! why do such good men love me! At times, it would be more delightful to me to lie in the Kennel, & (as Southey said) 'unfit to be pulled out by any honest man except with a pair of Tongs.'—What *he* then said (perhaps) rather unkindly of me, was prophetically true! Often have I wished to have been thus trodden & spit upon, if by any means it might be an atonement for the direful guilt, that (like all others) first *smiled* on me, like Innocence! then crept closer, & yet closer, till it had thrown it's serpent folds round & round me, and I was no longer in my own power!—*Something* even the most wretched of Beings (*human* Beings at least) owes to himself—& this I *will* say & *dare* with truth say—that never was I led to this wicked direful practice of taking Opium or Laudanum by any desire or expectation of exciting *pleasurable* sensations; but purely by *terror*, by cowardice of pain, first of mental pain, & afterwards as my System became weakened, even of bodily Pain.

My Prayers have been fervent, in agony of Spirit, and for hours together, incessant! still ending, O! only for the merits, for the agonies, for the cross of my blessed Redeemer! For I am nothing, but evil—I can do nothing, but evil! Help, Help!—I believe! help thou my unbelief!—

Mr Daniel has been the wisest of physicians to me. I cannot say, how much I am indebted both to his Skill and Kindness. But he is one of the few rare men, who can make even their Kindness Skill, & the best and most unaffected Virtues of their Hearts *professionally* useful.

Anxious as I am to see you, yet I would wish to delay it till some

3 days after the total abandonment of the Poison. I expect, that this will commence on Tuesday next.—

Dr Estlin has contrived not only to pick a gratuitous quarrel with me, but by his female agents to rouse men who should be ashamed of such folly, for my saying in a Lecture on the Paradise Regained, that Milton had been pleased to represent the Devil as a sceptical Socinian. Alas! if I *should* get well—wo! to the poor Doctor, & to his Unitarians! They have treated me so ungenerously, that I am by the allowance of all my friends let loose from all bands of delicacy. Estlin has behaved downright cruel & brutal to me.—

I scarce know what to say or to bid you say to Mary or to Charlotte—for I cannot, of course, address myself to the reason of Women—& all that their common sense, their experience, & their feelings, suggest to them, must be irreversably against me. Nevertheless, strange as it must appear to them & perhaps incredible, it is still true, that I not only have loved ever, and still do *love* them; but that there never was a moment, in which I would not have shed my very blood for their sakes—At the very worst, I never neglected them but when in an hundred fold degree I was injuring myself. But this I cannot expect women to understand or believe—& must take the alienation of Mary's & Charlotte's esteem & affection among the due punishments of my Crime—

I am as much pleased as it is possible I can be at present in the present state of my body & mind at the improving state of your Affairs. Nothing would give me truer delight, than being recovered, to be able by my exertions to aid you: and assuredly, either this will [be] the case, or my Death.

I ought to say, that Mr Daniel is *sanguine* respecting my total recovery: tho' he admits, that after the Laudanum has been totally discontinued, there must be a long process to remedy the ravages in my constitution, which it has caused, & to bring down my carcase to something like a bulk proportionate to my years—

Allston has altogether forgot me: but I have not forgot him!—but I am an Englishman, & he is an American!—I was in my bitterest affliction glad to hear that his Picture had been noticed, however unworthily & by such a scurvy set of Judges. I intreated Bird to call on him and intreat him to write to me, tho' but *two* Lines—But I fear, Allston, tho' the very best & prime, is an American!

I dare not ask you to give my Love to Mary—it is sufficient, that she has it.—As soon as I am better, if I do not come over, I will write & ask you to come over hither after Miss Brent's Return from London—

Your affectionate Friend
S. T. Coleridge

929. *To Miss Cottle*

Address: Miss Cottle | Brunswick Square
MS. Mr. J. Graham Eggar. Pub. E. L. G. ii. 114.

2. Queen's Square.
19 May, 1814.

Dear Madam

In my yet unconfirmed Health (a specific irritation, moreover, of the lower part of the intestinal Canal affecting by nervous sympathy my knees with frequent, scarcely tolerable, achings, and with *quite* intolerable restlessness—almost, Heaven's Master be praised, the only relict and sediment of my Illness) the Walk to Brunswick Square & back is too much for my strength: or I should not have suffered so many days to pass without having called to inquire after my good friend's State of Body. Barnard will pass by your door, & you will be so kind as to let me know by him (do not trouble yourself with writing) how your Brother goes on. I hope, that finally this distressful accident may prove in some degree serviceable to him by removing or lessening the inflammatory ferment of his Blood & consequent turgescence & weakness of the Vessels. But I wish, he could sit in a more aery room: and still more, that he had a small riding Chair, which a Lad might with ease push along thro' the open air.—

My affectionate respects to Miss Anne, & be assured, that I am, dear Madam, | with unfeigned regard | Your friend & servt
S. T. Coleridge

930. *To William Allen*[1]

Address: William Allen, Esqre. | Plough Court | Lombard Street | London
Post-pay'd
MS. Mr. John C. Hanbury. Pub. Through a City Archway. The Story of Allen and Hanburys, 1715–1954, *by Desmond Chapman-Huston and Ernest C. Cripps, 1954, p. 291.*
Postmark: Bristol, 19 May 1814.

19 May, 1814
2. Queen's Square, Bristol.

Dear Sir

I take a great liberty which yet, I trust, your Humanity will excuse in consideration of the calamitous state of my Health: tho' Heaven's Master be praised, by the skill and kindness of my Physician, who has attended me twice & three times a day for months past, almost the only relict and sediment of my Disease

---

[1] William Allen (1770–1843), Quaker, scientist, and philanthropist, was a strong abolitionist. In 1792 he entered Bevan's chemical establishment at Plough Court.

consists in an excessive irritability of the lower part of the intestinal Canal, whenever the Bile (so long locked up in it's ducts by the fatal use of narcotics) or the watry secretions, trickle over it: and which by nervous sympathy affects my knees for the time with an indescribable & intolerable aching, weakness, & feverish restlessness. Now some years ago you were so good as to procure for me (tho' not in reality for myself) a *Clyster Machine* of most convenient construction for self-injection—& when last in London, I settled the Bill with your young Man.—I well remember, that in *appearance it was an elegant Cylinder of polished Brass*. You would not only oblige, but *actually & importantly* SERVE me, if you would condescend to drop a line or two at Everall's & Wilson's, St James's Street, (formerly, Savigny's) describing *what* it was, & at what place you procured it, in case they should not possess the same—requesting them to send it, as soon as procured, to their Correspondent, J. and J. Gilbert, Cutlers &c, Bristol.

Should you chance to see Thomas or Mrs Clarkson, be so good as to inform them that I have been for many months *worse than nothing*; but that by the Grace of God, who has answered my fervent & importunate prayers for mercy, and for increase of faith and fortitude, & (instrumentally) by the great prudence, skill, & gentleness of my medical attendant I am almost miraculously restored, and (as it were) *emancipated*. Mrs C. will understand the phrase in respect to *me*.

I pray, hope, and trust, that our friend, Sir Humphrey Davy will bring back himself safe from his extensive Tour, with *new* stores of practical science, & his *old* English Heart & Understanding!

What scenes, dear Sir! have we not lived through! What *centuries* of aweful Events condensed into twenty years! I could not help applying to Buonaparte this stanza of an obscure Poet of the reign of Charles the first, (Habington)

> 'The Tide, which did it's banks o'erflow,
> As sent abroad by the angry Sea
> To level vastest Fabrics low,
> And all old Trophies overthrow,
>   *Ebbs, like a Thief, away*!'

Dr Young says, 'An Undevout Astronomer is mad!'[1] I am sure, we may now with at least equal truth apply this to an undevout Politician.—

Excuse this freedom, | dear Sir, | from your obliged | humble
Servant
S. T. Coleridge—

[1] *Night Thoughts*, ix. line 771.

P.S. Should it be in your power conveniently to send down more directly the Machine, by the Bristol Coach, addressed to me at my friend's, Josiah Wade, Esqre. No. 2. Queen's Square, Bristol, with the Bill—the amount shall be remitted with most unfeigned Thanks by return of Post.—

931. *To Henry Daniel*

Transcript Coleridge family. Hitherto unpublished.

May 19th 1814. 2 Queen's Square, Bristol

Dear Sir

Not for the Poetry, *believe* me! (though as the lines have both sense & logic, there *is* worse stuff going under the name of Poetry than *even* these) but as an exact and most faithful portraiture of the state of my mind under influences of incipient bodily derangement from the use of Opium, at the time that I yet remained ignorant of the cause, & still *mighty proud* of my supposed grand discovery of Laudanum, as the Remedy or Palliative of Evils, which itself had mainly produced, & at every dose was reproducing, the lines may not be without interest to you, both as a *thinking* medical man, & under God, I trust, as one about to be entitled to my life-long, affectionate gratitude for my emancipation from a Slavery more dreadful, than any man, who has not felt it's iron fetters eating into his very soul, can possibly imagine.

God bless you.

S. T. C.

'Diseased Sleep', a fragment from a larger poem, composed 1803.

Written as a letter & of course never intended to be published, and which, I trust, never will be.

O, if for such such sufferings be,
Yet why, O God, yet why for me?
From low desires my Heart hath fled,
On Beauty hath my Fancy fed;
To be beloved is all I need,
And whom I love, I love indeed.
My waking thoughts with scorn repell
Loveless Lust, Revenge[ful] spell:—
O why should Sleep be made *my* Hell.[1]

[1] Except for lines 5 and 6, this excerpt from *The Pains of Sleep* differs markedly from the poem as Coleridge published it. See *Poems*, i. 389–91. See also Letters 516, 521, and 524.

The above was part of a long letter in verse written to a friend, while I yet remained ignorant that the direful sufferings, I so complained of, were the mere effects of Opium, which I even to that hour imagined a sort of Guardian Genius to me!

Another Fragment on the Night Mair

O Heaven! 'twas frightful! Now run down & stared at
By shapes more ugly than can be remembered!
Now *seeing* nothing, & *imagining* nothing,
But only being *afraid*—stifled with Fear!
While every goodly or familiar form
Had a strange power of breathing terror on me.[1]

932. To J. J. Morgan

Address: J. J. Morgan, Esqre. | Mrs Smith's | Ashley | Box | near Bath
MS. Lord Latymer. Hitherto unpublished.
Postmark: ⟨23⟩ May 1814.

Monday, 23 May, 1814.

My dear Morgan
    On Friday I dined at Hood's after a very silly, yet to me somewhat serious, affair. Mr Eden met me walking with an old Maltese Acquaintance, Captn Skinner (who from disgust quitted the Navy for the Merchant service, & has christened his Ship *Sir Alexander Ball*)—and with much eagerness told me that Mr Russel was packing up & to set off to meet his father Sir Richard W. Russel who has been 18 years in the E. Indies, & begged, I would send back the Books, I had borrowed from him. Accordingly I hastened home, sent all, I found, & begged to know if there were any more. Answer: Yes! a 3rd. Vol. of Milton—To work I went—emptied two chaos chest[s] of Books, looked into all possible & all impossible places—then called up my factotum, Boy Barnard (I wish, you knew him!) & looked over again—examined my linen Drawer &c &c—& just as I was nigh fainting, & wet thro' with perspiration, Barnard says—'Perhaps, Sir! you may have left it at Mr Hood's.'—Aye! to be sure, I did—quoth I—but I wish, your memory had been so good as to have come half an hour earlier. This so knocked me up, that I was forced to coach it to Hood's—at Hood's I unconsciously in the earnestness of talking to his Partner's Nephew just entered at Brazen Nose, Oxford, drank Port Wine (which was Hood's fault, who had promised & stipulated that a Pint Bottle of Madeira should be put beside me, as my Quotum)—& tho' I got home before

[1] *Remorse*, IV. i. 68–73.

9 o/clock, yet as Hood accompanied me, & we sat with my friend
Wade talking & laughing till near 12, the exertion &c &c threw me
back terribly—Daniel perceived it instantly the next morning, &
has layed an embargo on Hood (to use his own phrase)—& yesterday I was still worse, & the puffiness had returned in my right Leg.
One Half of the effect, however, Daniel attributes to the East Wind,
acting on the surface of my Skin—& to day I commence the tonic
Regimen with Soda, Gentian, &c—and all Spirit is given up—but
an addition allowed in Wine. I cannot express, how kindly as well
as wisely Mr Daniel conducts himself toward me. After a journey of
20 miles from Bristol ergo, 40—he contrived to spend two hours
& more with me Yester evening, because he heard at home that I
had *sent* for the medicine. His great Object appears to be, to keep
up my spirits, & to prevent (& to desire all about me, to prevent)
any painful or depressing circumstances from coming into contact
with me. I have no hesitation in declaring him the most of a man
of genius, and of genius too chastised by unaffected good common
sense, of any medical man, I ever met with—& I have known, &
respected, many—

Thus, you see, that it was quite out of my power to meet you at
Bath—But I trust, that by exact care another Week may enable
me to report Progress *in person.* But I am feeble beyond your conception, not indeed in momentary strength, but in constitution—
Yet I have not been altogether idle for the last fortnight.

I have my doubts, whether this pantomime Trick of pretending
to give a British Constitution to those Hypanthropes, or quasi-
humans, the French, will proceed even thro' a first Trial. But our
Parliament at home, or the faction of Landholders, are mad or
ideotic—. The Corn Law Debates are more disgraceful than even
the Bullion—I again affirm, what I have often affirmed, that take
away from the Legislature the Merchants & Manufacturers, & I will
stand on Blackfriars or Westminster Bridge, & take the first 800
decently drest men that pass over, & would pledge my life for more
intellect, more real knowlege, than is congregated in the two
Houses.—It cannot be otherwise.—I should like to know, what
Rickman says on the Subject—The Papers, I understand, preserve a profound silence on the subject—

Should you find in any of the circulating Libraries at Bath the
Life of the Revd Mr Richard Baxter (the famous old Baxter)
written by himself & edited by his colleague, Sylvester,[1] by all
means take it home with you—It is as cram full of wisdom,

---

[1] *Reliquiae Baxterianae: or Mr. Richard Baxter's Narrative of the most
Memorable Passages of his Life and Times*, ed. M. Sylvester, 1696. A copy of this
work with annotations by Coleridge is now in the Harvard College Library.

information, & interest, as an egg is of meat—Indeed, no man can have a just idea of the Period from Charles the first to James the 2nd, who has not read it—
My best Love to Mary.
God bless her, you, Charlotte, | & | poor |
S. T. C.—

Does Mary know Mrs Daniel—Miss James, that was? She appears to me an open-hearted good-natured Woman: & spoke to me of Mary in high terms of admiration.

They have a pretty little *she-kingdom-of-heavenite*, six months old, with very fine eyes & eye-lashes. Mrs D. told me on my second call very good naturedly, that she had longed to see me, tho' she was very angry *at* me: for that the few Hours, that Daniel used to be able to give her of his company, 'he must go & sit a little with Coleridge.'—

I mention these things, simply because I know it will give you pleasure to learn that spite of calumny, & spite of afflicting & degrading Truths, there are yet those who are kind to me as much beyond my expectation as my deserts.—

933. *To Joseph Cottle*

Address: Joseph Cottle, Esqre. | Brunswick Square
MS. Yale University Lib. Pub. with omis. Letters, ii. 619.

Friday, 27 May 1814
My dear Cottle

Gladness be with you for your convalescence, and equally at the Hope which has sustained and tranquillized you thro' your imminent Peril. Far otherwise is & hath been my state—yet I too am grateful, tho' I can not rejoice. I feel, with an intensity unfathomable by words, my utter nothingness, impotence, & worthlessness, in and for myself—I have learnt *what* a sin is against an infinite imperishable Being, such as is the Soul of Man—I have had more than a Glimpse of what is meant by Death, & utter Darkness, & the Worm that dieth not—and that all the Hell of the Reprobate is no more inconsistent with the Love of God, than the Blindness of one who has occasioned loathsome and guilty Diseases to eat out his eyes, is inconsistent with the Light of the Sun. But the consolations, at least the *sensible* sweetness, of Hope, I do *not* possess. On the contrary, the Temptation, which I have constantly to fight up against, is a fear that if Annihilation & the *possibility* of Heaven were offered to my choice, I should choose the former.

This is, perhaps, in part, a constitutional Idiosyncrasy: for when
a *mere Boy* I wrote these Lines—

> O what a wonder seems the fear of Death,
> Seeing, how gladly we all sink to Sleep,
> Babes, children, Youths, & Men,
> Night following Night for threescore years & ten![1]

And in my early manhood in lines, descriptive of a gloomy solitude,
I disguised my own sensations in the following words—

> Here Wisdom might abide, & here Remorse!
> Here too the woe-worn[2] Man, who weak in Soul,
> And of this busy human Heart aweary,
> Worships the spirit of *unconscious Life*
> In Tree or Wild-flower.—Gentle Lunatic!
> If so he might not *wholly cease* to BE,
> He would far rather not be that, he is;
> But would be something, that he knows not of,
> In Woods or Waters or among the Rocks.[3]—

My main Comfort therefore consists in what the Divines call, *the
Faith of Adherence*—and no spiritual Effort appears to benefit me
so much, as the one, earnest, importunate, & often for hours
momently [repeated], Prayer: 'I believe! Lord, help my Unbelief!
Give me Faith but as a mustard Seed: & I shall remove this mountain! Faith! Faith! Faith! I believe—O give me Faith! O for my
Redeemer's sake give me Faith in my Redeemer.'

In all this I justify God: for I was accustomed to oppose the
preaching of the Terrors of the Gospel, & to represent it as debas-
ing Virtue by admixture of slavish Selfishness. I now see that what
is spiritual can only be spiritually *apprehended*—*com*prehended It
cannot be.

Mr Eden gave you a too flattering account of me. It is true, I am
restored as much beyond my expectations almost, as my Deserts;
but I am *exceedingly* weak, & need for myself solace & refocillation
of animal spirits, instead of being in a condition of offering it to
others.—Yet as soon as I can, I will call on you.

S. T. Coleridge

P.S. It is no small gratification to me, that I have seen & conversed
with Mrs H. More[4]—She is indisputably the *first* literary female,

---

[1] These lines were not printed until 1829, when they were prefixed to the
Monody on the Death of Chatterton. Poems, i. 125. See also Letter 1194 n. 1.
[2] heart-sick [Cancelled word in line above.]
[3] See *The Picture, or the Lover's Resolution*, lines 17–25, *Poems*, i. 369–70.
[4] Hannah More (1745–1833), religious writer.

I ever met with—In part, no doubt, because she is a Christian.—
Make my best respects when you write—

934. *To Charles Mathews*[1]

Address: —— Matthews, Esqre | to be left at the | Bristol Theatre (To be
forwarded to Mr Matthews)
MS. Huntington Lib. Pub. Letters, *ii. 621.*

2. Queen's Square, Bristol.
Monday Night, 30 May, 1814.

Dear Sir
   Unusual as this Liberty may be, yet as it is a friendly one, you
will pardon it, especially from one who has had already some connection with the stage, & may have more. But I was so highly
gratified with my feast of this night, that I feel a sort of restless
impulse to tell you, what I felt & thought.
   Imprimis, I grieved that you had such miserable materials to
deal with as Colman's Solomon Gundy,[2] a character which in &
of itself (Matthews, & his Variations ad Libitum put out of the
Question) contains no one element of genuine Comedy, no, nor
even of Fun, or Drollery. The play is assuredly the very sediment,
the dregs, of a noble Cask of Wine: for such *was*? yes, in *many*
instances *was* & has been; and in many more *might* have been,
COLMAN's Dramatic Genius. A *Genius* Colman IS by *nature*—
what he is *not*, or *has* not been, is all of his own making. In my
humble opinion, he possessed the elements of dramatic power in a
far higher degree, than Sheridan: which of the two, think you,
should pronounce with the deeper sigh of self-reproach, '*Fuimus*
Troes! And what *might* we not have been?'—
   But I leave this to proceed to the really astonishing effect of
your Duplicate of Cook in Sir Archy Mac Sarcasm[3]—To say that in
some of your higher notes your Voice was rather *thinner*, rather
less *substance* & *thick* body, than poor Cook's, would be merely to
say, that A. B. is not exactly A. A.—But on the whole it was almost
illusion—& so very excellent, that if I were intimate with you, I
should get angry and abuse you for not forming for yourself some
original & important character—The man, who could so imper-
sonate Sir Archy McSarcasm might do *any thing* in *profound*
Comedy (i.e. that which gives us the *passions* of men & their endless modifications & influences on Thoughts, Gestures, &c, modified in their turn by Circumstances of Rank, Relations, Nationality

---

[1] Charles Mathews (1776–1835), comedani.
[2] A character in George Colman's *Who wants a Guinea?*
[3] A character in Charles Macklin's *Love à la Mode.*

&c, instead of mere transitory manners—in short, the inmost man represented on the superficies, instead of the Superficies merely representing itself.)—

But will you forgive a Stranger for a suggestion?—I cannot but think, that it would *answer* for your still increasing fame, if you were either previously to, or as an occasional diversification, of Sir Archy, to study & give that one most incomparable Monologue of Sir Pertinax McSycophant,[1] where he gives his Son the History of his rise & progress in the World.—Being in it's essence a Soliloquy with all the advantages of a Dialogue, it would be a most happy Introduction to your Sir Archy McSarcasm, which, I doubt not, will call forth with good reason the Covent Garden Manager's Thanks to you next season.—

I once had the presumption to address this advice to an Actor on the London Stage. '*Think*, in order that you may be able to *observe! Observe*, in order that you may have materials to *think* upon!—And 3rdly, keep awake ever the habit of instantly *embodying & realizing* the results of the two: but always *think*.'

A great Actor, comic or tragic, is not to be a mere *Copy*, a *fac simile*, but an *imitation*, of Nature. Now an *Imitation* differs from a Copy in this, that it of necessity implies & demands *difference*—whereas a Copy aims at *identity*. What a marble peach on a mantle-piece, that you take up deluded, & put down with pettish disgust, is compared with a fruit-piece of Vanhuysen's,[2] even such is a mere *Copy* of nature compared with a true histrionic *Imitation*. A good actor is Pygmalion's Statue, a work of exquisite *art, animated* & gifted with *motion*; but still *art*, still a species of *Poetry*.

Not the least advantage, which an Actor gains by having secured a high reputation, is this: that those who sincerely admire him, may dare tell him the Truth at times, & thus, if he have sensible friends, secure his progressive Improvement: in other words, *keep him thinking*. For without *thinking* nothing *consummate* can be effected—

Accept this, dear Sir! as it is meant—a small testimony of the high gratification, I have received from you, & of the respectful & sincere kind wishes, with which I am

Your obedt. &c
S. T. Coleridge

[1] A character in Macklin's *Man of the World.*
[2] Jan Van Huysum (1682–1749), Dutch painter.

935. *To J. J. Morgan*

Address: J. J. Morgan, Esqre. | Mrs Smith's | Ashley Box] near Bath.
MS. Lord Latymer. Pub. E. L. G. ii. 115.
Postmark: Bristol, 1 June 1814.

2 [1] June, 1814
2 Queen's Square—

My very dear Morgan

I have been so almost alarmed by neither hearing from, or seeing, you, that I should have come over to Box, but for the most unfortunate *Burthenment* upon me of Lady Beaumont's Sister, Mrs Fermor, who has taken lodgings close by us, in order, forsooth, to have the comfort of my religious openings & consolations. The Lord has deserted her, she says.—A good innocent woman, as ever lived, but doleful as a dull Tragedy, or as the Miss Cottles. It is really a direful Burthen, which the *usual* Wisdom & Delicacy of Lady Beaumont have imposed upon me.

However, before this week is over, if I continue but as I am, I will be with you. By the bye, Jo. Cottle, who is *fizzling* & desperately disposed, spite of all poetic Decency, to *let* a third Epic, called Messiah[1] (O such an Epic! ! !) he gave me 10 pounds for reading thro', and correcting seven books out of TWENTY FOUR! & never galley-slave earned a penny so painfully and laboriously. (Confound the Pens! I can scarce write with them.)—Well, poor Jo. has burst a small blood Vessel in his Chest; but is convalescent—& instead of applying his Conscience to himself he has taken into his skull (heaven knows! there is *room* enough for any alien guest) to turn it all on me—& I have had some 4 or 5 letters, arm's length each, & (except the occasional bad spelling, very finely *sentenced*) the object of all which is to convince me, that it has not been Opium, quoad Opium, that has injured me; but—(what think you?—) the DEVIL. Yes, says he, the Devil, depend upon it, has got possession of you. It is the Devil, that is even now within you.—'A strong man armed (that is, this said *Devil*) has the mastery of you; but a stronger than he will not suffer him, I hope, to keep possession.—Do not deceive yourself about opium &c: it is the evil Spirit, it is the DEVIL, that is in you.'—Now is not Jo. a rare Comforter to a poor fellow in dreadful Low Spirits?—I verily believe, that Wade would have gone & setting fire to all his Mss. have suffocated him in his own poetry, if I had [not] prevented it—& poor Jo. had not burst a Blood Vessel.—

God bless him! he is a well-meaning Creature; but a great Fool.—Not a line from Allston!—tho' I had so EARNESTLY intreated

[1] Cottle's *Messiah* appeared in 1815.

him to write to me, & especially begged him to get The Friend from Wallis.[1] It is the improved Edition, & the whole is quite out of Print—so that this is of importance. I ordered it from Bulgin,[2] & the answer from his London Correspondent was: 'Out of Print, & the Publishers, Gale, Curtis &c, have long given over the hope of inducing the Author to prepare a second Edition'.—How my good qualities diffuse themselves!—Bul[gin] did not know me, which was lucky.—I am prof[essedly] better. Love to Mrs M. & (if she be with you) Miss B.—*Dear* Morgan, your *very* friend

S. T. C.

P.S. Quere. As I COULD not have swallowed the Devil with his antlers dispreading, whether it does not follow, that he must have *pocketed his Horns*: consequently, that the Devil is a poor cowardly Wittold? Indeed, I never had a good opinion of him.

936. *To Sir George Beaumont*

Address: Sir George Beaumont, Bart. | S. Audley Street | Grosvenor Square London
MS. Pierpont Morgan Lib. Pub. with omis. Memorials of Coleorton, *ii. 171.*
Postmark: Bristol, 9 June 1814.

Thursday, 10 [9] June 1814
2. Queen's Square, Bristol.

Dear Sir George

A forgotten Exile, as I seem to be, from the Love of those, whom I most dearly loved, I am in doubt whether to deem it a Palliative or an Aggravation, that I remain myself unaltered. My Esteem & Affections were in their good old age, some ten years ago. What was, is; and, alas! old Trees, they say, rarely permit new Grafts on them. When however I turn from others to myself, I have abundant cause both for Wonder and Gratitude, that having been what I was, I am even as I am: tho', but for the comparison, even this is sufficiently humiliating. Nihil e nihilo factus, tantùm in hôc aliquid sum, quòd *scio*, me nihil esse—sine Christo. Alii disputent! ego mirabor.

Enough & more than enough of myself, which indeed I should not have referred to at all, except as a sort of Preface for the avoiding of apparent abruptness. The sole subject of this Letter, and my only Object, is the state of Mrs Fermor's mental & bodily Health. After having accorded with her wishes for a private Inter-

[1] G. A. Wallis, painter, whom Coleridge had met in Italy.
[2] William Bulgin, bookseller, whose business in 1814 was at 28 Corn Street, Bristol.

view with one of our most eloquent Preachers in Bristol, which I
the more readily did, because he is constitutionally a chearful, and
by study & reflection (some few Recrements of Calvinism forgotten
or forgiven) a rational & judicious Man: I then, but not without
difficulty, persuaded her to call in, and *once* at least to talk with,
my excellent friend, Daniel—who truly is & merits the high &
honorable name of a MEDICAL CHIRURGEON—i.e. a practical
Thinker, who combines Hand with Head, thinks in order that he
may observe, observes constantly & steadily in order that he may
have substantial materials to think on, and keeps alive the habit
& facility of applying & realizing the Results of both. The sum
total of all intellectual excellence is Good Sense & Method. When
these have passed into the instinctive readiness of Habit, when the
Wheel revolves so rapidly that we can not see it revolve at all,
then we call the combination, Genius. But in all modes alike, & in
all professions, the two sole component parts even of *Genius* are—
GOOD SENSE, and METHOD.

Mrs Fermor has seen him twice, & yester evening I had a long
and detailed communication from him on the subject. I will dare
confess, tho' at the risk of appearing arrogant, so fully had I made
up my mind on the case, that I received satisfaction and confirmation, rather than any additional Light, from the coincidence of my
opinions with those of so quick-eyed & experienced a Practitioner.
It is, perhaps, one little symptom of the inherent nobleness of our
human Nature, that in all cases in which both mind & body are
affected, we would still refer the *whole* effect to the *former*. Nay, if
our misfortunes from without, Death or Alienation (the moral
Death) of Friends, or other incident calamities, will not suffice, we
will often seek a cause even in imaginary *Guilt*, rather than condescend to believe that the Afflictions of our nobler Being have
their source in the mere disturbed functions of our bodily organs;
which are not *we*, and scarcely *our's*.—This I perceive daily in
Mrs Fermor. She clings to the belief of the exclusive *mental* Origin
of her Complaint, as a Limpet to the smooth Rock, hardly removable, tho' by mere force of voluntary adhesion. Desunt
Retinacula: adsugit tamen.—And doubtless whichever may have
begun the affray, the other is sure to carry it on—& a cycle of
Re-actions is the result.—Still however nothing can be more manifest than that the greatest part of this excellent Woman's Sufferings are connected with the state of her alimentary Canal; with
abdominal congestion; & the disproportioned Health & Vigor of
her *Stomach* to that of the lower *Viscera*. Hence she digests so
quickly, that the very activity of the Gastric Juice, left too soon
without materials to work on, is one & not the smallest cause, of

her morning Disquietudes. Because she has daily a natural relief,
no matter what or how scanty, she deceives herself (as thousands
do, especially delicate Females of the higher Class) that she needs
no assistance in *this* respect. Yet when Daniel had at length overpersuaded her to take a few aperient pills, the *Scybala*, which
[were] brought off, put the truth of the case beyond all doubt. I
could almost pledge whatever is most dear to me, that she would
(& tho' of course slowly, yet in a far shorter time than she now
imagines possible) be restored to at least a comfortable state of
mind & body, could she be induced to settle at Bristol for six or
eight weeks, under the care of Daniel, & having at the same time,
which at Bath she cannot have, always something to look forward
to as mental occupation, *Lectures*, *Preaching*, & rational evening
Conversation Parties. I need not say, that more needing to be
cheered, than in a mood to cheer others, this advice is something
more than disinterested on my part: except indeed that it is [at] all
times our Interest to feel & to realize Gratitude. Mildest, but for a
certain time systematic, Depurgation, with gentle & varied Tonics;
these accompanied by a circumspect regulation of her Diet,
especially for the six or seven first Hours after she awakes; would
doubtless form the Basis of her medical Treatment.—But I must
not conceal from you, dear Sir! that this & all other things will be
alike profitless & vain, if she perseveres in having on all these
occasions an opinion of her own, founded on her own fancies.—
'*Oh! I could not do this, Sir!—O Sir, a Spoonful of Coffee would
stimulate me dangerously.—Pray, Sir! say no more on that: for I have
an irremoveable objection against such & such medicines—&c.*'—
Just as if it was not the Business & Duty of her medical attendant
to watch minutely the real effects of each Prescription: or as if
(should any peculiarity of Temperament baffle or pervert it's
usual operation) he would be fool & rogue enough to persevere in
it. In short, Sir George! Mrs Fermor must be induced to place
herself out of her own management, & to give up *thinking & having
opinions* on matters, concerning which, without any detraction
from her knowlege & good sense, she is herself (& because it is
herself) least capable of judging aright. I here advise nothing but
what I have myself submitted to: & that in a tenfold more humiliating form, than there is the least intention or necessity of recommending to *her*.—But if this be not done, either here or elsewhere,
it becomes a painful but peremptory duty to express to you my
full conviction & that of Daniel's that she will become worse &
worse: & that a state of *absolute Melancholia* will in a few years be
the final sad Catastrophe.—Of course, this letter is entirely for your
private Perusal—but your Influence must needs be great—& so

truly amiable & [exe]mplary a woman merits to have every possible effort emplo[yed for] her Happiness.—

S. T. Coleridge

P.S. Mrs F. quits Bristol tomorrow. To day she has had an interview with the Revd Mr Day, the least gloomy of our Bristol Evangelicals of the estab. Church. Her spiritual Confidant must have *unction*, or she will not be interested; must be cheerful, or he will do her Harm.—

937. *To J. J. Morgan*

Address: J. J. Morgan, Esqre | Mrs Smith's | Ashley | Box | Bath
MS. Lord Latymer. Pub. with omis. E. L. G. ii. 117.
Postmark: Bristol, 11 June 1814.

11th June, 1814

My dear Friend

I should have been with you ere this, but for an ugly erysipelatous inflammation on and round my right ancles, and toward night, when the leg has been for many hours down, a puffiness in the instep: which Daniel looked graver at yesterday than he has done at any thing for some weeks.—I believe, however, that it was brought on, first, by staying out till past eleven at George Kiddle's with Hood & T. Castle: which was more their fault than mine, for I had ordered Haberfield, my Keeper, to come for me at ¼ past 8—& made strenuous efforts to go, but they all rose up in arms & forced me back to my chair, under pretence that Mr Daniel had said, I might stay till 9—then in came Wade, who did not however approve of it—and so it spun on till ½ past eleven—2. A few evenings after I stayed till 12 at Daniel's own House, & after supper Mrs Daniel made a jorum of Hollands & Water, & I looked at Daniel— & said—Is this lawful?—Why, why, (quoth Daniel, the master of the House casting a veil over the Doctor) 'once now & then'—I believe, his conscience sorely misgave him, as he uttered the words— but the Conversation was mantling like Champagne—& Laughter, as I have often observed, is the most potent Producer of Forgetfulness, of the whole Pharmacopoeia, moral or medical.

During Convalescence, and as the System begins to restore itself, every the least deviation betrays itself at once, & *tells* against the Health, tenfold more than it would have done or appeared to do, in the heighth of the Disease.

I dined with Hood yesterday: and tho' I drank no wine at dinner, & confined myself rigorously to the Pint of Madeira prescribed me, yet such was the stimulus of Conversation (there was a Devonshire Family, the Grangers, Hood's Relations by marriage, who are intimate with my Relations by Gore) that both Insteps were swoln at my return—tho' I left him at ½ past 7, & both went & returned in a Coach. This morning the puffiness is entirely gone: and the Blush much fainter; but the *small* of the Leg still remains a misnomer: & makes it's fellow Leg for the first time in it's Life look quite genteel, by the comparison.—The etymology of the word erysipelas is clearly this; the first man in England afflicted with it was called Harry—a great Toper. Every time the Doctor visited him, he said to Him—Harry! sip the less—which being constantly repeated by the man's friends became the name of the Disease, & by quick pronunciation got corrupted into Erysipelas. Indeed, if I recollect right, this Harry was a Staffordshire man, where they use & omit the H by the rule of Contraries.—Those who are fond of far-fetched Etymologies may go to the Greeks for one.— Poor Kiddle too is confined with his old complaint, erysipelas in the Face.—

Allston called on me yesterday; but there was [such] a Levee in my Bedroom that I had no opportunity of talking to him, till I was too much exhausted to ask any questions of any Interest. I was very glad to see him, tho' he ought to have written to me.— Wallis[1] after repeated Intreaties, to which he payed no attention, has gone off with the Friend: & where or how to procure a Copy with the reprinted Numbers I know not. What makes it more provoking is, that to a certainty Wallis will never read five pages of the Book. He is either a bad man or a mad man; but I believe, the last positively, & the former only negatively.

I am as much disposed, as you, to think with at least comparative respect of the New Englanders; but I cannot explain or altogether get over, the almost uniform Experience of all who have had any concerns with any Americans.—

Should my Leg be entirely reduced by Monday, I will take the stage, & be with you—if not, yet as soon as it is. It will give you pleasure to see the doses of Laudanum, I shall bring with me.—

My kind Love to your Wife & Sister. There is a coolness between me & Porter—I will tell you the Particulars when we meet—but all common friends highly approve both of my feelings & conduct. There is, I hear & fear, some danger, that Porter's Head will be turned by the flatteries & evening Lady Parties, of his Parish.—

God bless you | &
S. T. Coleridge

P.S. I have not been altogether idle, of late—& hope to make my Industry keep pace with my Convalescence. I have been perfecting

---

[1] In this and the following sentence the name Wallis is inked out in the MS.

myself in the Spanish: & am reading with high Delight the minor Works of Cervantes, (in a lovely Edition), his Persiles, his Galatea, Novels, Voyage to Parnassus, & Numancia, a Tragedy—and the Trato del Argel (Algiers) a Comedy.[1]—

Lady Beaumont's Sister (Mrs Fermor) left Bristol for Bath yesterday—Poor afflicted Dowager! she clings obstinately to the Faith, that the whole Source of her Sufferings is in her Head & Heart, tho' it is evident that [the] mischief lies a foot or two below the one, & 8 or 9 Inches below the other—. For tho' 'alimentary Canal' & the 'lower digestive and eliminative organs' are handsome-looking synonimes for Guts, yet they cannot stand the competition with Desertion from Heaven, want of genial Grace, the *mind*, Sir! O the *mind*—

938. *To J. J. Morgan*

Address: J. J. Morgan, Esqre. | Mrs Smith's | Ashley | Box | Bath
MS. Harvard College Lib. Pub. Chambers, Life, 356.
Postmark: Bristol, 16 June 1814.

[16 June 1814]

My dear Friend

This ugly Complaint in my Leg, which as the Devil is no *Uni*corn, has brought on a Stomach Sickness & a perilously (for good manners, I mean) sudden Elimination of the Ingesta after meals, without previous nausea, present effort, or after pain. I tell Daniel, that I have a schirrous Liver: & he laughs at me for my Information. The angry Itching, which I dare not appease except by the continual application of wet Cloths, keeps me awake two thirds of the Night. Pumping on it 5 or 6 times a day for 5 minutes together seems to be most effective—but as it vanishes in an instant, so in an instant does it return—& sometimes the convex of the foot, especially about an inch & a half from the Toes, pits hydropically. But Daniel assures me, that it is mere Wind & Weakness, from the rapid Diminution of the poison-dose—which he has now so reduced, that *he* thinks all my bodily uneasiness *before*, & tranquillity after, taking the modicum, is *mental*—that I *make up my mind* to be quiet, because there is nothing more to look forward to for 12 hours; and therefore *am* quiet. That there is *much* Truth in this, I cannot doubt; but not to the Extent, Daniel believes. He overlooks an obscure but most important fact of physiology, that in

---

[1] Coleridge refers to the following works of Cervantes: *Los Trabajos de Persiles y Sigismunda*, 1617; *La Galatea*, 1585; *Novelas Exemplares*, 1613; *Viage del Parnaso*, 1614; *La Numancia*, c. 1585; and *El Trato de Argel*, c. 1585.

From a portrait of Samuel Taylor Coleridge painted by Washington Allston in 1814 and now in the National Portrait Gallery

certain cases (more especially in irritable Constitutions convalescing from Complaints of Stomach, Liver, or Kidneys) injurious Substances seem to act by pure abstract *Quality*, diminish the *Quantity* as you will. We have an analogous fact in Night Shade, the very smallest conceivable Doses of which appear to produce nearly the same effects as the largest—and this on all animals, on which it has been tried—& with myself 6 grains of Calomel produce the same effect as one, & one as six. If in addition to his natural quickness of eye & mental Intuition, & to his unaffected Good-sense (one proof of which I was delighted to learn, on the occasion of my having written a marginal Note in a book, he lent me, (Willan's Synopsis of Cutaneous Complaints edited by Bateman)[1] in which the Author having scouted the idea of Mothermarks, I had written—'Επέχω,[2] me nimiâ experientiâ invitum cogente, i.e. I *hesitate* &c. Daniel was quite delighted—I have suffered myself, says he, for some years to be laughed at by my Brother Surgeons, because I will not '*lie* for the honor of Philosophy.'—In the multitude of Infants, I have help'd, or witnessed, Nature bringing into the World, whose Mothers I had previously attended, I have had such repeated facts, that I hold it presumptuous Pedantry to reject, because our present state of Science is inadequate to explain, them)—if to these I can add (as I am adding) habits of psychological analysis, Daniel will be one of our first men, in the medical Line.

In head & vigor of mind I am not amiss—in disposition to activity much improved—but subject at times to strange Relapses of Disquietude, without apparent cause or occasion—For instance, all Sunday last I was thoroughly *be-belzebubbed.*—Still however, I hope (especially if Daniel should determine on *bandaging* the small of my Right Leg) to be with you by Tea on Friday; but you dare not positively expect me.

I have had long & affecting Conversations with poor dear Allston. As to Sir G. B. I had given *him* up long ago—& nothing has happened of which, as he well remembers, I did not distinctly warn him, except the envious Duplicity of his Countryman, the wretch who *preys* on fair fame by *side Hints*—thence appropriately called Prey-side-Hint—and put on a Protégée, 'whom like a young Dove, he could not but warm at his very breast'—'whose goodness was equal to his Science and Genius'—these were the old fratricide's very words to *me*, verily, *a merry Cain* sort of treating *Abel* Folks (Spelling, avaunt!)—this I did not (God

---

[1] Thomas Bateman, *Synopsis of Cutaneous Diseases according to the arrangement of Dr. Willan*, 1813.
[2] Underlined once in MS.

forbid, that I should) anticipate! All else has been better, rather than worse, than I had feared. Allston has not yet learnt all, he will learn, of the excessive meanness of Patrons, of the malignant Envy & Brutality of the Race of Painters!—The first Hour, I was with him after his re-arrival in England, I told him what a Devildom they were all members of—from three Causes, 1. & least, the necessity of living for the greater part in the Metropolis—2. from the double competition of Bread & Reputation—3. & chiefly, from vulgar Birth & want of all the Discipline of classical & gentlemanly education—Be assured, if you do not see me on Friday, it will not [be] a want of good will, or the effect of Indolence—your Effusions must be therefore not *satirical*, but L E G iac.—

From mine, & Wade's Friend, Hartley, I can procure you gratis the very best *Advice*—He is one of the acutest Attorneys in Bristol, an honest man, & in full practice—and all the rest in the least possible expensive way.—

I looked over the 5 first Books of the 1st. (Quarto) Edition of Joan of Arc yesterday, at Hood's request, in order to mark the lines written by me.[1]—I was really astonished, 1. at the school-boy wretched Allegoric Machinery—2. at the transmogrification of the fanatic Virago into a modern novel-pawing Proselyte of the age of Reason, a Tom Paine in Petticoats, but *so* lovely!—& in love, moreover!—'*on her rubied Cheek Hung Pity's crystal gem*'! 3. at the utter want of all rhythm in the verse, the monotony & dead *plumb down* of the Pauses—& the absence of all Bone, Muscle, & Sinew in the single Lines.—His Carmen Triumphale![2]—Is he grown silly?—The Courier for the last 2 years has been repeating me with a thousandfold Echo in it's leading §§s; & S. has bedevilified into vilest Rhyme rhythmless the leading §§s of the Courier.—

My best Love to Mary & Charlotte. Repose, and a wine glass of Infusion of Senna with three tea-spoonfuls of Epsom Salts, as soon as she awakes, 3 mornings in one week, will make a *Hebe* of her—or to pay a yet higher compliment—her own prettier Self.—In Bristol they will have it, that Mary is handsomer than Charlotte—how provokingly obstinate!

S. T. C.—

[1] Coleridge contributed 255 lines to Book II of Southey's *Joan of Arc*, 1796. Late in that year he proposed to 'alter' these lines and include them in a separate poem on which he was at work and to which he gave such titles as 'the progress of European Liberty, a vision' and 'the Visions of the Maid of Orleans'. In 1817 this fragmentary poem, which includes the contributions to *Joan of Arc*, was published in *Sibylline Leaves* as *The Destiny of Nations, a Vision*. See Letters 146, 163, 164, 178, and 194.

[2] Southey's *Carmen Triumphale, for the Commencement of the Year 1814*.

939. *To Josiah Wade*

Pub. Early Rec. *ii. 185.*

Bristol, June 26th, 1814.

Dear Sir,

For I am unworthy to call any good man friend—much less you, whose hospitality and love I have abused; accept, however, my intreaties for your forgiveness, and for your prayers.

Conceive a poor miserable wretch, who for many years has been attempting to beat off pain, by a constant recurrence to the vice that reproduces it. Conceive a spirit in hell, employed in tracing out for others the road to that heaven, from which his crimes exclude him! In short, conceive whatever is most wretched, helpless, and hopeless, and you will form as tolerable a notion of my state, as it is possible for a good man to have.

I used to think the text in St. James that 'he who offended in one point, offends in all,' very harsh; but I now feel the awful, the tremendous truth of it. In the one crime of OPIUM, what crime have I not made myself guilty of!—Ingratitude to my Maker! and to my benefactors—injustice! *and unnatural cruelty to my poor children*!—self-contempt for my repeated promise—breach, nay, too often, actual falsehood!

After my death, I earnestly entreat, that a full and unqualified narration of my wretchedness, and of its guilty cause, may be made public, that at least some little good may be effected by the direful example![1]

May God Almighty bless you, and have mercy on your still affectionate, and in his heart, grateful—

S. T. Coleridge.

[1] Although the Coleridge family bitterly opposed the publication of this and other letters concerning opium, Cottle included them in *Early Recollections* three years after Coleridge's death. Cottle defended himself by citing Coleridge's own injunction in the present letter; ten years later, in reissuing his work as *Reminiscences*, he quoted freely from Southey's letters to show that Southey had encouraged him to publish. One must agree with E. H. Coleridge, however, that Cottle had no 'right to wound the feelings of the living or to expose the frailties and remorse of the dead'. Furthermore, a letter from Wade to Henry Nelson Coleridge of 26 Sept. 1836 shows that Cottle misrepresented the facts in order to obtain possession of Coleridge's letters to Wade. See *Letters*, ii. 616 n., and E. L. Griggs, 'Robert Southey's Estimate of Samuel Taylor Coleridge', *Huntington Lib. Quar.*, Nov. 1945, pp. 89–94.

940. *To J. J. Morgan*

MS. Lord Latymer. Hitherto unpublished.

My dear Friend   Wednesday Noon. [29 June 1814]

On my return the improvement of my Health and appearance was so manifest and striking, that all my friends triumphed in me. —Le Breton and Hood had separately intended to have gone to Ashley on the Sunday in a Post Chaise & taken me back if I had not returned on the Saturday. It was lucky that Wade did not return till Sunday Night from Portsmouth.—I have been a little thrown back by the Bustle of the Proclamation Day,[1] but still more by the *imminent* danger which our own large Transparency[2] ran three or four several times of Conflagration from the Obstinacy and Self-conceit of the Lighter & Frame-maker—so that from the time it was lit till ½ past 11, when I persuaded Wade to put all the Lights out, we were in continual alarm, with three of us constantly watching the abominable Lamps.—I saw Allston's last night—it is a truly Michael Angelesque Figure, & of course beyond all comparison the finest in the City—but the meaning thereof greatly resembled my old story of Guy Vulpes, frigidus, calidus, postquam omnia capit, attamen inventus, *Ille* recepit eum—It was 'Ille, the Constable' with a vengeance.

All the People are mad—or rather this is the first day of their convalescence. I have appointed tomorrow for an hour's Conversation with Hartley, who has promised me his best advice & assistance. After the Interview, I will write immediately, if I do not come myself instead.

I hope, I left my Razors at Ashley—if not, they are gone.

1 Proclamation Day, to which this letter refers, was 27 June 1814. J. Latimer, *19th Century Annals of Bristol*, gives a description of the celebrations: 'The intelligence of the conclusion of a definitive treaty of peace, closing a war with France which had lasted, with a brief interval, for twenty-one years, was received with transports of joy. The mail coach conveying the news was stopped at Totterdown by the populace, who removed the horses, and dragged the vehicle through the streets amidst a whirlwind of cheers. The customary proclamations were made by the civic authorities on the 27th of June, the details of the ceremony being identical with those of 1801. In the evening the city was illuminated. A lofty triumphal arch, erected in Corn Street in front of the Commercial Rooms, was, when its pictorial embellishments were lighted up, an especial attraction; but the inhabitants of the chief streets appear to have vied with each other in the production of fanciful allegories, the description of which fills many columns of the newspapers. Probably the most picturesque and effective displays were the illumination of the battlements of the tower of St. Mary Redcliff, and the huge bonfire on Brandon Hill.'

2 For a description of Coleridge's design for the Transparency see Letter 964.

Queen's Square on Monday Noon was quite sublime from the immense multitude of Men, Women, and Children: when they moved all by one impulse across the Square, I could only compare it to a vast deep & rapid River with the tremulous motion of Sunshine on it's Waves—& the contrast of this with the thing to be seen! A red Wheelbarrow on men's Shoulders with no one in it— without exaggeration an old Petticoat on a Broomstick would have made as fine a Shew.—O man! man! ever greater than thy Circumstances.—

My kindest Love to Mary & Sharlet. Daniel told me, he was glad to hear, I had gone, tho' he could not resist Wade's Importunities & Uneasinesses—for that he saw clearly, I had been on the Gridiron for the last Week, and that it was injuring my Health.

A shocking Event happened yester evening. Young Shepherd, Daniel's Pupil, who used to bring over my Medicines, & whom I particularly liked, fell into the water at the end of Princess Street, while he was attempting to frighten M'kenzie, a stupid young man, his fellow-Pupil, whom he & Day were in the habit of making Jokes of—& never rose till taken out from the Mud, irrecoverably gone! His Parents live at Bath—Daniel & Leech went over to them last night—I have not seen D. since.—

God bless you, | My dear Friends, | and your ever | affectionate

S. T. Coleridge

I dine with Hood to day.

941. *To the Morgans*

Address: J. J. Morgan, Esqre | Mrs Smith's | Ashley | Box | Bath To be left at the Farm House, on the Hill at Ashley—where they will be so good as to send it up to Mr M. immediately.
MS. Cornell University Lib. Hitherto unpublished.

My dear Friends

Thursday Morning [30 June 1814][1]

This small Salmon has just this moment been sent me by Le Breton, but Sally says, it *must be drest to day*. I have determined to risk it, however, by the 12 o/clock Coach—After I have sent it off, I am going to Hartley's.—I continue well—that is, as well as I ever am—for I am almost certain, that there is a source of Disease of 25 years' standing at least, much more serious & which, if curable at all, would be of incomparably more tedious Cure than even old Blacky, alias, Opium.—

God bless you &
S. T. Coleridge

If you don't eat it, Cook it as soon as you receive it.—

[1] See next letter.

942. *To the Morgans*

Address: J. J. Morgan, Esqre, | Mr B. Morgan's, | Chemist and Druggist, | Bath
Double To be forwarded to Ashley to Mr J. J. M. as soon as possible. 4 July, 1814.
MS. Lord Latymer. Hitherto unpublished.
Postmark: Bristol, 3 July 1814.

> Thursday Night, 11 o/clock
> 30 June, 1814

My dear Mary and Charlotte
The highest Compliment, I can pay you, and it is no higher than,
I am sure, you deserve, is to tell you (should you happen to open
this Letter in Morgan's Absence) that the inclosed contains
Hartley's Opinion on my friend's Statement, which, I foreknow,
M. will think clear, well-digested, and as far as the case permits,
satisfactory—but that the overleaf part of this Letter is for Morgan
alone, respects *me* alone, & is fit for Men alone—And now I would
pledge my Life, that you don't read a Line beyond this page:
so compleat is my reliance *on that*, which spite of the unevenness
of *your* Tempers contrasted with the dulcet uniformity and almost
insipid regularity of MY never-to-be-disturbed Humour & inirritable
Spirits, has yet forced me to love you both very dearly, *very* VERY
dearly: to wit, on your *good* & *honor-full* Hearts:—Your (if you
chance to see this Scrawl, or whether you do or no) most affectionate Friend, Brother, Lover, my dearest Mary & Charlotte,

> S. T. Coleridge

N.B. Porter called *once* before my entire confinement—then never
called for 8 weeks, viz. till the last time, when he thrice *commissioned* Wade to deliver his Invitation—& left with Sally an *apology*
for his having *never* called during my Illness from his having been
occupied concerning his Brother! !—

P.S. I took all imaginable precautions to secure the arrival of the
Salmon this Evening—the fellow, whom I shillinged, pledged himself most solemnly for it's Delivery—but should you smell before
you see it, I shall be more vexed than surprized—but when I come,
I shall bring one with me, I trust. Should you like a young Turtle,
all alive, & if not kicking yet *finning*?—God bless you.—

> J. Wade's, Esqre., 2. Queen's Square, Bristol.—
> Thursday Night, 30 June, 1814—

My dear Friend
I gave you a Hint that I had latterly from increased knowlege
begun to suspect a Source of Disease in myself anterior to, & even
more serious than, the OPIUM; & which had been from it's constitutional effects the *cause* of my resorting to that Drug: tho' from
never having had any '*Complaint*' in my whole Life, and having

since my twenty second year never had any illicit connection, I did not till lately even *suspect* it—from the *mistaken* supposition, that Strictures in the Urethra always originated in some vicious Cause.—But since I have read Sir Everard Home's two Volumes on Strictures,[1] & Whately's milder Plans, a mass of Evidence has crowded on me; & this morning I took courage & communicated my Fears to DANIEL: who very judiciously replied, that whether so or not, it was highly improper that such a Dread should haunt my mind, when the Point might be settled in a few minutes by attempting to pass a probe-βουγίε thro' the Canal into the βλαδδερ. Tomorrow morning this is to be done: & you may well imagine the state of my mind at present, in expectation of the Event, the distressful feelings οφ μοδεστὶ and a crowd of indefinite sensations connected with ΜΟΔΕΣΤΥ put out of the Question: tho' God knows, they now agitate me so as almost to overwhelm the Dread of having the Worst, I suspect, ascertained.—I write now merely to give an outlet to my anxieties—merely to be *doing* something— After the Operation I will, if I can, finish this Letter, and inform you of the Result.—Chiefly in consequence of the evidence of a Stranger, a Captn Kidd, poor Shepherd's Death has been brought in after long, very long hesitation by the Coroner's jury, *accidental* —just as it ought to be.—But both myself & D. have (*privately*) our melancholy Doubts. It is odd; but for the two last times I have been in his Company, the Conversation has happened to turn on Suicide: & Daniel has endeavored to collect the various arguments, I used, to prove it's guilt & it's exceeding irrationality, as '*striking a blow in the Dark*, independent of it's rebellion to the Laws of God "Thou shalt *not* murder" in an act aggravated by the foreknown certainty, that no repentance producing a change of Habit could take place, & no compensation be made to our fellow-creatures— independent of all this, there does not exist the slightest probability, that the act would answer the end proposed: that of putting one out of one's misery!—On the contrary, every analogy tends to establish the Belief, that the Body & the Senses are the means of *sheathing* & shielding the Soul, & drawing it off by perpetual Influxes of Images & Sensations from it's own Disharmonies—so that the probability (Religion out of the Question) is, that the Soul would pass into the state of [horri]ble Night-mair, *concentered* to the dominant pai[nful] Thought.'—There is no doubt, that he struggled hard to save himself, & twice on rising called out for Help—& Kidd swore that he fell sideways with his shoulder fore- most.—12 o/clock.—

S. T. C.—

[1] Everard Home, *Practical Observations on the Treatment of Strictures in the Urethra and in the Oesophagus*, 2nd ed., vol. i, 1797, vol. ii, 1803.

P.S. My God! what if in some whim of mind I had palliated, or attempted to defend, Suicide! It proves how *careful* we ought to be.—If I had done it, it might have made [me] unhappy for my Life-long.—Tho' I look, and in many respects am, so much better, yet mark my words! I am much nearer the narrow Bed of 6 feet by 2 than any of my friends imagine.—I hope, however, to see you & *you* (i.e. M. & C.) before my Finale. Believe me, I am not ᾿ypped; but have *grounds* for my presentiment—Coffin grounds black as Coffee Grounds.

Saturday Night.

I will not delay sending this any longer. A most curious, pressing, and unexpected Money-demand from a Reverend of our Acquaintance so agitated me, not for the sum or the money, to which there was no other answer but '*I can't*' (&, which is not *my* opinion or design, *all* HIS *former* friends tell me, that I ought to add '*if I could, I would not*'), but *purely* and *merely* for the *baseness* of the act, so that Daniel thought it unfit to agitate me yet more.—The Trial is therefore deferred to Monday Morning. Since I have read on the Subject, I myself have no doubt of the melancholy fact. I am *quite certain*, that I have not deceived myself as to 9 Symptoms, & it is scarcely possible that these should co-exist without στρικτῦρς unless some thing, if possible still worse, affects the βλαδδερ— Whatever be the result, I will see you in a few Days: & explain whatever is mysterious in this Postscript.—

943. *To J. J. Morgan*

Address: J. J. Morgan, Esqre | Mrs Smith's | Ashley | Box | Bath
MS. formerly in the possession of the late A. H. Hallam Murray. Pub. with omis. E. L. G. ii. 120.
Postmark: Bristol, 7 July 1814.

Thursday, 7 July 1814.[1]

My dear Friend

Suppose, I borrowed Hood's Horse for a fortnight, to ride over myself, in order to give you a little Horse Exercise, is there any stable near you, at either of the Farm Houses, in which it could be properly & safely stabled? Be so good as to let me have an immediate answer. Ten miles & back again every morning from 11 to 3 would do you a world of good: & let me persuade you to leave off the magnesia, unless where you are *certain* of an Acid on your Stomach; and instead of it have Pills made in the proportion of 2 grains of Calomel to a proper quantity of the Pillula Rufi in every

[1] Coleridge began this letter on Wednesday morning.

3 Pills (your Cousin will make them up, so as to be mildly laxative) and take three 3 nights in the week—& give a trial, a fair trial, for one week at least, (& should it agree with you continue it for 3 weeks, or a month) to the following superoxygenated Sulfat of Iron—viz—on half an ounce of Salt of Steel let your Cousin pour two drachms of Nitric Acid, wait till the Orange Fumes have evaporated, and then add an Ounce of Water—and of this take two Drops in a small Tumbler of Water twice a day, an hour after Breakfast, and an hour before Dinner—and increase the Dose gradually to 5 drops twice a day, for (say) 10 days, & then as gradually decrease for the next ten days. It is well worth trying & will not cost you sixpence. If it should agree with you (& it is nothing but an austere pleasant Lemonade) it, joined with the Laxative, as above, & horse exercise will do you a great deal of good—& I begin to hope confidently, that I shall be able to work *profitably*, & somewhere or other to renew our former Relations. I can at all events get six guineas a week: & that in a country Cottage would be ample for us. As I have nothing to say, I shall shut up this Letter till I return from Allston's, Merchant Tailors' Hall, to which I go (please God) at 12 o/clock—& will fill up the Letter with my Impressions from his Pictures.—God bless you— & let Sharlot kiss her crooked little finger for me—& Mary (if she can) the dimple on her chin.

S. T. Coleridge

Wednesday afternoon, ½ past 3. Too late for the Post.—Had taken Mrs Daniel & a female friend of her's together with small *Sore Throat* who unexpectedly popped in on me, to Allston's. If disappointed in finding only the great Picture at the Merch. Tayl. Hall (opposite to Guild Hall in Broad Street, up one of the Bristol *Urēthras*) I was more than gratified by the wonderful Improvement of the Picture, since he has restored it to his original Conception.[1] I cannot by words convey to you, how much he has improved it within the last Fortnight. Were it not, that I still think (tho' ages *might* pass without the world at large noticing it) that in the figure of the Soldier there is too much motion for the distinct Expression, or rather too little expression for the quantity & vehemence of Motion, I should scarcely hesitate to declare it in it's present state a *perfect* work of art. Such Richness with such variety of Colors, all harmonizing, and while they vivify, yet deepen not counteract, the total effect of a grand Solemnity of Tint, I never before contemplated.—I must defer seeing his other pictures, which are at

[1] Referring to Allston's *The Dead Man Revived by Touching the Bones of the Prophet Elisha.*

his Lodgings, till Friday when I expect to go with Daniel, first to the M. T. Hall, & then to the *good bad* little Hydatid's.—The same game in Bristol as in London—A. can visit *me*; but his own House & real Feelings belong as exclusive Property to his 'Countrymen', as he called one of the Beasts last night: when to Wade's great Delight I gave him a justly complimentary, but from that very cause a most severe reproof. 'Countryman?' (said I) 'Live the age of Methusalem, & you *may* have a right to say *that*, Allston!—At present, either the World is your Country, & England with all it's faults your *Home*, inasmuch as it contains the largest number of those who are capable of feeling your *Fame* before the idle Many (the same in *kind* in all places but better (even these) in *degree here*, than in any other part of the world) have learnt to give you *Reputation*: or you are *morally* not worthy of your high Gifts, which as a Painter give you a *praeternational* Privilege, even beyond the greatest Poet, by the universality of *your* Language: and you prefer the accident of Place, naked Place, unenriched by any of the associations of Law, Religion, or intellectual *Fountaincy*, to the essential grandeur of God in Man.'—I said it loftily, & tho' mildly yet not without perceptible Indignation: and it faintly tinged his Cheek, tho' the increased yellow was the predominant Hue.—Good Heavens! that such a man with such a Heart & such Genius should be—not *an* American, but downright *American*, & I do believe, 9 parts in 10 owing to the little Hydatid. O that (if only his Health could have been preserved) instead of being a *good* little Hydatid she had been an absolute Sarah+Mary+Edith+ Eliza—*Fricker* (Christ! what a *name* for *Coleridge to be transferred to!) with all the discontent, and miserableness of the Angel of the Race, self-nibbling Martha!—Then perhaps he might have hated her, & been a fine Fellow.

* If I know my own feelings, it was no arrogance that prompted this admiration of the name in any the remotest way connected with myself; but in & for itself I think, that the word Cō lĕ rĭdge (amphimacron = long on both sides) has a noble *verbal physiognomy*—Ex. gr. Suppose me married to little Megrim, & that a Brentus Coleridge should discover the North West Passage, or (he being by the Mother's side of a ship-building generation) a power & machinery capable of rendering a Vessel on the open seas independent of the Winds—can you conceive a nobler Sound than Baron Cōlĕrĭdge of Cōlĕrĭdge, in the County of Devon?—But if Charlotte prefers it, he shall be a Baronet, Sir Brentus Coleridge, of Coleridge Hall & Hundred, the Son of the celebrated S. T. Coleridge lawfully &c on the &c of Charlotte Brent of *Brain town*? Brent is very well: & so is Morgan; but I appeal to both Mary & to Charlotte, whether there is not a peculiar indescribable Beauty of the lofty kind in Cōlĕrĭdge?—For it is one of the vilest Belzebubberies of Detraction to pronounce it Col-ridge, or Cŏllĕridge, or even Cōle-ridge. It is & must be to all honest and honorable men, a trisyllabic Amphimacer, – ᴗ –! S. T. C.

11 o'clock, Wednesday Evening.

I have dined out at York Place with Clayfield—: Turbot, Lobster Sauce, Boiled Fowl, Turtle, Ham, a quarter of Lamb, Tatas & Cauliflower &c—then Duck, green Peas, a gooseberry, & a currant Pie, and a soft Pudding. Desert, Grapes, Pine Apples, Strawberries, cherries, & other more vulgar Fruits & Sweetmeats. Wines—? he is a Wine-merchant!—Champagne, Burgundy, Madeira—I forget the Commonalty!—Company? not one to make such a dinner less unendurable to me, except a very lovely Woman called Mrs Grove, the Wife of a Major Grove. Further I know not.— On my return I found your letter—your Letter (*Brief*, as the Germans call it). I want no money. Would to God, I could send you 10,000£ instead of having 10£.—Whether your Suspicion is right or wrong, I request you earnestly not even to give it a thought, till I have in person told you the whole. Be assured, that had no previous respect, or rather sympathy with the respect felt by those, I dearly love, interfered, it was a thing to laugh at, & for the miserable Reverend's sake to *pity*! Whoever it be, he has incurred the *contempt* (not merely forfeited the Esteem and Regard) of all his oldest Bristol Friends. I will bring you my answer, of which I (for once in my Life sacrificing Indolence to Prudence) made a Copy.

I am still improving in Health & Spirits; but that Lignum vitae Leg of mine, will not go Partners in the *thinning* Line with my Body, or in the *prettying* Line with my Face. An ugly obstinate Son of a Thigh Bone! it is downright Forgery for him to *lignify* before amputation, and mismetamorphose before Putrefaction. *Right* as he may flatter himself, he is, I must inform him, that it is a *sinister* mode of Proceeding; but, however, I don't wish him to be *mortified*, & indeed would dispense with his hot *Blushes*.

How sweet the tuneful Bells' responsive Peal!—This, you know, is Thanksgiving Day.—God bless you all three—

J, M M, and C B,

And likewise me,

S. T. C.

I send this to Ashley direct—In your next tell me, which is likeliest to bring it soonest to you.—

944. *To J. J. Morgan*

Address: J. J. Morgan, Esqre | W. Allston's, Esqre
MS. Lord Latymer. Pub. with omis. E. L. G. ii. 124.

[Late July 1814][1]

My dear Friend

An hour after dinner I was taken very ill and sick, and I am sorry to add not without some Botherment of Thought at every effort of attention. The Elimination of a large Quantity of Bile (for the production of which I am obliged to Mrs Daniel's excellent Glass of Punch last night) has indeed relieved me; but I am so faint and feeble, tho' with no disquieting feelings, that I dare not undertake the Walk to Portland Square—especially, as I am enforced to give one of the Actors (whose name I know not) a meeting at ½ past 8 this evening at Mr Ambrose's, he having to enact some part in the Remorse: & tomorrow morning at ½ past 8, Mr Bengough, the Ordonio, is to breakfast here & have the part read & commented on to him.

I will take care, if God grant me Life, that this unlucky Indisposition shall be no injury to Allston—I should have done more, had I not been so anxious to do so much. I could not bear the Thought of putting in an ordinary Puff on such a man—or even an *anonymous* one.[2] I thought, that a bold Avowal of *my* sentiments on the fine Arts, as divided into—Poetry—1 of Language —2 of the ear—and 3 of the Eye—& the last subdivided into the *plastic* (statuary) & the graphic (painting) connected (& as it were *isthmused*) with common Life by the Link of Architecture—& exemplifying my principles by continued reference to Allston's Pictures—would from the mere curiosity of Malignity & envy answer our friend's *pecuniary* Interests best: his *Fame* he will make for himself—for which indeed (& you may tell him so from me) he has but *one* thing to do—Having arrived at perfection, *comparative* perfection certainly, in colouring, drawing, and composition, to be as equal to these three in his *Expression*, (not of a particular Passion but of the living, ever-individualizing *Soul*, whose chief & best meaning is *itself*) as even in *this* he is superior to other artists.—He will remember the Galatea of Rafael in the

---

[1] This letter must have been written not long before *Remorse* was produced in Bristol on 1 Aug. 1814. See *Shakespearean Criticism*, ii. 258.

[2] On 6 Aug. 1814, the editor of *Felix Farley's Bristol Journal* announced 'the commencement of a series of Essays upon the Fine Arts; particularly upon that of Painting; illustrated by Criticisms upon the Pictures now exhibiting by Mr. Allston'. Coleridge's essays 'On the Principles of Genial Criticism concerning the Fine Arts' appeared 13, 20, and 27 Aug. and 10 and 24 Sept. 1814. See *Biog. Lit.* ii. 219–46 and 305.

Farnesini [*sic*] which we saw together—& understand, my dear Morgan,

Your faithful & loving Friend
S. T. C.

P.S. WOULD TO GOD, there were a place as cheap & pleasant, ½ a mile from Bristol as Ashley! I know no other way to reconcile 2 Irreconcileables, both necessary to my moral Being!—

945. *To Robert Southey*

MS. Mr. William Roethke. Hitherto unpublished.

2. Queen's Square, Bristol—
10 August, 1814—

Dear Southey

The young Gentleman, who may probably deliver this, is Mr Henry Biddulph, the Son of a respectable Clergyman of this City, celebrated as a zealous Preacher, and a man of evangelical Benevolence & active Beneficence.—I do not myself know Mr H. Biddulph; but he is dear to several of my best Friends here, and therefore (tho' I know, how much at this time of the year especially you are over-loaded with recommendations) any little Instructions or *verbal* Cicerone isms, you can give him, would oblige me: tho' I dare say, the desire of seeing you, & having to say, that he has seen & talked with you, is his main Object for wishing a Letter. Before this, you will have received from me an answer to your last—God bless you | &

S. T. Coleridge

946. *To John Murray*

Address: Mr Murray | Bookseller | Albermarle Street | Piccadilly | London
MS. Sir John Murray. Pub. Letters, ii. 624.
Postmark: Bristol, 23 August 1814.

J. Wade's, Esqre., 2. Queen's Square, Bristol.—
[23 August 1814]

Dear Sir

I have heard from my friend, Mr Charles Lamb, writing by desire of Mr Robinson, that you wish to have the justly celebrated FAUST of Goethe translated;[1] & that some one or other of my partial friends have induced you to consider me as the man most

---

[1] *Faust. Ein Fragment*, 1790; *Faust. Eine Tragödie*, Part I, 1808.

likely to execute the work adequately, those excepted, of course, whose higher Powers (established by the solid & satisfactory Ordeal of the wide and rapid Sale of their works) it might seem profanation to employ in any other manner, than in the developement of their own intellectual organization. I return my thanks to the Recommender, whoever he be, & no less to you for your flattering Faith in the Recommendation: & thinking, as I do, that among many volumes of praise-worthy German Poems the Louisa of Voss,[1] and the Faust of Goethe are the two, if not the only ones, that are emphatically *original* in their conception, & characteristic of a new & peculiar sort of Thinking and Imagining, I should not be averse from exerting my best efforts in an attempt to import whatever is importable of either or of both into our own Language.[2]—

But let me not [be] suspected of a presumption, of which I am not consciously guilty, if I say that I feel two difficulties, one arising from long disuse of Versification added to what *I* know, better than the most hostile Critic could inform me, of my comparative Weakness; and the other, that *any* Work in Poetry strikes me with more than common awe, as proposed for realization by myself—because from long habits of meditation on Language, as the symbolic medium of the connection of Thought with Thought, & of Thoughts, as affected and modified by Passion & Emotion, I should spend days in avoiding what I deemed faults, tho' with the full pre-knowlege, that their admission would not have offended perhaps 3 of all my Readers, & might be deemed Beauties by 300— if so many there were:—& this not out of any respect to the PUBLIC (i.e. the persons who might happen to purchase & look over the Book), but from a hobby-horsical, superstitious regard to my own feelings & sense of Duty. Language is the sacred Fire in the Temple of Humanity; and the Muses are it's especial & Vestal Priestesses. Tho' I cannot prevent the vile drugs, and counterfeit Frankincense, which render it's flame at once pitchy, glowing, and unsteady, I would yet be no voluntary accomplice in this Sacrilege. With the commencement of a PUBLIC commences the degradation of the GOOD & the BEAUTIFUL—both fade or retire before the accidentally AGREEABLE—. OTHELLO becomes a hollow Lip-worship, & the CASTLE SPECTRE, or any more recent Thing of Froth, Noise, & Impermanence, that may have overbillowed it on the restless Sea

---

[1] See Letter 457 for Coleridge's earlier plan to translate the *Luise* of J. H. Voss.

[2] In replying to this letter, Murray offered 'the sum of One Hundred Pounds for the Translation and the preliminary Analysis, with such passages translated as you may judge proper of the works of Goethe'. *A Publisher and His Friends*, 118. Nothing came of this plan.

of Curiosity, is the *true* Prayer of Praise & Admiration.—I thought it right to state to you these opinions of mine, that you might know that I think the Translation of the 'FAUST' a task demanding (from *me*, I mean) no ordinary efforts—& why.—Next, that it is painful, very painful & even odious to me, to attempt any thing of a literary nature, with any motive of *pecuniary* advantage; that I bow to the all-wise Providence, which has made me a *poor* man & therefore compelled me by other duties inspiring yet higher feelings, to bring *even my Intellect* to the *Market*—And the Finale is this—I should like to attempt the Translation—if you will mention your Terms, at once & irrevocably (for I am an Ideot at Bargaining & shrink from the very Thought) I will return an answer by the next Post, whether in my present Circumstances I can or cannot undertake it. If I do, I will do it immediately; but I must have all Goethe's Works, which I cannot procure in Bristol— for to give the Faust without a preliminary critical Essay would be worse than nothing—as far as regards the PUBLIC. If you were to ask me as a Friend, whether I think it would suit *the General Taste*, I should reply—that I cannot calculate on Caprice & Accident (for instance, some fashionable Man or Review happening to take it up favorably), but that otherwise my fears would be stronger than my Hopes.—Men of Genius will admire it, of necessity; those most, who think deepliest & most imaginatively—The Louisa would delight *all* of Good Hearts.—I remain, dear Sir,

with due respect,
S. T. Coleridge

947. *To John Murray*

Address: Mr Murray | Bookseller | Albermarle Street | London.   Single Sheet.
MS. Sir John Murray. Pub. A Publisher and His Friends, *119*.
Postmark: Bristol, 31 August 1814.

Wednesday, 31 August, 1814
Josiah Wade's, Esqre. 2. Queen's Square, Bristol.

Dear Sir

I have received your Letter. Considering the necessary Labor, and (from the questionable nature of the original work, both as to it's fair claims on *Fame* (the dictum of the good & wise according to unchanging Principles) and as to its Chance for *Reputation*, as an accidental result of local and temporary Taste) the risk of character on the part of the Translator, who will assuredly have to answer for any disappointment of the Reader, the Terms proposed are humiliatingly low: yet such as under modifications I accede to.—I have received testimonials from men not merely of genius according to *my* belief, but of the highest *accredited* reputation, that my Translation of the Wallenstein was in language & in metre superior to the original—& the parts most admired were substitutions of my own, on a principle of Compensation—Yet the whole work went for waste paper—I was abused—nay, my own remarks in the preface were transferred to a Review, as the Reviewer's sentiments *against* me, without even a Hint that he had copied them from my own preface.—Such was the fate of Wallenstein! and yet I dare appeal to any number of men of Genius—say for instance, Mr W. Scott, Mr Southey, Mr Wordsworth, Mr Wilson, Mr Sotheby, Sir G. Beaumont &c, &c—whether the Wallenstein with all it's Defects (& it has grievous defects) is not worth all Schiller's other plays, put together—But I wonder not—It was *too* good, & not good enough—and the advice of the younger Pliny—aim at pleasing either *all*, or *the Few*—is as *prudentially* good as it is philosophically accurate. I wrote to Mr Longman, before the work was published— I foretold it's fate, even to a detailed accuracy, and advised him to *put up* with the Loss from the Purchase of the MSS. and of the Translation, as a much less evil than the Publication—I went so far as to declare that it's Success was in the then state of public Taste impossible—that the enthusiastic Admirers of the Robbers, Cabal & Love[1] &c would lay the [blame] on me—& that he himself would suspect, that if he had only lit on *another* Translator, then—&c. Every thing took place as I had foretold, even his own Feelings—so little do Prophets gain from the fulfilment of their Prophecies!—

On the other hand, tho' I know that executed as alone I can or dare do it, that is, to the utmost of my powers (for which the intolerable Pain, nay, the far greater Toil & Effort of doing otherwise, is a far safer Pledge than any solicitude on my part concerning the approbation of the PUBLIC), the Translation of so very difficult a work, as the Faustus, will be most inadequately remunerated by the Terms, you propose; yet they very probably are the highest, it may be worth your while to offer to *me*. I say this, as a philosopher: for tho' I have been much talked of, & written of, for evil &—not for good, but—for suspected Capability—yet none of my works have ever sold. The Wallenstein went to the Waste—the Remorse, tho' acted 20 times, rests quietly on the Shelves in the second Edition, with copies enough for 7 years' consumption, or 7 times 7 —I lost 200£ by non-payment, from forgetfulness & under various pretences, by the *Friend*—and for my Poems I *did* get—from 10 to 15£!—And yet, forsooth, the Quarterly Review attacks me for neglecting & misusing my Powers!—I do not quarrel with the

[1] *Die Räuber* was published in 1781; *Kabale und Liebe* in 1784.

Public—all is as it must be—but surely the *Public* (if there be such a Person) has no right to quarrel with *me* for not getting into Jail by publishing what they will not read!—

The Faust, you perhaps know, is only a *Fragment*—whether Goethe ever will finish it, or whether it is even his object to do so, is quite unknown—A large proportion of the work cannot be rendered in blank Verse, but must be in wild *lyrical* metres—& Mr Lamb informs me, that the Baroness de Sta[ë]l[1] has given a very unfavorable account of the Work—Still however I will undertake it, and that instantly, so as to let you have the last Sheet before the middle of November, on the following Terms—

1. That *on the* delivery of the last Mss Sheet you remit a 100 guineas to Mrs Coleridge, or Mr Robert Southey, at a Bill of five weeks—2. that I, or my Widow or Family, may any time after two years from the first publication have the privilege of reprinting it in any *collection* of all my poetical writings, or of my Works in general—which set off with a Life of me might perhaps be made profitable to my Widow—and thirdly, that if (as I long ago meditated) I should re-model the whole, give it a Finale, and be able to bring it thus re-written & re-cast, on the Stage, it shall not be considered as a Breach of engagement between us: I on my part promising that you shall for an equitable consideration have the Copy of this new Work; either as a separate Work, or forming a part of the same Volume—or both, as Circumstances may dictate to you. When I say, that I am confident, that in this *possible* tho' not probable case, I should not repeat or retain one fifth of the original, you will perceive that I consult only my dread of appearing to act amiss: as it would be even more easy for me to compose the whole anew.—If these Terms suit you, I will commence the Task as soon as I receive Goethe's Works from you. If you could procure Goethe's late Life of himself, which extends but a short way[2]—or any German *Biographical* Work of the German living poets—it would enable me to render the P[reli]minary Essay more entertaining—

respe[ctfully,] dear Sir,
S. T. Coleridge.

[1] Southey introduced Coleridge to Madame de Staël in Oct. 1813. 'It was after this interview that Madame de Staël said of Coleridge: "Pourtant, pour M. Coleridge, il est tout à fait *un monologue!*"' *Southey Letters*, ii. 332 n.

[2] J. W. von Goethe, *Aus meinem Leben. Dichtung und Wahrheit*, Part I, 1811; Part II, 1812; Part III, 1814.

948. *To the Morgans*

Address: J. J. or Mrs Morgan, Esqre | Paul Street | Portland Square
MS. Lord Latymer. Hitherto unpublished.

Sunday Evening, 8 o/clock—[4 September 1814][1]
My dear Friends

I called both at Mr Kiddle's and at Mr Hood's—and both were, it seems, at the Revd. Mr Edwards's at Bedminster—but Mrs Hood told me, that Kiddle had not received the expected Letters; & I told her, and explained to her, that it was quite out of my power to wait longer—that I felt it *absolutely necessary* to the fulfilment of my Engagement with Murray the Bookseller to retire from Bristol immediately, from the deep Conviction that it was impossible for *me* to labor effectually there—that therefore if Mr Hood should go into Wales *tomorrow*, I still held myself his promised Companion—but if not, I must give up the pleasure altogether.— She very much wished, that Mr Hood should go: & begged me to wait till tomorrow morning, when he would call upon me.—In the mean time I will have seen Mr Daniel—& before you go, will introduce Morgan to him for a private Conversation without Megrim. I have done what I can, without ungratefully making Enemies—. But should you be uneasy to return home, all I can say is, that I will follow you as soon as possible—tho' I would rather go with you—

S. T. Coleridge

N.B. I *cannot* well go from Bristol for good, till I have waited for T[uesday's] Post for Murray's final answer. I expected it to [day—] tomorrow there is no Post—

949. *To the Editor of 'Felix Farley's Bristol Journal'*

Pub. Felix Farley's Bristol Journal, *10 September 1814.* In the *Bristol Gazette* of 1 Sept. a critic signing himself 'Cosmo' attacked Coleridge's essays 'On the Principles of Genial Criticism'. The present letter was Coleridge's reply. Subsequent attacks appearing in the *Gazette* on 15 and 29 Sept. were ignored.

[10 September 1814]
Sir,

An ambitious Sign-painter* has been disturbed in stomach usque ad nauseam (eheu! quantum valet invida Bilis!) by my

[1] This letter was written on the Sunday following Coleridge's letter to Murray of 31 Aug. 1814.

* Such I believe him to be, though by the exquisitely ludicrous Personification of Music, worthy of Holofernes! and by the no less exquisite blunder in the

having presumed to elucidate a Principle of Painting by reference to the Works of a resident Artist, whose genius has been accredited by far higher and more public testimonials than mine. He has in consequence discovered an intolerable deformity in my Essay on Beauty, nay, in the very introductory sentences, and presented me unasked with a sort of Caffrarian *Cosmetic* for its removal. Should any of your Readers be desirous to have the like made up for them, the following is the recipe:—Stercoris anserini q. s. adipe anserino bene permissi. Fiat COSMIANUM. Which last word Ainsworth cites from Martial and explains by 'a sort of Pomatum of a rank scent made by one Cosmo.'

I return him thanks; but till he has acquired a knowledge enough not to mistake the Acanthus of the Corinthian for the Ramshorns of the Ionic Order; logic enough not to confound the genus with the species, and the species with the genus; modesty enough not to talk of books, which he never read, was never able to read, and probably never saw; (but why should I tire you with a detail of ignorancies and misstatements, at least equal in number to that of his sentences?) in short, till this Nauseist of 'mere mechanic ingenuity' shall have proved himself capable of writing three periods consecutively without some offence against either Grammar, Logic, History or good Manners; I must content myself by admonishing him, Nil, nisi lignum, oblinire; which may be interpreted, keep to thy own Ladder Friend! (on which Hogarth in his Beer Street has immortalized one of thy Predecessors) and pray Heaven to preserve thee from Envy, Hatred, Uncharitableness and all the vices, that might finally translate thee to a far less honourable one.

Aristotle, Mr. Editor! tells us, Cytharizando fit Cytharoedus. Si quis huic miserrimo (ipso quod habet extracto) aliud superimposuerit Cerebrum, forsitan Criticando fiet Criticus. There is no danger of Cosmo's suffering any pain from the preceding sentence, unless the School boy, who furnished his Letter to the Editor of the Gazette with the thousand times quoted quotation from Ovid, should be mischievous enough to construe it for him.

With sincere respect, I remain, dear Sir,
Your obliged,
S. T. Coleridge.

reason which he assigns for preferring this omniform 'She' of his, to her Sisters, Painting and Poetry, he would fain mislead us into supposing him a *Fidler*. But this I regard as a mere *ruse da* [sic] *guerre*. [Note by S. T. C.]

950. *To John Murray*

Address: Mr Murray | Bookseller | Albermarle Street | London   Single Sheet
MS. Sir John Murray. Pub. E. L. G. ii. 125.
Postmark: Bath, 10 September 1814.

[10 September 1814]

Dear Sir

I cannot persuade myself, that I can have offended you by my openness. I think the 'Faust' a work of genius, of genuine and original Genius. The Scenes in the Cathedral and in the Prison must delight and affect all Readers not pre-determined to dislike. But the Scenes of Witchery and that astonishing Witch-Gallop up the Brocken will be denounced as *fantastic* and absurd. Fantastic they *are*, and were meant to be; but I need not tell you, how many will detect the supposed fault for one, who can enter into the philosophy of that imaginative Superstition, which justifies it. I have shewn to the full conviction of no small number among our first-rate men that every one of the Faults so wildly charged on the Hamlet by the Decriers of Shakespear, and palliated even by his admirers only on the score of their being overbalanced by its Beauties, forms an essential part of the essential Excellence of that marvellous *Plenum* of the myriad-minded man—a bold phrase, which I have transferred from a Patriarch of Constantinople, to whom it had been applied by a Greek Monk.[1]—In my Essay I meant to have given a full tho' comprest critical account of the 4 Stages of German Poetry from Hans Sachs to Tiek and Schlegel, who with Goethe are the living Stars, that are now culminant on the German Parnassus.—In reference to the *Labor* and to the quantity of thoughtful Reading I deemed the price inadequate; not as less than you were justified in offering.—I trust, however, to hear from you at all events.—I have left Bristol for a Cottage 5 miles from Bath, in order to be perfectly out of the Reach of Interruption.—

There are, however, two Works, which I could dare confidently recommend to you for Translation—the first, the minor works of Cervantes, namely, his Novels, his divine Galathea, his Persiles, Naumantium, a Tragedy, and his humorous Voyage to Parnassus —6 volumes in Spanish, but which might be printed in 3 sizable Octavos in English. I will not say, that they are equal altogether to Don Quixote. What indeed is? What can be? But I will dare affirm, that in their *kind* they are equal, and of most consummate Excellence. A middle thing between the Novel and the Romance, they are more natural than the latter, more elevated and of more permanent Interest than the former—and with all the charms of the

---

[1] Cf. *Biog. Lit.*, ch. xv, and *Anima Poetae*, ed. E. H. Coleridge, 1895, p. 21.

most delicious poetry in the most unaffected melody of Prose they may be re-perused for the 20th time with additional pleasure.— The second, the Prose Works of Boccaccio, excluding his Decameron —these too are of the same class as the above mentioned of Cervantes, but I dare affirm them far more interesting, affecting, and eloquent than the Decameron itself—and if less amusing, yet (if there be no contradiction in saying so) more entertaining.—Either of these works I would undertake at any moderate price.—Pray, let me hear from you—

Your obliged
S. T. Coleridge

Direct to—Mr B. Morgan, | chemist | Bridge Street | Bath *for Mr Coleridge*
I am at a Mrs Smith's, Ashley, Box, Bath.—

951. *To Daniel Stuart*

Address: D. Stuart, Esqre | Kilburn House | near | London   To be forwarded if Mr Stuart should not be at Kilburn.
MS. British Museum. Pub. with omis. Letters, ii. 627.
Postmark: 12 September 1814.

Mrs Smith's, Ashley, Box, near Bath—12 Septr, 1814

My dear Sir
   I wrote some time ago to Mr Street, earnestly requesting your address, and intreating him to inform you of the dreadful State in which I was, when your kind Letter must have arrived, and during your stay at Bath. All Letters, and even the information of their having been received, it was deemed necessary to withhold from me—for some months the Doctor was with me from four to six hours at different times every day, and I could never be left alone. Even now, that both in mental & bodily Health I am on the whole better than I have been for at least 12 years, the very Retrospect of what I suffered is often such, as leaves me struggling against the immoral Wish to have died at the commencement of my Sufferings. Sooner or later my Case will be published—a case not much less instructive to medical men, than to the too numerous class of Patients suffering similar *soul-&-body* Blights from similar Causes. It ought to give, tho' assuredly it will not give, a profitable Hint to such as Carlisle, that Kindness, Gentleness, and Patience are as much prescripts of medical Skill, as dictates of moral Wisdom. There is a spiritual *ossificatio cordis*—& in the case of Carlisle the causes may be easily traced. The ultimate or predisposing Cause a

restless craving videri quam esse, even to themselves—2. thence
a seeking from others for a confirmation of that, which, if it had
had any other existence but in the Wish, would like Light have
been it's own & only possible Evidence—3. thence unquiet & insolent Positiveness, the infallible symptom, because the necessary
Effect, of inward Uncertainty—4. and thence as the proximate
Causes, pompous and irritable Vanity, with vindictive *Envy*, which
before the occasional Looking-Glass of Conscience tries to hide it's
own face from it's own Eyes by assuming the Mask of *Contempt*.
Had Carlisle behaved towards me even with common professional
Honor (me who had been duped by Fool plus Fiend, i.e. *Basil*+
Mrs M. to travel 300 miles solely to put myself under his care)
instead of eagerly seizing the opportunity of avenging himself for
an offence, of which I was wholly unconscious, that of having, 3 or
4 years before reduced him, neither wittingly or willingly, to play
the second fiddle at a Wine Party—good God! what unspeakable
miseries should I have escaped!—What might I not have done!—
But let me not complain! I ought to be, and I trust that I am,
grateful for what I am—having escaped with my intellectual
Powers, if less elastic, yet not less vigorous, and with ampler and
far more solid materials to exert them on. We *know* nothing even
of others, till we know *ourselves* to be as nothing! (a solemn truth,
spite of the Point and antithesis, in which the Thought has chanced
to *word* itself.)—From this *Word* of Truth, which the sore Discipline
of an almost friendless Sick-bed has compacted into an indwelling
Reality; from this article formerly of *speculative* BELIEF, but
which Embarrassment, & Grief, and Miserableness and Desertion
have *actualized* into *practical* FAITH; I have learnt to counteract
Calumny by Self-reproach—and not only to rejoice (as indeed from
natural disposition, from the very constitution of my Heart, I
should have done at all periods of my Life) at the temporal prosperity & increased & increasing Reputation of my old fellow-
labourers in philosophical, political, & poetical Literature, but to
bear their neglect, and even their detraction—as *if I had done
nothing at all*—when it would have asked no very violent strain of
recollection for one or two of them to have considered whether some
part of *their* most successful *Somethings* were not among the
Nothings of my intellectual No-doings.—But all strange things are
less strange, than the sense of intellectual Obligations. Seldom do
I ever see a Review; yet almost as often as that Seldomness permits, have I smiled at finding myself attacked in strains of Thought,
which would never have occurred to the Writer had he not directly
or indirectly learnt them from myself.—This is among the salutary
effects even of the Dawn of actual Religion on the mind, that we

begin to reflect on our Duties to God and to ourselves as permanent
Beings, and not to flatter ourselves by a superficial auditing of our
negative Duties to our neighbors, or mere Acts in transitu to the
transitory. I have too sad an account to settle between my Self that
is & has been & my Self that *can* not cease to be, to allow me a
single Complaint, that for all my labors in behalf of Truth, against
the Jacobins first, then against military Despotism abroad, against
Weakness, and Despondency and Faction and factious *Goodiness*
at home—I have never received from those in power even a verbal
acknowlegement—tho' by mere reference to dates it might be
proved, that no small number of fine Speeches in the House of
Commons & elsewhere originated directly or indirectly in my
Essays & Conversations. I dare assert, that the science of reasoning
and judging concerning the productions of Literature, the characters
& measures of public men, and the events of nations by a systematic
Subsumption of them under PRINCIPLES deduced from the Nature
of MAN; and that of prophecying concerning the Future (in contradiction to the Hopes or Fears of the majority) by a careful cross-
examination of some period, the most analogous, in past History,
as learnt from contemporary Authorities, and the proportioning of
the ultimate Event to the Likenesses as modified or counteracted
by the Differences, was as good as unknown in the Public Prints
before the year, 1795–96.—Earl Darnley on the appearance of my
Letters in the Courier concerning the Spaniards[1] bluntly asked me,
whether I had lost my senses—& quoted Lord Grenville at me—
If you should happen to cast your eye over my character of Pitt,
my two Letters to Fox, my Essays on the French Empire under
Buonaparte compared with the Roman under the first Emperors,
that on the probability of the restoration of the Bourbons,[2] and
those on Ireland & Catholic Emancipation[3] (which last unfortunately remain for the greater part in Manuscript, Mr Street not
relishing them) & should add to them my Essays in the Friend on
Taxation, and the supposed Effects of War on our commercial
Prosperity, those on international Law in defence of our siege of
Copenhagen[4]—and if you had before you the long Letter, which I
wrote to Sir G. Beaumont in 1806,[5] concerning the inevitableness
of a War with America, and the specific dangers of that War, if not
provided against by specific pre-arrangements—with a list of their

[1] See *Essays on His Own Times*, ii. 593–676.
[2] Ibid. ii. 319–29; 552–85; 478–514; and 532–42.
[3] For Coleridge's earlier essays on the Catholic Question see note to Letter
828. Coleridge's *Letters to Mr. Justice Fletcher*, which deal with the affairs of
Ireland, were soon to appear in the *Courier*. See note to Letter 952.
[4] See *The Friend*, 1809–10, Nos. 12, 24, and 26.
[5] No such letter has come to light.

Frigates, so called, with their size & number & weight of metal, the characters of their Commanders, and the proportion suspected of British Sea-men (I have luckily a Copy of it—a rare accident with me—)—I dare amuse myself, I say, with the Belief, that by far the better half of all these would read to you now, as *History*. —And what have I got for all this? What for my first daring to blow the Trumpet of sound Philosophy against the Lancastrian Faction?—The answer is not complex—Unthanked and left worse than defenceless by the Friends of the Government and the Establishment, to be undermined or outraged by all the malice, hatred, & calumny of it's Enemies—& to think & toil, with a patent for all the Abuse, and a transfer to others of all the Honors. In the Quarterly Review of the Remorse (delayed till it could by no possibility be of the least service to me, & the compliments in which are as senseless & silly as the censures—every fault ascribed to it being either no improba[bi]lity at all, or from the very essence & end of the Drama no *dramatic* Improba[bi]lity, without noticing any one of the *real* Faults (and there are *many* glaring and one or two *deadly* Sins) in the Tragedy)—in this Review I am abused, & insolently reproved, as a man, with reference to my supposed private Habits, for *not publishing*—Would to Heaven, I never had—to this very moment I am embarrassed & tormented in consequence of the non-payment of the Subscribers to the Friend —but I *could* rebut the charge, & not merely say but prove—that there is not a man in England, whose Thoughts, Images, Words, & Erudition have been published in larger quantities than *mine*— tho', I must admit, not *by* or *for* myself.—Believe me, if I felt any pain from these things, I should not make this Exposé—: for it is constitutional with me to *shrink* from all Talk or Communication of what gnaws within me—and if I felt any real anger, I should not do what I fully intend to do, publish two long Satires in Drydenic Verse, entitled Puff and Slander[1]—but I seem to myself to have endured the hootings and peltings & 'Go up, Bald-head!' (*II Kings*, *C. 2nd. v. 23, 24*) quite long enough—and shall therefore send forth my two She-bears to tear in pieces the most obnoxious of these ragged *children* in intellect, and to scare the rest of these mischievous little Mud-larks back to their crevice-nests & lurking Holes—While those who know me best, spite of my many infirmities, love me best, I am determined hence forward to treat my unprovoked enemies in the spirit of the Tiberian Adage, Oderint modo timeant.—

---

[1] E. H. Coleridge suggests that these satires may have found partial realization in the autobiographical lines entitled, *A Character*. See *Letters*, ii. 630 n., and *Poems*, i. 451. See also Letter 1092.

And now having for the very first time in my whole Life opened out my whole feelings & thoughts concerning my Past Fates & Fortunes, I will draw anew on your patience by a detail of my present Operations—My medical friend is so well satisfied of my Convalescence, and that nothing now remains but to superinduce *positive* Health on a system, from which Disease & it's *removeable* Causes have been driven out, that he has not merely consented to but advised my leaving Bristol for some rural Retirement. I could indeed pursue nothing uninterruptedly in that City. Accordingly, I am now joint-tenant with Mr Morgan of a sweet little Cottage at Ashley, half a mile from Box, on the Bath Road. I breakfast every morning before nine—work till one—& walk or read till 3—thence till Tea time, chat or read some lownge-book—or correct what I have written—from 6 to 8, work again—from 8 to Bed time play whist, or the little mock-billiard, called Bagatelle, & then sup & go to bed. My morning Hours, as the longest and most important Division, I keep sacred to my most important Work, which is printing at Bristol, two of my friends having taken upon them the risk.—It is so long since I have conversed with you, that I cannot say whether the subject will or will not be interesting to you. The Title is: Christianity the one true Philosophy—or 5 Treatises on the Logos, or communicative Intelligence, Natural, Human, and Divine:—to which is prefixed a prefatory Essay on the Laws & Limits of Toleration & Liberality illustrated by fragments of *Auto*-biography[1]—. The first Treatise—Logos propaideuticos—or the science of systematic Thinking in ordinary Life—the second, Logos architectonicus, or an attempt to apply the constructive, or mathematical, Process to Metaphysics & Natural Theology—the 3rd—ὁ Λόγος ὁ θεάνθρωπος (the divine Logos incarnate) a full Commentary on the Gospel of St John, in developement of St Paul's doctrine of preaching Christ alone, & him Crucified—the 4th, on Spinoza, and Spinozism with a Life of B. Spinoza—this entitled, Logos Agonistes.—5th and last, Logos alogos, (i.e. logos illogicus) or on modern Unitarianism, it's causes & effects[2]—. The whole will

[1] Chambers suggests that the *Biographia Literaria* presumably grew out of these 'fragments of *Auto*-biography'. *Life*, 270.

[2] Coleridge first publicly referred to his projected work on the Logos in the third essay 'On the Principles of Genial Criticism': 'I am about to put to the press a large volume on the Logos, or the communicative intelligence in nature and in man, together with, and as preliminary to, a Commentary on the Gospel of St. John.' *Felix Farley's Bristol Journal*, 27 Aug. 1814. *Biog. Lit.* ii. 230.

In 1815 this abortive work received the title, 'Logosophia: or on the Logos, divine and human, in six Treatises' (Letter 976); and in the *Biographia Literaria* (i. 92) it is referred to as 'on the Productive Logos human and divine'.

During the remainder of his life Coleridge was to make innumerable references

be comprized in two portly Octavos—and the second Treatise will be the only one, which will, & from the nature of the subject must be, unintelligible to the great majority even of well-educated Readers. The purpose of the whole is—a philosophical Defence of the Articles of the Church, as far as they respect Doctrine, or points of Faith.—If Originality be any merit, this work will have that at all events from the first page to the last—The Evenings I have employed in composing a series of Essays on the Principles of *genial* criticism concerning the Fine Arts, especially those of Statuary and Painting—and of these 4 in title, but six or more [in] size have been published in Felix Farley's Bristol Journal—a strange place for such a publication; but my motive was originally to serve poor Allston, who is now exhibiting his Pictures at Bristol. —O dear Sir! do pray, if you have the power or opportunity, use your influence with Taylor of the Sun not to continue that accursed system of detraction & calumny against Allston—The articles, by whomever written, were a disgrace to human Nature—and to my positive knowlege argued only less ignorance than malignity. Mr Allston has been cruelly used. Good God! what did I not hear Sir G. Beaumont say with my own ears! Nay, he wrote to me after repeated examination of Allston's great picture, declaring himself a compleat Convert to all my opinions of Allston's paramount Genius, as an Historical Painter. What did I not hear Mr West[1] say —After a *full Hour's* examination of the Picture he pointed out *one* thing he thought out of harmony, (& which against my urgent advice Allston altered—& had reason to repent sorely) and then said—I have shot my Bolt! It is as near Perfect[ion] as a Picture can be.—What did not Mr Carr, what did not the Marquis of Stafford both say & promise after repeated Visits! They absolutely forced him to stop his exhibition after all the heavy expences of the Room &c &c—and made him *such* promises, that West said —You *must* comply with their wishes—they have bound themselves down to buy your Picture—nay, he mentioned to *me* what ought to be the Price!—And O good God! with what shameless Cruelty, partly because he was an American, tho' in his Principles as deep an Abhorrer of Maddison, the Congress, & the War as any English-man of us all—& partly, from the intrigues and envy of West him-self—did they skulk out of their Engagements.—And Allston just rescued from Death with a constitution shattered by almost un-heard of Pains—his little property lost by a London Bankruptcy—

to his unrealized *magnum opus*. See Alice D. Snyder, *Coleridge on Logic and Learning*, 1929, for a discussion of the surviving MSS. of Coleridge's projected work and for the text of excerpts from them.

[1] Benjamin West (1738–1820), historical painter.

&c &c—and he himself the most quiet, inoffending, unenvious Being in existence!—But to return to my Essays.—I shall publish no more in Bristol—what they could do, they have done—But I have carefully corrected and polished those already published, and shall carry them on to 16 or 20—containing animated descriptions of all the *best* pictures of the great Masters in England, with characteristics of the great Masters from Giotto to Correggio. The first 3 Essays were of necessity more austere—for till it could be determined what *Beauty* was, whether it was Beauty merely because it pleased, or pleased because it was Beauty, it would have been as absurd to talk of general Principles of Taste, as of Tastes.— Now will this Series, purified from all accidental, local, or personal references, suit or serve the Courier in the present Dearth? I have no hesitation in declaring them the best compositions, *I* have ever written—I could regularly supply two Essays a week—and one political Essay.—Be so good as to speak to Mr Street—I could send him up 8 or 10 at once—. Make my best respects to Mrs Stuart—I shall be very anxious to hear from you—Your affectionate & grateful Friend,

S. T. Coleridge.

952. *To Daniel Stuart*

Address: D. Stuart, Esqre | Kilburne House | Kilburne | London
MS. British Museum. Pub. Letters from the Lake Poets, *233.*
Postmark: Bath, 17 October 1814.

16 Octr 1814.

Dear Stuart

I thank you for your very kind Letters, the latter of which I should have felt as too flattering from almost any one but yourself. But as I have a hundred times myself said of you, that I was never in your company in my Life for an hour together in which I did not acquire some rememberable instruction, of more or less value, & all of that kind which I most wanted & which was most useful to me— & added that I could assert the same of no other man—it would be unreasonable indeed to expect that I myself should be deemed sincere to the very Syllable, and yet entertain the least doubt of the sincerity of the Praise, high as it is, in a Letter of your's—who, thank God! in all the changes & contrasts of your fortune have preserved that best of the products of sound good Sense, Simplicity of Language, manners, & character.—Now I must tell you what has prevented my answering them—I happened to walk with the Morgans to Corsham House, P. Methuen's, Esqre—the father of the M.P.[1]—to see the famous or rather far-famed Collection of

---

[1] Paul Cobb Methuen (1752–1816), formerly M.P. for Great Bedwyn, was

Pictures—it was not the Shewing Day—but I sent in my name as one not regularly resident in the Neighbourhood—and was not only admitted—but a servant begged to know whether I was *the* Mr Coleridge, *the* great Author—You may suppose my answer & given *as* gravely as possible—I was received with every possible attention by the Family who sent off the Servant & accompanied me throughout the Rooms—and afterwards engaged me to spend a few Days at Corsham House—which I did—. At the Races the Marquis of Lansdown[1] expressed to them a Wish to meet me—I accordingly went again—met the Marquis—& rather suppose that he was not displeased with me—for he invited me home to Bow Wood—I went —& was prest to stay for a week or more—which I could not do for various reasons—but he left me with assurances that he would find me out either at Ashley, or at Bremell at Mr Bowles's.—

This has been the sole Cause why I have delayed likewise my 3rd Letter,[2] which I send off with this. I hope, it does not fall off— indeed, I think, it does not.—I requested Mr Street to be so good as to send me the Courier during the time, I was writing for it—at least, those that contained my own Essays—but I have seen neither of them in *Print*. Will you be so good as to speak to Mr Street— *they* should be directed—Mr B. Morgan, Chemist, Bridge Street, Bath—but *Letters*—to me, Ashley Cottage, Box, Bath. He may depend on having the 4th & 5th in the course of this Week—& till the Paper fill again with Parliament reports I doubt not, I shall be able to give the Courier one political and one critical Essay, weekly—after I have finished the Fletcher Letters—which (if Mr Street should chuse) I should carry on into a full & fair view of the whole Relations of Ireland to Great Britain, including the Catholic Question—Should it be convenient to you to send me, as soon as possible, a few Pounds, I should be served by them especially—for Murray, the Bookseller, has treated me in a strange way—about a translation of Goethe's Faust—but it is not worth mentioning except that I employed some weeks unprofitably—when it was of more than usual necessity that I [shou]ld have done otherwise—

My very best respects to Mrs Stuart and believe me, dear Stuart, with unfeigned Esteem & affectionate | Regard | your obliged Friend

S. T. Coleridge

the father of Paul Methuen (1779–1849), at this time M.P. for Wiltshire and later Baron Methuen.

[1] Henry Petty-Fitzmaurice, third Marquis of Lansdowne (1780–1863), statesman and patron of art and literature.

[2] Coleridge's six *Letters to Mr. Justice Fletcher* appeared in the *Courier* 20 and 29 Sept., 21 Oct., 2 Nov., and 3, 6, 9, and 10 Dec. 1814. See *Essays on His Own Times*, iii. 677–733.

953. *To Daniel Stuart*

Address: D. Stuart, Esqre | 9 Harley Street | Cavendish Square | London
MS. British Museum. Pub. with omis. Letters, *ii. 634.*
Postmark: Bath, 29 October 1814.

[29 October 1814]

Dear Stuart

After I had finished the IIId Letter, I thought it the best, I had ever written; but on re-perusal I perfectly agree with you. It *is* misty, and like most misty compositions, *laborious*—what the Italians call *faticoso*. I except the two last paragraphs ('In this guise, my Lord!' to—'aversabitur.')[1] These I still like.—Yet what I *wanted* to say is very important, because it strikes at the *root* of all *Legislative* Jacobinism. The view, which our Laws take of robbery and even murder, not as *Guilt* of which God alone is presumed to be the Judge, but as *Crimes*, depriving the *King* of one of *his* Subjects, rendering dangerous and abating the value of the *King's High*-ways, &c, may suggest some notion of my meaning. Jack, Tom, and Harry have no existence in the eye of Law, except as included in some form or other of the *permanent Property* of the Realm—just as on the other Hand Religion has nothing to do with ranks, estates, or offices; but exerts itself wholly on what is *personal*— viz. our Souls, Consciences, and the *morality* of our actions as opposed to mere *Legality*.—'Ranks, Estates, Offices &c were *made* for *Persons*,' exclaim Major Cartwright[2] & his Partizans. Yes, I reply, as far [as] the *divine* administration is concerned; but *Human* Jurisprudence wisely aware of it's own weakness & sensible how incommensurate it's powers are with so vast an object, as the Well-being of Individuals as Individuals, *reverses* the position—& knows nothing of Persons other than as Proprietors, Officiaries, Subjects. The preambles of our old Statutes concerning aliens (as foreign Merchants) and Jews, are all so many illustrations of my principle —the strongest instance of opposition to which, and therefore characteristic of the present age, was the attempt to legislate for animals by Lord Erskine[3]—i.e. not merely interfering with Persons, as Persons (or with what are called by Moralists, the imperfect Duties—a very obscure phrase for obligations of Conscience not capable of being realized (*perfecta*) by legal penalties) but extending *personality* to *Things*.

In saying this I mean only to designate the general Spirit of Human Law. Every Principle on it's application to Practice must

[1] For these two paragraphs see *Essays on His Own Times*, iii. 694–7.
[2] John Cartwright (1740–1824), political reformer.
[3] In 1809 Lord Erskine (1750–1823) introduced a bill for the prevention of cruelty to animals. The bill was defeated in the House of Commons.

be limited & modified by circumstances, our Reason by our Common Sense—Still however the *Principle* is most important, as Aim, Rule, and Guide.—Guided by this spirit our ancestors repealed the Puritan Law, by which Adultery was to be punished with Death, & brought it back to a civil Damage—So too, actions for Seduction.—Not that the Judge or Legislator did not feel the guilt of such crimes; but that the *Law* knows nothing about Guilt—. So in the Exchequer common Debts are sued for on the plea, that the Creditor is less able to pay our Lord the King—&c &c—. Now contrast with this the Preamble to the first French Constitution, and I think, my meaning will become more intelligible—that the pretence of considering Persons not States, Happiness not Property, always has ended & always will end in making a new *State* or Corporation infinitely more oppressive than the former— and in which the real freedom of Persons is as much less, as the things interfered with are more numerous & more minute. Compare the Duties exacted from a United Irishman by the Confederacy with those required of him by the Law of the Land. This I think not ill expressed in the two last Periods of the fourth Paragraph, 'Thus in order to sacrifice—confederation.'[1]

Of course, I immediately recognized your Hand in the article concerning the Edingburgh Review: and much pleased I was with it—and equally so in finding from your Letter that we had so compleatly co-incided in our feelings concerning that wicked Lord Nelson Article.[2] If there be one thing on earth that can outrage an honest man's feelings, it is the assumption of austere morality for the purposes of personal Slander. And the gross Ingratitude of the attack!—In the name of God, what have we to do with Lord Nelson's Mistresses or domestic Quarrels? Sir A. Ball, himself exemplary in this respect, told me that of his own personal Knowlege Lady Nelson was enough to drive any man wild—He himself once heard her at Nelson's own Table at Breakfast when two Lieutenants were present as well as Sir A. B. reproach & worrett him about his '*beastly infidelities* in the Mediterranean'. She had no sympathy with his acute sensibilities; and his alienation was effected tho' not shewn before he knew Lady Hamilton, by being *heart-starved* still more than by being teized & tormented by her sullens. Observe that Sir A. Ball detested Lady Hamilton. To the same enthusiastic sensibilities, which made a fool of him with regard to his Emma, his Country owed the victories of the Nile, Copenhagen, & Trafalgar—& the heroic Spirit of all the officers

---

[1] See *Essays on His Own Times*, iii. 694.

[2] In Sept. 1814 the *Edinburgh Review* contained a review of *The Letters of Lord Nelson to Lady Hamilton* . . . 2 vols., 1814.

reared under him.—When I was at Bow Wood, there was a plan suggested between Bowles and myself to engage among the cleverest literary characters of our knowlege six or eight—each of whom was to engage to take some one subject, of those into which the Ed. Review might be aptly divided—as Science, Classical Knowlege, Style, Taste, Philosophy, Political Economy, Morals, Religion, and Patriotism—to state the number of Essays, he could write, and the time at which he would deliver each—& so go thro' the whole of the Review—to be published in the first instance in the Courier, during the Recess of Parliament. We thought of Southey, Wordsworth, Crow, Crabbe, Woolaston—& Bowles thought, he could answer for several single articles from Persons of the highest rank in the Church & our two Universities.—Such a plan adequately executed 7 or 8 years ago would have gone near to blow up this Magazine of Mischief.

As to Ridgway & the Essays, I have not only no objection to my name being given; but I should prefer it. I had just as much right to call myself dramatically an Irish Protestant[1] when writing in [the] character of one, as Swift to call himself a Draper.—I have waded thro' as mischievous a work as two huge Quar[tos, very] dull can be, by a Mr Edward Wakefield, called An Account of Ireland.[2] Of all Scriblers these Agricultural Quarto-mongers are the vilest. I thought of making the affairs of Ireland in toto, chiefly however with reference to the Catholic Question, a new Series; and of republishing in the appendix to the 8 Letters to Mr Justice Fletcher[3] Lord Clare's (then Chancellor Fitzgibbon's) admirable Speech, worthy of Demosthenes—of which a copy was brought over from Dublin by Rickman & given to Lamb—it was never printed in England, nor is it to be procured. I never met a person who had heard of it.—Except that one main point is omitted (and it is remarkable, that the Poet, Edmund Spencer, in his Dialogue on Ireland, is the only writer who has urged this point) viz—the forcing upon Savages the Laws of a comparatively civilized People instead of adopting measures gradually to render them susceptible of these Laws, this Speech might be deservedly called, the Philosophy of the past and present History of Ireland.—It makes me smile to observe, how all the mediocre men exult in a ministry that have been so successful without any overpowering Talent of

---

[1] Coleridge's signature to the *Letters to Mr. Justice Fletcher.*

[2] Edward Wakefield, *An Account of Ireland, Statistical and Political,* 2 vols., 1812. Coleridge cites this work in his sixth *Letter to Mr. Justice Fletcher.* See *Essays on His Own Times,* iii. 732.

[3] There were actually six letters, published in eight instalments in the *Courier.*

Eloquence &c. It is true, that a series of gigantic Events like those of the last 18 months will lift up any cock-boat to the very Skies upon their Billows; but no less true, that sooner or later parliamentary Talent will be found absolutely requisite for an English Ministry.

I perceive, that this affair of Colonel De Quentin has made the Regent unpopular—Even those, who justify and applaud the sentence of the Court Martial, and see even the Regent's additions in a favorable Light in and for themselves, do not hesitate to reprobate the Prince's private Manoeuvres with Col. Palmer as dishonorable & treacherous.

It must be uncomfortable for the Courier, except on great points, to express dissatisfaction with Ministers—but really Vansittart's Assentation to the Retrenchers, Banks &c is very humiliating—while the Brewer, by pure force of pertinacious Bullying is actually Lord of the Ascendant. I can easily understand how the Country might be richer by the proposed Improvements, Palace &c—especially now that so many thousands are thrown back on society —but why it should impoverish the Island, & extort a threat of Resignation from Vansittart, I cannot see—.

My best respects to Mrs Stuart—. Do you think of spending any time at Bath this winter?—with sincere regard & esteem

Your obliged
S. T. Coleridge

P.S. I confess that the *Principle* would lead me farther than I might wish to go; but in the Friend I have at large shewn that no Principle can be applied practically without exceptions, limitations, modifications—in short, without a compromise between Science & Prudence. Yet in the very strongest instance, that of the Slave Trade, I should plead now on different grounds, from what I did.—
Please to tell Mr Street that J. J. Morgan will draw for the 20£.

954. *To John Kenyon*[1]

Address: J. Kenyon, Esqre | 9 Argyle Street
MS. Mr. Carl H. Pforzheimer. Pub. with omis. Letters, *ii. 639.*

3 Novr. 1814.
Mr B. Morgan's, Bath.—

My dear Sir

At Binns's, Cheap Street, I found Jer. Taylor's Dissuasive from Popery, in the largest and only compleat Edition of his Polemical

---

[1] John Kenyon (1784–1856), poet and philanthropist.

Tracts.[1] Mr Binns had no objection to the §§ being transcribed any morning or evening at his House: and I put in a piece of Paper with the words at which the Transcript should begin & with which end —P. 450, line 5th—to P. 451, l. 31—I believe.—But indeed I am ashamed, rather I feel awkward and uncomfortable at obtruding on you so long a task—much longer than I had imagined. I don't like to use any words that might give you any *un*pleasure—but I cannot help fearing that like a child spoilt by your & Mrs Kenyon's great Indulgence I may have been betrayed into presuming on it more than I ought.—Indeed, my dear Sir! I do feel very keenly how exceeding kind you & Mrs K. have been to me—it makes this Scrawl of mine look dim in a way, that was less uncommon with me formerly than it has been for the last 8 or 10 years—. But to return, or turn off, to the good old Bishop—. It would be worth your while to read Taylor's Letter on original Sin, & what follows. It is the masterpiece of Human Eloquence—I compare it to an old Statue of Janus, with one of the Faces, that which looks toward his Opponents, the controversial Phiz, in highest Preservation—the face of a mighty one, all Power, all Life!—the Face of a God rushing on to Battle; and in the same moment enjoying at once both Contest and Triumph. The other, that which should have been the Countenance that looks toward his Followers—that with which he substitutes his own Opinion—all weather-eaten, dim, noseless, a *Ghost in Marble*[2]—such as you may have seen represented in many of Piranesi's astounding Engravings from Rome & the Campus Martius. Jer. Taylor's Discursive Intellect dazzle-darkened his Intuitions—: the principle of becoming all Things to all men if by *any* means he might save *any*, with him as with Burke, thickened the protecting Epidermis of the Tact-nerve of Truth into something too like a Callus. But take him all in all, such a miraculous Combination of Erudition broad, deep, and omnigenous, of Logic subtle as well as acute, and as robust as agile; of psychological Insight, so fine yet so secure!—of public Prudence & practical *Sageness* that

[1] Jeremy Taylor, *ΣΎΜΒΟΛΟΝ ΘΕΟΛΟΓΙΚῸΝ: or a Collection of Polemicall Discourses. . . ,* 3rd edn., 1674. A copy of this work with annotations by Coleridge is in the British Museum.

In this volume Coleridge wrote an unfinished note to Charles Lamb on the verso of the title-page of Taylor's *Of the Sacred Order and Offices of Episcopacy*:

I wish, my dear Charles! you would look in the Biograph. Britann. (if there *be* a tolerable Life of Jereme Taylor that adds any thing to his Funeral Sermon) and attach to each of his Works (I think, you have all but his Latin Grammar) the date of the original publication.—I remember your saying, within a year after I first Io noctes Atticae at the Cat and Salutation, Blood Alley, Newgate Market, when Butchers grasped their steels, and listened to our knock-down Arguments—

[2] Cf. *Aids to Reflection*, 1825, p. 275, and *Literary Remains*, iii. 328.

one ray of *creative Faith* would have lit up and transfigured into
Wisdom; and of genuine Imagination, with it's streaming Face
unifying all at one moment like that of the setting Sun when thro'
one interspace of blue Sky no larger [than] itself it emerges from
the Cloud to sink behind the Mountain—but a face seen only at
starts, when some Breeze from the higher Air scatters for a
moment the cloud of Butterfly Fancies, which flutter around him
like a moving Garment of ten thousand Colors—(Now how shall I
get out of this sentence ?—The Tail is too big to be taken up into the
Coiler's Mouth—) well, as I was saying, I *believe*, such a complex
Man hardly shall we meet again—.

You may depend on the Wakefields—(crepitus post Tonitrua!
foetor, articulatus post fragrantia murmura, et musicos odores
Zephyrorum e paradiso—) on Tuesday—I shall fag all tonight &
tomorrow at him—& shall try *my* Hand at a Review—Aid me,
butcherly Muses! and sharpen on your Steel my cleaver bright
& keen.

May God bless you & your's!— | Your obliged
S. T. Coleridge.

P.S. My address after Tuesday will be (God permitting) Mr Page's,
Surgeon, Calne.—

955. *To Daniel Stuart*

Address: D. Stuart, Esqre. | Courier Office | Strand | London   To be forwarded
to Mr S.
MS. British Museum. Pub. Letters from the Lake Poets, *237.*
Postmark: Bath, 23 November 1814.

Ashley, Box, Bath.
Wednesday—[23 November 1814]

My dear Stuart

Monday after next I expect, as far as so perplexed a Being dare
expect any thing, to remove to Calne, Wilts—at a Mr Page's,
Surgeon. I suppose, that the Press of Parliamentary & American
Matter has prevented the insertion of my communications: for if
there had been any thing offensive in them, I should have heard
from Mr Street.—My next will conclude, making up 8 distinct
Letters: & I almost confide, that you will like the last better than
any but the second. One of them sent off by Morgan from an imperfect Copy, while I was at Bow Wood, by mistake—for I had
myself rewritten the Letter & left a Press Copy—was either from
this cause or from the carelessness of the compositors so misprinted
as to be scarcely intelligible—I mean, the Letter in which the Bible

Society is introduced.[1] I had greatly softened it—& in every respect amended the Style. It was in truth merely my first rude Sketch.—

The question on the state of Ireland, & it's causes, involving the Catholic Question, I have thought would be better treated in a separate Series—I have been, I may truly say, indefatigable in collecting information, from men as well as from Books—and my object would be to produce such a work, as would compel even an Emancipator, if a man of an enlightened mind, to admit, that I had not omitted, or weakened any one argument that could be adduced on either side, with any shew of reason. The more, however, I think, the more *unsceptical* my dread of what is called Catholic Emancipation becomes.

I have now to request your kind advice—first of all, acknowleging the receipt of 10£, which I was authorized by you to draw for—. The 8 Letters, of which Mr S. has the 5th & 6th, would form a pamphlet of about a 100 pages, with the notes which I should add in the appendix, and the insertions made in the correction of the whole—Now would you think it 1. adviseable to republish them— & 2. do you think, that Ridgeway, or any other, would reprint them, on any terms that would be likely to be of any pecuniary advantage to me—by giving me so much for the Copy-right, if such a bargain could be made, which I should prefer tho' it should be only 20 or 30£—or by taking the risk of an Edition, and giving me a portion of the Profits?—At the same time you would oblige me by asking, whether a collection of political Essays on the most important political Subjects from 1795 to the present Date, partly selected from my Contributions to the M. Post & Courier, & partly MSS— including the Characters of Pitt, Wyndham, Burke, Fox, and Buonaparte, would be purchased. With exception of my Letters to Fox, which I have not been able to procure, I have them already prepared for the press—

Since I have received the Courier, I have submitted to the painful & disgusting task of reading the Quarterly & Edingburgh reviews for the last year—& every day have noted down short observations—but more especially, on America & the American War, concerning which I wish, I could converse with you. I have seen many witty & some very just observations; but I have not yet met with any work, which appears to me to have done any thing like common justice to the Subject. In order to understand the Subject as a truly great Statesman ought to understand it, we ought first to consider the *colonial* character, in genere—then the [col]onial character as modified by the circumstan[ces] of

---

[1] Coleridge mentioned the British and Foreign Bible Society in his fourth *Letter to Mr. Justice Fletcher*. See *Essays on His Own Times*, iii. 704–7.